Autograph Page

Autograph page continued

Dear Taylor Swift,
A Year in the Life of the Artist Rush Whitacre
Through his Letters

Disclaimer: I love my college and grad school experiences. I would never change them for a minute. Ohio University and the University of Cincinnati are amazing schools and everything written in this book about them should be taken with a grain of salt. My experiences with these schools should be read as my experiences, not as what everyone should expect to experience when attending them.

Also, due to a death-threat I received on my voice mail shortly after selling my fourth copy of this book I did end up editing and cropping out some names, sorry to do this, but some things must be done in order to survive.

***This Book Contains Original Letters As They Were Sent Out To Taylor Swift. There are Errors that the Author is very well aware of. A later edition will be published with the errors corrected, making this a limited edition, limited to the number purchased before the errors are corrected.

© 2011 Rush Whitacre

All rights reserved.

ISBN 978-0-578-09954-5

No portion of this book may be reproduced, stored in a retrieval system, or transmitted in any form except for brief quotations in printed reviews without the prior permission of the author.

Special Thanks To:

Victor C. Whitacre, Dad
(Words missing), Mom
Vicki, Sister
Ricki, Brother
David, Brother
Randall, Brother
(word missing), Brother
Clark, Brother
Lauren Purje, Close Friend
Carley Lowe, Close Friend, Designer
Alan Gaynor, Photographer
And to all my friends
And to all those who I may have forgotten

Front Cover

Photography by Alan Gaynor, 2011

Designed by Carley Lowe, 2011

Hair is Taylor Swifts from fearless Album, buy her music today in stores and on itunes

Back Cover

(top and bottom): first step in a 15 painting series of the bridges in New York Central Park

Middle(Sunflower): LifeCycle IVb, Oil on Canvas, 11 feet by 24 feet, painted by Rush Whitacre

Copyright 2011

First Publication 2011

A LifeCycle Production

Letters Project #1

This is for my dad, for you are the unmoving stable ground in my life,
And without you mom I fear I would never have had a single creative bone in my body.
I love you both very much.

A special thanks to Lahoma Williamson:
I truly believe that love makes us want to live, and I thank you for loving my Dad.

Letter 365 is the first letter in my book. I did this because this book is also acting as the last letter I am sending to Taylor.

11-14-11, Letter 365

May this letter act as the foreword to this book as I have not the strength to write one after it.

Dear Taylor Swift,

Someday I want to say that I matter. That my work, my effort, mattered. That someday someone out there, out here in the world will look at what I have done and want to learn more about me, or maybe a person will see me, really see how much energy and passion I have brought to my work. Maybe my work will be touching enough that my life will bring a tear so someone's eyes. I cannot say, for I am still alive, and I am still making work, and I am still struggling. Like many others, I am laughing, and happy, but in a world of pitfalls and traps, I am also broke, in debt, and working until I cannot even stand anymore. Despite all the downfalls I am still here, still alive and here in this world. I have achieved what I have because I have worked long hours and have planned things out far in advance. I have worked hard so that I could move to have the opportunity to create artwork in the greatest city in the world, New York City. I am here and making artwork in spite of all the things that are working against my art, like my day jobs, the under the table job, the rejection and being ignored by galleries, the rejection from professors, the rejections from friends, the unreturned phone calls where I could have made money or that ever important connection but didn't. I am still here, and hungry for life.

I am an artist despite the two divorces, the family tragedies, my mom and dad's failing health, the car problems, and despite my broken heart from so many relationships gone wrong from cheaters and thieves and downright haters and liars. I am here in New York flying in the face of all those things that could have,,, and probably should have,,, kept me back; I am here making my art. I will never give up as I am relentless in my pursuit, and I will never ask for permission and I will not apologize for my art or ask to be apologized to. If there isn't an opportunity in sight, I will create the opportunity, and I will take chances. I will not wait to be rescued and I will not think twice about begging if that is what keeps me here and able to create. And, I will keep creating no matter what. I will not let myself down, and hopefully I will be a role model for others to see, for others to be inspired by, for my friends, for my enemies, and for the in-between people who may or may not know anything about me, for my past students, perfect strangers, and for all those who are lost or lonely, I love you, and never forget that you are loved.

This book is just about a life, mine, my story that I am sharing with you. My journey through this past year, through my finishing up of Grad school, to the events that led to my reoccurring dream(the one that started me down the path of writing these letters in the first place), through some of the saddest moments of my life, and some of my happiest. My downfalls and triumphs in my move to New York City, and to the near death of both my parents in the same week, I have laid it all out on the table, uncut, uncensored, and unedited. This is my life, and here in these pages you will see my flickering flame dart from almost smoked out, to forest fire rage with enthusiasm. Sometimes it was simply the 'knowing' that I would be writing one of these letters at the end of the day that would bring me through. With these letters I was able to remain alive inside even when everything faltered and crumbled around me. You may find yourself in my pages, my poems, and sometimes wrapped up inside my arms crying with me as I did upon my work countless times. For everyone that has helped me, loved me, and loves me still, this is for you.

For this being my last letter to Taylor, I just wanted to say, thank you.

This Poem is for my family, friends, students, and loved ones

"Monthly Pass"

Ladies and gentlemen on the subway of my life

I never planned on becoming an artist

I just am, and always will be

And I have never known and nor will I ever know

Another you, another brother or sister or friend

Like I know you as an individual, as family's do

Compassionate and compelling and honest to a fault

I have my hand out to you

But I am not a beggar, and I am not a bum

I am sensitive to your needs, your wants, your dreams

And I offer you my hand, myself selflessly

Together we can and will make this moment a memory

Thank you for your patience, your trust, your compassion

I may always be indebted to your kindnesses

But I know without a doubt that I will never be alone

And I thank you for this.

I toss this letter into the void, the abyss between us, this space that keeps conversation from happening.

Sincerely,

Rush Whitacre

740-336-9169

Pre Letter-Project:

    Six days before my first letter I reinjured my back working in my studio for hours on a very lightweight model made out of foam core. This model was to be the main selling point for me to get my Masters Degree. I was bent over just ever so slightly for a couple of hours, and the next day when I woke up I could barely move without screaming in agony… One of my peers drove me to the Hospital and I was prescribed pain meds and muscle relaxers and in my anguish I misunderstood the doctor. I thought he said to 'double' the medication, when what he really said was take double the amount the first time. So, I consumed a 10 day supply of meds in a five day period. What ensued was a five day span where I slept all the time, and upon waking up every 6 to 8 hours I had the same vivid reoccurring dream. The dream lasted probably seconds for all I know, but it led to these letters, this year of time recorded.

    In my dream I am in a large gallery. A video projection is in front of me but I cannot make it out, and then I start to panic and the walls fade out. Throughout it all I am unable to move my head or eyes to look around the gallery, I feel simply trapped. Then something happened in the dream that I cannot explain. From my left an arm would come into view, then a face, and that face would say to me, "Color, Which Color?" and Poof, I wake up. That face was Miss Taylor Swifts. Up to this point in my life I hadn't paid any deliberate attention to her life/career/music. I was not a fan, but not a foe either. I had seen her on TV at a glimpse between changing channels maybe once or twice(as I do not watch cable TV), and maybe on the front of a magazine or something a couple of times, but that is it as far as I know. Then I saw her in this dream, so you can imagine my bewilderment. 10 or 12 times this dream came to me. Call it the pain meds talking if you want, because I have no idea why. In five days I ran out of all the meds and I laid in bed and thought about what I should do with this dream, this question, where did it belong in my life's work. Being the kind of artist I am, one who draws energy from his life's experiences to create, I just knew that this event had some place in it. On the 6th day I decided to write Miss Swift, and answer her question of 'Color, which color'. On the seventh day I realized that my journey wasn't over, that I needed these letters, this recording of history… There is a short letter about my day, and a short poem about whatever I felt like writing about in that moment, one for every day for a year. So, without any further delay, from my lonely room in the socially awkward city of Cincinnati I tossed the following into the void:

11-15-10 (First Letter)

Dear Taylor Swift,

So, I don't know you at all. I never listen to country music, unless it happens to 'pop' onto a top 40 radio station, and even then I guess I really don't think about it. I am not saying that I don't like country music; I just don't seem to turn to that channel… well, anyway. There is also another twist to this letter, and I am sure you get hundreds of thousands of fan mail letters a year, and I am most certain that you don't read them all because that would take a lifetime, or several lifetimes. I guess what I am trying to say is, I am not necessarily a fan so much as a curious artist who has had this recurring dream about you. Please, dear lord don't think that I am some kind of creepster or something, I just decided to write you, to maybe make sense of it all. I am almost certain that you won't even get this letter, rather some other little old ladies in a giant room whose sole job is to open your junk mail. Well little old ladies, here is the deal. I don't have a clue as to why I had this reoccurring dream, and the only time I have really even seen a picture of Taylor was about 2 or 3 months before I had them. My (related person who is not named) was watching TV, some kind of special on Swift; I was too busy to care at all about anything she was saying I guess I hadn't thought about this event until this dream, no offense to Taylor.

   In this dream, which was very frightening at first, and not because you were in it Taylor, but because of my back pain I am sure. I think as I was waking up my back pain was at its most severe, causing me to panic in my dream,,, Anyway. In this dream I am in a gallery, I think at the CAC in Cincinnati, which is odd because I have only been there like once and as much as I liked it I can't fathom as to why my brain would choose it. So, in a large gallery I stand looking at a massive wall with some video projection on it. It is blurry and I can't make it out. The walls fade out to a blurry white just as blurry as the video is and then you (Taylor) come in from my left with just your arm, then the rest of you, and your face stops in front of me and you ask the question: "Color, which Color?" And Poof I wake up… now, I have had this dream about 10 nor 12 times and I am quite certain that I don't know what it means. I blame it on pain killers I have been taking for my back here for the past 5 days. Long story, bad bad back.

Anyway, I don't want to just leave you without an answer, so, pick Baby Blue. Here is a poem.

Possible new poem:

And I was the one who danced,

And I was the one who sang you that song,

And I filled you all up with my words,

And then you left without one and down to the ground crashed letters, letters.

There spilled out for all of my friends who all spelled out this lining,

This end, and I regret not listening to them,

So I scoop them all up and I send letters,

Letters to fill you all up with my words,

To let you know from afar that you filled me all up and I felt so alive,

So many lines in my head so I wrote them all down and your gone.

I cry, and I still cry letters, letters, tears full of letters,

And I watch them all fall to the floor and the wall and they fill up this room to the top of my head.

Now I scoop them all up and pretend I see text,

But they make no sense so I'll put them in place

Where they'll be waiting for the next.

And then, I'll use letters letters to make all the words

To fill them all up with my song.

I cast this letter into the void, this abyss between us, this space that keeps conversation from happening.

Rush Whitacre

11-16-10

Dear Taylor Swift,

 Ok, so about this dream….. So, I don't know you at all, and I don't know your music really. I just recently decided to do some investigating of it because I can't understand why my brain decided to have this strange reoccurring dream… I never listen to country music, unless it happens to pop onto a top 40 radio station, this I mentioned yesterday in my letter(and I am sure I am going to repeat myself here but that is ok because the dream repeated so many times why not parts of my letters here at first… ha ha. well, anyway. There is also another twist to this letter, and I am sure you get hundreds of thousands of fan mail letters a year, and I am certain that you don't read them all because that would take a lifetime. I guess what I am trying to say is, I am not necessarily a fan so much as a curious artist who has had this recurring dream about you. Please, dear lord don't think that I am some kind of creepster/stalker/ or anything else along those lines, I just decided to write you, to maybe make sense of it all. Maybe this letter is the cure to making this dream feel like it can rest, or go away finally. I am almost certain that you won't even get this letter, rather some other person who works for you. Actually, I have this funny vision of a small room of lovely women opening your mail and reading each one, silly I know. This is not like me at all, and I am really embarrassed by the fact that I am even considering to write this and send it off into the world, but I must, something is telling me I must. Maybe if nothing else, the dream will begin to make sense to me.

 Dream:

 So, in this dream I am in a gallery here in Cincinnati Ohio, I can't tell exactly which one, but I am leaning towards the CAC because the giant white wall in front of me reminds me of a giant wall at the CAC. I am simply staring at the wall, not able to move, in the longest of these reoccurring dreams I remember mingling with people, looking at art, there is a hum of talking about the work all around me. Then, I end up suddenly in front of an interactive video installation, at least I think that is what it is, and everything suddenly gets very quiet. I have had this dream enough times to know that this is when you are around somewhere, so I start looking but I can't move my head side to side, just my eyes and the room gets hazy, and then I can't move my eyes. I move, but I actually don't use my feet, it is more of an odd hover of sorts, and I can't look down, or at least I haven't in the dream. The video disappears; I end up with nothing but a wall of misty white nothing in front of me. To the left of me an arm stretches out until it is in front of me and then your face. And I know it is you because you have a very distinctive face. In almost every case you only say one line to me, that is unless I somehow manage to wake up before it is over, which happened once. You ask, or say: "color, which color?" or just "which color?" You have probably said other things, but the one that seems to stick with me is color. Lol, must be the painter side of me coming though putting words into your mouth. So, I am going to answer your question; baby blue, you should choose baby blue, for whatever question you are having in regards to choosing a color. I hope this helps. Smiles.

If telling you about the dream doesn't seem to make the dream go away, I might make a poem about it, or song (that one works for you right…). You don't have to read them, I expect nothing in return, and I might just keep them to myself, no need to bother you.

I toss this letter into the void, the abyss between us, this space that keeps conversation from happening.

Sincerely,

Rush Whitacre

11-17-10

Dear Taylor Swift,

Well, I decided that I might as well be formal for at least one of these letters that I am writing. Well, anyway, I have these two dogs, a Doberman and a great Dane, I walked them last night wondering what I would do if I had that dream again after writing you all about it. My back is an awful thing sometimes,, keeping me from doing the work that I love to do… I reinjured it this time by simply working on a maquette of a gallery space for a couple of hours. I am pretty sure it was me standing for hours slightly bent over that screwed me up. I will survive.

So, my (related person who is not named) wants me to write poetry so that she and I can publish a poetry book together. So, I might as well keep in practice with these letters. Here is my next installment to the void, the space that keeps conversation from actually happening. If nothing else, I will entertain one of the lovely ladies who get to read your fan mail and who get to decide its fate. Smiles.

This poem is for being the chosen one,

'M'

I can't remember the last time I felt this way
This hum of satisfaction, your highs and lows and over-reaction
A moment passes onto the next, and I'm so happy.
I work and work and never end where I should
These distractions that I can't distract take me to places
Where my heart goes, leads me, teases me apart
And I sing this melody, this poem, this epic tragedy
About a moment, a field of lost souls, where I have been sent
Will you hold me and never let me go
Show me open arms and I'll wrap me up inside
And make all my smiles smile and all my laughter's cry
Because you loved me, love me still
Love me and I will
I can't remember the last time that I felt this way
On the way home I let the wind in through my window
And on the way home I heard our song on the radio
I arrived so unexpectedly, to see you with another,
There my heart goes
And my heart goes, leads me, teases me apart
Will you would hold me and never let me go
Show me open arms and I'll wrap me up inside
And make all my smiles smile and all my laughter's cry
Because you loved me, love me still
Love me and I will
Yeah, Love me and I will
But I must turn away my eyes and see a different you,
A different you a different me
Still I go into the blue,
A sea of uncertainty
Wandering and wondering where I went wrong
Where she went right, and was I ever right

>And my heart goes, leads me, teases me apart
>
>You said you'd hold me and never let me go
>
>You'd show me open arms and I'd wrap me up inside
>
>And make all my smiles smile and all my laughter's cry
>
>Because you loved me, love me still
>
>You Love me and I've lost my will
>
>Yeah, Yea. Love me and I will
>
>And I will

I toss this letter into the void, the abyss between us, this space that keeps conversation from happening.

Sincerely,

Rush Whitacre

11-18-10

Hello Taylor,

      Well, here I am again. I had a really good day. I hate to even bring this up again, but, I wrote down what exactly you said to me in my dream this time, this morning I mean. Which I must add, I must be doing something to get my dogs attention when I am having this dream because this time when I woke up they were both just staring at me, it was sooo cute. Anyway, you just looked at me; there was absolute silence, haziness all around. Your arm swung in and you looked me right in the eyes and said, "Which color?" What is just funny is I woke up with a smile on my face, not because I figured anything out, but because somehow between the dream world and this real world my mind somehow put it together that soon, or at least hopefully soon you would have the answer to that question due to my previous letter; 'baby blue,' whatever it is this question is supposed to mean, pick and use baby blue. I sent this answer to your lovely ladies who get all of your fan mail (joke from previous letter where I assume all your mail is opened by some lovely ladies in some mail room in Nashville.) If it works out, like I said in my previous letter, please call me and tell me what it is that needed this serious critique from me. Lol, really though. Because I believe in fate, that things for the most part happen for a reason, I want to believe that this recurring dream just has to be a way for the world wanting me to get this message to you. Geez, here I go again, sounding sooooooooooooo silly. Anyway, my number is 740-336-9169. Maybe in my next dream I will get more info, rather than just a short statement/question. Maybe then I can say exactly when, with whom, on what date, with whatever it is that is supposed to be this color, or maybe it will just go away.

Anyway, I am going to give you another quick poem/song/whatever. I am sure I will just make it up; I seem to think I work best that way, and sometimes I do.

Here is my fourth attempt at sending something off into the void to you Taylor, this space that keeps conversation from happening. Smiles. And for the lovely ladies reading this, bless you.

Sincerely,

Rush Whitacre

11-19-10

Dear Taylor,

  Again, this is more formal, I guess if for no other reason that I started with 'dear'. First of all, I have to confess something; I just absolutely love songs where a piano seems to waltz some magical tune, not recognizing its own throne, its power, its destiny I guess I am saying this because I was just listening to Stephan Moccio; October. Of course, I don't listen to this kind of music all the time, just when I want to be reminded... that my fingers were meant for other things, like painting, sculpting, installation. And that I should let the genius skill for music remain there for me to thrive on, and use as my emotional palette from which I can reflect back my own reaction to its energy. Or, whatever.

  Another poem, or song, or simple words, that I again toss into the abyss. This time, a rhyme (and I usually write about love, or lost love, or just being broken, so please don't take them personally, it's just How I work. And again, in case you didn't get my earlier letters, I am writing this crap (trust me, I don't think my writing is that great), but anyway, I am writing this stuff because of the dream I kept having about you, where in it you show up then a hazy fog makes the walls of this gallery disappear, then you say or ask, "color, which color". I am pretty sure it is a question by the look on your face. I know that sounds really really messed up, and it is, for me just as much as it is for me to write it to you and for you to have to see this and read it, that is, if you read it... smiles, I still think that you do sign your signature, but you probably also have an army of lovely older ladies opening your mail to see what's what. I may never know. If baby blue does work out for you, call me and let me know, just because I am curious, 740-336-9169) Anyway, here goes;

'Better Off In Tennessee'

Darrel
Had a girlfriend
Her name was Denise

Too bad, he was a little boy, never got down on his knees
To give her the love, and show her what he had
Well now he's in Maryville Tennessee
With his heart in her hands

Now
Back to Scotland, where the romance first ignites
There was something magic in the air
10 Long days and endless, sleepless nights
Darrel found the courage, to hold her by his side
And she felt like home and she felt so right
Then in the end she disappeared and she lied

Darrel had a girlfriend
And he tried to love her right
And inside he was torn up and an awful sight
And if he could have stopped time he would
But he knows, he's better off in Tennessee
Where he can dream of her at night

Denise, a diamond in the rough
Every guy who's tried to please
Too bad, they're all just little boys
Who never got down on their knees
And give you the love
Like the one who wished he had
Well now he's in Maryville Tennessee
With his heart in your hands
With his heart
In your hands

Denise had a boyfriend…. But he's better off in Tennessee

Rush Whitacre

This one I skip into the void, that space that prevents conversation from happening.
"Which color?" -*Taylor Swift*-
"Baby Blue" —*Rush Whitacre*-

11-20-10

Dear Taylor,

    Hi,

    So, for today's letter, I will simply just write out a poem. Maybe about the dream. I actually must tell you, I have made a decision about my writing of these letters. About what my intent is with them. Not to mention that dream that started me down this path. If I hadn't hurt my back again, I wouldn't have taken the medicine as I did, and I would be there right now writing these letters. I just seem to wake up so happy after having that dream, sometimes bewildered I suppose. And it is, now that I think about it, a rather odd thing to feel, especially since it is just me in this gallery setting, the CAC in Cincinnati, at least I am pretty sure it is the CAC. Not that it matters, what does matter is that the room fades away, like in a mist or fog and then your arm, your left arm appears, from the side, my left side or from below, and then there you are staring into my eyes with one thing on your mind, to ask me or say to me "Color, which color", or sometimes you just say 'which color.' And I will tell you again, baby blue is my answer, if you must choose a color, you should choose baby blue. I don't know what you are having trouble picking a color for, so, lol, I guess that's that. It's just a dream I suppose, and yet, as an artist I find myself oddly *drawn* to still continue to write you. Or your lovely ladies who read your mail, assuming that's the case.

I know; I will write a poem about the color baby blue, forget the dream poem.

'Baby blue'

When I look into the sky I am reminded of your face

Photo albums of my memory, leafed through pages, hard to erase

I turn into the back, into the dark, vacant lots, the emptiness

I've filled them all with fantasies, delusions left wanting of themselves

And dreams left to come true

And the waiting in the dark is the hardest part

I would have missed you sooner if I had only knew

That you still loved me

Please come back to me, my sweet baby blue

On the heel of this November I dreamt a dream of you

Faded walls and a masquerade ball
And dreams are dreams unless you really want them too
And if the fog in the air is the breath you breathe
My baby's blues, your eyes shine through
And dreams I left to finish are waiting for you
left to come true
And the waiting in the dark is the hardest part
I would have missed you sooner, but sooner wasn't soon enough
if I had only knew
That you still loved me,
I would have let you know, that
I love you too
Please come to me my baby blue
All types of hues across the land
And you stared into my ocean
Your rivers and streams push against my will to let go
Push me, rushing are the currents
Hurried by your somber brow and intuition
You know where I belong
And our dreams, I leave empty like the rest of this album
And the waiting in the dark is the hardest part
I would have missed you sooner
But sooner will never come, and if you only knew
That I still love you
Please come back my baby blue

-Rush Whitacre-

I pitch this letter into the void, this chasm, this space that keeps conversations from happening.

Pick baby blue.

Sincerely,

Rush Whitacre

11-21-10

Dear Taylor,

    So, my roommate is hilarious. His name is Louis and he tells the funniest stories, and he records everything he says, which is good, because he is a writer, and not good because he also records my infectious laughter, it is so loud. I inherited it from my dad.

    Ok, well, anyway, here is my next installment into this venture I decided to get into, these letters, these stories, and this dream of you. I swear, I wish this dream wasn't real. Not because you aren't worthy of me having a dream about you, but now it has given me purpose. You sing, and I can write, well, ok, my writing sucks, but I can still get it to you, or you lovely ladies who read your mail. Smiles, I will still continue to believe that. So, my hat is off to you lovely ladies for being so lucky to open such an abundance of mail from fans, and… me, the dream guy.

    Here is a poem about the devil and thanksgiving. Enjoy.

"Feast"

One thanksgiving when I was dating the devil

The food was cooking and I looked awfully besheviled

The devil passed me a cup and said drink this son

If you want to hear a story then I've got you one

He took two sips and smoke came from his lips

He turned with a mic and his leg on a bike

Such a scene as it was, and

Then I looked passed the devils peach fuzz

I was convinced that someone had spiked the chips

Because the drink I didn't drink at the crack of his whip

Smelled only of cinnamon and spice

So it had to be lovely, it had to be nice

Then I put down the basket and ran to the phone

Called up my mother but no one was home

Then I called up my brother

Because I could think of no other

Who would believe what I'd say

About what I'd seen this cold November day

So sitting all alone, I laid down my phone

I heard some kind of beeping, a familiar tone

Out of some kitchen came the devil running fast

> A turkey leg sticking up like a hopeless ships mast
>
> My phone now dead, the devils butter was spread
>
> And I gave in, my hopes wearing thin
>
> Besides it was only food, how is that a sin
>
> So I tasted the food and thought not the least
>
> "Devil pass me a plate, so I can join the feast."

I cast this letter off into the void, this place that keeps conversation from happening. Enjoy.

Sincerely,

Rush Whitacre

11-22-10

Dear Taylor,

    I don't know how the weather is where you are, but it has been really nice here in Cinci.

So, I could hardly sleep last night. I had some tea, not thinking about the caffeine and oooops, I was up really late. I can't stay up too late tonight, early morning class tomorrow, 8 AM actually. I'm not having that dream anymore, you know that one, me in a gallery, I am fairly sure it is the CAC. The walls fade away into a haze and your arm comes in and then your face. I looked up a picture of you because I didn't want to doubt my reasoning skills in saying you are the one from my dreams, otherwise these letters would really make me feel silly instead of just silly. Lol. Anyway you come close and say/ask, "Color, which color," or you just say, "Which color?" Is it a statement, or a question, I don't know. Either way, as I have mentioned before. Pick baby blue.

    Ok, here is another poem/song/whatever comes to my mind. This may simply be stream of consciousness, so here goes… (Again, I usually write about love, or lost love, or pain from loss, so don't take these personally. I can't help it, when I decide to write a poem, it usually is about love or pain or loss. So that's it.)

> "In a Pinch"
>
> How long has it been since I've been draped around you
>
> How long will it be before you realize I'm gone
>
> Out of all the order, where are you chaos when I need you most
>
> When all that I know flutters away like dandelions in a storm
>
> And all the warmth from your body is not beside me anymore
>
> Where will I go

> I'm left here waiting
>
> Where will I go
>
> I don't want this anymore
>
> Don't go, so choose and don't go
>
> And I'll be here waiting in the cold
>
> Not long ago we were best friends and I believed you
>
> Now nothing was ever perfect, but now nothing was ever real
>
> How long will it be before I realize I'm gone
>
> Out of all the things I need, I thought I needed you most
>
> Like everything I know, it breaks loose and floats away
>
> And all the heat dissipates into this empty space inside me
>
> Now where will I go
>
> I've been here waiting
>
> Where will I go
>
> I can't take this anymore
>
> So go, I choose and I want you to go
>
> And I'll be here waiting in the cold

There you go,

I toss this letter into the void, this space that keeps conversation from happening. I hope the lovely ladies(the ones who read your mail. Ha ha) enjoy my work.

Sincerely,
Rush Whitacre

11-23-10

Dear Taylor,

    Hello again Taylor, Tis me. So, I spent the whole morning with my students, they are good. I mean, they really listen to me. With them knowing that I am a grad I have been worried that my students wouldn't take me seriously. But, I actually think they want to learn from me, or maybe that is my dream. But I did give them a work day today which meant that they didn't have to be there and all of them showed up, except for ten. Ok, so 17 showed up, more than half, which was still surprising. So, being a grad isn't that bad, and teaching isn't as scary as I thought it was going to be, it actually feels really good, for the most part.

So, here I will state again my intent with these letters. I am an artist, who somehow doesn't listen to much country, but still manages to have a reoccurring dream about Taylor Swift. It is not every night, but it was at least 10 to 12 times in a week, the one where I was on meds for my back pain. The dream itself doesn't last long. It is simply me in a gallery at the CAC (at least I am sure as heck it is the CAC, I will scope out the location next time I go there), the walls fade out, or a fog or mist comes in and then Taylor's arm comes in from the left side and she says/asks; "Color, which color", and sometimes she only gets out the words, 'which color'. Either way, I like to write poetry, I may not be good at it, but writing Taylor is reason enough, she asks me which color, and I write her poetry. So, enjoy.

Here goes, another poem for your lovely ladies to read, that is, for the lovely ladies who open your mail when you are busy singing.

'The Thread of Time'

A needle, see

Yes I say a needle I need

For I am mending

Mending time, and time is mending me

I need two needles

One for night when all is dark and lonely

And one for day when I can see

Time is a thread

Passing through me, passing through me once only

I need three needles I say

One for the hours I lose

One for the minutes that I don't notice

And one for the seconds that beat away my heart

A terrible thing to bruise

I need a needle

Yes, pass me a needle I say

For Time is in need of mending

In need of Mending you, and mending me

Quick, thread the needle, for time is passing away

I cast this letter into this abyss of not knowing the end result, into the void that keeps conversation from happening.

Sincerely,

Rush Whitacre

740-336-9169

Remember, if you find yourself in conflict with which color to choose, I suggest baby blue. But that is only my suggestion.

11-24-10

Dear Taylor,

    I came home for Thanksgiving, but my father did not let my dogs stay in the house, instead he built an outdoor house for them. In less than an hour my Great Dane and Doberman were shivering to death, so, I bundled them up and drove to my (related person who is not named)'s house. They are warm now, and I am exhausted. So, either way, I have decided that I won't bore you about my dream of you anymore. It is getting to be old news, and talking about it isn't making it go away or answer any of my questions. So, here is another poem, into the abyss of mail.

I was robbed the other day

It hardly took me by surprise

I actually expected to be taken advantage of

Since my vulnerable spot I put before your eyes

And all is different, yet nothing ever changes

The sky still fills with my tears, clouding my view

The stars twinkle behind them, I know they do

For they will never leave me, even when does you know who

Like Cassiopeia and her true love Orion

You will follow me, and I will blindly march forward

Searching for that which I do not know

Filler for an empty space, a key hole, a voice to record

And yet, I am not satiated by any taste, or sound

A world barren of emotion, motives, ambition, light

Awaiting the dawn of a new sunset

A new day that is awaiting a new night.

    I toss this letter into the void, this space that keeps conversation from happening, a distance too great, two worlds drifting side by side, unaware of each other.

Rush Whitacre

11-25-10

Dear Taylor,

      Today is thanksgiving. I came to my (related person who is not named)'s house the night before, four hours away from Cincinnati. I spent time with my (related person who is not named), my two (related person who is male and not named)s, and an old laptop, not this one that I write to you with, but a different one that stopped working. My younger (related person who is male and not named), (related person who is male and not named), is a magician with computers. It is like he can touch them and know what they need. Well, anyway, I was with my (related person who is male and not named) during the night while he fixed the laptop and then I got thirsty and came down from his room and got a drink. My (related person who is not named) was enamored with the TV, I checked it out. It was you on the screen, and a flood of strange and bizarre feelings of coincidences ran through my mind. I froze, then I heard you say, "speak now", something like, "it is not about the right time, or the wrong time, it is about speaking now." I can't agree more, so I will continue to write you. When it came to the program about you, I couldn't watch it, it sent chills down my spine and gave me goose bumps, I guess I have been thinking about these poems I write you, and how you are this mystery to me. Then there you were entertaining my (related person who is not named), lol. So I am here to say that I simply can't learn about you, I can't do it Taylor, I can't learn about you and feel right about writing these letters and poems, so I left the room after I asked my (related person who is not named) why she was watching you. I don't know how to learn about you and not feel somehow ugly, and I never want to come across as ugly to you or anyone, just like I never want to be an ugly person to my friends or family. So, I will keep you a mystery, just as I am a mystery to you. Who knows, maybe someday we will meet, and then you can ask me about my poems, about my art, and I will tell you about the color baby blue, and ask you about your amazing life, I guess that is a better way to get to know someone anyway. Until then, I dream.

So on a different note, as I said in all the letters before, pick baby blue when there is a color you can't decide on. I mean, you asked me in my dreams, a recurring dream which I have had several times and which is the spark for these letters, these poems. You said/ask, "Color, which color", so I will answer you again, baby blue.

      I can't think of any other kind of poem to write you tonight except one of an apology, for not wanting to learn about you. I am sure you are a wonderful person, and I am sure I will learn about you in time, I just can't now because I am not writing you as a fan, or an obsessed fanatic, I am writing you because I dreamed you. Ok ok, here it is. Remember this is not for you, as I only write for myself.

'I'm so sorry'

I've let my heart write my words and I'm so sorry

But I can't know you, and feel good about this story

I know somehow deep down inside that you are all that is good

You are all that my mother said, and you are all for me but understood

I write myself into the wrong and all along you're with me

But if all you see are my words, my wit, you are without me

You will know that I exist and you will know that I am strong

But that which you will never learn are the same things that make this belong

I'm not asking for forgiveness because I haven't seen the wrong

I haven't seen lost innocence, nor have I lied or strung you along

I'm not saying that I am right, I write to understand

About this dream I had, to learn about you not second hand

And as silly as that may sound, it is not as silly as it may seem

I live my life as close to real, and not some short-lived dream

And even if you never cross my path, or see my art in some New York Gallery

You will know that I exist, and that one day in our past we had this little story

About some boy in Ohio, writing to some girl in Tennessee

About his dreams, his thoughts, about everything he could be

And someday you will look up into Van Gogh's night so starry starry

And see why that boy was unable to know you, and to why he had to say

I'm so very sorry sorry

I toss this letter into the void, this abyss between two people, this space that keeps conversation from happening.

Sincerely,

Rush Whitacre

11-26-10

Dear Taylor Swift,

    I am sure you are too busy for a pet, so, I will just tell you what a trip mine are. I'm sure my Great Dane thinks that I am her boyfriend because she always is so protective of me and so jealous of my Doberman when I pet him. Well, at 8 am this morning, after a night of watching movies and talking with the family, the cable guy shows up and my dogs just go crazy, especially Sienna the Dane, she jumps up onto the couch and wakes me up out of a very peaceful sleep which causes a domino effect of me being pushed onto the floor. A barrage of barking ensues and as I come to my senses I can't help but wonder where I am and what's going on. As I try to settle the dogs down I hear very meager voice from the slightly cracked open door say; "Hello, it's the cable guy, did you call for service." He had such a scared look on his face. I couldn't help but snicker a little, because if people only knew what babies my dogs are they would be the ones laughing

    So, I have an interesting venture coming up this December. A few years ago my (related person who is not named) gave me her stamp collection because she always wanted me to have it and she moved into a small condo and couldn't take it with her. Now, this morning, my (related person who is not named) tells me that she wants me to not have to worry about my school loans and she wants me to sell the collection rather than have the burden of moving it from place to place and having to be afraid of something bad happening to it. I am kind of relieved, and kind of shocked all at the same time. I have no idea how to go about it really, she has been collecting for the past 50 years. She tells me it is worth somewhere between 250,000 and 300,000 dollars, and to be quite honest, I am sure it is, just because it is HUGE. She even collected every princess Diana stamp possible. Well, anyway, that is my interesting story for the evening, and I have no idea how to even begin to search for a way to sell it. I always thought I would be stuck with it forever, or just simply have enough stamps forever for mail! Lol... wish me luck! or at least the lovely ladies who open your mail can wish me luck, assuming that you have some lovely ladies open your mail when you are not able to.

So, here is a poem about Wishing,

'Behind the Glass'

I'm waiting

I'm waiting, hoping to see the light that you let me see

Looking for the touch that sets me free

I know that I am small

But inside I'm filled from wall to wall

I'm not some missing son or lonely lass

I am the one behind the glass

Rub, rub away and shine me on and on and on

Rub, and rub until I'm there and the smoke is gone

Rub, and rub you will feel a little childish

Rub and rub, hold your breath and make a wish

I'm waiting

I've been waiting for so long

That I can't remember the words to any song

I can't remember how to remember how to think

> Without knowing how to remember how to unthink
>
> I may seem overlooked
>
> But those could be my best qualities out of all
>
> I don't mean to be mean or short or crass
>
> Just so long as you understand, I am the one behind the glass
>
> So rub and rub and end my anguish
>
> Take my hand and make a wish
>
> Or maybe two.

I send this letter into the void, the space that keeps conversation from actually happening.

Pick baby blue.

Sincerely,

Rush Whitacre

740-336-9169

11-27-10

Dear Taylor Swift,

So, I saw 'Unstoppable' with my (related person who is male and not named). There were a couple moments where I wish I hadn't gone with him because of the moments in the movie that tugged on my little heart strings. I am a sucker for movies that have some kind of plot where two people want to be together but there is something keeping them apart, and then a huge event happens that brings the two people together stronger than ever thought possible. I had tears streaming out of my eyes; I had to keep wiping them away. Also, because it was based on true events, and knowing that the two people were really still together. But anyway, maybe it's just me; I always get emotionally involved in sappy movies.

One more week of school left and then I only have 2 quarters until I have my Masters degree. I am nervous, not about graduating, but what next. I want to move to NY and try my hardest to become a professional artist, maybe designing things for the rich and famous, or making installations for the city or for cities around the world. Yeah, I am totally dreaming when I make statements like that I assure you. I miss painting. I have been working on installations for some time now, but the canvas is calling to me. "Paint another flower Rush, Paint on me another flower." Oh well. I will paint again, I will.

So, after careful consideration I decided that today's poem or song would come out of an experience I had with a young woman named (I will call her Caldwell girl) Caldwell girl. I wouldn't say that we dated, but the moments, just simply magical moments still call to me from my past, reminding me that I am not here to solve every equation. Kim's brother died at the hands of a drunk driver years before I met her, and she was unable to visit her brother's grave because of how bad it hurt. She told me that I could go visit if I wanted to, so I did, thinking that I would understand her better. All it did was cause me to lose her. Some borders you shouldn't cross I guess, even if you have permission.

So, here is the poem, this is for the love I have for the girl:

"Dear Brother,"

"Dear Brother, I never got to say Goodbye"

My world crumbles when I allow the thought of what we were seep in,

And what we could still be.

I fall apart; tumble inward upon myself like a house of cards,

There is no foundation, only empty rooms that we never got to fill.

My memories of you are beautiful, as you are.

You will never be ugly to me,

Because you will never grow old or ill fated,

And I forgive you for this loneliness

For this hole that I keep looking to fill

This hole in my heart that I allow you to de-scab over and over because of your memory.

Because of your memory I am bittersweet.

I love you, but I am sensitive.

I must let you go, and I must let you leave me...

Please let me go.

For I have no choice except the choice of letting you know.

So I choose, and I say I love you

And I say goodbye.

May you find Peace Caldwell girl.

I toss this letter into the void, the abyss between us, this space that keeps conversation from happening.

Sincerely,
Rush Whitacre

11-28-10

Dear Taylor,

What a day this has been. I got my artist statement written, my Resume written, and I worked on my web page for hours. So, yes, I can say that today has definitely been productive, even if it really didn't start until after noon. Well,,,,, I came across some videos today that I have been looking for- for awhile. In my undergrad school, OU in Athens Ohio, I built a home within the school of art. There was an abandoned loft that at one time housed the graduate students, but then it was abandoned because it had plywood floors and wooden stairs. A fire hazard because the wooden floors would absorb any dropped chemicals. Anyway. When I discovered it, it was a WRECK. I mean, trash and dust from 10 years worth of abandonment had accumulated. I tossed it all out, mopped the place, painted the floors and walls, and then hauled up about 6000 pounds of lumber (with the help of my friends, great friends). When all was said and done, we had an amazing place. Even if we had to climb up to the loft using tables that were stacked up on one another. We had four beds, 7 couches, carpet, and plenty of tables, doors with dead bolts, and even a loft above the loft. Anyway, I had video-taped the loft several times, and I thought I lost them until now. I was sooooo happy to see them, and all of my friends once again.

     Here is the kicker, in the winter quarter after I graduated, someone left the hot plate on and the heat from it set off the fire alarm in the loft... there was no fire, but the fire dept, and police dept showed up and they freaked. Then when they pulled the director of the school into the loft, he really freaked...... obviously we weren't suppose to be living there... That incident occurred on a Wednesday, on Thursday the director hauled all the teachers up into the loft to see who knew about it. Four of them knew, but everyone kept their mouths shut. About 100 students knew, but they kept their mouths shut too. On Friday night and Saturday night, my friends who were still going to school there cut the entire loft that we had built into little 1 foot pieces and pulled the whole thing down... they had to, one of the teachers who knew about it gave my friends inside information that they had better do it.. I couldn't make it, too much snow and I was 3 hours away. I guess the OU campus will never know just exactly what they lost. What they lost was the most amazing artist lounge any college campus could ever ask for... All fields of focus, ceramics, photo, graphic designers, sculptors, painters, art historians, etc. could get into the loft and totally have debates and conversations, and just simply share their knowledge about the art world, and their experience of it. Seigfred Hall will never be the same. Anyway, it kinda made me sad to see the videos and know that the loft doesn't exist anymore.

     So, here is a poem about how you can never go home:

          "Risky Loss"

All the people here are different,
Yet all the street names appear the same
And all I can do, is but walk around, unnoticed
And feel so much in the way
Like everyone kept on moving
And I stayed so much in place
All of my friends have gone,
And no one here knows my name.
For all the times that I have spent
Wasting away here in this town
And all my friends who would smile back at me,
All I can do is frown
How I would give anything
To bring back the past
But all I have are memories
Something that isn't real enough to last
I hate it just the same
Now after all that I have done
After all the places that I have roam
And all the friends I want to see
But they say you can't go back home
So I sit here
Waiting for you to call
And let me know just how far I've gone
How far did I fall
Before I hit the darkened bottom
Before I hit the oily wall
And after all where I did roam
Nothing in here's the same
And you can never go back home
I toss this letter into the void, this space that keeps conversation from happening.
  -Pick baby blue-
Sincerely,

Rush Whitacre

11-29-10

Dear Taylor,

Oh man, I am so ready for this break. I need to rest my brain. I really don't feel like I accomplished much, but I know that I spent a long time thinking,,, and thinking and planning. Mostly about my thesis. I think I am going to make a giant knitting/weaving machine using twenty students as performers. Well, anyway. I spent the day working on my website again. I didn't realize that I had so many different installations. I actually surprised myself as I kept on finding more and more of them. I actually have more installation work than I do paintings… that makes me sad, because I really miss painting. I am going to paint some over the break, along with work on my book. My editor keeps on asking me how it is going, and I just tell her that I am too busy with school to work on it right now.. lol. When I met her my book was 1244 pages long, which is waaaaay too long, and now I have it edited down to 675 pages, and maybe by the grace of god I may have it down closer to 400 by the end of December… I am keeping my fingers crossed, let's see, that is about 24 pages a day I will have to edit in order to get it done. I think I can do it...

So, today was my last day in graduate critique, and I am sooooo happy about that fact, it was the worst class I have had at UC. They put the class into effect at the last minute and none of the teachers had any idea as to how it was to function in our education. So, it simply didn't work out, at least not for me, and they made it mandatory. Yuck, and it has to be taken every quarter, double yuck.

Separately from the stupid class, I wonder what dogs dream about, have you ever wondered that. My Doberman is here beside me just dreaming away, kinda whimpering and slightly growling. He is cute when he sleeps. I bet he is dreaming about squirrels, he loves to chase them.

Today's poem comes from my choosing to flip open the book *Eragon* to a random page and point blindly into it. The line I pointed at read; "I am trusting you not to do anything stupid."

"I Trust"

And you've never let me down,

All the while goin'round town talking jive to all the strangers.

Spending all my thoughtful words of how much I love you

Buying nothing you can show me, having reasons less to stay

Yet you stay, and I stay with you anyway

And I wish, I hope that I may make you happy

For all that I have are your actions, sprinkled like angel-dust

And even though I feel so stupid you still give me a reason

You keep holding me and I hold on and trust

I trust without a pause, and I trust for I can't see the flaws

And even if you break my heart into pieces

I will know that I can trust, and that I could trust again

That I could let my heart go, and reel it back in,

S l o w l y.

And so I Trust

I trust with my eyes closed, walking forward,

tears flowing

And you guide me into the open

Into the vulnerable field of not knowing

Whether you love me, or love me not

I will always be by your side

Because I love you, even if you forgot

And even if you break my little heart,

into a thousand littler pieces

There will be a thousand little reasons

For why my trust for you is ceaseless

And so I trust,

That I will trust you again

For you Taylor, pick baby blue.

I toss this letter into the void, the abyss between two people, this space that keeps conversation from happening.

'And so I trust"

Rush Whitacre

11-30-10

Dear Taylor Swift,

    Ok Ok Ok, so, again, my dogs have somehow found another pair of my shoes and chewed them into bits. And when I came in the room they just were so excited to see me… so funny. I can't get upset at them, because it is my fault that they were able to get to my shoes. Anyway, I went to a movie tonight with my friend Amanda, 'love and other drugs'. Nah, it really wasn't that great, I actually like the 'Unstoppable' movie with Denzel Washington better. Love and other drugs wasn't moving, wasn't emotional, it was just slap stick humor and a frail attempt at drama. Even if critics call Unstoppable stoppable, at least it had true emotional tension between the guy who stopped the train and the woman he loved, as she was watching the whole train-thing happen on TV. Maybe it is just me, but heartbreaking moments in movies just get me good…

This is how my day went; got in bed around 2 am, woke up at 6:30 am, taught at 8 to 11, had class from 11 to 12:30, then walk the dogs, eat, and then rush back to school for a meeting with my thesis committee at 2, then an artist lecture at 5, and then walk the dogs again at 6 something, and then rest for minute before my roommate shows me that the radiator from above us is leaking down through the ceiling onto his wall and bedroom floor. They recently redid some things on the valves on the entire apt building. I think someone didn't turn the wrench hard enough. After waiting for an hour for a landlord who didn't send help I got on facebook and discovered that my friend Amanda was bored and wanted something to do, so, I cured her boredom, at least I think I did. It was hard to tell from all the texts her boyfriends kept on sending. Trust me, we are just friends, I don't roll with the whole idea of trying to take girls from their guys. I guess in all of my relationships now that I think of it, I am the guy who has the bad things happen to him that end the relationship. Well, I don't need to, and simply won't bore you with my personal life. Just know that I have had my share of broken hearts, and I can sympathize with the Hathaway character in the movie and how because she is sick, guys have broken her heart because they don't want to be with a sick girl. I don't know if you have had your heart broken, I mean really broken to where you call you mom crying. Well, I have, twice, and it sucks. Lol, why am I talking to Taylor Swift about this… Well anyway, I am sure that letters like mine keep life just a tad bit interesting. But back to the subject at hand, the whole broken heart thing, and I've kept telling myself to keep on being a good person, keep trusting, and keep working hard and I will find her, or she will find me, or somehow we will find each other. And I am sure that will happen, well, actually no, I don't think that will just happen, but I am still positive that it very well could. See, I don't know if you've had your heart broken in the past, but my guess is that you have and I am sure it hurt a lot, and I am sure the person who did it has regrets, most likely a lot more than he realizes.

So, here is another poem, it's about connectedness, kinda.

"This End for That End"

When the wind blows

The pines outside my window

Beckon my eyes to their sway

And I am helpless, I am ensnared

I am captivated as the pine

Rocks its limbs as a mother

As a mother rocks her baby

Soothing repetitive motion

Like an ocean that laps upon the shore

As the wind blows her hair

Adrift, flipping like paper in a fan.

When the wind blows

I am free of all the worries in the world

I know that I am not alone

That all the air that touches me

Is touching you, and you also

Can't help but be moved,

You can't help but be connected

To the pine, to the ocean, to me

I Toss this letter into the void, the uncertain trip it makes into the abyss for whose eyes I do not know, to a place that keeps conversation from happening.

Pick baby blue,

Sincerely,

Rush Whitacre

12-1-10

Dear Taylor,

    What an interesting day today has been. Besides the walking of my dogs, I have gone to the bank twice, post office twice, soon to be a third time when I go to mail this to you, I have acted as a guard watching over the apt building as the HVAC guy filled up the heating system in the building. Of course, my apt had three of its newly fixed radiators leaking all over the place and through the floor to the basement (twice)… and it is freezing in this place. My roommate Louis is wearing 4 to 5 layers of clothes. He is hilarious. I don't think he is as cold as he lets on.

    Yes, one more day of school and I am free for the winter break. Thank goodness too. I keep thinking about all the pages I have to edit and it makes me excited… I never thought I would say that I am excited to edit written work. Yeah, that is weird I guess, but, I keep thinking about getting my fantasy book finished and printed, even if it is self published, either way it is what I am aiming for at the moment, to have that little bugger finished and on its way to being published by this summer before I move to New York. I hope so anyway.

Well, I just got off the phone with my (related person who is not named), I had my (related person who is male and not named) show her my website, my (related person who is male and not named) was impressed, he is the computer guru and he doesn't even have a website. This has been a good day, no classes, no worries, just dogs and an indoor sprinkler system called the radiator heater.

Ok, I feel a bit behind the times most of the time because I don't watch TV, I have one, but use it for watching House on DVD, and some other movies like Serendipity, my fave. Well, I never knew about this guy named Butch Walker until a couple of years ago and he sings this song called "The best thing that you never had," and I am convinced that he wrote it because of how his record label screwed him over and not because of a girl. So, This poem tonight I dedicate to Butch Walker.

"I Know who Doesn't Have the Best Thing"

Oh Walker

Why does your heart break so easy

When all of the eyes upon you love you so strong

Like the will of the label, the chill of the cold

How can you hold such a low and yet so below

You keep down inside dreams, dreams, dreams

Like fantasies, they dream, and their offspring

Spring-fourth from your lips to a mic

To the ears of the one who screams,

I love you, please.. play,, more.

Oh Walker

Don't fret about that day, you could'a slept it away

but the next would have opened that door, like a window

Only you would ground, like you floored, an audience

To a place you couldn't see, beyond the lights

Beyond the darkness behind the curtain, a gypsy sign

Wandering through with a message that you and only you

Thought was for you only, then closed your eyes

And the moment waited not for you,

but for the eyes of another

Oh Walker

You were wrong, as we were wrong and it all got wasted

And you lost as we lost, but you lost big and we lost all

So your name was lost, erased from the wall, our wall

So you took down all your loyalty and lost your royalty

Maybe making your worst day worse

And my best day, your last day, bad

and you were wrong about that day

I was the best thing you had

and now you are the best thing that I gave away.

-Oh Taylor-, pick baby blue

I toss this letter into the void, this abyss, the place that keeps conversation from happening.

Sincerely,

Rush Whitacre

12-2-10

Dear Taylor,

     YES! I had my last class for this quarter, and now I am free to do whatever for at least a month. Well, actually, what I mean to say is, tomorrow I begin round 10 of editing for my book… I wonder if I am actually going to pull off doing 25 pages a day. I don't see why I won't be able to, so long as I have nothing else to do right… suuuurrre. I'm gonna try anyway. I have to.

Did I ever tell you that my Doberman has a foot fetish. Everytime I dangle my feet off the end of the bed my Doberman comes over and begins rubbing his body and face all over my feet. It is actually kinda nice because it is like having a really soft foot massage. He is actually doing it right now, which is why I mentioned it.

My (related person who is not named) called me and wants me to come home, and my dad is having his 87th birthday tomorrow, the 3rd of December. So, another pretty exciting Christmas break. I think I am going to split my time between my (related person who is not named)'s house and my dad's house, that or just stay at my (related person who is not named)'s house. I guess it really depends on where the environment is best for editing this time around. In the past I just spent my days at Subway editing my novel. I don't think that I will go there this break. I need a new environment. Soo, I will work on that on Saturday after I get home.

I have to tell you, I am hooked on this Maroon 5 song, 'give a little more', I really like it. The lead singer's voice is like a gummy bear, soft and sweet.

Anyway, I am going to get a little extra sleep tonight since I can and not have to worry about getting up at 5 or 6 to get ready to go to school.

This poem/song I dedicate to the Sunflower:

"Sunflower"

From something so small you spring fourth

Delicate, writhing within a dark place

Waiting, growing, and then pop

You are in the sunlight

Your spotlight of life

Your stalk grows course as sandpaper

Head so heavy that you bow

The world is yours to have

And yet you serve the servants

The little workers, they'll die to protect you

Growing so fast that nothing can keep up to hide you

Or keep you from reaching your sweetness

But worse yet, you don't wait

Your life is fast and fleeting

but somehow, you will be remembered

Your greatness is only outdone by your strength

And your strength only outdone by your weakest weakness

That weakness is my desire

And I desire to pluck you out

and put you in a vase

to live with me

your last days

Pick baby blue,

I toss this letter into the void, into this abyss of uncertainty, this place that keeps conversation from happening.

Sincerely,

Rush Whitacre

12-3-10

Dear Taylor,

Today has been a day of highs and lows for me. This morning I graded my students final projects with a certain satisfaction, then took my roommate Yangue car shopping for a used car, and I had a ball watching him look about on the different car lots. When I got back my dogs had somehow magically gotten into a bottle of aspirin, and I don't know how many they ate. Fortunately I know that they only had about a ten minute span where they could have eaten the pills so I was able to give them hydrogen peroxide to get them to vomit them back up. They are doing just fine not. Then, I checked my email and the head of graduate students took away all of my freshman interns who were suppose to help me with my thesis, and then right after that email I got one from my painting teacher explaining that since I didn't meet with him on the last week of this quarter he would give me an incomplete, which wasn't explained to me, and I thought was irrelevant since I had already met with him three times this quarter. So, my world started out so great, and then came crashing down here at the end of the day. Kinda bitter-sweet I guess.

Oh yeah, and I forgot that my students had also been photo-shopping me into pics of themselves all morning and then, which I thought was a flattering thing for them to do. Well, anyway, I am sure tomorrow will be better. Things always have a way of working out.

So, I go back with my Chinese roommate to help him buy a car tomorrow. I am partially excited, and partially scared to death because he doesn't have a lot of experience driving, so, I hope that I am not helping him into trouble of some kind, like a wreck or something… that would not make me very happy. So, I will focus on the fact that I am going to help teach him how to drive better before sending him out into the world.

Here is a poem about a subject I know well;

'Colors'

Cover me with your

Garments of scarlet

Your blanket of fire and might

Cast away all hues of blue

And scare away my blacks of night

I long to be comforted with

Your warmth and dispel

All the cold and icy death

All hot and burning hell

Color has its effect

On all who it touches

And on all who wear it

And on all bad obsesses

Love is always the red rose

Yellow is never as hot

Violets are for a love long gone

And daisies for love me, love me not

When professing my love forever

Your cheeks get rosy red

I like to see that color

And end my day in bed

Everyone should have someone to love

And everyone should have a color meter

To call their own

And life would be so much sweeter

Not so alone

I cast this letter into the void, this abyss, this chasm whose depth I cannot imagine, into this space that keeps conversation from happening.

Pick baby blue

Sincerely,

Rush Whitacre

12-4-10

Dear Taylor,

    Well, My roommate didn't buy any of the cars we looked at today. The one that showed the most promise was a little blue Saturn car and the dealership was unwilling to budge on the price and he didn't like that, so, he told them no and got up and left. I was proud of him, but now he doesn't have a car to drive still. Lol. Oh well. We all decided that it was best if he spent the rest of the holiday searching out cars to buy, and when I come back from the holiday we will go searching again. What a trip he is, Yangue that is, my roommate, he is Chinese and he just acts so funny.

    Snow, we have 5 inches of snow, well, maybe four in places. But still, I am not driving home right now because I am sooo tired, the roads might freeze, and well, simply put, I am just too tired to want to stay that focused for four hours.

(little side note here) Lol, I can hear my roommates arguing as to why Yangue should be going out to the bar with Louis, and Louis is really good at getting Yangue to go out, but I don't know if it is going to work tonight because of everyone's tired factor. I will go, because there is a pool table, and I like to play pool once in awhile, Louis goes to drink and make fun of people and to get Yangue out of the house. Gosh, what a trio we are, kinda like the three stooges.

Anyway, back to what I was saying, I am not going home, just not going to do it. Not until tomorrow anyway. I reach a point where there is no way that I will drive 4 hours, and I reached that point 3 hours ago. So, I am staying here in Cincinnati for the night, hopefully playing pool, just for fun.

Ok, so earlier tonight I saw a street walker, she looked so sad and lost and lonely. Actually, I think she is a stripper who wears her attire all the way to work. I have seen her walk past my apt building several times now, I am sure she lives in the apt down the street on the corner from me as I have seen her get dropped off there while I am walking my dogs early in the morning. So, I dedicate this poem to her.

"Walker of Telford Street"

Oh girl, what will you do

When all your tears outweigh the money

When you come home

and you don't remember who you are

You look so sad behind that colored mask you wear

And you stumble stand and stumble land

On a floor, to a drink that wasn't really a drink at all

Oh girl, do you wish for a better life

When those strippers shoes

Don't keep your toes from being frozen

Like the hearts of those

Who buy your pain and sell you ugliness

Oh girl, people watch you pass by on the sidewalk

They look upon you with such disdain

As if they would rather see you in the street

Dodging cars, or see you in a dark alley

Chasing the dragon, meant for the lost, the broken

My heart reaches out for you

But you are blind

For the drugs you work so hard to get

Rob your brain of its most precious ability.

To feel wanted, to feel love.

So walk on by and try to imagine my thoughts

For you will be wrong, for I am not judging,

I am praying, that love finds you

Before the dogs do.

    I toss this letter into the void, this wondrous uncertain abyss, this strange space that keeps conversation from happening.

Taylor, pick baby blue

Sincerely,

Rush Whitacre

740-336-9169

12-5-10

Dear Taylor,

    So, here I lay again, at my (related person who is not named)'s house, Ivan my Doberman(thinking he is a small dog) is squeezed onto the couch down towards my feet and my Dane is carefully hoping around the living room patiently waiting for my (related person who is male and not named) to bring her an ice cube. My (related person who is not named)'s cat somehow was outside and I had to get her in past two giant curious sniffing dogs that have yet to have their first real encounter with a cat. Let's just say, I quickly let go of the cat once I got her inside because she went bazurk. My dad is going to be upset that I didn't stay at his house, but that's life. I can't have my dogs freezing to death in a wooden box.

    So, one of my exgirlfriend's added me on her facebook page as a friend. I was really surprised because I broke the relationship off because she was hooked on smoking marijuana, and told me that she loved me, but loved me even more while she was high. I don't smoke, and I told her that I couldn't be with someone who felt they had to smoke pot in order to feel that they loved me 'more'.. whatever that is supposed to mean. Well, she told me that I ruined her life, and ruined her chances of being with another man because I have made her not be able to trust anyone. She told me that she still loved me but would never take me back. And on and on. Sad thing is, she looked up her soul-mate's birthday in 3 different books(I don't honestly remember which books they were, but they were some that had to deal with horoscopes and things like that.) and, in all three books her soul-mate was born on February 20th, which is my birthday. So, of course, I assume her connection to me hasn't changed, but instead has weighed on her mind. Soul-mate or not, she is still into drugs, and I am still not(and will never be). Don't get me wrong, being with my soul-mate sounds amazing, and is something that I think all of us strive for, even if we don't believe in it. I understand my Ex's desire and wants, but I am going to have to sit this one out, and continue to not be with her, even as sad as it may make her. I will say this about her, and I won't say her name, but there really was something she and I shared. I can't put my finger on it, like there really was some mysterious bond lurking beneath the surface, something I think is still with me. Lol, silly huh.

I dedicate this poem to those who have met their soul-mate but can't be with them.

"Divided"

I was all alone

Like a lone swan, my world was desperate

Always looking for love, we were strangers

And the sadness was like a shadow, it followed

I was alone, and then you found me

I brushed you off, I over looked you, I ignored

I had grown blind, I couldn't see love

Even your beam of joy, a projection unnoticed

Then I looked up, you had stayed

Something inside me wanted you to stay

But I couldn't make it happen, make something do something

To keep you near, but you stayed anyway

You laughed, and my surprise, was your curiosity

For I had become so good at pushing away

That I had forgotten how to pull, how to reel

How to make you closer still

Then you told me that you loved me, a moment too soon

And I knew right then, I knew we would end tragically

That we would end, ironically

And I knew that I loved you,

And that I would lose you,

And I would have to learn how to love you

From where ever I may be

But for now, I will relish this moment

And hold you close to me

I toss this letter into the void, into this abyss of uncertainty, this place that keeps conversation from happening.

Pick baby blue

Sincerely,

Rush Whitacre

12-6-10

Dear Taylor,

It never fails, every year my (related person who is not named) finds a way to buy gifts for my (related person who is male and not named) and I, and in her ritualistic way, she found a way to buy a gift for my (related person who is male and not named) and I to share, which usually means, we can share it, but it stays with my younger (related person who is male and not named). Lol, and I don't mind in the least, I am just glad she cares so much and that we can all get together and make memories. What she got was the new Wii, a red one. I laughed so hard watching my (related person who is male and not named) box. He is so out of shape, but he so badly wanted to box and so every other word out of his mouth was some form of gripe about how his arm hurt, or his elbow couldn't take much more. Yet, he kept on boxing and boxing, and then golfing, which was even funnier because he couldn't get the club on the screen to line up with the controller in his hand. So funny to see his arm twitch back and forth, back and forth.

Oh, the holidays, so many things to be grateful for, and so many things I will never understand. Like the mass crowds all lined up for WOW. The people lined up outside of stores because of some fantastic sale, only to find out the store only had 3. Nah, that's just me being cynical, I really like the holidays.

My (related person who is not named) wants me to sit and do some drawings while I am home. She wants me to make some drawings so that she may try and sell them. Mmm, I can't say that I don't object to the making of some drawings, nor the selling of them. I do however believe that she will have a hard time letting them go for the price that they will bring. I mean, come on, I know that I do not have a name established, at least not nearly enough. And therefore I can only surmise that my drawings may bring 50 bucks, if that.

So, today's Poem is about me, the artist, the one drawing.

"A Time to Sketch"

Across the paper

A pastel pencil marks and moves

Mysteriously a

Beach scene slowly grips the grooves
And the moonstone charcoal paper
Disappears by the touch of a finger tip
The boom box occupies the
Top of the drawing by the clip
There are flip flops underneath
There are headphones
And sand molds, sunglasses sheathed,
Shells and brochures
The artist carefully
Sculpts each objects mold
With shades of charcoal
Dark to white and warm to cold
Each tone covering the paper
No color because the gray's bold
As the subjects begin to arise
The artist studies in satisfaction
His meticulous work to revise
And when completed
And when no finger
Can make a difference
He rests

Taylor, if you find yourself trying to figure out a color, pick baby blue

I toss this letter into the void, a strange abyss of vacancy, this space that keeps conversation from happening.

Sincerely,

Rush Whitacre

12-7-10

Dear Taylor,

    Today I traveled to my Dad's house in Beverly, ate lunch, and then chased the neighbor's dog for 2 hours… and I am freezing. I felt sorry for the dog I think more so than the neighbors. I think the neighbor's aren't too nice to their dog. The dogs name was Patches and he did not like me at all. Every time the dog got close to me he growled and snarled, he even lunged in my direction to see if I was scared. I was scared, really I was, but I knew I had to not move or else the dog might think I was either being aggressive, or really in fear. I don't know how dogs think, but I would like to think I do. I guess I will leave that up to the dog whisperer.

Now I am back at (related person who is not named)s, it is 7:57 pm, and I am put up all the holiday decorations. They look ok, just a few Christmas lights on the front of a condo, twinkling for an audience of other condos. My dogs are sleeping on the floor, occasionally being woken up by my (related person who is not named)'s cat as she tries to sneak to her don't food bowl. My (related person who is not named) keeps going to the kitchen getting out her own little snacks, and juice.

Ok, now my great Dane is standing over top of me, just standing here, and now slightly stepping on my side,,,, and there she has accomplished her goal, of pushing the Doberman off the couch so that she can lay next to me… sooooo funny.

So, I have been thinking a lot about a person who I wrote one of my poems for already. I think I am going to write another in memory of them.

"Heartbreak survival"

I have repaired most of the damage you did

There are still some things left,

I cannot trust anyone I date

I drive them all crazy with my jealousy
and I have no more patience which they also hate

I no longer care much about anyone except myself.

I have to admit, I still have a super low self esteem

and a wisp of faith, confidence, and bravado.

I isolate and all I want to do is scream
These things, not all your fault.

I was weak to begin with,

and you preyed upon me.
It still bothers me to feel like this

Like I lost a chance to have something real.

I always felt like things between us would be

evolutionary transcendent

and just so damned lovely.

I tried so hard

I can honestly say I tried with everything I had

to make it work between us.

I literally gave up my sense of worth...
I still love you.

I love you like a junkie loves his poison

But I don't plan on doing much about it.

Love matters very little

When you have to just concentrate on survival.

Taylor, pick baby blue

I toss this letter into the void, this strange abyss of curiosity, this space that prevents conversation from happening.

Sincerely,
Rush Whitacre

12-8-10

Dear Taylor,

      There are so many new scientific discoveries going on right now. Reverse aging of mice, the keplar telescope looking for planets that are like our own, and the search for wormholes using the world's smartest physicists and most powerful computers. I just have to say, we may very well be living in the age of immortals. We very well could be living in a time where some form of medicine allows people to never grow old, stay healthy, a freaky world is ahead.

      Ok, my friend Gari just called me and told me that I would make 'bank' if I moved to shrezeport Louisiana and got into working on film sets. He is talking to me right now actually. He says that I am the most intelligent artist when it spatial relationships. Oh, and Gari is drunk. Ok, I had to stop writing because he just needed my full attention. Gari is going through a really bad time in his life, he screwed himself over by being a jackass at some point, which is really too bad. And I can't help him, I don't have the power.

This poem is for Gari

"Into Darkness"

I watched you slave away

On a canvas that choked your soul

It robbed you of your smile

And the sunflower towered over you

Blinding me of your pain

Of your desire to make something moving

Something meaningful, something real

Beyond the sad layers you kept covering up

You were also the one in control throughout

Then an angel fell for you

Fell all the way down, keeping her eyes fixed on you

And only you, but you denied her

And you burned your bridges

And you walked away, staying with your gun

The devil who brought you nothing but shame

Brought you anger, brought you down

But you are loved, like air to lungs

Like tears to sadness

Like laughter to comedy

You are loved by the angel

And the angel follows you, kneels for you

And you can't see her worship

Her sorrow for your trouble, your pain

Don't deny that you couldn't feel the wings of Love

The draft pushing away your pain, your fires

And lifting you up into the night

Into the arms of an angel

Out of fire's light

And Into darkness

Taylor, pick baby blue

I toss this letter into the void, the abyss between worlds, this space that keeps conversation from happening.

Sincerely,

Rush Whitacre
740-336-9169

12-9-10

Dear Taylor,

 Well, today has been rather uneventful. I worked on my video, and for some reason my computer program, adobe premiere pro decided to malfunction and not work anymore. So, with my (related person who is male and not named) sleeping, or sick, if that is the case. I am left with just working on my book, spending time with (related person who is not named) at her house, and dad at his house. Maybe tomorrow when my (related person who is male and not named) is feeling better I can get him to check out my computer problems.

 Today my (related person who is not named) had some visitors, two young girls who came to talk to her about the changes in her health care plan. They loved my dogs, wanted to take them home actually. I sometimes wish I had as much charm and love factor as my dogs. Lol, not really, I can't imagine being pet on my head as often as they get that. My great Dane has a new boyfriend, my (related person who is not named)'s shih tzu thinks that Sienna is his girlfriend. It is so funny, this giant dog being hit on by such a very small floppy haired ankle biter.

 I stayed at my (related person who is not named)'s house today, but my dad came to Marietta to play bridge with his bridge club. They play bridge at Shoney's, so, I got invited by the club to eat with everyone. They almost had me stay to fill in a spot, but then the last person showed up just as they started to play. So, no bridge game for me today, but that is ok, I am sure I have plenty of time for games. At least I hope.

 This poem is for Ivan

You stand

Waiting by my side, ready to protect me

Armed with a k9 pride, pointy ears, a panting tongue

And a whine of sadness

When I don't let you sleep, on my bed

Your lover knocks you down

And behind your back runs around

Yet you hold firm your belief

That no matter what, you will succeed

Your belief that tomorrow will come

That you will wake to another grassy field

That you will run free and safe

Even if that freedom comes with uncertainty

But, until tomorrow comes,

You sit, staring, looking for my eyes

To cross the path of your eyes

Until tomorrow you will stare from your seat

And I will listen to you, from my bed

As you whimper and whine, talking to me

Telling me of how badly you want to lie

At my feet, at my side, on my bed

Telling me that you are just waiting

For me to fall asleep

To make your move

Pick baby blue

I toss this letter into the void, this abyss between us, this space that keeps conversation from happening.

Sincerely,

Rush Whitacre

12-10-10

Dear Taylor,

    Today I visited with my grandma. She recognized me, and I was sooo happy. The last time I visited she had a hard time remembering my name, so, today was a good day for her. Her name is Ruth, and lived a very interesting life. Maybe sometime I will write some stories that I know about her, or maybe I will interview her, yeah, that is actually a great idea.

    My (related person who is not named) took my (related person who is male and not named) and I to Bob Evans for breakfast, a friend of the family just happen to be working there and she served us, Her name is Carrie. When Carrie wasn't at the table my (related person who is not named) told me about how Carrie had become a Heroin addict and how she had her kids taken away, and how Carrie disappeared for 3 years and then one day showed up sober, got a job, and eventually got custody of her kids again. I am guessing that Carrie hit rock bottom at some point during the end of her three year binge, something powerful. Maybe she lost a friend, or maybe she almost died, or maybe she simply had a really bad trip. Either way, she straightened up her life. I really hadn't seen her since I was real young, like 11 or 12.

So, after a day of running around and walking through Wal-Mart to just stare at all the Appalachian red necks shop for goods that keep our economy going. I ask myself how this country really keeps afloat, because we are so close to being flushed down the drain due to our desire to have our cake and eat it too.

Subject change. My (related person who is not named) just found some old papers that my grandfather wrote, quite amazing all the work he did, hand written in cursive, beautiful cursive for a doctor. My (related person who is male and not named) went up stairs, in his habitual way so that he can avoid the family, or watch wrestling, or to see what else he can download for free.

So, today's poem is for Carrie.

"Carrie"

Oh Carrie,

Can I hold you, wrap you, slip you into

Find you, blind you, push you out through

A door into another room, another because

A drug to feel, an empty vessel, a bitter buzz

Where is mommy, asks the girl

When will she be home, is she at the door

Where is mommy, asks the boy

Will she find us, doesn't she love me any more

"Mommy", says the grandma

Mommy will only be gone awhile

For now you will stay with me and grandpa

Oh Carrie, have all your lessons learned you

Have you all your troubles troubled

Or all your dues still over due

Because no matter what the bubble

you will search for that same high

 all the way come kingdom come,

Or hell's angels wicked thumb

At the end of the day, it will pop, decay

You will have your life your way

And when your high's bottom have bottomed out

You will cry for the lie that you did live

But you will save yourself

And you will be rewarded

With the love of a child who doth give

Pick baby blue

I toss this letter into the void, this abyss between us, this space that keeps conversation from happening.

Sincerely,

Rush Whitacre

12-11-10

Dear Taylor,

    Today was a rather odd day. I started out my morning with breakfast with (related person who is not named) and my (related person who is male and not named), and the middle of it with my dad at the farm where he and I had lunch, and then back to my (related person who is not named)'s house where we had dinner. So, that was my short version, here is the fun version!!

    At breakfast my (related person who is not named) started an argument with my (related person who is male and not named), I stayed out of it, because it was just silly. And of course, my dad called me and pretty much save me from the firestorm of words. The farm experience was nice yet funny. My dad thought that by putting a 200 watt light bulb right up against a pvc pipe would keep it from freezing. Well, he was right, in fact he was so right that he melted the main water line into the lodge, which consequently drained the cabin and drained the water source of all the water. Of course, all of this happened before we got there, and… we had a good laugh. Then, on my way back my ex, (the one who firmly believes that we are each others soul mates) called. She called randomly again to see what was going on in my life, do I have a girlfriend, have I had my heart broken yet, do I want her back. I have to admit, I did do her wrong in the way I told her it was over, but at the same time, all I did was get rid of her – tell her to go away because I didn't want someone in my life who was addicted to drugs. And she just couldn't understand, just couldn't understand that I didn't want to be with a person like that. I guess it is a good thing that she has a boyfriend to keep her busy, preoccupied so to speak so that I don't have to worry about a surprise problem, or visit. Oh well, I wish her well, and love, and happiness. Ok, then the grand finally is that after I got home I was good and helpful as always, and then my (related person who is not named) started again in on my (related person who is male and not named), being mean to him and telling him of all the things he was doing wrong, and then I got involved because I asked my (related person who is male and not named) what he did wrong this month. Well, needless to say, only my (related person who is male and not named) found that funny. Now, I am here in the living room, all by myself, which usually doesn't happen until much later. Oh well, it's the holidays, and in my family that means drama, or, no drama. I guess this holiday, there is going to be drama. And I was hoping not.

So,, This poem is for those who think they are in love, but lust continually gets in the way.

"Lust of the Butterfly"

Growing, evolving, changing

You are eager to gaze upon me

I dangle before you like a pregnant raindrop

I feel your eyes press upon me

My delicate chrysalis obeys your eyes

You want what you see but are afraid

Am I an uncertain thing, not done until finished

I want you to get to know me

See, my insides how they change

They change for you, for you, I change

But you will never know me through

All you see are my outsides

It is not enough, because you don't know who I am

You are still only looking at my shell

I wriggle, squirm, flex my body

My shell pops open, and you have gone

My tears leave me wet, but soon

Soon I will dry, and I will recover

Soon I will forget you, those eyes

Soon I will be floating, fluttering, flapping

And you will wish you had stayed

Taylor, pick baby blue

I toss this letter into the void, this abyss, this space that keeps conversation from happening

Sincerely,

Rush Whitacre

12-12-10

Dear Taylor,

   Well, it happened, my (related person who is not named) raised the bar. She got my (related person who is male and not named) and I very upset today, and when she is in a mood like she was today there is no reasoning with her. I am staying at my dad's house for the rest of my break. So, I guess my day started out with a great breakfast, which quickly dissolved into a mess, which resulted in my removal of myself, then transplanting myself to my dad's house in Beverly. Good ol'Beverly, a village, not enough people to be a town. It is only 7:44 pm and I keep thinking that I want to go to the movies with my (related person who is male and not named) tonight, but maybe that kind of thing is better suited for another night. Yeah, better for another night.

   My dad's girlfriend is sooo good to him. I firmly believe that she is the reason he is still alive. He always took good care of himself, but now he just seems to have so much more reason to want to stick around longer. I don't remember if I already said this, but I will write it again, there is 20 years of age difference between my (related person who is not named) and dad's ages, and so, when I was born my dad was 56, he is now 87, and I am 31. I don't figure he will be around too much longer, it makes me sad to think about it.

   So, I promised myself that I would work on my book during this break, but being at my (related person who is not named)'s house proved to be way too stressful and I can't operate in a writing mode under a roof with so much personal drama going on. But, now that I am at my father's house I am all alone, and I feel so free. I have been editing away for the past two hours, it is great! I plan on editing all day tomorrow, with a brief 4 hour break to play bridge in my dad's bridge club. I just can't tell you how much I love the game bridge, I just wish I were a better player. Yep, edit until noon, and then edit again from 4:30 until I fall asleep. Such a daunting thing, to edit over 600 pages in the hopes of getting that number to around 400. I just keep telling myself that it will happen, and it will happen, just not all of it during this break, but I will have it done by this coming summer for sure. I want to be able to go around New York and sell copies of my book to various book stores and maybe put on little acts for schools. Who knows.

Until then Taylor, pick baby blue

This poem is for those who are alone like me during this holiday season:

"Holiday puzzle"

Go

Don't let the wind stop you nor the snow

Enjoy the movies, the mall, and all the miles

Enjoy the bells, the drop of change, and all the smiles

Watch the lovers love

Their cold hands glove

> The mistletoe they don't miss
>
> Isn't a holiday enough reason to kiss
>
> Enjoy the kids playing in the snow with all their roars
>
> And stand in awe as carolers sing loudly through open doors
>
> Savor the smells of holiday food
>
> And embrace people that seem simply rude
>
> For this is the season of good cheer
>
> A time to have loved ones near
>
> So if you find yourself all alone
>
> Then look up a friend and give them a phone
>
> Laugh, cry tears of happiness, and smile
>
> For these holidays will only be here awhile

I toss this letter into the void, the abyss between us, this space that keeps conversation from happening.

Sincerely,

Rush Whitacre

12—13-10

Dear Taylor,

    Well, bridge was cancelled today because of weather. Actually, I personally think that it was cancelled because an 8th player couldn't be found, but that is neither here nor there. The point is, I didn't have to play, so instead I went to Marietta and spent the day with my friends Pancakes and Wester, they are brothers. It was Wester and Pancakes who I filmed in a movie this past summer, the zombie movie I filmed in Marietta Ohio. They are hilarious, and so much fun to work with. I have no ambitions of our movie making big bucks, but I do foresee it being something the four of us can be really proud of. Hell, I am the only one editing it together at this point, so, if nothing else I am proud of myself, and of my friends and brother. They are the greatest people I know.

    So, anyway, I drove to Wester's house because that is where Pancakes works, he is a telemarketer and he needs internet, Wester has internet, thus, Pancakes works in his brothers basement. As soon as I got to the house Pancakes and his friend Rob invited me to eat at KFC. I went. Problem was, I had just eaten before I left, and so, I just had a pop. We laughed and laughed, so much that Pancakes was 23 minutes late back to work and we didn't even know. And then, when we did get back to Wester's house we find out that Pancakes place of employment was having internet problems and no one was able to log in to work for 35 minutes, so he didn't miss out on anything and still got paid. A cherry on top moment.

I really can't explain to you how important my friends are to me. I just love my friends to death. So, after reminiscing on all our times together I had to leave so that Wester could spend time with his family. When I arrived home I spent an hour piling foam and mattresses around my dogs giant dog box so that they might stay a little warmer, because it is getting pretty cold out there. So, 8 inches of foam and 4 large dog treats later the dogs were in dog heaven.

A family friend is living in my dad's house. Kind of funny actually, because no one lives at my dad's house anymore but this family friend. His name is Bob and he is a savant piano player, but he doesn't pursue anything with it, nothing. It kills me to see someone with the piano skills that he has, and could have even more, and then brush them off like it doesn't matter. Well, I guess if he is going to brush it off, then maybe it doesn't matter.

Good news, my dad just called and told me that the dogs could come in because it is just too dang cold outside.

Ok Taylor, Pick baby blue

This is a poem for frosty.

"Winter Wonder"

Have you ever wondered about the magic of snow

Sometimes it falls straight down,

sometimes it blows

Snow comes in all different varieties

Some big, some small

Some so tiny you barely see them fall

And when it comes to packing

Snow makes all the calls

Wetter snow is better snow

For rolling into balls

And once you've stacked your snowman into rows

You need charcoal eyes, a smile, and a carrot nose

So grab a hat, some twigs, a scarf that's red

And decorate your snowman's head

Through the snow you'll see him play

You'll see him run and laugh throughout the day

Just be aware and not to cuddle

For your snowman could go to puddle

So keep him cold and keep him neat

And he will not melt from all the heat

I toss this letter into the void, this abyss between us, this space that keeps conversation from happening.

Sincerely,
Rush Whitacre
740-336-9169

12-14-10

Dear Taylor,

      All day today I spent time working on the movie at my friend Wester's house. Pancakes and Rob were working away, Pancakes trying to give away Stone-bridge insurance to people with JC Penny's credit cards, and Rob is also a telemarketer and he was trying to get people to make pledges to the New Jersey PD. Every so often we all three took a break, most of the time they came to my computer to watch or listen to the various out-takes of Pancakes doing or saying the wrong things, or just screwing up his lines. This was a great day, and now, after I write this letter I am going to work on my book. I really need to edit 6 chapters tonight, so, I shall be up late, later than I want to be up anyway. I was listening to the radio today and a song of yours came on, December I believe is the name. Nice song, I believe the transition from individual to universal worked well with it. Of course I am no song writer as I have mentioned before. Anyway, the radio mentioned that you just turned 21, congratulations. I hope it was a good day, actually, I am sure it was. Birthdays are usually good, usually.

      I am avoiding answering any phone calls from my phone tonight, unless my dad calls. I really get distracted when some people call, like some of my friends, they want to talk to me for hours, and I want to talk to them for hours, but tonight I need some focus time. So, book here I come.

This poem is for my (related person who is not named):

"All that I am"

Looking back on all my memories

And all the angry things between us

I only hold onto sweet sweet moments

Like all the times you came and watched me play

And all the track and field meets so far away
I remember the times you laughed at my jokes
And called my brother stupid as he smokes
I can't remember a tear I cried
Or all the times you may have lied
I do remember endless cub scout meetings
And faraway retreats and farm animal feedings
And all the songs that you would sing
As I drove the van from our Disney fling
I love you (related person who is not named) for all that you have been to me
And I love you (related person who is not named) for all that you could never be
So even if we never see eyes to eyes
I know that not forever are our goodbyes
So I take this life you have given me
And with all that I have use it wisely
So this life is for you (related person who is not named) and all the stake I have in it
And all the joy even if only for a little bit
This poem is for you (related person who is not named), for all you have made me
All that I am, and all that I will be

Taylor, pick baby blue

I toss this letter into the void, this abyss between us, this space that keeps conversation from happening.

Sincerely,
Rush Whitacre
740-336-9169

12-15-10
Dear Taylor,
     Today I finished the editing of the 'Sacra Via' scene for my zombie movie. I can't help but laugh every time I work on the movie… Does that make it a flop of a horror film? I guess you could say yes, but in a different regard, making a funny horror

zombie comedy documentary may be better anyway. Let's just say, I have plenty of out-takes for the funny parts at the end of the movie. For instance, in the Sacra Via scene every time Pancakes went to start his lines he would screw up, 4 to 7 or 8 times and it is just so funny. Even Pancakes laughed today at himself, I played some of his bloopers to him, he had forgotten. Priceless. I didn't finish the scene until about 2 hours after Pancakes left, so I was left laying on the cold basement concrete floor editing away, which by the way, I haven't rendered or exported any of the scene yet, just edited it. While I am lying on the concrete floor I guess Wester's babysitter came down to see if I was there, but she looked right over me, and must have been very quiet because I didn't even hear her. This led Wester to believe that I had left with Pancakes is his car to do whatever, and of course, he was let down. And, to top it all off, Wester didn't come looking for me, so when I finally did finish and go up stairs to tell Wester what I accomplished he totally thought that I had been with Pancakes out to eat or something. Too funny. He laughed, I laughed, and then his wife didn't laugh too much. Oops, I guess I stayed too long. Then I left.

My (related person who is not named) called while I was at Wester's house. She is trying to help me find a doctor for my back. Long story about me, a car accident that wasn't my fault, and I don't feel like regurgitating it right now. I am enjoying a nice roaring fire, warm toes, typing fingers, and two dogs who are wiped out and sleeping on the couch, don't worry, it is a huge four piece sectional, I could fit 11 Great Danes on it! Not that I want that many great Danes. One is plenty. I just knocked on a wooden shelf to see how my dogs would react and they first looked at me and I said 'gett'um' and they went barking straight away to the kitchen. So funny they are, like they needed my approval first.

This Christmas break is halfway over. I feel like I haven't accomplished much, even though I keep working 15 to 16 hour days. I go to bed around 2 to 3 am, and get up around 8:30, depending on which alarm I decide to listen to. Video editing, I understand why some of these animated movies have teams of a hundred just to make the characters hair. Me by myself, I get the job done, but if there were ten of me it would be finished already. I can't even imagine ten of me... I am sure you would get tired of these letters ten times faster. I hope you aren't getting tired of them, actually, part of me hopes that you never get to read them because I must sound pretty silly! Smiles.

Pick baby blue,

I dedicate this poem to sadness

"Forever loves me, Forever not"

Why am I all alone

My chest hasn't felt this empty is such a long time

My fingers feel numb and senseless

And the memories rob me nothing, an easy crime

So this is my space, my place to start living my life

I've done wrecked these ships at the end of relation

And baited these hooks knowing my line's not strong enough

So please can you see, I've only got a little of me

Living in the moment, feels so cold, feels so right

I just want one close, a hand to hold tonight

And if you've ever seen someone else love another

You know that your forever doesn't have an other

You are alone, all the world and the people in it; blind

They walk past you, but they don't see you, they've already seen your kind

They see they can't walk through you, but around

In desperation you say 'I love you' to each person who's in frown

And still, you are rejected, you are indeed a bit desperate

So keep looking, don't give up, and don't even a little fret

You are just alone, and alone isn't forever strong

Because forever in itself turns out to be too long

I toss this letter into the void, this abyss between us, this space that keeps conversation from happening.

Sincerely,
Rush Whitacre
740-336-9169

12-16-10
Dear Taylor,

    We have 5 inches of snow outside! My dogs love it, they run around eating it like some treat. I didn't get to work on the editing of the movie, but I didn't drive all over Marietta re-filming all the various spots my crew and I filmed last summer. I figure that it doesn't hurt to have two different seasons just in case I want to let the viewers see Marietta in the winter. When I got to my friend Wester's house I discovered that I was the only one there, I spent longer in Marietta than I had suspected, oops. So I came home, and here I am once again. Me, my two dogs, and another fire in the fireplace. That's kind of a funny word: fireplace, quite literal, the place of fire. Unfortunately, the fire place doesn't heat this house too well. The way my dad built this house makes it beautiful, but the cold windows seem to let the cold fly in! the kitchen and living room on both the front and back of the house are just two massive walls of glass, nice for the views.

So, this friend of mine, her name is Maggie(I am changing the name because the internet is way too easy for finding people.) She lives in Columbus Ohio and graduated from OU the same time as me, only she was in the photo major. Most of her portfolio is of herself naked in various poses, nothing perverted that I ever saw, just tasteful nudes. Anyway, she asked me if I had found my 'lucky' lady. And of course when I said no she razzed me about it for at least 20 minutes, maybe thirty. I laughed at most of the things she was saying, most. Now that I think of it, I hope she wasn't hinting around that she wanted me because that would never happen. Sorry, but Maggie and I are just way too different. I remember in our last year at OU she slept around on her boyfriend, multiple times with several guys. Then of course he found out from her and didn't care, but the point is, that's not the kind of girl for me. In the end I most likely have no one else to blame but myself.. This kind of thing has happened to me all the way back to my first girlfriend of 5 years. In the end she cheated on me with my best friend, I lost them both. Occasionally I run into that friends mom at a store, or at the mall, if I ask her about her son(the friend I lost) she still says; "You know Rush, he hasn't gotten over that, he stills says that it was the most stupid thing he ever did in his life." I don't know how to feel about that, I moved on. I have had other girlfriends, but not a fit. I mean, I am not picky, I just want the one, but more importantly I want to be her one.

I dedicate this poem to my one where ever she may be,

"You Know Me Already"

Dear One, I haven't been looking for you in awhile

It has been so long

I think of all the times I was wrong

Reckless with the love that I peddled

And I am ready, and not wanting the just settled

They say that love comes when you least expect it

And if you rush you'll always wreck it

Sadly, searching only makes you wait

So I leave you clues hoping you take the bait

Just keep following in my well laid track

Because Love's like a pendulum, I'll come right back

Like a ghost you are to me haunting

I'm wanting the one and the one wanting

So I stopped the search and tried not dreaming about it

> A warm glass of milk, a little prayer and 'I've had it'
>
> But in my thoughts is where you'll stay
>
> I'll wait for you, I'll wait for you to say
>
> Dear one, I love you
>
> And I hope you feel it too

(Hey Taylor, if you see my one, point them to Ohio)

Pick baby blue

I toss this letter into the void, this abyss between us, this space that keeps conversation from happening

Sincerely,

Rush Whitacre

740-336-9169

12-17-10

Dear Taylor,

    Today has been rather boring. I spent the day working on Sacra Via, finishing up a few blips, and started Turtle Mound scene. I am amazed at how much time it takes to put a film together,,, and I am only an amateur, if that. If anything I would call myself lucky to have such good friends who I could push around for an entire summer filming and refilming scenes. And then re-refilming(I know, don't ask). What a mess. First we filmed and then had to return the equipment to UC, so then I was forced to go way further in debt and buy equipment so that we could finish. THEN, we thought we bought a crap shotgun mic, the NTG2, so I had to buy a Seinheiser(this spelling is wrong I think, but it doesn't matter), what matters is that at the moment when I was going to mail back the NTG2, Pancakes checked out my professional digital recorder and discovered that it was on the wrong setting for the NTG2, I felt like such a doofus. I ended up with two mics… oops. It was a good laugh, and sad because of all the scenes who's sounds weren't any good. Nonetheless, I can still use the video to some extent, and that is what matters to me, being able to use what I've got.

    I injured my back earlier. I don't even know what I did, but I have pretty much been doing not much work besides the lay down on the bed kind, therefore, all the computer work I've been able to do today. Yippie. Now I will finish this letter and work on my book.

    My friend Gari called me again last night, he wanted to know if I would have a place for him to crash if he had to move to Cincinnati. I don't really have any room, but I told him I would do whatever I had to, to make sure he had a place to live if he had to make his move to be trained for a new job. Now, I just have to figure out how and where…. Lol, it will work out, things in my life always do, for the most part.

Well, a dealer will be here this coming Tuesday from Spinks Auction house. He is coming to look at my stamp collection. Along with all the hundreds of thousands of stamps from all over the world, I think I have every princess Diana stamp ever made, which I am hoping will be worth something besides face value since William is getting married. Gosh, I hope so, I just want to pay off my school loans and not have them hanging over me. Wish me luck, or I guess, wish my stamps luck. Ha ha…

This may sound off, but, I dedicate this poem to Earth

"Home"

Breathing, waiting for stars to exhale, birth

She calls to you from the night sky, a raven

Words on a breeze, melody in her rain, dance

I call her light, faint, and indiscriminately severed

Her skin bathes me, feeds me, breaths my air

I travel around her wrinkles, her dimples, and cracks

Her water consumed, betrayed by clouds, air waves

I am her star, her star dust, her dirt, her life interrupted

Without her, I would not exist at all, not a verb, not a letter

Without me, I doubt she would notice such a vacancy

She is not time, space, nor dimensions set in place

Her face tells a story, burdened and broken, seared

Full of fools and emptied nothingness, fairies

A rage of oxen, a murder of crows, an elephant's tongue

You watch her heal, decay, envelope, release

She is love, life, and of death, a cycle recycle, then cease

We are her surgeons, her police, her principles, and thieves

She sees us succeed, and blisters where we fail

We are tied to her, tethered like bees to a stinger

We shall never know another home, another great love

As that of our earth and her heavens above

Like a beautiful summer morn, pick baby blue

I toss this letter into the void, this abyss between us, this place that keeps conversation from happening.

Sincerely,
Rush Whitacre
740-336-9169

12-18-10
Dear Taylor,

    Well, Sacra Via is done, only 3 minutes and 10 seconds long, but done nonetheless. I am really seeing how this movie I made is really just a high end home movie, I think so anyway. It makes me laugh so much to work on, just all the different things that my friends stumbled over.

    Ok, so, I rode my stationary bike today for ten miles, something I haven't done in probably a year. I am going to be sore tomorrow I think. Actually, I was thinking of riding it again before going to bed, maybe do 4 or 5 more miles, and then jump into the hot tub to let my muscles get hot and relaxed, and then of course, eat a banana. I've only ever gotten one major muscle cramp, and it was terrifyingly painful. I was laying on my bed after track practice in high school and my calf muscle seized up into one giant knot. It was like I was knocked out or something because all I remember is coming to screaming bloody murder. My (related person who is male and not named) ran in and yelled asking what was wrong. I was unable to process what he was asking, then my dad came in and could tell what was wrong by the way I was grabbing at my leg and by the way my foot was locked in the down position. He grabbed my foot and pushed it up and pounded on my heel. My calf muscle finally relaxed, and I was sweating from the pain. Even funnier was when my (related person who is male and not named) handed me the phone. I guess I had been on the phone with my high school sweetheart and totally forgot because of the cramp attack. She was sooo worried, she thought I was being murdered. To be quite honest, I think that the pain I was going through was probably a pretty good comparison.

    My dad is amazing. I have written about him before. I wish I had the money to erect a statue of him here in Beverly. Anyway, at 87 years old he is out on our hundred acre woods(yes, with Pooh Bear and his honey pot) staying in the cabin that we built preparing to go deer hunting tomorrow(Sunday). He just called me. He wanted to remind me that the Whitacre Christmas party is going to be tomorrow at Golden Corral at 1 pm. I have to go, my niece threatened me, telling me that she hasn't seen me in years and that she was driving in from MN just because I am going to be there. So, yeah, I am going. Lol. My (related person who is male and not named) isn't going. He just recently got off of drugs, oxycodone, because the last family gathering a few weeks before thanksgiving he was sooo doped up that he kept falling asleep at the dinner table, and he caused quite a family-wide discussion about what to do about him. I want him there so that people can see how different he is, but I don't want him there if someone in the family is going to be mean to him. He is still too fragile to be put through an emotional ringer.

      This poem goes to a dog's nose.

"Obedient Sniffer"

A dog's nose is quite a thing I'd say

They're always sniffing out things all day

A dog's nose can find you when you're in trouble

And it likes the feel your legs or chin when there's stubble

And when you think you have a moment alone

You hear a dog's sniffer and then a 'let-me-in' groan

A dog's nose knows the scent of your clothes

The scent of your toes, and the scent of your elbows

A dog's nose will always have you beat

Especially in trusting strangers that you meet

And when your hands are washed and clean

Into them goes a wet dog's sniffing machine

But even better than when they are wet

Is when they get wetter and then they want pet

A dog's nose can find where you hide your shoes

So they can enjoy them like their rawhide chews

A dog's nose is cute in a sneeze or cough

Or sometimes as its rests in your palm so soft

A dog's nose will be with you in the end

Because it is attached to man's best friend

Taylor, pick baby blue,

I toss this letter into the void, this abyss between us, this space that keeps conversation from happening.

Sincerely,
Rush Whitacre

740-336-9169

12-19-10

Dear Taylor Swift,

    Today was the Whitacre Christmas party. My sister's entire family showed up, her three kids and then her husband's three kids, even Anita and her husband George who flew in from Rome at the last minute. My niece's Natina and Natasia got to see me, and I got to see them. I was surprised to find out that Natina was pregnant with her second baby. And Natasia had bangs for the first time in her life, she was so pretty. So many surprises around the holidays, great surprises. We were there for 3 hours just eating and talking and showing each other things from the past year. My (related person who is male and not named) didn't show up for Christmas. I didn't figure he would, but everyone asked about him, if he was ok, how he was doing. I will have to get hold of him and let him know. That is, if he will ever answer his phone... I am hoping to make plans to go to Rome this coming June during the hot season and go sightseeing and stay at Anita and George's house. That is something I love doing, travel. I went to Venice for one day a few years ago, but I didn't get to see much. It's hard to see that many things in just one day.

    I gave my dogs a bath after I got home. I don't know how Ivan(the Doberman) does it, but he can find something stinky to roll in just about everywhere he goes. While we were gone I put him into the giant outdoor kennel we made for him and Sienna. When I got home one of the dogs had flipped over their food bowl, and Ivan smelled like he had rolled in his food. I tell you, he is priceless, just full of personality. I got to thinking about what I am going to do with them while I am in New York... I hate to think about getting rid of them, I really do, but I don't know if I will be able to support myself and two giant dogs, not to mention, a place for them to live. I don't think a big city like New York is the right place for giant dogs. Big dogs need space, a yard or field to run in, not a concrete megaplex.

    I was in a really good conversation last night with a friend of mine on facebook, and then my battery died right in the middle of it. I have to sit in the parking lot of the library to get wireless internet. I'll tell you why again if I haven't already told you that is. My dad is living at his girlfriends, and when my (related person who is male and not named) moved out my dad had the internet turned off, no one was here to use it. So, yeah. A bummer, but also kind of fun. Sad thing is, if our house was a half a block closer to the library I wouldn't have to go anywhere, it would reach me...

"Horsing around"

Oh whirling wind passing by my ear

My stead gallops, trots, now gallops and I steer

A blazing sun bears witness of the day

A creek, a grassy meadow, a horse's buffet

The cracking of my whip
And clicking from my lip
Rev my horse up to speed
Trampling through the meadows weed
And I feel the firmness of the saddle beneath me
Giving me something to grip, giving me security
I need to keep a strength-filled grip
As I make him jump, as I crack the whip
I listen to my horse's heart beating
His breathing fast, and sprint is fleeting
And the joy and happiness of the one ridden
Makes me cry tears for his freedom forbidden
Now daydreaming as we walk between the courses,
Fences chase the road, encircling the white horses
I feel a certain rush as I am thrown from my saddle
I open my eyes and my world is rattled
I am awake, and behind me sits my father's ford
A dream, and I return to the reality of my blue skateboard

Pick baby blue.

I toss this letter into the void, the abyss between us, this space that keeps conversation from happening.

Sincerely,
Rush Whitacre
740-336-9169

12-20-10
Dear Taylor Swift,

     Hello again! I am up to chapter 24 in the editing of my book(28 more to go, lol), this chapter's name is "Passage of Nim". It is pretty much a water path that my characters have to take in order to get where they have to go. It is a treacherous journey. And then on my movie, I am up to a scene called 'Capitolium'. It is the documentary portion of an Indian mound and how Marietta didn't realize it and built their public library on it in the early 1900's. So, I am getting there, maybe if I continue making movies, maybe this first one will be available to the public. Lol, gosh I hope so, it cracks me up.

Today was the make-up bridge day since last Monday the bridge group was snowed out. It really is my dad's bridge group, I just get called in when they need someone, and if I am available. I enjoy the game, the only thing that sucked about it today was my back and the hard seats at Roger's Restaurant. I finished with the highest amount of points, this was the second time since filling in that I have had the top score. Of course, score doesn't always mean that you are great at playing the game, because you could be a great player and just get crappy cards all night, which happens from time to time.

I am nervous about tomorrow. I have a guy coming from Spinks auction house out of New York and London. He is coming to assess the stamps I want to auction off. God, it is ridiculous, there has to be a quarter million dollars worth of stamps. I just don't want to be ripped off, and I don't want the guy coming to be some sort of con-man, that would suck even worse, because then he would know where I live, and he would know what I have to be taken… lol, actually, I am pretty sure this guy coming is the real deal. My friend Pancakes called the Philadelphia philatelic society and then that society called this guy, his name is George, at least that is how I think you spell his last name. I guess I will find out soon. I think the guy is in for a big surprise, simply the amount of stamps that there are…

I dedicate this poem to a person who I fell in love with, and who got away,

I will refer to her as, 'the cold well girl.'

"In the Wake"

You stood in front of me and wouldn't walk away

You simply just stood there waiting

I think you wanted me to kiss you

But I was the one who needed holding

I was broken, stripped naked, exposed

And you standing there before me,

Made me realize just how far off I was

My judgment impaired, and in my folly

I knew the end would come sooner than I wished

And still, I chased you like a wind I would never breathe

Like a wave, your energy set in motion

Rolling to me, rolling through me,

And rolling away, leaving me to bob in your swells

        I don't regret our meeting and how it happened
        You in one world, and I in another
        Bumping together to become one, and then many
        Like my heart back then, I revisit unwillingly
        It beat from many pieces, many times over
        And our embraces continue in my memories,
        Like whispers from a cloud to a lightning bolt
        They flash across my mind, a tropical brain storm
        Passing through just to leave behind its trace
        But then the weather passes, going somewhere new
        And my ocean is again calm, and I wait patiently
        For another wave, only this time at the ready,
        Poised to jump, prepared to ride.

I toss this letter into the void, the abyss between us, this space that keeps conversation from happening.

Sincerely,
Rush Whitacre
740-336-9169

12-21-10

Dear Taylor,

      Well, George came, he thumbed through all the stamp albums, looked through all the shoe boxes, and then packed all of my stamps into his Jaguar and drove off to Maryland. And, I, am left with a contract stating what I can expect and how the auction house is going to be contacting me, and how I can watch the auction over the internet. I guess the auction will occur this coming march, so that gives me plenty of time to wonder if my stamps are really going to auction or not. I am sure the auction will go off without a hitch. At least I sure hope so. I have been trying to decide what to do with the money. I would pay off my school loans, but then I would still have a broken back… and working with that just does seem to make any sense. So, I think what may happen is that I will use the money to get my back better so that I in turn can do more good faster and longer for other people. I mean, sure if I pay off my school loans I won't have that lingering over my head, but then I will be miserable and in pain.

I am kinda jealous of my dad right now. He is at Glenwood retirement home playing bridge for the second day in a row. There is something about that game that is just so enticing. It's like you will never have the same hand twice, nor the same game twice because there are so many combinations of hands when four people each have 13 cards to hold in their hands. You should take some time and learn the game, and the rules. It might seem impossible at first, but, once you learn a little, enough to get yourself in trouble that is, you too will be hooked.

Today's movie scene that I worked on is Capitolium, and I am in no way near the completion of it. I discovered that the mic on the camera that my (related person who is male and not named) had strapped to his helmet for his helmet cam shots would do to use the audio from for some of the scenes when I didn't have a great shotgun mic. I was actually surprised at how well the camera's mic picked up sound, and left out other sounds. So, with any luck, I will have twice as much footage to go through because of that camera's mic. Granted, the sound is in no way shape or form anything near movie quality, it is great for this purpose. I bet you never have mic problems.

I don't know if I will ever know what it is I am going to do for my thesis. I just don't know.

This poem is for an angel:

"So Yo Know"

Tomorrow you can tilt your halo

You can take it, and off with it throw

Or bend it into a circle rainbow

For now though, you should know

That I am falling, wingless and low

Weighted down, hooked at the elbow

Unable to reach for thy out stretched glow

And your eyes watch, they see through me so

Please don't take too long, or be too slow

Or I will soon hit bottom down below

I need you angel, so don't leave, don't go

I am faster falling without you in tow

It's like you are aware, it's like you know

my plan was simple, well thought, and thorough

I jumped, I leapt, the potion I did swallow

You caught my foul, and found me foe

        And I gave you my heart to stow
        My crime so heinous, a below the belt blow
        But not my fault, as a hit from cupid's bow
        Dear angel, my crime was my love for yo.

Pick baby blue.

I toss this letter into the void, the abyss between us, this space that keeps conversation from happening.

Sincerely,
Rush Whitacre
740-336-9169

12-22-10
Dear Taylor,

    I did something today that I haven't done in for so long that I can't imagine when it was. I woke up feeling refreshed and ready to go, and I had somehow slept in until 1… Yes, that is 1 pm. Oh my god. I was so flustered when I looked at the clock that I didn't believe it, I had to turn on my cell phone to check. So, I had a great morning I guess, sleeping and dreaming. As for the rest of the day. I finished editing the Capitolium scene. Actually, it is rendering right now as I am typing this.

    So, my (related person who is not named) found out about how much the Spinks guy thought the stamps would sell for she was not happy. Then she told my older (related person who is male and not named) (related person who is male and not named) and of course he called me all upset. She had obviously told him a lie, because he thought I had sold the stamps outright to the guy for $15,000. He then thought that I could have gotten 300,000 dollars out of them and that he was disappointed in me….. wow, the trials and tribulations of living in a family where one member has the ability to make other people miserable. Luckily for me, a few years back my older (related person who is male and not named) (related person who is male and not named) saw the 'light' so to speak and discovered my (related person who is not named)'s absurdity for bending the truth, and sometimes out-right breaking it. So, I told (related person who is male and not named) the truth about the whole situation and he agreed that I had done the right thing about the stamps. Taylor, do you have any crazy people in your life? I hope not, life is too much fun to spend it being miserable because of someone else.

     I just got off the phone with my friends Wester and Ruby, they invited me over for Christmas, and I am sure I will end up at their house at some point. They are the closest friends I have right now, so, I will be there with them and their three kids. I just love kids, always so playful and energetic and ready to learn anything. Their middle child has a speech impairment. What I mean by that is that their son has refused to learn to talk because he has been allowed to simply make noises and point at the things that he wants instead of learning the words he needs to in order to be able to communicate with the world. Simply put, his learning disability was partially self-taught, as well, as environmental.

This poem is for the bottom line,

"Bottom Dreamers"
All my life, I have been fed a lie
That there was the one, the only
This 'someone' who was meant to be by my side
I have to admit that my belief was not ill-founded
But raised in me by an age of entertainment
And dreams instilled in me by hero's well-rounded
By songs bathing me in words
Melodies of melodrama's
And images that wreak of the 'absurds'
Relationships designed by designers
Nothing left to chance, no turn wrong, and no truth
No need for purification, or for refiners
Because in the eyes of the dream
And in the realm of make-believe
A relationship formed on a silver screen
Or in the hiding from a press so pressed
Means a lie must be created, paid for, and well kept
And for the viewers of this youth have hearts at unrest
And unrest at its best is no exception to treat the fools
Who's lives breed work and bleed economy
Only to be unknowingly treated like carriers, like the mules

Pick baby blue,

I toss this letter into the void, the abyss between us, this space that keeps conversation from happening.

Sincerely,
Rush Whitacre
740-336-9169

12-23-10
Dear Taylor Swift,

    Today has been a long day… I went to Wester's house to work on my book and export Capitolium for a second time, because I had to fix a blip or two. Pancakes wasn't working, but he was there just fooling around, updating his Wii. He has his Wii mod'd so that he can have every game ever made by Nintendo. Then, we all got geared up to go to the Griffith Christmas party. Wow, there were a lot of people, but there didn't seem to be much intermingling amongst the different 'clans'. Everyone just seemed to stick to their own. At least, that is my take on it. Of course, the kids all played together, as kids do. Running around and having a great time. Sometimes I wonder why we ever grew out of that stage.

    Then, after opening presents at the giant family get together, the three Griffith (related person who is male and not named)s, and their families, and myself all went back to their parent's house so that the kids and their parents could open their other presents. These kids had such a ball, just a ball I tell you smiles everywhere, and especially Wester's daughter, she was sooooooo cute. She picked up a buzz lightyear car that got all worked up when you shook it, and then when you sat it down it would spin its tires and drive off somewhere and bounce off of things and that little baby girl just laughed and laughed. Priceless…

    Then of course, I spent the night hiding my pain in my lower back. I am desperate. If I don't find some form of permanent relief that doesn't involve painkillers, and or permanent surgery on my back then I don't know what I am gonna do. I just can't take the pain. I almost, almost found myself falling to the floor at Wester's parent's house. I somehow got my feet back under me and turned around and knelt down on the couch. I don't wish back pain on anyone, and I mean no one. The car accident I was in really did a number on my back, and I refuse, absolutely refuse to let it hold me down, so I just have to find the solution. I am going to look into the experimental procedure they are doing down in Cincinnati when I get back there after the holidays. I saw some commercial about how they can inject something into the disc space and make that area regrow or somehow become padded again. I will do anything, anything to get this pain to go away forever.

I dedicate this poem to a wreck of a young man.   Kinda dark and mysterious… Smiles, I like it.

"Man at the Tower"

Pebble

Of a hate

Come forth,

Penalize the

Indifferent for the

Lack of understanding

Of the rest. With weary eyes,

A look as the visitors reveal their gaze.

Whispers are not quiet enough to keep secret,

Each word thrown at the victim. 'Look down' I say…

'Look at your own feet and see they're just as dirty or worse'

'Probably worse than those showcased in the box in

Front of them.' They're footing is misplaced,

Then their mouths close tight and the

Frustration is buried. Look at

The clouds, Cry for the

Heavens, my darling,

Very soon it

Will all be

Finished.

I toss this letter into the void, the abyss between us, this space that keeps conversation from happening.

Sincerely,

Rush Whitacre

740-336-9169

12-24-10

Dear Taylor Swift,

  Today is Mound Cemetery day. That is, the scene for my movie, the scene titled Mound Cemetery. This is the scene where the 'ground zero' accident for my movie takes place. I was importing the files that I have to edit together. Wow, so many. I am waiting for them to be fully on my CS5 so that I can begin. Anyway, I am sure I will come back to this letter later to finish it, I just wanted to get this letter started a little earlier than usual. I am going to the movies later with my dad, he wants to see 'true grit'. The remake, or, from what I hear it is not necessarily a remake as much as it is a redo, then again, that was the comment of only one critic. And I don't listen to critics, I just go and make the best of a bad movie, that is, if it turns out to be a bad movie. I doubt that true grit is going to be a bad movie though.

  Well, I just got home from the movie, I know by reading this letter that you simply went from one sentence to the next, but I have been gone for hours, kind of making this letter like the oddness of a time traveler. I was here, then gone for some time, then back again and even though you couldn't tell that I was gone you can tell that something is different, something has changed. Well, in this case I have actually been to see the movie True Grit whereas before I had not, and now I can tell you about it, whereas before I could only speculate… lol, and now I sound like a bumbling idiot, rambling on about time travel…

  So, the movie was good. I couldn't go as far as to say great, but I do like Jeff Bridges, and I did like asking my dad questions as to how he thought it compared to the original with John Wayne. From what he could remember, it appeared similar. Now, I find it hard that Holly Wood would remake something and not change it up in a classical Holly Wood style. So, I guess if I want to see the difference for myself I will just have to see the original for myself, or maybe I will wait 40 years for the next remake to come out and then compare it to this one… lol sure. Why not.

  Well, here is a Christmas toast. May all of our loved ones have a very merry time this Christmas.

I say, pick baby blue,

  This poem is for the hard workers who don't have someone to be with this holiday, may instead love find them.

      "Four Legs to Stand On"

Dear Rider,

Everywhere you go you are surrounded by smiles

And you feel happy inside, but alone you are

You approach, and backs turn to you

The smiles were masks, like the mask over your heart

The necessary unthinkable become drawn

And you draw, firing away neurons inside your brain

A depression, an impression, a recess without a bell

Tolling not, because it is not your time

So you ride on, and your horse runs dry

Along with the oasis you thought would be waiting

A life lived for the love that has abandoned itself

Collapsing, the trail is beneath your horse, crumbling

You dismount and let your horse go free

And yet, your faithful companion

Leaves not your side.

Maybe you

Are not

Alone.

I toss this letter into the void, the abyss between us, this space that keeps conversation from happening.

Sincerely,

Rush Whitacre

740-336-9169

12-25-10

Dear Taylor Swift,

    I pulled one of my brilliant moves. Last night after I finished working on the mound cemetery scene for the day I didn't save it. I didn't turn off the program obviously, because I would have been prompted to save. So, when I went to work on my laptop today the screen is frozen and I have to turn off the computer the hard boot way. Thus, losing all of my work from the day before. I wouldn't have hard booted if I had known that I didn't save. Silly me. Oh well, I am well beyond the point where I was yesterday.

Well, I had decided to go to the movies with my (related person who is male and not named) tonight, but, he turned out to not want to go, and then I lost track of time and then here I am again, working on my movie and book. My (related person who is male and not named) told me that tomorrow he and I would go see the new Tron movie in 3D. I hear it is suppose to be the movie of the year. I saw the first one and actually liked it, so I am looking forward to this new one. I don't know what to think about this strange technology, the 3D TV that is. I mean, sure, it is another form of entertainment, but seriously, do we need 3D news where the bad things of the world visually come into our living rooms to get us, I don't think so. Soon we will have holographic TV tables and then projectors that make an entire room into an interactive environment with sights and smells making your couch the only place you feel safe.

And, to top it all off... We are teaching our technology to be us, think like us, work better than us, understand us, and be able to read our every move. Like the kinects for Xbox, and the computer that is set to participate in Jeopardy, and then the ridiculous company that put a satellite up into the sky called skynet... We have amazing artists and writers out there who come up with fantastical ideas, and then we have scientists who come along and pose the question "hmmm, I wonder if I can make it real..." and then they set off to do so. Cloning, fountain of youth, terminator, invisible man, etc. the list goes on and on. Of course, with the invisible man I am referring to the combat camo that is the equivalent of Harry Potter's invisibility cloak. Either way, we are on the verge of many things amazing, one of which is that of machines becoming aware of their existence... lol. Just kidding. I don't think they will become aware, that would be quite a feat. But, the idea is still there to make a computer that thinks for itself, how lazy would that make us... "Umm, yeah, computer, I need a 12 page paper on the subject of the great wall of china, with 5 sources. You have 5 minutes." And in the time it takes to brush your teeth and comb your hair you would have your paper... I hope computing doesn't get to this stage, we could become so dumb as a species. We already are becoming stockpile, do we need to become overstock...

I dedicate this poem to the game.

"A Sure Bet"

It took me a long time to realize

How I dealt you all the wrong cards

Then checked you into a corner, and in

Doing my bidding, I watched you squirm

Second guessing all the moves I made

Trying to figure out if you went wrong

And in thinking yourself into the right

You made your call

You put your heart on the line

And I bid you until your commitment

Pushed it in with all the others that I collected

When the final card was laid

You realized that I had you all along

That I knew exactly what I was doing

And how I knew you would follow me.

You trusted someone caught up in the game, and

You lost, and your loss I soon learned was my loss

And now, the game over, you gone

I'm counting down the days, the months, and the years

When I once again will be at your table

To win back my heart that I slow bid away

Pick baby blue,

I toss this letter into the void, the abyss between us, this space that keeps conversation from happening.

Sincerely,

Rush Whitacre

740-336-9169

12-26-10

Dear Taylor Swift,

    Well I didn't work on the movie, instead I waited for my (related person who is male and not named) to show up. I waited and waited.

    So, my (related person who is male and not named) bailed on me for the second time in a row. I went to the movies anyway, and did a little shopping. You know, they have been talking about how Tron is suppose to be the movie of the year, but, I saw it and I wasn't really that impressed. First of all, it was classified as a 3D movie and they didn't seem to utilize the possibilities of 3D very much. In fact, I was down-right disappointed with the 3D in the movie. The preview for the new Pirates of the Caribbean had much much better 3D effects in it. I thought I would be able to reach out and touch some parts of that preview. Anyway, that is my rant on the movie I saw today.

Most of the time when I go to a movie I think about it, or discuss it with whoever is with me. Tonight though, I didn't think about the movie I saw tonight, I thought about a movie I saw with my (related person who is male and not named) a few weeks ago, 'Unstoppable'. I keep coming back to the scene where the young guy, who is trying to stop the train and who is also being watched by the woman he loves from a TV in her home, how he nearly falls to his death right in front of her on that screen. And she just keeps on hoping and saying come one '__' whatever his name is. And then he makes it, he hadn't fallen to his death under the trains wheels. So she and their son, and her mother all jump into a car to find him, to be with him. I got to thinking about it, the name 'Unstoppable'. The reality of the runaway train, the courage of the two men who brought it to a rest, and the bond between that man and the woman he loves, the woman he has a child with, their 'Unstoppable' love. I want to believe in that. That out there, somewhere is a woman whose love for me, and my love for her is unstoppable, and will bring us through and together no matter what. It's a dream, but it is my dream.

I dedicate this poem to that which is unstoppable.

"Speechless"

I drove past your house today

And you were sitting in the yard reading

I now wonder what you would have done

If you had seen me in my pick-up truck receding

I broke down and cried like I never meant to

In a block or two I stopped and waited

And to this day part of me is still sitting there

Thinking about my life, my words so baited

and why I didn't just stop and ask for forgiveness

Maybe that is my one last wish on my wish-list

Because I would go back and ask for It now

Even though you will never hear this

"Please, please forgive me for not holding you tight

And not kissing you longer

I am not here to argue, I'm not here to fight

And I'm not here to just spend the night

I just want to love you, I just do

I just want to hold you and always you

>   And if deep inside you can't forgive me
>
>   Then help me what should I do"
>
>   The floor creaked behind me, she heard me crying to myself
>
>   For she still had a key to my father's old place
>
>   And how foolish I felt
>
>   And how my heart raced
>
>   And she said,
>
>   Come home you fool
>
>   I've been waiting there since two
>
>   And I love you .

I toss this letter into the void, this abyss between us, this space that keeps conversation from happening.

Sincerely,
Rush Whitacre
740-336-9169

12-27-10

Dear Taylor Swift,

     I worked on the Mound Cemetery scene today. Then I went with my dad to the doctors. He had to be seen, and he wanted me to be seen for my back. I was seen, and now I have an MRI at 7 am tomorrow morning at Marietta Memorial Hospital. Dr. Krupidev decided that if my back hadn't been seen in 10 years that maybe it was time to see what was going on in there. Joy joy. I bet I have had at least a dozen MRI's in my life so far, at least. I had several when I was having surgery on my ankle, before and after shots. Gosh, I don't even want to count, so I won't.

     I was really glad to go though because my dad never tells me how his health is really, and in front of the doctor he had to tell him straight up what was going on with him. He never said anything to the doctor that bothered me. On the way home I asked him if he could be made to look 60 years younger, and made to feel 60 years younger would he do it. He followed that with "Do I get to know what I know now." I of course said yes. He replied: "Yes, I would do that." You know Taylor, he is never going to see the medical advancement that allows us to stay young forever. I am not ok with that, but my father is. He knows that eventually our science will unlock the fountain of youth at a molecular level, and that he won't be around to read about it. I am not saying that people should become immortal, not by any means, but I do think something like long distance travel through space might require abnormal life spans. Lol, the thought of someone being alive and inside of a little capsule flying through space. Who wants that as a life goal.

    The other day when I went to the movies to see Tron I ate Chinese food. I love the Chinese food at the food court in our mall, but anyways. I got this fortune out of my fortune cookie that just made me laugh and laugh. I gave it to my dad so that he could give it to his girlfriend. I told me to tell her that he was much happier today than he was yesterday. The fortune read: "The key to happiness is a bad memory." Lol. Too funny. He laughed and said. That works in two ways.

This poem is for my broken heart back in 1997

> As stories go,
>
> This breakup
>
> Was like a movie.
>
> I loved her with all my might
>
> But on a warm June fourth night
>
> I left for Europe,
>
> And she left with my friend
>
> That was where she made
>
> Her first decision not right
>
> I traveled and my life changed
>
> I saw things I had never seen before
>
> And did things that still make me laugh some more
>
> And all that time that I was enjoying
>
> Back home without me there
>
> It was my heart she was destroying
>
> When my trip was over, in short
>
> She was there to pick me up at the airport
>
> I could tell that something wasn't right
>
> And it wasn't just the jet-lag from the night
>
> She told me about her doings with my friend of all my life
>
> And in my bewildered state I lied, said it was ok,
>
> That I had planned on breaking up anyway
>
> She cried all the way home
>
> And I cried all that night

For I lost them both,
I lost them, right?

Pick baby blue.

I toss this letter into the void, the abyss between us, this space that keeps conversation from happening.

Sincerely,

Rush Whitacre

740-336-9169

12-28-10

Dear Taylor Swift,

    Early morning for me, that is, while I am on a long break anyway. I had my MRI this morning, and I wait for the results. I am supposed to call my doctors office just after 4 to see what they think of my back. I may do that, or I might wait until some other time. I am not sure I want to know right now how bad my back is. All I know is that I don't want it to hurt me anymore. I can't afford to miss any more of my classes in grad school.

    I had forgotten just how loud the MRI machines are. They are incredibly loud, and they make all kinds of weird sounds, like video game sounds. I thought the sounds were loud, even through two ear protection devices. One was ear plugs, and the other was ear protection ear muffs like used at a gun range. I heard every blip, bleep, and bloop.

    I finished the Mound Cemetery scene, it is exporting right now. It was just under 9 minutes long. I need to add up what I have so far as time goes. I would like to have just over an hour of time... I am doubting that I will have enough video to make that goal, but it is going to be close. This Cemetery scene is one of the crucial parts of the video. This is the part where we end our day of Geocaching and my (related person who is male and not named) gets hurt on the mound. This is the beginning of something very very very old, something from the ancient Indians infects my (related person who is male and not named) at this point, but it doesn't reveal itself until later that night. See, the next two scenes are, Pancakes, Wester, and I go to a bar to "celebrate" the ending of the Geocaching documentary, and while we are there my (related person who is male and not named) (related person who is male and not named) goes to Wester's house to work on his helmet cam footage and the website... Ok, ok, I feel myself telling too much, and even if the movie is a C+ movie, I still don't want to give much away. I am more excited to just work on it than what I think it will accomplish anywhere. I actually don't see it making any money, none. For starters, the sound is crap, just crap. Oh well, that part doesn't matter to me, what matters to me is the experience of getting a group of people to do what I asked them to do, and in some fashion, succeed in putting all the scenes together to make a coherent film. Yep, that's pretty much it.

      I dedicate this poem to rock climbing

"Faithful Falling"

There are few words that need to be understood in the challenge to follow the leader

Slack, rope, and falling are necessary, these few to say the least

Where foot holds disappear on vertical faces,

Hand holds can too

Leaving you with two options

Learn to spin a web

Or learn to place your gear well

Because if you fall

You fall on faith

Faith in the rope you are tied to

Faith in the gear you place

Faith in your partner

Climbing means something special to me

Down there the world is corrupt,

And violent and people are, well, just people

Some you can trust,

Some you want to trust, and some, no thanks

Up here I climb only with people I trust

Up here life is simple

Up here I am happy

I am free.

Pick Baby blue,

I toss this letter into the void, the abyss between us, this space that keeps conversation from happening.

Sincerely,
Rush Whitacre

740-336-9169

12-29-10

Dear Taylor Swift,

    Today I drove back to Cincinnati. I arrived and unpacked and my Chinese roommate was so happy to see me. And he was surprised because I didn't tell him I was coming home. He and I went shopping after I got home. I didn't have any groceries, and I also didn't have any dog food. I love my dogs, but I have to sell them. I don't want to wait until the last minute and sell them before moving home and then to NY, plus, I don't want to burden my pets with my family, they don't have the means or time to take care of them. It makes me sad to think of them being gone, but, I just have to do what is right for them too. I can't have two giant dogs in a small apt in NY either. Plus, when I am in NY I am sure I will be busy with work and making deals for better position in life, or better shows, or better galleries. Who knows…

    In the last 20 minutes I have found myself to be actually rather sad. I think I know why, a combination of things. Realization of having to sell the dogs, so many bills tossed my way by my roommate who collected the mail while I was gone, thinking about my back and the pain it causes me, I hate feeling like I am out of shape(although I am sure I am), and the sudden missing of my family, friends, neighbors back home. I guess I never realized how much better I feel around the people who genuinely care about me. Huh, how about that.

    Ok, enough of that. So, as soon as I got back to Cincinnati the first thing I did was take the dogs to the open grassy area on campus and they ran around like wild animals, well, yeah, wild. Then I had to visit my studio and water my plants. I have a small collection of exotic plants that I had a friend water once for me while I was away. He did a good job, only two of them I think are going to die, they were already on their way out, so to speak… One of my Succulents grew so much that it ran into a self and the top of it got malformed and turned sideways, so it has this four foot body and then the head of it is weird and crooked. I am curious to see if over the next few months as to whether it straightens itself out… Maybe it will, maybe it won't. either way I will love it.. Now it has a memory of my studio.

This Poem is for the joker rider

"Implied Diamond"

I

And you

Are always thinking

Wondering about the world

Questioning the bad and good

> Looking at others to check ourselves
> If they're smiling does that mean happiness
> Or does their smiling represent long lost retribution
> Some dissolved karma form meant to dissatisfy
> Nothing really meant to hurt, illusion
> Just trickery played on minds
> Leaving you feeling odd
> And sometimes lost
> Never broken
> Whole

Pick baby blue,

I toss this letter into the void, the abyss between us, this space that keeps conversation from happening.

Sincerely,
Rush Whitacre
740-336-9169

12-30-10
Dear Taylor Swift,

    Today was a rather quick day. I woke up in my bed in Cincinnati and before I knew it, it was 2 pm and I had to go to the studio to do some work. My professors would like to see my model of the space where I will be having my thesis show. So, I printed out all the walls of my show area and assembled them together, tomorrow I think I will fix them into position on the walls I have made out of foam core. I guess I had better be focusing on what time my classes are this quarter. I haven't even thought about looking up there times, I will do that tomorrow. No need to worry about that until the last minute I suppose…

    So, I posted my two dogs on craigslist today, and put out a cry for help on facebook for help locating a good home, or homes for my dogs. I hate to see them go, but, it is better this way, better for them, and better for me. I have already had two people say they will help me out on facebook. That site is so ridiculous, a social network of social networks. I hate it, and I love it, I guess you could say that I have a love/hate relationship with facebook. Wow, my (related person who is male and not named) just got onto facebook and asked me why I was selling the dogs, I think he is going to get upset with me, maybe. That is ok though, they are my dogs, and he has never taken care of them, nor does he have a responsible bone in his body.

My roommate Louis just left to go to happening down at northside tavern. He has so many friends it is great. I mean, great for him because he gets out and they can drive him where ever they are going, and he is a really funny guy, and I can see why people want him around. And he does dress well. He told me that he stopped buying t-shirts years ago so that he could only have nice dress shirts to wear. I guess that makes sense, then again, I like to relax once in awhile, so a T is for me during those times. Speaking of T's, I think I will put on right now.

Ok, let me see, I covered the dogs pretty good, and my day at the studio, and my facebook adventures. Now, it is time for a poem.

This Poem is for a Wimer…

"Waiting for the Fall"
Oh little lass of fallen embers
Whose mothers heart of glass never remembers
And oh the boys will treat you right
When their gone the bugs will bite in the night
Smiles while telling lies will all be seen through
Because a reputation is gone with one false due
And collecting hearts in autumn is like a rock against a wall
With a little touch they all begin to fall
So straighten out your affairs and do this wisely
Before long your days will be short and you will smile nicely
And all the leaves that you've collected
Will disappear, fade away, never inspected
And with this loss of hate, love, dissatisfaction
Comes your personalities panicky reaction
So smile dear and don't hold your breath in long
And don't wait around for leaves to fall in the wrong
Wait my cherried piper and the right one will fall at your shoe
And in his walk, and with his talk, you will think he always knew

Pick baby blue,

I toss this letter into the void, the abyss between us, this space that keeps conversation from happening.

Sincerely,
Rush Whitacre
740-336-9169

12-31-10

Dear Taylor Swift,

    Long day at the studio, and all I got done was collaging photo's together to make the walls and floors of the space where my thesis will take place. It was quite an ordeal too. A few years back I found a dozen or so laser jet printers out by a dumpster at Ohio University. I picked up four of them, and took all the other cartridges thinking that I would have quite a supply to print with, well, I do actually, and thank goodness because I do a lot of printing… well, the other side of the coin to the free printers is that I have found out why they were being thrown away. Lol, almost every time I try to print I have to open the printer up and act like I am checking for a paper jam, and then when I shut it up it will print once page at a time… how about that for a day of printing out many many pages… yeah, funny ha ha, not funny fun.

    I can't stop laughing, I have all the episodes of House, and he is just soooo dang funny. There are a lot of doctors in my family, and I have been around doctors all of my life, and to see a brilliant doctor like House going around doing whatever it takes to get the answer, and in most cases, he saves his patients lives. House is so funny with his turn of phrases, and his funny wit, and then there is his friend Wilson, who he tests most of all out of everyone. Poor Wilson. House does everything to keep Wilson from ever getting one up on him. I think any way, except maybe there was an episode where House fell to the floor because Wilson had sawn House's cane in almost in half and then in one of House's rampages towards the end of the show Wilson is beside him and the cane snaps in half and House drops to the floor, wham. Victory for Wilson. Lol.

    Well, it is new years eve, and I have a group of friends waiting for me down at a place called Grammers, at least I think it is. So, I will make this quick, or maybe quicker than usual.

    This poem is for is for love at new years,
                    Ring the bell
                    Ring the bell

> And lean in close dear
> Come here close, come here near
> And throw confetti, and keep on dancing
> Look at all the people, the people romancing
> The laughing people, the happy people
> Now, join me, hand in hand beneath the steeple
> And kiss me, and never let me go
> And hold me, and make the time go slow
> Because I want to start this thing we have right
> And I want it to start tonight
> And Oh, watch as the ball drops in fits
> And these seconds feel like minutes
> And we turn, you smile, and I soar
> And to this day want to kiss you more
> A night so full of fun and cheer
> Everyone should have a happy new year

Pick baby blue,

I toss this letter into the void, the abyss between us, this space that keeps conversation from happening.

Sincerely,
Rush Whitacre
740-336-9169

1-1-11
Dear Taylor Swift,

    Today is a case for all ones I guess. Happy New Year Taylor. I am positive this year is going to be another great year. I am hopeful anyway.

    So, I was supposed to hand off my Great Dane today, but my (related person who is male and not named) couldn't come to pick her up. Maybe tomorrow they are talking. I hope so, because I would rather see my dog go to live with my (related person who is male and not named) than anyone else. Now, as far as the Doberman goes, I don't know who is going to end up with him. My older (related person who is male and not named) who is a vet is also advertising for me to see if we can't get the dog in with a good family. I really don't someone to take him who is going to abuse him.

Today has been a lazy day. I didn't end up going to Grammers, I honestly just wanted to hang out here at the house. I have been working for awhile and thought, 'you know, tonight is just for me, and I am going to enjoy it!' and, so I did. I surfed the net and found a Natasha Bedingfield song called 'Strip Me', and I really like it. It kind of reminds me of me a little. Here I am, just this little voice amongst millions, aiming high, chasing rainbows and hoping that at the end of the day I don't come home empty. I decided awhile ago that if I keep thinking that I can't have something great then I won't. Since that moment I made the decision that, 'why not me,' why can't I aim for something amazing. I mean, if I am not going to succeed then I am not going to succeed, but I will do everything in my power so that in the end I can say that there simply wasn't anything else I could have done, and therefore I didn't fail, it just simply wasn't meant to be. Like Natasha sings: "Take what you want, steal my pride, build me up, or cut me down to size, shut me out, but I'll just scream, I'm only one voice in a million, but you ain't taking that from me" sometimes all it takes is one voice.

Today is Saturday, and Monday I start school up again, teaching and making my own work... I am lost in the middle of a sea of monster, professors whose goal is to push me, but all they really are doing is pushing me to the side, actually one in particular is pulling me down, when all my ideas are on such a grand scale, and that is what I do, grand scale. I then also go back to an environment lacking of compassion, love, a tender-side. There is not a woman at UC for me, I have looked, searched, and found myself running in circles, actually almost caught up to myself once, like I had time traveled... just kidding about the time travel, but that would be cool though.

This poem is for the 'one' voice, thank you Natasha for the advice.

"The Search"

A crowd of faces, try to keep me hidden

And out of all the gray, I am the color, loud and under ridden

You can't see me though, because you aren't looking

But you can hear me, lost amongst a sea of chatter

And these walls confuse you, as I echo to your ears

Making you think I am 'others' as you look into the mirrors

But the 'others' won't satisfy this void

I am determined to be heard, because I am free

                And all I can do is keep screaming until you hear me
            And when you do it won't matter if you understand the words
               Knowing I exist will give you a taste, a scent, a vision
                 A recognition of what you have been missing all along
              Your eyes and ears will act as one, leading you to where I am
             And our worlds shall combine as our pupils pass over each other
              And taking your eyes away only result in an immediate yearning
                For when two hearts are tied together as in soul mates are
                 The bond is unbreakable no matter what the interference
                   From one life to the next, one energy to another
                      They will always search each other out
                         Not always finding one another
                              But when they do
                                 A Forever
                                   Ensues

Pick baby blue

I toss this into the void, the abyss between us, this space that keeps conversation from happening.

Sincerely,
Rush Whitacre
740-336-9169

1-2-11

Dear Taylor Swift,

     Today was a rather eventful day all around. Worked from 12 to 4 on cleaning up all the class rooms with my grad friends, and then had a sub at Jimmy Johns. I have to tell you, I have this major thing for Jimmy John subs, their number 9 with extra cherry peppers is just to die for. I think it is their bread, their fresh French bread that they serve all of their sandwiches on. But then again, I would say that everything they have is fresher than subway, and they definitely make their subs faster by a long shot. I don't care what time of the day I go in there, or how busy they look, from the moment I tell the person behind the counter what I want, to the moment I get my change and cup and take three steps to the other end of the counter,,, they have my sub done and ready do eat. They smile and tell me what it is and I am always just astounded. One of their slogans say "Sandwiches so fast you'll freak" and there is a reason for that. They do make them very fast, huh, I wonder how fast their delivery system is by car or bike… I will have to try it out sometime.

So, after a great sandwich I went home and waited for my (related person who is male and not named) and (related person who is not named) to show up to pick up the Great Dane, Sienna. But before they arrived I discovered that I wasn't signed up for any of the classes that I had signed up for before the break. I was shocked… not a single class showed up on my class listing. So, I had to sign up again. Unfortunately, I was only able to sign up for three of the classes, the other two were closed. I just have to hope that I can show up to class and get the teacher to let me in. I am not worried, things like this happen all the time, and I am not in the least concerned.

So, then my (related person who is not named) and (related person who is male and not named) show up. I cried because this was the first time my (related person who is male and not named) has been anywhere to see where I am living, and because I knew that it meant Sienna would be leaving very soon. They had a surprise for me… an amazing surprise, they stopped off at a best buy and purchased a net book for me to carry around instead of this giant 11 pound laptop of mine. They know that it will be easier on my back, and I will be able to go around and show people my portfolio a lot easier and the battery life is so much longer, 9 hours verses my large one of only 2 to 2.5 hours… I can't thank them enough.

One of my Ex's called me tonight, she found out about my plan of moving to New York and was concerned. Ironic really if you think about it. Anyway, I broke up with her because I just couldn't get past her cheating on me. I guess that is just something I will never tolerate…

This poem is for mistakes that some regret,

"peering over the Shoulder"

It was cold out on the porch that morning when you left

I nearly frosted off my toes, stealing away my heat in theft

And you never did return, so I went back to bed

And I went searching through my mind for all things we said

And all the things I'd like to give you,

Are all the things inside me that I've minced beyond askew

A past is a place we can visit only in the mind

Only in our heart, our dreams, a wishing place you'll find

But all the words for wishing have been bid

They don't matter now you're gone, I wish they did

<blockquote>
Because wishing is for the sad, the lost and lonely

For the days I wished you would just hold me

And all those little things we've left undone

I don't wish for them anymore, but one

And I know it's a bit selfish, but its true

I just want to hear you say once more, I love you
</blockquote>

Pick baby blue,

I toss this letter into the void, the abyss between us, this place that keeps conversation from happening.

Sincerely,
Rush Whitacre
740-336-9169

1-3-11

Dear Taylor Swift,

     My first class was interesting, it was graduate studio which is a mandatory class, and as such they are always interesting because every grad is in the class every quarter…. Blah. I would like it better if I didn't have to re-crit my work again in another class. Fortunately, I am not taking any studio classes this quarter so I don't have to re-crit,, ha ha,, I just realized that.. how awesome. I have to be honest, I actually woke up this morning thinking that I was going to have to drop out of school and focus on getting something done with my back. I walked my dog earlier and I was in tears from the pain of trying to walk up and down the block… then I want to class and sat on a couch, took a muscle relaxer and by the end of class my back was doing pretty good. Then I went to jimmy johns,,, again, and while sitting there I noticed on the wall one of their funny signs, or sometimes, serious signs; it said: "If you do the things you need to do when you need to do them THEN SOMEDAY you can do that things you want to do when you want to do them…. This sign was like the number thirteen to me… Usually when I am questioning where I am, as to whether I am where I am suppose to be in life, or whether I am questioning a decision I am about to make, or just simply am I suppose to 'be'. It is amazing how many times that number will show up to comfort me, to let me know that I am at the right place, or with the right people, or whatever the case may be as far as my doubt on something goes… I guess I started noticing the power of this number in my life in 2000. That was a strange year.

Well, my second class was alright. I was taught by the director of the school of art, Marcus. He is funny to me, so many people seem to be scared of him or something, I don't know why. He is a man from England with a very deep accented voice, skinny, large Adams apple, slightly balding on the top and a smile that just won't stop when he smiles. It is a reading intensive class. Marcus handed out at least 25 pages during class for us to read, and then another 20 to read for the next class. I am sure in the next class we will have more readings handed out to us. Wow, between his class, two art histories, grad critique where I have to start writing my thesis, and the Grad thesis class itself I am sure my fingers are going to wear out this keyboard…

This poem is to me getting through the next two quarters and graduating without having a bad back problem…

"Beating"

I raise my eyes to you ladder

And all your rungs, covered with uncertain travesty

Brittle boards, and splinters fight against my grip

And I don't look down, not even slightly overtly

For I know that my courage cannot afford a fear

So I keep climbing, sometimes slow, sometimes fast

Sometimes up, sometimes over, but never down

Along the way, I've found friends I once passed

Family to console me, to encourage me, to ask,

Are you ok, can I help you, can I make things easier

In my brain I am unsure of what to say

So I say nothing, or my pain hurts me until I am crazier

Just let me work this out, ok, let me try to heal

But the ladder is tall, and steep, and I am falling apart

Determination pulls me from places that I can't say

And my will power is driven by a beating heart

That only knows the world's most upbeat song,

It knows it well, for it practices every day that I can tell

And sometime down the road I am sure that it will slow

But I know it will pump out happiness as its flow

Pick baby blue

I toss this letter into the void, the abyss between us, this place that keeps conversation from happening.

Sincerely,
Rush Whitacre
740-336-9169

1-4-11

Dear Taylor Swift,

    I am in class, I have yet to go home, and my silly Doberman is probably thinking that I have forgotten about him.. worse of all, is that my cell phone died earlier and I called my roommate and all I got out of my mouth to Yangue was, "Yangue, can you take the dogs out." And then my phone died.

So, now I am on break, had to help the teacher make her class available online to the rest of us. Such a weird thing that blackboard has done, place their activation under several links verses right out there for everyone to see, that and the grades area, it too is buried under a series of links…. Come on blackboard, make your stuff a little more user friendly.

    Ok, so, I started this letter earlier and in the midst of me trying to get the projector to work I had to restart my computer, thus,,, erasing the letter because I had forgotten to save it… yup, that is what I did. I know because I just realized that I had already started this letter earlier today and I spent 45 minutes searching through folder after folder looking for it,, then, it dawned on me, my computer asked for me to force-end word in order to restart the computer. Lol, so, ha ha ha on me.

    I guess what I had talked about earlier was the Japanese prints class I had in the morning, the teacher told us that she is using a book that isn't in print anymore and to not going looking for it on Amazon because the last time she checked it was 500 dollars….. and still, she expects us to read it somehow. There are 40 people in the class, and two books on reserve in the library… lol, I am laughing, this is going to be a funny class, to see if anyone really really reads the material. I am sure about half will get it done between now and Thursday.

    So, I am way in over my head this quarter… I am pretty sure that I am going to not get everything done, but I am ok with that, because when it is all said and done I know that I will be able to say that I really tried my best. Actually, I think I will get everything done, but I don't think that I will get it done gracefully…lol. So many classes, so much reading, I mean, wow a lot. So many presentations, so many tests, blah blah blah. I can't even think about it right now because it is making my head spin. Gross sick to my stomach just thinking about it… ok enough of that.

This poem is for the angel upon my shoulders:

"Results Up-lifted"

Please do not rest upon me
For I am heavy laden with worry
And the weight I have collected on my table
Although heavy at times, is manageable
If anything, please lift me up and raise my eyes
Because in front of me there's beauty in the skies
And I long to see it as I curve through this maze
For now, doors and raging storms prevent my gaze
My legs tremble towards the end of a corridor
I step forward as my target is teasing me some more
It is a destination that I have worked to reach
Or maybe it has worked on me like a leach
Determined, choking in the last bit of air
To energize muscles, invigorate heart layers
And I bust through the window, a phase,
Between me and a peace, a necessary longing stays
My angel, I feel her, lifting me from a certain hell
A pain, a rooster crows, and the ringing of a bell
Let me know that I too have succeeded
A retaliation, a rebellion, a re-through proceeded
For I am sure that my new path is much more relaxed
Ancient, well traveled, but grown over it are well turned backs
I continue, Angel upon my shoulder of concern,
Hoping to get noticed, hoping that heads will turn

Pick baby blue

I toss this letter into the void, the abyss between us, this space that keeps conversation from happening.

Sincerely,
Rush Whitacre
740-336-9169

1-5-11

Dear Taylor Swift,

    One class for the day, then lunch, then I went home to walk Ivan, My dad is picking him up tomorrow because I feel bad for him. I really don't have time to spend with my doggy and therefore, he has to go… I think my dad is going to find a home for him because my dad doesn't have time for him either.

    So, I have spent hours now working on printing out more pictures of the space where my thesis is going to take place. Mmmm, I don't know, I think I would like to see it in color, but then again, time and money run against me. They want something like 70 cents per page for color prints,,, so, yeah, no color. I guess it doesn't really matter, the place I am showing in is an old school, the colors are so…. Well, school tan-drab. Worse of all, I cannot alter anything, nothing, that is, in the school, not in my maquette… duh. I guess I don't care, I have the largest space, so I will make the largest thing I can think of. I have been thinking that the important thing is that there is freedom within my controlled environment. Like school has. I have some freedom within the constraints of all the mandatory stuff they want me to do. Actually, I personally don't feel much of the 'free'dom within my major since they have made so many classes mandatory… lol, I am not trying to complain here, just explain. I really like it here at UC. Thumbs up.

    I am listening to the radio Q102. I can remember when I was little we had this radio station back home near Marietta Ohio. And they use to say as their slogan: "Q 102 Lock us in and rip off the knob" it was great because I have a memory of a guy named Mark who use to work for my dad as a helper around the house. Well, he picked me up one day on my older (related person who is male and not named)'s car and on the way home Q102 did their little slogan thing and Mark said it too and then actually grabbed the radio knob and he really ripped it off..He didn't mean too, and then he turned so red in the face, I mean red. I was only in the 4th grade. That memory is a good one. I laughed and laughed and laughed, and Mark was so worried, he asked me to not say anything, but I knew it was ok, so I did, and my dad laughed at how hard I was laughing.

    Oh, that radio just announced that I should check out a video on youtube about a homeless man from Columbus with a golden voice…. I just watched it, you should too, the guys name is Ted Williams.

This Poem is to a girl, I don't know her yet, because I haven't met her, I don't even know if she exists.

"Eyeless"

I love you, at least I think that's it

Is it impossible to love someone if you've never met

Maybe I am only fooling, or maybe I am for real

    Or it is my heart that has led me down this path I feel
    Towards a fantasy, a dream, a lover, a trick
    One of a fountain of declaration by raid pursues quick
    You caress across my mind like toxic toxicity
    And all my thoughts are shredded, a labyrinth of electricity
    Words cannot be made in such times,
    And the letters aren't letters, their rhymes
    All I can do is stare, daydream, an across the room look
    I am a fool, a romantic, a lover, a crook
    Stealing away my thoughts to pad my fall
    And I keep looking into the eyes of an eyeless wall
    Maybe it knows the answer,
    Or maybe like me it is longing for a partner
    A partner who is staring into something eyeless too
    Something that will never truly see you
    Because they don't know how
    And fate does not allow

Pick baby blue,

I toss this letter into the void, the abyss between us, this space that keeps conversation from happening.

Sincerely,
Rush Whitacre
740-336-9169

1-6-11

Dear Taylor Swift,

    What an amazing day. Day started out with me not wanting to go to Japanese prints class and then I didn't go…. It was great, why didn't I go, well it is because Bryan found in sitting outside of his class and asked me if I were joining his class. And, then I did, and I am going to get grad credit for it!!! I am really happy about this, because I was so regretting the Japanese prints class, really regretting the Japanese prints class. There was just something about the class that was making me sick to my stomach and I just couldn't stand the idea of being in it any longer. The class that Bryan teaches is designed for freshman, but there are three grads in it, several adults, and it is team taught, and there are about 150 students in it, half of which either are, or were my students. So, right before class started I stood up and some of the students gasped in air and said 'RUSH', and began waving madly. It was a good feeling, to have student like the way I taught them, and remember me for that.

After my morning class I had a small break and prepared for my next class, and while I waited two of my previous students sat with me and showed me some youtube videos that were just great.. one of them is; Extreme Sheep Led Art. It is really quite something. And then, I had lunch and my class started. Teaching this class was really quite easy, it was a work day and everyone got to work, and I went around and discussed ideas and how to make their pieces stronger. And yeah, that was just about it, then I had to rush my Doberman to my dad who drove all the way to Cincinnati's 275-32 intersection.

Now for the best part of my day, I decided to be the designated driver for my friend/roommate Louis who was going out to celebrate his friend's birthday at the bar. Oh, my, god, I haven't laughed that hard and for that long in such a long time… It was karaoke night and Chance, Louis's friend got very intoxicated and danced like nothing I have ever seen a person do, he was just so wasted, and I am just not going to try to describe what he was doing. Sarah, Chances girlfriend(I think), had to at one point rebutton and zip up and put Chances belt because they had all come undone and were falling off. It was just one amazing act, like a skit, just not planned. Then they got chance on the stage to sing some rap song with really fast lyrics, and he did it, followed by a round of applause, I think mostly because no one thought he would be able to do it. It has been an amazing day/night. And then, Louis got drunk and the whole way back to the apartment he kept asking me if I were drunk, and I replied, Louis, I can't get drunk on Coca cola…

I dedicate this poem to the one who turned themselves purple, green, blue, and red

"A Boatman's Anker"

Above everything else that I wish for you

I turn my back on disregard, and sadness

For what would a world be

If all air exhaled sounded like sirens

And all your eyes could see, flashing lights

Brittle raindrops come apart even as they fall

Sometimes disappearing

But you are not a magic hat

And the white one is late, very late

> And down the road he runs
> But disappearing he does not
> Just as you my dear cannot be divided by zero
> No matter how imaginary your world
> Or how real the unintentional
> The balance is unwavering and set
> So blow into your sails
> And feel the resistance against the sand
> There is no move made
> Beyond a boat docked in a tackle box
> Like a lure, my wish has been cast
> And I wish you happiness
> And I wish you love

Pick baby blue,

I toss this letter into the void, the abyss between us, this space that keeps conversation from happening.

Sincerely,
Rush Whitacre
740-336-9169

1-7-11

Dear Taylor Swift,

    Today has been a rather slow day for me. A meeting with Bryan about the classes the first week, and then lunch. I guess since lunch I have been working a little here in my studio. Mostly listening to music on youtube videos, writing on my thesis paper, and trying to figure out what exactly it is I am trying to say with my thesis piece. 'Freedom within control, or boundaries, or rules, or something along these lines. I just need to keep 'wording' up the paper and I am sure it will come together. Well, I hope anyway.

    I have made arrangements to go to a show tomorrow night and that makes me very happy. Because then I get to accomplish two things at once. I get to see a show, and I get a show under my belt for to write about for a class… only 5 more months, that is what I keep telling myself, when June comes I will be done and I can travel the world, or move to NYC, or do whatever. Traveling might have to wait until I make a little money, but NYC is not out of the question, something about it tells me that my destiny lays there. I just have to get there and do what I do best… which is,

    Ok, so, I think I am onto something here. I keep on pissing off the dean of students here at UC, but with the schools best interests in mind. Ok, so today I applied to be in a freshman class as a 2nd year grad,,, with the stipulation that I be allowed to take it for academic credit instead of studio credit, and I be allowed to take it for 4 credit hours instead of 3… So, you can imagine the conversation I had with the dean over why I should be allowed to take the class… She said that she would talk it over with the undergraduate assistant dean and see what they can come up with. So, with a great big giant bowl of luck I might be able to take this undergraduate freshman class as a 2nd year grad and change the way the school sees learning on some small level. That learning isn't about number of years you have been in school, but more about your interests… actually, let's get real, I am too small and the university is too big to be moved by me… I mean, I think I am charismatic, maybe, lol, I don't like to judge myself, it makes me feel like I have to make myself sound better or something. I just like to be me. Anyway, like I was saying, I don't know what I am capable of getting accomplished.

I write this poem for the one who stole a kiss in the woods.

"Kiss Bliss"

My feet felt lighter than air

The silly trees, naked and bare

Watching us as we walked

Listening to our feet crumple their leaves

And then you and your unique way

Suddenly stopped

And waited in the quiet of the forest wood

And when I finally noticed I stopped and stood

Your smiling face cracked into laughter

Followed by words interrupted

"I am heeding you, I am heeding you."

And not knowing what you meant

I stayed in place, lost, curiosity spent

Heeding you say, I rather questioned

As such, you walked close

"It means that I am getting you to stop"

And as naïve as anyone in my position could be

> I took one step closer, just for me
> And you pulled me in by surprise
> Kissed me on my lips,
> Taking away all my reason
> And I knew I would never be whole again

Pick baby blue,

I toss this letter into the void, the abyss between us, this space that keeps conversation from happening.

Sincerely,
Rush Whitacre
740-336-9169

1-8-11

Dear Taylor Swift,

    Well, unfortunately I did not set my alarm, so when I woke up and my room was still dark and I was really rested ready to tackle the morning… to my surprise, it was the afternoon, and my sudden fully rested feeling was that of a guilty one. I hate waking up late when there is no reason for it, except for when I really need the rest. And I guess I needed the rest. Then I got my two apt. mates up and we went to the Asian market to do some shopping. We decided to go out to eat first because the last time we ate after and all the dumplings that Yangue and Louis bought thawed just a little and then refroze in the freezer into one giant dumpling. When Louis told me the story on the way I had tears in my eyes from laughter. He really is a funny guy. Yangue needed to buy a new wok, and Louis and I just investigate all the different kinds of Asian foods at the market. Then, as we were checking out I picked up some drinks, so Leechee, and Sarsaparilla. I like those ones.

    Gosh, I really don't have time for sleeping. I have so many articles I need to be reading and I can't even imagine how I would catch up if I ever got behind. Naah, I would probably just keep plugging away like I always do. Keep working on my project, reading, and getting out of them what I can, and that's that. I am only one man, I haven't perfected magic, or slowing of time, and nor do I have an entire cast of people helping me out along my way in this life. I don't know. Maybe I will some day. I guess that depends on what happens.

    So, there are more mandatory things assigned to us grads revolving around the class 'Grad Studio'. We now have to go to at least three art openings and then do a write up of a paragraph for each… Now, I am totally for going to the openings, I love art, I love going out to an art opening and visiting with other artsy people, and seeing new stuff. But, us Grads are laughing at the idea of treating us like we are freshman or something with the stipulation of a paragraph of the work. I would rather the stipulation be, go to the show and take a picture of your favorite work, pass it around in class and say why it is your favorite work, end of story. None of this writing stuff when the class is not about shows, it is about your thesis, your ideas about thesis, and well, input from everyone about the work… it all helps in the end, I feel myself coming across too hyper-critical, and I don't mean to be. Smiles.

I dedicate this poem to Emilia, yeah, she works in the office of the DAAP School of art, she is awesome.

"Pens for Wandering"

Oh Emilia

I don't know if you saw

But I rearranged all your pens and markers

And now they mingle with each other

And your slip about your self-mades

Are not like your lost puppy faced charades

And a laugh that brightens even your lowly lit cubicle

Blinding your personality is, streaking through the lives

Of all those who need your attention

And don't fret about not going on the New York trip

For I talked your friend into this thing

A crowed bus filled with students to the max

And all the booz and sleeping pills that some take to relax

And you said you would miss this trip and all

Because you know who's names fill the roll call

And all the people that you will never see

And art you shall never know the name of

They too shall be missing you

And the students, they will never know

That they were the reason you wouldn't go

Pick baby blue

I toss this letter into the void, the abyss between us, this place that keeps conversation from happening.

Sincerely,
Rush Whitacre
740-336-9169

1-9-11

Dear Taylor Swift,

(Rant time, sorry) Ok, all I want in this life is for someone to love me for who I am, what I have to offer, and be understanding that my time is filled with busy things, but not always. To find someone who I can love, enjoy, laugh with, travel with, share everything with. Someone who can look at me and just laugh because they are so happy, leaving me confused I am sure. Does that sound so wrong, or like it should be hard to find…. Well, it is hard to find, I am still looking for it. Sorry, just my rant on my love life, or lack thereof. Anyway, onto other things.

You know, it is funny how every time my Dad talks to me he asks me if I saw something on TV… and every time I tell him, dad, I have a TV, but I don't watch TV. I mean, I guess I have never tried to get any channels from the air, not that I would watch it anyway. I don't know, I guess since 2001 I just lost the flavor for TV. I watch videos and check almost everything I want on the net, and then I also have movies and TV shows that I have purchased, like House, I just love that show.

Well, my doggies are doing good at their new homes. Ivan at my Dads for now, and Sienna with my (related person who is male and not named). He is just so happy that he has her, I am too. Well, today is Sunday, and I am reading, working a little, and reading some more. I have a small team of professors working on trying to figure out if I can take a class at school. I think I mentioned this to you before, but, I am trying to get into a visual concepts class with my friend who teaches the class. I sat in on one of the classes and I just loved it. It shall be interesting as to what happens. My guess is that they won't let me in the class, but I will still go anyway, because I know I will learn a lot from the class just by being in it.

So, I just finished putting all the last pictures into my little maquette for where my thesis will be held, the CCAC. It is getting tough for me to decide what to do. I have the largest space, and I am seeing how my finances could suddenly be sucked into it like into a black hole.. lol. Ok, not that funny really, but I still have to focus on this because it is important, probably more important than most of the readings, because without this, I don't graduate.

Ok, I have been feeling a little down today. I walked passed that movie theatre by my place and thought I would go, and then realized that I would rather see all the movies on the list with someone special, so, here I am, at home in my apt. just thinking about it…

Here, I dedicate another poem to the Cold Well Girl,

"Salt Swept Shores"

Follow me

I want to take you back to a gravel road hill

Leading to a grassy field,

By the school where we met

And the spot where I said, "I don't know about you

But this grass looks soft and I must try it"

In and among the blades of green I learned a novel

A page turning, risky, carefully planned synopsis

Your life, and loss, and hurt that continued, continues

I was a boy, devastated by a realm of broken mirrors

Each shard reflecting a past, hurting me with each bright flash

My self-indulged mind, trapped within its own sad state

Unable to appreciate the you it could have seen otherwise

Melted inside by your words, I became aware of my own

My voice that I hadn't been able to use

My story that I was unable to share

And you standing, not leaving, turning away, then turning back

Hurricanes aren't this powerful, such forces as tidal gravity

I was your shore, and you the wave who crashed upon me

And then you retreated

Stealing away bits of my soul, like sand to the seas

I toss this letter into the void, the abyss between us, this place that keeps conversation from happening.

Sincerely,

Rush Whitacre

740-336-9169

Maybe I will go buy a fortune cookie, see what it has to say.

1-10-11

Dear Taylor Swift,

Another day of classes, another day of learning. Grad studio and Critical theory class. I spent 4 hours with three of my friends at the local coffee shop studying. We had a good time, laughed more than we read. Turns out, when it comes to a critical theory class it isn't as important to know the material as it is to know of it, and understand it just a little. I had a little bit of all the bases covered. Not to many people did, it was 117 pages of reading, and it was really thick stuff. I have this weeks reading downloaded to my computer, about the same amount to read……. Here we go.

I had a bad meal day. Up until 9 something tonight I had only had a rice crispy treat, and a single carrot stick… So, yeah, it sucked, I didn't have any cash and my credit card was maxed out. I just haven't made it to the bank to cash my check, so, I am a broke little puppy until then. I will tell you what didn't suck though, swimming followed with a nice giant hot tub at the Rec center. I just love that place. Oh, and we had a teacher cancel class today, not my class, not my teacher, but the teacher cancelled and the class decided that they would hold the class themselves,,, in the hot tub… of course that was earlier today before I went… but, the point I am working towards here is that once the teacher found out what his students were going to do he decided that it was a great idea joined them… Now, I am not sure, but something about this thing that he did just doesn't sound like it was an ok thing to do. I don't know, just something about it screams,,, 'NO'.

So, some good news is that I have overloaded my schedule so much over the past year and a half that next quarter I only have 9 credit hours I need to take my final quarter,, well, I guess I have 13 credit hours to take because I dropped my 4 credit hour Japanese prints class so that I could sit in on a freshman class called visual concepts. It is actually going to become a freshman/grad class. Which I would agree with, since it is like a little magical nugget that is going to allow my brain to relax and become that much more creative.. I think that every artist needs that in their life, some special place where they can feel their brain being happy, relaxed, growing..

This poem is for Leah, a friend I had lunch with today, she lives 45 minutes away with her husband and kids.

"Café Frappe"

Leah, the weary warrior

Cautious, and yet always battering

Waging wars with friends not enemies

Keeping that smile as your secret weapon

Persuasion of the gaze,

And a dark sense of humor,

like the wall you have built up around you

I know you can hear me through this concrete and stone

Yet you are curiously ignoring every word, every laugh

Every conversation that you could have had

Talking is all over now,

We have all gone our separate ways

Learning nothing of each other

Believing in everything that we read

Placing screens between us

And the coffee, frozen chai tea, and Kalua

Only make flavors flavored

Not wars won, nor battles battled

So smile Leah, and let your charm wash over us,

Making us think what you are thinking

Making us enjoy, that which you have to share

Convincing you are, with that smile

I toss this letter into the void, the abyss between us, this space that keeps conversation from happening.

Sincerely,

Rush Whitacre

740-336-9169

1-11-11

Dear Taylor Swift,

Haaaa, so, they wouldn't let me take that Freshman class for credit, but, I am getting Graduate assistantship for it… what that means is that I will get a letter from the two teachers who are teaching the class saying that I assisted them as a graduate student… How awesome is that. Well, I think it is awesome, just an added bonus I didn't think I was going to get. I am sitting in the class that I am teaching right now, it is a work day, and I am pretty much supervising. Last class period I had a boy cut his thumb and need three stitches, and then today from the same area of the room I had a girl cut through her cardboard and then through the power cord to her hot glue gun, setting off the breaker so that the electricity to all the outlets went out. Fortunately the electrician reacts quickly to electric problems, it was fixed in less than ten minutes.

    I have been having a little sick feeling from my stomach area all day. I just don't know why, I haven't eaten anything weird, or strange. Maybe I am just beyond the point of hungry and need to eat something. Maybe that is it.

    Yup, that was what was wrong with me, I was just hungry. Hey, good news, my night class was cancelled and now I can go do other things, like print out the next 100 and some pages of my Critical theory class. I have two weeks this time to read it all, and that makes me happy, because that means I can read them today, then forget about them for about 10 days and then read them again a day or two before. I don't know, I may never fully understand theory when it comes to art because it seems that there are many reasons to have extra comma's, many reasons to repeat ideas in twenty different ways, and more than one reason to try to solve that which we don't understand, love, hate, reason, difference, unstoppable questions and consequences without actions. There, I said part of it, and the other part, can't be said, it can only be felt.

I dedicate this poem to my heart, as of lately, it has needed a beat of its own.
  "A dedication of plenty, less served by a subtle raining drone without consent"
                      Racing, chasing a dream
               Looking past a wall into another space,
        A world that I can only see through with self-vision
           Thumping at the thought of dream fulfillment
          Or dream derailment, into a sect of happiness
    For there are always, and at the same time, two different paths
       and at every intersection there is a fork in the road
     and for the same reason, a need to look long down either
         beating, drumming in my ears as I day-dream
            As I purr and reach out with my claws
          Flexing and yawning, blinking with love-eyes
      Choosing something that I cannot justify with reason
       Only with this, a moment that no one can understand
     Something that even I only justify with my drumming
    My thumping, my beating flesh, a sixth sense of awareness
       As my heart knows things that no one else knows
           Tearing away layers of my emotions
       Revealing still frames of who I am, who I am not

> Thumping, faster when she enters the room
>
> Upon leaving: dialed down into a muted somber glitch
>
> A scratch in a well oiled machine
>
> She breaths, and I drown
>
> An unfortunate state of affairs.

I toss this letter into the void, the abyss between us, this space that keeps conversation from happening.

Sincerely,

Rush Whitacre

740-336-9169

1-12-11

Dear Taylor Swift,

    I keep forgetting how few classes I am actually in this quarter, even though I am volunteering my time in a freshman class, I sill have so much time free. I am blown away. Today was Grad studio day, and that is it. Next Wednesday I am presenting my ideas for what I am going to be doing for my thesis. I am excited. I spent the afternoon making 48 little miniature desks that were exactly 1/12 the size of the original sized desks. They are so cute, and even have metal legs and everything. I have to remake all of the found objects, desks, chairs, chalk boards, etc, within the Clifton Cultural Arts Center to exact dimensions, only 1/12 the size so that I can accurately depict how I am going to make my maze with all of their things that no one is using. Kinda sad actually. The school is full of all kinds of stuff that their board can't decide what to do with it and so it sits around in rooms,,, just waiting for me to come along and organize it into some kind of assemblage, which I am going to call my educational maze. I was also trying o tackle all the questions I think I am going to be asked, one of them being, how are you going to get people to enter into the maze. So, I decided that at every door that enters into the room I am going to have some items there that a person has to pass through just to get into the room, so upon entering the room they are already in the maze, and I don't have to make them. By shear consequence of entering the room you will have interacted with my piece whether you like it or not. I am actually really liking this idea, it seems so simple it just has to work. I am sure I will be asked all kinds of questions and be told all kinds of things to make my piece stronger. Truth is, I don't see how my ideas can be made stronger given my concern, the materials I am going to use, and how I plan on using them

Did I say those little desks are cute, cause, wow, they are so close to real life only smaller that I don't know how I am going to be able to make the other founds objects to be as nice and real.

Well, our IGA is still closed that is just about 3 buildings away. Tisk tisk, I guess this is what happens when you don't pay your taxes, you get shut down.

Well, tomorrow I have a crit with my class. I am sure all of my students are nervously at school working madly, and probably will be there all night. Lol, they just need to be better planners. Oh well.

I dedicate this poem to failed relationships.

"Parallel lines divide"

What is happening

I can feel this end, this sudden twinge of empty

And why has this happened to me

I am so confused

My mind keeps running, tripping over this moment

Tripping over this moment

I close my eyes

Or I cry

And all the world appears to peer

All my outsides turned towards them

All my insides turned away

And why has this happened to me

I played by all the rules, watched for all the signs

And in this end I stood between the arm bars

They came down and I realized this almost certain fate

Train upon me, suddenly upon me

Your trap of an offer by your knowing, and my not

I decline, and step aside, leaving you instead; behind

I don't know what has happened to you

But I do about me

I toss this letter into the void, the abyss between us, this space that keeps conversation from happening.

Sincerely,

Rush Whitacre

740-336-9169

1-13-11

Dear Taylor Swift,

    A long fun day. Class with Bryan, where I sat in the back and checked out the atmosphere of the class in the back. They were more tame than I thought, just a little more talking than that from the front. I did notice that it was harder to hear Bryan, I might tell him about that, maybe. Right after Bryan's class I sat in the class room where I teach and watched my students run around like chickens with their heads cut off trying to finish their pieces. Kind of funny because while I ate some food they would all once in a while look in my direction to see if I was watching them, especially those who obviously didn't spend enough time on their work. I guess they will find out their fates when I dish out their grades. Some students don't get it from their Crit, but they do from a D letter grade. Hopefully anyway.

    I guess I didn't think about it too much, but the dates will be the same backwards and forwards from 1-11-11 to 1-19-11. Just a fun little fact.

    Tonight there were two art openings, one was at a gallery called Meyers gallery, and the other was a recital that took place at the CCM building on campus. The art opening was interesting, it was a room full of gizmo's that at one time were used to make molds, or make prints on t-shirts, etc. waffles were being made, and with a little bit of whip cream they were delicious. I only heard about the recital at the CCM because of a student who asked me to go to check her sister playing the piano. It was the first time I was asked to go to anything by a student, and, I thought it was wise to go to instill in my students that if I am invited to see a art show, that I will go. It was a great time. I love listening to piano, and violins. I remember last year going to the opening symphony orchestra, there were 42 violins. I had never heard a symphony in person before. When the violins started in on our national anthem at the beginning of that night's performance tears streamed from my eyes, it was an amazing moment that I will never forget. It was like my heart was being lifted right out of my chest, like they were playing music just for it. Absolutely amazing.

    Well, for tonight's poem I thought I would try something different. I have always loved the song Iris by the Goo Goo Dolls. But what I have always wanted was for there to be a third part during the long musical break.

I dedicate this poem to the missing third

"Two Thirds Iris"

And all of those words have been missing

But I know that I've felt them before

      It's the strangest thing that I'll ever feel
      Such a beautiful song cut short by a score
      And all of this waste for what moment
      Maybe a second wind just to breath
      Faster and faster we get there
      To the words that aren't there to read
      Now you can't fight my reason without me
      Nor the truth of the space simply bare
      Then something comes washing over you
      Yeah, you can't read them they're not really there
      Because they don't want the world to see them
      And I know someday you'll understand
      When everything's done and left open
      I just want you to know they were planned
      And all of this time I've spent waiting
      For a moment to be by your side
      When all that I've lost has now found me
      I just want you to hold me tonight

I toss this letter into the void, the abyss between us, this space that keeps conversation from happening.

Sincerely,
Rush Whitacre
740-336-9169

1-14-11
Dear Taylor Swift,

  Gosh, what a day what a day. I am sure my daily activities are pale in comparison to some of your days, but today was a busy day for me. Early to the CCAC for a meeting which lasted 2 hours, then to my studio to work on my Maquette. My intern came today and she made little chairs while I worked on making shelving units. Her name is Meghan and she is a hard worker. I learned that she works at some club in the downtown area, I guess she gets paid by the number of names she takes in. I have no idea what that means, other than she must take names and numbers for some marketing kind of thing for the business she works for, I have no idea. She made about 20 chairs and then had to leave, and I left to go to an opening at the school. It was a night opening, there were snacks, and every piece was able to light up, or had some light component to it, hence the reason for night opening. It was kind of nice, but, it was what it was, snack time!

Something upsetting happened to me at the show. I had this friend last year, her name Saneeya, she is from Pakistan. She and I were the best of friends, the very best of friends. We did everything together. Then, at the beginning of this year she and I went to Wal-Mart once, and then she just disappeared off the face of the planet. I called a few times and she never answers, I text and she doesn't text back, when we talk it is only hello, that is if we even see each other. And we never see each other anywhere. I guess you could say that I am just really confused by the whole thing. Normally I know why things happen, but in this case, I have no idea. Then at the show tonight she shows and says hello, talks to the two artists and then leaves, moments before she showed up my other friend, Andre left saying he had to go meet a guy he might want to date, then he came back in and asked me for another grads number and while he talked to me Saneeya left. Then Andre left. I left in a moment or two, and as I left I saw Andre and Saneeya and the other grad all walking up a hill laughing and having a great conversation I am sure. I looked longingly up the hill at them, wishing one of them would look back and notice that their third amigo was left behind. I am only kidding myself I guess. I would never treat anyone like that, it is awful that there are people in the world like that who can come into your life, use you for a little bit with a plan to leave you once they have gotten what they wanted. Oh well, better to not dwell. It just goes to show, you can't make someone fall in love with you, and you can't make someone be your friend no matter how much you would like it. Not that I am trying to make anyone do either, it is just a phrase I have heard before. Saneeya is just not my type, was just a really good friend.

This Poem is for Meghan, for choosing to be my intern and helping me out.

"MegBar"

She was eager to take over where I left off

Questioning my questions

Changing the curve of my results

Laughing at my mis-cuts

And at the same time

Spinning tales about work in strange places

And chairs too small to sit in

Un-named singers bouncing my speakers

Electricity for eardrums that aren't paying attention

Hot glue dripping, pulling, sticking

> Connecting paper and metal
>
> Resulting in a fixation for repetition
>
> Leaving nothing undone
>
> Raising something of an atmosphere
>
> For a place that only one twelfth can imagine
>
> Miniature suggestions pushing major conceptions
>
> And in her mind, it is but a doll house
>
> A place for play
>
> A world worth returning to
>
> If only to correct my incorrectness

I toss this letter into the void, the abyss between us, this space that keeps conversation from happening.

Sincerely,
Rush Whitacre
740-336-9169

1-15-11

Dear Taylor Swift,

    Hello hello hello, from Ohio. As I heard someone say once, 'Round on both ends and hi in the middle.' Hello Taylor.

    Studio time can be a bothersome some times, especially when things don't or won't come together the way you want them to. My intern didn't show up, and then I seemed to have technical difficulty every time I turned around, kinda funny actually. It was another maquette day, me and all the stuff I am using to make many different kinds of furniture, only in miniature version. I guess I have about half of the shelving units done, and I started on the table portions of the installation. I am slightly worried about my next Grad Studio class because this is a new quarter and I don't know how my presentation is going to be taken. We will see, or at least I will see.

    I just came from a Wes Anderson party, where everyone dressed up like a character from a Wes Anderson movie. I will just come out that admit it straight out that I have only seen one Wes Anderson movie… and that was last night. It was, ironically, the movie Rushmore… Ironically because Rush is my name. anyway, I thought I had better see one before going to the movie themed party… It was a funny party because it was a stopping point for some guy's birthday party as well.. so, in the middle of the party a giant group of drunk birthday revelers come marching through our party and steal the show because they were so loud and so animated that everyone couldn't help but pay attention. Anyway, the night was filled with entertainment and laughter and good friends. So, to end the day like this was a magical thing. I might not have my one and only, but I do have a great group of friends. I hope you too are ending your days with happiness, love, and the company of someone special.

I found out today that my dad found a home for my Doberman. Some man in West Virginia who has two sons and about 200 acres of land for the Doberman to run on if he chooses. I feel good about it. I just didn't have enough time to spend with the dog, and as much as it makes me sad to see Ivan go, I know that he is going to be in a better place, or at least to a place where he will be surrounded by a lot more attention that I could give him.

This poem is for the 'D' in DDT

"A Chair not Named"

I approached you like a mouse to a trap

Curious and hopeful for the tiniest scrap

I never knew that the journey to love could hurt so bad

This lesson you taught me, now isn't that sad

You watched me walk around you

Like an elephant wearing glass shoes

I put up defenses not knowing why

Like a fox you snuck in, you were so sly

And you discovered my tenderness

Your blue eyes hypnotizing I confess

My defenses crippled, drawn and quartered

I guess at the time that's what I preferred

You showed me what it was like to be afraid

And then I caught on that I was played

I cried, got angry, furious, enraged, deep breath, be calm

And I stood to leave and you battered me with your palm

Yelling loudly, stay, stay, you must please hear me out

I paused, but my heart walked on, it already lost this bout

It knew better than the rest of me

Before you, I was happy, but you couldn't see

I toss this letter into the void, the abyss between us, this space that keeps conversation from happening.

Sincerely,
Rush Whitacre
740-336-9169

1-16-11

Dear Taylor Swift,

    I have never seen so many people crammed into a laundry mat before. I go to a laundry mat because I am such a people watcher, and because I like their giant laundry machines that actually work, unlike the ones in the basement our apartment. People are so funny about not wanting to make eye contact. I mean, don't get me wrong, when I think that someone is staring at me I avoid their eyes. I guess that when I am the one doing the people watching I have a tendency to be the one staring, but not on purpose, more as a means to understand what is going on. I guess it is a bad idea, but, if you are just innocently watching from afar, like in a food court at a mall, I see no harm in it. I think I was pushing my people watching skills to a max at the laundry mat though, everyone was in close quarters with each other, everyone was waiting for a dryer, except me cause I got there early. So, behind me were about twenty other people waiting for a dryer. No, don't get me wrong, there were a lot of dryers, but they were all taken, and the anxiety for the others desire to get a dryer was palpable. So, being the artist I am, the kind who likes to give people an experience with my work, I walked over to my five dryers and popped in an additional quarter and could hear a sigh from someone in the back. I waited for about one minute and then took all my clothes out. I got more thank-you's for leaving my time in the dryer.

    I worked today in my studio again. All the desks have been made, all the square tables, most of the shelving units, and about 1/3 of the chairs have been made. My Intern came and she and I busted out about 70 to 80 chairs, it was great. She asked me what I would do if I had a best friend talking to an ex-girlfriend every day. I of course told her that it would depend on whether that friend was already friends with my ex, and would also depend on the circumstances. I told her that she had to talk to her friend and find out what exactly was going on, because if Meghan, my intern, thinks that lines have been crossed that she would have to find out the truth first before making any rash decisions. Poor girl, the last thing she needs in her life is drama, and it sound very much like that is exactly what she was going through. Meghan is a good worker, has a good head on her shoulders. I am really glad that I have her on my team as an intern.

    I watched 'House' after I got home, I just love that show. If ever I am having a bad day all I have to do is put on an episode of house and I begin to feel less bogged down. Of course, there are some sad times on the show, but for the most part it is a pretty upbeat, fast paced experience.

This poem is for the thief, yes yes you know who you are..

"conundrum"

Slithering into my somber relaxed state

Your voice and posture were alluring

And my guard down, as I trust you

I mean trusted

For it is always a paradox

That only those you trust will ever deceive you

In front of my eyes

Blinded by the kindness

And all the promises and lies

I graciously let loose my innocence

A loss not of body or mind, but a loss of self

Of self doubt no doubtless and doubtful

And my brain, unable to rest, burned

Ashes fell, peppered the floor, the wall

Like pencil shavings

Only less valuable

And I reserved the right to not mention your name

Because it is a name that gives a thing power

And you shall not have power over me

Not a little, not at all

I toss this letter into the void, the abyss between us, this space that keeps conversation from happening.

Sincerely,

Rush Whitacre

740-336-9169

1-17-11

Dear Taylor Swift,

    I bet I looked at over 100 journal articles today, probably reading at least half of them looking for a couple of articles that have anything to do with the ideas I have been working with. I found three, and only within them did I find about a paragraph of anything that I can talk about. This, 'Freedom within restrictions/rules/regulations within an institution,' and I am unsure as to how my professors and class mates will receive my ideas, considering this is my fourth thesis idea since I started at UC. I have four by choice, because I thought, 'you know, I am only in grad school once, and therefore get the most out of my peers as I can while I can. I mean, it makes perfect sense to me, but, my peers are kinda not getting it, they see me as using them, which is not the case, I swear, I just have ideas I want feedback on, so that later down the road I might create these other ideas, or put them to use in other works. I don't know, let's see, today is MLK day, and I give my presentation of ideas and present my maquette this Wednesday, soooo, I need to practice some form of talk or something between now and then to show that I know what I am talking about.. there are always so many questions. I guess I will just have to take them as they come.

    My roommate Louis has been gone for days now… He left this past Friday because it was his and his (related person who is not named)'s birthday. I guess they share a birthday, something I didn't know. I guess I am not totally surprised, he doesn't have a car, and he hasn't called for a ride back to here, which he calls home, I guess I never have thought of it as home, more like an apartment between homes really… Does that sound strange?

    Meanwhile, my other roommate never leaves his room. I mean, he does to eat, but 99.9 percent of the time he is in his room writing up journal articles, trying to get published. I understand that it takes a great deal of effort to make a journal article, but the brain also needs time to relax and kick back so that it can reminisce on the past, maybe if for no other reason so that the brain can put 1 and 2 and 3 together so that it might be able to figure out how to put 1 and 3 together, not just 1 and 2… If that makes any sense, well, it does to me.

    I've been listening to something corporate today, there is something about their music, I can't put my finger on it, something about "Hurricane" that takes me to a place, one that I can almost grasp at from my past…

    I dedicate this poem to a Scotland trip, a girl, and avoidance lost.

"My Advantage"

A plan on a plane

Lost as it was loaded

A joke without a punch

Every turn I made you laughed

I tried to hide, swallow my insult and run

But the wings of a plane are only so wide,

And thirty-six thousand feet of air is not a jump

It is a leap of insanity, a flightless suicide

And my desire to be apart from you

Was secretly a lie

I wanted you like I wanted to lose it all

Loss of my will power, loss of my heart

A beating disaster not hard to find

Something I was hiding on my sleeve

And like a fool, I kept it there, wondering

Wasting away

Wanting you to notice and take advantage

And you didn't

So I took advantage of myself

And lost

I toss this letter into the void, the abyss between us, this space that keeps conversation from happening.

Sincerely,
Rush Whitacre
740-336-9169

1-18-11

Dear Taylor Swift,

     Looooooooooong day. I am sitting here in my studio in Scioto Hall just thinking about how sore my feet are from all the standing, standing, standing, and then a tiny little bit of sitting. I think my class is doing great, the one I am teaching. I gave quite a nice little PowerPoint that I made, and then lectured on their new assignment, combining elements of other products into one product that solves another person's needs/wants. I personally think this is a great assignment, even though I didn't come up with it, I did modify it for better learning. Bryan, the guy who is overseeing all the grads who are teaching is a great guy, and has great lesson plans, it's just that sometimes things need to be adjusted. Maybe more work is needed, or maybe the assignment needs to be different,, blah blah blah, enough about all that, I have had enough today. During my last class I thought I was going to have to get on the floor and sleep. There is something hypnotic about the teacher's voice. She gets louder, and then not so loud like a speaker with a short in it, and the class is so boring.

I had dominoes for dinner. I waited around while my friend Chrin Sand cut some boards to make stretchers. He is a really good guy. He found out right before the quarter started that his wife had lung cancer. I was stunned, all I could do is keep saying, 'he is such a great guy, and so is his wife, why them…" fortunately, it was a cancer that could be treated and be made to go away. She has already had her last chemo and her immune system is back up and running great. She was at the studio tonight, wearing her beany had to cover up the lack of hair. I just love the two of them, I really do, and I envy the love they have between them. Maybe me someday.

Tomorrow is Grad Studio. I am a little nervous. I haven't planned a whole lot to say, but I have a lot of work to show, so, I guess I had better get on the ball and come up with what I want to say, or at least write down what it is I have had on my mind this whole time. Too bad I can't hire someone to just sit in and do it for me, I don't like feeling this nervous about something so small. Yeah, why am I so nervous. I should have been more nervous last quarter when I was making up ideas to fill in the gaps. Oh well. I will have to let you know how it goes tomorrow

I have been listening to Tegan and Sara today, 'Where does the good go.' A good song, some of their other songs are ok, but for the most part, this one of theirs I like the most, 'call it off' is a real close second, real close.

I dedicate this poem to my friend Alexis, a grad student

"Printed WaterWall"

Katrina couldn't wash away your dreams

And all the miles of sand

And all the ocean ponds left behind

Only remind you that there is much ado

Like an inspector

I've watched you grace across the DAAP floors

Mission statement stamped across your forehead

Everyone knows that you are powerful

That you are intelligent

And that you will succeed no matter what

Yet you hide under your hat

All you insecurities

A well printed map

All roads leading you to doubt yourself

To dead ends, and work without friends

> Yet in your stride, this you have found a way to hide
>
> And before you,
>
> stand your peers,
>
> Eager to learn your way.

I toss this letter into the void, the abyss between us, this space that keeps conversation from happening.

Sincerely,

Rush Whitacre

740-336-9169

1-19-11

Dear Taylor Swift,

    Well, everyone loved my idea for my thesis, now, I just have to meet with my thesis committee three times, and have three more critiques in these grad studio classes, look good in front of the dean of students, and then a massive thesis, and then graduate, and then….. who knows. I think it is going to happen really fast, unfortunately.

    When I got to school I set up my maquette at the opposite end of the building, and then frantically started to arrange the hundreds of items my intern and I made. Then, anxiously waited for class to start. A waste of emotions I guess, because people loved it. Then I began building my show in the pipeline gallery, I am turning the entire gallery in to a giant cardboard box with no light, you enter from one way, and at this entrance it will be a ripped open entrance as if you climbed into a giant box. The only light allowed is that of cell phones. Uuuuh, well I guess it is a show, last minute you could say. My intern loves it, she must tell her friends all about me, because her and her friends have decided to make me cookies every week… lol, I blame it on my big art... maybe my flower paintings.

    I don't know, maybe you should check out my flower paintings on my website and see for yourself. I would love to find a place for them to live, maybe at a nice airport, or on someone's large wall, etc. but they need large wall space, like my sunflower, 11 feet by 24 feet.

    There must be something wrong with me, because I am mesmerized by the video for Tegan and Sara called 'call it off'. Something about their facial expressions and accents and use of language, "Call, break, it, off. Call, break, my, heart. Maybe I would have been something you'd been good at. Maybe you would have been something that I'd been good at." I just don't know, these words, with accent, and facial expressions,,, there is something really really beautiful about the whole scene, the melding of the mix...

I have a couple of past students who decided to research me on the net, and then come to me with their findings… I was actually not surprised, because all the articles on there about my work I knew about, and the school stuff, and well, all of it really. They thought they were some real investigators… It is true about what is said about the new generations, they know less and less about privacy and boundaries because everyone information is right there on the net to be gone through… I actually say, embrace the revolution, and keep what you want private locked up, or in your mind, cause otherwise. It will be everywhere.

This poem is for Jacki, my student from a recent past, she made excellent work, big work.

"Jacki's Remedy"

I knew from the moment you entered the room

"You all have much to learn." I said

You were a girl, pale, skinny

And always wearing something on your head

Covering that delicate, ready to fight attitude

Fight when you have to Jacki

Leave the rest for your friends to take care of

Because your friends have your back again

Leaving you room to be sane

And my ability to teach you

Wanes

In comparison to your ability to learn

Your ability to call me out

To make my weakness stern

Keep track of my every miss-move

Maybe that was where you learned the most

To remember everything just to prove

And then spin

A tiny

Grin

I toss this letter into the void, the abyss between us, this space that keeps conversation from happening.

Sincerely,
Rush Whitacre
740-336-9169

1-20-11

Dear Taylor Swift,

    Today, was a snow day. I woke up and started to get ready for school, and just as I was getting ready to start out the door I got a text message stating that school was closed today. Such a nice surprise. Then one of my students started to text me and I got her to come in and help me set up a show. It was great. Then I learned that this student needed volunteer hours in order to keep their scholarship and that made me even more happy because then I was able to get help and give help at the same time. And it also gave me someone I can call on for help/volunteer time. She and I got most of all the cardboard hung up… I don't know where I am going to get more cardboard, I need about 30 to 40 boxes more, and there is about 5 inches of snow on the ground, so any that was left out is most likely ruined… mmmm, I just don't know what is going to take place for me to get cardboard… ahhh, maybe a subway.. I remember one of my students telling me that they got some from subway once. So, yeah, I guess that is the ticket, my cardboard ticket that is.

    After all the cardboard gluing Jacki and I had a youtube fest in my studio. Funny stuff out there on the youtube I hadn't seen some of the things that she showed me. Some of the things she showed me weren't that funny, like the Potter puppet skits. I showed her some of my favorite fake movie trailers, like titanic 'two the surface', and while doing that I found out that there was a titanic 3 trailer. I was happy, because there are so many people out there with their desire to make funny things that are just there for free for anyone. I actually would like to see some director try to take some of the fake movie trailers into real movies…. What a challenge that would be… or even for someone to make one of the combo fake trailer movies, like 'Broke Back to the Future'… the idea of the Back to the Future characters falling in love and then there being this whole series of 'future' films… Oh, and then there is the whole "How it should have ended…" series. My favorite is the "How lord of the rings should have ended".. I admire the people who made this series because of all the different takes on the easiest way out for some books, directors, plots. I like to think about what might have happened if even the ending plans failed within the 'How it should have ended' version of movies. I don't know, maybe that is silly, but, the idea is still there that any version of anything can fail, every relationship has the possibility of failing, or succeeding, it all depends on who is doing the editing/revising/ cooperated thoughts. Roll the dice.

"Unexpected Message Delivery"

Everything I have ever known

Has just come crashing down

And all around me are things that I do not recognize

Pieces of a world I use to call my own

And now, I have to become something new

A beggar, a seamstress, perhaps a magician

The wanting of a heal for a break never felt so necessary

And all of this that I think the same fades into different

I whisper, but these words never grow up

And never become texts or instant messages

Or even emails

They were only meant for ears

Coming from breath drawn in my lungs

Exhaled from a body whose heart

Once pumped them throughout

Giving them purpose

Giving me life

Taking from me

A part of who I am that I give to you

Sounds, distractions, motions of emotions

Sentences for circulation

For that smile

Exhale

I toss this letter into the void, the abyss between us, this space the keeps conversation from happening.

Sincerely,
Rush Whitacre
740-336-9169

1-21-11

Dear Taylor Swift,

    I just love my life. So many good things that out-weigh the bad. I skipped my trip to some packaging plant this morning because I got a text that woke me up at 5 am telling me that school would not open until 10,,, and the trip was suppose to start at 9, and so, I figured that that trip for our class was cancelled, and I was grateful because I couldn't get to sleep until about 3am and when I got that text I just unplugged my alarm with a great big smile… then I woke up hours later, went to the bank, got a haircut, and went to my studio where I messed around for a little while and then finished off the walls with cardboard in the gallery where I am having a show… I think that I am going to videotape myself inside the giant cardboard box violently tearing it apart from the inside as if I am inside a present trying to get out…. I guess, it is kinda like I am trying to be a present who is trying to make himself known to something, to the art-world through the gallery??? Maybe, that is how it can be perceived. Anyhow, I think it is going to be neat, now I just have to figure out what to wear, hmmm.

    I couldn't spend all my time at the studio, so I left. But,,, before I left I noticed at the elevator that there was a can of paint with a sign that read free… Awesome, or so I thought, turns out it was a funny, not so funny trick, mostly on my part. I picked it up and thought, hmm it has to be at least half full, cool, nice, free paint, and then before I even thought twice, I gave it a little shake.. MISTAKE. The lid wasn't on tight, and that paint spilled out all over my jacket, shirt, face, hair, shoes…. And it was old paint that smell like, well, nasty old paint… lol… I couldn't get mad, I knew that it was my fault. Luckily, the bathroom was right behind me and I could get the paint washed off before it stained my jacket and shirt… I don't know about my shoes yet because I kinda neglected them in my fear for my jacket, my only winter jacket. I can't go without it…

Then I came home and my roommate Louis wanted to go to Kroger's, so, we went to Kroger's… I love to go to Kroger's with Louis because he always sounds like he doesn't want to stay very long, and then he finds himself roaming all over the store just checking out all the different kinds of foods. He is funny, just the way his mind operates, how he sees the world. He is laughing right now actually, he has a really genuine laugh. I have a loud laugh, inherited from my father no doubt, because my father has a really loud laugh, loudest laugh I know. I love that man.

    Today, I have been listening to Tegan and Sara, 'The Con'. I really have been listening to them lately, I guess I just start down a path and can't find my way back, it just twists and turns.

    This poem is for the photoshoping girl who hasn't taught me anything about photoshoping, yet..

"Carlee"

Fair game like your fair complexion

A smile against a ribbon

Focused on kneeling, curling

Folding around the sharp edge of scissors

Cutting, but only fraying edges

Thinking that everything I ask, say

Is somehow misleading, leading

Creepy without a pretext of texting

Or asking questions out of innocence

Which was broken by years of development

Or velopment of a creation of decreaction

Because humans can't just trust anyone anymore

A past dictating a future of sameness

New rules for old flaws

And she is lost in the upkeep of knowledge

Lost by the fact that more rules doesn't equal safety

New rules only means less freedom

Less creativity, less room to breath

And that is why she is an artist, to stretch

To break the rules

To exhale

I toss this letter into the void, the abyss between us, this space that keeps conversation from happening.

Sincerely,
Rush Whitacre
740-336-9169

1-22-11

Dear Taylor Swift,

    A shopping day today. Since the IGA closed down my roommate from China has been hurting, because he isn't as willing I guess to walk to get food, and I can understand that, so, I am the chauffeur for my two roommates when it comes to going to the Asian Market, I guess to anywhere, but mostly to the market. We didn't eat at our favorite Chinese rest, but that is ok, none of us were hungry. We have this method for bringing food into the apartment which is nice. Since we are on the first floor one of us goes into the apartment and the others lift the food to the person who is inside,,, and the kitchen is in the right place, food comes in the window and right into the pantry.

I wasn't going to bring this up, but, I kind of told you I would if it happened I think… So, I told you before in one of my first letters that I wouldn't go out of my way to learn about you because doing so just made me feel creepy in some way, so, I haven't. Then, last night while standing in line at Kroger's my roommate Louis pics up some magazine with you and some guy named Jake something on the cover. Maybe I should also say that Louis doesn't know anything about these letters, he just doesn't, I don't know how, hmm. Anyway, he didn't read anything to me, but I did see that the cover said that you were in tears… Now Taylor, I know that you don't know me, or anything about me, so I guess you will have to trust me on this, I am a pretty darn good friend, and I don't like to see my friends sad, or hurting because they have been taken advantage of. If someone has taken advantage of you then I am sorry for that. From all of things that have been exposed to me about you(which hasn't been a lot really) via radio, TV, and now a magazine by others like my (related person who is not named) or Louis, or, just by happenstance, you come across as an amazing heart, one deserving of love in the first degree without any need for bail. May your conviction, take you by surprise.

Anyway. I haven't found any more cardboard so that I can finish my gallery show… it is rather amazing because there is always cardboard here and there, and now, nothing. It is like the snow has decided to hide it, all of it in Cincinnati. Nah, I am sure it will come out of the woodworks soon. It is a capitalist society, and a capitalist society needs boxes so that products get moved… lol

This poem I dedicate to the Villain in the fantasy novel I wrote

"Hex Wrecked"

All this time you were hiding right in front of me

Concealed behind layers

Masked behind a face that I could not see

I trusted you, helped you

And I would have done anything to fix you

And this you knew

I travelled to the farthest reaches of this world

Faced death and your demons

And my life unfurled

As I pushed forward

My feet skidding back through the sand

And Magic not on board

I held my own, but lost everything I knew

My father, my friends all turned to stone

And across the square I heard you

Laughing, cackling, and then cursing me

And then it hits you, a crippling choke

You don't have power over me

Your spells are all broke

Now it is my time

It is my place

And I will not stop until all those I love

Are also free from your wicked embrace

I toss this letter into the void, the abyss between us, this space that keeps conversation from happening.

Sincerely,
Rush Whitacre
740-336-9169

1-23-11

Dear Taylor Swift,

    Such a lazy day. Just me, some reading material, my facebook, my cell phone, some House episodes, and a few hours of siesta. My dad called today. He wanted to see how I am doing. I talk to him about every other day. His most worrisome feelings are that I will go without money for food. He cracks me up, because trust me, if I thought I was going to starve the first people I would go to are my family. I am pretty sure that there is enough money in the united states that no one should go hungry, ever.

    So, today's reading was about time and space in the postmodern cinema. The two films being discussed were Bladerunner, and "Wings of Desire". Very interesting I must say, because I had never seen Wings of desire before, and City of Angels had to copy from it… The reason for discussing this movie was to use them as the cinematic coloring palate from which we are to discuss postmodernism in cinema in our philosophy class tomorrow. Blah blah blah. I have to discuss this reading in front of everyone, like I am teaching the class. What fun this should be. I can see it now, me fumbling through my notes and my friend Patty who is also teaching a part of tomorrow readings looking through her notes, and finally we look at each other and shrug and then just wing it. Probably for the best anyway.

This week I meet with my Thesis committee, and I am sure that is going to be a breeze. These things are kinda like a formality in my mind because I work hard, and I feel that my plans and ideas, and philosophies are good, I just am hoping that they are solid. Time will tell. I must say that a lot, time will tell, or we will see. I guess time will tell is better, because we implies an other as a witness. I don't think I have any witness's on my life really.

My friend Jacki has been buzzing in on me all day with one text after another. She says she wants to be able to read my mind. I told her that the only way that can happen is if she is my friend for a long long time, and those kinds of relationships are hard to come by sometimes.

Tonight's poem I dedicate to Jacki's desire to read my mind.

"Powerless Mind Reader"

Questions questions questions

You have so many questions for me

And I am sorry that all I have in return are not answers

But more misleading statements

And words like elbows bumping from one point to the next

Without regard for steadying the mast

Or clearing the way for something bigger to come along

But that is just who I am

My secrets are my secrets and are not there to harm

And I am no one special with my personal privacies

So bring your armies of questions

And your tests to see if I am wholesome

Or to see if a liar lurks beneath my brow

Because like you, I have all my processes intact,

And I will not be broken easily

And my mind will not be read like a book

Or like a receipt, or like some script

If you want to get to know me, and learn how to judge my motifs

Then you will have to listen, talk, walk, ride, and stand by my side

As someone who will stick up for me,

As someone I could lean on,

As a friend.

I toss this letter into the void, the abyss between us, this space that keeps conversation from happening

Sincerely,
Rush Whitacre
740-336-9169

1-24-11

Dear Taylor Swift,

    Well, two classes today, two classes down. Grad studio and Grad Seminar on philosophy. I got to teach part of philosophy class, it was actually really cool. I think I discussed this yesterday, but if I didn't I will reiterate. I did the parts on postmodernism of cinema, with an article from Harvey on Bladerunner, and Wings of desire. It was a hit, or rather, what I talked about was a hit, according Marcus, he said he enjoyed class today. I can't decide how the day could be any better.

    Oh yeah, I forgot, I was surrounded by most of the class I had last quarter, well, most of the girls because they don't feel they are getting the educational experience they need in their drawing class… Uh huh, I know what you are thinking, there must be another reason. No, actually, I don't think there is. And, the girl to guy ratio at the undergrad level is like 5 to 1, so, it is no wonder that the girls are having a problem trying to figure out the lessons. From my experience of teaching the students who want to learn the most are the female students, at least at this freshman level. Not to say that the male students do not want to learn, they just don't seem to go searching for a different way, or better way to learn, they seem to be preoccupied with other things on their minds. So, what started out as me getting some Photoshop lessons is actually going to get me into teaching drawing class outside of all the other things that I am doing… I am down with that, so long as those I am teaching will listen to me and not just come to me to goof off. I don't have time for that.

    Oh, and now I have to grade the first assignments that my students did. Aren't they going to be surprised, because I think I am going to naturally start low so that they will get the hint that their work is crap, because, actually, it was. Problem is, I don't think it is all their fault, these assignments they are doing I don't think are in the best interest of the students and their learning, their critical thinking processes. What do I know, I just can see a trend, and it isn't leading down the path of student learning, at least not one that is the most beneficial…

The following poem I dedicate to the one bobbing in the ocean,

"Wave Rider"

You were adrift

I could feel your ripples.

In my eyes, you were drowning

I watched you, followed you, I was intrigued

Your every word inspiring like due upon petals

Like rain into the waves, you absorbed me.

Now my musings are interlaced with my intrigue

My desire, my love, are happy at your whim

My love, which I am afraid to say in practice, like a fate

Fear of a karma, who's wrath I wish not to reap too soon

So I do not speak of love

Not a whisper

But I enjoy you bobbing in my ocean

Like dancing, pouring sweet nothings into my ear

Tempting as you are to easily love, I will not tell you direct

Even as my world rocks yours and we combine

And our inter-tangling leaves no trace of our separateness

I still will not speak of love

Night comes, and then the dawn

The ripples that led me to you have ceased

I search far and wide, deep and shallow

I was wrong about holding back

My plan I let play out like a game, and like any game

There are losers, and I just lost

Where have the waves taken you

I toss this letter into the void, the abyss between us, this space that keeps conversation from happening.

Sincerely,
Rush Whitacre
740-336-9169

1-25-11
Dear Taylor,

Its Tuesday again, my long day. I want to talk about the paper that I either forgot about, or I wasn't made aware of that I didn't have for class in my last class, but instead, I will start at the beginning. I did a silly thing yesterday. In the middle of fooling around with a bottle of five hour energy and messing around on the internet I drank the five hour energy, and then couldn't sleep… Oh yeah, I drank it while doing work on some of my students grading… I guess I must have really been into it because I didn't even realize it until I was turning the bottle in my hand and it felt lighter than it should… I actually didn't think that it would keep me awake that much because it really doesn't have that much caffeine in it. Well, let's just say that around 4 am when I still wasn't feeling sleepy, and I was tired of just laying here, I learned my lesson…

My first class really wasn't a class, it was the freshman class that I am sitting in on. It was kinda hard to sit through since I hadn't slept much, and the lights were off for most of it. We watched old commercials from the 80's and 'Yo Gabba Gabba' as a way of bring about the idea of what advertisers were trying to do, and what shows were trying to do, and that is, get you hooked using the very basic drives that attract the minds of very very creative people, the youngest of kids. After Bryan's class I had a brief 2 hour break where I went to Chipotle. Two of my students from last quarter wanted me to eat with them, well actually, they wanted me to help them learn some color theory, but then their hunger overtook them and decided that I could show them a thing or two about color theory after we ate. Just as well I suppose, I got to eat, and I got to teach some.. a win win situation. It was actually pretty amazing how good I felt about teaching color theory. I had never taught it before, but I know what it is, and for the most part how it works. Pretty easy I guess, unless you have no idea how it is suppose to work.

Then, I taught my class. Mostly it was just me watching as my students made their foam prototypes. Yeah, and then all through the class I was bombarded by questions because foam sucks to work with. Really it does at first, but then it gets better the more you work with it. By the end of my class that I was teaching I was so ready to go home. I was going to skip my class and just go home. Then something made me stay, probably my inability to not do something just because I am tired routine. Anyway, I am glad I stuck around, because I learned that I had missed the writing of a paper for my exhibition and planning class. Ugh, not something that made my night….. fortunately, when I told my professor that I flat out did not know about the paper, and how it wasn't listed on the assignments page on blackboard, she was very understanding. She said it was no problem. I must tell you, this class is a real push over. And it isn't the professor's fault, it is just because I have had so many shows that I just know what is going on, well, most of the aspects of the whole ordeal.

I dedicate this poem to a girl in Maryville TN, I'll call her 'accent'

"A Carrying Accent"

After my battle with the dark side's emotional trap

I wandered in and out of security

        Thinking that alarms would not go off
        And then they did
        And coming from the light I heard a voice
        Something foreign to me, something southern
        Something that rocked the foundation of my level
        Releasing me from the ensnarement,
        Giving back to me a heart worn out by its battle
        That which no one should be able to greedily keep
        Your hands lifted me, giving my weary legs a break
        Saved my life,
        Saved my heart from being bruised, scarred
        And unable to beat again for another
        Occasionally, it drums a beat for you
        Saying thanks
        Whittling away to the core of what we were
        Shear intensity

I toss this letter into the void, the abyss between us, this space that keeps conversation from happening.

Sincerely,
Rush Whitacre
740-336-9169

1-26-11

Dear Taylor Swift,

    One class today, Grad studio, it was lame again. Not because of my peers, just the format is screwed up. It was thrown in at the last minute as a course, the professors are still feeling their way through it, and it is mandatory every quarter, which screams, hey, we can't fail you in it because you can't take it twice in the same quarter. Other than that, it is still really messed up. I have the solution for the Grad studio, but I won't waste my time typing it up on here. The two professors did take time to talk about the paragraphs we talked about from the galleries we visited, they took 3 minutes,,, literally 3 minutes.. really funny if you ask me.

Some of my students from last quarter took me out to lunch today, it was a pretty good time, and I got to eat some of the 'cafeteria' food again. The food was pretty ok. The salad bar was actually amazing, so many choices. While at one of the bars waiting in line one of my students from last quarter disclosed something to me that took me by such surprise that I almost lost my plate onto the floor. I won't dare repeat it to anyone, or even on here. It was just something that I did not expect to come from this girl to me… shocking.

After I got to my studio I registered for classes, and then grabbed my swimming stuff and went swimming at the pool, the highlight of my day. After that another student of mine, Jacki, which I told you about before, she asked me to eat somewhere. We went to Wendy's, and it was a good thing to because I needed cardboard to finish the show I am putting up in the pipeline gallery, and on our way back from Wendy's we stopped at a Kroger's and they had lots of cardboard for me to finish my installation. Now all the walls, floor, and ceiling are totally covered with cardboard, I am happy. OH, lol, I forgot, just like fate to make things funny, a fire inspector came through today at the studios and noticed all my cardboard everywhere and told my friend Chris that it was a fire hazard and Chris said, Oh. And that was the end of Chris talking to the fire inspector. Chris is so funny. I showed up just after the fire inspector left.

After Jacki and I got all the cardboard we glued like mad until it was done… I took her back to her dorm at 1 am, what a job it was. She is a trooper.

This poem is for my (related person who is male and not named) (related person who is male and not named), he is a year and a day younger than me.

For you (related person who is male and not named),

"Dear (related person who is male and not named), I love you"

One day when you read this

You will know that my love for you is greater than you imagined

We spent years fighting, arguing, crying when we were young

And I have spent years feeling guilty

Lost by the frustrated past

The one that keeps you from being close to me,

Like a brother should

I spend minutes, and hours daily

Wondering how you are

Hoping that you are in a happy moment

That is what I wish for you, happiness

If there is one thing that you should never question

It is that I love you, unconditionally

And if there were a second

It is that I will always have your back

And if there were a third

Again, I love you, and I will never know another brother,

As I know you.

I toss this letter into the void, the abyss between us, this space that keeps conversation from happening.

Sincerely,
Rush Whitacre
740-336-9169

1-27-11
Dear Taylor Swift,

    I have thought about tomorrow all day today. I have been trying to think about what I am going to say to my thesis committee about my presentation. I guess all I have really been focusing on is the fact that I have to meet with the committee and not what I have to meet with them about. Oh well, in the end, I will know what to say and do when the time comes, I hope, if not, I will just keep telling myself that now to prepare my mind to be blown away. Ok, so, in the visual culture class today the entire thing was about how important it is to be aware of the dangers of facebook, and how everything that goes onto facebook is there forever because someone out there has it on their page and so on and so forth. I didn't think I would like the facebook lecture, but then, what Kerri had to say was actually pretty impactful, and the statistics were staggering.

    During the class I taught today I passed out the grades from the last assignment and discussed with them why they got what they got. Some of the students were not happy with their grade, I actually graded the students rather hard on their assignment and upon giving back their grade to them I could see some of their faces change from a semi happy looks to some of them changing to downright dumbfoundedness. I know why, because they couldn't understand that my grading curve starts at a B+ and an A can only be earned at the end of the quarter by showing me throughout the quarter how they have learned from their crits by improving on their future works. Seems perfectly reasonable to me.

After class I wandered the campus, weaving here and there, thinking about my life, and what it means, where I should go, how I should go about making something of a name for myself in New York. It is a huge city full of people, artists, randomness and beauty. Time will tell I suppose.

This poem is for Irony,

"Poetic Citeop"

Poems aren't meant for dinner appetizers

Their spirit runs like a butterfly in the wind

Vowels counted in a 100 meter dash, crawl

Words fight for importance in piece

Space is irrelevant as it does not exist

Periods, commas, and all the other fun symbols

They aren't even necessary, unless. You care@

And just when you do care, the poem cares not

All the world is a ballot, and all the people are pages

Poetry is that of a permanent marker

Leaving its traces, its tales, its fantasies, its mundaneness

Letters curving around minds, through hearts

Pulling out anxiety, and raising awareness of blank page

Text type decisions

Not font cues

And certainly not words meant to distract

Meant to avert the eyes into up-right thought

Into day dreams about fantasies of fantasies of delusions
Because those my friend, inspire poetry.

I toss this letter into the void, the abyss between us, this space that keeps conversation from happening.

Sincerely,
Rush Whitacre
740-336-9169

1-28-11
Dear Taylor swift,

    YES, my thesis committee meeting went excellently. Actually, it was the best meeting I have had since I have been back to school this year. Now I am looking forward to the rest of this year. And, I am actually going to paint this next quarter, maybe make a couple of paintings about something beautiful. God, I am excited about that, especially knowing that I have my thesis planned out and I don't have to feel guilty about painting and not getting my thesis in order… But, now because I have a grad studio and a thesis committee and both of those fulfill my need to keep on going and going with thesis working. Painting can once again be consumed with painting and not other ideas towards getting me a MFA.

    I had a meeting with Bryan today as well. Since he is the one who overlooks all the grads who are teaching and I haven't had a meeting with him all quarter I figured it was my time to pay him a visit and get some input and then I ended up spending about 4 hours with him looking up videos on all kinds of things from giant toys to Disneyworld to animatronic animals. And I saw videos of some of the Muppet things at Disney that just blew my mind, like dinosaurs who walk on their own on only two legs and Muppets who ride around on a strange contraption that looks like a segway, and it appears that the muppets are actually running and keep the segway contraption upright and level and running. I have to admit, it was a lot of fun.

    Then, I went back to my studio and nearly fell asleep. So, I called it a day and went to Chipotle and then home to enjoy an episode of House or two while having dinner. Lol, and then after eating I suddenly fell asleep and lost time. It was great, really really great. And then I woke up at midnight and realized, huh, I wonder if I am going to be able to sleep tonight, and, maybe I will, maybe I won't. we will see. It was quite a nap after all, and then I woke to the theme song of House playing over and over. And it was an instant message that woke me up from my old student Jacki, who I am going to start calling my friend instead because she really is a good friend to me.

This poem I dedicate to my friends

And I laugh
I laugh with you, beside you, because of you
And you because of me
But I am too much of a goof for accidently acting
My door is always open
And my phone is charged, most likely on silent
Still, I want to hear you tell my machine what you think
What you want
How you feel about everything
How you hate talking to the nothingness
Wondering if I will ever call you back
Or if any of this matters
Keep an eye peeled,
For I am sure I am playing a harmless joke somehow
And here I am waiting
Watching
Gleaming at the chance
To witness one of my many pleasures
A small gift from me to you,
A prank
A reason for contemplation
A reason to look at me, my smile,
To see my love for you, and my desire,
To see you happy.
To laugh.

I toss this letter into the void, the abyss between us, this space that keeps conversation from happening.

Sincerely,

Rush Whitacre

740-336-9169

1-29-11

Dear Taylor Swift,

    I actually woke up today not knowing what to do. Lol. I called off my meeting at the CCAC because I was way too tired, and the other two helpers agreed that I needed some more sleep. It is Saturday again, just another lazy day for cleaning and relaxing before another busy week. I never thought I would say this, that is if I haven't said it already, but I am really liking the Blackboard site where I can communicate with all of my students, and even hold an entire class if needed. I hated it when I had to first use it at my first college. It just seemed like an inconvenience that I didn't want to have in my life. The idea that after leaving class I would have to be in class longer via the internet at home. I guess today's college student grew up with blackboard and they are use to it and now I am happy to be on the other end of the deal, the one posting everything for the students to get online to see my goals and plans for them

    For the last 6 hours my roommate Louis has been playing music as loud as his speakers can play it. The sound is almost deafening in my room, so I can't imagine how loud it is in his room. His music taste is so random, mostly loud alternative, but then there is the occasional " what the heck is he listening to" moment. I think it is great, just wished he didn't play it so loud, for his sake, and mine. My friend Jacki is back to her texting mayhem again. She went with her boyfriend to the aquarium today and I got a play by play. What she saw, sharks she pet, etc. I think tomorrow we are going to the movies, her and her friend Kat and me. Black Swan, that is on the agenda, I don't even know what it is about. So, I had better see the trailer before we go so I can decide if I can steer them into another movie. Lol, not likely.

    I just checked out the movie 'Never Let Me Go', it really looks good, I am going to see when it comes out. I don't go to the movies that often, and I should because they are good for my visual brain. A new environment, big screen, strange quite atmosphere like a library where everyone is avoiding everyone else. It's just a nice vacation from the everyday.

    I dedicate this poem to Leah, another friend who I tease and say she has a crush on me, but that isn't true at all.

"Stained Flesh"

Frame after frame

Sample sheets filling walls

And the naked truth of nakedness

Reveals to you a world of confusion

And critiquing isn't bathing you in solution

Only your pictures get that treatment
The people in them are washed clean by flashes
And your eyes drip of visions not seizable
Your camera not capable
Then the sun sets along with your shutter
In the night you are caught in a paradox
A moon, stars, and a crush on a strip of film
A rush of light stains across your memory
And all unsaid things are just not exposed
Angles weren't decided, cap unremoved, battery dead
And the soft moonlight offers no solace
No solution, no reason
Only magic
Mysteries in the machine
Dubiously fraught with doubt and uncertainty
As each frame like the casting of a rainbow
Brilliant and never in the same way
Show your true beauty

I toss this letter into the void, the abyss between us, this space that keeps conversation from happening.

Sincerely,
Rush Whitacre
740-336-9169

1-30-11
Dear Taylor,

    Today I film my tearing down of my giant box room, I need to do it today because this coming Thursday is another opening that my friend Michael is having with his drawings. So, I am betting I will have a lot of fixing of the walls, painting, rewalling, we shall see, or at least I will. I am here in my studio waiting for my cameras to unload all of their contents onto my external hard drives so that I don't lose the data on them. I had recorded that stamp guy because I wanted a record of the guy and his doings at my house in Beverly just in case he turned out to be some kind of fraud. Of course, I am not sure that a video of the guy taking all of my stamps really matters, just a reminder that they are gone if nothing else. Oh, crap, I have a whole lot of video to transfer to my hard drives…. So, I guess this will take awhile.

Ok, so, I filmed myself doing all the tearing down of all the cardboard… unbelievable, 4 days to put up, and 20 minutes to rip all down, and then almost an hour and a half to de-glue all of the ceiling of hot glue… thank god for razor blades. You know, I am almost certain that I would never get all that glue off, let along in only an hour and a half without a razorblade… hmm. I tried a scraper, didn't even touch the stuff, and wouldn't even make it budge. Chris, who runs the gallery was really surprised at how fast I got the glue off(so was I, I used hot glue without even thinking about the consequences.) I got off easy.

Now of course, I am working on putting the video together so that I may show it somewhere someday… Me as the present, in the present and now past, tearing my way out of a giant box like that of a present opening itself up to the gallery, like I am a gift to the art world only able to reveal myself because no one else is going to put me on that pedestal, in that limelight, in that moment. I long for a moment where someone out there falls in love with my work, and through my work fall in love with me because of and/or in spite of my desire.

This poem is for the one who is sewing, there is a piece of love out there for you,

Eye

Hole of metal

Gaping not, as though it were

It is not, like the boy who's watching

Or like the thimble

The protector of flesh so what's the point

A pregnant pause, and then one aborted

Threading the gap

Missing, and missing time, again

Try once more, wet the end

And all is focused and shaking

Wiggling, pushing

Victory

And pulling subsides at the end of your rope

At the knot two become one

At the loop

Lives the eye, the point you avoid

A travesty un-manipulated by cloth

Broken by machine error

Fixed not by human sorrow

Only pitched

A singular

Shiny

Darn

I toss this letter into the void, the abyss between us, this space that keeps conversation from happening.

Sincerely,
Rush Whitacre
740-336-9169

1-31-11

Dear Taylor,

    Slept in till' ten, class at eleven, I almost decided to not go, like it was my job to make such decisions as to whether I could or don't have to go to class. I have no option. Lol. Besides that, I only have two times I can miss, and I would rather miss them by my selection and not by sheer dumb luck or laziness... There were three crits, and all three were rather the same as so many other crits with nothing important being said, nothing beyond the surface. Ed tries to talk beyond the piece and in his attempt he fails for the shear fact that his words from the beginning to the end most of the time are contradictory, and he talks about the piece in such a way that he maintains the focus and attention of everyone on the work in front of them rather than calling attention to himself as a contradiction. It is actually all too funny sometimes and therefore he even prefaces this thoughts with something like, "you may not like this idea", or, "This may have nothing to do with anything." Which I then inside think to myself, hmmm, then maybe I don't have to think about your "nothing to do about anything", anymore. Not really, I really do like Ed, he is a good guy, and I just don't always understand him.

    I spent the afternoon listening to music, and then working on a paper with my grad friend Gretchen for our Exhibition and planning class. It was a group paper, so, two of us met in person, and the third in the party participated via email. So, that is how it goes with groups. Can't be everywhere all at once. I then went back to my studio, listened to more loud music from the radio, and called it a day. I haven't used my brain at all today I don't think, well, maybe when I was having a discussion with Andre about Postmodernity. That subject is like condensed pea soup, good luck to all those who have decided that they are going to focus their lives on discussing it. I am looking forward to the next phase of art, 'Ultramodernity,' which is not pluralism, but more like this analogy, if modernity is a controlling father telling you all the things you are to do and not do, then postmodernism is more like the grandfather, the one who is laid back and knows the rules but doesn't mean that you have to follow them in a way spoiling your, and then Ultramodernity is the like the mother-n-law where all rules are emphasized and all rules are ignored. Good luck figuring that one out.

This poem is for Bryan,

"Leader of the Little"

A 'Jack' of all trades

Living behind a smile and shakes

Your peers are not your equals

And your followers do your bidding

But that's only because you have power over them

And no amount of electricity

Could ever fuel your computer enough

So that you could enjoy everything ever created by Disney

Your sheer joy placed into what you do

Can be seen by all those around you

Like a kid you jump around, and yell, and celebrate

All the little things

May you someday be rewarded

Celebrated, laughed at, laughed with, and then admired

We are thankful

that you not only leave your mark on institutions

but in the scheme of biological imperative

You will be remembered,

And cherished

Laughed with.

I toss this letter into the void, the abyss between us, this space that keeps conversation from happening.

Sincerely,
Rush Whitacre

740-336-9169

p.s. I will write more poems about Bryan, there are several facets I would like to touch upon.

2-1-11

Dear Taylor Swift,

    I had a different method for doing critique today with the class I am teaching. An artist lecture was going to start an hour before our class was over and I really wanted to hear this guy talk. I had the students put a sheet of paper out in front of them so that every student could go around and make comments about everyone else's piece. This actually proved to go way faster than I had thought it would. Because at the end of it we still had an hour. So, we visited the site for the next projects that the students are going to do their next pieces. 12 foot giant toys blown up from smaller toys made out of cardboard. It's going to be a fun project, or at least I would like to make this kind of thing if I were in their shoes. The only problem is working in a group, as far as 'group' projects go. You can come across problems where someone isn't pulling their weight… I remember last year there were a few students who were not pulling their weight and all the problems it caused the groups. I hope that doesn't happen this year.

    Exhibition and planning was a good class tonight. The teacher talked a lot about exhibiting and planning of shows for inside of a museum setting, imagine that, and she went over all the guidelines for labels for pieces and all the different types of labels and how many words can be on each on each. I really had no idea all the rules placed on so many little things in an exhibition. I just thought that a label was done when the person who was typing up the label had said all that was needed to be said. I never thought about word limitations on such things, nor the effect on putting two spaces after a period instead of one and how that consumes so much space over the course of a wall. Blah blah blah. I don't really care that much about it, but it was interesting. I am sure somewhere down the road I will use the information somehow to make some form of reaction art work about museums and their stringent rules with stuff that really shouldn't matter or be so tight, but it is.

    My friend Jacki has been texting me again all day, this has been a Jacki-a-thon ever since I invited her to come over and help me set up a show that was all about cardboard? She told me her boyfriend was getting concerned because of all the texts she was sending, I told her to tell him to relax, I am not at all interested. I think she told him.

This Poem is for Jennifer, she is a first year grad

Oh, infectious smile

Matched by a laugh and glistening eyes

May your charm spread

And all those who part from your presence

Take with them a bit of your happiness

A hint of your smile

A dash of cheer

Because I too want to be infected

I too want to see through your eyes

Into the world that you see with all its wonder

To feel the same breeze on my face

Lifting the corners of my mouth

To experience my friends as you do yours

Opening my mouth in laughter

And saying out loud how much I love them

How much they mean to me

And continually smile

Even as you are drawing, painting, printing

You are happy

That message written across your face

Read by others

Absorbed by everyone.

I toss this letter into the void, the abyss between us, this space that keeps conversation from happening.

Sincerely,
Rush Whitacre
740-336-9169

2-2-11

Dear Taylor Swift,

  Well, I had an interesting visiting artist crit today. A guy named Ryan Kelly came to my studio. He is a gay man from Philadelphia and he makes a lot of work not necessarily about sexual identity, but in connection with the idea of his discovery that he was gay. Now I know that it is said that people don't choose to be gay,,, but at some point they do discover that they are, so, there is a difference for what I am saying… not that any of this conversation really matters that much anyway I am sure. What does matter is that I filled Ryan Kelly's mind so full of stuff that at the end of his visit I could see his eyes searching all over the place for some level field place to land his creative thought plane so that he could give me some advice… in the end we decided that his best advice was for me to consider the idea that maybe it is not the content that matters but the scale. I already knew this, but it was a nice thing that someone else picked up on it… personally, I think I need to pick a slight manipulation of my large ideas so that all the things that I do can be considered an extension of myself and not just my signature… I am not going to be able to place my signature on large works, so, I really do need to come up with something that designates my work as my work without being some quite obvious sell-out option. Lol, we shall see my choice, or now depending on my fate.

So, after my artist meeting I ran to Verizon to meet up with my fried Gari… I know I wrote a poem about him. He shares my birthday and birth year… if you look through your letters I am sure you will find our history together… well, he has finally moved to Cincinnati and he looks great, he really looks great. I hope he is able to keep up his progress… I really want to include him in the artist revolution in NYC, making art and me writing art critic write ups for the papers across the nation, hoping for a chance to make someone out there pay attention to my idiocy, or my intelligence, or my ambivalence towards certain kinds of art, or art practices… or maybe I am just talking out of my butt, with the idea that this is what I want to do…

This poem is for the person with dyed hair that everyone copies, you know who you are… "C"

"Carlee, part II"

You walk around every day

Uncertain, yet knowing that you are the baseline

That everyone is going to mimic you in some way

You don't smile, unless with your sidekick

And your sidekick makes you feel smart

Even if she is smarter, and she makes you laugh

Even if you are funnier than her most of the time

A brief break in the red reveals a small light streak

A moment for questions, for revelation

For a crush to form between the lines

A squeezing of ideas, of wrinkles

Your every move is dictated.

Your every decision can be read like brail.

> A literal tactile surface for feeling,
>
> For discovering the truth behind your ultimate unspoken end
>
> And Just as you don't feel loved
>
> Those who you discover to despise the most
>
> You learn to feel sorry for, or embrace
>
> Because those people, yes they.
>
> Who at the last moments who would make you think…
>
> Who would change your mind
>
> Who make you question who you are
>
> These people are the ones copying you
>
> The ones desperately trying to become a Carlee,
>
> The greatest of all forms of flattery.

I toss this letter into the void, the abyss between us, the space that keeps conversation from happening.

Sincerely,
Rush Whitacre
740-336-9169

2-3-11

Dear Taylor Swift,

    What a great day turned into a horrible day. Last night I got my new phone, all day today I feel it has been playing with me instead of the reverse. Then I sat in on Ryan's class and then gave another student some tutoring in color theory that was very appreciative, and then I graded papers, annnnnd then gave a PowerPoint presentation to both my class and the neighboring class, Susan's class. Even Susan liked my presentation of the PowerPoint images. I was nervous, especially when I had no idea of what the name of apiece was.

    Then in my class I got a phone call about some horrible news and here I am 5 hours later back in my home town. I don't want to talk about the problem right now because it is ridiculously stupid, and very dramatic, and I don't like drama in my life, really don't. if nothing else, I have a roaring fire at my side, a comfy bed, and excellent pillows. Only thing I am missing are my dogs, but, then again, I gave them away, so, I guess all I am missing is someone to enjoy the fire with.

Jacki is still texting me a lot. She is worried about me, I told her to worry about her boyfriend before I do and form a triangle of worry, lol. Wow, the fire is really popping tonight, must be full of water or maybe it is just really hot. Whichever the case may be, I am getting quite a show. I haven't seen my dad yet, I see him in the morning, along with a lawyer and the chief of police, and then I go to see my (related person who is male and not named). And after seeing my (related person who is male and not named) I am going to see Wester my friend. Wester is worried.

I hate the long drive from Cincinnati to Beverly, and vice versa. There just seems to be so much dead time, or worse, you can catch the beginning of rush hour if you leave Cincinnati at the right time to catch the rush hour in Columbus! Not fun. Luckily I take all the by-passes possible, or then again, there is old route 32, about 136 miles of in from Cincinnati to Athens. Quite a scenic route, unless it is night time, then it is watch out for the deer time. Yeah, and I have seen quite a few, actually more closer to Athens really.

This poem is for cracks in the sidewalk.

>Tap, tip, toe, tiptoe, Tap
>
>As I walk down the walk
>
>With my stick and a pack.
>
>As I walk down through places
>
>I keep my eyes peeled for crevices,
>
>Or small cracks for shoe-laces
>
>My boots are loose and shabby
>
>My shoes are short and flabby
>
>But when it comes to missing cracks
>
>My high heels can tip the tabby's
>
>These walks of sides, sided-walks
>
>Are all like my listening of your talks
>
>About my walks, and cracks
>
>And avoiding their stigma, their luck
>
>That my mother too would agree
>
>If you are to walk down a strip of pave
>
>Careful where you tip your taps
>
>And foot your steps
>
>Because beneath your nose
>
>Down past your shirt and slacks
>
>Grows the reason for the game

Step on a crack, break your mothers back

I toss this letter into the void, the abyss between us, this space that keeps conversation from happening.

Sincerely,
Rush Whitacre
740-336-9169

2-4-11

Dear Taylor Swift,

    I guess I am staying at my dad's old house again tonight. I got my truck checked out earlier today, the check engine light was on, and has been plaguing my eyes for about 3 weeks now. And…. Guess what the light was about. I would have never guessed. My fluids were just a little low. So, they added a little and reset the light. I am glad that is all it was, because I have had this truck now for about 115,000 miles and it hasn't given me any troubles.. knock on wood for real. I was actually relieved, I can't afford a major problem with my truck right now. It has been a really really good vehicle. I am debating whether I am going to take it to New York when I move there, or whether I am going to sell it, or have someone take care of it while I am gone. Wow, this is actually making me a little depressed, the thought of not being able to drive my truck, or having to sell it… it has been so good to me.

    I spent the day at my friend Wester's house. Pancakes was working and he and his wife and I went to KFC to eat for dinner. I bet we spent 2 hours there just laughing and having a great time. It appeared that everyone who came into the restaurant knew Pancakes or Whitney somehow. They just kept waving and saying hi to everyone. While we sat we came up with at least 12 different kinds of apps that should exist for cell phones. I can't say what they are because I don't think that anyone should be allowed to steal the ideas of others, not to mention, we would like to either make them using a program on the internet, or try to sell the ideas to someone who will then make them. I don't know, maybe just making them for fun for everyone is the thing to do. There are so many different kinds of apps out there, I would rather one I make get out there for people to have fun with than sit on a screen with a 99 cent price attached to it and everyone pass on it because there are so many other free ones.

    After KFC we went back to Westers house where I got to see Westers nice new furniture and learned that they took their house off of the market because they couldn't seem to satisfy the realtors and they got fed up and just took down their for sale sign. I think that maybe the new furniture was a way to smooth over the loss of not being able to find a place. Well, it's none of my business, and it was really nice furniture, so, to each their own.

I was thinking a lot about poems today, and all the other poems I have written to you, and I thought I would write one more on the dark side tonight.

I dedicate this poem to the guy who sanded off many layers,

"His Dark Side"

Alone,

Quiet in a room of solitude

Death contemplates

Tempting vials so viscous

So breathing becomes laden

His couch a home for sleep

His sleep a shed

A storage of unfinished business

Answers fighting problems

Unsung heroes

Haven't battled this hard

Mind waging war

Heart waging peace

And in the middle lives a voice

Trepidatiously vocalizing song

Air from lungs passed through a body

Flowing over flesh

Vibrating cords

Casting out the demons

I toss this letter into the void, the abyss between us, this space that keeps conversation from happening.

Sincerely,
Rush Whitacre
740-336-9169

2-5-11
Dear Taylor Swift,

Well, I went to a home show today with Wester and Pancakes. It was rather a disappointment. Then I drove back to Cincinnati and met up with my friend Gari. He is like my (related person who is male and not named), like family. We spent the whole after noon either at his work, or at Chipotle, or at this little watering hole where we reminisced about our undergrad days, which weren't that long ago, and all the people who we love and wish we could still have around us. Yeah, we are all spread out all over the place now, and I am not sure if we are better for it or not.

Right now Gari is playing a video game, call of duty something or other. I have no idea what it is all about other than the cool version called Nazi Zombies, which to me is just hilarious, the combination of two strangely different things into one game. I don't know, maybe it is just me. And then, Gari tells me that the game is not about winning anything, just about surviving levels, that there is no win, only, how long can you live. I don't know, I guess that is a good thing, just the feeling of making it so far, and I guess if it is a zombie apocalypse,,, there most likely aren't any "winners" in the end, just all dead people.

I was going to drive home, but, wow, I just checked the time, it is 4 am, and I am about to call it a night, maybe watch a little more game, and then disappear into a couch and sleep until the afternoon. I have to tell you, these zombies really do make scary noises, and they are just creepy as hell.

Jacki texted me several times today, and she wants me to teach her some color theory like I have been teaching some of the other students. I don't mind it, but it would be nice if I could coordinate it so that I tutored all of them at the same time so that I wasn't saying the same thing three different times, I will have to mention it to them all.

This Poem is for the Innocent

"Blind-Sided"

Bring me your whipped back

And your blistered feet

Let me wash them

And wipe them clean

Bring me your leathered skin

From a sun's sun,

Who's relentless beams,

Have been wearing on you.

Let me shade you,

With my wings that

Keep me afloat

Make me able to watch,

Over you

Bring me your keeper

Your burden, what weighs on you

Bring me your anger and frustration

Let me soothe them with my whisper

Bring me your heart,

Your soul,

The innocence

That you have been robbed of

Let me remind you

That I too feel your pain

Your suffering

And I love you

I toss this letter into the void, the abyss between us, this space that keeps conversation from happening.

Sincerely,
Rush Whitacre
740-336-9169

2-6-11

Dear Taylor Swift,

    Gosh, what a night that was. Gari and I were up sooo late. I woke around 2 pm, still tired, but knowing that it was worth it, because good friends and laughing and having a great time is where it is all about. Today was a good day... I got all of my students binders graded, and I went to Wal-Mart with Jacki and Katie and had fun watching them shop. They bought hot glue guns for the cardboard project, and I almost bought one, but, I just couldn't bring myself to buy something that I just don't need right at the moment, it was going to be an impulse buy, and I just had to set the items down... I saw a picture of you in Wal-Mart, I don't remember what it was about, just that it was you, I think it was in the makeup isle if I am not mistaken, but since I was with girls who weren't looking for makeup we didn't hand around and gawk at the things in the isle, nor the pictures of things, so, I rightly couldn't say that you were advertising. We went to eat at Wendy's after Wal-Mart. It was late, and the food at Wendy's was kinda tasting like it was almost past it due date to be served Gross.

Back at the studio Jacki and I sat and talked for about 2 hours, shooting the breeze and then we got to talking about beat boxing and I told her about Beardyman and his chaos pad. Wow, I had totally forgotten about Beardyman. I am actually listening to him beat box right now. There is something quite different about beat boxing with just your body, and then with a machine that samples your bodily noises and repeats it for you. I didn't get any work done for school for myself, and I have a grad crit this coming Wednesday that I desperately need to go to the CCAC to make some designs for my thesis piece using the actual furniture from the building. Without using the actual furniture I won't know what I am getting into, nor what possibilities there are. I am really feeling like I am behind now. I will just go there and play around with all the furniture and make something up. I don't really care what everyone else thinks, just that I have something to show as if I really have been doing work of some kind, I mean, I know what I am doing in my head, I have so much worked out in my head, it is just a matter of making some physical things for others to see.

This poem is for the one with the very lacey shoes to the knee

"Lacey Legs"

You are all around me

Silent and pondering a rosy cheek

A sudden blush

Marked by the one peering into your heart

You don't think you are noticed

And in your silence,

You don't speak,

Because no one has taken the time,

To listen

You work to figure me out

But all your tempting curiosities bar you

Chain your mind in place

Caressing your ego's id

Blatantly outright open in all its intent

To learn

And still I fetch you into another wood

A brief intermission for salvation

But the trees get in the way.

There is no path

Only more forest, more secrets.

Less certainty.

A wall of nettles

Would offer you more answers

Unlike the man who knows you

And will keep you

Un-Martyred

I toss this letter into the void, the abyss between us, this space that keeps conversation from happening.

Sincerely,
Rush Whitacre
740-336-9169

2-7-11

Dear Taylor Swift,

    LOL, let me start off with a little laughter. I didn't get out of bed until 2 pm, because I was working late, and my alarms weren't obviously loud enough to wake me from my devices of being able to tune out loud cell phone noises. Either way, I didn't make it to my first class, and I almost decided to not make it to my second class. However, I have already missed two of those classes, but for really good reasons which I don't think are needed at this time. I can assure you, that my attendance has been pretty perfect up to this quarter.

    I am home, watching Die Hard, the original with Bruce Willis. Nothing like a good classic to cap off the night. Well, not much happened today, so , I guess I don't have much else to say… My class was boring, the aftermath of it was minimal, and even at the studio there wasn't anything happening. So, what I am trying to say is, maybe tomorrow my stories and news will be more interesting, and worthy of story, so, for now, here is the latest poem

This poem is for that second chance,

"Please look"

I wanted to say so many things that I couldn't open up to

And your back now seems so far away

And you keep walking, and stepping stones are a guide

My voice is so little, but my heart is wide

And now it beats loudly, faster than it should

And I can't cry anymore

You took advantage of me, and then I robbed myself

This I cannot blame you for

My solitude, my silence, my very presence of soul

Bids me to lay horizontal

Oh soft ground

Green grass, comforting my skin

Awakening my senses to a world I am unable to understand

Break off a piece of my lips and make them talk

Make them know a soft touch

For I am not long for this universe

And the emptiness of this sidewalk,

this grass,

this hole in my heart

Are diluted like a fresh spring through gravel

Tainted by a bathing bird

Sensitive claws clinging to scales

Lifting up flesh for feeding

For another tomorrow

And a turn

A look

A return

I toss this letter into the void, the abyss between us, this space that keeps conversation from happening.

Sincerely,
Rush Whitacre
740-336-9169

2-8-11
Dear Taylor Swift,

I am laughing at how far behind I am. Or, maybe I am ahead, because it seems that right when I think I am behind I am actually really ahead. I think I am behind, and that is all that is necessary for me to know.. I have a grad studio class tomorrow for which I have nothing prepared, yeahhh.. yes, this quarter is going wild…

Ok, today the visual culture class was actually team taught meaning that Bryan and Kerri shared the stage and worked things out to where they bantered back and forth for a little bit. It was kinda nice… of course, I was busy writing a paper while the class was going on, but still I got a lot out of it, and I should do more work like I did in that class. I should work on writing more while I am in that class. Maybe if I focused more on writing in that class while listening to Bryan and Kerri I would have more of my thesis written. Maybe the problem I am having right now is that I really don't care about the thesis, or the writing for it. I think I have lost all desire to even finish this year out… and that is bad. I need to find my focus and fast, that or I just need to sleep more. Sleep, I don't even know what that is anymore. Jacki is still ringing my text messaging sounds off the hook. She is nice, but her boyfriend is not so nice to her. I am sure they won't stay together much longer, at least from what I am hearing from her side. I guess that is how it goes sometimes, boy meets girl, boy falls in love, girl falls in love, and then someone falls out of love and it all falls apart… too bad for either side.

I got to watch all the students working on their giant toy projects today. I have a group who is trying to be sneaky and make a piece that attacks one of the other classes giant toys… this could be interesting. I told them they could make the piece but they had to show up at the critique for the other class to show how their piece is meant to attack the other piece. I think that this class to class interaction will be good.

This poem is for that which we can't have, but want

"Between Realms"

Over your shoulder you look

A past beyond reach lay there

Staring forward at you

Wondering what you will grow up to be

A yes, or a no.

A true or a false

Neither realm is able to know the other

Neither know the other exist

A pitty that you still reach out

Trying to grab onto something you can't see

A something that felt so good

And now only a feeling you search for

A feeling written in a book

      Someone else's emotional trials

    Chapters labeled in love, lust, hate, forgiveness

        And yours not labeled

    Not reread, not spell checked, nor corrected

     And your wind blows around the pages

        All your thoughts

    All your tears, and all your visions

        A jumbled mess

I toss this letter into the void, the abyss between us, this space that keeps conversation from happening.

Sincerely,
Rush Whitacre
740-336-9169

2-9-11

Dear Taylor Swift,

  Gosh, I must tell you, my grad installation class has never been so bizarre. I presented the most abstract thing to the class, something so conceptual that they had no idea of how to approach the topic. In fact, the two teachers, Kevin Matthews and Chip(Chuck) were not even considering my idea as art, in fact Kevin Matthews said, "So What." And of course other students jumped on him, not necessarily backing me up directly, but making statements and dispensing ideas here and there, and I guess sticking up for what I was trying to point out to the rest of the class, and that is, this class isn't really set up to be that helpful for us in the long run, and that my ideas are the only ones breaking the norm and showing that this class could be so much more than just a, "Oh, yeah, this is an object, and this is what I want you to see and feel and understand and this is my idea and my wants and desires and blah blah. I want my classmates to be free, really free, and able to explode their ideas into the world, and in the class room. But everyone is so worried about bullcrap like this little paper, and that little paper, and guidelines, and rules, and deadlines too early… deadlines are a good thing, but they are not a good thing for anyone if they are ridiculously early.

  I am sorry, but I spent hours laughing about my crit, and I just can't get it out of my head, all this confusion swirling around in my head. Jacki is here in the studio, painting a castle and a dragon.. I think she is trying not to acknowledge the fact that I am not helping… actually, I enjoy watching other people do things, like play video games, or sing karaoke, or do whatever so long as the person is really into what they are doing, or I guess no doing that can be fun too. Yep, me the people watcher. I wanted to get to the bottom of Jacki's like or dislike of me, even though she has a boyfriend. She told me, that she would date me if she didn't have a boyfriend, even though there is a little age difference, she said it is what it is, but since she has a boyfriend, she said that was not possible. I have to admit, I was taken with her frankness, her ability to just step out and say it to me.. and, then I was put in my place and made to understand that I had no chance,,, lol, even if I wanted. Now, I am confused a little.

So, on that note, this poem is for Jacki, for different reason.

"Strange Understanding"

Ears are waiting for you

Lessons leaving port when you are not on board

And all you want is for a nickel

A quarter, a dime

Just a little piece of land

Some quality moments being heard this time

And not like some tickets being sold

To some one sided show

Or a two way looking glass

With no way for looking out

Your soft somber hair lets you know

For how could it not

It has seen your tears drip drop

To a floor that reflects not a moment

Not a kindle of a thought

And your ideas still fall on repurposed ears

And so you keep looking

And talking

Will anyone ever listen to you

Can they hear you

Or are all the dogs in the world only after one thing

And deaf to all others

Patrons in a line that never moves

A weasel pruned

I toss this letter into the void, the abyss between us, this space that keeps conversation from happening.

Sincerely,
Rush Whitacre
740-336-9169

2-10-11
Dear Taylor Swift,

    Another day, another work day for my students. I actually like having so many different students working on such large projects, it kinda makes me feel like I could have that many people working on my work, or my projects. It is like oxygen to me to think of having so many workers working for me, doing things to help make my ideas come true. My friend Dustin and I walked around checking out all the different undergrads, seeing what they were doing, helping out where we could… I really enjoyed the having Dustin around because I never get to spend time with him, I find him really interesting, and he really enjoys my ways of messing around with the university and its rules and regulations as far as the classes are being run.

    Later, after class I grabbed a meal at the Tai restaurant, had the tai spice chicken and vegetables, they were delicious. I had them made extra hot, but they were really that hot, they were actually kinda boring as far as spice goes, but the flavor was amazing. Tonight, I am watching Moulin Rouge the movie with Nicole Kidman. This is really a great movie, and I never knew that Nicole Kidman could sing they way she is. I actually can see it as almost like a parody of a parody of entertainment upon music upon musicals, upon Madonna…

    It is getting late, and I should let my mind wander off to dreamland, who knows what I will be dreaming about, hopefully something relaxing.

This poem is for change

"On my 'Queue'"

Switches

Make things different

Have pushing buttons

Left you calloused

Turned off, turned on

Make light, make dark

Electricity, and dumbwaiters

Stop their living upon thy click

                    Upon thy turn

                    It is not easy,

        And twisted knobs will do you no good

                  For all your wishes

                  And all your dreams

                      Waste away

              Fail at the moment off

         Cease as the turn is downward

            Keep looking for the cure

             Angled away from eyes

             And looking for pieces

               Connected by lace

                     Left open

                       But off

         No one knows the darkness

              Knows not of a path

            Broken like virgin ground

               Unable to recoup

                    To regain

                    To return

I toss this letter into the void, the abyss between us, this space that keeps conversation from happening.

Sincerely,
Rush Whitacre
740-336-9169

2-11-11

Dear Taylor Swift,

      Two eleven eleven, a neat date, nine more days and it will be my birthday. Feb 20, the six days a lover day, that is, 6 days after valentines. I am a Pisces, but I am not altogether sure how to feel about that, because I don't really know what that means. I have several different friends who are also Pisces, like my friend Gari, who was born on my birthday and birth year, and he and I are similar, but we are really different in so many many ways. I can't even tell you. He is a really cool guy, scares me with his ability to use his body as a weapon. I don't really know how explain a Pisces. If I were asked I guess I would describe myself I would probably say that I was shy in the presence of large groups, melancholy but not sad just contemplative, intense personality with intense ideas and forward moving motion in my step, I don't seek thrills they tend to know where I am most of the time, and my favorite thing to do is be in the arms of the one I love,,, that is of course, when I have someone.

    I just got done watching the movie 'the curious case of Benjamin Button.' What a good,,, looooong, movie. And I kinda figured out that it was Brad pitt's voice before Benjamin actually turned into him. I would have never guessed that the movie was about a man who grew younger as he went along in life. I just clicked on it to watch on netflicks without reading about it. And, before I knew it, it was two hours later and I was thinking, my god, how much longer can this thing seriously go for, so I checked, and 45 min was still left. I really liked it, kind of reminded me of several different movies all rolled up into one. Hmm, Bicentennial man for the epic adventure part, forest Gump for the 'I'll try anything I'm asked part, Meet Joe Black for the how calm can Benjamin button be part(and because brad played that part as well), etc, etc. I could keep going, but there really isn't any reason to.

    I am making tomorrow a big day for me. I need to spend time at the Carl Solway gallery doing some investigation of their current exhibition. I have to make up a 15 to 20 minute PowerPoint presentation of all the different things that the curator did to make the show happen, it should be interesting. I have no idea what I am doing in this exhibition and planning class, part of me thinks that I have lost my mind and need a vacation from school… but, then, I am so close to being done, I must finish, I must. Then of course, come the sucky loans that need to be paid back,,, and,,, how,,, that,,, sucks. It's like, here is all this money to go to school so that you can become a teacher, and so that you can fund other teachers, and when you get out,,,, we will be here waiting for you Muh ha ha ha ha.

    This poem is for lessons learned too late.

"walking with a fine 'line'"

You stared into my eyes

Subtle grin,

A green squint I had not expected

Your hands folded

Not at all ready for another

And I envious of the mat laid

Not able to overcome

Nor walk across

> To see you is like to spoon out a heart
> One small dollop at a time
> And now the bed lays bare
> Your scent too soon gone
> A phone silent
> And my head spinning
> Thinking about the loss
> And how the next time
> I won't be so careless with my heart
> With my secrets
> And with my hands I will hold on tight
> Instead of letting go so easily
> I will be ready
> I will be aware.

I toss this letter into the void, the abyss between us, this space that keeps conversation from happening.

Sincerely,
Rush Whitacre
740-336-9169

2-12-11

Dear Taylor Swift,

    There is a reason I avoid girls with boyfriends, because they have boyfriends… Drama is something that I hate. Ok, so, Jacki who has been working off her volunteer hours with me while working on my thesis project has a boyfriend who has become insanely jealous of me because she has been working with me in my studio, and sometimes at my place. So, I am now kicking her off the list of people who can work with me. Last thing I need is some guy coming around to cause me trouble and grief, not to mention, possibly be looking for a fight. Totally not necessary, and uncalled for. She just texted me and told me that she was allowed to talk to me and to work off the rest of her volunteer hours to help me put together my thesis this spring. I smell the stench of trouble, and I aim not to step in the pile of it. I do want a good girl in my life, and I am sure Jacki is, but she is also a really good person, and I am not a cheater, or a cheater-maker, so, in the words of Mick Jagger, "You can't always get what you want."

    My dad just called in the middle of my texting. I don't know what kind of motor was put in that man when he was made, because he just seems to continue to go and go. At 87 he regularly hunts, goes out into the woods to cut and collect fire wood, and he just told me that he just came back from Seneca rocks where he use to rock climb all the time. I just hope to even live that long, let alone be that active. He likes to call and check in on me. He found out this time that our Duke bill came four months late. I don't know how a gas and electric company can just not send a bill for four months and then send it and say 'Hey, you have to pay this amount or else… I just don't get it. I emailed the company and told them they would have to charge us the bill over another four month period and make sure they send us a bill in the mail every month, not just in email.

    I got around to two different galleries, one of them inside the museum. My friend Rabsu went with me and we had a good time, and then had Wendy's to eat in downtown Cincinnati. Rabsu is from India, and he is looking for a 'hot' India woman… The Irony, he is in America, not India, and he wants a girlfriend who has likeness's like those from the women in his country. I laughed and he laughed as he told me this, and then I told him,,,, go to your home country, you will find one there that suits you. He then asked me what kind of woman I was looking for, I told him, 'I am looking for something like magic'. He really laughed then. That was an experience, it was the largest Wendy's I have ever been in, and there was only like 2 people in it at dinner time. It must be one of those lunch type of places, because judging by their lack of customers at dinner I would say they wouldn't last long.

This poem is for magic, the magic I am looking for.

"Single Point Perspective"

Out there in the world

Getting your heart broken, as I am

Telling yourself that if you just keep loving

Like you've never been hurt

That you will be true and open for the next

Again, leaving yourself open to being hurt

And like the life I live parallel alongside yours

We believe we will find each other

Like magic finding the rabbit at the bottom of the hat

We keep pulling up wild birds, talons scraping

White gloves with nothing to show for it, maybe pain

Maybe a crushed dream, and family plans lost

One broken heart after another

And to you these lines never appear to get closer between us

But like the artist I am

I know where the vanishing point is

Where our paths cross

Where everything in our worlds come together

Where everything makes sense

Where you will find me

And I wait for you

I toss this letter into the void, the abyss between us, this space that keeps conversation from happening.

Sincerely,
Rush Whitacre
740-336-9169

2-13-11

Dear Taylor Swift,

  Well, (a deep subject with water in it) I have had a great day, and got a lot done! Despite my up until 3 am from all of Jacki's texts, I got up at nine and had all of my laundry done by, and the Yangue and I went to the Asian Market so that he could get some groceries and so that he could flirt with the cashier as far as I could tell. I have no idea. Yangue was having a problem with the smell of the grocery store and he was complaining to one of the bag boys in Chinese. Sometimes I really wish I knew what he was saying, like today, he looked like he was upsetting the people at the store. Yangue is really funny, just the things he says and the things he does, like make weird decisions that I don't understand. We ate at chipotle before going to the market and Yangue ordered a burrito and then sat down to tell me that he hated burrito's… lol, Laughed so hard. I just kept hearing him say, this sucks, I hate the smell of burrito wraps.

  After we got back I immediately began working on some writings that I have needed to get done for this week. Mostly for Grad Critique. I was going to work on a PowerPoint for exhibition and planning but that got put on the back burner because I was having a grand ol'time writing about a different project involving lots of paper and folding it many many times. Besides, the grad studio stuff is due tomorrow, and the PowerPoint isn't due until the 22nd of this month, priorities. I still can't believe that I am so close to graduating.. and the time is only going to speed up from here on out. I guess I am going to have to put myself into overdrive if I am to make art to make a living. I just keep asking myself, what is something I can do, or make and then mass produce that millions can buy. Well, I am not musically inclined, and my ability to make a movie is quite frankly terrible, and no one buys poetry anymore… it is all over the internet, and despite my best efforts to write it, it will always end up on the net, not that I have any there right now, I guess it is just how the world is going. If it can be made digital, it will be, and then it will be everywhere. And old friend of mine named Lyan told me that in one of his artist statements he wrote that his greatest ambition was to sell out as quickly as possible… I am not saying he is right about that, but he does make a compelling argument for reasons, or ability to make money… now, what is it exactly that a fine artist in the field of painting, drawing, installation, etc do to sell out… I will get back to you on that.

This poem is for love when cupid's aim is off,

"Burning"

Fire

Barely breathed out

An unexpected heat desired

Flanking my moves with yours

Making my reasons difficult to avoid

Its warming in the world

The embers from past flames are gone

And all I feel is this heat

This burning inside

This dawn turned to dusk

Nights left wanting for more

Days of clouds, drips of snow and rain

Washing away almost everything

Except this picture set in motion

A big screen, a pillow, and a smile

Not a word, just breathing

Just warmth

Just this fire

Set ablaze by our flame

I toss this letter into the void, the abyss between us, this space that keeps conversation from happening.

Sincerely,
Rush Whitacre
740-336-9169

2-14-11

Dear Taylor Swift,

      Valentines day, another day for celebrating love, and togetherness, and friends and family, and designed mostly for your special valentine. I decided to start typing this letter in class because I want to get a head start on it, and because we are having a discussion about a rough draft of a rough draft of a animated video about a farmer whose going to kill himself because he can fee his family. Which, to me, is a very strange thing, although it is happening in places in the world like India. Ok, after a little tiny bit of heated debate, and Ed starting a conversation/argument for the sake of argument, which in itself is masturbatory, as well as always ending with, "I just wanted to do that for 'doing's' sake" C'mon man, say something in that realm that is useful and constructive. Dan, my hero of the day, pointed out under his breath the inquisition that is taking place, and the artist isn't allowed to talk. Then the little dangerous one takes over, and she fights for her stance/opinion to the n'th degree, no matter how separate someone else's ideas might be similar.

      Zach is sitting next to me again. He is a funny guy. I am in Marcus class now, I spent hours going around helping my students by answering their questions on the giant toy projects that are due tomorrow… I better not type too much in this class because Marcus is a little more attentive, and he is the director of the school, and he has a British accent, and he knows one heck of a lot about philosophy, so, I will finish this later.

      OK, FLASH FORWARD… It is now 5 am and I just got home after helping my students get their plane off the ground and hanging in the cafeteria area of the University. The plane is really cool I must say, along with the Wall-e, and the Rock'm Sock'm fighters, and along with the star wars snow skidder. I haven't actually see the snow skidder, but I am pretty sure it is going to be amazing because I saw all the different individual pieces, and I am sure the whole thing will go together well. So, after I get about two hours of sleep I think I will head back to school to see what people think of my students work. I like to brag about my students and their abilities. Besides, my students are the only ones to ever hang such a large piece in the school above an area where students congregate all the time. This is going to be a great two weeks of seeing all this work all over the school.

Well, since I technically started this letter on Valentine's day, I can only think that writing a poem about something valentininish to be appropriate. Imagine that.

"Ribbons, bows, and a little bag"

Tissue paper sticking up

Crinkling with every move

It is like a jungle in their

And all the presents like animals

They call out for you

This forest is dense though

Secretly concealing

Hiding within a shielding cloak

Inside, a token of myself

A piece of love that I wanted to give

And all you have to do is open it, embrace it

Hold it tight and never let it go

Smile

And look to me and see my smile

My joy of seeing you happy

Suddenly,

The movie ends

The fantasy collapses

A room lights up and all the audience walks out

Beside me is the popcorn I didn't eat

And a lonely cup of soda

Was this a dream

I toss this letter into the void, the abyss between us, this space that keeps conversation from happening.

Sincerely,

Rush Whitacre

740-336-9169

2-15-11

Dear Taylor Swift,

      I slept in today until I woke up and noticed that my clock read 1:30 pm exactly… I freaked. I teach at 2 on Tuesday and Thursdays and it takes ten minutes to drive to my parking garage, and then ten minutes to walk across campus… so, you can see how fast my gears were working in my head… luckily, I had taken a shower before going to bed, otherwise it would have been a bad day, a very bad day.. ha ha. I made it to class with 2 minutes to spare, and all of my students were so very very tired, and so very very exhausted. You wouldn't believe what these kids were able to pull off. There is actually a Star Wars snow speeder in the commons area of DAAP, there is a full sized plane, Two Wall-E's a huge connect four game, a light bright, a furby, a giant jack, a set of rock'm sock'm robots, two Lego men, a large Nintendo gaming system with controllers and a game and the game battleship, all giant at least 12 feet in one direction. I am so proud of my students, I actually had to not think about the amount of work these students had to put into their projects because I could feel the tears of joy coming to my eyes… really, I was so amazed and pleased with my students that I had to not think about it.

      Tonight's planning class was almost like it didn't happen, I was so tired that I was unable to think about anything that was being said, or even care about it for that matter. Then after class I spent a few hours with Jacki in my studio working on painting a dragon on the wall of my studio. I think that her art skills could be improved if she would just take the time to really hone her skills in on the details, and then also spend more time on her projects. I know it is hard to do when in school and everything you ever knew is different and far away from you, but you still have to get organized. The more time I spend with the students of DAAP the more I understand the amazing difference there is in their way of life because of technology. For instance, today, almost no one actually talks on the phone anymore, it is almost entirely done in text messaging. I think that this move to no talking and all text is making society very very different. I am not saying that we are going to learn how to not be able to talk to people face to face, but doing so will have a very different meaning than it does now. My guess is that all this texting is actually dulling down emotions and heated angry conversations… it is harder to keep your mouth shut while talking to someone than it is to send a text, one that you have to spend many seconds typing up making sure it says exactly what you want it to say. Off subject, I really need to do some work on my thesis, really, really bad… I have been putting it off. Oops

      This poem is for the "Maybe"

            "Short Sleeved"

              All my days

    Spent thinking about those looks you give me

         Those little hints of wonder

And my mind sizzles

The knowing of our next time together

Is like seeing that surface of the water

And knowing that when I get there

I will breathe again

I will know that I'm alive

And all my little curiosities about you

Will come streaming back into my mind

Through a door

Or an open window

Maybe a crack in the wall of the heart

The heart that for you

I so easily wear

On my sleeve

I toss this letter into the void, the abyss between us, this space that keeps conversation from happening.

Sincerely,
Rush Whitacre
740-336-9169

2-16-11

Dear Taylor Swift,

      Ok, so, today in Grad Studio we started off with slightly changing the critical analysis papers, so, I am going to rewrite my critical analysis paper again so that it fits their even tighter wants, because it is my need to make this class my trial ways of the slippery slope. This class is bizarre, experimental, and actually redundant as hell. I am bringing in my A-game of chaos, of changing up the norm, of making people think abstractly. I am still processing the words that my professor Kevin Matthews said at my last time of presentation, "SO WHAT", he said that with such vigor… and he is the head of my thesis committee… this shall be an interesting 4 to 5 months. So what, he said, here is my so what: are we here to talk about ideas or things,,,, the answer is, both, depending on what the student wants.. well, I want to present just enough chaos, just enough ideas that a student has to be forced to think a lot about ideas, not only about my ideas for a 'thing' but also for the class, and what is the nature of the class, what are we doing in this damn class anyway… And in my last crit, I succeeded in my aim, everyone was forced to stop, look around at each other, then look at me and ask me what are you doing, and then look back at each other and think, "what am I doing for that matter", "what are we doing in this class"… of course, it won't be until after I have graduated that I was right, that my way of presenting.

Ok, so this is to be the time around where we as the presenter is not suppose to speak…so, during Fix's presentation Ed says so many things that he talked with Fix about his work, so it was almost as if Fix had talked, and then he led us down a path towards the wrong direction, and so, we had this massive discussion based off of Ed's words and now Fix is allowed to talk and he has to go back over the entire thing everyone said and we are having an entirely different conversation… this is great, this is what I present in all of my presentations, enough chaos so that what I do have is thought provoking, idea provoking, thing generating provoking. Oh well, onto the next class.

I had a surprising thing happen to me this afternoon, a student, named Lawly, who I taught last quarter texted me and we met up and talked about books and art and she and I are going to meet up again this coming Friday for her to show me her work that she didn't finish from a class I had taught her from last spring. I have no idea what to expect, because I don't remember anything about what she was doing. She was home schooled and I can really tell that there is a real difference in her personality compared to all of those who were put through the machine of public schooling. Lawly seems to walk around with some weird form of innocence, but I know for sure that she is not because of photos she has had come across the facebook news feed. Anyway, she is a good person, and a good artist, so, she will be ok.

This poem is for Carlee,

"Inner Valley"

A red and gold palette

Used in the making of her hair

And her personality,

Like a rocket, sure of its destination

Calculated by so many,

And a trajectory precise enough

That not even the heavens can shift it

An honest happy smile

Spread across her pale skin

Pure as the eyes connected

And all you see is not

And all you feel is stared upon

> Ridiculed by the ridiculed
> Savored by the passing of light
> And a little laugh
> And a little stare
> All bodes well in the eyes
> Of the in-between

I toss this letter into the void, the abyss between us, this space that keeps conversation from happening.

Sincerely,
Rush Whitacre
740-336-9169

2-17-11
Dear Taylor Swift,

    Today was a rather interesting day… I sat in on Visual culture today and we watched Grizzly man. I had seen it before, but seeing it a second time was better because I was able to analyze it in a different way, I was able to enjoy it for the scenes, and the guts that Tim had to get so close to such giant animals, ones that could just as easily eat your face off as they could walk away. Well, either way, I am glad that no one will ever hear Tim's death, his screaming, his moaning, his girlfriend hitting the bear with a frying pan. He really did love those animals, and it is amazing that he survived out there in the wild for as long as he did. I really like it for a second time… I might even watch it for a third time.

    Class went well, other than the crit, it went well. My students are in love with this new assignment, it is like a virus or bacteria that keeps growing and growing. I changed their assignment from the other classes because I thought it was way too boring for them to just keep themselves in two hallways, so I gave them the reigns and they now have the power for their 'diseases' to spread to all parts of the building.

    It is now hours later, and I am sitting here with Jacki, she has asked me to help her cut out letters, so that she could hot glue them onto elastic stretchy cord to help her to make her 'disease' piece. I have no idea what she is doing, really, I don't, but I am sure it will be good, she is pretty creative. Right now, she is to my right, and she doesn't know that I am writing about her, she knows that I have been writing to someone every day, but she doesn't know who, and it is driving her crazy. I think it is funny, and I am not going to let her know because it is just not any fun anymore is she knows…

I think that Jacki is going to breakup with her boyfriend. She told me that she told him that they were just good friends, not boyfriend and girlfriend… I just sit here thinking, poor guy.

Tomorrow is Friday, a meeting with Bryan in the morning, and listen to him talk about how great everything is, and how wonderful everything is, and then ask us how are students are doing, and how the crits went, and pretty much it is like a business meeting. We are suppose to have one every week, but I haven't been to one yet, so, I had pretty much make this one since it is the end of the 7th week.

This poem is for the walk to the rainbow.

"Eluded"

One day during a certain rain

The sun came out

And in my view appeared a rainbow

Red, orange, yellow, green blue indigo and violet

Beautiful as it was

I wanted more, I wanted to touch the rainbow

Feel its beauty

Be coated in its wonder

An urge of an uncontrollable kind

And so I walked toward the bow

Thinking all along the way of the stories I've heard

The tales of fortune

Of becoming rich

Not just in wealth, but of the heart

A heart of gold

I walked, and pondered, and days passed

And all the while the bow eluded me

Moving farther and farther away

But I persevered, and now crawling

I thought to myself

I am in love

And there had better be gold at the end of this rainbow.

I toss this letter into the void, the abyss between us, this space that keeps conversation from happening.

Sincerely,

Rush Whitacre

740-336-9169

2-18-11

Dear Taylor,

    Ok, this has been by far the most lazy days of my life… I slept in until 2 something in the afternoon, and then watched movies on netflicks all afternoon, eating pizza, and drinking diet cola. How sad is that. I just kept sleeping and sleeping, and then I looked at thought, well, whats the point of actually getting out of bed to do anything today… it is Friday, I have no classes, and I have no girlfriend, and I have no dogs anymore, and I thought, what the hell. I will rest the whole day and then sleep tonight, and then spend the whole weekend making up for it… we shall see…

    Sunday is my birthday, I turn 32. I am starting to see a cycle here,,,, lol, every year I am getting older and every year I am seeing a pattern. The longer I stay single, the harder it will be for me to find someone to be with, to spend my days with… etc. and I don't want to be alone, I don't want to look to my side and have an empty seat. I want someone who I can make laugh, someone who I can say things to-to make them want to poke me in the side and then playfully chase me, or vice-a-versa. Surely it can't be that hard. I just have to figure out where, because I don't go to bars, and I don't go to church, and I don't do drugs. I will just have to join some clubs, or, stay in school the rest of my life… lol yeah, I don't think I will stay in school for the rest of my life. Not going to happen.

    My two roommates were at it again earlier, playfully yelling curse words at each other, and Louis had just finished taking a shower and was yelling for Yangue to go into the bathroom to dry him off… Their friendship/roommateness/encounters make me laugh so hard. You would just have to hear Louis boisterously yell out profanities at Yangue. He does it all in jest, but, it comes out sounding so serious, and that is the part that makes the whole thing so funny, and then to top it all off Yangue gives it right back to Louis. Earlier before Louis went out with his friends he and Yangue were having a cursing encounter and then Louis kicked an empty box into Yangue's room hitting the ceiling and then the top of Yangue's head, and then Yangue punched the box at Louis, and then immediately following that they exchanged very nice parting exchanges. It was a surreal moment.

    I forgot to mention, I was suppose to have a meeting this morning with Bryan, the guy who I guess you could say was my boss?!?, and of course I slept way in, and a little bit ago I got online to email him to find out what I had missed and he had sent out a message yesterday evening cancelling the meeting… so, I caught a break. I was so lucky. I have been lucky quite a bit lately.

This poem is for wanting something that you can't have.

And I run

Scraping along all the sides

Pushing off the walls

Quickening my pace

Altering my route

And taking all the shortcuts

Still ending on an empty street

Glaring

Just standing, wondering

'should I keep chasing,

Or let it slip out of sight

Out of my life'

The mood is sullen and still

And the moment passes

And comes full circle

This time deeper, quieter, and more hollow

A kind of space that leaves a person wanting

I wait

Looking at what I want

Ready to hold on tight if the chance arises.

I toss this letter into the void, the abyss between us, this space that keeps conversation from happening.

Sincerely,
Rush Whitacre
740-336-9169

2-19-11

Dear Taylor Swift,

    Well, I got some work done on the maquette I started for my exhibition and planning class. Such a silly class, I just don't know what the goal of this whole class is besides giving people a chance to set up a show who haven't done it before… and, my opinion is that if you have not made art work, nor set up your own show, then you probably shouldn't be in the class. The other day we went over how to measure a wall to be able to put a work of art on the wall at the height that you want it at... the four of us who are fine arts majors just stared at each other with expressions of,,, 'are you kidding me, are we really going over how to measure a wall.' Then I thought about it later, there are four people in the class who don't make work, but who want to work in museums and galleries... kinda a weird idea really, wanting to be something without the experience of being it.

Well, today is Saturday, tomorrow is my birthday. My friend Gari and I are going out tonight, Sunday is his birthday, and he wanted me to go out with him to celebrate with him.. this might be interesting, might be really interesting. Time will tell. Gari lives with a friend of his right now, and this friend left and went to OU in Athens Ohio to celebrate some other guys birthday who's is also on the same day as ours. But, that friend of Gari's left his girlfriend here, so she is going out with us, and Gari said to me that this should be interesting to see guys come up and hit on her, he says that she is something like a supermodel... I will be the judge of that. Gari wants to get really plastered, and I will be driving, so, I will be sipping on my coke, maybe one beer at midnight because it is my birthday. I don't see any harm in that. Well, I don't know what the plans are, but it is sure to be an interesting night.

I need to call my (related person who is male and not named), his birthday is on the 21st of this month. A year and a day younger than me. He is still sending me pics of my old Great Dane. She is growing up and looking great and I can't wait to see her again and see her run around. Sienna, my doggy no more.

Grace says to not drink diet coke because it is very bad for you, because of the false sugar quality of it, whatever the name of it is, false anything in a drink is bad for you and you should not drink it... a part of me believes that, but, at the same time, I would like to lose about 25 pounds of what I have on my body and the only way I know to do that is to just simply starve my body of all of its excess nutrients, which I am not doing, so, this is a conundrum...

This poem is for Gari on his birthday:

"Dear Gari"

Oh dear Gari

You think that you are special on this day

And that you are the only one

That not a one shares your birthday

But, then out of the wood works

Comes a sleuth of participants,

A group of rebel forces

To squash your melody of uniqueness

I know your simple desire
Your individuality,
To be a one amongst all the zeros
And I am still aware of your wants
Your knowledge of a future
Of a world of only you
Of only me
Of oneness
But I've known since I met you
That there is not such a thing
That I am not alone in the universe
You are a selfish being
A being of repetition
Of sameness
And like you
I too will search all others
Like us
Who search a greater truth.

I toss this letter into the void, the abyss between us, this space that keeps conversation from happening.ds

Sincerely,

Rush Whitacre

740-336-9169

2-20-11

Dear Taylor Swift,

    HAPPY BIRTHDAY TO ME!!!!!!!!

    Ok, so, I mostly celebrated my birthday last night, but that is ok, because today I am working on a maquette of the space where the freedom show will be exhibited. Jacki decided to join me in my studio, she is working on her virus/bacterium/disease piece that she is making for space class. I have no idea what she thinks she is going to make with puzzles, little slinkys, and little army men. I have a feeling that she is going to have to cut the things she bought into little pieces. I would use a blender and set it to slow chop and see what happens to the little men, maybe even use an old blender and throw in some paint so see how it affects the little army men. But that is just me, exploratory art.

Jacki's music is playing like mad all around the room, and I haven't decided if I like it or not, I am leaning towards indifference, because anything I listen to ends up turning into background noise in the end. My maquette is almost done, the flexi-cardboard is really helpful for curved walls and flat walls. I wish I had heard of it before, I would have been making maquetts faster and better with this stuff.

This morning Gari figured out that he had lost his keys, gone, not in the apartment. He and I tore the apt apart looking for them and came up short in all regards. We figure that he left them in is friends girlfriends car and that they are in Columbus at come modeling convention where she is getting signed. I have no idea what is happening… I told him to call me once he found out where they were so that I would not worry any more about them. See, I sometimes like to play little pranks on people, little jokes, and so I made sure that Gari searched my coat to make sure the keys were not in my jacket, I wanted him to have no doubt that the keys were not with me. That kind of trust is important to me, I want my friends to know that I don't mess around with someone's things to the extent that it is damaging to them, or to the extent that they lose all trust in me. I only play 'ha ha' jokes/pranks, not the kind that make a person say to me that I am a jerk or something like that. Oh well.

Good news, all the grads have discovered that the Grad Studio that we all hate is actually just a performance class where we bring in things that really doesn't have a whole lot to do with anything, just something to do, to perform with… which has been all my crits.

I dedicate this poem to indecisiveness,

"Clueless"

Puzzled pieces

Two puzzles, not fitting, not together

Colors of vibrant orange, red, and yellow

But rough edges don't match the smooth

And try as you might to keep them separated

The pieces mingle, the pieces clash

And all the while, nothing makes sense

You push and pull and smash

And your confusion, your choices

Are not being made, not settled on

And the answer is right there before you

Smacking you across the face with its glow

Its curiosity in nature, and its fit is magic

> But your eyes won't connect to your brain
> And your brain won't process image
> Nor what your mouth wants to say
> And that which will ease your emotions
> Is that which you cannot see
> And you are blind
> Because you don't
> Or won't
> Or want to

I toss this letter into the void, the abyss between us, this space that keeps conversation from happening.

Sincerely,
Rush Whitacre
740-336-9169

2-21-11

Dear Taylor Swift,

     Another Monday another day of Grad Studio. Today was another day of not talking, but nodding and looking like I know what I know, and would say something, but don't really care. This class sucks.

     Now I am sitting beside Jacki in the foundations room. She has a little virus piece to make, and I have a 10 minute video to make about the Carl Solway gallery... This day keeps getting better and better. I just left the philosophy class with Marcus and all the grad students who are mandatorily must take the class because if it were mandatory no one would take it.. and I mean no one. Yes, it is a great class, and there are a lot of good lessons to be learned,,, but, over the course of a year. There is literally enough reading to be done for a year's worth of reading and comprehension. And, there are several grads who have said that they are not reading the readings out of spite, kinda interesting to me.

     Now, I must venture off into the world of powerpointlessness for a class that racks my brain through the shear fact that I am fighting to stay awake. I just keep thinking, please, please, something happen.

     Ok, so, I am obviously having a day where I am tired and not wanting to be here, and my day was not that bad, but, I just need to nap and I can't because I have all this work, these little things I need to do, hoops I have to jump through. So, ignore the negativity.

Ok, so, it has been 3 or 4 weeks now since I did anything to help myself with my thesis, my work, and my piece that is suppose to help me graduate… How about that, and my intern is suffering because I never talk to her and let her know what I am doing, which is my fault… I actually forgot I had one for about a week, I just didn't think about her. Megan,, and I am sorry Megan for not contacting you.

Ok, so, I have been trying to talk Jacki into sending you a poem, so, she might do that. Of course, I have to ok it, so, we shall see what she comes up with… she also writes poems, kinda like mine, but more dark, mysterious, and I am thinking that some of them are subliminally contented… but, then again, I haven't read those…and she won't let me read them.… M

So, this poem is for strategy.

"The Roman Traveler"

Grids, Patterns

Ellipses, and graphic representation

All rigid and unplanned

And your poor eyesight

Can't see beyond your astigmatism

Your unnaturally curved eyes,

And in this sense even your body

Lies to you

But your body

Doesn't lie to me

You always let me know

How I should tread along your curves

The path is not always clear

And the signs vague

But when the moment comes

And I ease forward into an unknown

The subtle right

The signs are sure and vivid

And all our energy is set on a course

Me as the driver, you as the navigator

Destination unknown

I toss this letter into the void, the abyss between us, this space the keeps conversation from happening.

Sincerely,
Rush Whitacre
740-336-9169

2-22-11

Dear Taylor Swift,

  Well, I am going to preface this letter with,,, This is letter one hundred, and I am mailing this to 4 places just celebrate the fact that I am to letter number 100, and because I am sure you are not getting these letters…. I am not saying that 4 letters are better than one, but, maybe this method for the 100th letter will cause a seek and find to discover of the other 99. Don't worry, the letters are going to keep coming, and even if your little old ladies who open your mail have thrown them away, I am sure you will have some more interesting reading to come in the future.

  Soooo, with that out of the way,,, my classes today were rather uneventful, and rather,,, well, sad. As you know, I am sitting in on a freshman class, for the heck of it. There was one good thing that happened, I didn't have to sit by myself, two of my past students sat by me, so, I was like an island in the back of the room, and two survivors from a ship wreck migrated to my shore, and well, it was Carlee, and Copy-Cat-Cami,,, ,,, ,,, and, Carlee is hilarious, and Copy-Cat-Cami is just a pain in the butt. Actually, I think that Carlee sat by me so that she could play angry birds, and not pay attention to class… Ironically, Katie, who teaches the class, just as I was receiving a text from Jacki,,, Katie demanded that people in the front stop texting… and I thought it was Jacki, and so I immediately texted back to wreak havoc. Plan didn't work, fail.

  My students worked on their projects, and I worked on a PowerPoint that was due in my night class. Then, my students kept me preoccupied and I didn't get my presentation done, and I meagerly finished it just in time to present it to the class… I was proud, and so was the teacher, since she had seen me cramming it together at the last minute… After class she asked me what I thought of the Jun Kaneco show at the Carl Solway Gallery and I replied, Huh, it was ok, and then I watched her face change from delight to an expression of 'WHAT', because she loves ceramics and most of the show I did my presentation was displaying ceramics.

  On a different note, I asked Jacki is she would mind including a poem that she wrote, and since I don't really know anyone else here who writes poems, I decided that the two of us would do for a 100th letter/poem combo… I hope you enjoy.

This poem is for passion

"i is for imaginary"

Over and over and despite

And despite repeated

Making my way through a mix

A sudden urge to stop fails

And my wants are small

And my will is great

So judge me as you may

I will see this through

Anguish, pain, suffering;

Things that my pride ignore

And still pounding – beating

Beating

Like this heart

This flesh, my 'will' connected

Alone Together

Separate in dilution and haste

Measuring up to an i

An unsolvable equation

Measured only by the absence

The product

The solution

I toss this letter into the void, the abyss between us, this space that keeps conversation from happening.

Sincerely,
Rush Whitacre
740-336-9169

2-23-11
Dear Taylor Swift,

Just one class today, Grad Studio. Actually, today was a good day in this class. For some reason Chip(Chuck) was in a good mood, he was making fun of Randy's paintings, asking us if his work could do without his awful frames. I actually didn't understand the whole frame thing that Randy was trying to pull off. He picked some god-awful gold frames that looked like they had been picked up from a flea market and then used sharpie marker over all of the glass to make them look like little stain glass windows. Most everyone agreed on one of them as having some qualities that could make it the most successful piece out of the whole group. I actually was thinking it moments before a girl named Kat who opened her mouth to declare it as the most successful pieces, I was having a moment myself when this happened, I thought, wow, how surreal.

Later I picked up some subway to eat with Jacki and her friend Katie, different Katie. Subway was good, and I learned that Jacki had broken up with her boyfriend, and then today was going to get back with him, and I have no idea, I just need to steer clear of it all… Too much drama. While in DAAP I walked around and admired all the different viral works that all the students were working on, They really seem to be into this work. Except for the part where the hall doesn't look like it has had much work done to it… I am hoping that my students are all working at home or in their dorms on their pieces because I am expecting to see some really nice pieces when they do end up arriving tomorrow…

It is late, and I am tired, so, I am going to wrap this letter up. I leave for New York this coming Wednesday, and I should be there for three days going around and hitting all the different art places, museums, Chelsea, armory show, etc. I have gone to New York every year now for four years. Not a great expanse of time, nor hardly an achievement worth mentioning. In fact, I don't even know why I bothered to write about it.. oh well. If you haven't seen the Armory show before, you should get a good disguise and hit it up sometime. There is art from all over the world from all different kinds of gallery's going to be there.

Here is a poem for Alice(the one from Grad Studio

"Katie's Mouth"

The 2 in the back are always waiting

Ears perked

Eyes forward

All listening to the artist

The one who's full of hot air

The one with the work

On the wall

And as the artist talks

They are interrupted by a familiar sound

> The lips of a boisterous giant
> And as rude as her interruption was
> Her words more than make up for
> Her lacking in manners or raising of hand
> And the two in the back are now talking under their breath
> Pointing and talking and glaring
> Seemingly amazed at a recurring theme
> The cutting off of one artist from another
> I expect to see this behavior again
> In two days

I toss this letter into the void, the abyss between us, this space that keeps conversation from happening.

Sincerely,
Rush Whitacre
740-336-9169

2-24-11

Dear Taylor Swift,

  Another day watching my students working on their work. Today I missed my Visual Cultural class because of being up all night working on making up the sheet for the entire freshman's final project. Gosh, 4 am rolls around really quickly, let me tell you.. last night I didn't even feel sleepy, I just kept writing and writing, and when I finished I looked at the clock and about fell over. Then I moved and my body said to me, "Oh, yeah, you haven't moved in quite a long time. Kinda like driving for a very long time, you get up from where you are and you think,,, ohh, did I just step out of some kind of a mold of some kind, like you were slightly stuck in place and even your clothes appear to have wished you had moved hours before. Of course, I am sure you don't have this problem. For you have people drive you around… must be nice, and also kinda restrictive at the same time.

  After the space class I went to the TUC to get some Chic-Fila chicken. And, like usual, It was overpriced, and it still tasted like chicken. I will say this much though, they do have some of the best sauces to dip the chicken in.. I would say that is what makes a place if they are going to specialize in chicken, sauces… without some kind of special sauces to dip chicken in there is no real way to set yourself apart from the crowd.

Chic Fila only lasts for so long, and then you find yourself outside of Chrin Sands Studio talking to Chrin Sand about art openings that are coming up. The Keith Haring show is tomorrow, Friday, at 8 pm. I think that I am going to take some students from last quarter because they don't have transportation, Copy-Cat-Cami, Hogan, and some other girl who I have never met. I am just glad that I will have some company to join me on the ride to the show. I don't like going to places by myself, especially since I don't know who is going to be there and I don't want to go and just stand and observe works with no one to talk to.

Copy-Cat-Cami is a livewire, comparable to Keisha, some would say anyway, I don't get the whole Keisha comparison, and then Hogan is a guy who tries to come off as innocent and not a trouble maker, but in reality he is probably the leader who is being kept hidden. Either way, I am sure the trip to the CAC, and maybe the MGGM is going to be a great time… MGGM stands for Museum Gallery Gallery Museum. It is quite a tacky name, but a rememberable one. So, she said she would get another student of mine to come along, Hogan, and maybe yet another one… we shall see. Tomorrow shall be fun.

This poem is for not knowing what to choose,

"Undone, Unknown"

Undecidedly I decide to not know

Up or down, left or right

Or to just stay put

My meager food supply begins to suffer

And my reflex response slows

All my knowledge

Of who what when where and why

Dissolve

I am not able to make a decision

I am not able to feel

Or taste

Or understand why I am even confused,

In the first place

I look to my sister for answers

To a ream of paper that is yet to be typed on

To a cloud that has yet to form

And they too

Will not answer me

> Do not understand my standstill
>
> My inability to decide
>
> My moment that I let pass
>
> For I do not know where the spinning wheel stops
>
> Just like I don't know where this poem st...

I toss this letter into the void, the abyss between us, this space that keeps conversation from happening.

Sincerely,
Rush Whitacre
740-336-9169

2-25-11

Dear Taylor Swift,

    Lol, today was certainly interesting. I was woken up to a phone call about how the giant toys were supposed to be taken down the day before. Well, I said to the other Grad student on the line... "Huh, what are you talking about, are you crazy?" she laughed, I laughed, and then we said that we would see each other at school to move the toys. There was almost no one there except for maybe a hand full of kids, and I got them to help Susan and I to move toys and clean up tape off of the floor. We moved two 12 foot tall Lego guys, one with a helmet, a giant slinky dog from toy story, a snow speeder from star wars, a AT AT from star wars, and a regular Nintendo system that was huge. We only broke one of the feet off of the slinky dog, not too bad, but enough that it can't be hidden, oh, and I guess we had to cut the spring off of the slinky dog as well. Unfortunately, that was also the group that had the most inner turmoil I guess.. oops.

    Wow, I got around and saw a lot of art tonight. I went to the Museum Gallery Gallery Museum and saw an exhibition of pictures of pictures of painted areas where the pictures were there placed to show that the area that the pictures were then display in was also the very same spot that was photographed... it was a redundant show. Like seeing a movie in a theater with a TV in front of you also playing the same movie and then you also having a droid phone playing the same movie on it in the palm of your hand.... Unnecessary, and after awhile, ridiculous. I couldn't wait to get out of there. Oh, I forgot to mention. I took two of my former students with me. I took Copy-Cat-Cami, and Hogan. They were hilarious. After leaving the MGGM we were directed to the pendelton Final Fridays show... this was quite worth the going to. Final Fridays is held in a building where there are about 50 artists working, and on the last Friday of every month all the artists open their studios and gallery doors to show off their work and to hopefully make some money on their stuff. Wow, there was a lot of art there, but I wasn't impressed with any of it except the work of one little cute old lady, her work was beautiful. She really knew how to work with color, shape, and toy with my imagination. Her work grabbed me, and held me in place. I made my two students look long and hard at her work. After the final Fridays show I took my two students to the CAC opening of Keith Hering's work… wow, what a huge party, what an amazing little DJ service that came to do the show. Harings work to me wasn't that impressive, not to say that I didn't go around and look at it cause I did, because I wanted to see what my students were up against.

This poem is for Macki, one of Jacki's friends,

"Something Obviously Baited"

Confused by the gap

The difference between knowing and not

And all your strange confusing thoughts

Owned by you

But belonging to only a part

That which itches

Slowly driving you mad

And the girl you talk of

She is waiting for

Longing for

Love

To be loved

To be held in the arms

The strength

You worry about her

You want what she wants

And you want to be happy

Do not worry

You will be

I toss this letter into the void, the abyss between us, this space that keeps conversation from happening.

Sincerely,

Rush Whitacre

740-336-9169

2-26-11

Dear Taylor Swift,

 Yes, it has been two weeks since our last visit to the Asian market, and so, today we went. This time we, Louis, Yangue and I went to a new Chinese buffet called Grand Buffet. This is the same Buffet that Gari and I went to a couple of weeks ago, and there food is soo good, the best Chinese Buffet that I have ever eaten at, and for only $6.25, an amazing deal. After we at Louis proceeded to do this hilarious thing where he tried to pronounce the Chinese words on the back of the fortune cookies to Yangue to see if he could understand what they meant… It was absolutely crazy hilarious. Louis just kept on pronouncing the words in several different ways over and over and over maybe 30 to 40 to 50 times, and every so often Yangue would repeat the sound that Louis made and Louis and I would listen intently to what Yangue was going to say the word meant and he wouldn't, he would just sit there with his eyes wide and a pursed look to his lips and Louis or I would ask what the word meant and Yangue would only shake his head no.. and then say, I don't know. It was so funny… I can see that this type of event would only be funny if you were there, so, 'you had to be there'…

 We did our usual trip around the Asian market aisles, Yangue buying up all kinds of weird vegetables and dumplings, and Louis looking around at all the things with any kind of Chinese character on in. that boy is obsessed with Chinese culture and history, and with being hilariously rude to Yangue, and Yangue with the way he reacts to Louis. I am so glad that Louis and Yangue are so close. I am going to miss them when I am gone. I don't know what is going to happen to me when I graduate, I just don't know… the reason I say that is because my back has flared up again today, really bad, really really bad. I took some muscle relaxers and a hydrocodone, things I haven't taken in months, and they don't seem to be making much of a difference. I am about to take my second round because it has been 4 hours, and the package says I can take once every four hours as needed. So, I will hopefully be ok to sleep tonight… actually, I was starting to think that I might have the dream again that I had the last time I was all drugged up on this stuff for my back the last time. I have been laying here for hours watching movies on Netflix, just had a spoon of Mint Chocolate Ice cream, delicious. Tonight is sure to be good to me.

This Poem is for Randy(not my brother), for you have been writing on my facebook page as of late, and your side of the game,,, is losing.

"Ran Slo cal dow"

Peering under his bladed cap,

The anger of a sycamore

Frustration of an ecosystem out of balance

This his mouth and fingers

Always two steps ahead of thought

Of reason

Of choice

Importance is missing.

Teeth laid to rest in a glass of water,

All the world is a stripe,

A thin line,

Like his work

His time spent demanding of color

Forcing a single-file

Like cars on the auto bon

A thread through the seam

Or plane's soaring off to the same destination

A jet stream across a baby blue ocean,

Dissipating clean out of history,

Out of memory,

Lost for the better of all creation

I toss this letter into the void, the abyss between us, this space that keeps conversation from happening.

Sincerely,
Rush Whitacre
740-336-9169

2-27-11

Dear Taylor Swift,

    I am going to bed early tonight. I just don't feel like reading any philosophy tonight. Marcus's class is interesting, more on the level of just listening to the man talk about philosophy and less on us reading it to figure it out. I would think that if all anyone is going to remember are a few paragraphs from the readings and class discussions then why not just give us the summarization of all of it that is important, just the basic understanding of the philosophy verses some long drawn out reading that we aren't going to remember no matter what. I am not lazy, just don't understand burning out my eyes with unnecessary text.

I walked to school earlier. It is such a nice day, besides the rain and the little bit of humidity, it was a really nice day with a nice small cool breeze. My students were working on their wall/ceiling projects. The guys on the 5th floor like it when I am there because they think I am a goof ball, while at the same time I am able to be very smart and articulate about my job. I must say though, this project is actually a really ridiculous project. A grad named Christian designed it, but it really doesn't have any purpose, it is just a 'here you go, you have to make this thing and I am not going to tell you what you are suppose to get out of it, or how to go about making it. Actually, to be quite honest, It has not really been stated in any of the objectives of this courses assignments as to what the kids were suppose to be learning. Last quarter I was able to put into the assignment sheets what it was they were supposed to be learning because it was clear to me then what I thought each assignment was suppose to be teaching he kids,,, but this quarter, I have no idea for the most part. I feel kind of dumb giving the assignment and not having a clue of what to say to the kids as far as to what they should be getting from the assignment.

I just remembered, I have to make it to the bank tomorrow morning, or my checks I have out are going to bounce. And that will suck.

I leave for New York this coming Wednesday and won't be back to Cincinnati until Saturday or Sunday. I am really excited to visit the big city again. My friend Laura-girl is there and she is waiting for me to get there so she and I can do the town up the right way. I am not exactly sure what she means by that, so, hopefully a really good coffee from some random coffee shop or something.

This poem is for Taylor's look-a-like

"Jacki's Ironic clue"

Blushing

Red in the face with a little laugh

A little smile

And a brilliant idea from one into the next

Insecure

Unsure of choices made and decisions, decisions

Decisions are always in the present

They are always a thought

Like your blushing

Occurring sometimes without any reason

Your blonde curly hair, short

> Like your stature compared to the original
>
> But it can't be denied that you have an original
>
> For in thy copy
>
> There is perfection
>
> There is room for nothing less
>
> Everything was made for you
>
> The mold, the trial and error,
>
> and the mistakes,
>
> So that you would never be

I toss this letter into the void, the abyss between us, this space that keeps conversation from happening.

Sincerely,
Rush Whitacre
740-336-9169

2-28-11

Dear Taylor Swift,

    I slept through my first class, there was a huge storm last night that cut off all the electricity to the building. My alarm was blinking, can't remember the time it was blinking, I just know it wasn't the right time. The funniest thing happened though while the storm was going on. First of all let me set the stage. Flashes of lightening every sec, because of the mixture of real lightening and heat lightening. Thunder crashing every 3 or 4 seconds, and wind blowing rain in through all the windows. It was a really wild storm. I woke up in the middle of it when there weren't any lights on and the room was hot, no cool air was coming into the building through the windows. When I went to the window rain blew in all over me, so I shut the window and realized how crazy hot it was in the room, and opened it again. I lay back down and listened to the rain and watched the flashes of light. Then, in the middle of all the storm noises I hear two distinct noises, my roommates. Yangue had apparently needed to go to the bathroom and was in there doing his business, and then Louis I guess also had to go to do his business in the bathroom. So, as Yangue comes out of the bathroom Louis scares the ever-loving wits out of Yangue. All I hear is Louis yell BAAH, and Yangue scream and then yell at Louis in Chinese, or English, I couldn't tell because of how fast he was talking. Then the infamous Louis Laugh followed and then a slamming of Yangue's bedroom door and Louis laughing as he entered into the bathroom. Now, I was really tired, but upon hearing the scenario that took place in the pitch black of our apt, at 5 am in the morning, I laughed uncontrollably, so much so that I forgot all about getting up to set my alarm so that I could get up for my first class. So, there you go, laughing really can make you sleep in.

Now, I did make it to my second class, that is after a series of errands and taking my roommate Louis to the bank. Speaking of Louis again, I am really getting tired of him complaining about money problems when he doesn't have a job. The dude doesn't even have a job and he is complaining.... Come on man, I think that if you don't have a job you shouldn't be allowed to complain about money problems. I have been wondering where his money comes from in the first place. The guy has no money, and I am pretty sure his mother and father don't pay his way, so, where does it come from. The guy has no job... I am sure he isn't a drug dealer. All he does is sit and play video games all day and watch movies. Ok, enough of a rant on Louis, hey Louis, love you man, like a bro, I just want to you stop complaining about the bills and start coming up with solutions for how to pay them.

This poem is for Hamerlein,

"Angered, Crazed, and Blistering"

A man with the crusty scarf

standing in the woods

opened his mouth to talk

but nothing came,

no noise, no squeek,

the empty gap, silenced

by choice or by not choice

the gap struggled

Jawing up and down

Motioning for something to happen

then smoke drifted out,

a fireless smoke,

smoke bubbles,

filling the spaces, the emptiness

and as they popped

the craziest things erupted out,

the noise made all who heard it high

The louder the noise

The more intoxicating the sound

Addiction was inevitable

I toss this letter into the void, the abyss between us, this space that keeps conversation from happening.

Sincerely,
Rush Whitacre
740-336-9169

3-1-11

Dear Taylor Swift,

  I was so worried today about crit with my students. I had no idea on how to crit them. It was actually funny how the crit presented itself. Small random groups that neither grew in size, nor shrank in size, students came, and then they left and more came. And then, it was over. I guess I didn't want to do the individual crits because I just didn't know how to do them, I was afraid of having this entire class in the hallway following me around and me saying the same thing over and over. It was a great crit. I wouldn't have missed it for the world.

After crit, was my last class before finals week in exhibition and planning. All we pretty much did was listen to four people talk about show they went to and then talked about what we are doing for our final week in the class. I have a meeting at 9 am tomorrow morning with my group from the class to discuss our plans for what we plan on showing for our work down at the National Underground Railroad Freedom Center, or NURFC as we sometimes call it.

  After class I went down to visit with Jacki and her roommate Katie. I ended up getting caught up in a little childish play/fun/thing and the next thing I knew Kat had her hand soaked in green food dye and was pushing it upon my face… I was sooo upset, I had no idea that such an atrocity was going to befall my face. I had to leave the school of DAAP and walk to my studio and wash off my face. I was actually surprised that the green food dye washed out of my face after only 10 minutes of scrubbing with harsh chemicals meant to dissolve oil paint. I was really glad though because I leave tomorrow and riding on a bus for 12 hours with a green face, with undergrads a lot of whom I have taught, not fun. I would have just cancelled and not gone on the trip. I would have also missed tomorrow's class because not showing up is much better than showing up with a face that is half green. Thank god I got it all washed out.

  I am at home now, there wasn't any mail. I am only saying this because there is always mail, there is always something in that darn box yelling out, hey, hey you, you need to pay attention to me or I will be a bill and you will be charged extra!!!.. really though, I Have never been charged extra, lol, not that I can remember anyway, not that it really matters anyway

This poem is for Gretchen,

"The Vertical Line"

A mirror

The worst judge

Worse that those eyes

The ones that can't look me in the eyes

The ones that are always looking just below

To my identity, my mark

The one I shall leave upon the world

As the world left it upon me

We listen to you

Your laugh is infectious

For we see you smiling at life

And we shall never know its meaning

As you know what it means

Your smile

Creates many smiles

And strikes up many conversations

About many things

That have

No meaning

Unlike your purpose

Your life

The permanent mark

I toss this letter into the void, the abyss between us, this space that keeps conversation from happening.

Sincerely,
Rush Whitacre
740-336-9169

3-2-11

Dear Taylor,

Today's crit in Graduate Studio was amazing. First, we started off with Susan's ceramic stuff that she keeps making. She is working with clay in a non-traditional way where she is laying it out and everyone is suppose to walk on it. I am not convinced that Susan has thought out her idea of how she is going to get people to walk on her piece. I for one will not walk on her piece what so ever. I simply will not walk on her piece, not now, not then, not ever… mostly because I come to a gallery, or a show to look at art, not to walk on it,,, unless the artist has been sneaking and gotten me to walk across it without me figuring it out in the first place… It is possible, there was an artist a few years ago at the Columbus Art Museum who put a giant sheet of one inch thick steel like they would use on the roads to temporarily cover a hole and it was placed in front of a door to a gallery so as to make you think that you should walk on it because it looked like it should be there to keep you from seeing work being done or to keep you safe from a hole.. then, when you came out of that particular gallery, that is when you discovered that you had just experienced the artist's work.

Dustin's piece was also then very amazing. He sent out his artist critical writing part in a word document but set the text to the color white so that it looked like it didn't exist, even though all of the class could plainly see there was a word count, and that the file had a file size, they still couldn't figure it out that all they had to do was highlight the text to see it. I didn't even look at the text in the first place, so, seeing it in class was great for the first time…. I was so happy that Dustin went so far as to show his disdain for the class by doing what he did. Randy, who is quite a character, called Ed a waffle,,, and we all laughed so loud. It was great, but then Dustin was told he could talk and he did, that was a bit disappointing to me. I just wish for once that one of the grad just decide to not talk, just listen to everyone else and then not explain anything at all. Seriously, when I go to a gallery I am not there listening to the artist explain their piece, I go there and I have to maybe read a little label, but for the most part I am experiencing the artist's work first hand though how I see it in its location. I have to decipher a piece of it from all of the experiences that I have had in the past, and I prefer to have my own little experience with whatever tour I decide to take through the space/gallery/museum.

I followed Ed for about 2 hours today. I told him what I was doing and he said it was ok. So, I followed him as closely as I could for about 2 hours, and it was great, because I never spend any time with him, and I think he liked having a big sidekick who talked and listened.

So, this poem is for Ed,

Walking and looking down

Standing and smiling

Waiting in line to get money

And nervous, very nervous

About the man standing behind you

He might see your pin number
Walking and talking
Sitting and reading
And a class that waits
And waits
For you to talk
For you to respond to anything
But you don't
You toss out excuses,
And preface them with more excuses
And even the professor laughs
And even I laugh
At the professor
An inside joke as it appears
And only you and I
Are in the inside

I toss this letter into the void, the abyss between us, this space that keeps conversation from happening.

Sincerely,
Rush Whitacre
740-336-9169

3-3-11

Dear Taylor Swift,

    Ok, 58 kids, 13 hours, 2 gas station stops and then cracker barrel for breakfast and now we are back on the road to NYC… I think I heard that there is at least 1.5 hours left to go, and then we drop our stuff off at the hotel and then off to the MOMA… I sat by Alex all the way, well , so far. I am glad because he is much smaller than me and we don't feel like we are crowding each other, well, I am sure I am crowding him because I am big enough to crowd without meaning to… He told me that I could call him Alex the Great, so, I think that would be a great place to start a poem.

"Alex the Great"

<pre>
                    Hours, and hours of battle
                       Battery's deadened
                   And fingers calloused and tired
             Eyes fighting against a glare that is never ending
                         Hark, it is the isun
                   And its battle against the ipod
                      The intensity in your play
                    And confusion from every loss
                     And the game is a tricky one,
                          Always defending
                           Always waging
                         Always trying to win
                         Or make you retreat
                 Your face never changes with emotion
                        But the sounds you make
                          They tell a story
                     Elaborate and destined for ears
                   For the contemplative mind of myself
                    To enjoy, to independently decipher
                    To look back upon and be nostalgic
                About a time when I knew a guy named Alex
                     Who like to play star wars games
                     And do everything he can to win
</pre>

    Ok, many hours later, many floors of the MoMA, hundreds of paintings later, about 10 miles of walking, a giant free pizza dinner, a brisk walk into Chelsea to see a show because Bryan knew the people who were putting the show on, actually, the woman who was putting on the show promotes him somehow here in NY, I don't know, because all the shows of his I have ever seen seem to get destroyed after me makes them. So, I will assume for right now that Bryan has some alternate work that I haven't seen that he somehow gets to NY to be circulated,,, maybe. Bryan does have an absolutely beautiful baby, he is just the cutest thing, and Bryan is so very very happy. I wish you could see how he talks about his baby, he is such a good dad.

    My legs are so tired. They always get really tired on trips like this. Long sleepless trips though the night. Miles and miles of walking through the cold and careful to not step in odd potholes from the winter's plows. Something happened on this trip that hasn't happened on other trips, well, actually two things. One, I bought a poster, I just had to, it was actually one of those things that the universe was opening up to me and telling me to do, like these letters I am mailing to you. Lol, I will leave the story of the poster for another day. In fact, I will leave it for a conversation we could theoretically have in person. So, if we ever meet, ask me about the poster from the MOMA Museum. You will totally understand.

The second thing that happened is that Erica and I were walking back from the Museum and got wrangled in by a street salesman who was peddling tickets to a comedy show... Erica and I caved. For one, I have never been to a comedy club, second, I have never purchased from any of those guys because I don't trust them. And third, that guy threw in a bunch of things we could get for free, mostly bar drinks, so, I guess it will be fun to hang around with a bunch of drunk grads. Lol, we shall see.

I toss this letter into the void, the abyss between us, this space that keeps conversation from happening.

Sincerely,

Rush Whitacre

740-336-9169

3-4-11

Dear Taylor Swift,

Oh, I slept pretty good in this little old hotel. I was late to the Armory show by an hour, and thank god too, it was just the same old stuff pretty much as that from last year. I really wasn't too impressed only because I felt like I had already seen most of the stuff in there from last year. I mean, there were new things, but, for the most part as I was walking up and down the aisles I just kept thinking to myself, really, really, is this mostly the same kind of things I saw before, or am I mistaken...

Afterwards I followed some of the other grads Tilley, Michael, and Babyboo into soho and ate some of the best food, I don't remember the name of the pub we went to, but they had some of the best fajitas ever. Sooo good. Then we walked to the financial district and gazed at the WTC buildings that were going up. Tilley and Babybooand Michael just stood there and stared in awe of what was still an absence amongst the giant towers that were going up. I actually was expecting there to be more work done in the area, but the one tower that I saw really had only maybe gone up 7 more floors from what I had seen. I guess there is still a lot to be done.

Then, after a long day of my legs just aching like hell, I got to do what is so nice, and that is sit on the subway and just ride, sit there and ride and listen to the people and watch peddlers try to get change from all the riders by announcing that they need it. I just love to people watch. I am getting ready to go and meet up with my friend Laura-girl who I went to undergrad at OU in Athens Ohio with. She moved up here after a year of saving up money to do it and she has been making art and working jobs to get by. I am so proud of her. Anyway, I will write more, I am off to 5th street and Ave. A to a 'cherry tavern' is the name of the pub. Maybe I will get a good poem out of tonight.

Well, I don't know how the poem is going to turn out, but I can say that that I had a great time out and about with Laura-girl. She is so funny. She and I really don't have chemistry together, meaning I don't think we are compatible to date each other. Actually, she isn't like a sister to me, but more like a really really good friend. At least, I don't think she has ever had any romantic feelings towards me, and if she did, well, that would just be odd for her.

This poem is for Laura-girl,

"Heart Breaker"

Smiling that smile

And laughing that laugh

Your drink is almost gone and another is already coming

You date guys who don't end up hating you

After you have broken up

And you laugh another laugh

And whisper into my ear

These guys are nerds, I use to date that one…

And now I laugh a little laugh

And we both have a drink

And a look

And a smile

And we both know in that moment

That our friendship is a one of a kind

Now you dance

You are so funny Laura-girl as you hop around

Do you realize that you are drunk

Or are all the chemicals in your head

Keeping you afloat

Oblivious of the drought that your liver

Is about to go through

And the heartbreak
That this guy is about to experience

I toss this letter into the void, the abyss between us, this space that keeps conversation from happening.

Sincerely,
Rush Whitacre
740-336-9169

3-5-11

Dear Taylor Swift,

 Wow what a day so far. I saw the Whitney Biennial, then spent 6 hours in Central Park, I just love the park, I could spend all day there, I guess you could say I did pretty much. I bet I walked at least 12 to 14 miles from one end to the other. I was trying to make it my goal to see all of the little bridges. My feet were killing me, but then I came across this amazing little white bridge near the reservoir and I couldn't figure out why it would be where it is because it was probably the most beautiful bridge in the entire park. I sat on the center of it for, gosh, what seemed like an hour, and just smiled and smiled thinking about all the people walking by. They stared at me, probably wondered why I was smiling. It was weird. There was no wind all day and then as soon as I got to the top of that little bridge, which I don't know the name of, but anyway, as soon as I got to the top of that little bridge the wind blew so hard I thought it was going to blow me right off the top to the dirt path below. A passerby who had been jogging stopped and asked me if I was ok, laughed and said 'that was a close one wasn't it.' Then he and I talked a little bit about the park and all of the events in it. I guess I never really knew exactly how big the park was until today, spending all day walking around in it. Wow, so much to see… I had to hike over to the 96 east street subway line because there was no way I could make it to hotel Latham on 28th street, no way after all my walking.

 Tonight myself and four of the girl grads are going to a comedy club, the one that jerry Seinfeld got started in, and the one where Chris Rock was discovered. So, I guess that tonight is going to be a fun night of laughing and carrying on. At least I hope it is. I think I already said this, but I think the girls want to go drinking afterward… that should be interesting, and I shall be watching out like a bodies guard for them. Or at least sober so that I can get them all back to the hotel safely. Actually, they would be fine without me, I wouldn't want to mess with three female art students from DAAP, they are creative people, even in defending themselves…

    This has been a really great trip. I have gotten to do some things that I have wanted to do for a really long time, mostly that walking around in the park thing, I may do that tomorrow after checking out the new painting exhibit at the met, especially since it is right there anyway. And then I can also pick up some food from the street vendors too. Ha ha, street meat.

This poem is for my walk around central park, my friend was suppose to meet up with me but we never could find each other, so we gave up and just walked around separately.

This is for my journey in the park,

"A Happy Moment"

I'm right here

Walking around without you

A long path

A bridge with a breeze too

And the sun is shining.

I go all day

Wearing these soles through

Laughing out loud

Watching all the birds chew

And the bread will last only awhile

Friendly people

Ask if I need help

Light hearted

I say yes and I please do

But they don't know

That I have been lost for quite awhile

Going round circles

Hoping that I find you

Faking myself out

Looking at the trees-through

And then a bridge stops me

And I stare

And rest and smile for some while

I toss this letter into the void, the abyss between us, this space that keeps conversation from happening.

Sincerely,
Rush Whitacre
740-336-9169

3-6-11

Dear Taylor Swift,

Ok, it is 3 am and I decided that I would start this letter early because I have to ride a bus back tomorrow for 12 hours, and I am not about to type this letter on the bus…

So, wow, the comedy club was amazingly hilarious, and I would do it again in a heartbeat. The acts were amazing, and the last guy that went up was so incredibly on top of his game, it was like the crowd was tailored to his routine, just hilarious, just really freaking hilarious. The three grads who I took with me laughed harder than me at all the jokes. Especially Jennifer, she laughed so hard that she caught the attention of the comedian, and he makes a couple jokes about it. It was too good. Then after that we came back to the hotel and I was thinking about calling it a night because all the walking and then all the laughing nearly killed me. But then we all went out to a dancing bar and danced until 2 am. What a crazy crazy time. So, I am about to get off of here and crash. I will most likely write more about this later.

Ok, so, here it is later today, and let me tell you that it is raining, and this is great because I have never been in New York when there has been any other kind of whether other then nice weather. Needless to say, I also want to experience NY in the winter to get a good snow storm in, but, I won't get that until I move there. So, for now, I will just have to imagine. Today is the day we go to the Met and see the Cezenne exhibit. I went, I saw, and I really liked what I saw, but I just wish there were more paintings. It was nice to see how Cezenne went about his practice and all, but I still would have like to have seen more. One of my favorite parts about this trip was being able to walk some of the undergrads around so that they could see some of the particular works like Van Gogh's Starry Night, and Chuck Close's before and after paintings. The students were really impressed with the Close picture before he had his unfortunate stroke. His after paintings were very impressive as well, but just to be able to see the precision, and photo quality that an artist can put into a painting is just brilliant in Close's paintings before.

After the Met, I walked Makinley over to the Natural History Museum to see the Dinosaur exhibits. She loved them, and we actually got to experience the Tropical Butterfly exhibit, the butterflies had just hatched and there were dozens and dozens of butterflies flying around and mating. I don't why I was surprised at the notion that the butterflies could be mating and were, I guess the thought just never crossed my mind. They were quite beautiful in their little mating stances hanging upside-down. Together they looked like one giant butterfly with two heads.

      Now, here I am on the bus to come home, I am exhausted, and a 12 hour bus ride is not going to make it any easier for me to feel like I slept. Oh well, I had just make this poem quick

For Makinley and her butterfly,

"Blue Wings"
No Flash, thank you
Said the attendant
As watchful as ever from her position of power
The girl pouted as she fiddled with buttons
Turning so as not to give that satisfaction
The one of knowing that she was made embarrassed
Made to feel unaware
But why not a flash, the girl thought
They are but butterflies
And a flash certainly won't dull their wits
So the girl flashed again
And again came a scolding
Then fluttered down a pair of blue wings
Landing on the attendant's nose
In all its glory, and all its delicateness
The butterfly gently flapped
Then irony came in the form of a question
Dear, dear girl, would take my picture with the butterfly
The girl turned, leaned in close, finger on the camera button
And blew with her mouth the butterfly off

I toss this letter into the void, the abyss between us, this space that keeps conversation from happening.

Sincerely,
Rush Whitacre

740-336-9169

3-7-11

Dear Taylor Swift,

    I told myself last year that I wouldn't do the New York trip this year and now I remember why, that bus trip is killer. Got back to Cincinnati and felt very sick to my stomach, aching all over from sleeping on the hard bus floor, and just plain wanting to shower and sleep for all day, even though I knew that I had class at 11 and shouldn't skip it. Well, I did anyway, just somehow slept right through it. Now of course, I am afraid that I may very well not get a very good grade in that stupid grad studio class because I have missed one too many classes, oops. I guess I will get what I get. The trip to NY was totally worth it, and no one can tell me otherwise.

    So, when I finally did wake up for the day I checked out the mail box and was reminded of the reality of the bill situation, bills must be paid, and bill late fees must be taken into account,,, not fun. But, who cares, not me, I am simply too tired to care about being charged an additional 10 dollars to pay my bill. So stupid. My roommates were happy about having to pay bills, they never are, especially Louis, he becomes so winey around bill time, it is just sad. I have to listen to him go on and on about the bills, and how he doesn't like how our land lord does what he does to charge us for heat… blah blah blah. Ha ha, who knows, maybe I should give more of a crap, but the simple thing is, I just don't. I see the bills, I know for sure that I have no power over the heat situation and I just take it, well,,,, that is not entirely true I guess, because this month, I really don't have enough money to pay all the bills, so, this month the land lord is going to have something to complain about. Irony, I wonder how the land lord will complain, I wonder if it will be in the form of a letter, or by phone?? Hmmm, I bet by phone at first, and then by letter, and then by lawyer… but here is the thing, they still haven't come in to fix the faucet, the ceiling, or considered even telling us the truth about how we are being charged for heat… so, I am totally confused. Anyway, enough about this crap. If all else fails, I will move into my studio, kinda like I did when I went to school at … well, maybe that is better for a story in person, or at least it is more fun to tell in person anyway.

This poem is for Claire, I just found out that the guy you are dating doesn't like it when you look good, because he has a low self esteem. Pity

"Treads"

Tall, towering over the short men

And legs that reach the ground

From the stars

When I met you, you were beautiful

You danced across a room to me

> But, something happened, you changed
> As you fell apart I began to worry
> Is she depressed
> Is she sick of trying
> Has her world fallen apart and the reason not apparent
> Oh Claire, you shouldn't have to be less than perfect
> Less than you are when you aren't trying
> Because I can tell that you are trying
> But not for the better
> You are trying to look worse
> To hold onto your severed flesh's dignity
> His lacking has become your undoing
> And I fear that if you allow him to
> He will devour you entirely
> Slowly to rot
> Decay
> Slime of the earth
> And then there truly won't be much of you
> After being stepped on
> By his boots

I toss this letter into the void, the abyss between us, this space that keeps conversation from happening.

Sincerely,
Rush Whitacre
740-336-9169

3-8-11
Dear Taylor Swift,

    I slept through my first class again today, well, really it was just the freshman class that I am not enrolled in, so, it really didn't matter really… nonetheless, I did make it to my meeting with Gretchen to go over our plan on how to make our presentation for exhibition and planning. The meeting went well, and so didn't my class with my students. None of them really like their final project. I don't know, I guess I don't like to many of the projects that they are being made to do. I guess I don't understand what it is they are to be learning from their work, other than learning that they have to make something, and that making something is what is to be done.

Just one and a half weeks and I won't be teaching any more, that is what I keep telling myself, one and a half weeks and I can go back to being a full time student myself, making work and focusing on my stuff. I can't wait, paintings, I am going to be making paintings this coming quarter, how exciting, really exciting. Marcus, the director of the school of art is teaching the painting class, and I heard that he has plans for lots of reading for us painters… now, I don't mind reading usually, but I haven't really sat down and just painted in a while, so, he is going to meet with some resistance from me when it comes to the readings. I just want to put some good ol' globs of paint onto a canvas and push it around. Yeah, just to play with color.

I spent my night class at the NURFC, the National Underground Railroad Freedom Center, plotting out the layout for the first time ever art show of the inmates who were freed because of the exoneration program that have been freeing wrongfully arrested and jailed individuals by using DNA testing and proving that the imprisoned person wasn't the one who committed the crime. It is quite a show, so many emotional stories, and letters, poems, and some paintings and drawings. I can't help but to think of the how that person's life was ruined, lost from all those years behind bars. There is not taking back 17 to 20 years of wrongful imprisonment.

This poem is for my friend Wester, and his weird food or alcohol making ideas

"Just Funny Ideas"

Cookies, and cups

Alcohol from chocolate covered cordials

And maple bacon in no bakes

My friend Wester has tried it all

With back sweetening

And filtering, filtering, and carbon filtering

How many things must you get your fingers into

How many baths must you run

To cool down that brew

Does your wife know that you drink

Does she know that you love me like a brother

No matter what the offense

Smiles

And all your days of formulating

> And all your hours of deciding on a new mix
> All have led you to this solution
> Start a brewery, winery
> To make thy one spirits,
> That is what you crave
> To make something great
> So that your kids won't have to worry
> So that you won't have to worry
> Because in the end
> Money is what you really want
> Money
> For a better life
> For your kids

I toss this letter into the void, the abyss between us, this space that keeps conversation from happening.

Sincerely,
Rush Whitacre
740-336-9169

3-9-11

Dear Taylor Swift,

    An early morning, bank stuff taken care of, and I met with my Grad Studio class. YES, I received the best news from my professors, but first, let me tell you about the students who went today, because it was amazing. First we got to talk about Leah's work, which were prints who's methods for making were started back in the Victorian age, and so therefore were scrutinized for all the wrong reasons. I just love to see Leah smile, because then I know that the world is where it should be. Anyway, there was this moment amongst all the chatter when Randy broke in and asked a question. I don't remember what the question was, and I can't remember what Leah said in response to it, but that was because before she answered there was this 4 to 5 second moment where she slowly grew this amazing smile across her face and it really didn't matter what she said from that moment on because her work was done, right there. Then of course Randy kept on going on and on about how he didn't understand why everyone kept on calling Leah's work Victorian, kept on making the comment that 'just because it is done in the style like they did back then doesn't make it so, because none of the material used in the photo's said anything about it being so… God bless you Randy. Leah's crit was followed by Anna from Russia, and her crit was ok. The really great thing about Anna is that she can't speak English the greatest, and so rather than talk about her work at the end of her crit she danced. She simply blew everyone away. She usually walks around very still with her boots on, like a person from the military.. But in her dancing she was so very elegant and smooth, took everyone by surprise. She received clapping that was so loud, very loud, loudest I have heard since I have been at UC. Funny really. Then came the best news about the class, this class that everyone including myself is struggling with to understand has been reduced to everyone getting A's, let me say that again because it feels so good, "Everyone gets A's" I nearly jumped out of my skin with great exhilaration. I hate to say it, but I really should be getting an F in the class just from shear missing classes. Not that I would miss classes on purpose, but because I just couldn't drag myself out of bed for one reason or another, legit reasons. A's for everyone,,, awesome.

Then in the afternoon I sat in on a different class's crit, the installation's crit. I just love Matt, I think he would let me sit in on just about any of his classes just because I think he thinks like me, the more the merrier, so long as I don't cause a problem.

The inner-workings of the university of Cincinnati are rather an odd one. I can see how the university works, how the people work, but I can't understand how these people decide as a group of professionals come up with random mandatory classes that don't appear to have much to do with the advancement of our education. I mean, really

This poem is for love part M

"Temperature of a moment"

I wonder if you will ever know my love

My choices around you,

To be close to you.

The air you breath is slow

And the uptake, it is like a flash of smoke

I am coughing, choking, taking too much in

Like my ideals, flesh, dream, and sin

You make them all appear like gravity's foe

A repulsion that defies the law of physics

Not like the physical interaction,

Or the chemical reaction between us.

Like a moment in-between realms

The secular section of a second sanctum

> Why, oh why, is there a need for a number two
>
> When all that is needed is a first
>
> A second would be admitting to the not knowing of a know
>
> The underlying falsehood of self, or self's mirror
>
> A self that is not self, but other
>
> A temporary relationally aesthetic moment
>
> Meant only for the right person,
>
> At the right time,
>
> Right place.

I toss this letter into the void, the abyss between us, this space that keeps conversation from happening.

Sincerely,
Rush Whitacre
740-336-9169

3-10-11

Dear Taylor Swift,

    Hello, and how are you. I taught class today, if you can call it teaching that is. I really didn't need to be there other than to help out my students and give out a few grades. My students were really quiet today. It was like they really didn't want to be there. I should have told them to go home if they really needed to work outside of school. It wasn't fair that they had to stay there if they didn't need to. I was too caught up in helping those who needed it, and grading everyone's last project. I actually developed a great way to grade their last project, it is quite brilliant. It is almost impossible to describe on here in less than a page, so, I will spare you the details. Just know that it involves simple lines and circles around the lines… how funny is that.

    After class I went to my studio where I started the gross job of writing my artist statement for Marcus's class… I did come up with a fairly brilliant way of solving the dilemma, here I will give you the rules behind my reasoning:

"Not only will I create an artist statement that makes sense for the kind of work I have been documenting as of recent times in the form of letters to a famous person every day, but It will also be the creation a type of artwork that is temporary and can only be made from this past quarter based on readings and the order they are in, thus like a relationalistic work which I will then read to my peers, let them experience it, and most likely discuss it in a letter to my famous person. My words will not be used within the artist statement because that would detract from the purpose of keeping the quotes wholesome and prime.   Quotes are chosen in the order in which they appear on blackboard as of 3-10-11. All quotes are taken from the portions that were uploaded for the intent of our reading, and not from the extraneous portions either at the beginning or end of such sections. All quoted sentences were chosen only if they were a prime number starting with the prime number 2 from the first article and this continues through the articles in order until I reach 1250 to 1500 words, or until I reach the end of the last article and then go back to the beginning continuing the counting of sentences until 1250 to 1500 words are reached. So, an example for selecting my sentences I will choose the 2nd sentence from the first article, the 3rd sentence from the second article, the 5th sentence from the third article, and so on and so forth until word count is sufficient. This is my artist statement and will act as itself as an art object for this class. Prime, as in it stands solid alone, indivisible by only itself or one. Quotes will be designated as (article #/sentence #)"

Well, anyway, that is the gist of my paper, be a judge if you want. I think it will speak volumes to Marcus…

I dedicate this poem to surprise kisses

"Irony's web"

You are like a snow out of nowhere,

Surprising

And all I can do is wish and wonder

Can I have you once again, and

Will we share that moment that I remember

Will I notice

Or will my attraction

Be my distraction keeping me from you

And I hear the piano

Keying away my life

My heart's cord sprung

And I love you with all my heart

And all my soul

And my life's a life not worth living

If kissing you isn't like the air I breath

Like the arms I want wrapped around me

Like your warmth through those tears

That make me love you even more

As you smile and say

Kiss me, come here you

Kiss me, I love you

I toss this letter into the void, the abyss between us, this space that keeps conversation from happening.

Sincerely,
Rush Whitacre
740-336-9169

3-11-11

Dear Taylor Swift,

    More work and work, I love when there are so many things to do, it makes my day worth running around for. Sitting in my studio I can't help but imagine what it will be like when I am gone, seeing that now I only have one quarter left, three months, and then a month at home and the moving to New York. Gosh, I wonder what that will be like, me in NY. Most of my family, and extended family know about my plans, I wonder what they think. Doesn't matter, I keep telling everyone that my most recent trip to NY was the best ever and that I can't wait to live there for awhile.

    You are so lucky. Stars are born, and this statement is truer now than in any other time in history. People who are born with genetic dispositions for greatness are more easily discovered and further developed sooner than ever before. This kind of thing is for sure to not stop any time soon. Strangest thing is that this kind of behavior is also leading to a selective kind of breeding that puts the fastest runners in contact with other fast runners, and those really good at math with other mathaletes, and so on and so fourth that just enough of those people with similar qualities, or genetic dispositions for one thing or another are going to breed and have offspring, when in turns makes the gene pool in that area usually stronger, thus slowly altering human existence into weird possibility pools, genes.

    OK, enough of that weird stuff, I am back home now, my roommate is watching something funny, his laughter is penetrating through the wall. Louis really has a nice laugh. One of those laughs that make you happy to hear, I don't know, there is just something to his laugh. Yesterday I heard him loose it laughing and I rushed into his room to see what was going on that was so funny and he pulled up this video that his friend sent him. The video was one of a reporter asking Charles mansion a question and Charles Mansion did use any words to reply, he just made the weirdest strangest, whacked out facial expressions I have ever seen anyone make. Louis was totally right in laughing like he did, it was Hilarious, with a capital H.

I am going to confide this in you. I don't know if I will ever find someone who can match my ability to love, be understanding, patient, loyal, romantic, laugh and be laughed at. I just don't know. I have hopes of this happening, but doubts as well. I just know that the people who I thought were going to be a good thing weren't, or they simply gave up, or fizzled out, or downright cheated on me. And, I also was told by my most recent ex that the reason the others took advantage of me was because I was an easy target. Funny, I always thought that simply being myself and loving like I've never been hurt meant that I was simply being me, a human being looking for something real. What do I know. So, I keep looking.

Until then, whoever you are, this poem is for you,

"A Head's Up"

I want you to see everything

And I want you to experience what it is you need

Before you meet me to understand what is coming your way

Because this world is designed to throw us at each other in ways we can't imagine

In ways that break us apart before we can understand and learn

What is a broken heart if all you are is left with is confusion

I want to know, and I want you to know why I love you

Not just why I feel, or why you feel this, this is important

And I will never know you through as I hope you never me

For I want to never be left with nothing left to learn

As I want to spend the rest of my life with you, a gravity

Pulling me in harder, as attraction is attraction on any level

And I will love you like an endless wave never crashing

Never reaching a shore, I'm sure of that as I am sure of air

As I breath in, breath out, smelling your scent you left me

A memory bringing me tears, as a memory is there when you are not

And I will see you again soon, as a spring to its fall

As I spring for you, and there is no up to this temperature gage

Hot is hot, and bad in my life is something you are not

This truth is not my doing, and it is not your fault.

I know that you fall for me, as I spring for you.

I toss this letter into the void, the abyss between us, this space that keeps conversation from happening.

Sincerely,
Rush Whitacre
740-336-9169

3-12-11

Dear Taylor Swift,

  An all out work day for me. I spent 2 hours at the CCAC today with Meghan rearranging the furniture that I will be using to make my thesis show. I don't know how I am going to pull this off, but I am sure I will figure something out, most likely a last minute thing. I still have Kevin Matthews's voice ringing in my ears about me telling him that I might not be able to even write my thesis paper about my thesis project until I make my creation, and in front of everyone he said loudly, "You have to do better than that." I shut down and let him talk for a little while. Ok, I am seriously done talking about that day, it was total crap.

  So, after working at the at the CCAC I drove straight to the Law building where I matted and framed works of art for almost 12 hours straight, and we only got halfway done. I think tomorrow I am suppose to meet at the law building around 12 noon to finish up the job… I hope it doesn't take too long, I have work to do of my own, 2 papers, writing a syllabus from scratch, and writing an artist statement using only quotes from critical theory essays and books that we read in Marcus's class. Ugggh, I am almost to spring break, I am this close… I was the only DAAP student who showed up to help the Law students with the matting and framing of the art. I turned into the brains of the operation almost immediately because no one else there could cut matte board. Another uuugh, which means that I am the only one able to work while everyone else waits for me to finish cuts so that the rest can be assembled.

  Jacki is texting me telling me how she is hanging out with her ex, and how he is breaking her heart little by little… hmmm, this type of behavior sucks for two people. She broke up with him, but still loves parts of him, and then she hangs out with him and he is out to be mean to her. And I am sitting here typing to you, feeling weird, helpless, and unable to communicate to her. No matter what I say she will not be able to see what is best for her, and that is to just walk away. I am just a friend, and I feel that any advice I would give would be taken with a grain of salt, or sent over her head and not comprehended. So, I resort to being a master listener.. Me just listening is probably the greatest thing I could do right now.

This Poem is for a "Shorr",

"Social Scientist"

There she is, a figure to be reckoned with

A moving force, unstoppable, and direct to a point

To a flaw
To the ends of which her 'rights' meet 50 % when she is wrong
And her wrongs have yet to be recorded
They are there, but overlooked, and joked about
Because when they happen
It is a wrong in the realm of a comedy of errors
Mattering as much as a drop of water to the ocean
A tear to an eternity of rain
And she knows she is loved, because everyone laughs,
Behind her back, and then in front
And vice versa.
When there is a serious matter to be debated
Watch-out, because she will skewer any doubt you have
With her knowledge, wit, and stamina
And if she tries to hide anything that takes her by surprise
She will tell you plain and clear
For the red hue that fills her cheeks
Will never lie about her state of mind
Or the words she is thinking, screaming on the inside
While on the outside she is stammered, or reserved
Just remember, her back will turn to you soon enough
And you too will have your chance
To toss your wad of paper,
Aim carefully.

I toss this letter into the void, the abyss between us, this space that keeps conversation from happening.
Sincerely,
Rush Whitacre
740-336-9169

3-13-11
Dear Taylor Swift,

Another day here in Cincinnati where it was freezing this morning, and then the sun came out and the day warmed up and jackets came off and everyone had a smile on their face. My day started out with Louis at Kroger's… I am telling you, that guy is hilarious. I could listen to his stories all day long. I told him how much I love to his stories and now I have my own entertainment whenever I want it. All I have to do is be around him for a little bit and he starts into one of his small stories that ends up having 50 little side stories and tangents thus making the story so complicated and interesting and so much worthwhile to listen to.

After the trip to Kroger's I dropped Louis off here at the house and bolted to the Law school building. Yeah, I had another 6 hours of matting and framing left to do and I had to meet Jodi, the social scientist, so that she could let me in so that she and I could get to work. That poem I wrote I sent to her in an email earlier and she was so flattered by it that she has since then told me that she wanted to read the other poems and even help to edit my other things. She has sent 5 emails today, I was really flattered, but I had to gracefully decline her wanting to edit my things… I think that she would be a bit too harsh on me at times and she doesn't understand me and my wants. After spending time with Jodi for two days I know that she would simply tear apart anything I do, which is a good thing, but if that is how it would be all the time I fear that I would worry too much on being perfect and less on being creative first, and perfect secondary.

Right after finishing up the framing job I ran to school to see how everyone was doing as far as my students go.. Only about a handful of them were there, which was good, because there wasn't much room for them to work in anyway after the ones who were already there were there… now that I think about it, it really was quite a thing that only about 10 total people from all the classes were there, because there is about 120 students in all in this year's freshman class… so, I guess there were 7 of my students, where was everyone? I just hope that everyone gets there piece done, that is all I hope. Two of my students were texting me all day about what was going on with what for the show… and of course, I think the one girl only typed to tell me that she bought new shoes for the occasion, I laughed, and then thought about how great it was that she decided that it was a big deal that she gets to have a show at the CAC, even if it is only for 3 hours.

This poem is for the dragon lover,

"Dragon"

Quiet

Her secret is like a privilege

Seeing it like the slits of her eyes

You feel her as she gleams into your soul

Tearing you apart

Emotion by emotion

> Tail gouging grooves, a crushing sound
>
> The left over mayhem
>
> The darkness
>
> Poignant and enduring
>
> She is slow to inhale
>
> Bringing in her world around,
>
> The smell of moist cave walls
>
> Puddles,
>
> The sound of a drip
>
> Scales cling to cracks
>
> A fire from deep inside brews
>
> Exhale
>
> And all the cave comes to life
>
> Light in this world
>
> Never felt so cold

I toss this letter into the void, the abyss between us, this space that keeps conversation from happening.

Sincerely,

Rush Whitacre

740-336-9169

3-14-11

Dear Taylor Swift,

    Today was the last day for my students to be in my class. We held an art opening at the CAC for three hours for all the students to show off their work. It was a good time, at least for me, I really enjoyed teaching this year. It a change from last year in that last year I only got to teach for one quarter and it was broken up into 2.5 week workshops that meant that I wasn't guaranteed to have any of the same students from workshop to workshop. So, fall of this year I was presented with my first full quarter class. It was awesome, I will never forget any of my students. The CAC, or Contemporary Art Center gave us three areas for the students to present their work, one dark large room, the open foyer area, and then the lobby on the ground floor. It was a really great show. Today was weird a little in that I feel like I got nothing done but running around and putting money into meters. One of the students earlier had a moment of crisis where she had torn apart another student's older work of art, with permission to use the piece, just not tear it apart, and then that student got really angry… Then, she couldn't get the dang thing to fit in her car, so she called me up balling, telling me the whole story. It was great, nothing like a little drama to pretty much start your day. That was reason number one as to why I lost my first parking space where I just put 4 hours of quarters into the meter… pretty funny actually, I laughed and thought, really, I mean really, talk about fate. It was fun, Carlee's Cousin had a good little trip to Kentucky to get the crib for her latest project.

Once I got home I started working on my final project, get this. I got to my apt around 10 pm, and still had to make a syllabus and finish my 2500 work artist statement for my critical theory class… magically, I just finished about 20 minutes ago, it is 4:30 am, and I am not tired.. this is a bad sign. I am half afraid to go to sleep because the assignments are due by 9 am this morning… mmm, stay up and be really tired tomorrow, or, get some three hours of sleep and pray that one of my 5 alarms gets me up… yup, a hard decision indeed. I guess I could always just put some Netflix on and watch some movies. Lol, a bad idea, surly I will fall asleep then. I am slightly disappointed that I haven't heard back from Jodi, the person I helped to matte and frame all those artworks up for the Show at the NURFC. Oh well.

I just realized that I have a bigger dilemma, I just realized that I have a 3 page paper due tonight by 5:30 pm via email to the professor for the exhibition and planning class. I guess this letter is the pusher for me to not go to bed tonight. Oh Boy, here we go.

I dedicate this poem to the naming

"Check Please"

Lemon

Used to describe a car

The flavor of sour

Scent of cleanliness

And my favorite addition to a diet cola

Yellow, not a flavor, a color

A decision not made by man

But by nature

Are we to assume

That yellow means sour

That yellow means fruit

Human nature says yes

As we search for answers

Search to name the unnamed

> Because we like to talk,
>
> We like to gossip
>
> We like to prove our intelligence
>
> But all we really do
>
> Is limit our ability to think
>
> To solve problems
>
> To creatively make choices
>
> To sever, to cut clean
>
> To know

I toss this letter into the void, the abyss between us, this space the keeps conversation from happening.

Sincerely,
Rush Whitacre
740-336-9169

3-15-11

Dear Taylor Swift,

    Well, I got my last assignment in to Marcus, and instead of having it in before 9 AM,,, I got it there around 9:20 AM and Marcus wasn't there yet, so, I consider that as being turned in on time, why not, he isn't going to know one way or another. So, after a night of not sleeping I hung out with some of the other grads in the sculpture department just talking about the break. I felt so out of it this morning, and I hate feeling so tired that I am useless.

    I am here at home now, chilling and watching some movies and thinking about what I want to do on St. Patrick's day. My friend Chris, and Babyboo and this other guy name Jonathon want to sit at Scioto, our studio building, and watch the show Twin Peaks all day long starting at 9AM. They asked me if I would buy some snacks since they are buying the drinks. St. Patrick's day is starting to sound like it could be quite a barf fest for some of the guys involved. I don't know, I think it will be fun to watch everyone getting drunk and laughing at a show that I have never seen before, I don't even have a clue as to what it is about. I don't care, I just want to be a part of something on St. Patrick's day, something fun, something with my friends. I think that tomorrow night I will go home to spend some days with my dad, and visit my (related person who is not named). I miss them, I haven't been home at all this quarter and that is a first for me, to be away this long since I have been to Cincinnati.

I think that Jacki is coming over later today. She and I are going share a pizza and watch a movie to celebrate the ending of quarter. She and I would never work out as dating partners because, well, just because it just wouldn't work out right now. She needs some time to grow, and I need some time to establish. Now, as with all things, if I win the lottery, my mind might change, seeing that I would have all the money in the world to do for her that she wanted and needed. For now, I will just keep my head low until I get out of this University.

Ok, flash forward, I just took Jacki home. We watched the new Karate Kid movie with Jaden Smith in it. This Karate Kid version can't even compete against the original Karate Kid.. in fact, they are on two completely different levels, not even on the same level. I think that the original Karate Kind should be showed right alongside the original so that the costumer doesn't go wanting. We then watched the classic Labyrinth movie with David Bowie. I keep forgetting how much I really do love that movie, it is timeless, too bad Jim Henson died too soon.

This poem is for Fire and Ice

"Toyed with"

Amazing

That a production house

Full of sweatshop workers, slaves

Could produce from the same mold

Such differences in personality

In stare, Emotion, in Heart

One of a longing sadness

And the other of amazing fierce determination

As much as she can see

And as much as she wants to make them equal

They are not

One is obviously a boy

The other a girl

And amongst the loving caress's she gives their backs

She too can't help but want them to be a pair, one love

Like the boy who wishes to be hers

A reality blunted by walls and waves of despair

Like a reality you awake from

Something of a dream

Her passionate love like Fire

And his broken heart like ice

I toss this letter into the void, the abyss between us, this space that keeps conversation from happening.

Sincerely,
Rush Whitacre
740-336-9169

3-16-11
Dear Taylor Swift,

    Today has been a long day. Just relaxing here at the apartment, that is, until I got a text message from my bank telling me that my checking account was over drawn by 47 dollars and some odd change. I hate that it was overdrawn, but then again, I hate paying overdraft fees, so, I quickly ran to the bank and make the account good. Today has been a Jay Z kind of day. I have been listening to Jay Z most of the day, wondering what it is like to be one of the greatest rappers of all time, I mean, he is obviously talented, and he is obviously loved by millions of fans. When I was in New York his music was blasted in all the bars and clubs. Now, do I think he is the greatest performer ever, no, it is no doubtedly that that title goes to Michael Jackson. It is still not clear to the extent to which Jackson has altered the direction of music, for we will not know within our lifetimes completely, or we might if we live long enough.

    I want to rant about facebook for a minute. What about facebook is it that makes everyone go so hog wild with all their private everything. I was contemplating the deletion of my account today because I really don't have a need for such a thing. All I do is get on the net and when I get to the facebook page of mine there is nothing but some kind of bull-crap either about me, or about what ever. Also, can I please get on my email and not get any more requests for friendship on my email account that doesn't have anything to do with anything.

    So, I guess tomorrow will be St. Patty's day. My friend Chrin Sand has some party planned where we all show up and watch the show twin peaks all day. I Have never watched it, and I am sure I am not going to like it by the explanation that Chris gave me. I will see. More than anything I would really like to go home over the break, so, tomorrow night I will be doing such a thing.

    So, my roommate Louis got me started on the series Battlestar Galactica and I can't stop watching it, it is really good. I am up to episode 9 now from the first season. I guess there are four season's, so yeah, I will most likely be watching them all during this break, how sad is that. Anyway, it is that good, and no, I can't watch it all during the break, because there is a thing called sleep, and a thing called a thesis paper that I have to write, and I will write it. I have to, or else I will not be having a good next quarter.

This poem is for the wounded,

"Horizontal Bandage"

Just hiding isn't going to make it so

And you can wish

Or flip pennies into a well and close your eyes

Or stare into a night sky

Praying for that tiny flicker of hope

To glance in front of you

Running away will fail too

As your wounds are always right there

On you like the frown upon your face

The freckle on your cheek

Everyone around you can see the body language

But only you can see the drops

The tears that dribble down your cheek

To the floor, to the bed, to that pillow

The one you lay your head upon

Night after night

In an attempt to nurse your wound

The gaping hole

Your broken heart

I toss this letter into the void, the abyss between us, this space that keeps conversation from happening.

Sincerely,

Rush Whitacre

740-336-9169

3-17-11

Dear Taylor Swift,

I am soooooo tired, so tired, and my roommate is wanting me to go out tonight and I am ready to do that only because we never hang out, and this will be a good time to hang out… him drinking, and me drinking diet something having fun, watching everyone drink and slowly get more and more loud until the end which is pretty much a mass exodus upon the bar tenders screaming at the people to get out of the bar and leave. At least the past two times I have been there this is how it has happened, and I don't have a problem with it, I just will not drink because I have to drive, so, I really just want to have a good time and not be harassed to drink. Period

So, earlier today I spent all day watching Twin Peaks, and like I mentioned yesterday, I didn't like it, at all. I am not really into twin peaks, it is just too much like a days of our lives show, and I am not into soap operas. Literally, there were five other guys, and two girls at the showing of twin peaks today. Let's see, Jonathon, Dustin, Chris, and BabybooClaire and Sarah were there watching the show, and Claire ducked out early, and everyone had been drinking since 8 am and they were laughing at everything. I wasn't laughing at everyone who was just plain drunk and silly stupid.

Then, 7 hours later, while I am really really engrossed in the sub plot of the story where everyone is having an affair with at least one other person. Yeah, I allowed my bored mind to get engrossed in the story line. Silly me. Then, we took a break and pretty much just plain quite watching the show and stepped outside to enjoy the nice weather, and it was so nice to have the sun shine on my face and feel the warmth of the environment, and not to mention, great conversation and laughing amongst peers

I don't think that people understand that amount of exposure that I am going to try to get in New York. There are things that I have planned, public events to get people rallied together to make large art experiences, 'Art Experiences' for anyone who can do it to do it, will do it, to do it… Now, I just have to get 6 close people, friends, probably coworkers who I get to know while working at some crappy job to make it by while living in New York… probably at Blick, we will see. My friend Laura-girl works there, so, yeah, I will hopefully get the job based on her recommendation, which I am sure I will. Gosh, so many artists in New York to work around… I shall see………

This Poem is for the Storyteller,

"Casey"

So many interruptions

And questions and chaos keep you humbled

You realize your voice, your body language

Can be over-thrown at any moment

By the mouth of anyone seeking more

Asking who, what, why from others

And as you wait to take back your pedestal

Your argument placed on hold for a show of craft

> For images, pictures, art of a screen
>
> And then you are noticed in your pouting
>
> And again you are handed the torch, flame flickering
>
> A smile upon your face, mouth open to talk
>
> And again you are cut off
>
> Your voice stammered by the two who laugh at you
>
> In a private joke, like a mini series, short story
>
> And the critics slow to a halt
>
> And your voice loud and clear continue in your story
>
> All the while waiting for the interruption
>
> The mouth that you debate with
>
> Is silent
>
> For now
>
> Pick your fights well
>
> Because in the silence lurks a monster

I toss this letter into the void, the abyss between us, this space that keeps conversation from happening.

Sincerely,
Rush Whitacre
740-336-9169

3-18-11

Dear Taylor Swift,

Well, I am back home, and my dad has been busy getting the house ready to sell. The living room where I slept during the Christmas break has been fully redone with new wood flooring and all the shelving units are empty and bare. This is a pretty sad little setup here in this house. I am not sleeping in my room again, I'm in the living room. This room is just too nice to not sleep in before the house is gone.

Back to this morning. I woke up and packed everything I thought I was going to need for my trip home. Of course I forget one thing that would have made my nights here at my dad's better, my favorite pillow, but then again, I do have a lot of pillows at either place, and so, I will manage. I also forgot that I won't have internet here at my dads, so now I have to decide when I am going to post my students grades on the internet. I have a feeling that I am just going to have to sit in the library parking lot and post them using their free wireless internet. Yup, that will be my job, my last and final blip as a teacher at the university of Cincinnati, but not my ultimate last I am sure as a teacher as a whole. I am sure I will be teaching some while I am in New York, maybe get a job with some artist as an under-study or something. I feel the world opening up to me slowly, and I am sure that after I graduate from UC I am sure that the doors to the world will swing wide and I will get lost in the abundance of choices. Life, too many choices, too many chances to be taken, to be possible choices at times. I just have to figure out with ones will lead me to the right doors.

    The drive home sucked. It rained the whole way, all the way to my (related person who is not named) house. When I got there I guess that (related person who is not named) had just gotten home from where ever it was that she had been. She wasn't pleasant at all, she must have had a bad week. The dog that I gave to my (related person who is male and not named) was at first very uncertain of my being there at the house, but then I think that she remembered me after she smelled me for a little bit. I think that made my (related person who is male and not named) jealous, but then again, my (related person who is male and not named) has been jealous of several things that I have. There is no need to go into detail about these things, that would be silly. All I really want to say is, It was so nice to play around with Sienna again, she really is a lovable Great Dane. My (related person who is male and not named) (related person who is male and not named) I don't think knows how lucky he is to have her. And,,, I brought home some rooster's wings for my (related person who is male and not named) to eat, he loves Rooster's wings, he and I both eat the flavor called Killer, and let me tell you, this time around they were almost hot enough to be killer for real, phew.

Well, I am going to dedicate this poem to the foolishness of falling in love,

"The Wading Game"

How have I come this far

This path obviously has lead me astray into this land

And I am lost

I am heart deep in this muck

And there is no way out

Just to be, or to be broken

And I really don't want to be broken

All I want to do is keep up this illusion

This false reality that I have developed inside my head

Like a self planned, self executed, and self trap

Sprung and slapping me around and around

Making me start to see the waste, the drama, the despair

And I am still heart deep

Still waiting while wading,

And then I see there isn't a way out but to be broken

To sink, to learn to swim, or to surrender

And my heart sinks deeper

And deeper I fall for you, I know not of drowning

Yet I am not loved back, making me motionless

Questioning which air I should breath

The above which is free, or the below which is trapped

And in my waiting, my inability to move

You have moved on

I toss this letter into the void, the abyss between us, this space that keeps conversation from happening.

Sincerely,
Rush Whitacre
740-336-9169

3-19-11

Dear Taylor Swift,

    Nothing like a small lazy little town to slow a person down when they have been moving at the speed of art for so long.

    Ok, I want to say, that this morning's breakfast at Rogers restaurant was absolutely delicious, and that I am looking forward to another tomorrow morning, unless the IGA has something that can persuade me otherwise. My dad is really dead-set on selling his house this coming summer. He talked on and on today about all the things he wanted me to move out of the house so that it was just that much closer to being done. I was almost fed up with hearing about it when the check came and we got up to leave, then his attention shifted to wanting to go get the mail. So, yeah, that is how that is going down I guess. I just wish it were all over already.

    I think I spent 2 hours fixing up my bike, putting new innertubes in the wheels so that I wouldn't have to worry about getting a flat tire, that would suck. Carlee told me that she wanted to go bike riding with me when I came back and I told her that a bike ride sounded great. We will see if this bike riding things pans out, I don't know, because Carlee is a bit flakey at times. We were suppose to meet several times this past quarter for her to learn more about color theory, but then she only showed up twice, so, I guess I will believe it when I see it. I think that for the most part my students really enjoyed my classes and that is why they want to be my friend outside of school. I guess they can all be my friend now outside of school since I am not a teacher at all anymore. Hmm, interesting.

So, tonight I as suppose to hang out with my friend Wester at Buffalo Wild Wings and what the UFC fight, which of course I am not into at all. I could really give a crap about two guys pulverizing each other until one of them just simply can't do it anymore. I guess that I am just not that kind of guy. I guess I don't watch any sports now that I think about it, huh, oh well. I do watch shows and movies on Netflix though, I love Netflix. I wish my dad still had internet here at the house, I soooo wouldn't get much done, and I really need to work on writing my thesis.

And, to top off my night, my (related person who is not named) fell and broke two bones in her wrist today. I don't really have anything I want to say about that other than I feel bad that I couldn't be there to help. She said that she tried to call everyone she knew and that she was met with answering services with everyone. Yeah, that is all I have to say about that.

This poem is for the one who's eyes are bigger than his stomach

"Half Yard Friend"

In a dead stare in a conversation

Your words are hard to listen to

Like darts you throw them to my ears

They miss their target sometimes as I flinch

Your stories are like icing to a cake after it has been burned

Funny, ironic, and always covering every subject

You are like a diamond to me friend

Like a one in a million chance find

You are my greatest fan, and hero all tied into one

Will I ever know a friend again like this one

No

And I can live with this fact

Because I know that you will always be my friend

You will always have my back

And you will always know more than I

And know how to prove it

With a few simple key strokes

And the click of your mouse
Instantaneous satisfaction
A half a yard to the mile

I toss this letter into the void, the abyss between us, this space that keeps conversation from happening.

Sincerely,
Rush Whitacre
740-336-9169

3-20-11

Dear Taylor Swift,

    Ahhh, I slept in and feel pretty rested. My dad surprised me today. I thought we were just going to go out to eat but he found out that I wanted to go visit my grandmother at the pines of Marietta. So, we went to Marietta Ohio and had breakfast and then zipped over to see my grandma. She is getting so old, I think she is either 94 or 95. Fortunately she still remembered who I was. I am worried that someday I am going to walk into her room and she isn't going to know who I am. My (related person who is male and not named) (related person who is male and not named) is the one who is preaching how we should all go see her while we still can and while she can still remember who we all are.

    Since I have been home from Marietta I spent hours at my neighbor's house shooting breeze with him, Josh, about one thing or another. I told him about the war that has broken out in Libya and how we are dropping all these bombs and how t the people in Japan are going through some crazy stuff right now. Actually, the irony of the whole this is even more bizarre,,, An earthquake occurs in Japan which send a tsunami roaring across the ocean towards Hawaii, and after that there is a major nuclear explosion in Japan…. Oddly familiar. I mentioned this to my dad and he too found it ironic, only that this time it was a natural disaster copying a part of history. Like the idea of art mimicking life mimicking art, which came first, the chicken or the egg or the chicken. But honestly, that whole thing in Japan is really a serious thing.

    Anyway, Josh had set up a new trampoline for his kids to play on. Those kids were having such a ball jumping around and making all kinds of noises showing off. Josh is a really good man, and a good dad. While at Josh's his sister-n-law showed up, she is the last girl I dated, from last summer. She was looking pretty good I must admit, but I am pretty sure that there isn't a round number 2. Anyway, as all their guests showed up I kinda ushered myself off to my house. McDonalds was my dinner, kinda gross and greasy, but yet again I am home on break from school, and in Beverly

Ohio after 6 pm on a Sunday the only thing left open is McDonalds or subway, and I am all sub'd out for now. So, while I am eating my food I get a texted on my phone, which isn't anything unusual because Jacki texts me dozens of times a day sometimes because she is bored. This time was different though because it was Ashley who was writing me. She wrote me to tell me that her boyfriend had cheated on her... Now, what does a person say to that really... I said that I was sorry to hear it, and asked her if she was ok. And that is where I left it.

This poem is for revenge

"Passively watching with popcorn"

How do you know

Where your misfortune comes from

Especially when it comes out of the blue

No warning, no signs

Just a blind-siding problem, accident

A stinging sensation in the back of your mind

A single thought of, "did someone plan this"

Or, "How could this have possibly happened"

Or, "I know who did this, but how can I prove it"

You can search, and you can dig as many holes as you want.

You will know the someone who has made you a fool

Not karma, not happenstance, and not shear dumb luck

And as you look back through the years

At memories of those you have hurt

Too many memories, too many people

And the lies become the truth become the lies

What is the truth, when all you see are lies

You will never know your villain

Because letting bad things are way worse and easily hidden

Passive aggressive revenge

Means simply doing nothing

Just let it happen

I toss this letter into the void, the abyss between us, this space that keeps conversation from happening.

Sincerely,

Rush Whitacre

740-336-9169

3-21-11

Dear Taylor,

    Wow, I am assuming that this letter is going to be short, although, I can't be for sure since I just started it. My dad started off with my dad telling me that he was going to go to the hospital for some kind of tests, and then our housekeeper showed up and woke me from a nap. Quite pleasant to be woken up by the scent of lemon fresh cleaner all in the air and as it drops down on your face… Of course, I wouldn't have this problem if I weren't sleeping the living room beneath all the book shelves.

    Ok, so, still no writing on my thesis, which is a number one priority of mine and I find myself delaying it for some reason. I don't think I am delaying the writing of my thesis on purpose so much as I am just simply not doing it. I quite frankly don't really care about it that much and therefore find it hard to have it pop into my head as a 'thing' that I need to do. What my brain is actually telling me that I need to do is to work on my book, get it done, and get it published. I am simply not putting in the time needed to get it done and every time I think about it I can't help but wonder if it is waiting for me, or if I am waiting for it. I guess I won't know until I get there.

    There has been a thunderstorm running through the sky here all day. I equate it to the style of a storm in Florida, short, racing across the sky, and anywhere from a few annoying drops, to an amazing array of lightening, wind, and rain. The lightening was quite spectacular, so much so that I found myself running into the house for cover. I actually thought it was going to get me on the porch. Part of me wonders what it would be like to be struck by lightning. I wonder if you feel it as it is happening, or do you only feel the after affects, that is if you survive it. Hopefully, I will never be able to say.

    I napped this afternoon, slept for at least an hour or two. I guess you could call that part two of my spring break, catch up on some much needed sleep. Tomorrow I am hoping to cut some canvas to take back to school so that I can start painting. Actually, maybe what I will do is measure all of the canvas I have left and see if I need to order a new roll. I have been having a funny idea roll across my mind about making a painting that is 100 feet long and 11 feet wide, which would be the full length of the room minus 4 feet at each end for door clearance, and one foot for ceiling clearance. I honestly think that this would be an amazing painting. I would just have to decide at the beginning that this is what I want to do and I would have to haul ass on it all quarter… I am not sure I want to put that kind of money, or time into my thesis, honestly. I mean, I know I could do it, I am just not sure that it is worth my time. Better to stick with the furniture sculpture.

This poem is for hope.

"Staring into the Haze"

Signal fire

A seamless stream of smoke

Into the sky

A prayer bracelet

Filing its way through fingers

Through closed eyes

The rocking of the desperate

And the yelling of the fraught

Bringing closer the yearned

The desire of the worried

Hope

Just another four letter word

Laced with a reputation for drama

Of regret

Of deceiving those who's dreams simply won't come true

It is never lost

And not always there to be found

It is a place to rest

When no bed is present

I toss this letter into the void, the abyss between us, this space that keeps conversation from happening.

Sincerely,

Rush Whitacre

740-336-9169

3-22-11

Dear Taylor Swift,

     Interesting hearing your name on the radio and the announcer saying that you goofed on the national anthem... I don't know any more than that though, remember, I said that I wouldn't go out of my way to learn about you, but if the world spoon feeds me things, then I have no choice because it is there before me without my causing it. Which is cool in a way, cause I can only imagine that the things I learn about you will be very very gossipy things, verses very personal private things. I guess the two could cross a line somewhere, maybe, I guess it depends on the moment. Anyway, maybe someday you will have to share your story of this anthem goof with me, until then, carry on.

    I had a really good day today. I woke up at noon, zipped off to Marietta to spend the afternoon with Pancakes and his friend Rob, then I went for a walk with Ashley, and then bowling with Ashley and her friend Monica. All in all, this was a good day. I think that the best part was the bowling part. I haven't been bowling in such a long time. Somehow we got placed next to a group of four or five people who must have been in a league or something because they all consistently scored above 160 every game they all played, and many times above 200, up to the 250 to 260 range. Ashley and Monica kept on telling me that they hated me for getting my little scores of 120 to 154. I just laughed at them. Monica's goal for the night was to get a strike, but she never did. She kept knocking down all the pins but one, it was rather comical by the middle of the third game. I will bowl again, soon.

    A little bit ago I was sitting at the library in the parking lot using their internet to give my students their grades. I for the life of me could not figure out how. I scanned over the blackboard site and tried to follow all the directions,,, but it was just really really stupid ridiculously messed up, and hard. I was forced to give up as my computer battery reached a 7% power level. Right before getting off though I emailed Bryan, my "boss" with a lowercase 'b' and told him that I just needed him to simply the directions because either I was messing them up, or the computer was screwing with me, either way my students were not going to receive their grades at the rate of my understanding of the site.

This poem is for 'controllers'

"Thumb Driven"

Fits in the palm of your hand

Like my heart

And you know it well,

Your controller peppered with buttons

Like my buttons, and how you push them

And thumb sticks

Meant for moving, looking

Changing my beat, my tune, even my vision

And around my buttons do you wrap your hands

Fingers resting in place

Until it is time for action, for movement, for sight

> And then a little jab
>
> A button for you, a twitching, reflex, movement for me
>
> Like your hand poised to tickle
>
> I reach to fold
>
> And you flinch
>
> You cover
>
> You blush
>
> And my recognition of your moment
>
> Brings forth baths of laughter for me
>
> Embarrassment for you
>
> So keep your hands wrapped
>
> Your fingers rested and poised
>
> I am ready for my jab

I toss this letter into the void, the abyss between us, this space that keeps conversation from happening.

Sincerely,
Rush Whitacre
740-336-9169

3-23-11

Dear Taylor,

    It has been just a great day. This morning my Ex-girlfriend Mandy called at 8:45 AM and asked me why I had left a DVD on her car window, she was asking nicely. I of course told her because I already had a copy of it and I wanted her to have a copy of it, because I thought it was the sweetest thing, I mean, for when she did it. Then we talked for about an hour. I made her laugh so hard, she seemed like she was in a good place in her life and I am happy for her. She is getting married this coming summer I guess, getting engaged after knowing the guy for only a month or two. I think it is all rather soon, but then what do I know.

    I got a haircut, and then spent the rest of the day cleaning up one thing or another, mostly carpets and rugs with a rugdocter machine to make them smell good. Then I cleaned my truck and my dad's trailer with it, and then my dad's girlfriends house with it, so, it got a good working over. And after all that I am getting cleaned up to go to the movies with Bob, one of my good friends who actually lives here in my dad's house. After his dad sold their house Bob moved in with us and has been here ever since, so, he is family. Bob's dad 'Chef' is the one who works on our house, he too is a really nice guy. He was here today working on replacing the flooring in one of the closets to help my dad get this house ready to sell. I just don't know anyone who would ever want it because it is the biggest house in Beverly, and it is a bit of a money trap because it takes so much money to keep it heated in the winter, and so much to keep it air conditioned in the summer.

So, I have to get a shower now to go to the movie, I will write more on here later once I have seen Battle LA. I hope I make it back alive. Ok, I am back, and that movie was predictable and it was corny, and the computer generated graphics were outdated and already done before, and there were so many corny lines and moments. I found myself literally sitting in my seat saying, "What, are you serious, did that seriously just happen?" My friend Bob who was with me probably got really annoyed at how I kept on leaning over and interrupting his fun time of watching and experiencing. Oh well, I think I enhanced his experience if you ask me.

This Poem is for blindfold race

"Unexpected Journey"

But a decision to speak

And a motion from the opposite sex

Leading me

Tempting me into a room

A cave, or a castle

I do not know the difference

As I am being led by my ego

Deceived by my id

Traveling by foot, shoeless

And the volcanic rock slices, tears

And I do not feel a thing

At least not until I get to the salty sands of your ocean

Your horizon

Indefinitely out beyond my reach

Beyond my ships blazing mast's pull

Yet I push forward

Turning my wheel, changing my position

But it doesn't matter

I see you everywhere I look

My distant love

I toss this letter into the void, the abyss between us, this space that keeps conversation from happening.

Sincerely,
Rush Whitacre
740-336-9169

3-24-11
Dear Taylor,

    Still at home, it is Thursday and all is well, except a bitter cold snap has swept into the area. I could see my breath all day. Despite the cold I have enjoyed a nice roaring fire while here at the house, I always love having a fire. The smell, the sound, the flames, nice. All morning I spent talking to 'Chef' about all kinds of things, mostly about what it would be like to win the lottery since the mega millions is up to 312 million dollars. 'Chef' told me that if he won a lottery that big he would still work for my dad but he would do it for free because he needs something to fill his time. I laughed and told him that he was absolutely right, a man needs something to do, something to fill his time other than simply waiting to die, or that which he must do, eat, sleep, etc(must do's).

    I spent many hours at Wester's house, first with Pancakes looking up funny Youtube video's, and then Wester showed up and Pancakes left. I don't think that the two (related person who is male and not named)s get along that well. In fact, if I had to say it, I would say that something is up between the two of them. Pancakes sounded terrible. He really sounded like he had pneumonia or something. Pancakes told me that he was having trouble breathing to the point that walking from his vehicle to his chair where he works in Wester's basement. His chair is usually no further away from his parked car than 75 feet. Pancakes is in trouble with his weight, and I fear that if he doesn't seek help he is going to be in a lot of trouble. He is like 5'9"or 10" and weighs 440 to 460 pounds. I really feel sorry for him. Wester and I spent hours together after Pancakes left just messing around and looking at all kinds of other videos and talking about the movie we shot last summer, and possibilities for new movies in the future, and then he needed to run to the gas station where Ashley just happens to work to pick up hotdog buns. So, we went to the station and I formally introduced Wester to Ashley. Wester embarrassed her so badly that she turned bright red in the face and I had already walked away from her and Wester stayed there saying things like: "Oh, I just found out that you are single and I am really glad that we are meeting and I was wondering if we could get together sometime……" Hilarious things, and I came and was really surprised that Wester had done this, I didn't know that he had it in him to pull off such a funny joke.

      Then, tonight, Ashley came over and we watched JackAss 3, she picked it out, and then for a really long time she seemed disgusted with her choice of movie. Throughout the movie whenever there was a scene with a penis in it, or some form of vulgarity that was absurd I looked at her and said "Ashley, what kind of girl are you to bring such a thing into my life" lol, it was fun. I learned tonight that Ashley will be 21 in 6 months. She seemed rather excited for that day to come, especially for someone who doesn't drink. Anyway, today has been a great day.

This poem is for the straight off,

"Turn Me On"

Words, oh words and how they are read

Like physical sensations

Earthquakes worth repeating

Changing my mind's ability for rationale

Ability to choose, to be in control

Is lost, and I am mastered by you

By your sway, your bodies motion

This wreckless action damaging no one

Making me cry from pleasure of word

Of physical joy, to pain deceived

To a touch of tongue in places

That only temptation can fantasize about

Will I ever know another mouth's word

I know never, as thy moves with my stillness

And my verbal agreement

Flashes a smile across your face

Through your body's rocking

And I am left at your mercy

Completely exposed

Vulnerable beyond vulnerable

A pose worth repeating

repeating

I toss this letter into the void, the abyss between us, this space that keeps conversation from happening.

Sincerely,
Rush Whitacre
740-336-9169

3-25-11

Dear Taylor Swift,

Man, this is Friday and I have no plans and I have not worked on my thesis at all,,, and I don't plan on doing any of it today, this is my day of doing nothing… Jacki told me that I should just rent movies and chill out in front of the TV all day. Her idea is winning me over, I will be back in a minute, I will be back with some movies.

Ok, the movies I picked up are Due Date, The Social Network, Hot Tub Time Machine, and The Other Guys. This is quite a selection. Ok, so, I picked the other guys because Wester told me to watch it because it was funny, I picked Hot Tub Time Machine because John Cusack is in it, and Due Date because one of my students from fall quarter told me to watch it for the actor show last name is something like Galifanakis, or something like that, I am sure I could get the movie out of the player to spell his name correctly, but I just got comfortable and don't feel like moving, I will just push play.

So, since my movies look like they are going to take me all day to watch I probably won't have much to talk about besides whether the movies lived up to the expectations that either I, or my friends have told me they should be. And Wester told me that 'the other guys' is supposed to be hilarious, so, I shall see. I will let you know…

Ok, flash forward to after all the movies…. Alright, so, Due Date was ok, it was strange, and the character I was told to pay attention to doesn't look or act anything like me, I think my student was simply being a smartass. I do like Robert Downey Jr. though, so, I did enjoy the movie as a whole. There were some just plain strange moments, like the phone call jr. makes to his wife while at the gas station. Ok, my favorite out of these four movies was the social network, let me just say wow, and then I also watched the making of scenes and those made me love them even more. I am into making movies and so I am always watching the making of for movies that I think are really amazing, and the social network is simply amazing. Hot Tub Time Machine was neither good nor bad, and the other guys had just a few moments that I would consider to be funny, I mean I am sure there are people out there who would consider it to be really funny, just not me.

This poem is for The Man with the tie before me:

"I'm a salesman"

And that smile you wear

Is as fake as the plastic you wear around your neck

As false as the statements you make to make a sale

Maybe you are more alone than anyone knows

Inside that heart of yours

Like an ashtray, where others put in

To be put out

Like a planeless air traffic controller

Hand motions like a magician

Entertainment for one, for the costumer

For the bottom line

And it is all you can do to not laugh

To not lose your concentration

As you know I am devious

And my plan is to trip you up

To make you laugh

To smile

And per chance to give you a moment

A memory to look back upon

To be happy

Now

And when you remember this

This moment when I make you forget

I make you trip

I toss this letter into the void, the abyss between us, this space that keeps conversation from happening.

Sincerely,
Rush Whitacre
740-336-9169

3-26-11

Dear Taylor Swift,

    I slept so well, and returned my movies in time.. which is really important because I didn't the last time and in my small town they are due the nest day regardless of when you rent them by 5 pm, and it sucks to return movies only to have to pay for them again the next time you go to rent something... Sucks...

    So, I packed up and left to come home in Cincinnati today. Oh, and I also treated my leather on my car seats... they do smell rather like funny smelling leather... Oh well, that is how it is every time I treat the leather. I really didn't think it through though because after packing up the truck I had to driving sitting on the treated leather for four hours and now I am at Gari's work place, smelling like leather conditioner and someone who has sat in the same place for four hours. Oh well. I think that Gari and I are going to get a drink at applebee's or somewhere. Gari is cleaning off a cell phone right now to put a protective cover on the cell phone. Right before we left the store Gari gave me a free protective cover for my phone, one that would break if I dropped the phone, one that would absorb the fall so that the phone doesn't break. Gari is awesome, I can't thank him enough for helping me out. Right now he is passed out in front of a TV where he was playing a game called call of duty black ops. I am pretty sure I would not play this game because, well first of all I don't play games, and second of all I get motion sick and anything that has to move as fast as this game apparently has to be played must certainly make you motion sick..

    I am always wondering how Gari is doing, he seems to be ok when I hang out with him, and he seems to be happy, but the last time I hung out with him he expressed to me that he hated his job and wanted to find something else to do. This of course is unlike Gari, he usually knows how to deal with life's obstacles and find a way to make a good in a difficult time, like he always has. I guess that selling phones is just not as cracked up as it would seem to be.. I will never know, maybe, we shall see. Until then, Taylor, keep doing what you love, creating your art, your magic that somehow moves the hearts of millions. I am envious and humbled.

    So, Gari and I just got back to his apartment where he is fighting Nazi Zombies again on his TV. I wonder if he will ever work on art again, because he has time to play video games, therefore it is only reasonable that he should have time to make a drawing, or starting a painting, or make something that could be considered a Gari masterpiece. I guess I will just have to hope that he comes around and is able to make his job his job time, and learn to make some art time amongst all the video games.

This poem is for trying to say goodbye

"Self Heart Breaker"

My dear

I have spent so many days,

And wasted so many hours

Attempting to mastermind my way into your life

But now all I have are moments of thinking of how to say goodbye

I just can't keep falling for you

When all you want to do is leave

And leave, run.

For the one you loved before is biding

And time is on his hands, you have handed him the clock.

At the same time as you wait for the romantic gesture,

I wait for my heart to be crushed

I remain in the limbo, destitute

Unsteady, worried, and knowing my days are limited

For you will get back with him

And I will just get back far enough

Enough to step out of the picture

Photoshoped out like a transformed 'Carlee'

Visually out of your life

But not out of your memory

I wave goodbye

I toss this letter into the void, the abyss between us, this space that keeps conversation from happening.

Sincerely,
Rush Whitacre
740-336-9169

3-27-11

Dear Taylor Swift,

     Woke up at Gari's apt.... I forgot that I was there, and then I was awoken to Gari tripping on something in his living room where I was asleep on his friend's uncomfortable couch. Then Gari took my cell phone and started messing around with it, changing things on it, making it look like something I am sure he would want in a phone. I trust him with it because he sold it to me, and because he is learning all kinds of new things everyday about phones and what they do, or what could be done to them, like mine. I am assuming that he will be good to my phone, as with me since we are such good friends. Anyway, he gave me a free screen protector and a free skin for my phone because it was returned with a phone that some girl didn't want, so, yeah, he is a really good friend.

Since I have been gone I guess Yangue and Louis have not been talking all because Louis owes Yangue 30 dollars. Louis Louis Louis, you are a sloppy sloppy mess and I am worried about you. Louis has become quite a drinker, and he never cleans up after himself in either his room nor in the kitchen. I just don't eat here anymore therefore taking myself out of the equation. I have three more months and then I am out!!! I will be out of Cincinnati, and back into my home village for a little while, and then into New York, at least that is the plan as of right now. I was asked today by Yangue what I was going to do, he would like it if I stayed for another year, I just can't see that happening, at least not right now, I feel New York pulling on me like gravity of the earth to raindrops, and I am falling for that place.

My nephew is getting married this coming Sunday in Columbus, it is a double wedding, so, that should be rather interesting. I have never been to a double wedding, at least not to one with someone close like David Moose, my Sister's middle child. Funny, I have 5 brothers and one sister, and the four oldest ones are all in their late 50's and 60's, because my dad had a family before he had a family, sometimes complicating if you don't know the family very well.

I really need to just give up on finding a great girl. I am seriously having a "ghost of Christmas past" thing happening only with ex-girlfriends,,, I guess it would be called "Girlfriends of years past" three of my past ex's have contacted me in the past 2 weeks and of course none of them want me, which is good because the feeling is mutual. I mean, we are not enemies, just not matches, but each has something going on in their lives that makes me wish I could find someone to share with, someone who needs a closeness, not needy, just a true closeness, someone who just wants to be held just to be held. What can I say, I am Pisces and I need extra closeness time. Lol

This poem is for just being honest with one's self.

"Wanting you, but first"

I just realized that I have to let you go

You are hell bent on not seeing me

For me

And I can't allow my heart to be toyed

So, good bye, I won't try to think about this

And I won't write poetry to escape you

So don't notice these words that are written

I can't promise they're not for you

And memories of you won't make me cry

So please don't notice my tears

> As they fall and splash out your name
> And I can't wait for you to become wise or grow up
> Because I can't be with you and raise you
> So please get hurt by someone else
> So that you can know who I am
> So please go,
> Have your heart broken into a thousand little pieces
> By the one who you think you love the most
> So that if you ever find me again
> You will know what love is.

I toss this letter into the void, the abyss between us, this space that keeps conversation from happening.

Sincerely,
Rush Whitacre
740-336-9169

3-28-11

Dear Taylor Swift,

    First day back to school, this is it, I am really going to graduate and be out of school, for real… I got a reminder to apply for graduation and the deadline is in like 8 days,, and to top it all off the stupid site is offline and all I get are errors when I try to apply. So annoying. I guess I will just have to pray that the internet allows me to get through so that I can graduate. Naaah, I am not that worried about it. First of all, there has to be some backup plan for this kind of problem, who knows.

    I worked out earlier today. Today is the day of my new self. I have created a workout schedule and everything, three days a week. I don't know, I just want to go to NYC with a set in motion healthier lifestyle than I have now… so, since I only eat out I am only eating either subway, or chipotle. And am only eating a 12 inch sub a day, or I am eating a 6 inch sub and a burrito bowl a day… I have a feeling that on Tuesdays and Thursdays I will be doing the 6 inch and burrito thing in order to keep going, because those are my busiest days.. this diet I feel is going to be something that helps to define me, something that I can use mentally to direct my future actions by… I mean, if someone can keep control of their own intake of anything, then they certainly should be able to think themselves through other life problems, or situations.. not that I can't do that, I just really haven't been that interested in keeping up with my health in a small way, and I decided that if NYC is calling me then I had better be ready.

My class tonight was rather short, only about 45 minutes, and Babybooand Tilley were both in it, and I must say that Tilley was looking rather like she could tackle this class and swallow it easily. Meaning that she looked ready for it. My professor is so nice, she didn't know how to get her class to register as available online, which is a common mistake, and I helped her out and she was very grateful… the stupid blackboard site is so complicated…. There are actually two places where you could consider that you have made the right selection to make your course available to all the class. Only, one is easy to find and it is the wrong on, and the other is harder to find and is the right one to click on to make your class available to everyone in the class. Her name is Maria, and then she has a hyphened name.. it should have never been allowed for names to be hyphened, names should have been either from one or the other… I am not saying that one name is better than the other, just that it is silly to worry so much about something so silly, something that we put so much importance on

This poem is for Jacki, as she gave the theme to me to write about.

"Burning Knives"

This rope on fire

Flames licking at the soles of my feet

And I sweat as the heat tires me

I can't feel through my blistered finger tips

And my heals aren't much traction to speak of

So I slip, and slide, and fall

A fire as sharp as the flash from a bomb

Quick, irreversible, and with cause

And I am murdered

Knifed before my time

A blade in flames to sever me from my life

My heart from the one I gave it to

And so what

It is not like they earned it anyway

They simply tried it on and put it back on the rack

A Love in a world of capitalism

Compassion sold to the person who wants the best deal

And who doesn't mind paying the highest price

Without knowing it.

I toss this letter into the void, the abyss between us, this space that keeps conversation from happening.

Sincerely,
Rush Whitacre
740-336-9169

3-29-11
Dear Taylor Swift,

I think that this is going to be a much better quarter than last quarter. This quarter I have 'Lady' and the sculpture teacher for Grade Studio, and the class appears to be much more planned out and the work looks like it is going to be much more fun and more helpful to us in the future. Thank you 'Lady', for I feel like her insight into asking her class from last quarter all kinds of questions paid off. I also had class with Marcus, the director, for my painting class. He again has about 50 readings for us to read on blackboard. I am actually glad that these readings are there for us because I feel like they are relative to current times and current thinking, and that is what I am most interested in learning about, and they are more like magazine articles than really heavy theory sections from books about theory. Yuck.

I am not laying in my bed thinking about the day's events.. I don't know if I have mentioned this before or not, but I have started a new diet this quarter. I have decided that I really need to lose about 30 pounds of fat and gain about 20 pounds of muscle. So, I have started this diet, two days ago I started it. So, I know it is early in the diet phase, but I am really dedicated to something when I decide on something. So, I decided that I would give the subway diet a chance. Only, my version is probably a bit more extreme. I have worked out a workout routine at the recreational center for Mon., Wed., and Fri. and every day I only eat one foot long sub from subway and all the diet soda that I need. I plan on doing the 1 foot long thing for two weeks, and then introduce maybe another 6 inch sub, or eating a burrito from chipotle and a 6 inch sub. I know, I am relying on food from restaurants… but, what can I say, I am in college and I am busy, and I am desperate to lose this weight before I move to NYC… I just want to be fit and ready for all the walking and all the life changes ahead. Defined body, controlled body, shows a mind that is just as sophisticated, right? Lol, who knows.

So, I just found out that one of my students from the past fall quarter is not going to be able to come back to school because her parents got a divorce… at least this is the story that she has given me, and I don't doubt her, but… last I checked, colleges set up money issues at the beginning of the year for the entire year without there being any reason for the money thing to change… maybe Cincinnati is different, but I don't think so, because if it were I am sure it would be the same for Grad School, and I worked out my money things at the beginning of the year and they can't change it no matter what because a deal is a deal.

This poem is for the poetic map of my mind

"Synaptic GPS"

Traffic jam

So many words flowing through my rivers

Flying in my skies and driving across the neural roads of my mind

That it is hard to make my way through my literary thoughts

I search for a taxi, a bus, or even a train to ride

To bypass all the clutter,

The synonym pile-ups, and rhyming-wrecks

These things only seem to make the making less makeable

And I am tired of wading

Standing in a mess of periods, question marks, and commas

Breaking up sentence's into fragments

And hoping that the left overs fit

Somehow come together to make sense

To be stitched together, glued, or nailed

So that when you read it you know

You feel this passion, this hate, this love, this rage

A hot shower, cold waterfall, snow storm of words

Something you can touch, and it touches you back

Changing it for a moment

Changing you for the rest of your life

I toss this letter into the void, the abyss between us, this space that keeps conversation from happening.

Sincerely,
Rush Whitacre
740-336-9169

3-30-11

Dear Taylor Swift,

Early to wake, early to realize that just a little longer in bed will do a body good and then,,,, oops, it is not 1 pm and I have way over slept… that is what happened to me this morning, and then I jumped out of bed, got a shower, and hurried to the Recreational center to work out.. I was supposed to be there by 1 pm because that is the time in which I set for myself. Oh well, I didn't have class, so, I guess I didn't feel like doing anything for school… this is a bad habit that I have to change or I will suffer greatly. I have to write my thesis, and work on coming up with my thesis plan for creating my sculpture out of all kinds of furniture from the place… Uggh, I only have one quarter left and then I guess I can take a break in my mind from school, after all, this is my last quarter in school ever. Wow, I never thought I would say that about myself, that I will be a master's graduate.

My workout today was nice and harder than that on Monday, I increased the amount of weight lifted on most of the machines that I used. I am worried about my right shoulder, there is something seriously wrong with it. I injured it awhile ago while swimming, like months ago, and it is still hurting today… weird. I don't what I should do about it, so I just keep working out thinking that maybe it will be better if the muscles are a little more in shape. I guess I will continue to work out until either my arm just simply won't let me, or until the pain keeps me from adding more weight. I just can't imagine that my arm would go for so long and either not heal itself, and not be painful until now when I start lifting light weights like I am to start out with. I have noticed that when I put my arm through the full range of motions that it isn't hurting, actually, yeah, not at all… hmm, only after two sessions my arm doesn't hurt… so, maybe this is a good thing…

I just got don't talking to Jacki earlier, and she won't say, but I am sure she is getting back with her boyfriend, and that is a good thing. I guess she has made demands of him though, that he has to ask her back out in some romantic way that is memorable, and then she told me that she doesn't see him being able to do that… Anyway, her conversation with me made me think about how much I wish I had someone in my life who wanted me, just simply wanted me in their life, romantically, and friendly, and I guess just about everyway there is to be between two people who love each other.. Through the doubt I keep telling myself that I will find her when I get to New York, the greatest city in the world..

This poem is for the Leak,

"Hoping"

Gaps formed where they should

By decay, and way before their time

A practiced line

From an emotionally compromised brain

Worn out nerves, and the slippery slope

> Beckoning you on and on
> Thinking that telling the wind to stop blowing
> Will actually make it so
> Thinking that it will do anything but make you feel
> Nothing shy of a fool
> You become the person who discloses
> The person who doors don't open for
> And the person on the other end simply doesn't react
> Deepening how stupid you feel
> For opening your mouth
> For letting your secret out
> There is no going back
> And all you feel you had to share
> Was actually only with your self

I toss this letter into the void, the abyss between us, this space that keeps conversation from happening.

Sincerely,
Rush Whitacre
740-336-9169

3-31-11

Dear Taylor Swift,

    This is my long day, Thursday… I can't believe I am going to say this, but, there is a possibility that I am going to like my grad studio class this quarter, but that is only because it is a completely different format. This quarter we are not talking about out most recent work over and over and over. And I am really glad about this because I am tired of making up work that I am actually not going to do for my thesis, or at Cincinnati's University. Instead I am going to be making a 20 min presentation about my work from very early on, on up through to what I am currently working on. I think that my presentation is going to be a pretty good one, maybe, I just have to make it accurate, fun to listen to, and just under 20 minutes. I am not worried about this grad studio at all. I have to present ¼ of a panel discussion, present a 20 thing on my work, and write about 2500 words as my part on the panel discussion,,, I think anyway. The class I am most worried about is my night class Thursday night, it is set up to be a survey, but I am taking it as an academic credit class, and it is another critical theory class… I found out that I have two presentations, two medium papers, and 4 short papers, one long paper of 10 to 12 pages, a whole lot of reading, listening to a lot of long boring lectures, and at the same time working on the writing of my own thesis. This class is going to make my quarter long and a pain in the butt. Oh well, it is my last quarter, and so long as I get a C, that is still passing. I really have had it with this school. It seems like their main purpose is to fill it with as many grad students as possible to get our money, but then their program for educating us, and boosting us to become better artists and art teachers is lacking, quite a bit I would say. I am fairly certain that there is no one person I would pin this growing problem on, except to say that their first step has been in the wrong direction and that was with the last minute addition of a class that they made mandatory to take but they still had no idea on how to teach and then put us through bull crap and make us frustrated to only then give everyone an A in the course. Everyone feels slighted when that happens, even those who know there was no way that they deserved it.

Well, I started two new paintings, a completely new idea involving an eye ball, and one that I started at the beginning of last year, one of my main character that I wrote about in my fantasy novel, Emarilda. The character painting is 6 feet high by 2.5 feet wide and she is leaning against a tree, I like it so far, and I can't wait to see how it turns out. The eye I am working on also looks like it will be pretty fantastic, it is for Jacki. I decided to make it for her because she has been so helpful to me over the past 3 months, it is kinda my way of saying that I am watching over her, even when I can't be there. Now I just have to finish it.

This poem is for the promise of wasted time

"Laptop Chained"

I know dear that you are soon to need my help

That your problems will overtake you

I can tell through your words that your certain uncertainty

Is building mass, the weight of a wrecking ball

Lingering over your head, over your foundation

You worry your inabilities are wasting other peoples time

Peoples time, what people

There is no one here but you,,, and me

And I am here because you are here

Your reasons don't always mean making sense

And your folly is creased like a paper airplane

Unfolded

Always pointing to the center and always too far left or right

You are not perfect
Your inabilities are there,
Wasting time for no one.

I toss this letter into the void, the abyss between us, this space that keeps conversation from happening.

Sincerely,

Rush Whitacre

740-336-9169

Dear Taylor Swift,

    Lol, oops, I just realized that I dated my last letter as April 1st,, kinda funny I guess considering that April 1st is suppose to be a day of fun jokes and pulling the wool over someone's eyes just so that you can trick them long enough to say, "April Fools!" Well, no one tried to get me! In fact I didn't hear of anyone getting anyone. Hmm, is the tradition wearing off?

    Today is Friday by the way, and I started my morning off with a meeting with all the grads about our grad thesis at the CCAC(Clifton Cultural Arts Center) in Cincinnati on Friday the 27th from 6 to 9 pm,,, I had to type that out, trying to commit the date to memory, I have to notify my sis about the date of my thesis show, and of my graduation ceremony. I am getting a little nervous. All I want to do is graduate, and get on with my life… I have this one quarter left, and everyone is counting on me. HELL, I am counting on myself. I just really don't need something to step into my life right now and pull me out of it, take me out of the game. Like my back, it would be awful to have to stop school right now because of a blowout in my back. I just won't think about it.

    I worked out again today. I extended my diet to either one foot long sub from subway a day, or one burrito bowl a day. I just divided it up throughout the day to keep food in me just enough so that I don't get crazily hungry and lose my will power, not to mention, I am sure that only subway subs all the time is not healthy. And when I go chipotle I get lemon slices, so, vitamin C should be a problem. Now, I just need to stay on task and get into a routine and start working on other things like my thesis… this is really important… really really important.

    Ok, so, I need to start wrapping this up, my nephew is getting married tomorrow in Columbus and I don't want to miss it, or be late. I think I mentioned this already, but it is the double wedding! I wonder how it is going to turn out.

    This poem is for the pirate in all of us,

"Hoist the Mast"
It was a black day
Black as the coffee grounds
In the bottom of me drinking glass
And the hoot'n and Hollering
Gunshoot'n, and bottles being broken
Don't shatter quite as nicely on the shelf
As they do over the heads of me enemy

Pirates

Rough, grungy, and always looking to loot

Steal, and take orders from the captain

After all, this is my ship

My Rum stored up in barrels in the brig

And my bloody parrot

"Land Ho!"

Yells the bird in the Crows nest

My spyglass drawn

Parrot mimicking everything I say

I command my band of thieves and scoundrels

"Hoist the mast, and turn her port-side"

I look down into my vessel,

My reflection in the black drink

I am reminded,

"We have no coffee beans aboard me ship"

I toss this letter into the void, the abyss between us, this space that keeps conversation from happening.

Sincerely,
Rush Whitacre
740-336-9169

4-2-11

Dear Taylor Swift,

    My nephews wedding was really nice, and I am sure they spent a lot of money on it because there was soo much food, and good food too. I am glad I spent extra time at the wedding because I got to visit with my nieces and their kids and I got to visit with my brothers and sister. I haven't shaved my goatee in so long that I can't even remember a time when I didn't have it. So, this morning after my shower I shaved it all off!! My face feels so weird, like, naked.

    I stopped at a half priced book store on my way home from Columbus and picked up a few books, one of which was a book called Phantom, as in Phantom of the Opera. I guess it is a rare book to find, at least the original first edition anyway. I just happened to stumble into the store right after someone gave away a box of books, and that one just happened to be in the mix, and in almost mint condition. I was excited. I also picked up some art books so that I have something to look at for inspiration, or to drop names in my thesis paper to compare or contrast my work. I just want to get this quarter over with, it is killing me, I feel like a caged animal at this university. I was meant to fly, soar with other great mind and hard working artists in New York City. I have my doubts about becoming famous, obviously, because that is really rare, but I do have my plans for making it into the Times for a show or two, and establishing myself a nice little studio where I can work/think/plan/brainstorm. Who knows, a lot can happen in three years, a lot can happen.

Gari seemed to be in a good mood. They made their quota of sales for Verizon this past month and he got a one thousand dollar bonus check, and his boss is taking him out tonight to celebrate, along with all the other new sales reps. I think he was upset that he just couldn't invite me to go with him, but I totally understood, and understand. And, I wouldn't be any fun, I am so tired and just not wanting to stay out late tonight, I just want to go to bed, mostly because I have to drive Yangue to a mall tomorrow so he can buy Makeup for his wife. I remember doing this last year for him right before I left to go home. He bought all kinds of makeup for his wife. I wonder if he is going to buy as much this year as he did last year…

Sirens, all kinds of sirens going down the street right now, I wonder what is going on in the little city of Cincinnati. There are always sirens, always, just not as many that just went by. I hope it isn't something major, like a Zombie Apocalypse.

This poem is for line not crossed,

"Removal of Doubt"

There comes a moment

In every relationship

Where a line must be drawn

It is this line

That can be the making

Or breaking point

The defining moment

Or the collapse of everything you hold dear to you

As you know it to be

In your heart

It is important to know which is which

Which lines you can cross

And which lines remove all doubt

All doubt of being able to tread back across it

Because once the wrong line is tripped over

There is no reason for retreat

No one will care how many steps

You take back across the line
It happened
And it obviously happened for a reason

I toss this letter into the void, the abyss between us, this space that keeps conversation from happening.

Sincerely,
Rush Whitacre
(740-336-9169)

4-3-11

Dear Taylor Swift,

    Well, here is another Sunday, a day before classes, a day for me to try to figure out what I am going to do to make, or write, or plan. After I write this letter I think that I will write some of my thesis, maybe, it depends on what happens in the mean time. Later I plan on going to school to paint for a little while, maybe that will take up some of my boredom. Ok, I will be back on here later, I need to focus on my thesis writing stuff.

    Alright, it is now 2 am, and I have yet to work on anything but two paintings that go with my fantasy story. I am finding my latest work to be more enjoyable than any of the other things that I have done and I would say that is because this is what I long to do, paint, and paint and paint…. I am sooo glad that I have decided to do my painting class as actual painting and not try to do some other kind of art in its place… and all the other guys who are painters are really excited to see how my work progresses. My friend Dan who is also a painter is so perplexed with how my paintings go from bizarre intense colors to brilliant correct colors. He just says that he will believe it when he sees it. I am hoping to have 10 paintings done this quarter, along with all of my other things I should be doing… hahahahaha,,, I am silly,, what a silly idea, 10 paintings done by the end of the quarter, I'd be lucky to fully finish three paintings I suppose.

    Dan decided that he wants to paint with me back here by my studio, he is working on some kind of fantasy painting, something of a mythological story of sorts, something dealing with a crow that is making noises for two travelers walking down a path and the crow trying to sound like a raven. I guess the moral of the story I guess is to not be an idiot, to not try to be something that you are not. A crow can't be a raven just because it wants to, it will always be a crow.

This poem is for the bare

I bare this small truth to you

And I bare my secret

My mind opens forth like a fountain

Making me crazy

I think things that aren't possible

And look through years

Decades

A Millennia of wishing

As time has pushed me into existence

Molecule by molecule

And I can feel these parts of me,

As they wish to stick together

Bond and work in some magical team effort

Forcing me to live

Begging me to feed

Atoms, cells, recalling stories

Fantastical recalls of stardust

Particles in space

For millions of years I floated around

And then one day I came together

I grew and developed

And I was born

Naked, and bare for all the world

And I shall leave just the same.

I toss this letter into the void, the abyss between us, this space that keeps conversation from happening.

Sincerely,
Rush Whitacre
740-336-9169

4-4-11

Dear Taylor Swift,

This has been a very very long day. I started out early, ended up at the Recreational center to work out and then had my night class which was long and boring, and I don't think I am going to get anything out of it. We shall see. Between the quizzes and tests and presentations I may just make it to graduation.

I found out earlier that my friend Chris had his drill stolen from the studio area, and I am so pissed about it. This is the third or fourth thing that has been stolen out of Chris's studio. He is such a nice guy, just the nicest guy you can think of and someone is stealing things from him left and right. I just don't know what to think, and I really don't want to think that someone from the studios took it. Why would anyone want to take his drill, I mean, it really isn't the greatest one you can buy, and you wouldn't get anything for it if you tried to sell it to anyone. Oh well, I will just keep it to myself I guess.

I just wonder if there is any way I can get through this quarter and not go insane. Lots of things going to happen in the next year. I just want to be happy, that's all

So, my paintings have figures on them with green, red, and blue skin as under paintings and it is totally making everyone question my ability to making paintings in the first place. So, I guess I will just have to be impressive with what I can do. It is funny, I can see more smiles on all the painters' faces by my shear decision to making paintings. Every time I am around the guys they just get these smiles on their faces. It makes me feel good.

I am watching Battlestar Galactica season 2.5 episode 4 I believe. This is really a good show, really addictive to watch. I just can't stop watching it.

Ok, this is the end of my show, and I am going to write another poem. I have no idea what this one will be or turn into, so, we shall see what comes from the nothing.

This poem is from the nothing,

"Essence of desire"

These Hands

As you couldn't hold me

As you held me before

You were weak

And I was unable to turn

My face framed in position

Glaring at the projection

The one I can't understand

And as it disappears

screaming

>   yelling
>
>   pitching our nest out
>
>   home lost
>
>   These hands
>
>   I couldn't hold you
>
>   My fingers unable to grab
>
>   Unable to grasp
>
>   And these hands
>
>   Were meant for you
>
>   And you were for me

I toss this letter into the void, the abyss between us, this space that keeps conversation from happening.

Sincerely,
Rush Whitacre
740-336-9169

4-5-11

Dear Taylor Swift,

  Today is Tuesday, now my long day. I traded up my Thursday night class for a Tuesday night class,, oh my gosh, I just realized what this does to my schedule. Now after the fourth week of the quarter I will be done with class for the week pretty much after my Tuesday night class, because I have no classes on Wednesday, and all my assignments for 'Lady's class will be done so all I will have to do is listen and talk some, and we don't meet on Thursdays for painting so that is clear. God, that is exciting. Lots of free time this quarter!!! I can't believe how great this quarter is turning out to be. It is just amazing to me, now I just have to work on my thesis, written and actual formation of the structure for the sculpture. Oh man, so much of that to do.

  My workout regimen is working out well. This is my second week in the gym and I can tell a difference especially when I take the stairs or have to open heavy doors. Things are just easier. I can't wait to see how much I have improved by the end of the quarter. My goal is to have a muscular stomach by summer, like a six pack, but I don't want to look like a monster full of muscles, just a healthy look, maybe like a swimmer just bigger muscles. I am sure that if I can keep up this exercise routine for two weeks that I should be able to keep it up all quarter. I will find some place back home for the summer to work out so that I can improve even more. Let's see, when I weighed in at the gym before the first workout I weighed 252 lbs, and at 6'3" with a fairly already muscular build I am not fat, just a stomach that I want to eliminate the extra fat from. I will succeed.

I guess we have an artist lecture tomorrow. I don't think that I will go because I just don't care that much to go. We all go to eat the food, whether the artist is good or not, and then leave because, well, we are starving art students in grad school. I guess I just don't care because I don't want to go knowing that I don't care about the visiting artist who is going to talk. I just don't want to sit there knowing that I am living a lie, eating food that I don't deserve.

Ok, it is now 5 AM, and I just got home after painting with Dan and Nicholas, I am exhausted. I will do what I can to write this poem.. lol, this should be fun.
This poem is for Dan Dean

"More than Expectations"

Chances are

Your plans won't work out as you think they should

And no act of god

Can make you pass

Chances are

You will find that you have more

Than one possibility

So, keep up your work

Stop worrying about your pride

Your voice moving

This train isn't just wheels on track

But chances

That roll away from you

Like little brush strokes

You pan away your glory in drops

Rather than in splashes

Your choices fray as you stay

And you stay to try

But keeping the ends close

Won't make you happy

And neither will pretend

Just the same.

I toss this letter into the void, the abyss between us, the space that keeps conversation from happening.

Sincerely,
Rush Whitacre
740-336-9169

4-6-11

Dear Taylor Swift,

    I woke up so late today, gosh, all from staying up so late with the boys. But I got so much painting done, it was great. I came across the music group while searching my name on youtube, it is called Big Time Rush, and I started to listen to their stuff, and it seems that the only song that I really like is one called Boyfriend, but it is a remix, the "Jump Smokers" remix I do believe. Anyway, I can dig that song a little. I just like the name of the band I guess. So, today I have to go and get my classes changed. I am dropping that stupid Historiography and picking up another art history class. I almost made the mistake of dropping my class first before adding the other class, this would have made me not full time and would have made the loan people and the pell grant people go crazy and think that I am no longer a full time student... so stupid. I remember at OU I did it and I was contacted by the school about me not being a full time student and how they were going to take away my grant. I simply told them to chill out and check me out in the system again. I will never know why some people are so cranky.

    I just got done working out at the Recreational center, it is wed. This Regiment of working out on Mon, Wed, and Fri is so nice. I can't believe that I didn't start this sooner. I haven't talked to my dad in a really long time. I wonder why... He usually calls me to check in on me, hmmm, I just know figured this out that he isn't calling. Oh well.

    Ok, the paintings I am working on are one that is of my main character leaning on a tree. She is in the woods right before she is discovered by Kadari, another character from the book. Another painting I am working on is of a scene from Briapol's cave, actually there are two of these, another one is of the city of Fantara in Fantaran Gulch, and then there is my eyeball painting that I am doing at random. I am having a small decision problem going on in my head as far as what I should do for my thesis. I know what I should do, and that is to build a large installation of all the furniture from within the CCAC, but I just can't help but to love my paintings.. I should have started them at the beginning of the year.. damn. Doesn't matter, I will still be able to show them at other places. So, that is what matters, now, I just have to figure out how to get enough done so that I can have a painting for each chapter… would be awesome.

This poem is for salvage,

"Before the Rats do"

All along this highway

You will see the bits and pieces

The finer portions of my heart

Now disregarded

Left to be blown around

Ran over

And shoveled to the side

Perfect for the pecking

By the scavengers

The ones who survive

By tearing apart

that which is already wounded

and I am wounded

My heart ran over

dragged to the side

Pecked apart by traitors

Only looking for love

So that when they get it

They too can tear their piece off

And feed it to the scavengers

I hope you find me

Before the rats do

I toss this letter into the void, the abyss between us, this space that keeps conversation from happening.

Sincerely,
Rush Whitacre
740-336-9169

4-7-11

Dear Taylor Swift,

    Today has taken such a turn for the worst. My (related person who is male and not named) called me up earlier to tell me that my (related person who is not named) fell ill suddenly to infection, went into a comma, and he told me that if her vitals don't improve that he is going to take her off of life support. This is hard for me to say, but she never even wanted to be put on life support. She is DNR. I really can't say much more in this letter. I just don't have it in me. I am really afraid that I am going to lose my (related person who is not named).

    This poem is for you mom

Drowning

Heart under water

And my tears can't bring you back

And I can't bring you back

Something inside

Broken

My heart stopping

And all I have I feel slip away

I want to tell you something now

That I have no problem leaving

But,

I do have a problem

When you let me go

Because I don't want to go

Not really

Not at all

I love you mom.

I toss this letter into the void, that abyss between us, this space that keeps conversation from happening

Sincerely,

Rush Whitacre

4-8-11

Dear Taylor Swift,

I guess later today I will find out how my (related person who is not named) is doing, she is about 7 hours away at the opposite end of Ohio and there is no way I can do it, I just can't drive there as an emotional wreck. Not to mention, my (related person who is not named) and I do not see eye to eye, ever. No matter what is going on in my life I am always aware of the possibility of my (related person who is not named) being there for me and at the same time not being there for me. Doing everything she can for me, and at the same time she also does things to betray all my trust.

All day today all I have done is watch Battlestar Galactica. I feel like such a bum, a giant bum, but I can't help it totally because I am just so worried about my (related person who is not named). I text my (related person who is male and not named) and get no response, my dad is not calling me back. I don't know what is going to happen, and that is something that no one knows.

This poem is for practice,

Cards drawn

No folding and chips laid

A fortune of faded corners

Easily read from across the table

Of the

Opponents well played deck

Beating the setup

Is like putting out the fire

With cigarette butts

I toss this letter into the void, the abyss between us, this space that keeps conversation from happening.

Sincerely,
Rush Whitacre
740-336-9169

4-9-11

Dear Taylor Swift,

Another day of totally ignoring the world, watching Battlestar Galactica and trying to ignore the fact that at this very moment my (related person who is not named) is dying in some hospital up north. The Battlestar shows are very very addictive and the keep my mind off of this thing that has plagued my mind. I am going to go and make a pizza, maybe a little food will make me feel not so empty and alone.

More Battlestar, this time an episode that is actually a movie called Razor. We shall see how this turns out. The pizza is good.

Ok, my (related person who is male and not named) (related person who is male and not named) just called me to tell me that our (related person who is not named) is awake and off of the ventilator and she doesn't have an IV in her anywhere. She is repeating words and or sayings over and over. (related person who is male and not named) thinks that she has had a stroke, that she is pretty bad, and they took her off of the ventilator and IV's because my (related person who is not named) wants to go, she doesn't want to live, she doesn't want to be ran by machines. I don't blame her, but it still hurts me so badly, I miss her so much. Like I miss comfort.

My roommate has been trying to get me out of the house for the past two days. I am really screwing up, I need to get some work done on my classes and assignments. I am just not able to do it for some reason, just too much going on in my brain… I have two presentations this week, and my thesis to write. Damn damn. I guess the reality of my not getting work done is setting in real hard, and even now as I am writing this letter I feel like I should be working on other assignments.

This poem is for the one memory,

She lingers

Out there in the world

A forgetful place

So many things to do

Plans to keep

Promises to make good on

Promises to break

And I can't stop forgetting her smile

A loss in a coat pocket

A small scrap of paper

Receipts, nickels, and holes

A ball of lint

Traces of the past left behind

Reminders of moments

Of places, events, shoelaces

You can pull and tie

Unfold and imagine words, numbers

> But if you don't double up
> You won't keep your mind
> Memories
> Directions on the lip
> The destination of home
> And it will be lost
> Repeated not.

I toss this letter into void, the abyss between us, this space that keeps conversation from happening.

Sincerely,
Rush Whitacre
740-336-9169

4-10-11

Dear Taylor Swift,

    I have had my butt beat into the ground today. I tried to catch up for this coming week, and this just isn't happening. I didn't even get any of my presentations done today. I spent the day working on both and neither have a saved location on my computer, I feel like such a loser… what is wrong with me, I never have problems like this, where I don't get things done, my mind is just not in the game!!!

    My exgirlfriend just called me because of something I just wrote on facebook, she thought it had something to do with her. So strange, because I don't ever write about exgirlfriend's, let alone think about them. I see no reason, and can't imagine any joy one would get out of being an ass to an ex. Besides coming out looking like an ex,,, and I don't want to come out of a relationship looking like an ass, let alone it being the goal. Her name is Mandy, and, she is getting married this coming summer, and I keep asking her if she thinks she is making the right decision, actually, I am telling her that it is the wrong decision.. that you just don't get engage to someone else after breaking up with someone else three months earlier. Then again, she does have three kids, and the do need a father figure, something stable, and so long as the man is a man and not a criminal, then I am ok with that. Her kids need a really good father figure because lord knows that their real father is not…

    Ashley just found out about my (related person who is not named), Ashley the other girl I kinda dated this past summer. She is simple, quiet, and trying to get an education and she must have found out about my (related person who is not named) through my neighbor Josh, her brother-n-law. Ok, I will deal with this and then get back to work on here.

Oh, previous students and their wants to not work on their assignments until the last minute. One of my students from last quarter just asked me what to do about not having started a drawing that is due tomorrow at 8 am. I laughed, said that they could sleep if they could find someone else to say up all night working on their assignments for them, but that would defeat the purpose of learning, because then you don't learn anything except that someone else can do your work for you, and that you are lazy. Now, if you could get a half a dozen to do your work for you however I would have to call you industrious and ambitious, and a hard working business person, but not a hard working artist, not at this level. You wouldn't be lazy obviously.

This poem is for missing the one you love,

"Deliberately Sinking"

Memories

Like flipping through photographs in my mind

Still frames from a shattered past

Present

And a future I long to reach out for

For now you are gone

And like a dream

I close my eyes and hope to see you there

Then I wake

And you never were, never could be.

Like a rainbow during the rain

I could never catch you

My eyes, my imagination, my heart

All playing tricks on me

Reaching for something solid

That only exists in air

Lessons learned in a mirror, blindfolded

Like the ocean, my idea of you is vast

Circling me, waving across my body

My thoughts of you run deep

And I am good at drowning.

I toss this letter into the void, the abyss between us, this space that keeps conversation from happening.

Sincerely,
Rush Whitacre
740-336-9169

4-11-11

Dear Taylor Swift,

    Wow, what a workout today. I usually don't feel tired this long after a workout. It is 11:37 pm and I can still feel the tired muscles in my arms and legs saying to me, "Rest, please rest us…" lol, gosh I hope they never really talk to me, how scary, I would never get any sleep. Well, anyway. I got my presentation done for my night class, piece of cake. I love little presentations, they are like a really good chocolate candy and dissolves just long enough for you to not need another one for a long time. I did my presentation on Jean-Paul Sartre's idea on Giacometti's break through and how he made sculpture like a painter would make paintings, at a distance.

    Something funny happened earlier today, I had my friend Les tell me that I should use twitter because it is a really good way to advertise art shows and openings and now the college is going to have some kind of twitter following for Grads so that they can be informed of whatever blah blah blah. So, I started a twitter account and it made me feel like I had to add 10 people… and there is only one person I know on twitter besides Les, and that is my friend Dominoe. So, I added Nathan, and then I couldn't find Les, so, I didn't get her. So, I figured, what the hell, I will add my favorite actors and music peoples. Funny, that when I when to type in,,, um, crap, now I can't remember which of my singers I typed in that brought you up as a person who I might be interested in tweeting to. So, I thought, what the hell, You, John Cusack, Katy Perry, Sara Bareilles and all the others that I added will just have to entertain my following feeds for awhile. If I see you tweet, I will just have to write you something, just because I am curious as to whether you will even recognize it is me from my letters, which would then make me wonder if you had even read any of them. Lol, ok, I will just type you my last line that I leave in all my letters. Not that you will understand what it is from, or who I am. Just because.

This poem is for the dreamer,

"The Dreamer"

In her own little world

Curious not about the future

Coming from a past she has forgotten

All she has is right now

A mirror in front of her

Reflecting the ever moment of present

She can see the future as it reflects

Shining in her eyes, capturing the moment

And then blasting throughout her body

In passing, leaving goosebumps, a smile, a tear

And with a tap the mirror breaks

Slowly letting light in through the cracks

And her eyes close to the reality

The absence of the knowing

The present moment passes

And a future unforeseeable

Dreams take over

Imaginary illusion of untrue falsities

A unnecessary doubling of time, place

And subject matter

No need to wake her

For her dream world is the same

As her real

Waking would feel like a dream

And dreaming is never ending.

I toss this letter into the void, the abyss between us, this space that keeps conversation from happening.

Sincerely,
Rush Whitacre
740-336-9169

4-12-11

Dear Taylor Swift,

    It is yet another Tuesday, only this time it is a long day until my night class because my first two classes were cancelled because of first year review for the first year grads… all of them. So, I walked around really quiet when I did walk around because of respect. Last year I was shown the same respect.

Side note: My computer does this thing that is so fast and so annoying because of the touch mouse pad thingy. Somehow the sensitive pad gets touched by the palms of my hands and then the computer just goes crazy that then either zooms way in or zooms way out… and this is both annoying, and funny. Mostly because it annoys me and then I do this funny thing where I somehow am surprised that such a thing could ever happen… lol, how about that for funny, I am actually surprised every time… I think mostly because I have to assess which has happened, leaving me with only two options, the obvious options, in or out… lol

My night class was both interesting, productive, and boring at the same time. I liked the subject matter being discussed, I felt like it was going somewhere, but the manner in which it was being distributed was rather boring. Of course, there is no other way to relay history, but still, nonetheless, it was boring. There has to be a way to make learning history more interesting, there just has to be. My guess is, that it would be really hard to judge a crowd in a class room so I can only imagine what it would take to make learning any kind of history really interesting. Still, there has to be a way.

Another side note: My roommate it over 500 dollars behind in paying the bills…. What does that mean to me, how should I look at him without thinking that he is screwing me over. Louis says that he is going to pay me, but I just can't believe him completely because he isn't showing me any sign of doing so. I ask him for money and he just says that he will get me money, not to call his mom, well, I have to say to you that I will if I absolutely feel I need toooo. Louis just needs some responsibility, I mean, if that is what it takes then I will just call his mother, and strange as that sounds.

I dedicate this poem to anger,

"Finished"

The rabbit said good bye

And I the turtle couldn't wave,

And I went about my life

Slowly walking along

Taking my time to look at all the world

To feel a blade of grass

And smell a flower

The wetness of a drop of dew water

Oh, but what is this

For it is the rabbit sleeping

Should I wake her, a little tap

No, for sleeping is where dreams come true

And who am I to stand in the way of dreams

So I mozzy on, walking down my path

I think a little about my dreaming friend

How does she dream

Happily, sadly, or just out of turn

I am sure she dreams well

In the near distance I hear a line

It calls me, pulls me toward it

And at this line I shall find an end to my curiosity

The cheering, and yelling has blinded me

I look back

And as I cross the line I see my friend the rabbit

Right behind me, sad, tears

upset

Back into the stream that feeds the ocean that feeds the stream.

You're a little full of myself.

I toss this letter into the void, the abyss between us, this space that keeps conversation from happening.

Sincerely,

Rush Whitacre

740-336-9169

4-13-11

Dear Taylor Swift,

    Do you ever get the feeling like you just made a really bad decision,,, only the decision you made was actually dictated by something you did weeks ago and consequently led up to the ultimate badness… yeah, that was today for me, starting out around 2 AM today and ending around 4 this afternoon. Anyway.

    I spent all day making a presentation to do tomorrow in my Grad Studio class. I love it, it is called: "DNA to BFA"… I just love it because it chronicles my doings in art school from the very beginning all the way up through to the end of my thesis in undergrad. The only problem I see is 'Lady' wanting to know why I don't have anything from grad school in this presentation,,, well it is simple, nothing in grad school happened before my BFA, so, it just doesn't belong. Smiles. Besides, I wouldn't want anything from grad school there anyway. Everything in Grad school is splintered, separate, and nothing really goes together other than it was all done for the effect of getting a degree, an MFA degree. I wonder how my presentation for being a visiting artist will be when I have to present my work from grad school, because my work in grad school is rather splintered to the point that I am thinking of just calling it random learning experiences. Each class being pulled in one direction or another, nothing really coming together to make a whole. It doesn't matter, I can tie it all together using humor if nothing else, or mass confusion. Yeah, either will do.

My (related person who is not named) is getting better every passing day. Her next step is to move into a nursing home for rehabilitation. I still haven't talked to her directly. Every time I do end up talking to her she continues down the path of trying to make me angry, and I just can't do that anymore. Not to mention, it makes no sense for me to call her and for her to get herself all upset for nothing. So I just won't do it. I love you move. Now that I think of it, I wonder who is going to take care of (related person who is male and not named) while she is gone, because he can't take care of himself, he just can't because he has been enabled into a black hole of no return. He actually makes all the right moves for bad things to have to happen to him. I feel sorry for him, he and (related person who is not named) both. I wish there was something I could do. What though…

This poem is a modification of one my (related person who is not named) wrote, for you Penny,

"Cape Cod flats, and the son who carried you"

I carry you out to the

Mud flats of life

We wait for the sea

An ocean of time

Ticking away our minutes

The tide at Cape Cod

Goes out three miles

And we walk the flats alone

We have to dig for our dinner

A clam or quahog

For there will be chowder

Tonight with the lobsters

I get distracted as a fish

Darts in the pools

A squid is seen now

> Propelling himself backward
>
> He dispenses a
>
> Murky black experience
>
> And I carry you home
>
> Over sand, over rocks
>
> A gull flies overhead
>
> Piercing are its crys
>
> Hunger pulls her to the water
>
> She searches for her supper
>
> We are glad that we are here today
>
> As rain threatens in the sky
>
> The tide starts to return
>
> We start back to our cabin
>
> A modified poem of Penelope Warren's, by Rush Whitacre

I toss this letter into the void, the abyss between us, this space that keeps conversation from happening.

Sincerely,

Rush Whitacre

740-336-9169

4-14-11

Dear Taylor Swift

    Taylor, I can't express to you how tired I am right now. It is morning and I am taking this moment to start this letter because I feel it will probably be good luck to start it now before doing my 20 min artist presentation. I feel really not nervous right now, probably because of how tired I am, but I know that while the girl going before me is doing hers I am going to start getting really nervous, I just know it. Ok, I have to get going.

    Flash forward: Ok, so, I think I did a smash up job of presenting, of course, I practiced the heck out of it before. But, then I was told by my friend Babyboothat he felt a very awkward vibe going around in the class, and I got attacked on several levels about my lecture only going up through to my BFA and not up through to my MFA.. lol, I thought it was a genius move, and my story in my artist presentation was brilliant, and even Christian mentioned that my method of delivery was a genius move. I don't know, I feel that what I did was excellent, and that is all that matters to me, I felt a little relieved after it was done. Just very tired now.

Well, it has been a week since my (related person who is not named) was in the hospital in a coma, and she has now been placed in a nursing home for rehabilitation. I honestly don't see her getting out of the nursing home. I remember when she was place in one before and how she didn't want to leave because she had people waiting on her hand and foot 24 hours a day. Of course, I also remember how she had to be transferred out and into a single room because she and her roommate just couldn't get along at all. It didn't surprise me. It usually doesn't take long for people to want to not be around my (related person who is not named), she has this way of finding a path to getting under your skin until you are pissed. I shouldn't be saying these things, but, they are the truth, and history shall be recorded as truthfully as possible.

My roommate has now been playing the same song over and over all day, the CEE-Lo Green song called F-You. He just loves it to death, I know this because he hates it when someone plays a song to death, and I can only judge that if he is willing to do it then the song must be something pretty special to him.

This poem is for the rain,

"Shower"

Clouds

A sky like a pallet

Paint smeared in circles

And a scent of fresh

A crisp sharp dash of light

Thunder rolls by

And my skin tingles

Drop by drop

Cold chills ravage my arms

My back, and shoulders

Speckled water like clear freckles

And I can't bear to wipe them off

I begin to soak

Water trails down my legs

Soggy soaks

And squishy shoes

Splashing puddles in my path

Smiling, ringing out my hair

Laughing at the sky

And the rain

Cleans

I toss this letter into the void, the abyss between us, this space that keeps conversation from happening.

Sincerely,

Rush Whitacre

740-336-9169

therush@hotmail.com

4-15-11

Dear Taylor Swift,

    Another Friday, and another day to work out, but I don't think I am going to go in and work out because this bed I am in is so comfortable right now. I only have a couple of episodes left of Battlestar to watch, that is what I will do. I am going to be really sad when I get the rest of the way through this show and don't have anything left in it. I am really stuck on the show, kinda like the show House, only with Battlestar Galactica I start to feel like I am in the show, like I am a part of the human race that is trying hard to survive against all odds. Ok, yeah, I am going to watch some Battlestar now.

    Well, that sucked, I have been waiting to find out what Starbuc is in the series and they never ever say. At the very end she just drops out of existence.. what the heck is that all about. What a secret, a mystery to leave lingering. There could be an entire other year in this series just about how Starbuc ended up on Earth, and how she died, and how she survived and maybe they could still keep her a mystery to a certain degree, but there is so much more that can be done with this series… Man, this sucks that it is over. Now I am going to have to find another show to watch. Got any suggestions?

    I am so bad, I am being really bad about my workouts on Fridays, I didn't work out last Friday either. I am going to work out tomorrow instead, I just can't not do it. My stomach is aching, but I don't want to eat, I am really getting serious about this losing weight thing. I hope I don't get tired of subway. That would suck, because that has been the baseline food. I guess there is always jimmy johns or chipotle. I don't know , maybe I am over doing it, maybe I should consult a nutrition specialist to see that I am getting the right vitamins and minerals… huh, maybe

    I am still in a little phase of awwww from that presentation I did. I keep thinking that there is some catch that I am not aware of, because this class I don't like, and this quarter I really like it. I must have lost my mind. Lol

Ok, I am going to go for a walk to get a snack, I will be back to finish this letter and poem. I am just too hungry to try to sleep in a little while.

Ok, so I picked up a frozen pizza, probably not the best choice if I am going to try to lose weight, so, I will only have maybe 2 pieces and save the rest for tomorrow. Gosh, I am just so hungry.

This poem is for Alex's blonde curly hair,

"Pulled over the Edge"

Curls,

And curls and curls

A trap for the fingers

Dense and turning in the wind

My eyes can't understand your length

As you are withdrawn

Simply a spring not sprung

Pushing me not away

And yet not pulling me in

I sit like a telescope

Gazing across the world

Across the city

Across the room

Wondering what it would be like

To be the man

Who got to run his fingers

Through that beautiful hair

Those curls

Rings of gold

I toss this letter into the void, the abyss between us, this space that keeps conversation from happening.

Sincerely,

Rush Whitacre

740-336-9169

4-16-11

Dear Taylor Swift,

    Nothing ever seems to go the way you think it will go. I spent the morning driving around my roommate Louis, and then right when I thought I would lay down to start reading I get a call from my sister to come to Columbus because she didn't know what kind of shape he was going to be in when he came out of the catch lab. Well, forget the studying, I left for Columbus. When I got there my dad still wasn't out of the catch lab, and everyone was worried, and then I got worried. I tear up so easily, and my dad is everything to me, everything. I know that he can't be around forever, and I definitely don't want him to suffer in anyway, but I am just not ready for him to leave me yet, not yet.

    So, I sat around in his hospital room, trying to read, and it was effort in vain. I couldn't stop eaves dropping on my brothers and sisters conversations. My brain was swirling around and around and not consuming anything that was before me in the book I was trying to read. Then dad came back from the catch lab and everyone got really interested in what was happening. He seemed ok, but, then came the obvious problem, he is faced with open heart surgery. There is no way out in this world, no science to save you from the inevitable death, there is only delay, that is if we are lucky enough to have that. My dad has been lucky up to this point, delaying as long as possible. My (related person who is not named) has kind of been doing the opposite, doing things to her body not really caring about her health, body, or emotional state. Hmm, what a strange way to grow up in a house with both extremes.

    Tomorrow I head back to the hospital to hear a doctor tell us all that dad needs open heart surgery.   My dad has been fighting the idea of open heart surgery for years, I think the fight is over, and the choice is either do the surgery, or not last much longer. Either way I don't think he has but anywhere from a couple of months to a couple of years. I wish I had the cure to aging, to make my dad young again. Lol, dream on Rush.

    I just now was having 11 conversations going on at once between my cell phone texts and facebook… really hard to keep up with. Ok, I am getting sleep, and I want to write this poem, and too bad I haven't heard from you, it would be nice for you to give me a topic for a poem sometime.

This poem is for the breaking of my heart

It is day one

And my world turns upside down

Tears flow, and anger ripples like a quake

Cracking the surface

Letting in the air of something shy

A prisoner like a tree to the vine

Being wrapped, strangled
Harder to breathe without you here
A cloud, sandstorm, hating me
Grinding me to pieces
Filling my cracks with salt
Burning me
And the rain won't wash me clean
This pain shall linger
Carrying through the years
Blending me to another whole
Another mix
And the divide created will remain
This love hate, hate love
Rapture
And my heart breaks
Divided.

I toss this letter into the void, the abyss between us, this space that keeps conversation from happening.

Sincerely,
Rush Whitacre
740-336-9169

4-17-11

Dear Taylor Swift,

    I woke up at my brother's house in Columbus this morning on the hardest couch I have ever slept on in my life. I am so glad that I am now back in Cincinnati laying here on my bed. I had a bed to sleep in at my bro's, but I was just way too tired for some reason to get off of that darn couch to walk up stairs. Emotionally worn out, physically worn out, worn out worn out. I am a little better now.

    At the hospital my dad seemed in better spirits while he was awake, and was always making funny little jokes with the nurses and picking on his girlfriend Lahoma. I just couldn't help but tear up, and I really hate to cry in front of my dad, as cliché as that sounds, but it is true. And I especially don't want to do it while he is in the condition he is in because I am afraid it would just remind him of his condition. I am on the verge of not being able to make it through this quarter… I don't know. I have to, I just have to make it through because I don't think I will be getting any more money from anyone anywhere to pay for the last quarter. So, yeah, this has to work for me.

I have been trying to figure out how to get a hold of my friend John Risque but he isn't returning my phone calls, and he isn't responding to my text messages. I am getting quite curious about him. I think that maybe we had a falling out and I am not aware of it. I haven't heard from him for such a long time, not since I asked him if I could interview him for a possible book that I want to write about the loft we all built, and lived in for the most part while going to OU in Athens Ohio. It is a long story, let's just say that I couldn't be somewhere when I really should have been, and this stunted my friendships with everyone who was involved with the adventures, and misadventures at OU.

I picked Yangue up at the airport a little bit ago, he took me out to eat as a treat for picking him up. He is a very nice man. Too bad he has to be so far away from home, his family, and from all the different kinds of food that he would rather be eating. He brought me home a bottle of Chinese liquor, which I am sure is very good quality, but I am just not into alcohol that much these days, now back when I was going to school at OU, it wasn't anything for anyone to be walking around with alcohol on them in some form or another. But now, nope, it just isn't my thing. Now Louis, my roommate, he drinks wine like it is going out of style. Louis owes me over 300 dollars, and I keep floating him money until he can get me paid off. I should have known that he was going to be good at helping with the bills when his (related person who is not named) said to me; "if my son cannot pay his bills, I will pay his bills for him." Lol, I thought what she was saying was a good thing, but really it was a warning.

This poem is for A.J.'s Obsession: Alex

"Obsession Depression"

The brunette hair stare

And a team of "I"s, and "Me"s

And bedtime stories of pisses off lads

A razor sharp laugh

Isolating him

To the desert of no oasis

Of no reprieve

Now she laughs at her decision

The fence, wall, blended orange peel

A defense against lips

Kissing

Not for the loud one

Or the lame

Brunette hair laughs again

A screen

A noise from speakers

Rakes across their ears

Then Alex realizes that the noise

The cackling, and yelling

And laughing

That was hurting her ears

Was coming from the very lad

Who she would call

One time date.

I toss this letter into the void, the abyss between us, this space that keeps conversation from happening.

Sincerely,

Rush Whitacre

740-336-9169

4-18-11

Dear Taylor Swift,

    Today started off with me in the director of the schools office crying. I told him that I just needed a pass on the test that I was supposed to take tonight. He already knew of my problems and how my family is going through bad health issues. I just couldn't hold it in. I just couldn't. I bet I spent at least 10 minutes in the main office with tears just dripping off of my face, I am sure that I looked like a mess, well, because I was a wreck, am a wreck. I have a lot of respect for Marcus, he gave me the week off to be with my family, to be with my dad, and to catch up on my studies. He is a very loving man, Marcus

    On a different note, my (related person who is not named) is still in a nursing home, my (related person who is male and not named) told me that she is sounding better, but not completely all there. Maybe she will get out and go home in 3 or 4 weeks my (related person who is male and not named) says.

    My dad is up in Columbus still, and won't be getting out of the hospital without surgery or a very low chance of living another 4 to 6 months. He has become a cardiac cripple. I am so sad just thinking about it, like right now I have two, now three tears running down my cheeks. God, I feel so helpless/useless/and so far away from love. I haven't felt love in such a long time, or at least felt like someone has loved me, or for someone to be there for me to love. Ok, I have this week off, I had better take advantage of it.

Something odd is happening, I can hear my neighbors above my apartment tonight. So strange, I never hear them and now tonight they are really making some noise, like they are rearranging furniture. Kinda refreshing, maybe someone is moving in, or moving out.

My roommate Louis is a real pain in the ass, he owes me money, and asks me for more and more. Lol, gosh, I feel like a sucker, but one who wants everyone to be ok. I think that somehow he will pay me for what he owes. Or not, it really isn't that much I guess, in the long run of things anyway.

This poem is for tears,

"Place to cry"

Why

What is the purpose

What is their purpose

And how can I see straight

If all I can see is sad

A mirror told me this

And the letter that followed

Only said that I was right

When everything else is wrong

I do not wish to cry

But in all the world

From all the places I could be

I can't imagine myself

In any other place

Than in the arms of a loved one

In the presence of family

Surrounded by friends

It would be there, here

In that place

Is where I would want to be sad

To cry, to have a tear

Or two run down my cheek

I toss this letter into the void, the abyss between us, this space that keeps conversation from happening.

Sincerely,
Rush Whitacre
740-336-9169

4-19-11

Dear Taylor Swift,

    Another day, another dilemma. Today I plan on writing out my entire thesis, for better or for worse, and once I have it completely written out I will place the sentences into a poem format and make parts of it rhyme, and parts of it not. They will all be clever decisions I am sure, for this is what I strive for, clever creative ideas to be turned into even better clever creative objects, etc. I have received no word from Columbus as of yet, as of any decisions that my dad will have, or might make. Thinking about that today would be a bad idea, I really need to get to work, to get something done towards my thesis. I am actually excited about this little journey, this new writing, this journal type thesis type poem time integration. A morphing of ideas. Oh bother, I hope it doesn't turn out to be floppy, not be able to stand on its own.

    Ok, I will get back on here in a little bit to share what I have done with my thesis, but first, shower time.

    Hours later. I have worked on my thesis and watched movies, and generally had good food. Mostly, I have been relaxing. I need to work harder and play less this week. I have already been given a week off from school by the director of the school and I really don't want to take too much advantage of this time off. I mean, this is probably the last week I am given off in my life for the next however long period of time it takes until I find that I can take a week off for myself.

    So, yeah, today was mostly thesis day as far as work goes for my schooling. I feel that I must finish this thesis first before studying for my test that I will have to take this next week, the one that I was allowed to put on hold this week, ok time to go to bed, tomorrow I will buckle down and focus hard on finishing my thesis, not matter how goofy I feel it is.

    My roommate just came in and I think he was drunk, he had his drunk face on and came in asking me all kinds of questions that were just weird and out of context. He came in all curious as to what I was watching and did I like it, so weird, so funny.

Aaaand, now he is singing very loudly, drunkenly. Oh Louis, you are yourself karaoke sessions. I will miss you.

This poem is for showed mysteries.

"A burning toss aside"

Flashlight

A fake fire in the woods

A motion of running

Fear lingering on your shoulders

And all the world feels behind you

As that is all you can do

And looking back while running away

Presents you with trips

And falls

And get back up again's

It's a party

A war

And love means confusion

As hate breads more moments

For love to seep in

For moments of kindness

To open up and breath

Suffocation

Yes, this is better that separation

The vanish of a warm body

As it once laid side by yours.

I toss this letter into the void, the abyss between us, this space that keeps conversation from happening.

Sincerely,
Rush Whitacre
740-336-9169

4-20-11

Dear Taylor Swift,

    Ok, I have been a complete bum today. I have lied around all day in bed working on my thesis off and on, and or checking out my facebook account, or twitter account, and I watched two movies. Got I am such a bum. I need to get my butt in focus and get this thesis written today and send it to my sister and let her check it out. I can't stand not having this thesis written..

    Hours later, still don't have my thesis written and I promised my sister that I would have it emailed to her today to be read and edited by her, or I guess it would rather be someone who has no idea what it is that I have written who could tell me how to make it more easily readable. Ok, part of the truth behind why I don't have my thesis completely written is because every time I have a snack, or a small meal I put on a show or a movie to watch because it is the only time that I do it. And well, if I finish my small meal and the movie is still playing I just keep watching it. This is a bad pattern, very bad, very addictive, lol. Tomorrow will be different, it has to be otherwise I am screwed, because I need time to study for my tests too!! Aaaaaah.

    I feel a little bad because one of my students contacted me earlier I told them that I would be able to help them with a project of theirs and then only 10 minutes later I told them that I just couldn't do it. It was stupid of me to think I would be able to, I mean, I was given this week off from school and I don't think it would be a good idea to march in there and just act like I can do anything I want, because I can't, I just can't march around and flash my presence around and just disappear for any reason I want. Not on campus anyway. I can do anything and go anywhere I want, I just can't do it where it makes me look like an ass, and I am not trying to pull one over on anyone, I just don't want to make what I am doing look like I am trying to pull one over on the professors, because I am not.. lol, why do I feel like I have to defend myself, lord I will never know.

    I will have to contact my (related person who is male and not named) tomorrow and find out how my (related person who is not named) is doing. I have to keep up with her, otherwise I am afraid that they will think I have forgotten about her.

    I don't know what I am doing for sure with several things in my life, one thing I know for sure that I know I am doing is writing these letters every day, spilling some of my guts out, and other times just getting things off of my chest. I guess sometimes I talk about my work as a grad student, but that hasn't been a whole lot since I decided that I am going to build a massive installation of furniture. Should be interesting, most likely a surprise for even myself.. lol, I hope it isn't a surprise for myself…

This poem is for the Dark brown eyes,

"Nothing shy of Given"

Shortly

At last in front of me

                    Dazzling bright whites

                Surrounding slightly oval ponds

                        Of brown and black

                So dark that not even a reflection

                        Nor light can escape

                            I am quivering

                        Lost and forgetting my way

                    I have to leave because I must

                        I stay because I want to

                        Forgetting all the world

                And everything that it is asking of me

                            I choose you

                              Brown eyes

                Erasing this essence of foreboding fear

                            Of losing you,

                            And losing myself

                    And all the world would know

                        That I left, that I gave up

                        A life I will not live

I toss this letter into the void, the abyss between us, this space that keeps conversation from happening.

Sincerely,
Rush Whitacre
740-336-9169

4-21-11

Dear Taylor Swift,

    Like another day on a week off from school, I slept in until noon and then woke up thinking that I am a complete lazy bum.. I mean, not in a bad way, just not in a productive way. I was immediately propositioned by Yangue to take him to the Asian market so that he could but some Chinese groceries. Its rather funny, because he really doesn't buy anything at the Asian market that he couldn't buy at a Kroger, or any other leading grocery chain. I think he just feels better thinking that he is still helping out his home China buy buying their products that are shipped here. Trust me, he knows that his country is heading to be the leading power in the world, money-wise, and people-wise. Well, definitely people-wise… China just has so many people. I don't know of anyone who can possibly take them on in sheer numbers. Soon here in America our national debt's interest will be larger than our nation can produce in taxes and then we are going to be screwed. When this happens China will just say it wants America's land in payment and we will be helpless to stop them, because they will have simply bought up all the land and businesses. There won't be a war, it will just be a memo: "Uhhh, we win" And then we will start receiving notice in the mail of all the new holidays we have to honor, and of the new internet address where we have to file our taxes. Lol, I hope I don't live that long to see that.

  After the Asian market I came home and received a message from my sister telling me that my dad is having surgery tomorrow at 11:30 AM. This news makes me sick to my stomach. It is something that I knew was coming, but it was the delay between the realization that it was going to happen, and the actualization of it happening was my slight safe haven. Now though, there is only fate. My dad is either going to survive the surgery, or he is not going to survive the surgery. Oh boy, here we go again, tears flowing out of my eyes making it really hard to type again… damn, actually, a poor damn at that, the tears are still making their way out.. anyway, so, I was packed up and heading on my way to Columbus to see my dad when I decided to stop and see my friend Gari just to update him on my dad's status. I ended up going out with Gari and talking and having a glass or two of wine and then I started to get to tired to make the rest of the trip and decided that there was no way that I could make it to Columbus, I was just too tired.

  Pray for my Dad.

This poem is for the silent thief,

"Forgive me Not"

Figuratively

It speaks to you

Even though its curtains

Are cinched by brass grips

Darkness falls on this mystery

And not a moment passes

Where he doesn't think about her

Forever

And that time limit still isn't long enough

She says she will wait forever and again

And a moment passes into the back

                Forgotten until the next bump

                      The next error

                      The next glitch

       Something that only memory's bond to

                      and it is the mind

                      who is its own master

              wielding the sword of words

                      as the saying goes

              Forgive, but never forget

                      Sounds more like

                      Never forgiving

I toss this letter into the void, the abyss between us, this space that keeps conversation from happening.

Sincerely,
Rush Whitacre
740-336-9169

4-22-11

Dear Taylor Swift,

      What a long long long long emotional day. Well, my dad had surgery all day today. I have just been biting at the bit worrying about anything and everything. Just sitting there in my chair, so helpless, not able to make a move that can make any difference in the world, and I all wanted was for my dad to come out of surgery and go home and be ok and live for a very long time and I can't fight nature, or fate, or run against a wind who's force is like the breath that was knocked out of me when the doctors asked us to come back to a family isolation room. It was like a fist in my throat, this vast empty space in my chest open up, and the waiting was like falling out of the sky only the ground never came, the ground just never came and I could feel my throat shutting, my heart stopping its beat, really it did and I thought I was going to explode, and then the doctor came into the room. I could feel all the eyes glued to this young man, this man who had my father's life literally in his hands for hours, and I mean hours. And even after the surgeon said that Dad did well the vast empty space just didn't go away, the fist in my throat went away, but not the empty space. It was only after sitting back in the waiting room for 15 to 20 minutes did I feel any kind of release, any kind of comfort.

Oh man, Taylor, I did everything I could to keep my mind busy reading to catch up with my studies for this test I will have this week, and it was really tough… luckily the reading of this theory was actually fun and nice to read, I am looking forward to reading more tomorrow. As for now, I am content with just writing you for a little bit.

Ok, the trick to hospital furniture is to find some from within the hospital that will fit your body, or, several pieces that will fit your body. I am 6'3" and I am stretched out over three pieces of furniture, not the most optimal situation, but I don't want to be very far from my father. He was so relaxed, and so many machines hooked up to him and so many fluids flowing into his body. And me standing there before him, so helpless, tears running down my cheeks, as they are right now. I just kept looking to the machines, those wonderful machines keeping my dad alive. He is a man worthy of being made young again if there ever was a man.

This poem is for Lahoma,

"Blended Petals"

Love,

I would like to think I know of love

I would like to think that I learned if from my father

For he has loved in his life

He has loved his sons, he has loved his daughter

My father had his ups and downs

His smiles and laughter

And when his father died, such a sad spell,

A sad frown

And as I found my dad

At his most depressed and saddest

I could tell that it didn't matter to him

If he died or made it through

And the situation I think made me maddest

But, later he found you

Or you found him, and thank god you did

Because you made him happy

You showed him love

You showed him and his kid

What it means to live

To want to live

For love,
Because he loves you
And I can't thank you enough

I toss this letter into the void, the abyss between us, this space that keeps conversation from happening.

Sincerely,
Rush Whitacre
740-336-9169

4-23-11

Dear Taylor Swift,

Today my dad smiled for this first time. Face changing, his smile is something that completely changes his face, and I go from crying about now being able to help him to complete and utter tears of happiness. It is soo good to be another day closer to having my dad back home, with Lahoma, where he belongs, where he is happy. Today everything that we were all worried about seemed to slowly go away and get better, except one thing that I won't mention on here because I am trying not record it, but just to know that it is something that he has had problems with during every visit to hospitals when he has procedures where they put him out.

    My brother and my sister were here again today. Lahoma and her daughter went home this morning, her daughter Donna, wasn't feeling very well and I think they both could use a real good night's sleep, I think we all could. I am here again, laying in the waiting room,(atrium as they call it) where all the patients families wait while their loved ones go through what ever procedure they need to have) and of course, lol, this furniture is only as comfortable as your level of exhaustion. If you are not really tired, it is not that comfortable. Tonight, I am going to sleep like a rock, I am drained to the max.

    I have had a certain amount of luck here tonight, my fortune cookie read, "Someone is interested in you, Keep your eyes open" lol, well, this man is going to be sleeping. I guess in the morning I will see if there is someone 'interested' in me here at the hospital... lol, highly doubtful. Maybe I should check my facebook right, see if there is someone interested,,, hmmm nope. Maybe on twitter, or on hotmail. Nope. I will just rely on the good old, 'if it happens, it happens' and I will just keep my eye open so long as I can keep them from making me sleep. You know, I have in the past have really taken stock in what fortune cookies said, only because they were fun to connect to life things happening in my life at the time. I actually have two taped to the inside of my wallet, they have a particular importance to me… Who knows,, maybe someone is actually taking stock in me… lol. I won't get my hopes up.

      Well, I am going to go back and see my dad for a minute and then come here to write my poem… maybe I will get something moving happen back there and I will just have to write about it. Be back soon.

This poem is for the Kiss Goodnight

"Kiss Goodnight"

I sometimes just stand there

The edge of your bed seems so far away

And I just stare out across your landscape

My mind wanders, puts up its sails

And I float along, knowing that you're here with me

You are sleeping

Dreaming I know by the way you move

I want to reach out to touch your face

To hold you

Because I want you to know I'm here

I'm still here

I love you so much

But your dreams are like the drug

That I dare not take away

So dream

I will wait for you, here

No matter the time it takes

And no distance can keep me

So I lean over

Whispering sweet dreams

And kiss you goodnight

I toss this letter into the void, the abyss between us, this space that keeps conversation from happening.

Sincerely,
Rush Whitacre

740-336-9169

4-24-11

Dear Taylor Swift,

0733 AM: It is early morning, very early. I was woken up by my sister, she was panicking because she couldn't get a hold of the nurse and I missed her first phone call. Then I called her back and she fortunately was talking to the nurse. When she called me back she sounded stressed, but better. I went back to check on dad and he is looking good. I think I mentioned this before, but, it seems like every hour that passes he gets that 1 percent better,, which to me is crucial, for me and him. I want this upward climb to continue, as I am sure so does everyone else, especially Lahoma. Ok, I am going to come back to this letter in a little bit, I want to have more of the day on it, as I am sure you want to know more about what is going on.

1045 AM: Ok, well they are not going to take out the ventilator or feeding tube until tomorrow, which is just fine with us. See, I guess as my sister informed me, because of my dad's small valve hole in his heart for such a long that he still had hypertension in his lungs from the pressure build up back into his lungs, well, as soon as he gets a little more revived his new valve should help to clear up the backed up pressure problems. So, we are aiming for tomorrow. Ok I will get back on here a little later.

3:01 pm: Dad is worn out. All the breathing on his own all night, that they let him do has just worn him out. Now they are trying to dry him out with lasics, I guess he gained quite a bit of weight fluid from all his swelling that they are trying to get the fluids out of him. There is a little worry that he could develop pneumonia from getting an infection in his lungs, I certainly hope that he doesn't, that would not make anyone very happy.

11:33 pm: Ok, so, the Nurse's changing of the guard occurred earlier and I have to say, I think my dad got the cutest nurse in the whole hospital, I think, at least that is what I told him and he just smiled. I can only imagine what is going through his mind. I hope that he doesn't remember any of the pain from this procedure. I can't tell you how many times I have wished for my dad to not go through any pain, being the person he is he should be exempt from pain from all the love and caring he has given throughout his life, and then being the human he is his human condition is unavoidable and as such he is subject to all of mans nature, mans words, mans nerve.

This poem is for taking a deep breath,(but first I am off to see my dad one last time)

"Panic Room"

No one

Can't anyone hear me

I am right here scared and alone

And all I want is for someone

Anyone

To come here and tell me it's ok

To say Just breath, just take a deep breath

Because I have forgotten where I am

And what has happened to me

Please

Please dear god

And I am strapped to this bed

I can't move my arms

I am crying

Crying

"Dad, Dad! Stop, don't pull on that wire"

"You are safe, just Breath dad"

"Take Deep Breaths"

"Try to relax, everything is ok"

"I am here"

I don't let him know

How scared I am

I toss this letter into the void, the abyss between us, this space that keeps conversation from happening

Sincerely,
Rush Whitacre
740-336-9169

4-25-11

Dear Taylor Swift,

    I am back in Cincinnati, working my butt off because I had forgotten about a presentation that I was suppose to plan way before this,, oh well, another night of very little to no sleep. So, I decided to take a break from making this crappy power point presentation. I swear to everything holy that if I get C's this quarter I am going to count myself lucky.(I know I have said that before already.)

Anyway, there is really great news!! This morning around 11:30 AM my dad got his ventilator and feeding tube out and I got to hear him talk and I just cried so many tears of joy. Several times this happened. It was so amazing, this was the first time that I have ever gotten so overwhelmed with joy that I just couldn't hold back my tears. It felt so good and made me that much more tired, so tired you have no idea, beyond belief. So, back to my work.

Fast forward: it is not 3:47 AM and I sent my PowerPoint presentation to my friend Chrin Sand because he for some reason was the person we were all sending our information to about the presentation that was based on Humor, and how humor evolves and it is incorporated into the art world.. blah blah blah. I just want to do my presentation tomorrow and get it over with.

Ok, I thought I was going to go to bed after my ppt was done, but, then I just had to do my paper too….. Now it is 6 AM. I am really afraid to go to sleep, because I don't want to miss and let my panel team down. So, I will go ahead and do this poem of quick fast.

This poem is for friends with connections:

"Of a feather, Together"

Tied

Hammer nailing foot

To the ground

And I hear the thunder

I pivot about

Not making much progress

The smell of rain is an addiction

And my fear, this moment

Lightening

A small drop

Then another

And I yell the word 'no'

And I yell the word 'help'

A Blue Jay hears me

And flutters to my voice

He sees me point and pull on my foot

And as he disappears, chirping

Laughing I think

The rain starts to hit near me

<blockquote>
I crouch

And the rain doesn't touch me

It is a breeze

I look

And it is my Blue Jay

And all his friends

Shielding me

As they flutter together
</blockquote>

I toss this letter into the void, the abyss between us, this space that keeps conversation from happening.

Sincerely,
Rush Whitacre
740-336-9169

4-26-11

Dear Taylor Swift,

    Ok, today started out terrible, just terrible. I really did sleep through my class that I was supposed to do a presentation in. I just completely slept right through it and all of my five alarms, 5 alarms, Cinco alarms….. I flipped out when I discovered that all the alarms were set and to the AM setting… three of them on my phone, and two on an alarm clock. I was dog tired, just too,,,, well you can imagine, and I am sure you have been that tired before.

    So, school today consisted of me going to DAAP to see if I can find 'Lady' to tell her all about how sorry I was/am for missing her class. Of course, I know that she is not going to be there, I just had this feeling that after her class she was going to leave and go home or something. And she did, she should, because she works hard. At what, I don't know, but I am sure she does. I unfortunately, or fortunately ran into Tilley, she was on my panel. I apologized to her and she consoled me and told me to not worry about it and that everyone understood and that 'Lady' was going to let me do my part of the presentation later. I broke down in tears… Oh, and let me tell you, this morning when I freaked out about missing class I ran to the shower and got in and thought about how I was a let down and how I didn't want to be letting down my panel and I just cried while shampooing my hair. Lol, wow, looking back on that right now makes me realize a little that I need a lot more sleep. I am most likely going to cut this short again tonight and do the poem part.

Earlier today I ran into Jacki. She and I have pretty much gone our separate ways as friends I think. She made a comment to me about my artwork being 'young', and I was pretty sure that she was talking about my body of work as a whole.. and this was during my phase of my (related person who is not named) being in a coma and me not knowing how I was to get to Akron Ohio to see her, and I was just blind in my brain. In my anger/frustration/confusion I snapped and told her that she would never make art work as well as I do, and that her opinion of my work didn't matter because she hadn't had enough schooling and that to call a body of work 'young' is inappropriate. Yeah, I regret this very much, because Jacki is a really cool person, a great friend. So, I saw her today and apologized to her face. Of course, it doesn't change anything, but now I feel a little better. And, now my (related person who is not named) is home in Marietta, in her home…

This poem is for passing the Buck,

"Let it in, Let it go"

He says to her, here, here you go

No, no thank you,

I am full

Are you sure

Because this dish is all I have to offer

I can not make anything better

Anything more sincere

I am sure, see; my plate is empty

I have had all I can take

And I don't want dessert, too sweet

Here, here you go

Maybe this time you will be ready

She replies again, No, I can't

Are you sure, for this is all I can muster

This heart saying sorry, and she walks away

Here, here you go

I am leaving this at the table for you

I forgive you and I will forget

Because forgive and not forget

Sounds a lot like

Never forgiving.

I toss this letter into the void, the abyss between us, this space that keeps conversation from happening.

Sincerely,
Rush Whitacre
740-336-9169

4-27-11

Dear Taylor Swift,

  I slept in until 2 today…. That cannot, and will not happen tomorrow.

  So, today I went to Kroger and bought groceries for the next two weeks. Even though Louis is a bit of a pain in the butt and is so far behind in bills I still can't not help but share things like snacks or other food stuffs with him because believe it or not he does have some amazing stories, or at least, he is good at getting stories across really well. Poor guy, he is so isolating himself in his room. This is his set up.. Louis sits in a lazyboy recliner, in front of him is a computer screen a keyboard, on his leg is a playstation2 controller and an empty ps2 game box with his mouse for the computer on top of that. Behind the computer screen is a television screen that has a ps2 game being played on it. The computer screen has facebook on it, but behind the facebook screen is a moving that is playing. This way Louis can be playing a ps2 game, be listening to the movie, and be waiting for someone to message him on facebook. While this kind of setup may sound really cool, and convenient, all it has really done for Louis that I can tell is made him really lazy and gain 40 pounds since he has moved in. He is also a really big drinker, around 1.5 liters of wine a night, and this drinking habit didn't start until he decided he had better start on a diet.. oh the irony.

  My other roommate Yangue has just become quite a hermit, so much so that I am now realizing that I hardly speak about him. Today I thought he would go to Kroger with us, but he didn't, he went to school instead. He made comments leading me on to believe that he wanted to go but completely bailed. Which is fine.

  I am losing my mind thinking about how I can get back the money that Louis owes me. I am just going to have to call his mother, as stupid as that sounds. Really stupid. But, she did tell me that she would help him out if he suddenly was unable to pay bills. Gosh, does that really sound that low… that I would have to go the extreme of calling a 29 year olds mother to say 'Hey, your son is slacking off and is not paying his bills'. Maybe I should ask myself if I am that person…

This poem is for my 'Dear G&F'

Like a code word

I use this as my sunglasses,

My mask

>   To hide behind
>
>   Instead of inside my shyness.
>
>   Social networks make me brave
>
>   Allowing me to type
>
>   And retype
>
>   And to rethink
>
>   Perhaps to dream
>
>   Whatever it is I want to say to you
>
>   About this, those, or that
>
>   Safe behind this network of virtual reality
>
>   This wired space
>
>   The thickest shield
>
>   That is if I can ever turn off my computer
>
>   And walk away
>
>   But I do not walk away
>
>   And I fight
>
>   And wield this sword
>
>   These fingers typing
>
>   60 words a minute
>
>   Minus 40,
>
>   Because of errors

I toss this letter into the void, the abyss between us, this space that keeps conversation from happening.

Sincerely,
Rush Whitacre
740-336-9169

4-28-11

Dear Taylor Swift,

    I woke up early today so that I could prepare to do my presentation and wouldn't you know that I didn't have to do my presentation. And then after class I got to help to break open a massive piñata that size of a VW bug. It was hilarious. There wasn't much candy, or whatever in side of it… but that isn't what mattered, what mattered was that it was made out of cardboard and a whole heck of a lot of fun to swing a bat at… I got to swing three times, like everyone else, and then when everyone thought it was all over Randy(a grad who's major is something like video or something) he grabbed the bat and began swinging it like there wasn't any tomorrow. Later I found out from others that I looked like I was taking out my anger on the boxes, but, I really wasn't, I was more worried about slipping on the candied floor. Lol, angry indeed.

  I really haven't done much since the piñata and I guess that is because I am just tired, or maybe my burrito from chipotle made me too full to want to do anything, or maybe I just kept finding things to preoccupy what I was doing, or maybe I was doing a couple of the things… I don't know, I just know that after today I only have three days to study for a massive test on Tuesday night… and I have readings I need to do for my Monday night class, oh, soon this will all be over. Smiles.

  Louis has been playing guns and roses all night tonight. He seems to get something stuck in his head and then he just goes for it, playing it over and over again until his mind is satisfied with whatever 'it' is. I bet I have heard him play November rain now 4 times, no joke. And then sweet child of mine. Maybe he is preparing his mind to remember the lyrics so that he can sing these songs. Ok, now he is playing sweet child o mine. I can only imagine what he will sound like singing this song. Louis does have a good singing voice, but his voice just isn't that of Axle Rose. I think that Louis lacks the energy, because he has allowed his out of shape self just go to waste in a lazy boy recliner… Oh Louis. Dear Louis, please start to take care of yourself.

This poem is for the changing of a will,

"Phantom Idiot"

Deceivement

A ban on making things right

And all those moments

Of working through the mist

And the least is the last on your mind

Who else could possibly hide in 'your' shadow

The raven

The knight

Or do I hear the scraping scrape

Of the chains

That keep you bonded

And I see that girl

The one who doesn't understand

How to be a friend

How to forgive

How to forget,

There is a pinch of stupid

And a dash of young making this dragon,

This dragon drawer.

Her dragon's days are numbered

As she will grow up

And they will simply

Disappear.

I toss this letter into the void, the abyss between us, this space that keeps conversation from happening.

Sincerely,
Rush Whitacre
740-336-9169

4-29-11

Dear Taylor Swift,

  Hello. The meeting for the graduate exhibition went well, for as far as I can tell anyway. I didn't have anything to add to the meeting, and the duo group for entertainment that I picked out was turned down by everyone in the group, so, I guess I am out of it. I just don't know anyone who would want to be the entertainment for the night. 'Lady' even asked me if the duo group would be free, and I laughed, haha, are you crazy, why would anyone want to entertain us for free… Oh well. I will rely on the other person in the group to come up with some form of entertainment. I am so over this graduate school thing. I just want to be out, just give me my diploma and let me go, I have plans, big plans, and better things to do than be led around by a finger under my chin.

  I fell into a deep napping sleep earlier. I was watching a movie and then the next thing I know I am completely asleep and being woken up to the sound of my cell phone ringing right by my ear. It was Hogan, he wanted to go to final Friday's and see all the art, he had gathered up Copy-Cat-Cami, Awdrei, Katie, and some other guy whose name I don't remember. Audrey is awesome, she just cracks me up. She has this very angelic look about her in the face and the way she walk and the way she prevents herself, but then out of the blue she will pull out some hilarious combination of slang and cuss words that you would never expect to come flying out of her mouth.

She is the opposite of Copy-Cat-Cami in appearance. Copy-Cat-Cami just looks like she could be trouble from the get go. Copy-Cat-Cami walks down the sidewalk and her attitude sticks out with every step she takes, and her mouth leads her attitude. She is what I don't need in my life as far as a girlfriend could go, only a friend. I don't know, if I had to judge as to whether I would date Audrey if given the chance I wouldn't either. All these kids just smoke to much pot, and that is something I could never get into. No matter how cute they may be, or how smart they come across, I just can't date a pot head, not again.

This poem is for the shadow.

Dark gray

And it is just there

Flat and attached

Chained to my feet, my body

I move and you move and I wonder

Are you watching me, scheming your escape

And I envision you in dark hair

Smart

Saying things to others behind my back

Making me feel smart, look sexy

But you are not, and I know this now

The sidewalk told me so

The wall, the light pole, and window sill

Said the same

And I am not bitter, sad, or hurt by you

For you are a part of me

And I don't dislike anything about me

And neither should you

But you should still be quiet

And flat

And dark

You should remain

Underfoot

Undertow

I toss this letter into the void, the abyss between us, this space that keeps conversation from happening.

Sincerely,
Rush Whitacre
740-336-9169

4-30-11
Dear Taylor Swift,

    I have a raging migraine right now, so tonight this is going to be a one pager. Here is the short jist of what happened today. I slept in, got leverage over my roommate who owes me money, ate meals, stopped in at my studio to print off all the study guide stuff and then came back here to the apt to try and study. Somewhere in the midst of studying, that is within the first 30 minutes I developed this damn migraine and suddenly fell asleep. When I woke up and had my legs dangling over the side of the bed and my right knee was locked into position and it hurt soo bad to straighten out. And... the damn migraine is still here. So, here we are.

    Oh, and my friend Laura-girl told me that she has a "room" opening up in her place that I could possibly start renting and move into this summer. So, things are looking like they may start falling into place sooner than I thought. This is looking awesome more and more. I just wish this migraine would go away already. So, I guess the room I would be renting would actually be a section of a living room, or rather, a living room which is part room and part living room... we shall see, I will come up to see what this space is really like.

Ok, this poem is for the good of it:

"Choosing So"

From where I stand

Looking down the road is hard

So many twists and turns possible

Traps lurking around every tree

Behind every cloud a rain drop

I don't see my fate yet

But for the good of it, I shall try

I shall leap into this hole

This path leading me where

I don't know

I will be happy
Because I will choose so

I toss this letter into the void, the abyss between us, this space that keeps conversation from happening.

Sincerely,

Rush Whitacre

5-1-11

Dear Taylor Swift,

    Study Study Study,,, that is my life for the past two days, except last night when I came down with a really bad migraine and this morning when I went to do laundry at the laundry mat. I really like the laundry mat. Today a woman and from what I could tell three of her daughters came in to do laundry. I have never seen the likes of laundry that they were doing. Bag after bag after bag. From the moment I walked into the place to the time when I left this family was bringing in laundry. Now, they obviously couldn't bring it all in at once, so I watched and they had simply just taken over an entire bank of washers and a wall of dryers for themselves. Quite an operation actually. I am still befuddled a bit by how a family could have so many clothes. Just amazing. I overheard the mother say to her oldest daughter that she was already eighty dollars into the laundry and expected she would need to make a run to an atm to get more money. When I left the place they were still hauling in more clothes. Impressive is the word I would use. And the way the mother was handling the whole situation was comical because she just drifted around the place like she was completely not aware of what was going on and not going on at the same time.

    Louis has become rather lonely lately I think. He wants to be around me more than ever to tell me stories and just simply be right here around me. He came into my room twice just to yell vulgarities at me because he finds it humorous

    Ok, this is hours later, and I have been studying the crap out of pics of artworks for my art history class on Tuesday night. There is some kind of test I have to take and I am not exactly sure as to how it is going to go down or anything, other than I know that it will be well worth my while to have all 200 images memorized. Some kind of wonderful I must tell you, this grad school environment. I stumbled upon the song again on youtube, Fett's Vette by MC Chris. I just think it is a lot of fun to listen to, it is something of a musical eardrum massage.

This poem is for the Battle noises

"Firm Grip"
Beep bop
And I click my thumb
And flex my trigger finger

And this control

Wireless and smokeless linger

And integrity

None

One thumb for go

And the other for, "Hey look at that"

Not to mention the power of my middle fingers

On their double trigger

This was just a game

But now I am running for reals

And my shoes have burned off their heals

Barefoot, and gravel make friends not

And I come out of my daze

Spilled a drink I just bought

And my TV is still making me blink

And the noises ring in my ears

Battle noises

My eyes and their tears

My thumbs still ready to fly

And I can't remember anything

Where am I

I toss this letter into the void, the abyss between us, this space that keeps conversation from happening.

Sincerely,

Rush Whitacre

740-336-9169

5-2-11

Dear Taylor Swift,

    Another day of memorizing more and more images of art. I just heard from one of my students from the past who is also in my history class that I have to also memorize the dates of these artworks….. WHICH I THINK IS WRONG. I have never known the importance of knowing the dates of when art works were made nearly as much as simply knowing the order of events. History seems to make more sense that way to me. Know less dates and just understand how one led to the next and so on and so forth. Well, there are some days that we need to remember, but for the most part, knowing every little date about every work of art just seems to be counterproductive to me. It would be just as well to know the years with which an artist lived versed when they made a certain work, unless it is a really big history changing piece.

I laid around in bed all day studying, I can't believe this. And, the worst of it is that I have totally gotten off of my workout regiment and diet schedule… this is not like me, but then again, I have been like this since my (related person who is not named) and dad had their near death experiences. After I get a little settled down I am sure I will get back into the swing of things. These images are just a pain in my butt. Soooo many to learn. And they are all from Europe since 1989… so, they are all really fairly new things. I know many of them, and then there are many that are not anything I am aware of ever seeing before.

I can't help it, I am listening to MC Chris's Fett's Vette song again, it is just so catchy. "My backpacks got jets, I'm Boba the Fett" lol, just a fun song. Here, as silly as this is I am going to past the address to the video I am talking about: http://www.youtube.com/watch?v=uILUCplfi-M

I am totally multitasking and should be studying for realz. I have this letter I am writing, three conversations on facebook, and texting a friend. This has to end soon because I am going to turn off my computer so that I am totally in mem-mode. Ok, time for something special

This poem is for the little pain

"Unreachable Itch"

Flutter

And opening of valves

Only remind me that I am alive

And here

Without you

Lubdub

And I feel it inside

And hear it in my ears

A twinge of the left kind

Shaking,

And my hands

Aren't the only things

> For I am lost behind these eyes
>
> Lost in an endless slide
>
> No ladders
>
> Pounding
>
> Fighting to get out
>
> Or to just get out of the way
>
> For I can't stand this endless nothing
>
> Left with nothing to choose
>
> But to make a choice
>
> I write goodbye
>
> I love you

I toss this letter into the void, the abyss between us, this space that keeps conversation from happening.

Sincerely,
Rush Whitacre
740-336-9169

5-3-11

Dear Taylor Swift,

     This is an amazingly stressful and long day. Not to mention it is Tuesday and Tuesdays are my longest days. Today though, takes the cake. My day started off with me getting up early so that I could get to school and have a bagel before class, and it was delicious, blueberry with cream cheese. Then, in Class four of my peers were suppose to give a presentation on vision. Well, only two of them could give their presentation because one of them was at the hospital with their mother, and the other suddenly could not function properly because of a sudden onset migraine from not sleeping much. Which this was fine because the two who did go did a pretty good job. Here is where the funny thing happened. I had my laptop out and was ready to take notes in it. I didn't type on it and I didn't type on it, but I had it opened up to a blank word document and then I decided to pull up my power point presentation just to be ready, you know, in case there was time for me to do my panel section that I missed from being with my dad. Well, 'Lady' was so concerned with me having my computer up and running that she made me put it away, and I just looked at her with a surprised look and she then whispered 'are you taking notes? Because you aren't typing anything, and to avoid a long discussion on what I was doing I just simply said, 'well, I was, but I will go ahead and put it away.' 'Lady' got the most angry look on her face, and I got even more confused. Why do people get all mad when you do what they want you to do??? Lol

Ok that was my first class, here is my second class,,, and to sum it up, Marcus, the director of DAAP here at UC was so angry that more grad students didn't come to a lunch lecture for a potential teacher for print making. Marcus was so upset because he said that only four grads turned up and it embarrassed him. Then Marcus spit on the floor and when person to person asking everyone where they were and why they weren't at the lecture. He got more and more enraged with every answer that was given him until he got to me and I simply told him that I didn't receive any emails with any such info. Then he asked if I got my blackboard email account activated yet and I told him I didn't know how. Marcus then threatened me, saying that if I hadn't figured out how to get blackboard to work with my email by the next email that he sent he would kick me out of the program. How about that for some bull crap.. lol. Oh Marcus,, tisk tisk. I think he was showing his true self today. Then I left to go to my final class for the day and take a massive test where I wrote 10 full pages in an hour. My hand cramped up pretty bad, but it was worth it. I am so glad that today is over

This Poem is for an Angry British Man

"Angry British Man"

Yellow Teeth

Or brown I do not know

For as you begin speaking

Or mumbling, as many have mimicked

I look down, or away, or pretend to be busy

Your intelligence suppresses learning

For you think you know better

You think you can teach

But you can't

You are a lecturer

Someone who talks at

Not with

So, keep to your not understood blubbering

Standing on a podium

Spreading your wisdom

And please do not include us in discussion

For disappointment can only follow

For we know not what you say

That is, if we can understand it

In the first place

I toss this letter into the void, the abyss between us, this space that keeps conversation from happening.

Sincerely,
Rush Whitacre
740-336-9169

5-4-11

Dear Taylor Swift,

    It is indeed a long day today, and when I say this, I mean that it is now 4:32 am, and I am just now starting this letter, I am really tired, but I still want to keep up with the times. My painting is coming along, especially since I simply dulled everything down to beautiful earth tones.

    This morning we had an artist lecturer who is applying for a job here at Cincinnati and she was a red head, and everyone thought she was rather boring and unqualified for what UC is looking for. Afterwards I should have gone home to my apt to sleep because I didn't sleep much last night let alone this one. I actually don't know how I have stayed up this late again and not pass out from exhaustion. You are not going to believe this, actually, I am quite flattered by my friend Dan Dean, he is painting a portrait of me and it is looking really good. I walked into his studio earlier to see if he wanted to go get a bite to eat and when I turned the corner to open my mouth I was blown away with a painting of me staring back at me. There is no other word than simple flattery. He told me then that he plans on painting every persons portrait in the program, and then, I felt a little less flattered, but still very much man-blushing, if there is such a possible thing to happen.

    But now I am here at my apt. laying here wondering when I will finish writing my thesis paper for my thesis committee to read. I am getting more and more nervous about my thesis and what I am going to do after I graduate. I mean, it is one thing to say, yeah I am moving to NY, but then it is another thing to do to get there and make all the adjustments and take all the losses I need to make in order to feel good about not leaving any loose ends or other crap for people deal with after I am gone. I guess one of my largest worries is theft, I have to admit that I am worried about being robbed by anyone while I am in NY, that would just be a very bad thing because I never want to have any bad thoughts about NY, ever. I love that city, I just love it.

    So, tomorrow, I think I will go home and pick up my trailer so that I can move about half of my stuff back home. Ugh, a long day for me tomorrow.

This poem is for the Trifecta surprise:

What is going on

I go days, weeks, maybe just hours

Lonely and sitting at a computer waiting

Checking status's, refreshing screens

And flipping through lists of friends on chat,

Is there anyone I want to chat with now

What about now, now, how about now?

Nope

Just my fingers, stroking over keys

Streaking across sensitive rectangles

Then tapping

Vibrating shakes me loose from my melancholy

Who is it, but Carlee, like an angel of many questions

And miraculously a message from Laura-girl,

And then Macki

And soon I am unable to keep up

Unable to type and switch and streak fast enough

I am happy

That is, until I realize

The strange irony in the form of a thought

"Does this really make me happy"

The answer

No

But only because it reminds me

That I am still alone

In life, and in front of this computer

I toss this letter into the void, the abyss between us, this space that keeps conversation from happening.

Sincerely,
Rush Whitacre

740-336-9169

5-5-11

Dear Taylor Swift,

Thursday, and I must say that I am impressed with how this grad critique is going. I think that I am jealous of how next year's class will be run because of how much more it will be organized. Last night's sleep was rough, I forgot to cut myself off from the diet Pepsi and the caffeine kept me awake another hour after I laid down. So, today was rough. I don't know what it is. The not knowing part of when I will do my panel presentation makes me really nervous, but only when the very moment arises that I think that I am going to be asked to get up and present it after others have presented their work. It is actually a really large rush of fear that comes over me, one that starts in my legs and hands with a surge of 'oh crap' tingling. Oh well, public speaking. I was told that of all the fears that people have, public speaking is number 1, and dying is number 2. Which I guess the irony of the situation is that at a burial, according to the results of a poll like this, the priest giving the sermon would rather be in the casket than standing on the earth above.

After class we had another visiting artist lecture and she was fantastic. Her name was Cynthia, and she is obsessed with wrestling, like hulk Hogan wrestling. I use to be when I was in the 6th grade, but something about it just wasn't interesting to me anymore. My (related person who is male and not named) loves the stuff, he can't get enough. My (related person who is not named) makes fun of him for it, actually, she is rather critical of him for it because when they watch TV together (related person who is male and not named) always wants to put wresting on, which he does during all of the commercials that happen during a show they are watching together. Oh (related person who is male and not named), you are quite a funny guy, and I miss you very much.

Well, I got a text message from my friend Wester, he told me that my (related person who is not named) was taken back to the hospital today. Funny, that (related person who is male and not named) couldn't call me, or text me. I wonder if she is doing ok. I couldn't get hold of anyone, so I am guessing that everything is ok, I am sure they would call me if it wasn't.

I am so bad with time this past week. It is now 3:30 Am. Carlee just got off of the phone with me. It was a nice surprise for her to contact me, we had a good conversation about school, art, her boyfriend, her sticking up for me when I needed it most. She is a great young woman.

This poem is for Dustin from sculpture:

Naked?

Why are you riding that rocking horse,

Naked?

You say you want to draw

> And you want to rock-n-sketch
> In paper cowboy chaps and hat
> And my mind is racing past all your pencils
> Galloping through marks
> And jumping right into the pool of
> 'What the Fuck'
> But liking your ideas
> Or idea nonetheless, and nonetheless
> Being repulsed by it
> Don't make me a video, please
> My imagination
> Will plague me just the same
> Probably worse
> So ride that horse
> And draw me a drawing
> For you will live on in infamy
> On my wall for all to see

I toss this letter into the void, the abyss between us, this space that keeps conversation from happening.

Sincerely,
Rush Whitacre
740-336-9169

5-6-11

Dear Taylor Swift,

    TGIF…. Chrin Sand, painting grad at UC and one of my best friends, he huh, stopped me in my tracks when he told me that there are only three weeks until our THESIS SHOW opening is…. Aaaaaah….!! So, now I am really freaking out because the amount of work needed to pull off my show is almost amongst me and I really need to go and buy the supplies to build my structure and then fill with 15 tons of furniture from within the school… and right now as I am typing this to you I can feel the nervous shakes creeping up into my fingers.. I just messaged my intern because I just realized that I really need to meet with her this weekend and go over the plans for the next three weeks. I talked Ruth into allowing me to take over the Lobby 13 days in advance before the show, and I am going to need every day… luckily the week right before we will have unlimited access to the building and I am so excited to spend the night at the Clifton Cultural Arts Center, CCAC, it will be sooo much fun. I just need to get started on this little adventure and I will be ok. So, tomorrow the adventure begins!!! I go to buy the lumber and bolts, and screws and anything, you can imagine, the kitchen sink is going into this piece, not really.

I went to my studio earlier, after going to the bank. My roommate just got his tax return back and I am really happy to say that he will be able to pay me back all of the money that he owes me. Nice. Anyway, I had to make some adjustments to my maquette, mostly gluing the middle three pieces together and cropping off one end. Then I made a video using my cell phone at the end of a stick and it looked like someone was walking through with a camcorder filming some bizarre form of what I am trying to accomplish. My intern just wrote me back, and she says that she is ready for crunch time… Good thing…

Tonight I went to red lobster and ate with my friend Mandy Castle. It was soo good. I had a NY strip steak with coconut butterfly shrimp. Mmmm, sooo good. I was skeptical about the steak, but it was totally worth it. I am actually looking forward to going back, although it was a bit on the expensive side. Either way, the company was amazing as usual, I just love hanging out with Amanda so much, she has such good stories, and such a cute dog. Actually, it was the dog that got her and I together tonight. I guess the dog got out of her collar and jumped down off of a 12 foot vertical embankment.

This Poem is for the franchise

Chain

Links needed for continued continues

A row of robots

Flesh handed conveyor

And a sway of motion at the hip

Or else a sharp stab in the back

And to the yelling

Notifying the flesh to turn an ear

And a nod

And another flop before the flip

And another yell

And then a final notice before the fall

Suddenly a plea

And the belt stops

> All the meat eyes gather to expose the error
>
> Error fixed
>
> The flesh conveyor rolls again
>
> And the sizzle burns
>
> But not those who stare like surgeons
>
> Down at the grill
>
> At five guys, burgers and fries

I toss this letter into the void, the abyss between us, this space that keeps conversation from happening.

Sincerely,
Rush Whitacre
740-336-9169

5-7-11

Dear Taylor Swift,

    WOW!!!! I spent over $1200, how did this happen. I went to the school excess sale looking to buy six digital projectors, three for my friend Wester and three for me, but,,,, they didn't have any worth, they were really old and the bulbs were broken, and usually the bulbs are really expensive. If I ever make enough money I will have a at home movie theatre where I will invite anyone and everyone to come and watch movies at my place.

    So, as I was saying, I did some shopping today. Instead of buying projectors I ended up buying three giant video cameras, with nice hard 'T Shock Stop' cases. I looked the camera's up online before I bought them. These Camera's I bought were originally $5,299, of course, that was back when they first came out about 12 years ago, and I talked the woman down from $750 for three to $500. I thought, well, if nothing else, I have three really nice camera cases for three other HD cameras' I plan on buying in the future. Which I will own someday. I want to make paintings and movies. I find that making movies is a very enjoyable thing, stressful at time, but, very enjoyable. I know now what these camera's aren't going to be anything near state of the art, and I am fine with that, because I bought them for the cases, and having them is just an added advantage. I realized after I got them home that the chargers were left out of the cases, or at least the chargers were, or maybe they were never meant to be a part of the package in the first place… I am sure that the chargers could be used for many other types of batteries for many other kinds of cameras like mine. So, the school most likely made a wise choice in keeping their charger portions of their camera kits… damn it!!

Lol. I would simply buy one but I can't justify buying a battery charger that is twice the price of all the equipment that I already purchased… I looked online, the chargers are anywhere from 800 dollars to 1400 dollars, how disgusting is that. Oh well, I am going to just go to school tomorrow and see if they will let me just charge my batteries on their chargers at the photo lab. It might even be a possibility that these cameras came from the photo lab in DAAP,,,, very doubtful. I am always amazed at how manufacturers don't take into account that it wouldn't be that hard to make the camera itself a battery charger so that if you lose your charger you can always use the camera itself. I guess that will happen after I take over the world… Oh, and all phones will have the same charger hole as well!!

This poem is for a mysterious dinner party.

Knock Knock,

"Come in, the door is open"

And I open the door

The smiles and questions begin

And when the door is shut she walks away

She stirs, and glances, and puffs

Water bubbles, lips pursed

And all I can do is stare into a screen

Motionless, avoiding the awkward

A pin prick of fear

A little voice in my head whispers,

"Beware, beware, watch out.

For the brunette dragon's smile is alluring

And I am weak against it

My brain wants to look, stare, gaze

But my eyes are being babysat

By the screen

My laptop is folded down

"Dinner is ready"

Says the dragon, my eyes stunned

The babysitter was gone

I toss this letter into the void, the abyss between us, this space the keeps conversation from happening.

Sincerely,

Rush Whitacre

740-336-9169

5-8-11

Dear Taylor Swift,

  Oh My, my, my… my roommate came into my room and has gotten hooked on the movie Kick-Ass. This movie isn't really at all what I thought it was going to be like. I thought that maybe they would pull some punches, but they really mess these kids up, getting stabbed and run over by a car. And there is this girl in the movie, she is like ten or something and she has this amazing part in the movie. Let's see, there is Kick-Ass, Red mist, hit girl, and bid daddy… what else does a movie need right, but some funky superhero types with funny names and funny costumes. I really enjoyed Kick Ass, and I do believe that I will be watching it again, probably soon because I am only here in Cincinnati for another 37 days and then I am out of here for good… How exciting is that!! Hopefully with my Master's degree intact. Ugh.

  So, I have a thesis committee meeting this coming Friday, and normal people would say that I made a bad choice but since I am 13's lucky person and this Friday is the 13th I feel pretty good about the whole thing. I just need to get my thesis paper finished by then, I have put it off and put it off and put it off for way too long now. I am only 276 words away from having the magic number of words needed to pass. What I really want to do is have about 500 words beyond that point so that if they tell me to cut out 400 words I would still be in the safe zone.

  I have been watching videos on youtube by the a cappella people who are making these really interesting videos of themselves making music videos using only their mouths and voices. There is this one guy named Sam Tsui who particularly caught my attention with his voice, it is pretty ok. I mean, for making their own songs and music videos they do pretty well.. I really like his a cappella version of 'King of Anything'. And I am also digging the two songs of his that I can find on youtube, 'don't want an ending' and …. Ok, I can't remember it off the top of my head, but that isn't the point, the point is that I like them very much.

  Oh well, maybe my music taste sucks to some, but not to my ears.

This poem is for Hogan,

"So What?"

Mischievous

That is the only word to describe you

That is, on a good day

I don't want to know about your bad days

Or about your really bad days

I am sure there is an ounce of sadness in there

An ounce of down trodden sorrow

Looking for a nest to land in

A place, a home, a corner to crawl to

Tell me that you laugh every day

And that you cry every week

Because no one seeks eternal happiness

For attaining that level requires a merging

A blending of tears and laughter

And you my friend

Are way too happy

Laugh way too often

For way to long

About anything you see

Hear

Or latch onto

And when you come crashing down

Just know that I am here

To be your friend

You cry, I cry

You laugh, so what

I toss this letter into the void, the abyss between us, this space that keeps conversation from happening.

Sincerely,
Rush Whitacre
740-336-9169

5-9-11
Dear Taylor Swift,

This is a day of simple things. Simple things like driving my roommate around and listening to him complain about how fat he is.. lol, I told him before we left the apartment that he should just walk to his bank like he use to do, that he would get some exercise and maybe feel better. He responded with, "I know right" which is his go to for things to say when someone says something smart or correct or just simply something he agrees with. I don't know, Louis seems to shoot himself in the foot. I only have 37 days left here in Cincinnati so long as I graduate from this god forsaken college. There are a lot of things to be said for it as a college, for instance, Melody Vank in the main office is amazing, and Emilia is just the biggest sweetheart in the world. I guess I would say that meeting Emilia has been the greatest part of coming to Cincinnati for Grad school. Her personality is the saving grace of the College office's grouping of personalities. Emilia still has a soul, she hasn't had it drug out of her and beaten into the canvas/pavement/desk/back of a skull smack. I guess you could say that I am counting down the days to when I leave. Gosh, I must be really having a bad day or something, I don't know about all of my negativity as actually being completely what I believe. I am just really tired, and cranky, and need a nap, a long awaited nap.

Tonight I had my night class with Maria, it is Art History III and we didn't have a test. Next week we have a test. So, at least this time I have some warning. I haven't gotten back my test yet, it is not graded. Which a fortunate thing because I don't want to know what my grade is, not yet, I have had enough crazy things happen to me. I guess you could say that I am tempered against being hurt, like my brain has shut off the pathways temporarily that allow it to feel being hurt. Don't worry, it is only a temporary thing I assure you. I am too sensitive of a guy to not feel everything around me, it is a part of who I am and it directs a lot of how I choose to make the art I do, and love the way I love, with all that I am and have to offer. Whatever that is.

This poem is for Megan S.

"Reflection Purpose"

A thank you is in order

Or disorder as the case may be

Look around my studio

Paint cans in disarray is all you'll see

Well, and maybe speakers, and plants

And even some art, if there is such a thing

And I thank you, for your help is nice to have

Even if I so rarely call upon you

For your help

Your words of wisdom

Of encouragement

Whatever encouragement means

                    I thought I knew

                    Help me to remember

            Reread those notes I had you take down

              For my world is turning upside down

                And I am grasping for reality

                   But its fringes are ripping

              Each handful separates and vanishes

                    Where I am I know not

                       Please, remind me

           And maybe from there we can step forward

                   And finish this monster

                          This cave

              This installation of epic proportions

                            Begin

I toss this letter into the void, the abyss between us, this space that keeps conversation from happening.

Sincerely,
Rush Whitacre
740-336-9169

5-10-11

Dear Taylor Swift,

    Yup, this is my long day, Tuesday. Nothing bad has happened today,,, yet. I am just wanting to get home and go to bed and sleep for five days. It is getting bad, people are noticing how tired I am, how exhausted I am, how out of it Iam. Me included.

    I actually decided to start this letter in class, my night class so that when I get home I have less to do before crashing. I really do love this class I am in, this is my art in Europe since 1989. I am not exactly sure what happened in Europe in 1989 that has caused for there to be a break in time for this course to exist, but oh well. I will ask The professor after class tonight to see what she says.

    All day I have been running around looking for anyone who might know anything about the batteries I have for my new cameras. without the charger my new(old school) camera's are relatively useless. I can power them using the power cord contraption that came with the camera but then I am tied down to only using these camera's near outlets, and also having the added weight of the power cord contraption box… Ok. I will call PBS and see if they have any chargers lying around in a junk closet they want to get rid of. I was actually told to go to thrift stores and good will, but I have to say that the size and kind of charger I need would be a 1 in a million chances that it would end up at good will, or in a yard sale, etc. I am just going to have to find one and pay for it… gross

I just went on break and went outside to take a break four of my students stopped me and asked me all kinds of questions as to what I am doing here tonight and why I am here. I am going to miss my students, and all their curiosities. That part of my being here at UC has been a very good aspect of learning for me. I think that if I get this letter done before class is over I am going to go to Buffalo Wild Wings. I haven't eaten wings in such a long time, yeah, It is time for wings.

It was funny, earlier today I was eating chili from the DAAP café and Bryan, my over-see'er, for when I was teaching, and all of a sudden he started talking about how his baby had to have poop dug out of him and then in his realization of me eating chili he just kept apologizing.. I laughed and said, "no no, it is fine, coming from a family with parents who are doctors it is amazing the conversations that take place at the dinner table.

This Poem is for the dash of white.

Below the seam

The ridge between perfect

And vertical

A drip onto the skin

A touch

Goose bumps

Follicles swelled to maximize reception

Of knowing the rhythm

Feeling

Above the bootstrap

Laces never untied

Removed only by zipper

And against gravity

A knee

A large wrinkle for bending

Legs

Bare and vulnerable to eyes

To sun

Covered for so long

That now exposed

Appear as white dashes

Purity in motion

I toss this letter into the void, the abyss between us, this space that keeps conversation from happening.

Sincerely,

Rush Whitacre

740-336-9169

5-11-11

Dear Taylor Swift,

    Ok, I just thought about it, and I haven't had that dream I talked about with you from the first week's worth of letters. Which is good, because I am sure I would simply have to be locked up for have the same dream for half a year, I think that would drive anyone crazy.

    Well, today was the second day of randomly having to move my thesis furniture from one room to another. I am going to keep track because I am sure there will be another move that is unnecessary I am sure. I moved furniture all morning, and then went to my studio and moved and cut lumber all afternoon. I am proud of myself, I think I got all the wood cut and all the holes drilled in that wood. I was thinking about it and how there needed to be holes drilled in all the boards to some degree and I only drilled holes in the 8 foot 2x8's.

    Well, I have a professor wanting to jump ship. Franklin, I can't ever remember his last name. He is a painting professor at UC. I heard my friend Chris talking about him once saying that Franklin is a multi-millionaire, that he has sold paintings for as much as 100,000 dollars. Now… I have seen Franklin's work,,, and I have heard him talk about his work and how he makes it.. and I have heard others talk about how Franklin described to them how he makes his paintings. I have heard from everyone that Franklin himself doesn't even know how he makes his paintings. He told Kim-the-awesome, when she asked how he made a particular painting that she liked, anyway, he told her "I don't know how I did that." Hmmm, I am sorry, but, I have looked at many paintings of Franklin's, and many of them look like someone mixed up colors and then just randomly started splashing them around on the surface of something, splashing, brushing, dabbing any old color until it looks like something that might be appealing. Now, don't get me wrong, I love color, and many of them have color. I guess I am hung up on the whole make the painting look like something other than just an old used pallet look. And, if you are going for the old used pallet look, by god be able to say why and not just shrug and say 'I don't know how I made that.'

    Ok, that rant went on too long

This Poem is for not wanting an ending

The days turn to hours

And this fear creeps up inside of my heart

And honestly

I don't want to push you away

But tonight's just another night

Like the count down

Ticking away until we are not around

There will come one day

And I will know the way

That you are not around

My heart seems to just be running

And empty doesn't get you far

And I feel with each beat

That I will give us one more day

Before I go

Before you let me leave you

And that thought just makes me sad

So say you won't forget

That love we had

Shared

Moments from a day

When I thought you were mine

I toss this letter into the void, the abyss between us, this space that keeps conversation from happening.

Sincerely,
Rush Whitacre

740-336-9169

5-12-11

Dear Taylor Swift,

Hi there. This has been the review day for all the sophomores, and I got to review 10 different students throughout the day. All of their work was about 2 steps below par. These students just either don't know how to work fast and smart, or they were not taught how to work fast and smart. My guess is that they were not taught how to work fast and smart. Who does that anyway, fast and smart.

Anyway, I heard back from my friend Laura-girl today, and it looks like I will be paying rent for June up in New York so that I can guarantee that I have a spot for the rest of the year. I just don't know what it going to happen to me. Here I am moving up to NY, no game plan, no strategy. Just me and my MFA. That sounds like a movie almost, 'Me and My MFA' Maybe I should video tape the whole venture, turn it into an actual documentary of my life from MFA to NYC… ha ha. Yeah, I think I had better stick to working on and thinking about my thesis right now, there is nothing in the world bothering me more than the fact that I haven't worked on that thing enough. I just dislike it altogether.

I found out today that 'Lady' really hates a person who I don't understand. 'Lady' gave the girl an F- because her notes were, I guess, really bad to say the least. I don't know, I am glad though that I don't have to take her Film Seminar,,,,, thank god. There is a reason for things, and that reason is Karma or fate or fortune cookies. Somehow everything levels out, the universe will balance itself. All the Hate will smash into all the love and there will be,,, well, quite a mess for one thing. Quite a mess.

I leave for home tomorrow. I am nervous, really nervous about getting my thesis made, built, and then taken down. So much energy will go into this thing that I can't even imagine how tired I am going to be. I am going to need to take a break… Because this is going to be quite a ride.

Everyone is talking about how much they really hate the Grad program, all the Grads just can't stand the Grad crit classes, nor all the mandatory classes and seminars. I will be so happy to say that I have my terminal degree. TERMINAL DEGREE… So happy to even write that on this screen/paper/whatever.

This poem is for the emergency brake:

"Black lines"

Locked brakes

Aroma of a sudden end

And the clink of door handles

And the bright light

And the hot fluid

From places from within,,, the vehicle

The smoke

The radio,,, still playing,, loud

A retching

Lurch

Fast paced steps

And ok'd ok's ok'ed ok

I turn from the hot pavement my face

I look to the stranger stranger

Who pulls you free

Who's life they laid down for you

And a breath

Then another

It is so quiet here behind my eyes

So deep

Presses

Then more presses

They are trying so hard to bring you back

But I know, that you were already gone.

I toss this letter into the void, the abyss between us, this space that keeps conversation from happening.

Sincerely,
Rush Whitacre
740-336-9169

5-13-11

Dear Taylor Swift,

    I have a lot to say in this letter, but I will try to keep it is one page. First of all I met with my thesis committee this morning and from the very get go they were completely against everything I had planned. Mind you, this was the 6th version of my thesis that I had created, the 6th time I have had to present my thoughts. This was the 6th completely different thesis. Lol, completely different. So, now, I am going to work on Thesis version 7.0. Now I am going to create a swirling mess of furniture to make it look like it were a vortex or a partial aftermath or in progress Tsunami, like the ones in Japan... I can't keep thinking though, isn't that a bit Cliché, wouldn't there be hundreds of artists out there doing the exact same thing at the same time, making some form of causal art, or remembrance art. I just don't want to fall into the "Oh, yeah, there was a lot of stuff like that that came out of that disaster" art. What happened was Kim-the-awesome made the comment that my piece that I was showing her made her think of being under water looking up at floating debris. From that statement everyone jumped on board with the idea that I should make a 'memorial-like piece'. I don't know, if that is what it takes for me to graduate, then so be it, that is what I will do.

After my stomach making sick meeting I ran all my stuff back to school and then just wandered around meaninglessly trying to figure out what just happened. I got kicked in the balls, ran over with a steam roller, and then chewed up and spit out and this all happened 3 weeks right before thesis... so now I have to almost make that entire thing at the place and not in my model because time is of the essence and I don't have time to waste on hot gluing foam core together. The idea is in my head, I just need to get it out there, at least I think it is in there.

Then I drove home. It was a long drive. I thought about how I Have an 8 page paper due in 5 days and I haven't started it. I also have a test this Monday night that I haven't looked anything up for. I am just a mess. Soooo many balls up in the air in this juggling gig, I just need to keep them up in the air or else I will fail. And I can't afford to fail!

I am home now and I got to go through all of my (related person who is male and not named)'s clothes and I found several things that will fit me. I was excited. Free clothes are always good. My dad looks like he has lost so much weight, but he looks good. I could also tell that he was really happy to see me. He made a comment to me that made me wonder if he was any depressed. Usually after someone gets bypass surgery they go through a spell of depression because of being so helpless for so long. My dad said that it was amazing how helpless he felt, and that made me wonder. Then I saw him and I don't think he is depressed at all. Thank God.

This poem is for innocent.

A key

The ratcheting of metal on metal

And rubbing of the wrists

A freeing moment for knuckle cracking

A 'thank you god'

And gazing to the ceiling

The trees

The smell of fresh air

And the drive home to a bed

A room

A loved one who missed you

Now so foreign

You have new firsts

New kisses, new hugs, new love

And the freedom

Oh the freedom

Is like air to the fire that kept you going

Everything

And nothing

Is different, nor the same

I toss this letter into the void, the abyss between us, this space that keeps conversation from happening.

Sincerely,
Rush Whitacre
740-336-9169

5-14-11

Dear Taylor Swift,

      Well, today wasn't as exciting as yesterday was. I drove down to spend time with (related person who is male and not named) and then I got a call from my dad that my sister was in town and she wanted to go through the house and have me point out everything that was in there that she could take, because she wanted to see all the things available. I just don't know how I could get any more stressed out right now. I have soo much going on in my life right now. I have a 6 page paper due this coming Thursday night, a test this Monday night, a thesis project that has been completely renovated and redone by my committee and now in my mind, and I don't have any time to make a model of what I am making, I just have to make it and make it fast. I pretty much have to make a couple of 1 to 2 min sketches to show to my intern and then I have to go for it… It is going to be awesome if what I have in my mind can be done in real life, then yeah. A tidal wave, not a quick upheaval of water like the tsunami in Japan, more like a quick moving large rolling wave like out in the ocean, and instead of water, it will be desks, tables, and chairs, and whatever else it is going to take to make it happen. I just need to make it look awesome, make it something my committee can look at and feel that I deserve to graduate.

    I am done trying to make something incredible that I know would be simply spectacular. My feeling in general about my thesis is that they really don't care too much, and only Kim-the-awesome has been putting in her two cents, really good coins I must add. So much so that I am pretty much only taking her advice for my piece, well, and a little bit from Matt , but only because it was something that I wanted to do in the first place, and that is give the viewer no choice but to have to walk through my piece to get from one side of the room to the other. Imagine, you are walking under a wave that is 50 feet long, 12 feet high, and is just getting ready to crash against the wall opposite where it started from. Oh please dear god let me pull this off. Even if I have to just barely pass a different class. I will prevail, mark my word, I will prevail.

This poem is for the Copy-Cat-Cami,

Mouth open

And curiously I wait

What is it this time

Why am I trying to anticipate

Why do I think I know what she will say

When everything you say is something new

Some new way of making a joke

Just to poke fun at me

But all for play

No harm done here

Just a warning that I press against

A shallow sifted blanket of dirt

A soft word

A secret

And everyone hears

But no one was really paying attention

For it is known what move you will make

Easily calculated

So Laugh

And we will laugh

How cliché

I toss this letter into the void, the abyss between us, this space that keeps conversation from happening.

Sincerely,
Rush Whitacre
740-336-9169

5-15-11

Dear Taylor Swift,

 Sunday Sunday Sunday,,, and today I was suppose to leave and go home between 10 and 2… did that happen… well I will let you decide after I tell you about my day.

 I woke up and had some of my favorite fried chicken our IGA… it is so delicious. Then I started organizing all of the climbing ropes by simply coiling them up for easy transport. In the middle of my coiling my (related person who is male and not named) shows up to go through the house to see if there is anything that he wants. Well, being the nice (related person who is male and not named) I am I walk him through the house, the entire house which is 9000 square feet of shear nightmare at this time with only walk ways within each of the rooms and hallway. Randy actually didn't take as much stuff as I thought he would take. I expected him to come into the house and try to take it over. I think he is giving in to the fact that the house he thought he would move into is actually going to be gone for good. That no Whitacre will live in it again… that is, unless I win the lottery and can somehow buy it back from the people who buy it. I think it is going to be quite a shock when dad finds out how little the house is going to sell for. Quite a shocker indeed.

 Here is a little tidbit I haven't told you before. About 2 to 3 years ago, maybe 4, I decided to try to make really good wines and beer with different recipes and kits. I made quite a bit, probably around 200 to 225 bottles of wine and just about the same amount beer… I am telling you this because what I did next was called my friend Wester and had him come to pick up my entire wine and beer making setup to take to his place for use and storage. I know, and hope he will take good care of it. I really do hope that he makes some pretty good wines with it. I had to drive to his house to unload the stuff there, then I left his house and drove to Cincinnati. So, do you think I left before 2 pm? I will just tell you – NO. I got here around 10 pm. Not bad I suppose, but not the greatest either.

 Still no studying for my test tomorrow night, and I am going to the CCAC tomorrow morning for start to move furniture up into the lobby area. I just had very fearful chills from the center of my back all the way down my legs,, they were heavy and the "I'm really really worried" type of chills. Deep breath.

This Poem is for Family.

"Alabaster Med Queen"

Bringing in the cold

The bittersweet emotions

About a rock, and stone not worth fighting for

And I was given it

And I can't stand the questioning

And pull that your voice has

On things that are not yours

An anchor just dragging you down

Cut it loose

Or pull it in

Before it takes you down

Or rips a hole

Separating us from each other

Because you sometimes sound a million miles away

And that is not too far

But far enough

That you will divide yourself

From me,

A choice only made by you.

I toss this letter into the void, the abyss between us, this space that keeps conversation from happening.

Sincerely,
Rush Whitacre
740-336-9169

5-16-11
Dear Taylor Swift,

    I have some exciting news. I got most of my furniture for my thesis piece moved into my space with the help of my friend Nate, and a cart I borrowed from Scioto our studios. I am feeling pretty good about thesis now. It is just a matter of construction is all, and I think I can handle that part. I hope so anyway. I mean, it is just a giant wave made out of furniture that is to be hanging over other people's heads.

So, after my furniture frenzy I showered and drove to school where I thought I would get about an hour of studying done… didn't happen, nada. Instead, out of the goodness of his heart Greg, a guy who is photographing the show gave me the numbers to all the pages where he found answers for the questions from the study guide. Then as I was leaving I told him that it was his fault that I was leaving earlier than him, he laughed a bit. And I left and here I am, done with the day's work and thinking about what to do about a paper I have due this Thursday… I guess spend all day working on it and not on my thesis project… boooooo.

I personally think that if I ran the DAAP school of art Grad program I would say that the grads only have to work on their thesis projects during the last 2 weeks of their school career, now doesn't that sound great. Imagine, you need two weeks to fully be ready for something big that you have to do a lot of work on and you are given time off for that two weeks to do whatever you need to do to make your "thing" is, or to do whatever it is you need to do to succeed. "why not me, why not me"

I just made lasagna from scratch… and it is finish and hot and smelling great. I forgot just how good a Garfield homemade, cheesy, tasty Lasagna is…. I forgot just how good a Garfield homemade, cheesy, tasty Lasagna is. Yeah you can admit it, you are jealous. Ok, I have to get you this poem now so that I can get back to writing my paper, the one I haven't started yet but have thought a lot about starting, but never started.

This poem is for peripheral vision,

Whip of the neck

Sudden little movements

A motion fan

A flip of hair

Maybe my reflection

I don't know

My mind thinks it knows

But my eyes say differently

Little mirages

And my tired brain can't decipher

So I whip my head

And look at the nothing

There is nothing there

And I can't help but wonder

Was there anything ever there

> So I stare
>
> Waiting for the movement
>
> Trying to catch the distraction
>
> Before it catches me
>
> And I give up
>
> Continue working on my music
>
> And I whip my head again
>
> Eyes daggered
>
> And still I can't see the movement
>
> The little distraction

I toss this letter into the void, the abyss between us, this space that keeps conversation from happening.

Sincerely,
Rush Whitacre
740-336-9169

5-17-11
Dear Taylor Swift,

    And, no I haven't started to write my 6 page paper yet, this is a Wednesday thing, and right now I am waiting for one of my previous students to come over to Audrey's house. Yeah, it is Copy-Cat-Cami, and she is brining over my fog machine so that I can maybe fix it, or put it out of its misery. I honestly don't know why she just didn't let me set it up in the first place. Secrets between artists I guess run deep from the beginning. I know for a fact that I have seen many great ideas that I could so totally borrow or just straight out use while I am NY, or even not in NY.

    Again, I have to say, after school is out I will have nowhere to go, just a storage unit. I am still trying to wrap this around my head. I just wish that I could find a famous person who wanted an artist on hand at all times just making artwork for them in exchange for a small wage, free place to stay(bedroom above the garage), a studio(large enough for me to do any and all works for the famous person) art supplies for the work, the right to seem my family 3 times a year, free food, and travel with the famous person to places with if that is ok with them… I just think it would be nice to be in a situation where I was in a position of not ever having to worry about food, water, shelter, some travel, and I would break out some of the greatest art ever. I worry about getting to NY and having to work 2 jobs and trying to mingle my way into the art scene and make art. I think that I will probably most benefit from making little maquettes that have the various installations that I could make in their spaces. I have discovered that it is the easiest way and cheapest way. Not to mention, if the gallery has the power to do it they may even have their small army of workers build the piece, or if I can make enough friends maybe I will have my own little art posse. A posse who work for each other when needed. That would be great.

I just found out that one of my previous students may be getting a felony charge for placing a fake bomb in the building… hello, it is an art building, and people should expect students to make stuff that is even a little controversial. Although, I do think that a person should get permission for things like placing a bomb, fake bomb I mean, in any building.

This poem is for addiction.

"Tracks"

Eyes following

Arm itching

Mouth watering

Thoughts and thoughts

And everything a reminder

The off button, what off button

There is no off button, nor enough anything

To satiate this so badly needed loss

And so my mouth waters

My eyes follow

My arm is itching

And my nervous twitch

Drags everyone around me in

They feel sorry for me,

Always asking if I am ok

Of course I am not

I am missing what I need most

I know this for my body is telling me

And my mind is going crazy

And my fingers

Oh my fingers can't finger it

And all I want to do is sleep

> Just sleep away the day
> The hours, minutes
> Seconds.

I toss this letter into the void, the abyss between us, the space that keeps conversation from happening.

Sincerely,

Rush Whitacre

740-336-9169

5-18-11

Dear Taylor Swift,

    Don't ask, I don't know either why I am still awake at 3:19 AM working on a paper I started at 12 noon today… I will tell you why,,,,, because I was slacking off all day, I was preoccupied in my mind, I was not really caring at all about this stupid paper because all I can wrap my mind around all day is the fact that I really needed to be at the CCAC building my thesis piece, not sitting on my duff typing away on some paper that doesn't really prove anything, and I think I can justly prove this fact with what I just wrote.

    And, because of how late it is I think that I will most likely go to bed early. I never know what it is I will be doing in my grad crit studio from day to day, week to week. I have a presentation I have to make up on the 31st, yeah, that humor presentation that I missed because of my parents and all the unfortunate things that went on with them.. I am both looking forward to getting my presentation over with because that class is,,,, yes you guessed it,, still ridiculous, and I am not the only one, there are many who see this class as really stupid and a waste of time. I know they are trying to make the class work, but even the first years see how much of a joke it is. I am counting down the days to getting out of this place. I can't even hide my disdain for some of the people in the program. For instance, there is this girl named Sara C. I won't give her full last name because she isn't totally deserving of that recognition. Anyway, I just found out that she has been complaining about me in her drunken rants, which mind you, she does get drunk quite a bit, almost every night, or at least that is the story that I have heard. I actually pulled that bit of information out of another grad student by accident, or rather, he kind of said it to me not realizing that I was the person that Sara was talking about. It was a bizarre moment for both of us.

    Ok, I have to get to bed now, so, this is sure to be a quick and possibly a short poem.

This poem is for Sara,

"Not Even Blindly"

I will not date you Sara

I will not look at you

Nor sing to you

Nor whisper sweet nothings into your ear

I don't even know who you are

Except that you find joy

In being rude to me

Making me look bad

To all my friends

And people who don't know me yet

But that is ok

Because the days turn to hours

And it will be soon that I am gone

And time will separate us

And your words will matter like a raisin

Not at all, shriveled

Lost amongst all the other flakes

And just like that

Everything said

Will turn to shit

So, no Sara, I will not date you

For you do not like me

And I

I could care less.

I toss this letter into the void the abyss between us, this space that keeps conversation from happening.

Sincerely,
Rush Whitacre
740-336-9169

5-19-11

Dear Taylor Swift,

    Well, this is Thursday, and I have class this morning. I couldn't wait to get on here and tell you about my day that lay before me.. This afternoon I am going to be at the CCAC working on my Thesis piece for the first day. And, I wanted to start my day off right by talking positively about my thesis instead of thinking about my Grad Crit/Studio class. I don't think I need to go into detail as to how that class is,,, it sucks. So, here in a minute I will simply get my show, take Louis to the bank,, that boy drives me crazy. He is always asking me to take him to the bank.. all I want to say is, dude, just take out enough money to last you for the week at least… lol. Actually, I would never say that, he always has the best stories in the morning. Either about his dreams, or about conversations he has had on facebook. I long to hear his stories, they are particularly good after he has had a few drinks, of if he is straight up drunk. Actually, if he is drunk the stories actually come to me, he will stagger into my room ranting about something or other about this or that and I know it is going to be funny by the way he is laughing on the way to my door. Yeah, the walls are that sound proofless.

    Ok, it is after class, I am standing here in the CCAC looking at this massive wall, this massive empty wall with nothing on it, I should take a picture of this wall, because this wall represents my blank canvas, or as Van Gogh would say, "It is taunting me." Ugh, Ok, I am simply going to start and see where all of this leads me.

    Hours later, judging by my unsure words before this I must have been pretty pessimistic about how my working would go… I would say that I am making pretty good progress, better than I thought. I really think that my show is going to suck, but only because it is not what I want to do. I really wanted to make my knitting/weaving machine. I keep thinking about how cool it would be to have people using my backpacks that are all spooled up with yarn ready to be used in my massive grid of 1 inch pvc pipes. With each turn the pipes would sway this way and that. I have this vision of 12 foot tall pipes swaying around this way and that as 30 people weave over and under each other as the walk around in my artwork. It will happen someday. Relational Aesthetics, maybe that piece would fall into that category.

This poem is for Alexandra, the indecisive

"Alexandra the Indecisive"

I don't know

I am thinking

Wait, I am not done

Just give me a minute

I don't know

What do you think

Uuuuuuuuuuum

                Don't rush me

              It is just going to take time

                This is tough

                Hold on

                Thinking

              Ok, here is my decision

                Ok, maybe not

                But,

                But, but

                Ok this is it

                Or that is it

            Hmm, I thought I already picked

                I guess not

I toss this letter into the void, the abyss between us, this space that keeps conversation from happening.

Sincerely,
Rush Whitacre
740-336-9169

5-20-11

Dear Taylor Swift,

    Hey, my friend Jeremiah is a really good friend. I am helping him out, and he is really helping me out. Of course, it is now almost 4:30 am and I am exhausted. I can't wait to get this project done so that I can move on with my life. I really am making some crazy installation. I don't know if I can finish this thing, but I will. Actually, I am more concerned with the clean up part. I Really don't want to take it apart and stick around to wear myself out and be useless. I refuse to be useless.

    You really should see this Thesis piece though. Thousands of pounds of furniture, thousands of pounds of lumber, thousands of screws. What a mess. It is certainly the largest of all the pieces at this thesis show. Chrin Sand told me that if nothing else, even if my pieces didn't turn out that great at least it was giant, and giant works of art are simply great by their giant nature… I don't share his philosophy, because I totally believe that someone can make a giant turd of an artwork, just a piece of crap.

So much is going to happen to me so suddenly. Major life changing events, and all of them seem fairly certain, all of them except the one about my being in New York, my safety, my work, my ability to sustain myself while living in the art center of the world. I sometimes wonder if this is the right thing for me to do. I wonder what leaving all my friends behind will be like, and what leaving my (related person who is male and not named) (related person who is male and not named) behind will be like. I wonder what kind of person I will become, or turn into. I hope I become a better person, I mean, better than I am right now. I must say, I don't really feel too proud about what I have been doing with Grad School this past year. Mostly I have been going against the grain and not doing what they want me to do and instead I have been just doing my own things outside of school. I haven't been getting bad grades at all, I just haven't been going all out for the school. UC has made some poor choices in its decision to change up some of the classes in its programs. Making some mandatory and others are simply a complete waste of time. Oh well, I am really enjoying this building of my thesis, so, I won't be knocking on anything just yet.

This poem is for the Laugh that just keeps going.

"New Grinder"

Oh Girl

You are simply a hot mess

You are your smoke

Whirling and whirling

You puff and breath

And drink your drink

I don't think you know how beautiful you are

Those soft luscious lips

Dark brown eyes

And a personality like a whip

SNAP

And in another moment

What you will have to say

Will surprise me

As you always do

And I only wish I could see into your brain

Your thought pattern

Your connections

I am sure there are super highways

>   Highways
>   And on some days,
>   Just highs

I toss this letter into the void, the abyss between us, this space that keeps conversation from happening.

Sincerely,
Rush Whitacre
740-336-9169

5-21-11
Dear Taylor Swift,

    It is really late again, and I just can't write you too much tonight, I am so whipped. And I really do feel bad for Jeremiah, he has been working his ass off and he won't even get to see my thesis finished. Let's just say, I have spent over a thousand dollars on lumber now, and tomorrow I am going to have to buy another 2 to 3 hundred dollars worth of wood, this is by far the largest amount of wood I have ever used on a project. This is ridiculous.

Anyway,

This poem is for Jeremiah,

>   Leprechaun
>   I thank you
>   I thank you with all my heart
>   For without you my thesis shall simply not exist
>   And all your strength
>   Spent
>   And like you
>   I am tired and aching
>   And all the skin on my fingers gone
>   Splinters, plenty
>   And I envy you
>   As you leave to sail around the world.

I toss this letter into the void, the abyss between us, this space that keeps conversation from happening.

Sincerely
Rush Whitacre
740-336-9169

5-22-11

Dear Taylor Swift,

    Oh Gosh, another really hard making day for my thesis. I am afraid that I am not going to have my piece done in time for this coming Friday. I am really afraid that I won't. I mean, what do I do if I don't get it done. Lol, what a silly concept – 'not get it done'. I will say this much, I am going to have a hell of a time taking my thesis apart. I might even just leave it there… ha ha ha. Then I surely wouldn't graduate, and that would suck just as bad. Tomorrow night I am suppose to give a presentation on something that I know nothing about, I haven't read anything, I haven't prepared anything, I have done nothing. I am not happy about this. So, I am going to get off of here and get to it.

This poem is for Healing,

So sore

Missed drills

Blistered heals

And this stupid hand

That I smashed

How it hurts

To bend this finger

That has a hole

Literally

Drilled into it.

I toss this letter into the void, the abyss between us, this space that keeps conversation from happening.

Sincerely,
Rush Whitacre

740-336-9169

5-23-11

Dear Taylor Swift,

    When it rains it pours. Now I am really scared that I will not get my thesis done on time. I spent 8 hours at a repair shop getting all my brakes redone, that is, my regular brakes well as my emergency brakes. My emergency brakes might as well have been called "Breaks" with as rusty and as bad as they were. I got to see them with my own eyes(bearing that they let me back into the place where all the dangerous things happen. It was a mess. I got to see so many people come and go. There was fortunately a woman who came in who was getting a second opinion about her tires. One place told her that she needed new tires because hers were dry rotted, and this place told her that she only needed one new tire, but then they kept on finding little things that needed replaced. First the tire, then a ball bearing needed replaced, then she needed to have an alignment. She was like me, the people at the repair shop just kept on finding new things that were wrong or needed fixed. She and I were in the same boat, at the mercy of the repair shop. There was no way they were going to let me drive away on no brakes, they could get sued for that if something bad were to happen, like me not being able to stop and hitting someone, or, well you can imagine.

    So, with my brakes repaired I went to Lowes and got my lumber so that I could once again get to work on my thesis piece. I have a small worry that my committee will not like what I have done, but then again, I don't care anymore. I really really don't care. If they don't pass me I seriously will sue the pants off of the school, and I will make my money back for my two years here and for my troubles for making the giant wave that is sitting at the CCAC. I mean it. I know is sounds so cliché to say that you are going to sue someone, but, seriously, you can't just take away someone's educational degree at the last minute because you don't like the work they have done(only because you were unable to have you fingers in their stuff every step of the way.) Now, I can understand needing a committee for those students who need help getting their buts together to make their thesis come together, but seriously, not all of us need that kind of babysitting. The way I see it, the thesis committee really is only an accessory to the thesis, some you can have if you need it, something that you can brag about later for having. I don't think they are as necessary as everyone thinks they are. They are fun though.

This poem is for chickened out,

Dagger eyes staring at me
A mouth questioning
Pondering
Worrying about the soon future
A voyage

<pre>
                An adventure of epic proportions
               Rain, sleet, waves, and a vast ocean
                       A mate amongst mates
                     A sail for a sail boat's mast
                             Salty winds
                           And giant whales
                         Dolphins, wild dolphins
                  And all around you there is danger
                 Storms, drowning, hurricanes, and scurvy
                   Only one of which really scares you
                         That and bad company
                             The worst kind
                                 Evil
                  But do not fret my friend Jeremiah
                           For you are a God
                          Amongst the Runes
</pre>

I toss this letter into the void, the abyss between us, this space that keeps conversation from happening.

Sincerely,
Rush Whitacre
740-336-9169

P.S. my bill for my new braking systems came to $1,480. Ridiculous!!!

5-24-11

Dear Taylor Swift,

  I feel like all I know is this wave that I am building at the CCAC. I have so many splinters, and so many bruises, and so many sore muscles. I am actually really amazed that my back hasn't given out. This is the largest installation that I have ever built. It is absolutely huge, monstrous. I wish you could see it Taylor, although I am still most certain that you have a group of little old ladies opening all of this mail, and therefore wouldn't even know that I exist, let alone that I am an artist, or that I have my thesis this coming Friday. Oh well. All of my days are starting to run together, and now I am going to resort to another short poem. Once I get time and don't have to focus so damn hard on this thesis I am sure I will get back into writing my longer letters and poems to you. I hope you enjoy them.

This poem is for the crash

"Ann"

How could I have known about your sadness

And my innocence robbed of me

As I stumbled into your arms

You still hadn't given any warning to me

That I should be aware

Of your love

And the twist that awaited me

This is for you

For your pain

And for myself as I give

And I give, and I hope you open those arms

To receive

I toss this letter into the void, the abyss between us, this space that keeps conversation from happening.

Sincerely,

Rush Whitacre

740-336-9169

5-25-11

Dear Taylor Swift,

    Today is going to be another long day, I can feel it in my bones. Actually, I mostly feel it in my eyes as they appear to dry out all the time… I hate dry eyes. Itchy, scratchy, and irritated. Ok, well, I am not going to come back to this letter latter I am sure, so I had better plan on telling all now, at least what I think will occur. I am hoping that Nate comes over today and helps me out because there is no way for me to get my work done otherwise. I hear back from a woman named Erica who works here in Cincinnati in a design firm of some kind. I guess that Ripley's Believe it or Not is looking for someone who can do shadow art, and so they contacted DAAP and DAAP contacted me. I am really excited about this opportunity. Who knows where making art for Ripley's could lead to, or not. I guess the pendulum could swing either way.

Have you ever had that happen to you, or do you always get the gig, get the date, and get the time slot? I am curious about fame, and power, and how much it takes to bend things to your will. Not that I want that or anything, because I am content just sitting here working and fighting for what is mine, doing whatever it takes to get the job done, to get what I need to feel good about what I do.

Today is Wednesday, at least I think it is, I hinder to look for I don't want it to be Thursday and I don't want to be so far behind… that makes me nervous, I will not look, I will just get off of here soon and start making stuff happen with the thesis. Thesis, HA, how funny.

This poem is for my Thesis,

"Emergent Sea"

Tables

Desks, hundreds of them

And chairs too

But what shall I do with all of you

Where do I begin

How do you end

Like my memory

And my skills to make you in my mind

Will you ever really exist

Exist

What does that really mean

To Exist

For you as furniture do exist

You are not used, acknowledged, or considered

Like the saying about the tree

There is one about you, chair

'if no one sits in you ever again,

Do you exist?'

And you table,

'if no one ever writes upon you again,

Do you exist?'

And you too desk,

'if no one ever sticks gum to your underside again,

Do you exist?'

After me

You will

I toss this letter into the void, the abyss between us, this space that keeps conversation from happening.

Sincerely,

Rush Whitacre

740-336-9169

5-26-11

Dear Taylor Swift,

      OH NO, IT IS ANOTHER NIGHT OF NO SLEEP!!!! Lol…. So I sleep during the day. Anyway, it is now Thursday morning, around 5 am, I just finished working on my thesis piece and I have called it a day. I can't wait to see what everyone has to say about it. The more I sit and look at it the more I appreciate it. I really never appreciated it while building it because I was just so dang focused on getting it done, that was all that mattered to me. Get it done. So, now I feel confident that even if I don't get anything else done I will have a really good thesis piece to exhibit at tonight's show. I am excited, and so isn't Nate, the first year grad from last year who dropped out of UC and didn't come back the second year. He is a really good friend, a hard worker, and he trusts me. Thank you thank you thank you Nate.

This poem is for Nate:

Long brown hair

And an uncertain attitude about oneself

Yes, that is my friend Nate

His golden eyes

And happy smile

Maybe he will put a hole in the wall

After all, painting is frustrating

And walls are easy targets

They are always staring at you

Oh Nate, keep painting

Your brush strokes are genius

I toss this letter into the void, the abyss between us, this space that keeps conversation from happening.

Sincerely,
Rush Whitacre
740-336-9169

5-27-11

Dear Taylor Swift,

    And,,,, my thesis show wasn't that exciting. I was exhausted, not as many people showed up, and,,, did I mention that I was exhausted. It actually didn't seem like any big deal. I hope that isn't how being famous turns out to be(not that I think that I will be famous by any stretch of the imagination", but I hope that I never get to a point where what I am doing just comes as a 'thing' that happens instead of a blessing, a wonderful great thing that I should be so happy to be a part of. Because I have to say,,, tonight's thesis show, because of how tired I was, really felt like something that I had to do verses something that really felt like something I wanted to be a part of.. and really, I blame that feeling on the fact that I haven't slept in so long

Either way, I am glad it is over. Now all I have to worry about is the taking down of my piece, and I am wondering how that is going to go. 'Lady' mentioned to me that she wants to be there during the taking down portion of my thesis. I think she wants to see how it goes together. That or get closer to me, something I don't desire in the least. Anyway, I am really looking forward to just sleeping and getting a lot of Z's. My hands are still vibrating from all of the drilling and screwing I did to my thesis piece, they are kinda numb I guess you could say, vibrationally numb. Weird.

This poem is for Tilly, I just love your laugh,

                  Staring at a shadow

                  A light through water

                Music from the sun itself

                 Math of mother earth

                 And all that you lack

                Is not in imagination

                    But in science

             The integrity of an Einstein

                        In art

                       In love

                    In a challenge

                A competition without competitors
                        Just a finish-line
                        Flipping in the wind
                        People cheering
                And you still staring at that desk
                Mapping out the future of a wave
                Something worth riding into shore
          And not worth watching on the 10 o'clock news
                    A death roll, a tsunami
         Something your music isn't able to choreograph
                    Not that you ever would
                  Keep working on that music
                          Wave grapher.

I toss this letter into the void, the abyss between us, this space that keeps conversation from happening.

Sincerely,
Rush Whitacre
740-336-9169

5-28-11

Dear Taylor Swift,

      The amount that I write about in this letter should be a good indicator as to how much I plan on doing today. I need to rest my entire body.

I love you Dad.

This poem is for my sister:

                            Dear Vicki,
                        There is a heart
                Something warm and caring
            Not edited by the mind of a doctor
                        Beating for you
                        Inside that chest

One of love, not science
So that you may beat
For others.

I toss this letter into the void, the abyss between us, this space that keeps conversation from happening.

Sincerely,

Rush Whitacre

740-336-9169

5-29-11

Dear Taylor Swift,

    Today is Sunday and I am sitting here in my studio thinking about working on my Thesis paper, but I just can't. I just can't find it in myself to do anything but rest and listen to music loudly. Well, not too loudly, but much louder in my studio than in my apt. bed room on my laptop alone. I don't know. I guess I just really don't care anymore, which is bad because I have a take home test left to take and a presentation to do… fortunately,,, I don't really have any more real work to do other than dismantle my thesis piece. I can assure you that the dismantling of my thesis piece is going to be a really gross procedure where I have to take a chainsaw to it to take it apart because I am refusing to unscrew all of the screws in it. That would probably be the end of me. Ok, I don't want to think about that.

    Tomorrow is a holiday,,, and a reminder that a week ago tomorrow I was ripped off to have new brakes put into my truck,,,, maybe that is something I should think about even less… lol. Lol again. I wonder how many times a day lol is typed really. I wish I knew the founder of lol, because I am sure that it really wasn't that long ago that lol was really used. I wonder if it was used during war times on morse code. Huh, yeah, I wonder if morse is the founder of lol… that is funny to consider.

Vertical dash ohh vertical dash.

    Before I go onto the poem I just wanted to say that I am caught up on my Stargate Universe series as far as Netflix is concerned. I know, I was hooked on Battlestar Galactica, and then when it ran out I found Stargate Universe, and now I am not having it either,,, so, now I am going to look on Amazon to see if the next season of House is ready for me to buy… maybe I am addicted to entertainment now… maybe I am just needing to give my brain a thoughtless rest and let a show entertain it.. yeah, that is more like it.

This poem is for a memory,

"Itchy attraction"

He works so hard

And it isn't hard to see

When he is thinking about her

As that light goes on in his mind

And he shows it on his face

Like the tears from his eyes

Glistening

Open to scrutiny

Yet so easily seen through

And all he wanted was a friend

But she wasn't but a scratch

And his itch only made things worse

So trying to forget

Only makes another memory

Or another line

Like the light I spoke of

The one from his mind

And the burning goes on

And he too

Remembers

He remembers her name

Scratch

I toss this letter into the void, the abyss between us, this space that keeps conversation from happening.

Sincerely,
Rush Whitacre
740-336-9169

5-30-11
Dear Taylor Swift,

Ok, so I have worked on my thesis paper all day today, and I finished it and decided to celebrate it by having some ice cream. How exciting is that. That is, until the first of June when I meet with my thesis committee and hear all the various things that they want me to do to make it better. Yuck. Well, I guess I keep forgetting, the only person that really needs to be reading my paper is my thesis committee chair, and that it Kevin Matthews , and Kevin Matthews I don't think is going to be that much of a pusher when it comes to the revising portion of the paper. And for that matter, he knows that I do a lot of writing between my five books that I am in the middle of writing, and my classes, and this thesis paper, he is pretty sure that I can write pretty well… of course, I do need revision from time to time as I have a really bad habit of not rereading my work to check for errors… especially on my stupid cell phone with its auto correct. That sill auto correct on my texting service on my phone is rather a crazy little piece of software. I would say that it was developed by a rather anal person

Oh, and I just did a count of the letters that I have sent you and this appears to be letter number 196… I am rather backed up on sending them to you, as my thesis has kept me from making the trip to the post office. I have assured myself though that before letter number 200 comes out I shall make the trip to the post office and have the letters sent. Gosh, so many letters. This is exciting. I am sure that you don't know anything about these letters as of yet, and that amazes me. I think that if I were to receive 200 letters in 200 days I am sure that I would be quite in a good mood. I think that letters are a good thing. Random letters from some random guy who had some random dream about you asking about some random color, which color. Soo funny. Anyway. Cheers. I am going to get that ice cream that I promised myself as a reward, so here is a poem.

This poem is for air conditioning.

"ZAP!"

There it goes again

That makes fuse number 8

And it is dark outside

No store is open

I don't mind the heat

It is the sleep that I miss

The warm covers

And cool forehead

My body is already telling me

No, not again

Not another sleepless night

Hot and sweaty

                        And unbearable
                  Do I risk the switching of a fuse
            The changing of one room for another
                Will my roommate believe me
               If I say that his fuse blew out
                      And not mine?
                          I think not

I toss this letter into the void, the abyss between us, this space that keeps conversation from happening.

Sincerely,
Rush Whitacre
740-336-9169

5-31-11

Dear Taylor Swift,

      Tuesday, my long day, the day before my last Thesis meeting with my thesis committee… how exciting is that… I have been counting down the days, and I am so happy that the day has arrived and that all I have to do is sit back and let my committee tell me either that they are proud of me, or that they are confused, or that they are whatever… I don't really care at all in the world.. I am prepared to listen and take in all of their advice. So, all I have left as of right now is the completion of my thesis paper with is due by the 10th, a paper for my art history class because I missed my presentation this past Monday, a take home test, and I have to buy my cap and gown, and I have to turn in my photos of my thesis piece along with my signed thesis committee stamp of approval… how lovely. It really isn't that much to do, but then it doesn't stop until I get moved into New York, and then my New York adventure begins. How exciting…

      Today I did my presentation in Grad Crit class, got out of doing my presentation in Grad painting class, and showed up to my night class long enough to find out that I didn't have to show up at all if I didn't want to… the take home test in that class actually was posted on blackboard on the internet and I didn't have to come to class to know this, I could have simply checked my blackboard account… I am glad I went to class though, I learn some helpful tips on how to make my take home test the best it could be. Gosh, I can't believe that it is almost over, that all the games and gimmicks are almost over, and for better or worse, I am a different more creative person for it.(I think???)

Ok, it is late, and my mind should be semi ready for tomorrow's bout with my thesis committee. I am fully expecting my committee to be a butt, and sign my paper and move on with their lives. I hope they don't want to go over my paper with me too much, they really don't seem like the group of people who really want to do such a thing. We shall see…

This poem is for the upright tractor trailer,

How idiotic,,,

Expecting a miracle

That a group of people

Would actually let you build a disaster

Dear M. you can't simply make

And make

And make,make,make

And not have math,

Or some mathematician standing behind you

Back you up and all your work

No one will buy your work

Shoddy at best,

Not complete

Wake up, smell the dirt

Because if you don't

I am sure you will see

that all you are left with are failed plans

ideas without brawn

brawn without mega-muscle

mega-muscle without extreme intelligence

because that is what you need

if you are going to upright

a big-rig

pass me that buck.

I toss this letter into the void, the abyss between us, this space that keeps conversation from happening.

Sincerely,

Rush Whitacre

740-336-9169

6-1-11

Dear Taylor Swift,

      I don't want to jinx it,,, but I think that today might be my day of things really looking up. Welllll, for the most part. This morning my thesis committee and I sat down and they asked me questions and I answered some, and we got along just fine… then they all signed the paper except my chair, and he didn't sign it because he wants to ask 'Lady' some questions about the paper and what not. I don't like this at all, I don't like this procedure at all. If he doesn't sign that paper before Friday at 5 then I will not graduate. I really do not like this at all. How can Kevin Matthews do this to me, how can he simply just hold this over my head. I am so upset about it… Ok, I know that I said that today was my turning point to going up, but that happened actually after this meeting.

So, after the meeting I met with Erica, who's last name I Never got because that just didn't seem important at the time. Anyway. Erica from a design firm here in Cincinnati. Actually, it was like an interview, She went over everything I needed to know about a project that is being done at the Ripley's Believe it or not in Hollywood, and I told her that I was extremely excited about making the work for the Ripley's Museum. That it would be quite a great opportunity. She told me that she was hoping to hear me say how excited I was for the project and told me that she had a great feeling that I was the right person for the job. Wow… wow wow wow… I also think that it helped that she too graduated from DAAP in Industrial design and it helped that I was local. Wow. I left the interview/meeting/checking me out thing feeling great. Feeling really amazing. Then I realized that my meter where I parked had been up for at least 20 minutes as I was standing at the elevator to go down to my truck… damn. But then I got there and no ticket was to be found… wow, how lucky, how lucky indeed.

Anyway, here is my countdown of things to do to graduate. I have to finish all the editing of my thesis paper, do a take home test, write a three page paper and talk about my thesis piece during painting class. Yeah, I am pretty sure that this is how that will work. So easy, so simply… and I just want it to be over so that I can begin the second phase of my life, the one that doesn't have school in it. I need this coming break, really.

This poem is for flowers,

                        Poking

              Growing from things dropped

                  From the dead

Pods bursting

A rupturing into soil

Into light

Into the fight of a lifetime

A rebellion against entropy

At least at first

Birth, life, death, return

The fantastic four

And all anyone really wants

Is to smell you

To see how pretty you are

To capture you on film

In paintings,

In the mind's eye

Poor flower

Don't worry

Soon,

You too will be picked

Packaged

And sent off to be loved,

Even if only for a little while

I toss this letter into the void, the abyss between us, this space that keeps conversation from happening.

Sincerely,
Rush Whitacre
740-336-9169

6-2-11
Dear Taylor Swift,
    Ok, so I think that I am going to just stay up all night and completely write a new thesis paper for my chair person of my thesis. I think that I will do that because I am absolutely sure that if I just write him a new paper he will be more happy with that

than an edition of the current one because the current one was initially written for my previous Thesis idea.

    Today was the first day that everything felt better. I worked hard for my thesis, and I don't mean my paper because I wasn't exactly sure what aspect my paper was going to entail. I mean, how can a person work for a year, edit his work for a year all the way up until the last couple of days before thesis and the be expected to write a thesis that makes the absolute power of the thesis make sense, one that doesn't fight against… so to speak

    I have spent the greater part of the day worrying about my thesis paper, so I am going to get off of there and start to make it look better for once. Talk to you later Taylor, as always.

This poem is for the challenge,

"Wind Whipped"

It is the stare

The look of determination

The pictures that can be looked at

Or admired years later

It is in these little victories that the battle is won

The one that a viewer wants to see

The look of "I can do this"

"No matter what,"

"I can make this happen,"

"And I will,"

"Just watch me."

And I look to these photos of confidence

These recordings of history

The power that some machine had to capture

To take my mind off of me

And onto the struggle of another

And to see them at their best

In the moment

Making the right decision

Second by second

Thought by thought

Do not question the photo of determination

> For you only have to look so far as recorded history
>
> To see the actual outcome
>
> The scoreboard of life
>
> The end
>
> For the absolute resolve

I toss this letter into the void, the abyss between us, this space that keeps conversation from happening.

Sincerely,
Rush Whitacre
740-336-9169

6-3-11

Dear Taylor Swift,

    I stayed up all night working on my thesis paper. I don't know how much longer I can stay up as we speak. I really overhauled the paper though, and I must say that I am worried about my chairs position as to whether he is going to let me pass on simply based on the fact that my paper is so different. I first gave him piece of crap paper because I simply had to, I just wasn't exactly sure as to how my project was to turn out. Now of course I have given Kevin Matthews a completely differ paper, probably only about 5 percent of it is actually from the same paper. Pretty awesome if you ask me.

    My friend Laura-girl is continually impressing me about her strides in her ideas and work to make a living, to make a go of it in NYC. I am sure she is having some difficulties about how to make ends meet, like the rest of us. Being a struggling artist is something that is rather foreign to me at the moment because I have been in school up to this point, and school has been the answer up to this point… now I am going to be relying on the market to being that which answers me back… I am wondering if the people will like what I do. I guess time will only tell.

    Today I worked on almost nothing, a little about my 3 page paper that is due to my art history teacher who I missed her class where I had to do a presentation. My stupid brakes… so much wasted that day, my time, my money, and more of my time because then my presentation turned into a three page paper instead of a 5 min presentation on a reading that was only .5 pages long.. but, whatever, I am not upset. I just want to make my professors happy and get out of this school with my skin still intact.

    This poem is short, and for Ben,

Seriously?

What are you thinking

Get your head out of your ass

And start to think about the last 70 years of your life

Do you want to be working at McDonalds forever?

I toss this letter into the void, this abyss between us, this space that keeps conversation from happening.

Sincerely,
Rush Whitacre
740-336-9169

6-4-11

Dear Taylor Swift,

    Well, it is Saturday night. I have a three page paper to finish, a thesis paper to finish editing, and a take home test to finish. I keep having other grads asking me to go out with them, but I am still busy with classes, and with all of the procedures of trying to pass my last class to get my MFA, that is, my last class that decided to make the final grade a take home test. Damn. C,, please, just let me get a C so that I can pass and move on with my life… there are too many little distractions going on at this place, to many little stupid things going on. I can't remember if I told you or not, but Saneeya, my old friend from Pakistan had her projector stolen from the CCAC, from the show. I was there while she was explaining the whole thing to Ruth, the director… Saneeya looked so pissed, and I felt sorry for her. Sara C. who I have never had a very good friendship with was there as well.. I could just see the contempt in her eyes. I wish I knew why she didn't like me as a person.

    So, being the weekend before my graduation, which is this coming Friday, I have my friend Mallz, Blits, and Lee coming down to celebrate. I am sure we will end up at my studio and just reminisce on the old days at OU when we partied in the Loft that I built. Oh the Loft…. How I miss that place. I miss my friends, the times we shared, and all the things that I was so certain about during that time,,, mostly about how much I knew my friends loved me, and I know for certain that my friends loved me at OU, for I have proof. Their actions(not to mention countless pictures and videos.)

This poem is for the word Awesome,

My words,

What do they mean if I can't back them up

If what I say doesn't count,

If my actions are the opposite

So, I keep true to myself

And to my words

So that you will believe me

I toss this letter into the void, the abyss between us, this space that keeps conversation from happening.

Sincerely,
Rush Whitacre
740-336-9169

6-5-11

Dear Taylor Swift,

And it is finally the first day of the last week of my college career. Yeah, I graduate this week but I am not sure how to feel about it, happy, sad, indifferent, or just light me and let me go, because I know for sure that I am ready to get out of Cincinnati for quite awhile. I am a little nervous about my dad coming down to see me graduate. I just don't want him to over exert himself. I mean, at 87 should he really be moving around that much after all the surgery he has gone through? My feeling is yes, but I don't want him to do it to show off is all… today he walked up two flights of stairs and immediately asked for a chair to sit in. I just love this man so much you know that I already had a chair ready for him.

So, I have this take home test to do,,, and I have this thesis paper to do… one is due on the 13th, and the other is due on the 10th… the thesis is due on the 10th. I have a grave feeling that it is going to get in my way if I am not careful. Of course, now all I have to do is work to not allow it to and it won't… more easily said that done. I have a feeling that Morri Thomas who is the teacher of my take home test is going to be a little leaniate on me especially since she came to my thesis opening and saw my work. I don't know.

I do have good news, I got the job of making shadow art for the Ripleys Believe it or not in HollyWood California. I will be making art works of Marilyn Monroe for their basement floor that exhibits several things about her, including dirty stockings that she took off and threw off after staying at some hotel. I guess the busboy picked them out of the trash. Too bad they didn't have ebay back then, probably would have made a lot of money off of them. Gross.

I think that I am going to pitch the idea to them that maybe I should only build my sculpture of Marilyn out of the various things they sell of her out of their own little gift shop, that would be a win win win situation. At least that is my opinion, right.

This poem is for making it through(I may have several of these in the next few days, or week… ugh)

"Webbed"

In front of me a shiny silver strand appears

And then another

For there are many ways to make these strange lines

And spiders are amongst the most likely

Once I was fooled while fishing

As I was caught in my line

But now I know

That when I am in the presence of a single strand of web

I am in the presence of a traveler

A spider who's landed as the wind died out

And who now is at this very second

Making a new home in the world

One next to you

Or your shoe

Or your hand propped on the floor,

Or perhaps the spider will sneak inside your door

Either way,

The spider is making it by on flys

And you shall not be caught

You are a web breaker

I toss this letter into the void, the abyss between us, this space that keeps conversation from happening.

Sincerely,

Rush Whitacre

740-336-9169

6-6-11

Dear Taylor Swift,

Ugh, it is Monday. I found out today that someone broke into the show at the CCAC and stole 50 dollars out of the donation bin for the place. Worse yet, the person who did it broke into the CCAC using a Graduate pin to get in and then unarmed the alarm system to do who knows. I have to say that I am getting more and more confused by the whole graduate program all the time. I can't wait to see what happens next year… what a mess that will be. I am sure that some new weird rules and regulations will be placed on the graduating grads next year. Oh well… after this Friday I am not going to care, I am simply just not going to care one bit… I am way to concerned with trying to graduate than I am with messing around with stealing money, let alone would I even consider such a thing.

So, from what I can gather, I have a paper due tonight, and a take home test, and then I have to finish my thesis paper and get it to 'Lady' by Friday. That thesis paper is weighing on my mind pretty bad. It is due on the tenth, and my take home test is due to Morri Thomas by the 13'th. Then after all of that I have to tear down my thesis piece… that is a must, I wonder how long that will take. I am sure it will take at least 3 days. I am almost certain of it. There is just way too much wood that needs to be unscrewed, and too many desks that need to be taken down and stacked and have their legs put back on. I am not sure that I can do it by myself. I just really don't think that it is possible, by myself. All I know is that I need to have the furniture removed and stacked and ready for the church to take away on Wednesday. They have to take it away, because I am not going to move it around anymore. I am done moving their stuff from place to place,, forget that mess.

Ok, so I really need to start and finish a paper for tonight so what I can graduate, and I also have my last class with Marcus tomorrow and I don't want to screw that up… It is my last chance to impress him with my ability to talk about my work. I think I will do a pretty good job. All I have to do is show off my thesis piece and tell its story in 5 minutes. I can do that..

This poem is for only having 4 more days.

Nervous

My fingers still have recovered

They are shaken

Swollen

And I don't know if everything is going to be ok

But it must be

Because I am not giving up

And I will never surrender

My will cannot be broken

> Yet everything is up in the air
>
> And if I am not able to play catch
>
> Or if I am not paying attention
>
> I may lose track of what it is important
>
> Or what it is that I should be catching in the first place
>
> And that is…
>
> You tell me, for I cannot make this decision alone
>
> I am simply too overwhelmed
>
> Be good dear and catch something for me
>
> And you can keep it
>
> Maybe I am not meant to have them all

I toss this letter into the void, the abyss between us, this space that keeps conversation from happening.

Sincerely,
Rush Whitacre
740-336-9169

6-7-11

Dear Taylor Swift,

    Well, I got my paper in on time last night… that means, only to finish my thesis paper, which I email to my chair person everyday with my new updates and fixs of the things that he is telling me to fix… I am tired of working on my thesis. Please, give it to someone else to make the small corrections and let me do all the big stuff, like writing my paper from beginning to end, or let me build my thesis piece in its entirety and then let me sit back and tell about a half dozen people what to do to make the last 10 percent of it amazingly detailed, or amazingly finished. Dream on Rush, you will never be that important.

    Today is Tuesday, which means three days until I graduate, and three more days until my thesis paper is due, and six days until my take home test is due. I really need to start that take home test. It is weighing on my mind. I feel like I am getting freed from a prison or something… 15 years in college,,, that is like 15 years in prison isn't it?? I hope that no one plans on throwing me a surprise party or anything.. I don't think that I can handle that right now.

I am realizing that I must be a really hard person to get hold of. I have had an away from home schedule for a long time, I have terrible cell phone service, and it would almost be impossible to set me up with a surprise party because everyone seems to think that my time is so important… well, I guess it is until I graduate, but after that It won't really be. I will have a lot of free time coming up. Part of me thinks that I should feel older than I act, or than I feel. I really act a lot younger than I should I guess. Oh bother.

Ok, back to working on my thesis. I see that Kevin Matthews has sent me another copy of my thesis paper back, again with no corrections on it, just a note attached saying that he wants me to fix certain things, but he doesn't say where they are in the paper.

This poem is for missing Sienna,

Oh Dog,

How is the world treating you

Better yet, how is my brother treating you?

Are you well fed

Do you still have a roof over your head

Roof

Yeah, I know, you bark like that

Oh, how it is to have a companion that howls

Or barks, or chews

That is you Sienna

A chewer, a cord breaker

Better than a deal breaker

And I am glad that my brother has you

For I get to see you often

Or maybe not often enough

But soon I will see you again

Roof,

That was me again

Saying

I love you too.

I toss this letter into the void, the abyss between us, this space that keeps conversation from happening.

Sincerely,
Rush Whitacre
740-336-9169

6-8-11

Dear Taylor Swift,

    Wednesday, Oh my goodness it is humpday, it is the middle of my last week in school and I have really nothing to say about it at all. Humpday, who decided that Wednesday was to be called humpday... why wouldn't Sunday be called Humpday, or Friday, or some holiday be nicknamed Humpday... it would make more sense for a holiday to have a nickname like that than every week have a day with that nickname.

    Anyway, two more days and I graduate. Five more until my test is due... I need to start it soo badly, but I just can't make myself do it when I am way too worried on my thesis paper not making it... again today I have emailed my thesis chair several times and he has me with a paper that looks the same as all the others that I have sent him.. I am thinking that he isn't really trying to help me out as much as he is claiming to others that he is.. Don't get me wrong, I really think that Kevin Matthews has some good qualities about him, but then again I don't think that his passive aggressiveness behavior is necessary. Not with me yet really, but with his students I have heard that he can really have a bad passive aggressive behavior with his students. Anyway, doesn't matter, I will worry about him being like that with me after it happens.

    There is no word on the whole stealing of the 50 bucks at the CCAC either... it is really weird. By now I was expecting there to be wild rumors about myself and the fact that I had my friend Dominoe help me out to build my thesis piece. There are wild stories about Nathan and stuff going missing that apparently happened during the first year of grad school, and apparently It was Nathan who caused these things to happen. I don't care what anyone thinks. Nathan is my friend. He has told me many times that I saved his life, and I believe that he would never do something so idiotic as to steal the money from the CCAC. That is not the Nathan I know, and it is much better that there is such short time before we all graduate and get the heck out of here.

Here is my curious thought for the day. I wonder if walking in graduation is going to be worth it...

This poem is for your feet,

"Touched Big Toe"
Pigeoned into position
Relaxed and not forced
And all they do is stare at each other

Day after day

Covered only by shoes and socks

And sometimes naked

Bathing in the warm sun

Toes,

Such silly little things

But so very important for balance

And for wiggling

And for all kinds of sands

My favorite part about toes

That they rhyme with nose

Or those foes clothes

Who doesn't like toes?

I toss this letter into the void, the abyss between us, this space the keeps conversation from happening.

Sincerely,
Rush Whitacre
740-336-9169

6-9-11

Dear Taylor Swift,

    Today's the day before the bid day…. I graduate tomorrow, and my paper is due tomorrow. I can't believe this, but for the past three or four days I have been receiving my thesis paper back from my chair, Matt , and he hasn't made any corrections directly on the paper itself,, just made suggestions in the emails about what to do. Odd. I wonder if there is something behind this action. For some reason I can't help but have this feeling that some of the faculty are out to get me, like to keep me from graduating… I guess I mostly thing this because I have been wreaking havoc with their class, Grad Crit. The awful class that has ruined the program as far as I can tell. I hope that whoever developed it learns the faults in the class and it failings before the next year. If they don't I feel sorry for the next years grads. I remember the idea behind the class, the idea of bringing us grads together, of having us do cross discipline critiques. Fail. Some of us, like myself have so much education across so many disciplines that this class was a waste of time. Yeah, I like to hear what other people have to say, but I don't like having to hear the same things over and over again. No one does.

Today my dad and my sister come down and we go out to eat. I think we are going to go to a steak house, which should be a nice change in pace. I haven't had steak in so long, I can't remember the last time I did, I think around Mother's day, or something like that. Of course, that reminds me of my grandmother, I wonder how she is doing at the pines. Life, I guess it goes on, as must I.

My sister makes me nervous. She is sometimes so intense, and so certain about some things that she can't look at what she is actually doing verses what she is meaning to do.. I mean, I love her to death, but sometimes I don't think that she see's that she can be concerned and controlling to a fault. I have a statue that I got from my grandfather, the only thing that I got from him, and she is so concerned that I may do something with it to lose it, or break it, or anything like that, that she can't see that she is actually coming across as not concerned about the statue with me, but rather a "I must have it, I will have it" kind of person. I will say this. That statue is mine, I am never going to give it up, and I was given it because I was the one to be trusted with it. Sometimes I just wish she would forget about the stupid statue. Lol, love you sis..

This poem is for White Marble,

So clean

And curves undeniably cut by an artist

Someone not representing life

But that which we want life to be

I toss this letter into the void, the abyss between us, this space that keeps conversation from happening.

Sincerely,

Rush Whitacre

6-10-11

Dear Taylor Swift,

Ok, I just want to start off this letter in a good way. First, I graduated, excellent awesome, great!!!! Secondly, I stayed up all night and got only 2 hours of sleep before going to graduation. Then twice today, on the day that my thesis paper is due, I have to send my paper to Kevin Matthews for the final touches, and then an hour before the deadline he sends me one last email for 5 very minor revisions… very minor to the point that 3 of them didn't even show up on word spell and grammar check. Lol. So, as I am riding my bicycle up the hill to school to turn in my last paper Kevin Matthews passes me in his van, honks and waves. I get into the office and just as I do he comes in and sits with his laptop. I think he was expecting to not see me come in to turn in my paper one last time. As if I wasn't going to leap through any hoop during the final hour before a deadline in order to graduate.. lol, Sorry Kevin Matthews Honey, you can't stop this. I am going to graduate, and I am going to go off into the world to make great art, and most likely I am going to get future art jobs before you because you are just not smart enough to play this kind of catch.

Sorry about that, it just really urked me that at the last minute Kevin Matthews decided to make a very minor change to my paper. And three times before this last email Kevin Matthews couldn't figure out how to send me my paper in a format that his changes would come through on to my computer… huh. Oh well, I am done now… that thank goodness.

I think that I am going to sleep for days now, just days, because I am soo tired. I just need a break. Wow, this is like losing a job. I have been in school now for 15 years straight… full time! Do they have unenschoolment benefits? Lol. Just kidding. Look out big world, here I come.

I am waiting for Ripley's to contact me. I don't know if they are waiting to still hear from the design firm, or if they are changing their minds, or what is going on, but I am getting really excited to hear from them. I think that one of the first things that I will do is make my sculpture out of trash in the mean time. Maybe I can have a shadow art showing at the Parkersburg Art Center some time. That would be awesome, maybe.

This poem is for the cheater thief,

You

Me?

Yes, I have been watching you

Your moves

Your ideas for fun

Little secrets

Big trouble

And the missing of a prize

Something that you didn't see coming

You didn't dream could happen

Three friends, at a cross roads

One a cheater, two thieves

And you standing back watching the tide come in

The tide of trouble

But when the wave crashes down

Where will you be standing

Laying and waiting

Running?
Or are you already untouchable
Touch

I toss this letter into the void, the abyss between us, this space that keeps conversation from happening.

Sincerely,
Rush Whitacre
740-336-9169

6-11-11

Dear Taylor Swift,

 Well, it is Saturday morning. I am going to pack up and go home today, I have to get as much stuff packed up into my trailer so that I can take my last trip with just my truck. What a mess this is. I also just remembered that my roommate Louis still owes me money for all the bills and rent. I have to keep on him about that. Otherwise I won't see a dime from him. Not one red penny. It's not that he won't pay me this time, it will be that he has too much going on in his head to remember t o pay me for the bills.

 My truck has been sitting three blocks away with a trailer attached to it taking up a good chunk of parking. I haven't seen it in a couple of days, because I can't drive it anywhere in Cincinnati and find parking for it, so I just have let it sit. I am wondering if anyone has towed it, or if it is still just sitting there safely waiting for me. Probably sitting here waiting for me. I have never had my car/truck towed before. And I have this fear about that kind of thing because I wouldn't know where to go to get my vehicle back, nor can I imagine how much damage would be done to it in the process of it being moved. I won't think about it, waste my time worrying about something that isn't going to happen.

 My dad was expecting me home early this afternoon, but I was just way too tired yesterday after all of the bullcrap I was put through, and all the last minute test writing and everything that I went through. Oh, well, it is over, and now I can focus on the next step of my life, moving home and getting ready to move to NYC. I need to call Laura-girl and let her know that I am still coming. I don't want her to worry about me not coming, because as I see it, I have to make this move if I am to further myself in my endeavor to become a known artist. I just need to keep my eyes and ears open and look for my opening. The blank portion of the art historical wall where I can sign my name. whatever that means, or whatever that has to do with moving I don't know, but

I do know that I cannot suffocate myself in Beverly Ohio anymore. Dreaming of something that just can't happen in a bubble.

This poem is for the thin shiny layer around my home town.

"She Red-Haired me"

Sheen

The glaring of truth

Of a safety only known by those living there

Miles and miles away from danger

From the dead eating live

The apocalypse of flesh eaters

Unable to make it the distance to get to you

And you are safe in this place

The location of strange

Simple moments

Quiet streets await your arrival

Are longing for you to travel

To settle

To discover the agony

The ecstasy of small

Freedom from being easily found

Yet everyone knows who you are.

And I will miss

The portal

The food court where I loved you

I toss this letter into the void, the abyss between us, this space that keeps conversation from happening.

Sincerely,
Rush Whitacre
740-336-9169

6-12-11

Dear Taylor Swift,

    Uggggh, I have to leave Beverly again to go back to Cincinnati one last time before moving away from Cincinnati for good. I just went to eat with my dad. He told me it was only the second time that he has driven since his surgery. I am so proud of him, he is doing so well. I hope that all the behind the scenes things that are going on with my dad and Lahoma are as good as everything I get to see of him and her together. They really are good for each other.

    Earlier today I saw that my neighbor put the pool up that I gave him. He has had the damnedest time with all the pools he has purchased for his family that I decided to give him mine. I am glad that he likes it. I am sure that when his kids see me they will go crazy, they always do. I don't know why, but his kids just love me to death. They loved my dogs, and last summer they really loved my pool when it was my pool. This was of course another reason for me to give him my pool. I figure if I am not able to appreciate it in NYC, then he might as well enjoy it. I hate mentioning my dogs, because it makes me realize how much I miss them. Maybe someday I will have some land that I can have dogs on. Some big dogs. Maybe. Anyway, I am looking forward to having some dogs again, and kids. I see my neighbors with their kids and I see such a wonderful family element that I want in my life. I will just have to wait for the right Miss's to come along to want to be that part of my life, well, at that point it would be a joined life. Yep, I am longing for that day, but I will be patient. Not need to make it up in my head.

    So, I have this feeling that I am not going to unpack my trailer, instead I think I will just back it into the back of the tractor barn until I come back for good, or, whatever, for two weeks, or three weeks. I really need a vacation. I am thinking about taking two weeks of July and staying in Seneca Rocks for some relaxation. Maybe rock climb for two days, and play in the creek, and swim in the swimming hole, and just relax, just chill. That is what I need before going to NYC. That is exactly what I need. Damn, that is a good idea.

This poem is for the Rocks

"View of Green"

Up here

I am free from the world

From the ties to congestion

Of roads

Of stress and unnecessary decisions

Up here,

I am free to choose my route

Free to laugh

Free to be with those I trust

Up here,
I only climb with my personal hero's
I climb with my family
My friends,
The loves of my life
The rocks are a love of my life
They are a member of the family
And the joining of my fingers
And the rocks
Is like the joining of
Iron and oxygen
Like the joining of
Sky and ground through lightening

I toss this letter into the void, the abyss between us, this space that keeps conversation from happening.

Sincerely,
Rush Whitacre
740-336-9169

6-13-11

Dear Taylor Swift,

    I would love to go home today. I really would. Just waiting on my roommates to give me the rent money. I feel like a bug in Louis's ear when it comes to money. He complained all winter, and now that summer has hit he is cool as ice cream. I don't think that he actually wants to help with the rent this month as much as he wants to get out of the apartment and get away from paying the rent here. I wonder what is going to happen to Louis. I wonder if he will ever make it as a writer. He has these grand ideas, but he chases nothing down. He fights for nothing but his right to do nothing. He is funny with how he talks about avoiding the sun. His fair skin, red hair, freckles, an all around fiery personality.

    Today is the 13th, I wonder what the day has in store for me. Like I said before about me and the number 13, I am 13's lucky person, not the other way around. Since today is a 13 kind of day, at the opposite end of the spectrum from a Friday the 13th, I am sure that today is going to be a good day. I have to take down my thesis piece today. I just got the lecture from 'Lady'. She is upset that someone apparently took the 50 dollars from the donation bin at the CCAC. She is fingering Nate Krier for it, but the only way he could have done it would have been to get the pass code from me, and I sure as heck didn't give it to him. Then 'Lady' made the comment that I had goofed off with someone else's paintings at the studios and that made me a suspect. I laughed out loud. Excuse me, but I didn't mess with anyone's paintings anywhere, there was graffiti on a wall and Dan and I copied the graffiti on to two other walls. I know who complained, and I also know that this person is a very sensitive person, so, I won't mention who they are(a waste of my time). I don't feel bad about my small little two inch by two inch painting of a piece of paper, but I am slightly offended that this person painted over it. That was simply not nice, I was trying to do something flattering, right, a copy is the sincerest form of flattery. Oh well. Maybe someday someone will write me letters everyday..

So, after I tear down my thesis I think that I had better get to work on packing to go home. I have some planning.

This poem goes out to those who can't stand me for some reason.

Too bad

I don't know why you don't like me

With your little mean comments

And your attitude that you are somehow better

Because you are not

You have bought into a lie, a bold face lie

Only an argument that you can win

Because the lie is with yourself

The hate stays with you, even if I notice it from afar

My friends love me, and they tell me all about you

And your hate for me, loathing, makes me smile

Because you don't know it, but I want you to talk about me

And your hate for me doesn't make me look bad

But good,

And I smile at the thought of your problem with me

Because,

That problem really is only yours

Not mine

and I will miss you

> and I will seal our loses
>
> with a kiss goodbye.
>
> Tomorrow I expect to hear from a friend
>
> That you still hate
>
> And all I can do is smile

I toss this letter into the void, the abyss between us, this space that keeps conversation from happening.

Sincerely,
Rush Whitacre
740-336-9169

6-14-11

Dear Taylor Swift,

    Less than 8 hours. I am still in shock that my thesis piece came down yesterday in less than 8 hours. It took well over a hundred hours to make, nearly 5 days straight. Of course, I did have three people help to take it down, and only one to put it up most of the time. Still, I am impressed that we pulled if off so quickly. And, I am done, I think. I will have to turn in my keys to my studio and move out of it. Uggg, moving out of my studio is going to be a pain in the butt. I don't know how I am going to get my paintings home without ruining them, on the top of my truck maybe? I should just leave them here for Dan to deal with, but I am so against just giving my work away without a great reason. They are still a part of me, and I just don't want to give a piece of myself away. That is why I gave Chrin Sand two of my dolls, because he traded one of his big paintings for them. That was an awesome deal. Not to mention, I love the intense colors that Land used in this particular painting, even if most of it is very what if and who cares, at least the colors are interesting.

    I didn't feel right trading with anyone else, my stuff is too big, and everyone else's stuff seemed to copied, to printed and reprinted. I am not a big fan of prints. I just am not.

    Today I helped Dustin move all the wood I gave him from my wave to his studio. He is a good guy, I think. I don't know what he thinks of me and all my doings here at UC, my fake presentations in Grad Crit, my books that I am writing, and my ability to get away with saying nothing in crit after crit in classes where 70 percent of the grade was participation in the same classes that at the beginning of the quarter the professors would say that they had no idea how to teach the class they were getting ready to teach because it hadn't been taught before. Class's like 'Lady's Video class that is graded on the notes you take, and then you are told how to take you notes better.. really? I paid for a class in Grad School where taking notes was the basis of the class grading policy? Not only that, but I have to alter the way I take notes, the way I learn, just to suite the prof? totally weird. I am glad I am out, Goodbye 'Lady', Oh, and thank you for the sneaky-rude comments and emails from the past two years. Trust me Taylor, this person needs to re-evaluate her ideas for the Grad program at UC(like stop having relationships with Grad students).

This poem is for the simplifier,

"Note Keeper"

You needed a change

But this one is making ripples you don't want

And you can't even swim, or float

Ironic, so just drown your mind

Like you do your liver

And see what can be saved after the surface settles

Don't worry

Ripples are meant to settle

Your memory of this place will change

As you will be forgotten

As will your unbeaten shorelines

You are not a tidal-wave, ripples, only ripples

And ripples change almost nothing

So drop in another coin

Make that wish, and watch your time

As it is wasted

And rolling away

I toss this letter into the void, the abyss between us, this space that keeps conversation from happening.

Sincerely,
Rush Whitacre
740-336-9169

6-15-11

Dear Taylor Swift,

Today's the day that the furniture is suppose to be taken away. I am keeping my fingers crossed. I really don't want to have to go to the CCAC and move it all over again... that would suck. I know that Ruth told me that I was supposed to leave it in the lobby, but there is always a possibility that the church won't take it. I will just wait and see.

I am feeling like a bum today. I still haven't fully packed up my studio, and all of its contents. I have to figure out what I am going to leave, and what I am going to take with me. I just don't know how I am going to get my paintings home, possibly strap them to the top of my truck, hmmmaybe. Let's see, I have my chair in my studio, my fold up bed, 50 gallons of paint, about 30 plants, 10 canvas's, giant stereo system, my maquete or mockete maquette(I never did know how to spell it correctly and the stupid spell checker doesn't know how to either.), I still have some tools left, and several large paint brushes. I know it doesn't sound like a lot, but my truck only has a 5.5 foot bed in it. I am soo glad that I decided to get my stuff out of my studio on the day that I did... I would have never gotten it out of there otherwise. All of my stuff now, well, most of my stuff now sits in a storage place at home in my dad's white building (pole building) I need to get my clothes out of it as soon as possible, otherwise they will mildew.

Ok, I need some motivation. I would ask my roommates what to do, but they would just give me some smart remark about what I should do with myself, and I don't really want to lay here and watch movies all day, and eating is something I haven't done since breakfast, so, I guess I will go get something to eat and maybe something will present itself to me then. Ok.

By the way, my dad is doing great. He is just doing great. He got to drive today for the first time since his surgery. I think that having that freedom back is going to help him recover just the much faster. I think that he needs that kind of freedom, and he also needs to get to go to the farm without having something bad happen to him. The last three times that he went to the farm he has had something bad happen to him health wise. He must have been getting excited to go out to the farm, getting his heart excited. Maybe when I get home I will take him to the farm, maybe he will be more calm with me. Lol

This poem is for the breaking up,

Desperation

And you are all I need

And you are all that I care about

My world, my home, my skin

And you aren't near any of them

And you are all that I say I need

My dreams have all but become this place

      And you are all but in it
      So stop shaking this word I give you
      And watch as it falls on deaf ears
      I wanted to be your everything
      Your ocean of salt water
      Your beach of white sands
      But, the nothing is listening
      It too knows that this loop is broken
      Broken is loop this that knows too it
      And my time-piece has stopped
      More than just second hand
      But knowledge
      Ticking away
      Ties broken.

I toss this letter into the void, the abyss between us, this space that keeps conversation from happening.

Sincerely,
Rush Whitacre
740-336-9169

6-16-11

Dear Taylor Swift,

  My dad called today, I can tell in his voice that he has been missing me very much. I am so grateful that he has Lahoma, his girlfriend. She is truly a wonderful woman. I just love to tease her about my dad going out to visit his red headed girlfriends(which he doesn't have obviously) That kind of thing just makes her smile big. I think she likes me. I am not sure though all the time. I think that maybe sometimes I am too much for her with my saying, "that's what she said" or other funny things. Maybe this is me just being paranoid. Probably.

  So, here is the bad news… that church didn't take but maybe ten tables out of all the tables that I used, which means I have to go back over to the place and pick them up and move them to the basement of the CCAC where I got them. This is going to suck. I am going to go do that, and then go to the school to pack up all of my things. I have got it in me now to get my stuff together and move home. I am missing my home town, it has been calling me for a long time. This means that I will have about a month in my home town, and then the move to NYC. What a month I have ahead of me. I just got goose bumps.

Mmm, fried chicken. Delicious. I can't wait to get home and have some of our town's famous fried chicken from the IGA, it simply is the best. I am sure though that it will take ten years off your life, lol. Anything that tastes good apparently is bad for you, what a cliché line.

Ok, so, I got all of my stuff packed up from my studio and all of the furniture moved back to the basement at the CCAC. I leave for home tomorrow, that is all there is too it. I sure do hope that it doesn't rain tonight, that would be a horrible bummer. I have everything out and exposed to the elements. All of my paintings just strapped to the top of my truck. I am sure if someone wanted to they could cut my stretchy cords and just take them, that would suck just as equally. They are not finished paintings which is what would particularly suck, because I want to finish them. They are of characters from the book I have written, Mabast. My dad's girlfriend keeps asking me when I am going to finish that thing. Sooooon, I tell her. Hopefully very soon.

This poem is for the finishing of my book.

Periods, and "what was I thinking" await me

As I traverse through my world again

For the tenth, twelfth, or one hundredth time

I look forward to it, envy these days that keep me busy

Busy from my world,

My editing of a place that is as perfect in my mind

But probably none other

It is mine through and through

And I need to, take out that comma,

I always put, in, too many of those

Not that it matters.

I also put in too many words

And too much story

And too little change in dialogue

Which is why I have the greatest editor

The greatest laugh, mind, voice in my head

I call her Kathy

Although she is a real person, and her name is Kathy

I shall still call her Kathy

Because Kathy is a pretty name

And no other name should ever suite her

So here is to my world

My adventure

My game

I toss this letter into the void, the abyss between us, this space that keeps conversation from happening.

Sincerely,

Rush Whitacre

740-336-9169

6-17-11

Dear Taylor Swift,

    Ok, so let me get this straight. I have now moved everything out of my studio that I want, and everything out of my apartment that I want, or at least I only left things there that I don't care about. I turned in my studio keys, I texted Dan that my old studio is his now, I hugged Emilia goodbye(secretary in the main office, she is awesome), I have written 'Lady' off(in fact, I think that she may even sabotage my chances of working with Ripley's Believe it or not, she has had the most jealous attitude about me getting the job, and she is pissed. I shouldn't have told her. I will keep you updated as to whether I still have the job.) and the last thing I need to do is to mail in my parking pass. I have to remember to do that otherwise they will try to charge me for it. I guess I can do the mailing of my parking pass later this summer. I think that I am pretty much done with all of my moving of stuff. I am leaving behind my kitchen stuff for Yangue and Louis to use. I started to pack it up and then thought about how I would be leaving them with nothing to eat off of and cook with. So, I just couldn't take that from them.

    Ok, so, no one knows that I am coming home today, and I should get there around 10:30. I wonder if my dad is going to be awake for me to surprise. I worry about him. I am sure he is doing as well as he possibly can, and I know that he has been through a lot and that he isn't meant to live forever, but I still am his son, and I worry that I won't get to spend some time with him before I move to NYC.

    Ok, onto a lighter subject. So, every time I drive to or from Cincinnati I get a package of beef jerky, usually the peppered kind because I think it is the best tasting. Well, I just walked out of the Flying J here on 70 with an enormous bag of jerky, and I am so hungry, and the smile on my face is classic I am sure, classic "Oh Yeah!)

This poem is for the hate waiting,

"Along Parallel Lines"

A horizon line is always there

Always tempting me to look

And I look

I look and envy the distance

The beauty of a simple concept

That ability that nature has to be artist and canvas

Simultaneously

Without regard to rules or skills

It is always a melody

Always aware of its next move

Aware of the future

Always pushing away from the past

Never looking back

Just what's next

Accepting of all things, all time, and all main

And it is the waiting that is killing you

For eternity has no clock,

No rules for keeping track

It just does as it always has

Moves away

Moment by moment

I toss this letter into the void, the abyss between us, this space that keeps conversation from happening.

Sincerely,
Rush Whitacre
740-336-9169

6-18-11
Dear Taylor Swift,

Here I am. Back in Beverly, back home, and unable to fathom how I can justify unloading my trucks contents on the inside while knowing that within days I will just have to pack all of my life up and move it to NYC. Gosh. This is getting serious. Lol. Listen to that, me, saying that my life is getting serious. I just need to get to NYC, get a job, and get settled down. Start saving back some money. Make loads of connections, friends, and start making plans for some serious large work. My life has a purpose in NYC, I hope it is a good one.

I actually have to be honest. I never dreamed that I would even be thinking about the notion of moving to a mega-city like NYC, not ever in my wildest dreams. I will be close to Laura-girl, and she will be very helpful in my making it as an artist in NYC. I hope she makes it big time. Maybe she and I can ride each other's coat tails, or push each other through doors that we can't individually get ourselves to on our own. I think we will make a good team. I am nervous, just a little. I have these emotions in me saying just do it, just move there and live there and work there and see what happens. What can possibly go wrong. I guess I could die a horrible death. I could lose my shirt and have to turn back and never return. But I am thinking that I am moving there with the best of plans. I will be moving in with Laura-girl, I will be applying at Blick, and at other galleries. Yeah, it just has to go well. I just have to keep up the running of a thousand miles an hour gig. That is all.. well, at least 999 miles an hour, after all, it is NYC. Lol

Tomorrow I am going to call Laura-girl and make sure that I have the right name and address to send my rent check to. I am getting really excited now!!! Really excited. I also should probably check into the schools around the area up there for space where I could use a studio on occasion to make work in. I would hate to have to drive from NYC to back there to Beverly, or OU in Athens in order to make my work... that would be no good. Where there is need for my work, there too shall be room for me to make it in.

This poem is for best things,

"Her Soft Lips"

Don't delay

And don't worry about me

You go that way

And I will go this way

I will find my way through this jungle

And I promise

I am going to do what is right for me

Thank you for opening up my eyes

I was way too close to the problem

My vision blurred

<blockquote>
And I would have never solved it

So as close as you were

And as hit-n-run-drunk in love

As I thought I was

I came in close

Kissed you

And you turned

You looked to the side

And said

"Oh, that was bad."
</blockquote>

I toss this letter into the void, the abyss between us, this space that keeps conversation from happening.

Sincerely,

Rush Whitacre

740-336-9169

6-19-11

Dear Taylor Swift,

    Happy Father's day! Today dad and I went to the farm that my (related person who is not named) owns. It is a little hundred acre wood that we have hunted on for over 2 decades. Believe it or not, my dad bush hogged the grass out there for 3 straight hours. I was worried, but, he did it. I rode that tractor and even broke a shear pin and got off the tractor and back on without my help. Sometimes, I think the fun of doing something you really shouldn't. like, ride a large tractor bouncing around in the thick grassy field at our farm moving it flat after having open heart surgery only 9 weeks earlier. There are other variables that play into why my dad shouldn't have been out there bush hogging, but, they are not that important to me to talk about, nor would this story become anymore interesting.

    While dad mowed I used a weed eater to clear out the area's near our cabin. My (related person who is male and not named) (related person who is male and not named) is now living in the cabin. My (related person who is not named) kicked him out of her place and he was allowed to move to the farm. The farm is his last resort. Next, he will be living on the street. I don't think that my (related person who is male and not named) knows just exactly how awful his life is going to become if he doesn't get his act together. Seriously. My (related person who is male and not named) (related person who is male and not named) has turned into something that really has me worried. I never thought that my (related person who is male and not named) would have allowed himself to get down this low. Wester, (related person who is male and not named)'s only friend, has told me that (related person who is male and not named) has made comments that have led Wester to believe that (related person who is male and not named) will do anything he has to so that he won't have to ever work again. I believe it. (related person who is male and not named) has found ways to use the system, the American system so that he doesn't have to pay for any of his medicine, and he gets food stamps, and he has applied for disability. (related person who is male and not named), has turned into something that I am not proud to talk about.

Onto a different subject, I have bug bites… If I had to make a guess I would say that the bites I have sustained on my ankles are from Noseeums. I am not sure if that is how you spell the name of them, but I guess they might be Chiggers. I am almost certain that the bites that I have are not from mosquitos. there were no mosquitos out there at the farm during the hottest time of the day, and my ankles aren't itching real bad like a mosquito bites would. So, yeah. Oh joy.

This poem is for all of my friends who are dads

"Recent Injuries"

You push

And sometimes paddle

And even sometimes pull

But you are never bad

And your kids know you well

Like they know their toys

Or their own hands

Today was made for you

And you shall enjoy it

Love who you are

And who your kids are

Let them copy you

And play all the games

The matches

The videos

And the stunts

Nothing compares to the real

The real of the moment

Between father and son

I toss this letter into the void, the abyss between us, this space the keeps conversation from happening.

Sincerely,
Rush Whitacre
740-336-9169

6-20-11

Dear Taylor Swift,

    Oh, my god… In ten days the end of this month will be here and I will be on my way to NYC(at least in my head that is how I would like this to play out.). I just want to get out of Beverly as soon as possible. I just want to move to the big city as quickly as my little feet can carry me. I have so much work to do and so many friends that want me to get with them before I leave.

    This is how I feel about my move to NYC. As far as I am concerned, Art history is being made in NYC. And, if I am to make it into the history books, it might benefit me to be where the history is being made, than to be in a little town that likes to stay in place. I am not saying that Beverly is a bad place by any stretch of the imagination, not at all. Beverly is actually where I would like to live down the road. It is a really nice little village where not much happens, and it is quiet, and a person doesn't have to many worries here. New York has more happing within once city block in one week than Beverly probably does in an entire year. Lol, wow, that statistic might actually be true..

    So, my goal is to get all of my belongings together and have them stored neatly inside of my father's pole building. It is my studio as of now, but soon will be like a graveyard for all of my worldly belongings. The stuff that I worry about the most will most likely be the least valuable in the end, my stupid baseball card collection. I don't think that even if I wait 50 years to sell them that they will be worth anything at all. I have one box in particular that I think I have all of my most valuable single cards in.. I am going to do what I can to keep it protected. I think that maybe the best approach will be to look up online how to make a storage area that is dry, or, something I can put into a storage container to keep the contents as dry as possible. I was thinking that plastic boxes from Wal-Mart and saran wrap, but then again, I am not totally sure how well that will keep the contents inside dry, considering that the objects may contain their own moisture. Uuggghh, not looking forward to this crappy way of storing my stuff.

This poem is a wish to become able to support myself enough to buy a house quickly. Lol

Luck
Magic
And pixies dust, please sprinkle me
Make this place love me
Make this place say my name
I just want to be remembered
I just want to limp away
And limp back
And make you smile
Laugh
Cry
Or feel that emotion
The one that makes you remember this
This moment
Yours, mine, ours, and this that and the other
For my goal, is your goal, is my point
Shoot, score, laugh, cry
Remember
And then buy me an ice cream cone.
A food from the carnival stand
A lollipop
Anything sweet
Sour, hot, or mild
Am I not deserving.

I toss this letter into the void, the abyss between us, this space the keeps conversation from happening.

Sincerely,
Rush Whitacre

6-21-11

Dear Taylor Swift,

    Tuesday, that is today. I am lying here on the floor of my dad's soon to be auctioned off house killing ants. Hundreds of ants. This is truly amazing. No one has had any kind of food in here for a very long time, including me, and there are ants,,,, loads of them. I bought ant poison earlier today, lots of it. It is the kind of poison that the ants pick up and take it back home to all the relatives and queen… what a concept. Think about it. If the ants really have a kind of Roman Empire under the ground that we don't know about, then this poison would be quite the perfect 'fall' for their empire. I am sure the poison is sweet, that it takes awhile to actually kick in and work, and that when the ants figure out what is happening, that it will all be too late… It is really fascinating if you think about it.. the ants are capable of creating an empire quickly, giant army, well protected defenses, and well organized. Then without even thinking about it, a lone murderer comes in, myself, and plants their decimation form within the house I am sleeping in. I don't have to do anything but put down a little pool of poisoned food and the ants systematically do the rest.. Now, take that same method of build up and destruction and apply it to the Human race… what is it exactly that is going to wipe us out if we could simply plug all the same figures into a equalizing equation… what would be out "poison". What is it exactly that we are going to do ourselves in with. I will give you a hint. We are making something right now that takes a long time to go away, and is harmful to every living thing on this earth. Think about it.

    Lol, anyway, enough of the doom and gloom. I just am tired of squashing ants with my fingers. They smell awful.

    Tomorrow is Wednesday. I am going to spend it at Wester's house if I can. He told me he bought a pool, and I am going to go and visit it and see if there is anything I can do to keep is running… Wester told me it was becoming quite the pool of slime and grime. I shall see I suppose.

    Ok, here is a question. What is it like to be so busy that you can't really do certain things that you really want to do? I am sure there are some things that you are preset to do that get in the way of things you really want to do, and I am wondering how you feel about not being able to do the things you really want to do what you want to do them.

This poem is for the second guessing.

"Ooops,"

Follow the little red brick road

See that it leads you to nowhere

That you will be surprised by

A little room, full of rectangles

Full of things more interesting than your abilities

> Come one 'Q' this 'R' has been waiting,,,
>
> On what you say
>
> For S to T U V
>
> And I can't make this more exciting
>
> Or less boring
>
> Just look out across your mixed agenda
>
> Your mixed idiot motifs
>
> And the Ryan of the situation
>
> Will leave you muligan'ed in the middle of nothing
>
> Warning or not
>
> The wall is too high to jump over now
>
> Sorry
>
> For I couldn't have warned you sooner.
>
> Miss
>
> Baker of the red bricks
>
> Lover of the crazy fake looking dogs
>
> I shall think of you often

I toss this letter into the void, the abyss between us, this space that keeps conversation from happening.

Sincerely,
Rush Whitacre
740-336-9169

6-22-11

Dear Taylor Swift,

    Well, I cleaned out Wester's pool. It wasn't as bad as I thought it was going to be. Really it was just a little green, and it didn't' have a cover. I remember that last summer, before I started talking to you about all of my life's events, that when I kept a pool cover on my pool it stayed clear of anything green.

    Wait, did I just say green

    Yes I said green. My dear Taylor, if you ever own a pool, just hire a pool boy/girl to take care of it. It is not that they are a pain in the butt to take care of or anything,,, it is just that you have to be relentless about the task of making sure the treatment you are using is the right one, and in the right amount, you just have to be relentless. Trust me. I would rather you be relentless in finding your true love, your better/best song lyrics, your reason for singing your heart out than I would you trying to figure out how to make unswimable water into swimable water… lol. Although, I am thinking about how much attention the media would give you if you if a rumor came out about you giving up singing for clean water, I am sure you would never do it, nor would I want you to. At the same time. I also don't want you to continue to write songs about guys who only seem to know how to break your heart. Granted, you do write one hell of a nice piece of art when it comes to the emotions of the heart… I just wish my flower paintings were albums… what words you would be hearing. Lol

    Anyway, tomorrow is Thursday. I am sure I will have to come back to Wester's house to check his pool. It is one of those things that need to be done. I love my friends, my close friends. Those I met in UC aren't really friends, or at least they didn't turn out to be like friends. I would say that they turned out to be more like 'not friends', which both sucks, and makes sense since the environment is more cut throat than when working towards your BFA… maybe the reality of how many, or few opportunities that are actually available to new graduates. America, the land of dreamers, the land of people who support the dreamers.

This poem is for "the long run"

"In the Gear"

Still moving

Moving, smiling, waiting

For you to see my name

Up in lights, up in the stars

Or perhaps just on some TV show

Why, because

Why, I don't know

I don't really care about you anymore

I never think about you

But still, it would be nice

To hear for once and for all

To hear you call

To hear your voice on the other end

And maybe, just maybe

You too will think about what it was like

To love, and be loved

By someone other than a parent

By someone other than a relative

By someone other than
An other than
An other

I toss this letter into the void, the abyss between us, this space that keeps conversation from happening.

Sincerely,
Rush Whitacre
740-336-9169

6-23-11

Dear Taylor Swift,

    Hello Taylor. I don't speak to you directly all the time, but today I want to. You see, these months of writing to you have brought me something that I have never had before, and that is a diary of sorts. So, I guess this is me saying thank you. You really didn't do anything for me to say thank you, other than get your name into my head I am sure. Not that I am downing this idea, this idea of getting known by putting your name into others heads… even if it is the radio station trying to make more listeners stop from changing the channel. Anyway. I just wanted to say… thank you. Your music is nice, and your ideas are pretty ok. All I know of you, as I have said before, is that which the world reveals to me… do you want to know what the world has revealed to me. I have seen your face on a magazine cover a couple of times, once I remember the cover saying something about you and a guy who broke up with your right before Christmas, and this next one about you being on some magazine, of which I don't remember the idea behind the advertisement, but I do know it had something to do with makeup.

    I do know this. The radio plays your songs, and they don't talk about you unless you are advertising yourself for the cure for cancer, or if you are in some relationship trouble. This is what I have heard from the radio announcers in and around the Cincinnati area. From what I have seen. You are really beautiful, and I would have to say the secret revolves around your nose-eyes combination. You should never have any surgery on your face, it is way too classical, along with your hair. If I could give you any suggestion at all, it would be for you to maybe pull your hair up a little like that of the Venus de Milo.. after-all, her hair has continuously been copied throughout the history of art since she was created. Her hair-doo just hasn't been literally copied onto a living person. And I say, why not. An icon is an icon is an icon is an icon. Live like your soul will be lighting the way for others to see.

So, I am really tired, it is about 1:30 am, and unlike when I was in school, I don't really have a reason for staying up this late. Speaking of school, I do miss it already. Not because of all the weird teaching pedagogies, and not because of all the different people I have met, but because I know it will be the last time that I will have to just think without caring about what my actions are.

This poem is for Erica,

> Little and short
> And I am not talking about you
> For I would never describe you as short
> … on anything
> Erica, I have seen in your heart
> A lingering worry
> Worry about your decisions,
> Worry about the importance of your discoveries
> And the likeness of what you show
> Verses keep to a lone audience.
> Free yourself
> As your decisions on hard decisions
> Will be like that to the walking of elephants on eggshells
> Impossible to comprehend
> Impossible to save if they come true
> So, just live
> Just smile, and above all
> Just know that the waves of love
> Are from me
> Are from those who know you best
> Can you feel them

I toss this letter into the void, the abyss between us, this space that keeps conversation from happening.

Sincerely,
Rush Whitacre
740-336-9169

6-24-11

Dear Taylor Swift,

What an Awesome day this has been. It started out with me being woken up by a person named Lori while I was sleeping.. apparently she came down to my dad's house, the one he is trying to auction off. She said that she was here to help me pack things up.. now, I must admit. I was lying in bed rather curiously covered up, and had she come in 10 minutes before I am sure I would have not been covered up.. Then 30 minutes after she left, the auctioneer came and I was so flustered that I had no idea as to what was going on. So, I showed them around and they were a cheery duo, father/son. Of course, why wouldn't they be, they get to see everything that everyone has ever been in their lives by looking at what there is to auction off after a family has gone through a house and literally decimated it by taking everything out of it that they want. I don't know, count it as a, "these are the kind of people that we are type of takers… if there really is any sort of thing.

Then, I spent all day packing a bunch of my art pieces of art that I have been unable to sell over the years… then I took them to the farm and piled them up high, about 20 feet high, with a diameter of probably 50 feet. I can't wait to set that stuff on fire. I am going to film it. Which reminds me…? I need to film my dad some this summer while he is still good in his head. I got to witness him today not at his best. He had taken a pain killer at 7 am, and for hours was rather goofy in the head.. He called himself slow, but he felt dumb. His personality change scared me enough that I couldn't hardly drag myself away from Lahoma's house, his girlfriends. Damn, I was worried.. but when I did drag myself away, I went to my studio here in Beverly and started to take everything out of it, all those art pieces I just talked about.. then I took them to the farm and unloaded them. My (related person who is male and not named) then proceeded to give me a downloaded copy of the Harry Potter Movie… I would love to know how he gets his entertainment. He is always getting the latest version of software, and movies for free. I wish I had his power, I wouldn't need to look for a job in NYC, I would just have to advertise myself as a super computer fixer, and then go at it…

Then I came home from the farm and found to my surprise that I had received another email from the design firm that I was discovered by. They just wanted to make me aware that Ripley's was indeed still wanting me to make some shadow art for them, that they were just bogged down with some other work at the moment. I am getting excited about this work.

This poem is for the peace of mind

Was I ever worried

Ever I was, because I was afraid

Afraid of what you ask, well let me say

A broom, a smile, and a wicked ninny

She shrieked about my wall

About my yarn and weaving machine

And all in return

With my favor in the good

Was it that she tried to melt me

A pool of rush, a hurry of nothing

And I just wanted to spin this web

This way wreck weave and just exhale

For this is close to the end

But not the end

Just the diagonal of the bottle neck

The slowdown,

Rubberneckers, and sideswipers

All who's eyes appear like glue

And the twisting of vision,

The crossing of eyes

Nothing like the finish

The crossing of t's,

Or dotting of I's

I toss this letting into the void, the abyss between us, this space the keeps conversation from happening.

Sincerely,
Rush Whitacre
740-336-9169

6-25-11

Dear Taylor Swift,

    There is a harmony in the world! And I call it,,, squash the ants.

Wester is getting out of town and taking his family on a much deserved vacation. He told me that he and his wife haven't been on a vacation for seven years and they were so looking forward to being away from Marietta for awhile. I would agree, I was at his house tonight and I could see the excitement in his eyes about getting out of town for a little while. I was, and am excited for him. He is coming down to your state, TN, to Gatlinburg/pigeon forge,(spelling is probably wrong on these, but, I don't care since I am tired and don't have the internet here at my old house. I told him to have a great time.

You know what I miss, a couch… I haven't had a good couch in my life now for about 3 or 4 years now. Can you believe that! Lol. I am going to have to get a good comfortable couch for my studio, when I get a studio.

I just realized that you must have not had a boyfriend for some time now… that is, I am only judging by the lack of any magazine covers with your picture on the front with a sad pose, a contemplative gaze/ that slightly open mind wondering what went right/wrong. Remember, I only read about you from the cover of a magazine, you life in lights, your heart spread wide open as the love-dagger comes down. And down, it goes. Maybe someday we will meet, then I will know what it means to be in the presence of a cool breeze.

Tomorrow is Sunday, a day of rest. Rest,,, what is that? I went to the store today and bought 30 plastic 'boxes' as I am calling them. All boring and gray, easy to identify as mine I guess, and easy to stack together in a corner, or wherever. I just have to build a well insulated closet in the middle of my studio here in Beverly, and figure out how to make the plastic boxes air tight/moisture proof. Why you ask,,, because I have this silly baseball card collection I feel I need to protect. Oh, and all of my books!

I need 5 of me…

This poem is for the love I have in my heart for this girl

Bubbling

And my heart pumping my pulse

Changing me, and I am a better man for loving you

I must ask myself that question, and many more

For my love for you never fades

Shining from within these cracks of this broken little thing

Still pumping, changing me

And I ask myself why I wonder where you are

If you are still into riding wild horses

Or are you just sitting somewhere reading

Waiting for a boy, silly, stop waiting

See, do you remember us sitting there

That stair case, people staring

And how I started to believe for once in my life

> I wasn't alone, and never would be
>
> And I said to you as I looked to the ceiling
>
> You were sitting there, staring into these eyes
>
> And my foolish mouth opened
>
> No more secrets, no more wonder
>
> And no more slack in this knot
>
> And for the last time
>
> I said that I loved you

I toss this letter into the void, the abyss between us, this space that keeps conversation from happening.

Sincerely,
Rush Whitacre
740-336-9169

6-26-11

Dear Taylor Swift,

    I woke up this morning cold… How about that for a summer morning.. It was rainy, the window was open, and I had a fan on me, but I never thought I would wake up cold under a thick warm red comforter. I woke up and went to see my dad bright and early.. I guess he had pains during the night and took another pain pill. I am expecting him to be a little goofy as one of his usual side problems with taking pain medicine.

    So, seeing as I didn't have any plans for the day.. I played it by ear. My dad opened up to me and started to talk to me about how depressed he is. He went through all the surgeries for his heart so that he might stay alive a little bit longer and enjoy life a bit longer, and now he has an ankle injury that has him down in the dumps. It is keeping him from walking well, and keeping him from being able to be independent. I can see how that would bum him out. Get through all the really dangerous stuff and have a little injury on the ankle about the size of a nickel keep you back. I felt really bad for him. I stayed with him all day and entertained him. I drove him to the farm and we lit a giant bonfire. It had all of my unwanted art in it, and all of my giant installations in it that I just couldn't find a place to keep. There were 40 foot flames.. I posted pictures to my facebook page, quite an awesome sight. My dad was happy that he got to be a part of my destroying of all of my art.

Today was really about sitting around watching the fire really. Luckily it had rained and everything was soaked. Soaked enough that the fire took a while to get started, it was actually quite little for a long time and then it just hit a hot spell and the flames grew crazily. I would say that we were sitting about 60 or 70 yards away and we could feel the heat off of the fire, if that tells you anything about how big and hot it was. I guess you could always look it up online.. every picture that gets online, stays online, there is no removing it no matter what. That is a fun, and scary thought all at the same time. I guess you can post pics of people you don't like online, and then you can always have them posted of you… share and share alike.

This poem is for Josh my neighbor

Wow guy,

You have so many kids

And look at them run, look at them bike

Maybe you should start a farm

Or start a football team, you have enough players

Just kidding, you only have four kids

But still, you could start a basketball team

You as the coach, and the largest player on the court

And don't mind your wife, she too knows me

And knows that you are in good hands

Or does she

As a door slams

And you disappear

I can see how much she means to you

And how important family is

And how your kids run

Play, swim, yell

Laugh

The important thing

The all important family time,

And how I envy you for your family

Someday, someday I too

Will have kids to chase around

And you will be envious

Envious but happy

I toss this letter into the void, the abyss between us, this space the keeps conversation from happening.

Sincerely,
Rush Whitacre
740-336-9169

6-27-11

Dear Taylor Swift,

    I spent the whole day with my dad. He is depressed, but I think I helped by giving him attention all day. Here is how it all went down. Breakfast at Mcdonalds, visit with dad and Lahoma's, she left to go to see her daughter, then dad and I left to go to the hospital, after that my dad and I ate Chinese food, then we went to the sheriff's office to give him some old coroner's report, then we went to Lowes to get the supplies to build me a storage unit in my studio, then we went to Wester's house to water the rabbits, then I came home to change clothes, unloaded all of my supplies, packed the truck with steak, clothes, speakers, and everything necessary to have a pool party at Wester's house with Pancakes, then I came home, it is not 3 AM and I am writing you!! How about that for a full day of messing around. Tomorrow I am going to hit the studio hard with deconstruction, and most likely derailing of boards that I have so that I can use them. What a lot of work…

    I think my (related person who is not named) is coming over tomorrow. That makes me nervous. She makes me very nervous because I never know if I am going to get someone who is reasonable, or completely unreasonable.. I am guessing that she will be ok. My (related person who is male and not named) told me that she is a completely different person since she had her incident with falling into a coma. We shall see..

    Speaking of (related person who is male and not named). I wonder how he is doing. I shall call him tomorrow and see how he is doing, and how his cats are doing.. He is running a Himalayan cattery and makes quite a bit of money doing it. Well, I am sure that he has A LOT of cat hair everywhere, because he doesn't have a vacuum last I checked, so you can imagine. 20 cats, no vacuum, and none of the female cats are fixed, so I am sure he has kittens, and probably 20…

    I do want to leave you on this note about the little pool party, cold, rainy, lightening… and amazing food. Sorry Taylor, but you really missed out on a great little time.

This poem is for the thief.

                      Shame on you

How can you sleep at night
Taking things that aren't yours
Making space in places that you don't own
And I hate you
Is that too strong of a word
Because I don't think that you hear me.
Read my words,
Karma has always been major in my life
And it always leans in my favor
Because I am unable to take advantage of myself
Nor am I able to sacrifice an ear
Or a lip
Or a voice that makes goose bumps
As you go, I go, and it empties
As I am empty
As my energy is fused with you
Or turned away
It is still acknowledged like a pointed corner
To an eyeball
To a well monitored turn
A path beaten
Keep your eyes on me
As I show you how to be close
As I will not be able to teach again.

I toss this letter into the void, the abyss between us, this space that keeps conversation from happening.

Sincerely,
Rush Whitacre
740-336-9169

6-28-11

Dear Taylor Swift,

 Loooooong day working. I denailed 136 boards, halfway tore apart the shelves I already built in my studio, and halfway babysat for my neighbor Josh because his two sons kept sneaking down into my yard to see what I was doing. His kids are soooo amazing. I mean, I look forward to the day when I plan on having kids. They really are what life is all about. Their personalities are all so different and so interesting. Josh is such a laid back guy, it is nice to see that his kids are so different and so full of energy to do things that I would consider things that are necessary for survival, like discovery, pushing the limits, and being relentless.

 Three times both Nathan and Austin, Josh's oldest sons came running down to hang out with me and try to explore in the other side of the white building where the tractors are stored. That Nathan is really interested in the tractors. I had him drive the yellow tractor that we have pretty much under his own control so that he could get a really good idea of what it was like to drive a machine. Josh kept snapping pictures of Nathan as I was telling him to straighten out the wheel and instead of straightening out the wheel by turning it he would instead just widen his stance with his hands.. it was a great experience for both of us. I haven't had that much fun in a long time. I am not saying that I can't wait to have kids, but, they are pretty amazing, and I am looking forward to them very much so.

 Ok, I am sooooo sun burnt. I just looked in the mirror, and I am red all over, my front, by back, and the only thing that isn't really burnt is the front of my neck and face.. I am funny-burnt right now, and hope to be tanned before I go down to Cincinnati to see everyone before I leave for NY. I just found out tonight that Dan, my friend from Grad School tore down a wall that I was suppose to tear down and this means that I can go down to UC and enjoy my time with friends verses trying to tear down a wall myself. Funny thing is, Dan tore the wall down by himself and with a screw driver in 45 min. If he would have had a battery operated drill he would have been done in under 10 min.. I called Dan and he told me that he borrowed a drill from a guy named Jonathon and his drill after 4 hours of charging died after removing 3 screws. I laughed and then apologized and said that I was sorry that I was not there to see it through, but that I would be there for Indian dinner on the 30th at 1 pm at Ambars, the best Indian food place in all of Cincinnati, bar none. And I don't care what others say, they are wrong.

This poem is for 'their smile'

   "Intimate seclusion of buds meant to replace fire"

    Looking around the room

    Seeing a certain happiness

    A certain knowledge of fate

    A knowing of the truth,

    Even if I am denying it all

And no red brick road
Made of clay as a means of faking
Faking all the energy of a falsehood
A major fake ascension of 'try'
As in not to complete,
But a simple have to
To show that you too can fail,
Even if at the end it was your result,
And not my transformation of your solution
Your true finally,
Your lie
As it was in the make believer of 'Hobs'
A hole of holies, of dirt from a digestion track
Yes, I called him that word.
A hole to his face as a means of understanding,
And his name, is just a vowel away from T T E

I toss this letter into the void, the abyss between us, this space the keeps conversation from happening.

Sincerely,
Rush Whitacre
740-336-9169

6-29-11

Dear Taylor Swift,

    Wow, what a movie. I just saw Transformers III dark of the moon. I hear a lot about how no one likes Michael Bay, but I don't know why. I guess I will have to ask Megan Fox if I ever meet her. I heard that she was fired from her role on the third movie because she called him a Nazi. I don't know if any of this is true, but it is funny to think that if she really was fired for calling him that then there might be something more to it than we know. My roommate Louis will be so happy to hear that she was not in this movie, he can't stand her. I remember right after he moved in I asked him what he thought of transformers the first movie and he thought that Michael Bay had ruined it, and that Megan Fox couldn't act, and that after 10 minutes he turned off the sound and he said it enhanced the movie's quality a lot. Then Louis said that if he ever ran into Megan Fox he would yell out to her for her to show him her 'tits', and it was in this moment that I just lost it, cracking up laughing. I could just imagine being near a crowd of people who all are wanting to interview her, or get her picture, or whatever, and then there would be Louis yelling out: "Show us your tits." Something about the whole scene in my head was simply priceless. Louis then told me that he is just upset that actors and actresses especially are being picked for their roles based more and more on their looks than on their ability to act, and this fact is really stupid.

I don't know what to think about any of it, or all of it, but I do have to say that I want to be there if Louis does in fact run into Miss Fox. He told me that when he worked in NYC he in fact did have a run in with Uma Thurman at some hotel when she was staying. I guess he was getting off of an elevator and she was getting on and he said that she was really drunk. Louis said that it was all really weird because she didn't say anything until just right before the elevator doors closed and he said that she blurted out through the crack of the doors, "Thank you." And then she was gone.

Well, anyway. My friend Eric and I went to the movies tonight and then parted ways. I have to get up early tomorrow to go down and move Louis out of the apartment, and to make sure the wall in the studio has truly been taken down. I was told it was taken down, but, in fact I want to make sure, because I don't really want to hear anything else from 'Lady' about it. I am so done with Cincinnati, graduated and out!

This poem is for sitting by the water,

> There is a ripple here
>
> And there
>
> And I start to feel something in these old bones
>
> Could it be love is coming
>
> Or a haunted past
>
> Or just my false hope in a bottle
>
> A wave crashes near-by
>
> Not close enough for me to get my hopes up
>
> But close enough for me to believe again
>
> And this water is heavy
>
> I float, but just barely
>
> On a raft long fallen apart,
>
> But I hold, grasping, clinging
>
> To a bundle of memories,
>
> My last thoughts of how I want my heart

> To not hurt
>
> To not stop or pound or crumble
>
> Beneath this silent darkness
>
> This night sky full of stars
>
> Twinkling away my life
>
> My hate

I toss this letter into the void, the abyss between us, this space that keeps conversation from happening.

Sincerely,
Rush Whitacre
740-336-9169

6-30-11

Dear Taylor Swift,

Ok, this has been a very long day. It always is if I have a full day planned and have to drive one way to start that day.

I had lunch with four of my graduate classmates, Dustin, Erica, and Dan. I guess 6 of the grads have formed a document to submit to the graduate program to try to get things changed for the better. Trust me, there is much work to be done to rehab the Grad program at UC. I just learned that since Marcus came into power the grad program has been transitioning into a thinking school instead of a doing(making) school, and yet the grads they are bringing in are 'making' students??? I know, doesn't make sense to me either. I guess Marcus is stepping down from director of graduate program after this year. I almost wonder if the program would be better with 'Lady' in the position verses just the Grads? Hmmm, I am thinking not. More power would probably mean more problems, this is only speculation, a guess since she came from less power into more power and things got worse.

The Lunch at Ambars was delicious as always. This time when I ordered a level 6 in temperature/heat/spiciness I actually got a 6,,, and it was so hot I couldn't finish. I was thoroughly impressed, and very much hot in the mouth.. lol

Ok, so, after lunch it was time to move Louis. I can't explain to you how unorganized he is, then he spent most of his time either drinking with Yangue or smoking cigarettes while I packed all of his things into, and onto my truck. Now, I am not complaining, just explaining. He ran out of cigarettes at one point and we had to go to CVS pharmacy and he didn't realize that I was in line a couple of people behind him and he was complaining to the cashier about how he was let in on the fact that Yangue and I were leaving the apartment and that he was going to be stuck with the place all alone…. And, we weren't keeping it a secret. I told Louis as soon as I found out. He is funny.

Well, I was suppose to have a dinner date with one of my old students who hasn't seen me in six months and she knows that I am moving to NYC and won't probably see me again. I couldn't have dinner with her because I was moving Louis from 3 pm until 11 pm.. unbelievable. It took many hours because he wouldn't help me, and only about 25 minutes to unload because he did help. Well, not to mention his stuff was already packed up at this point… but still.

This poem is for Louis's Mom, Terry,

"Brave, oh brave one"

I have dropped off at your doorstep the devils ex-boyfriend

And you hugged me, said thanks, and invited me in

And I stayed, swallowed in your time

Your energy, and conserved mine

Although, I must say, the ex

Did most of the taking

And the trap laid well, served in a two car garage

A concrete floor for holding

A small melody of whispers

A cold bedroom, a warm lover, and a single concern

When will this boy take flight

And you sleep, and dream, and drift away

And the devil is in a city

In a play, a drama, a heartbreaker

Thank you for saving the desperate ex,

The one who just wanted to be loved

And must.

I toss this letter into the void, the abyss between us, this space that keeps conversation from happening.

Sincerely,
Rush Whitacre
740-336-9169

7-1-11

Dear Taylor Swift,

It is now July! I actually planned on being up in NYC on this date, but, due to unforeseen events, my back, and several other terrible things,,, I am here in Beverly still. I just want to leave my stuff here in a safe place, somewhere where I know my stuff won't be stolen, or ruined by the weather. It is not easy, for I am all alone and I did that really stupid thing called working out in the sun for hours with not shirt on and I got sun-sick, or heat-stroke some call it. Let's just say, I have been sick for days now and trying to recover so that I can work. First my back, then this, and I can't imagine that anything should keep me from doing what I got to do, but then again I can accept surprises.

TGIF is all I have to say. Dang it! I need to cancel all my bills down in Cincinnati at my old apartment! Ok, I will do that after the 4th, but I have to remember otherwise it just won't happen until the bills haven't been paid for awhile and then I get a call, or worse, collections calling… that would suck!

I am getting so tired of being here in Beverly OH. I can feel this great adventure awaiting me in NYC, and I am desiring to be there now, not in a minute, not tomorrow, not in a week, but now. Laura-girl called and told me that she has talked to Blick and they know I am moving up there and they will be expecting my resume when I get there, along with some gallery's and hopefully I can find my niche, my people, the others like me, or those who want to work with me, those like my friend Laura-girl. I can't wait to see Laura-girl. I wonder how much she has changed since I saw her last, I wonder if she has another tattoo? Hmm, I wonder.

This morning I got to have breakfast with my student. We ate IHOP food, and it was good. Right after we went on a walk in a nearby park and just talked about everything. I got to see her new Tattoo, I really wasn't that impressed. I am not into tattoo's that much. I don't have any, and I can't see myself getting any at this point. It would have to be quite a special thing I suppose. Anyway, I had a really good time with Carlee, and I am going to miss her. She was one of my favorite students, she lost her ability to go to school because her parents got a divorce and lost her loans. She told me that she isn't poor enough to get assistance, but she is poor enough that she can't afford it on her own. I feel sorry for her, and wish I could help.

This is another Poem for Carlee, and her body art,

"Teardrops Won't Wash Away Tattoo's"

I miss you

Like I miss hugs from great huggers

And conversations from great conversationalists

I miss your smile

The one that tells me that you have it inside you

That you have a great sense of humor

A laugh worth listening to

And a brain able to comprehend a real funny thing

From something stupid

And I suppose I will continue to miss you

For how long, I do not know

No one knows how long forever is

And I shall not pretend

I just wish I would have held you a little longer

In that last hug

I wish I wouldn't have wasted my time thinking about it,

And just done it

This poem doesn't do you justice

So I shall continue thinking

Continue wishing

Continue missing you

I toss this letter into the void, the abyss between us, this space that keeps conversation from happening.

Sincerely
Rush Whitacre
740-336-9169

7-2-11

Dear Taylor Swift,

    Today I figured out exactly how I am going to store all of my stuff. I decided that on the overhang parking area attached to my studio is just going to have to become walled in and have a door put on it. I think it is a genius idea, because later I can turn that area into a little apartment, and use it as a place where I can stay when I come home to visit. Ok, I have lots of work to do, and very little time to do it in. I just hope that I don't spend too much time standing and staring and thinking about it instead of just doing it. I will keep you posted.

It is now 5 pm, and I have hardly anything done… Ugh. My neighbor came over with his kids, and they are very cute and adorable, but, they are also very good at distracting me with water gun fights and hose water fights!!! Yeah, I am all wet.

It is dark. I guess you could say that my distraction turned into an all day affair of distraction. I need more supplies. I need the metal to make the outside wall of my new living/storage area. I hate working on something and worrying the whole time that I might run out of something. Tomorrow, tomorrow I will go to Lowes and get the supplies to build on the walls. Right now all I have done is use my old 2x3's from a steal plant that I got for free to build the interior wall and exterior wall.. Um, I only got three short sections of wall done so far. Tomorrow is sure to be a much more productive day. Tomorrow I am going to go get the door, the metal, and all the trim need to seal off the room. I will have to measure so see that I have enough plywood to make the interior walls… Yep, that is something I will definitely have to check on. Wester told me it would be funny to make the walls bullet proof, to put a 3 inch area in the middle of the two walls that is just filled with pea-gravel. I laughed at him, and then thought, hmmm, bulletproof walls don't actually sound like a bad idea. I called to check on the pricing of the gravel and then realized that it was the weekend and the steel plant wouldn't be open in that department. So, then I came to my senses and decided that I had better just get the room finished so that I can get out of town! New York, New York.

This poem is for the hand print,

"Ha, Oh, it is Real"

She laughs

And lingers, but I don't let her close

The laugh was a bit much

And I can't allow her victory

Allow a win

A win by finding out the truth

A truth that most likely will leave me solitary

And my dear reader

I have an army that I cannot abandon

One that you cannot see, or hear

Or speak to

They are all of my imaginary friends

Real friends, neighbors, family, and a reputation

One that is amazingly unmoving

High for all to see

And this army, I call my life

My hopes, dreams, and ambitions

My support system

A canal of high fives, 'good jobs', and wtf's

A private party in public

A wholesome bad for you junk food

Like my mind a open container, a cookie jar

Do not take from me

Please ask first

I toss this letter into the void, the abyss between us, this space that keeps conversation from happening.

Sincerely,
Rush Whitacre
740-336-9169

7-3-11

Dear Taylor Swift,

    Well, it is Sunday, and I am back in Beverly. I have this thing in the back of my head that is nagging me to get all of my utilities cancelled and I keep forgetting to do it. I guess you could say that when I do remember to do it I have already waited too long and I really don't like waiting for a real person to get on the line. Actually, I hate having to push buttons on my phone to navigate through a menu because I always seem to get to the wrong area of the system and having to start all over again. That or I wait too long to decide which number to choose and get booted out anyway. Oh well, tomorrow is the fourth, and loud fireworks are sure to be a big hit.

    I started a new project today. Instead of building a storage area within my studio area I have taken the advice of my dad and I am just turning the entire overhung area(carport) into an apt/storage area and dad is turning the building over into my name. I just have to get to NYC and get a job so that I can afford the place. I hope it doesn't cost me too much, but I am sure it will. I am even thinking of turning off the water and electric water heater while I am in NY. No need to heat water if no one is there to use it…

    Ugggh, I have so much work to do to get his place ready for me to move into it. I have to build a double wall to make is as sound resistant as possible, put up the metal siding, insulate it, put the windows and doors in, put in the interior walls(plywood for now), and put in the wiring for the inside before putting in the inside walls. I am considering putting four deadbolts on it since I chose to put doors on the structure that have the hinges exposed to the outside of the building. I don't know why I chose those stupid doors. I just wanted to have a door you could kick in I guess, but now I am faced with the possibility of someone cutting off the hinges. If I put four deadbolts on each door then each door will lock similarly to that of a safe door, and I like this concept. I guess you can tell that I am a bit weary of someone breaking into where I will be storing all of my worldly items, cause I am. We had our building broken into before and had a generator stolen out of it, and I don't want to take any chances with something like it happening again. Hmmm, come to think of it, maybe I should do the same thing to all of the doors of the white building… that might be the best idea yet.

This poem is for tweeting,

"What is the Point"

Aimlessly

Advertising sentences

Arguing with single blurbs

Is anyone really reading all this wasted energy

What is the point?

Besides getting a single thought out to the masses

And getting online

On-phone, on the electricity of the world

In the end

As in all things that come to an end

This, that, and those tweets

Will matter not

Like I said

Wasted time, electricity

A point not sharpened

And dull like a broken pencil tip

Needing a newly cut edge

Something to make it stick out again

A motion pulled away from the body

And into the mind

Soul

I toss this letter into the void, the abyss between us, this space that keeps conversation from happening.

Sincerely,
Rush Whitacre
740-336-9169

7-4-11

Dear Taylor Swift,

    Boom, crack, pop… no, that is not my cereal. It is the fourth, and traditionally my (related person who is male and not named)s and I would go to buy fireworks, a lot of them and light them off all day. But today, only my (related person who is male and not named) (related person who is male and not named) is coming over and that is not until late and I am not sure if we are going to light off any fireworks at all. Which is ok, because I have a lot of work to do on my little living space that I have been working on. So much work.

    Ok, so, I did just say in the last paragraph, which I wrote hours ago, and I did get some work done on my space, but mostly just thinking about what I am going to do. I went to my (related person who is not named)'s house and discovered that my stereo from my old Camaro was there and I was excited to see it, and then I went to Lowes to buy more insulation. Yes, I have been blowing insulation into the attic area of the space I am working on for the past 24 hours. Today though was particularly nice because my father and his girlfriend helped me out. They fed the machine the 'green' recycled insulation while I held the other end and watched as it just went everywhere in the attic area. I couldn't see a foot in front of my face. If you ever want to see what a nuclear holocaust will look like just get into a confined area and run an insulation machine and watch as every bit of the air fills with particulate matter covering everything and making it impossible to see anything beyond a foot in front of your face. I kinda wish I had invented the insulation blowing machine, I would be rich. It is really simple, like a shopvac in reverse.

    I still have my bills on my mind from Cincinnati. I need to remember to call tomorrow to cancel them. I got a call from Louis today and he told me that he went to the old apt and grabbed the router for the internet and told me that he would return it. I hope he does because I don't want to have to pay for it. Besides, I am sure it is out of date by now anyway. How long does it take for electronics like that to go out of date anyway? A week? A day? They are most likely all out of date upon leaving the assembly line because something better/faster/prettier is always being devised right behind everything else. I wish my art career would take off like the internet did. Lol, what does that mean, right?

This poem is for Erica,

"Tiny like a Bud"

So beautiful

Your smile, nose, hands

Are petite and small,

But not your heart, or will to create

And create you do, photographs

I cannot imagine why you would be picked on

Not that you are a flower

For you are, just picked

And like all picked flowers,

You too are wilting

Withering

Drying at all the edges

And like all flowers

I find you beautiful, scarlet and bold

A red rose, a blue iris, a brilliant yellow sunflower

And I have painted them all

And in their final stage

Like you

They came to a high reign

A position of power

And then like all of us

You will end

And you will be remembered like the rose

The iris, the sunflower,

In a blaze of vibrant photographs

All but blurry

I toss this letter into the void, the abyss between us, this space that keeps conversation from happening.

Sincerely,
Rush Whitacre

740-336-9169

7-5-11

Dear Taylor Swift

    I think I got a lot done today, but my work isn't showing up in my structure. I don't know. I just feel like I am so exhausted but not much work is actually being done. It is a lot of work putting in sound-proof walls I guess because you have to pretty much put up two walls for every wall you actually build. Don't get me wrong, what I have put up really does look good so far. It is just taking a lot of time. My family can see in my eyes my desire to get out of here. Every day is trying on me as I am waking up and working at a pace of 110 miles an hour to get this 'room' finished for me to move into. I need to start thinking about buying a dehumidifier so that I can get the room moisture free for me to store all of my baseball cards in. Not that they are worth anything.

    I think I heard that you have a new boyfriend, but I didn't catch the name of the guy. It was a quick blurb for some Ellen show that I won't get to watch because I am too busy. Lol. Anyway, I just wanted to say, congratulations. I am single, and staying this way for awhile as I can see it. I am moving to NYC and maybe, just maybe I will find myself drenched in a new culture that takes my breath away. I am looking forward to finding my way around in the sea of people, the ocean of concrete buildings, the park, oh the beautiful park. NYC will surely be the best thing that has ever happened to me.(as far as moving to some place.)

    I bet my brothers and sister are a little upset with me as I have not taken time to come up and see them in Zanesville before leaving to go to NYC. This stupid auction, this stupid building of a replacement home, this stupid stuff that I hold onto that doesn't mean that much to me really I guess. I don't know why I am putting all of this work into this thing, it is kinda stupid actually. Time will tell, everything happens for a reason.

My (related person who is not named) goes in for surgery on her foot today. I won't be able to get down to see her for a day or two as I just have to get more of this building done beforehand. Plus, I don't want to see my (related person who is not named) in a bad way in the hospital. I don't want that kind of memory of her. We already have a sorted history, and remembering her in a bad way in the hospital would not make me a better person. If that makes sense.

This poem is for missing the holding of a hand,

"Reaching Out"

I always like holding hands

There is something very intimate about it

Something special

Like a connection that needs no explanation

A moment, a touch, a grasp
Endless
And you never expected me to be the type
The one to want to hold your hand
Your little eager fingers
That soft skin
And all I wanted to do was to let you in
To bring you close
And to not be driving this truck
And to not sit so far away
To raise up this arm rest
And pull you in
To keep you warm
To hold your hand

I toss this letter into the void, the abyss between us, this space the keeps conversation from happening.

Sincerely,
Rush Whitacre
740-336-9169

7-6-11

Dear Taylor Swift,

$2,500… that is what I have invested into my building project as of right now. 'what am I thinking… I should be saving this money for my NYC move… Oh well, sacrifices that have to be made will be made. I just have to do what I have to do in order to get where I need to be. I hate to say it, but there is a big part of me that just says…. F' this, and just burn everything and move as quickly as possible. But then reality checks in and I find myself building and building. All I am really doing is walling in a carport area you could say, but it is so much work, that is, if you want everything to fit just right, and all the doors to work properly, and the windows to open and shut properly… Ugggh, and it doesn't help when Laura-girl keeps calling me and tell me of all the awesome things I am missing out on while she is in NYC… damn

So, just like yesterday, and the day before, I have worked like one hundred miles a minute trying to make myself a place to store all of my worldly goods(aka, my crap).

The one really good thing that has happened is that my dad is giving me the building that I call my studio. There is no way that I would be able to afford to rent a place as big as this pole building up in NY. I am just going to have to come back here to make large work, and I like this concept, like a mini-vacation from the city. And the apartment that I am building onto it(I mean, it is just a little storage area for now, but could easily be upgraded into an apartment no problem), but the apartment I am adding on may actually increase the value of the building. Hmmm, I don't know if that is a good thing, or a bad thing. Time will tell. I keep questioning as to whether I need a building permit for it or not. I hope not, because I have not gotten one.

Ok, let me just say this, I can't stress enough as to how much I am looking forward to finally getting to New York. I hope that the first day I get there something really wonderful happens. I have chosen a date as to when I am leaving for the big city, the 20th of this month. I plan on leaving around 4 am, and it will mostly likely end up being an 11 to 12 hour trip because of stops, and because I want to take my time. Maybe I will see something along the way that makes me want to stop and smell the roses. Who knows.

This poem is for the fallen pine,

"Evergreen Devoured"

You are tall, and ominous

Your branches stretch out over my head

And I look at all the slaughtered limbs from the past

From harsh weather, and tall vehicles

Or perhaps the scars from chainsaws

I know you as my strong companion

Holding me up, my work, and helping to shelter me

I also know you as the weak one

The one whose limbs break off easily in the wind

Whose sap sticks to everything, everywhere

You are my reminder of the past

You stand together in groves

And die together in mass collective like a cult

Your smell is alluring, and your sawdust inviting

But above all

The shadow you cast across my yard

Is what I tend to enjoy the most

I toss this letter into the void, the abyss between us, this space that keeps conversation from happening.

Sincerely,
Rush Whitacre
740-336-9169

7-7-11

Dear Taylor Swift,

  More work. My work is never done. And when I want to take a break and go to see Wester I have to remind myself that he now has two full time jobs. One as a teacher(with only a 2 year degree), and one working with people who need dialysis I think. I am not really sure what Wester does as a nurse, I have never understood it. He really doesn't talk to me much about his nursing job, not that it matters. I guess I only bring that up because I have always enjoyed my parent's stories about their medical things, and I guess I would like to hear more about Wester's experiences with his work. I guess it really doesn't matter that much. He has become more and more involved with watching stuff about peppers, and learning things about how to be ready for different kinds of end of the world disasters. Now, personally, I think that it is a good idea to know that there are different end of the world things possible, but not necessary to be overly worried about it. Yes, bad things are possibly going to happen, yes if they do happen there will be loss of life, and yes you should be wary about different possible fall out problems.

  I am tired Taylor, lol, I keep laying my head down and dozing off to sleep with my computer here in front of me, and twice now I have woken up in a minute or two and each time I have accidently pressed a different letter leaving behind a trail of one letter. If it happens again, I am just going to leave the trail in the letter and you will know that I was tired and nodded off. Lol, probably won't happen in this letter though, because I am going to wrap it up quickly tonight. Maybe even leave you with a very short poem. Let's see,

This poem is for all of my hard working Z's

"'Z'ero unemployment"

As I sleep, all of my Z's are working hard

And all of my Z's Z's are working extra hard

Extra over time, less brain activity

Wash over me

I toss this letter into the void, the abyss between us, this space that keeps conversation from happening.

Sincerely,
Rush Whitacre
740-336-9169

7-8-11

Dear Taylor Swift,

TGIF.

That is a sentence all to itself, and in this letter TGIF is a paragraph all to itself. Here in about a week or two I shall be going to Kings Island to check out all the rides and new attractions… On Tuesday the 19th I believe. I hear that they have the most animatronic dionosaurs in the world or something right now… I can't imagine what that is going to be like. Having dinosaurs all over a park, moving around like they were alive. I wonder if any of them will be actually walking around the park or if they are all stationary. Hmm, time will tell.

Wester has me hooked on the epic rap battles of history. The latest one has been Napoleon vs. Napoleon. You should check them out if you haven't. I can see them catching on and becoming a big hit, or at least becoming very viral to say the least.

I am almost finished with my little apartment, of course, my work is never done and I am stressed out a little. I wish I had an entire entourage to help me out and to make my life a little easier. I just need about three good days of moving to get the rest of my stuff out to my little apartment. Maybe I could have it done in about an hour if I had ten of me…. Ha ha, dream away Rush, dream away.

My (related person who is not named) and I are still not getting along. I hate the relationship I have with her. We never get along and any time we are together some form of an argument happens to where that is what consumes our time, arguing. I don't know, I would just rather move to NYC and change my number and move on with my life at times, yeah, dealing with her can be that bad. My brothers and sister from my father's first marriage can't stand her to the point that they don't want to be anywhere near her. I don't blame them, she has bad mouthed them pretty bad in the past in letters and over the phone to other people. Oh well. Such is life.

This poem is for the spilled jar of Marbles,

"Pitiful glass of water"

Rotten,

To a core beyond the imaginable

To a distance not trekable

And my life has led me to this place

To this patch of grass

Where you dumped out my marbles

My life's work

Each marble a facet of my being

And you scrutinized each one

Stepping on them, pushing into the soil

The dirt that I had so many memories from

The land I have to now let go

You are a pinch of salt in my wounds

But you will not win

No victory, no celebration, no sleeping soundly

As the wolves of my memories

Howl

Bark, bite, snarl across your dreams

You will remember you deeds

And I will move on

I toss this letter into the void, the abyss between us, this space that keeps conversation from happening.

Sincerely,
Rush Whitacre
740-336-9169

7-9-11

Dear Taylor Swift,

This Saturday is the second to last Saturday that I will be here in Beverly… Kind of exciting, seeing as no one else knows of this fact. I guess I will have to tell everyone very soon. I just have to get out of this town you know. I am suffocating here. There is only a stale air about this place that I can't seem to survive on. I need a place where there is always a movement to ride, a motion that never stops, a love of loves, a death of deaths. As you know, my paintings of dead flowers are probably the most beautiful thing in my portfolio.. lol, or rather, as you don't know, as I am most certain that well after 200 letters you are still not reading these. Good for you, I am sure they would be boring and monotonous after awhile. I wouldn't know, for I haven't gone back to read any of them. ☺

    I have been thinking about the program at UC. I feel that my ability, my voice there didn't matter that much. And I mostly feel sorry for the incoming freshman mostly, as they will not know the difference between a great program and a so-so program in fine arts, which is what I would call the first year experience at UC, a so-so-whatever-happening. I am saying this from my two years of witnessing the place in working order, and listening to countless students talk about the program. Most of the time the students would say that they hate the program and don't know what it is exactly they are to be learning in the first place, but then they won't step out of their comfort zone and protest about the whole thing because they have never experienced a first year of college or anything near it ever in their life. So, they don't know that they are getting a so-so experience… but, since I have been in college for 15 years full time, I have a pretty good idea that they are.

    Well, enough of that… I have been moving and moving stuff into my apartment all day. I am so tired. I know that when I get to NYC that there will be lots of work to be done,,, but I doubt that I will be doing it all alone. I need to talk to Laura-girl about the working coming up here at the end of the month. She mentioned to me something about she and I moving a gallery from one street to another, but I am not sure what all that should entail. I hope I get to move a bunch of expensive artwork. That would be fun, moving say, 4 million dollars worth of paintings, or just one painting… wow, what a ridiculous imagination I have..

This poem is for the faint at heart

Needle

Prick

Blood

And my knees lock

I look, only because I can't look away

And I can't breath

Still can't breath

Still not

All my thoughts are bent around the rubber gloves

The conversation going no where

A distraction not working

Not working

Still not working

And then around my eyes forms a circle

Getting smaller

And smaller

And I look to the nurse

I realize what is happening

Still not breathing

Still focused

I open my mouth and say

I think I am going to fai__

And I did.

I toss this letter into the void, the abyss between us, this space the keeps conversation from happening.

Sincerely,
Rush Whitacre
740-336-9169

7-10-11

Dear Taylor Swift,

    Now a third of the way though this month… and I still can't figure out how I thought I was going to be able to make it to NYC by the beginning of this month…

    Ok, Taylor, here is the thing… you should come to Beverly Ohio and place the highest bid on my father's house. 'why' you ask,,, well, for many reasons. First, it is a great little town to spend time in, and even disappear in. second, it was owned by two legends, my (related person who is not named) and fathers the old time country doctors. My father delivered over 5 thousand baby's in his doctoring(that's a small city of people). Thirdly, the house could easily be put back on the market and flipped back to make a profit. Fourth, you buying it would simply triple the price of it, and headlines would be made. It is big enough to turn it into a museum dedicated to the practice of small town doctors and their stories. And the list goes on and one as to what could be done to this place… you might even be able to use it as a tax write off somehow.

    Ok, that was a completely stupid idea. Lol

    So, this is Sunday and I keep thinking that it is the Sunday before I go to Kings island… but, it is not.. that is next Sunday, and the next Tuesday after this one… I am sure that Kings island is going to be glorious that day. It is a Tuesday, not a weekend, and hopefully it won't be raining on that day… that would suck, kinda anyway. I am sure that I will still be going either way, to visit friends. Tell me, is it a stupid idea to go to Kings Island all day long on a Tuesday and then get up and travel to NYC the next day at 4 am??? Lol, because that is my plan as of right now. I am sure I will lose my mind, my energy, my sense of all sensibility. Sense, what is that?

I haven't decided if I want to be at the auction or not. I can't imagine that it is going to be a good day. Selling off the only home I have ever known. I know that my neighbor Josh is going to miss me. Lol.. He is a really cool guy, a little whipped, but a very caring and excellent man.

This poem is for 'right' moment.

"Passerby"

Blink

No don't you might miss it

You might not catch that clue

That cluster, that ball of the wicked

You say you weren't meant to

But, there is no one else, just a moment

The right moment

Positions, stances, and pedigree's matter

Sometimes

And sometimes it is just shear dumb luck

Simply being in the right place

Right time

Wrong place, wrong time

Double negative equals the opposite

And your brain just twinkled

A flickering of electricity

A clue that my words, thoughts, emotions

Touched you

Educated, plagiarized, skinny dipped without the plunge

Without the caught

The catch

The moment passed

And I am left

I toss this letter into the void, the abyss between us, this space the keeps conversation from happening.

Sincerely,
Rush Whitacre
740-336-9169

7-11-11

Dear Taylor Swift,

The beginning of a work week… yeah, and I feel like I haven't stopped working since the beginning of my thesis piece. I can't remember a day where I didn't have some form of hard labor to do… I have a permanent tingling feeling in my hands as of right now… it sucks, but my sister says that it should go away with some rest.. she thinks that it is from using my drill so much, for so long, and that once I stop screwing things that I will stop tingling. No pun intended, really.

I know I have mentioned this, I think anyway in the past few letters maybe, but I am going to bring it up again anyway. I am looking forward to Kings island. Why you ask. Well, let me tell you. There is this ride there that reminds me of a giant set of swings. Not traditional swings, but imagine swings that are like solid rods that run up into the air for about 300 feet. And that these rods have attached to them at the bottom a row of seats that face forward when they swing in one direction and don't turn. Then imagine that these long swings start to rotate you up into the air… and suddenly you are 300 feet in the air and facing straight down towards the ground feeling like you are going to fall out and plunge to your death…. Only you don't… I guess that is the major thrill of it all, to become completely helpless and at the mercy of the machine. Because, you are totally at the mercy of any ride I guess. I don't remember the name of this ride, just to say that it is by far one of the most thrilling rides at Kings Island,,, and one of the more simpler concepts as to how it brings out the scare you to death feeling…

I am hoping my friend Gari is still going to go with me,,, it will be a week from tomorrow. Oh, I am really really really excited. I keep calling Gari the most dangerous man I know, but really, that is only because of his martial arts experiences. Gari is a legit badass, and if I could afford to have him as my body guard I would,,, and I am sure he would want to be my body guard because at that point I would be able to pay him well. Oh Gari, may that day come soon.

This poem is for the 'house'.

"Always banking left"

Around here

Around there

This house, a foundation rattled

And I can't lower myself without falling

<pre>
                Without the struggle of a flight pattern, without the fuel
                            Without the plan
            Without the message in a bottle meant for my eyes only
                   A concept only the stars can be stellar about
                  A fortune that only a cookie would want inside it
                              And yet only in words
                         A prediction that you will falter
                               And I will succeed
                         And the sweetness surrounding you
                      Will be left at the table with the dealer
                         The card shark of all predators
                                  Teeth sink in
                        And my abyss is still constricting
                                Still ocean of air
                                 Let me breath
                                 Be free to fly
                       And I'll glide down into thy nest
                                Feathers ruffled
                                Talons clinched
</pre>

I toss this letter into the void, the abyss between us, this space the keeps conversation from happening.

Sincerely,
Rush Whitacre
740-336-9169

7-12-11

Dear Taylor Swift,

    I can't wait for the 20th to get here. That is that supposed day that I am going to try to launch my boat(truck) into the sea(the road) and sail(drive) to New York City(Brooklyn actually) Maybe I will even get time to stroll around central park with my two new roommates. That would be nice. Probably not, I can see myself having to spend all night unpacking and arranging my stuff so that I am ready for the next day.

Oh boy, what a next day that will be. Me, big city, and no plans… lol. Really, I have no plans… just get there and start looking for a job and start making strides towards making art(probably maquettes of spaces and the installations that I plan for those spaces…we shall see.(or sea rather, a little thesis humor.) anyway, I have lots to do before then. I Have to finish walling off the inside of this little apartment that I am making, have it ready to take in all of my stuff(which there is a hell of a lot of… waaaay to much stuff) and then I have to help to empty out the house and get it ready for the auction on the 6th of August… I am telling you, it would make for a nice little retreat. Lol. Yeah right, this little down is swirling down the drain as far as growth goes. I am afraid that when Ohio Power goes, I am thinking that this little village of Beverly will disappear. But then again, maybe not if another business takes up residence around here.

So, I am having these moments of stress that are not intense, I actually just chill out that think, oh well, if I don't get it done, I don't get it done. I am talking about my move on the 20th. I can feel this powerful pull to NYC, and I can also see this mountain here before me that I have to push my ball to the top of before moving on. Quite a large mountain. Speaking of mountains, that word reminds me of Seneca Rocks West Virginia. If you have never been there you should make a trip. Seneca West Virginia is my favorite place in the whole world. If I can retire there I will. The rocks, the smallness of the population, the friendly people, the roaring creeks when it rains. I have so many fond memories of that place growing up.

Uggg, so many splinters, so little time. The boards I used to make the studs inside the double wall for my "apartment" here in Beverly were actually shipped in from Russia… yeah, that's right, Russian 2x3s were used in the walls.. "how did I get them you ask." Well, that is a simple answer. I got them from Globe Metallurgical where I was a guard for a year. I got to see all the electrodes come in with all kinds of wood around them to keep them protected… yep, that is me, the scavenger. All in all, I got about 2000 2x3s. unfortunately, half of them have nearly rotted, and the other half have nearly all been used… oh well.

This poem is for insulation,

"Pink, Soft, Ouch"

Touch,

Itch

Grab, tuck, fold, pinch

Itch

And you keep me safe

All the while as you slowly cut

Sliver by sliver at my nerves

Like a cotton candy of pure razorblades

> Touch, itch
>
> You cut me, quietly, quickly, smally
>
> And I wonder where you will strike next…
>
> I guess I haven't learned to handle you right
>
> But I will
>
> And when you see that you can't hurt me anymore
>
> And all of the fiber of your being is stumbling to catch me
>
> You won't,
>
> And the warm feeling stays longer,
>
> Along with the cold
>
> Touch, itch

I toss this letter into the void, the abyss between us, this space that keeps conversation from happening.

Sincerely,
Rush Whitacre
740-336-9169

7-13-11

Dear Taylor Swift,

    13, what a day, and I am planning on leaving a week from today… how about that… one week and then NYC will be my home… Gosh, it seems to have snuck up on me so quickly… I think I will visit my favorite bridge while I am there. It is number 28. It is probably not the favorite bridge that everyone goes to see in New York, but it is one that I discovered in 2000 while I visited New York for the first time. I will never forget it, probably because shortly after I found out that the Starry Night painting by Van Gogh is also in New York in the Moma. Pretty cool.. Yeah, I will never forget that starry night painting. The first time I stood before it I cried a little. Mostly because I had previously read up about Van Gogh and his sad life, his small triumphs, but many many more disasters. Most people know him as the crazy artist who cut off his ear, when in fact he wasn't crazy at all. He was driven. Driven to the point of perfection, driven to the point of genius, which is also a fine line that if crossed leads you into madness. A fine line I say, a fine line indeed.

    His life story has had a major effect on many artists.. so many people decide to become an artist because they read about Van Gogh and his life, or they just fall in love with his paintings. I think that someone should try to actually go to where he lived and reenact his life. Not for film, but for the sake of trying to understand fully his intent, drive, etc. Nah, that would be a waste of time. Just enjoy his stuff, or don't. I enjoy it.

    I wonder what Laura-girl is doing today. I think she works all week and then has the weekend off. So, me getting to NYC on the 20th should put me in the right place to get settled in and then the weekend will hit and she and I can talk and maybe explore NYC a little. I wish I were there now. I just can't screw this up. I need to get there and get a job, and start making some money so that I can afford my rent and afford to eat, and afford to do the everyday things that I need to do, like travel from place to place. Ugg, I need to update my resume first... Ok, I need to get back to making a few adjustments to my apartment/storage unit before going to bed. A little caulking in all the cracks probably a good idea. This poem is for where the road disappears,

Signs,

So many signs

And I ignored them

I read, watched, and continued

My hesitation, my enemy

And my ability to fight thee

Gone

So I wait with my integrity in your hands

Standing on one leg, hands tied, mouth taped

Frozen in my shy little bubble

And your voice the axe against my will

My figure a statue against the cities wind

And my ego a beggar, a change rattled

Jingled, tuned for the ears of the deaf,

The ears of a hungry elephant.

Trunk held out wide

Like my ego

And you swing that axe

Singing a melody, chopping away

Stacking me up, pushing me over again

Timber

I toss this letter into the void, the abyss between us, this space that keeps conversation from happening.

Sincerely,

Rush Whitacre

740-336-9169

7-14-11

Dear Taylor Swift,

    Less than a week now by my calculations… I don't know how I am going to be able to get everything done in time for me to go… My dad occasionally asks me if I need someone to help me and I can't help but to feel some form of disappointment, even though I know I am working my butt off, and I am making giant leaps and bounds when it comes to my ability to build my own apartment. I double stuffed the walls of my apartment with insulation today.. I somehow bought enough insulation to do the walls twice as think as I previously thought I would be able to do. I think this is a good thing because now it won't take much to heat or cool my little place… awesome. One less thing to worry about I guess, freezing to death somehow in the winter time,,,, that is if I end up sleeping there in the winter time.

    My dad always tries to look so strong in my presence, and he always tries to look so ready to tackle any problem when I am around. I wonder what will happen to him once I am gone. He has a leg infection that he got from his surgery from his heart bypass. He told me today that he was thinking some more on suing the hospital. He told me that his leg has simply kept him from doing the things that he needs to do, and from enjoying life, and has caused him to go into the hospital so much, and worst of all it is still causing him to feel depressed. I think that maybe he needs to rest the leg more, he needs to take better care of himself. He gets so wrapped up in feeling like he needs to be doing something all the time that he doesn't think to be doing something just for himself…

    I was thinking about New York a lot today, and out of all the times I have visited there I have no ugly memories of the place, no moments where I could say that I wouldn't want to move there. There is something magical about New York, and it is in its people, it is in this streets, and soon it will be in me.

This poem is for the numb spots,

"Working Hands"
And you can't start a poem with and
Or end a sent with sent
Can you?
Will you show me how
For I am willing to break all the laws of gravity

> And all the skeptics will just melt
>
> And my hands work to the bone
>
> A splinter
>
> A nail
>
> And I started with and again
>
> And my alphabet bets that I fail
>
> And I fail to say what that I will miss
>
> For this is my only request
>
> And these scraps I look for under your table
>
> Don't exist
>
> They just don't fall anymore
>
> So I starve, and I am numb from your cold
>
> Lack of compassion, lack of rewording that now
>
> Lack of your ability to bring me up
>
> And all you do is down, down, down
>
> So I go, feeling nothing
>
> Portrayed as a sinner
>
> And you as the saint

I toss this letter into the void, the abyss between us, this space the keeps conversation from happening.

Sincerely,
Rush Whitacre
740-336-9169

7-15-11

Dear Taylor Swift,

    Another Friday, and I still have so much stuff left in the house it is ridiculous. Here is something else that is just ridiculous, I don't have much money left to support myself in NYC for very long, so I will need to be looking for a job asap after I get there… Gosh, so much to do. Now that I think about it I do need to have my resume updated, and I need to have my resume for galleries updated as well. So, Yeah. I have my masters degree, and I have no job line up, and I am looking at working with Blick as a means to sustain my living for a little while after getting to NYC… I don't know if that is the best idea or not. I mean, Blick is not actually that high of a paying job, only about 10 bucks an hour, and I could probably find a temp job through an agency for about 15 to 19 dollars an hour after fees are taken out. Maybe I should play the lottery and see if I can win it big… lol. I am my own lottery, I just need to make my numbers count is all…. That is how I see it. Or maybe my numbers are counting me… Huh, I guess I never thought about it that way.

So, today was another day of packing and moving stuff from the house to my new little apt. It isn't anywhere done, but that is ok, I just need to finish installing some walls. I was thinking about moving the electrical switch from its current location to a spot near the front door. Right now it is located up near the ceiling and part way into the room above my book shelves, and I can't seem to find the time to move it,,, nor the wire. It might be better to move it during a break, or during the time I move home to work on my Ripley's shadow art stuff. I shall see. It all depends on when I come home. Probably not until Christmas. And, if I don't come home until Christmas, then that will be kinda sad because that will mean that Ripley's somehow decided to not go with me and my shadow art skills, which are some pretty awesome skills if I do say so myself. Lol

First things first… I need to get moved to NYC…. Then I should worry about all the other details. So many things going on in my life at this second. Just too much to think about I guess. The city is like a giant robot, and I will be like a small electron moving along in its pathways, making it work, making it do things, and hopefully making it understand me.

I wish I knew more about you. I feel like an exposed fish that is going to be thown back. I will have this story to tell and no one will be there to hear it. :(

This poem is for the dogs I no longer have

"Panting"

I sometimes wonder where I would be going if I still had you

You and your beautiful coats

Your running, chasing, and protection.

I think that above all though

What I miss the most is your breath

Panting

Breathing hard after an amazing run

A pouncing play

A walk across the yard to see if you would chase a squirrel

I miss you sometimes

Mans best friend

I wonder if you are still playing

        Panting

   Running after things that mean nothing to you

       Only to your curiousity

       And my happiness soars

  As I close my eyes and pretend you are still here

        Waiting to be pet

         To be ran

         To breath

I toss this letter into the void, the abyss between us, this space that keeps conversation from happening.

Sincerely,
Rush Whitacre
740-336-9169

7-16-11

Dear Taylor Swift,

  This is my last weekend here in Beverly, and I don't think that it will be restful at all. My dad wants two rooms of carpet torn up and that means that I will have to have them cleared out and all of their contents so that the house is ready for the auction. I don't like the idea of this auction at all. My (related person who is male and not named) has the right idea I think, place the house on some nation-wide realtors site and give them 6 months to sell the house. If they can't make it happen then try to auction off the house. I hope my dad gets from it what he needs or what he wants, or at least he gets to say a proper goodbye to this big old house. I am going to miss it. It is the only house I have ever known.

  Today was another long hot sweaty day of hard labor and sore elbows. I am worried about all of my work with my elbows. I really have a problem with my hands starting to feel numb from all of the hard pulling and putting in of screws that have built my little apt./ storage unit. When I am laying down to rest I can feel the numbness creep in when my arms are curled up next to me, or next to my head. There is something to it. I think that it is that pressure of my muscles pressing or pulling on my elbows that are causing this feeling, or lack of feeling rather… I am not too worried about it. I just need to stop working so hard for a little bit and let my arms recover. I know that I will be ok once I get some rest… I just have to make it to NYC where, oddly enough, I will get some rest. How about that for a place to go to get some rest,,, in the city that never rests I go to get some.

  I am still worried about my fathers leg. It hasn't healed up at all. Instead he goes down to the hospital every day and has some form of treatment down to try to get it stimulated to heal. It isn't happening… I don't want to leave him so upset about it and all, but, I must go, I must go to find my place in this world. New York is that place where I will find where I belong, not to mention, I want to live there for a couple of years before things in the country get really bad. I certainly wouldn't want to be there during a major nation-wide, or world-wide problem or event. I don't think that making my way out of the city would be very likely, although I would like to think of myself as a survivor, I guess I wouldn't know until faced with the circumstance of such an event.

This poem is for the end of something bigger than humanity,

"Clasp Unhinged"

Clues

So many clues leading up to this point

So many missed chances

And a hand reached out

And a strong grip

To pull us out of this net

Will do us no good if we do not change our ways

Our plans as they are

Self destruct,

As we must fight each other

We fight ourselves

And there is nothing to stop the slice

The slippery slope of a mud hill

A dirty mind

A single cut of a strap

Shirt falls, and all is exposed

A bountiful feast for migrants

A song to for the song bird

And I am all but deaf

I toss this letter into the void, the abyss between us, this space that keeps conversation from happening.

Sincerely,

Rush Whitacre
740-336-9169

7-17-11

Dear Taylor Swift,

I got to thinking about the days of the week, and the whole thing about working for 6 days and then resting on the 7th… well, if we were to work the first 6 days, we would rest on a Saturday, but if you are extremely religious you might believe that you are to rest on the 1st day of the week… so weird.

Anyway, there is no rest for me. I have to help Lori move a bunch more stuff out of the house for my dad. He has so much going on with himself physically that I don't want him to feel like he has to worry too much about the house and all, all of the details going into the selling of a large house in a small town has him rather worked up a bit. I think that he doesn't want to sell it, but he can't afford to pay for it any more. He should have sold it years ago before he wasted so much money on keeping it up.

Looking back I can see how my father could have changed so many things about himself to make his life easier, but he just didn't because he,,, well, he probably just didn't think about them too much. I can remember how he would sometimes go to different schools and give talks about climbing. He loved climbing so much, it really is a part of his blood, as it is in mine. I am now up here in New York now though, and I haven't really thought about climbing up here as much as I could have I guess.. I just have too much going on right now to think about that. Like, packing, moving, finding a job. I worry about my dad.

So, my (related person who is not named) and I had a major argument about nothing again today. She and my (related person who is male and not named) came to the house to get stuff out of it that they wanted. One thing led to another and she took my marble collection out to the yard and dumped it out in the grass. She thought that her marbles were somewhere mixed in with mine. Lol, such a silly thing. I got upset, and then let it go. She has problems that are not mine. I just gave her my marbles, and found hers to give to her. What ever right…

Tomorrow is another day

This poem is for the distance I must go to make things happen

"shoe strings tied"

I can't make you read my poem

And I can't make you see my life

My story is that of two lives collapsed into one time

One place

And the element of my being

                    Is burning deep within

                    So cast me out of your life

                    And cast the first rock

                    Or stone, whichever is harder

                              heavier

                    I am glued to my beliefs

                    And you cannot un-stick me

                              By my gaze

                    I see 500 miles away

                    And if by your gaze you too can see that far

                    Then we shall see halfway

                              To the middle

                    To the heart of it all

                              To Ohio

                    From New York

                              To Ohio

                    From Tennessee

I toss this letter into the void, the abyss between us, this space that keeps conversation from happening.

Sincerely,
Rush Whitacre
740-336-9169

7-18-11

Dear Taylor Swift,

    Two days to go….. I can see now that I am going to fall short of my exiting of Ohio to New York… I still have so much to do, and I work myself into the nothing everyday. I literally am so tired at the end of everyday that I can't think straight, I can't make myself go any faster, further, for any length of time. My hands are tingly all the time from the vibration of a drill, the cutting of a saw, the lifting, cutting, gripping and gripping and gripping of wood to keep it in place while I put the screws in. I would say that the gripping and pulling with my hands and especially my left arm is what is hurting me the most. One thing that is for sure is that fact that the prednisone that I took for my back pain/inflammation has made my back pretty much immune to pain and inflammation... I am so happy about this... Now if I can just make it through to NY with no back pain. Please oh please let that be the case...

I still wonder what kind of work I will be doing when I get to NY... I don't have the much money to keep me afloat for very long. I also wonder what kind of doors my MFA will open for me where Laura-girls BFA could never get her. I have a feeling that my best bet is to apply at some employment agency where they can find me some job that I would really like. Who knows... I am just glad that I went through with my whole MFA, that I actually did it... I am still amazed that I was able to put up with so much bullcrap. I am not even going to get into it. I don't feel like wasting my time.

Anyway. My dads leg appears to be getting better... or my dad is getting better at hiding how his leg really is from me. Most likely a little of both. He is really upset about how the R--- Hospital treated his leg. Sure, they got his heart working in tip top condition, but his leg is not able to heal itself from the wound that the hostpital inflicted on him.. I know that I have talked a lot about this, but it really bothers me. He has that new heart valve, and if the infection gets into it, he may lose it,,, and maybe die. That would be terrible. Just not something I am prepared for, I guess who is prepared for such a thing???

This poem is for the giggle,

"Protection in a smile"

The baby is scared

So many faces looking at him

So many voices

And so many places to hide

But he can't move from his mother's arms

He just sits there

Snuggly held by two arms

And in his greatest fret

The baby smiles

And the onlookers smile

And the baby knows he has won

That he will survive,

That he has disarmed any predator

For that babies smile

Is a defense

A weapon against fear

Against death

Against all the cruelties of the world

That smile

Makes me happy

Makes me smile

And for the moment

I too feel at ease

I feel safe

I toss this letter into the void, the abyss between us, this space that keeps conversation from happening

Sincerely,

Rush Whitacre

740-336-9169

7-19-11

Dear Taylor Swift,

    It is now 4 am, and I have not slept at all… I have officially given up on the idea of trying to leave today to be in New York… But that is ok. It will happen and that is all that matters… I just hope that Laura-girl will be ok with me being a day or two, or god forbid three late. No matter what I will be there this weekend… period.

    My dad has been pushing Lori(our house keeper) onto me hard lately. I mean, he has been making her come down and work and work and work with me on all the things that I need to get done… I have so much work too… I can't thank her enough. Thank you Lori!

    Ok, because it is so late I am sure that I am going to get off of here and write this poem, maybe it will be short, or maybe it will be long, I don't know, It has been a long long long day and I just want to crash my brain onto one of my umpteen pillows. Huh, that is weird, umpteen is a word in my dictionary on my word,,, but Maquette is not… weird!!

This poem is for my memory of a friend named Pearly

You are sad

Some of the time

Most of the time

And you are also very very strange

As you hibernate

Or cut me out

Or have your hand out

Only to drop it at the last minute

Right as you need a friend the most

And you cry

But only fake dry nothings come

A lie in a basket of keys

And my lock belonging to none of them

Bare with me

As I peddle faster

Move smoother

And at the last second swing

And my hand will grasp yours

And you will see that I am still

Here

Still a friend

Still full of stories and laughter

Maybe that is why I am banished

Or you have banished yourself

I hope you are not alone

Or in the same apartment

For that would be sad

And a mistake

And a pigeon will deliver this message

A bird of many feathers

Kiss the wind

I am here

I toss this letter into the void, the abyss between us, this space that keeps conversation from happening.

Sincerely,

Rush Whitacre
740-336-9169

7-20-11

Dear Taylor Swift,

    Ok, I think that I already told you that I added you to my twitter, but if I haven't I will tell you that I did now. There is a reason for this, and I will tell you that as well. I added you because I mentioned to a friend of my at UC about all of these letters, but I didn't say who I was writing. Anyway, she, Les, told me that she had spoken to some famous people on twitter and she told me that I should definitely try it. So, that was months ago that I added you. But, what I am trying to say is that I found it interesting that on the same day that you were suppose to be in NYC I too was suppose to be there as well.. when I got your notification that you were going to be in NYC I couldn't help but to think about this connection of the 13 in my life. My goal was to be in NYC, and like always, me questioning if it was the right thing to be there, and then the person who has made the number 13 famous is there herself.. anyway, I just thought it was a nice little reminder for me that I am 13's lucky person.

    Today I organized all day in the whitebuilding(my studio, pole building) and it is a lot of work… Here is the funny crazy thing… if I had been ready to be in NYC I would have mostly definetly been in Central park, because that is the first thing that I was going to do with my friend Laura-girl when I got there… that would have been really crazy to see you there. I wonder if you have even laid eyes on any of my letters… oh well, fate as it seems has left me here in Beverly for another day, organizing, and slowly packing…

    More splinters, more back aching lifting, more more more… I wonder if when I get to NYC if my days are going to be filled so full of all this work stuff… lol, of course it will. I have to be relentless with my art, with my ideas, with my steam… I just can't afford to have a major problem with my back, that would be really bad… I would have to say that if my back went out I would probably have to move home and find someone(most likely a surgeon) to fix me. Knock on wood that that doesn't happen…

    I think that my dad is happy that I have not left today… luckily Laura-girl is ok with me not coming for a few days… I can see it now, I won't be ready to move until this weekend…. Gosh, I hope that I am ready at least by this coming Friday… please by this Friday…..

This poem is for the curious 13

"Why"
Why did you choose me?
I have been good,
And I acknowledge you as a clarifier

A notify'r that I am in the right place

That my problems will work themselves out

That what I am doing is what I should be doing

You show up, and without me knowing it

You comfort me

You make me smile, laugh, and wonder why

You, 13, are always there to show me the way

If I am ever in doubt, of any kind

You appear and all is well

I don't know what I shall do

If you ever lead me astray

Or leave me altogether

Like a building to the 14th floor

I would never skip you,

As I see no way around you

Like my shadow

Always present

I toss this letter into the void, the abyss between us, this space that keeps conversation from happening.

Sincerely,
Rush Whitacre
740-336-9169

7-21-11

Dear Taylor Swift,

    AAAAAAAAAAh. I am still here in Beverly… Oh well. I woke up this morning and trudged again through all of my things in the white building(studio, pole building, AWESOME) and I got everything in there sorted into three different categories as far as I can tell… 1. Tools, 2. Art supplies, 3. Everything else. Lol… my favorite is number 3 I guess.

    So, I wouldn't have been able to make it through everything without the help of Bob. He is a close family friend, and he is also someone who in the past I treated very poorly, but because of my treating him so poorly I grew so much as a person, and I have apologized so many times to him, again here, sorry man, I wasn't thinking at all. Not that it should matter too much, but what happened is this: No, I just had a second thought, and I don't think that retelling this story that it would make any difference. So, I will just say this, Sorry Bob, it won't ever happen again, and thank you for being so forgiving.

Anyway, I am sitting here listening to "Like a Boss" and I am thinking, yeah, the amount of work that it would take to accomplish everything that is said in the song… yeah that is the amount of energy I expel every day…

So, I told my friend Wester about all of these letters that I have been sending you, and, like any great friend he immediately started to picking on me about being a stalker… So, because that is absolutely not what I am, nor do I care about, I am going to simply say this; all I am doing is keeping track of my days with letters, and I only chose you, Taylor Swift, because of that reoccurring dream that I had. I guess that dream so many months ago was the catalyst for all of this… So, if I had dreamed about Leonardo DiCaprio I would be writing him, but, of course, that didn't happen. Lol. And, I like writing, and I especially like the writing of letters that I send out into the world about my life and not know where they end up, who reads them, and/or how seriously they are taken. So, yeah, this is where it is at. Writing letters to Taylor Swift, and then have great excitement about mailing them as I walk from my house to the post office, thinking all the time: "into the nothing, the nowhere, or as I mentioned the first week of letters; into a room of little old ladies who are reading all of these letters. I hope you enjoy them.

This poem is for that certain feeling of clean.

"Hot Enough"

So much sawdust

And so many screws

The sweat runs into my eyes

They burn

Like suntan lotion, they burn bad

I can't imagine that my shower water

Is hot enough

Nor flows hard enough

For me to be clean

So I stand there,

Lone and leaning

Soap running from hair into my eyes

A reminder of the day's work

The heavy lifting

The tired back

Aching for a chair

A stool, a bed, or a massage

None will make this better

like all dreams

I wake

I toss this letter into the void, the abyss between us, this space the keeps conversation from happening.

Sincerely,
Rush Whitacre
740-336-9169

7-22-11

Dear Taylor Swift,

    I feel sad in a way that I was not able to make it to NYC this past Wednesday… Let me just say this much. I have gotten so much done that I never thought I would have gotten done otherwise. Now when I come home to work on my shadow art I shall have a giant space open in my studio to work on the Marilyn Monroe piece for Ripleys believe it or not. Now that I have mentioned this, I also have to say that I haven't heard from Ripley's, and it is making me a little nervous as to whether I will hear from them… I am sure I will, because I am remaining optimistic, but at the same time, I wish I would have heard back from them sooner than now so that I could plan my days, or week or two around my schedule that I might have in NY when ever I get there and have some form of a job of some kind… I can't wait to have a job in NYC… there is something about having the job in NYC that sounds rather prestigious in some manner… probably just because I come from such a small community and NY is so big. Maybe that is all…

    Ok, I am really tired and I am going to be heading off to lala land here soon… speaking of la la land, I am sure that Laura-girl is tired of hearing me say that I am going to be moving up to NY and instead wants me moving literally… I could hear it in her voice tonight when she told me that I had better be up in NY by this Sunday or else… lol, I wonder what that means… she giggled after saying that. I am sure she is just wanting me up here to have a close friend nearby, and to be sure to have a truck up here for the move. Speaking of trucks,,, I wonder what kind of parking will be available. I hope that I have at least some form of street parking if nothing else. I will have to check with Laura-girl. I really don't want to spend to much time every time I want to park looking for a space for my truck. That would simply suck. Yeah, I am making a note to myself right now to call Laura-girl tomorrow to see about the parking situation. Once before Laura-girl told me that I could sell my truck after I got up here… Not a bad idea really. I am sure I could always hike my way home if worse came to worse. What is 500n miles anyway. I am guessing that I would be able to keep up an average of 10 miles of hiking a day, which means I would be home in roughly 50 days… Oh boy, what a month and a half that would be.

This poem is for the mother kissing her baby.

"Pressed against"

I see a look

Scared, unsure, terrified

And I am curious

What face am I suppose to make

Should I make a face

Or should I just watch along with all the others

Staring at you

Then looking away,

Then pretending not to stare while doing it

And then wondering why she just doesn't hold you

Hold you close

Close enough as if to breath with you

As to shhh you in your ear

As to swaddle you in arms

In a blanket of tightening arms

And to kiss you on your forehead

Comfort you

And make all the world a quieter place

A loving place

A place where everyone watches you

And knows more

About the power of a good mother

About love

I toss this letter into the void, the abyss between us, this space that keeps conversation from happening.

Sincerely,
Rush Whitacre
740-336-9169

7-23-11

Dear Taylor Swift,

I am still in Beverly,,, I am still in Beverly,,, and I am soooo tired. Physically exhausted from so much labor. Bob has been helping me to arrange my life in my studio and in getting everything together so that I can leave for NYC... I have my truck packed up now with all of my tools and I am going to work on packing all of my clothes today... I was going to pack them last night, but it was about 2 am before I go into bed and I simply took a shower and thought I would start to go through my clothes, but when I got to my bed I laid my head down and my body collapsed...

You know. I have a lot of thanking to do when it comes to the steroids that the doctor put me on for my back... I have been able to do so many heavy lifting things since I started to take them that it is really incredible. I am really amazed that I haven't had my back blowout or something... I guess I should knock on wood now.

Ok, today is packing of my clothes, and tomorrow is my move to NYC, period. I will write more later.

Ok, it was only a line ago for you, but now it has been 7 hours later for me... My dad sat here in my apt./storage area all day with me... I was really nice to spend the last day with him.. I am going to miss him so much. I think that I simply shall not be the same if something happens to him... I just hope that nothing happens to him for some years. I have no idea what he is thinking about any more... I can't imagine. I have tried to put myself in his shoes for weeks now and I just can't imagine being 87 and being on the verge of so many things happening to me all the time.... I am sure that my move to NYC is the least of his worries, at least I hope that my move to NYC is something that he is ok with... He has known for months now that I was moving.

Ok, it is getting very late, and I want to get up and leave at a decent hour if possible... I just keep walking around my little apt looking at all the things I will be leaving behind and I can't help but to think that I will be missing something once I get to New York. I haven't decided as of yet if I am going to take some canvas with me yet or not.. I have a small roll of the stuff that I plan on taking, but I haven't decided if I am going to take a nice piece from my giant roll of the stuff. I guess I won't. I can always buy some more when I get to NYC I suppose. I have no idea what to paint anyway, so, maybe I won't even paint at first... I actually plan on making maquettes of different galleries so as to make giant installations of stuff in them. I will just wait until I get there to see which of my ideas seem the most feasible.

This poem is for cold concrete and sockless feet.

> "Spy are my ankles and I"
>
> I jump and leap and land in my bed
>
> Covers fight me for the bottom
>
> My floor is cold again
>
> And my feet ache like my head
>
> Why can't you sleep asks the mouse
>
> And I answer into his little ear
>
> 'because I don't want to miss'
>
> 'Miss what?' asks the mouse
>
> I smile, and roll over
>
> The mouse in his curiosity now held my fate
>
> A sleepless wonder
>
> I pretended to not feel his tapping paw upon my back
>
> My snores barely rattled
>
> And my smile giving away my position

I toss this letter into the void, the abyss between us, this space that keeps conversation from happening.

Sincerely,
Rush Whitacre
740-336-9169

7-24-11

Dear Taylor Swift,

    I made it! I am finally in NYC and my two new roommates helped me to move my lighter weighted items up to our new apartment… it is going to be awesome. I am really tired and I want to get to bed because I want to go to the Park tomorrow and I want to check out some of the places along the subway along my route to the park and to Blick… that alone will be a full day of events…

    So, let me tell you about my trip up here to New York. It was mostly filled with me driving, and stopping twice to get gas, and changing channels once in a while to find music that was in my reception range. For the most part I kept on finding country stations. I think I have fallen in love with the song barefoot bluejean night. That song has me rolling, well, literally all day today I was rolling in my truck all the way to

NYC… I also listened to remind me a lot. The radio seemed to play those two songs a lot on the way up, and the pop song radio stations seemed to play so many commercials that I kept finding my self changing stations and always landing on a country station where the music just played and played. Oh, and just a kiss by lady antebellum, I think that is how you spell it.. well, anyway, that was my trip, driving and music, and singing like a person who's heart was on fire, and the love for the city pulled me in.

I am soooo excited to be here in this big old city. I also just found out that all of the utilities are included in my rent… which is sooo awesome. I didn't know that I wouldn't have to pay for utilities, and that makes all the difference.

Here is my first impression of Jesse, my newest roommate, so nice! And so cute. Lol

Anyway, after all of my heavy items disappeared from my truck, I was left with my heavy stuff, and the girls just disappeared out of sight… I had no idea where they went. It was funny. I could tell that they were tired of moving my stuff, but they were really grateful because I brought 2 air conditioners,,, and that makes all the difference. I am sure they were sweating a lot without them. Before I came Jesse told me that she was actually freezing wet towels to put in be with her so that she could finally fall asleep, and Laura-girl was sleeping with ice bottles in bed with her. So,, I am glad that I came when I did.

This poem is for pleasure moments

"Pleasure Moments"

Remember that

And tell me girl

That you only want me

That you only meant well

And that when this all comes down

You will be there

Like the support holding up this roof

This shelter

Because if the roof caves in

I don't know if I will know what to do

And you only meant well

So I see through all the darkness

And into the light

In through the rip

The tear, the mistake turned right

And I walk away

I toss this letter into the void, the abyss between us, this space that keeps conversation from happening.

Sincerely,
Rush Whitacre
740-336-9169

7-25-11

Dear Taylor Swift,

    My first full day in New York. I spent in it feels like mostly on the subway. The ride from my apartment in New York to my favorite bridge in New York, which I found out is bridge number 28, the bridge I discovered in 2000 when I first visited, anyway, I found out that it takes about an hour on the subway to get there…. Wow, I was amazed. I can remember all the times I visited New York and I can't figure out how I thought that the subway was so fast… I guess I didn't have to travel all the way from Brooklyn either though. Yeah, the ride from Brooklyn is actually about a half an hour by itself, so, yeah, I can see why I thought the subway was faster, cause I was closer to everything… yep.

    I am going to have a new adventure every day that I am up here in NYC. Every day is will present to me a new adventure, a new challenge, a new door to walk through… and I am excited for I know that I will never be alone up here in NYC… there are way to many people, way too many things to be doing, way to many ideas floating around in my head… but that subway, that is something else. I am considering what I am going to do with my truck while I am here in New York. I would love to keep it up here in New York, but I also don't want it to become a hassle to keep. I could probably sell it right away up here, but then again, do I really want to. There are so many advantages to having it up here, and then there is no reason to have it here for long periods of time. I don't know. Like everything else in my life, I am sure that the solution for this problem will present itself and I will have the answer handed to me. Or not.

    It is too late to call my dad, or my friends. They were worried about me and my driving up here. Oh well. I will call them tomorrow. Plenty of time for conversations. Plenty of time for all of the things that I need to do. At least for right now.

    Ok, this poem is for the motion of a subway,

"Enormous Cradle"

Steel and steal

Aluminum and numb

       And It rocks you baby
       And it rocks you to sleep
       Lulling you into submission
       Now I catch the sandman
       He is stronger in the midst of the tracks
       The uneven, shaky, unstable curve
       And you shall know him by name
       And you shall be claimed by him
       And I shall have it all
       As you sleep inside this hull
       So let the rocking take you over
       Let your mind wander
       And your body will tell you the truth
       And this is where you belong
       Within these arms of steel
       These naked metal wheels
       And this motion
       Oh, this motion and noise
       I miss you

I toss this letter into the void, the abyss between us, this space that keeps conversation from happening.

Sincerely,
Rush Whitacre
740-336-9169

7-26-11
Dear Taylor Swift,
  Day number two in New York. Yeah, this is awesome. Ok. It is setting in how badly I am going to need a job. I just have to find a job. There are so many things I could do, and so many things I want to do, but above all, I have to find a job. I need to find a way to make money, to take my skills and put them to use, to make myself useful.

I guess this coming Wednesday and Thursday I will be making myself useful by moving a gallery. I believe it is called the Viridian gallery. Sounds a bit, green.

Today I had an adventure into the subway and just rode it all over the place. I just love the rocking motion it makes. When I make enough money I am going to by a one month pass so that I can have an entire month to ride without having to worry about running out of time so quickly. I just love being able to get onto a subway and riding anywhere it goes. I consider it like a free ride, but in the end, I know that I have paid for it because I did, and that is all there is to it. I will say this much, if I had to pay each time I got onto a subway I would quickly go broke…. I really used the heck out of the subway today. And I can't wait to use it. The subway is literally like a giant cradle. I see people falling asleep on it all the time. It is great. I wished I trusted people enough to fall asleep on it. That would be awesome. I can see myself getting such a great sleep on a subway way car. Maybe.

It is just as hot up here in NY as it was back home in Ohio. This heat is amazing. I feel sorry for all the women who are here in NYC wearing burka's. I am sure they are really hot. I only say this because I saw two women wearing burka's as I was walking to the subway. They were wearing all black burka's… I can assure you, they had to be hot, sweaty, and uncomfortable. Yet again, I have never worn one, so, I can only imagine what it would be like to wear one…

Ok, tomorrow, I am going to look for a hotdog stand. I thought by now I would have come across one, but they are a little harder to come by than I thought. Oh well. I had a friend that loved the hot dogs in New York. He always told me that the best hot dogs were served by the dirtiest hot dog venders… I remember walking around NY with him while I was in my first year at OU and we happened to catch a hot dog vender spit on the ground. He looked at me and said,, "Oooh yeah, that is the stand to get a hot dog at." I just laughed, and then got a hotdog. It was desliscious.

This poem is for strange foods.

"Just Eat it"

Where did it come from

Where didn't it

And why does it matter

Or does it taste good,

Bad?

And you eat it anyway

Just watch it enter

As you smile

And are unable to keep it inside

Squeezed between your cheeks

Pushed out between your lips

And I laugh

And you spit

And I laugh even harder

Something I have taken for granted

Your spit

My shoes

And the inevitable walk away

I must endure

I toss this letter into the void, the abyss between us, this space that keeps conversation from happening.

Sincerely,
Rush Whitacre
740-336-9169

7-27-11

Dear Taylor Swift,

    Another day in New York,, and I can't believe that I am here. I am going to have so many adventures. Now, I just need to get a job so that I can make enough money to pay for rent and for my bills. I think I need to apply to 1 to 10 places a day, and that should almost guarantee me to have a position somewhere here in the city.. I am going to start to look into security positions around the city, and for a teaching position. There has to be an open teaching position for me here somewhere in the city. I don't really want to teach, but, if I have to I will do it so that I can have some money, and experience.

    I don't know. My thing is this. I want to teach, but I also want to get out here in NYC and do more of the starving artist thing for a little while so that I can get some experience trying to work for galleries and for museums first. I know I could be applying to galleries and things while I am working here as a teacher, but, it would be rather hard to work for a gallery and for a school at the same time since they keep similar hours. I don't know, I guess if I get accepted to teach as a art teacher at some pretty nice school here in NYC then I will count my lucky stars and I will teach. I am just so nervous right now about making money just to survive that I am wondering where I am going to get it from… Oh well. I do have a book I need to finish, called Mabast, I guess I should start working on it again. It is something that I know I could peddle here and there at happenings and other book stores. We shall see… but that is something that is going to take a couple of months to finish, and I don't know why I think it is so important, for it really isn't… well, that might be too harsh upon my own work I guess.

Tomorrow I think I will ride around in the subway and just cruise all over the place. I have this thing I am going to do at least once while I am up here in NYC, and that is I am going to beg for money at least once, at least just once. I want to be able to say that I experienced NYC from the seat on the sidewalk as people walk by looking down upon me and my sign. I am just curious what that feels like. I am not saying that I am going to try it tomorrow or anything, but I am going to do it sometime while I am up here. I am probably going to feel very much ashamed of myself, I shall see.

This poem is for the sad eyes.

"I don't see them crying"
They walk around the streets
Torn clothes and bumps and bruises
And a sign reading anything helps
So many eyes gazing down
And so many swinging bags
Purchases made for the feet, the back
The bodies of those not working
Just gaining, and gaining
And not looking down to see
What they are stepping on
The people of angles caves
Tired, poor, and unable to find a way out
The darkness of a dark place
Not charted
Known by the wrinkles of their hands
The missing light in their eyes
The words they can't say
As they sit begging for a better life
One dollar at a time

I toss this letter into the void, the abyss between us, this space the keeps conversation from happening.

Sincerely,
Rush Whitacre
740-336-9169

7-28-11

Dear Taylor Swift,

    What a day. This was day number two of my adventure of moving a gallery from one street to another. Susan, the president was there again today, and so was Vernitta, I think that is how you spell her name, she is the manager of sorts. We finished the entire gallery with three loads. The two guys who helped, Dave and Bob were very helpful. They were actually pretty funny, really. Instead of filling up the elevator with stuff first, they would grab a handful of stuff and take it down the freight elevator. By the last load I got them trained to fill the elevator first and then take it down to my truck… it was much faster. Susan and Vernitta were very happy that the job was done so quickly. I was too, for I wanted to walk around the artwalk… we didn't get to walk around in the artwalk though, for we had dinner. Or appetizers. I had a thing called a Nacholos from a place called the Half King… they were deliscious. Nachos and all the toppings to make them really tasty.

    Laura-girl forgot all about the fact that we had taken my truck to move the gallery. It was funny to see her face light up when she realized that we were not taking the subway… I was happy today, I found a route from Manhattan to Brooklyn, and from Brooklyn to Manhattan that didn't require me to pay $6.50 one way… On the way back Laura-girl and I took the FDR to the Brooklyn Bridge… It was an awesome experience to drive over the Brooklyn Bridge. I was soo happy. I got to drive over the other bridge that was built before the Brooklyn Bridge as a prototype in Cincinnati. The one in Cincinnati is 3 times smaller than the actual Brooklyn Bridge. I think that anyone who has driven over the bridge in Cincinnati should try their hand at the Brooklyn bridge. The drive just to get onto the bridge was worth it.. I just can't explain it, you just have to get in a car and do it.

    Tomorrow I am going to Blick to apply for a job, and I am going to Kelly's employment agency to see what kind of work they can find for me. I am sure they will find me something that pays pretty good money… the question is though, will I like it, will it give me the connection to the art world that I need… Maybe I will be able to work at both places, both Blick and at some other place that Kelly's finds me. I shall see. I think that Laura-girl is happy for me. She took a look at my Resume and was impressed with my work history. She mentioned that I should apply for a job at the Metropolitan Museum of Art at a security officer. I might just do that. I might just try my hand at Security at a Museum while I am up here in NYC… hilarious.

This poem is for all those Yellow Taxis.

"Hand out fluttering"

And I see her

I drive by, or walk by, so simply stare

And there she is

Hand out flagging

And all I can do is watch

There isn't anyone stopping

There isn't anyone looking to stop

'is it a shift change?'

Are there too many people?

Or have all the cabs decided

that they will only stop for certain types

certain flavors

certain mixes

and certain scents

which I am sure attract them all

my dear

keep that hand fluttering

keep it waving

and by all means keep yelling

soon

you too will be picked up.

I toss this letter into the void, the abyss between us, this space that keeps conversation from happening.

Sincerely,
Rush Whitacre
740-336-9169

7-29-11
Dear Taylor Swift,

Another Friday has come, and I am sitting here watching some movie on Netflix. I can see how my (related person who is male and not named) doesn't get up to do anything anymore, you can become so mesmerized about just getting involved into something so mentally and in your brain that you forget things like applying for jobs and trying to make a living. Gosh, I really need to apply for a job bad, I need to be making money this august to pay for my bills at the apartment… I would love to know how Louis made enough money that he didn't have to work this whole past year while living under the same roof as myself and Yangue. Louis literally didn't have to work at all for about 9 months… and I am still not sure if he has started to work… Oh Louis, I miss you.

I am applying for jobs. Mostly, I am applying for jobs over the internet. I don't know which is better, to go and apply in person, or to just do the whole internet thing. I am sure that in person is better, but then it is also something that apparently isn't happening as much and that businesses are just doing what I would call a raffle on the whole internet… for instance. If they have a thousand emails all with the subject line 'security' I am sure they don't search much past number 20, or maybe even 10, and therefore, I think that I will apply every week to maybe help my odds to be in the top somewhere where they might actually seem my name, my resume, my life's goals….. lol… yeah right, we are talking about the Met Museum.

I wish I would have been able to apply to Blick before moving up here. Truth be told, I wish I would have applied to teaching jobs up here before I moved up here… I guess I wasn't fully committed to the move during the time when I had a class that the assignments were to apply to different college for teaching positions… oops. Oh well, I guess I learned that lesson. Now I have to start to apply to different places and get a move on.

Ok, I am going to get off of here and go to the gallery to help move them the rest of the way.

This poem is for loud noises,

"Big Speakers, Little Voice"

This girl I know

Little as she is

Her voice always carries

Always screams out loud

As her microphone pulls in close

And her lips scrape across it

And my ears fight the deafening cry

Speakers burst

And all it was, is, and ever could be

Lost by the plug

The unplug

And power outage

And her smile caught in a flash

Of a camera

Of a screen

A stolen kiss

And my heart will never be the same

Or different

Or anything in between.

I toss this letter into the void, the abyss between us, this space the keeps conversation from happening.

Sincerely,
Rush Whitacre
740-336-9169

7-30-11

Dear Taylor Swift,

      My second full weekend up here in New York. I can see now that this year is going to fly by... I really need that work. Lol... I also wouldn't mind it if Alan, the man who owns an architect firm, or something like it, and who also does photography would hire me to do some work for him. I would love to do some work for him. I don't know exactly what I would be doing, but I am sure it would be worth it to do just about anything just to get my name started in the circulation of the people who need help like I can give help... We shall see

      I have a feeling that I am going to get a parking ticket , maybe several.. lol, and I can't help it really, I have to remember all of my parking times and the different sides of the street have different days and times as to when you can park there... and on most days those streets are.

      I have been doing a lot of catching up on the Idol show by simply watching the youtube videos. I just love the song Scotty McCreery sings, "I love you this big". It makes me want to write a song, and learn to sing, and learn to make better videos, heck, to even learn to play an instrument, yeah, that would be awesome. I keep mentioning to Laura-girl that we should make a film of somekind, just something a little small, a little fun, and a little bit uploaded to youtube... I think we should make a music video where we lipsink some other bands music.. I mean, it could be awesome.

I wonder what the rest of my life has in store for me. I know that is such an odd question, but, I have just begun. My journey starts here.

This poem is for the Journey,

"And When I See You"

He waits for the call

He works for a dollar bill

And he can't spend it on her

He waits all day for that phone

And the call is his own

But his breath is heavy,

His will strong

And he can't stay long

He works on keeping busy

He works on watching the day pass him by

And she is the day

There is no night as long as his

So many pieces, places, a treasure

A chest for his heart to beat inside

Live inside

Free from the path leading into loneliness

And the sun passes him by

Like the warmth across a face

A mountain, a ledge, a rope to descend

Bare hands

And the night comes, feathers fall

Drifting through the moonlight

Falling like dimes

Chained to the desperation of the angels

And she is his love, his time

Passing him by

I toss this letter into the void, the abyss between us, this space that keeps conversation from happening.

Sincerely,

Rush Whitacre

740-336-9169

7-31-11

Dear Taylor Swift

    Last day of July, and still no job… what I need is to go to the park, and that is what I think I will do. I am trying to get Laura-girl and maybe my other roommate to go there and make art in public. I need to get something started because I need some smaller works ready to show to galleries to try to have a show, to try to have something to sell, to add to my collection of works that no one can buy because it won't fit on their wall. Plus, I really really want to make nothing but paintings and drawings for a while. I am interested in expanding my skills, and my reputation into other venues other than just galleries. I am thinking that showing in restaurants is totally not out of the question. I can say this much, I really don't want to work in a restaurant, I really don't want to work with food… not that I wouldn't be good at it, but I just spent so much money on my education I can't stand the thought of spending my time asking "do you want fry's with that?"

    So. I guess my life must sound kinda boring, same things here lately… luckily, I have Laura-girl up here to keep things exciting… she is good at knowing when it is time to get out of the apartment and get moving to do something else other than sit and make art, or sit and write… That is something I haven't done yet, is work on my book, Mabast. I can almost hear my character Emarilda screaming out to me to finish editing her quest so that she can save her mother… Aaah, I guess I could also start drawing out the various characters and scenes, and maybe even the weapons and flowers, and etc. Yeah, I guess I could do that…

    Right now though I am working on am series of bridges from out of the Central Park. I am going to do a series of 20 of the Bridges and that should be enough to complete the series. I know there are more than double that amount, but, I am not interested in painting all of them, I am just interested in a select number of them… I can't say which, not on here, not enough room. I go tomorrow to take pictures of them, hopefully, unless something else happens, like I get an interview, or I get a last minute job working with the gallery.

This Poem is for my Friends of the Loft,

                      "Secret Society"

              I am aware of my conscious

            And my heart goes out to you

                        My friends

> The secret keepers of my love
> My joy can't be contained
> And my heart may explode
> If I don't get this out to all of you
> I love you, my lofty creators of moments
> Timeless smiles, hugs, and laughter
> Things I will carry with me forever
> I will never forget you, forgive me
> For I did not know that it would all end
> So
> Suddenly
> And inside all of you I know is a love
> A passion, a drive to make yourselves bigger
> To rise above
> To see that in those two years
> We lived like gods
> And like angels
> Sent out of the chaos, freed, wings flapping
> Be loved

I toss this letter into the void, the abyss between us, this space that keeps conversation from happening.

Sincerely,
Rush Whitacre
740-336-9169

8-1-11

Dear Taylor Swift,

Yay, it is Monday again, and I need to go out and make sure my truck is moved from the time of 11:30 to 1 pm…. Yay.. lol.. Actually, what this means, is, hey, wait a minute, let me go and check on it..

No, I don't have to move it because I am parked on the Tuesday side today, and I guess that means I don't have to do anything of the sort today.. wow, this is going to be a good day after all!

Anyway, today is another day for me to find more jobs and try to find myself a place to make money…. I am waiting on the Gallery to make up its mind as to whether I am the one to be making the shelves, or what the deal is.. last time I checked I thought that the idea was for me to build the shelves, but then again, what do I know. Laura-girl has been off work from the Gallery since it has moved locations because the room is still being worked on and it needs a lot of work. All of the walls need to be finished, and then I can start working on the shelves and racks, and is assuming that they want me to be the one working on them.. I hope so. Acutally, I just hope that they pay me for the moving, I haven't heard anything about it yet.

Laura-girl and I have been spending time on the porch just having a drink and talking and watching the neighbors across the street. I think we are pretty sure that they are either a whole bunch of kids whose parents are paying for them to live together, or they are drug dealers with not much cover… Because there are a lot of Chinese Kids, probably in their early 20's just hanging out over there all the time. I guess I would think these things except that they are always seaming to have cars stop our front of their place and a transaction always takes place, and quickly, then the car drives away. Then there is all the smoking that goes on after a transaction… so, yeah, I guess you could say that Laura-girl and I have been doing a bit of front porch staring, snooping I guess. But, it is not like we have to even try to see these things, they are right there in front of us.. lol

This poem is for Laura-girl,

"In my mind, you are famous"

I know you seek nothing of fame

And nothing of fame you want

But I can't help but watch you

From my chair

From my computer screen

Your eyes are the pens of your desire

And your paper a magical place

There are rabbits, and stars

And above all, there is love

And you are always welcome there

Always welcome to stare

Nobody cares

So, my dear dear friend

> Take this break from me
>
> Steal away my minutes
>
> And toss away myself doubt
>
> As I am taller than you, I still look up
>
> So keep leading the way
>
> And I shall follow you
>
> Where ever you may go
>
> Please
>
> Let me follow.

I toss this letter into the void, the abyss between us, this space that keeps conversation from happening.

Sincerely,
Rush Whitacre
740-336-9169

8-2-11

Dear Taylor Swift,

  Just another Tuesday, and I need to find myself something to do besides watching Netflix and looking for a job. Both of these things are breaking me down a bit… only because I have gotten addicted to Pawn Stars… Those guys are fun and easy to watch. They are in the business to make money, and they usually get their asking price for things that people bring in.. I am sure it doesn't hurt that the whole thing is being video-taped. If I go out to Vegas, I am sure to stop in and check their place out… I am sure it has gain a lot of attention since starting their show. Probably enough that they have had to hire a lot of people in just to watch the place and keep is safe. I am also glad that it is a 24 hour business. I don't know when I would visit, during the day, or during the night. I am sure it is busy at either time.

  Laura-girl is doing something that I think is a good idea, a thing she calls art for the people. She sells paintings for 20 bucks and you pick a theme, but if you pick anything beyond that it is considered a commissioned piece. And, I think I could make a painting for 20 dollars and make killing. Maybe. I tend to lean in the direction of putting 50 to 100 dollars worth of paint on everything. I could try it I guess.

  I wish there were more sites to look for jobs than NYFA. Well, I am sure there are, but I have not found any as helpful as NYFA. I am going to have to walk around and apply to different gallery's in person, maybe that will help.

I just want a job, just someone to work for, just enough money coming in so that I won't have to worry about food and shelter. That is not too much to ask for.

This poem is for not asking for too much,

"Hold my Hand"

Dear Dad

I have spent all my life

Looking up to you

Wanting to make you proud

And I try hard

But I can't seem to reach out for help

For those times that I need you the most

And now I am here

Standing by your side

Looking at you like I never have before

I smell the flowers

And run my hand across the wood

And my cheeks can't take another tear

And in this moment

I don't want the world to see me

I can't hold back my tears

And I know this moment won't last

But for now

It is all I have

So I will stand here

Holding your hand

And saying I love you

And saying I'll live a good life

Because you loved me

I toss this letter into the void, the abyss between us, this space that keeps conversation from happening.

Sincerely,

Rush Whitacre
740-336-9169

8-3-11

Dear Taylor Swift,

 Ok, so, I just woke up and I had another dream that involved you. Now, I can accept the fact that I had this dream about you, after all, I am writing to your fan-based mail sight everyday. Still, I want to tell you about this dream before I forget all of the strangeness about it.

 Dream: the setting is in a slightly stadium seated style theater. Not a movie theater, but a playhouse theater. Most of everyone sitting in the front two rows, 2 to 3 rows max are my friends, and there aren't that many other people in the theater, maybe a straggler or two or three, but not much. This theater to me is oddly shaped because the isle is about 2/3's of the way over from the left, and so isn't the exit/entrance to the place. This definitely is a theatre house, but apparently there isn't a show, so, now that I think about it I am slightly confused, because I can only surmise that the theatre is actually auditioning for actors for something, but that isn't happening either… the stage has an old worn looking floor, not that I really looked at it well or anything, just that I could tell out of my peripheral vision. Anway, about halfway back in the theater on the right hand side is your mother, yes, your mother. I only know what she looks like because of the world revealing to me what she looks like, I didn't search her out, lol. Anyway, she never looks up, but I know it is her, and I pass in front of the stage looking at all of my friends and I walk up the isle to where your mother is sitting. Here I sit in the seat diagonally in front of her. Then, in a moment you come up and sit in front of me diagonally to my left. Then, you Taylor proceed to take things out of your purse and hand them to me. I look at them and sit quietly while you giggle at my quandary as to why you have handed me such weird things, like glasses, and other random things that I cannot remember at this moment, but you did pass me back about a dozen things before I put it all back into your purse that you had at this point handed back as well. Then, I sat looking at the stage, it had lights on it, and from behind me your mother asked, "So, you like that twitter(or it was a word that sounded a lot like twitter anyway) do you?". For some reason I had this huge guilty feeling come over me, like I had just been caught picking my nose or something, and I responded with, "Yes, yes I do." And then I woke. Apparently, I was the butt of the joke… lol

This poem is for Rhyming,

"Why Should I?"

Of all the words

That I can think of

There are none so crazy

None so absurd

As those I must conjure up

And make up just for you

To appease this line

Sometimes two

And they are always mirrors

Life long fellows

Skipping rocks from different shores

Dropping to the ocean floor

Like my breath

Slow and patient

To the fault of a breaker

Broken bowed and bent

Caught up in my thoughts

Caught up in your imagination

And all my fights I've fought

Nothing as hard as in your creation

This seduction

Only in the mind, the edge of and angels wing

A fantasy for the neurons

Awake dear king

I toss this letter into the void, the abyss between us, this space that keeps conversation from happening.

Sincerely,
Rush Whitacre
740-336-9169

8-4-11

Dear Taylor Swift,

    Today was a very lazy day, I slept in until noon. And then I got up and started to look for a job again on the internet. I am also looking at videos of the most recent Idol winner, mostly because I really like this song, "I love you this big". I wonder if he wrote it, or if it was collaborated, or if someone else completely different wrote it all on their own. I may never know. I just figure it is one of those idol things.

    Ok, Laura-girl has been asking me, and asking me, and asking me to go to this free concert tonight, the band she want to see is Man Man. I have no idea who they are, but I am going to go, what the hell right, it is a free concert. Ok, I will be back later, probably much later.

…

    WOW, what a loud and fun concert. I mean, except for the fact that I couldn't understand any of the words that the music groups were saying, it was a great night. Everything was free, except the food, but it was a pretty good just the same. While I was waiting outside of the show I saw a familiar face, it was one of my students from Cincinnati, his name is BigMax. I think he was really surprised to see me there, he probably never in his craziest dreams thought he would see me there I guess. Oh well, the feeling is mutual. Anyway. During the show I watched as BigMax stood at the front of the show and as he got pummeled by crowd surfers as the crashed into his back. BigMax never helped to hold the people up, so they ended up getting shoved into his head, or back, or shoulders, and in his typical shyness he just stood there with the weight of a person on his head. It was rather comical from where I was sitting. Meanwhile, Laura-girl was working her way deep into the heart of all the mosh pit where people were being shoved and lifted, and shaken, and rolled around and around like dolls. I stepped out of the mess once I saw that the bigger guys were the ones being used as the objects for being shoved into other people. It was nice to finally get outside where I could get some fresh air.

    Ok, it is not 2:32 am, and I am really tired. Night.

This poem is for the night train riders,

"Blank stares across the board"

It is late

Very late

And all the long faces

They stare into the corridor

The weaving, rocking

And motion of a roller coaster ride

The long half empty train

All but leaving us asleep

All but like minded individuals

Just wanting to get home

And not off of a one way train

> Heading in the wrong way
>
> In the first place
>
> And we not aware
>
> In the second.

I toss this letter into the void, the abyss between us, this space that keeps conversation from happening.

Sincerely,
Rush Whitacre
740-336-9169

8-5-11

Dear Taylor Swift,

    Today I searched and searched for a job. I just kept on finding sites that wanted me to pay for the right to have them send me updates on jobs that come up for an offer to work… I am sure that maybe some of these sites are legit, but I just don't want to take the risk. I can't imagine paying for a site to do nothing when I am expecting so much to happen. I did see some nice jobs available online though. Like, working as the right hand person to a president of a gallery. Which I am sure is a pretty important position, but if I can't read about it, or apply for free and you are just going to dangle it in front of me like a carrot, then I am not going to spend money on your site.. besides, if it sounds too good to be true, I am sure it is, and I don't need some site to waste my time and for me to waste my money.

    After my exhausting search from galleries I spent about 2 hours fixing up my website with all of my artworks on it. I didn't change much, just how things were linked or not linked. I think that things flow better now. For some reason, when I built the site I forgot to link alike images together to make it easier to surf from one pic to the next. After tonight it is much easier. I will have to surf my own site tomorrow to see that everything is in working order. The site is acting all jenky. I didn't touch anything about the paintings or anything about them and they wouldn't come up at all when I clicked on their link, so, I am rather stumped. I spent about an hour trying to figure out the reason why. I erased the linkage and re-linked it and it still gave me an error page when I tried to click on the link… strange. I think that anything electronic has it out for me.

    Ok, so, today I tried calling a friend of mine who just will not answer any of my phone calls, and hasn't for at least 2 years. I called him using the *67 so that he wouldn't know it was from me. He answered, and then when he found out it was from me he said, "I don't want to talk to you." This hurt my feelings very much. But then again, I did make a mistake one night. One night he wouldn't come and hang out with myself and about 6 other friends, instead he went to a party where there was a certain girl he wanted to be with, meanwhile his wife is at home… and while I was out with my friends his name was brought up and I decided to call him and make fun of him in a fun-loving way for deciding to be at the party with the girl instead of with me… well, I guess I didn't think it through, because for some reason I saved his phone number under just his last name, and then his wifes number under his first and last name… are you getting the picture. So when I called and left my ornery message, lovingly harassing him about not spending time with me and instead of with the girl, I accidently left it on his wife's phone's answering service… even though this friend and I talked a couple of times since this disaster, I think that he probably had a therapist tell him to not talk to me… Oh well. My silly open mouth, his stupid ego.

I dedicate this poem to my lost friend

"Lonely Graphic Designer"

Your heart is as large as the prick of cupid's poisoned tipped arrow is deadly

Not as large as your ego, not as small as your id

And your sensitivity has betrayed you, and your brain

For I miss you, and I miss your voice, but I will not take back what I said

For I was right, and you need to accept that

You need to heal and not hide behind screen prints

And graphic designs, and stories that are not real, but flat

Raise up your johny bow, your chin, that laugh, that curiosity

And break away, chip away, flake away the black matte wall you designed

You screen printed between us, you've created this void

This empty path from there to here, from your barn to my city

And I still say that I will not take back my words, there is no Control Z

No Apple Z, just a forever flying arrow, tipped by the fancy of a blonde goddess

Poisoning your sense of husbandry, your sense of friendship

Your sense's are to over-thought, over-dramatic, over-zealous

And I cannot be here to hold your hand anymore, or anyless

Depending on which liars candle you have been blowing out lately,

Leaving yourself in the dark.

I toss this letter into the void, the abyss between us, this space that keeps conversation from happening.

Sincerely,

Rush Whitacre

740-336-9169

8-6-11

Dear Taylor Swift,

    A long day applying for jobs. Long long day. Let me tell you, about finally getting to talk to my friend Gari. I have been trying to get ahold of him for weeks and weeks and weeks and I have been so worried about him... I don't know why he has decided to call me tonight. I told me that he was, and has been having a really rough time lately, and he has been feeling like he is living in regret, and that he doesn't deserve friends like me.. I was so upset, because I knew that he was going through a rough time, and that he really needed a friend, and that I am that friend. Lets just say, I am really glad he finally called me... Love you like a bro Gari, miss you.

    So, this morning's conversation's with my roommates on this fine Saturday consisted of one of them started talking about how they wanted to have a 'C' section instead of natural birth and I got drug into this conversation because of my past and because my parents both being doctors. So, it was a rather interesting and fun conversation. I am surprised actually that 24 and 25 year old girls haven't done more research into what goes on with their bodies and what can happen, and what the risks are etc.. I love a good conversation about these types of things.

    Tonight, Jesse and I and her friend Rachael all got together and we were going to go to the Brooklyn Museum and see what was going on because I guess they have a lot of free things on the first Saturday of every month. We got there and there were hundreds and hundreds of people everywhere outside of the Museum.. we had just missed the chance to go inside to where the dance party was taking place, so, we all went to a park to see 'echo' a 44 foot tall sculpture of a face the is all white and really really creepy during the night. It really was something pretty spectacular to behold really. I enjoyed it. Then we went to a bar where I felt really out of place. The two girls just kept on talking and talking and I had nothing to talk to them about.. then the owner of the place came over to talk to us.. It was a bar inside of a really nice Italian resturante... If I ever find a girl to take on a date, know I will take her to this place, just a great atmosphere, and wonderful wonderful service. The place was called Stuzzi's. a definite must for anyone wanting true Italian cuisine.

    After that we said our good byes to Rachael, and then Jesse and I went to times square and just walked around, we each had some vendor food, and then some honey roasted nuts. This has truly been a really great New York memory making day. I can see a lot of things happening for the good.. I just need to get some business cards made, and find a decent job to make some money working at..

This poem is for is for the Street Solicitors,

"A Bargain, A Lie"

Hey you

Come here, don't you want this

Check out all of my shiny insides

My parts that make me,

Me

And hold me in your arms

You will see, I am beautiful

Come to my show, see me perform

Watch me talk, scream, yell, sing

Words I say, words I know, about you

About this little town, this new city

And all I can do is watch the time fly by me

And it flies

Feel my chest, my heart beating like a drum

Like a motor fueled by my love

And, now I see it, you're the one

Who's made me beautiful

Watch me dance

This little one-two

Is for you

I toss this letter into the void, the abyss between us, this space that keeps conversation from happening.

Sincerely,
Rush Whitacre
740-336-9169

8-7-11

Dear Taylor Swift,

    Sundays are weird days for me up here in NYC. I don't seem to get anything done, nothing. I keep wondering what I will do when I run out of Pawn Stars episodes to watch. My friend Rod has invited me out to Las Vegas to see him. I can tell you this much, if I go all the way out there I am going to go to the pawn shop and see all of the pawn stars. I just love them to death. Ok, enough about them.

About Rod. Rod is the man who is my good friend, who I discovered at OU. He came into the 3 dimentional studies room kinda awkwardly and late. And when he sat down beside me I knew that he was going to be a good friend of mine. Just the way he would listen to me talk and how he would make me laugh, I just knew that he was meant to be my friend. I guess I wasn't fully sure that he was going to be my friend until I built an installation art piece using a hose, a stiff piece of wire, and used a urinal that I propped up on a stand. I remember rod helping me to set up my piece and as I placed the pieces in the correct places it appeared to rod that what I was doing was hilarious. I had made the hose into a stick-like-figure of myself to my height and positioned it as if it were vomiting into a urinal. What was actually coming out of the hose where the mouth was located was a stethoscope, which represented my giving up on the idea of becoming a doctor, and a paint brush in a different place pointing up and representing the idea of how excited I was to make the choice of becoming an artist… As soon as the figure became clear to Rod he erupted into such a panic of laughter that the entire class just stared at him. Rod laughed to the point of distraction, and I just love him to death.

Some day, if I have enough money…. I told Rod if I make enough money some day I will hire him to be my body guard when I go out, and when we are in he will be surrounded by beautiful women, and I will pay him to do nothing but play the guitar for me. I remember all the songs he made up about myself and my other friends. Rod became an icon onto himself. So, that is my story about my friend Rod… I hope to see you soon in Vegas…

This poem is for Rod

"Better off in Ohio University"

Rod, had a girlfriend

Her name was Denise

Too bad he was a little boy

And never got down on his knees

To show her the love

And give her what he had

Well now he's in Ohio University

With his heart in her hands

Now, back to the loft

Where everything just made sense

And all those lonesome nights

Turned into parties

      Exclamation points and ampersands
        She held him close
      And took from him all he had
       His heart, his love, and soul
         All three
     And still, he's better off at Ohio University
        With his friends
      Who've never stopped believing
      Who never judged your jumping flare
       We'll always be there

I toss this letter into the void, the abyss between us, this space the keeps conversation from happening.

Sincerely,
Rush Whitacre
740-336-9169

8-8-11

Dear Taylor Swift,

  I was woke up by Laura-girl today. She reminded me that I needed to move my truck. We have a no parking rule on Mondays and Tuesdays on our street from 11:30 AM to 1 PM every week and I have to do the Truck shuffle so that I do not ticketed or towed. All in the name of cleaner streets. So, while I was sitting in my truck waiting for the streets to be cleaned I watched as Laura-girl passed by me on her way to work and we said hello and goodbye, and have a good day… then in about 25 minutes she came running up to my truck from the subway, it wasn't running… Which was good for me, because I needed something to do while I was waiting in my truck, and driving Laura-girl to her work seemed like a mighty nice thing to do.

  As soon as I got back, Alan, the architect who is a part of Viridian Galleries called me and wanted me to come down to the gallery this afternoon to check in on how the shelves in the Gallery are going to be built. I guess he heard about my idea for building a loft in the storage area because their space is limited and adding another level just for storage to me sounds like a great idea. Well, I guess Laura-girl leaked the idea to Vernita, and then Vernita suggested we go with My idea… Wow, I am impressed that such a small suggestion could go such a long way. See, I don't really have a job job, more like a job of odd-jobs where I have no given hours, I just get a phone call and get offered work… Maybe this is my way into the art world?? I don't know, but getting a phone call from an architect to come in to spec out my ideas for shelves in a gallery might be a very very very small step in the right direction. Very small step indeed. Or not, who knows.

      Well, I am back, and the visit to the gallery was a complete, almost complete waste of time, definitely a waste of gas, I wish I would have known about 30 min earlier that I would be going to the gallery, that way I could have taken the subway instead, it is nice to just sit and let it take me. Oh well. It would have been a waste, except that I got a visual map of the gallery, a ¼ scale map. So, I know what is going where, but I am being left to build the shelves myself… and that means,,, these shelves are either going to be great, or they are going to suck. I think they will suck if I am limited on the money I need to spend on them to make them……

This poem is for the loose grip

"I envy nothing"

You smile at me and I know you love me

You have given me so much

And for so long I thought

And then I realized just how short we lasted

How everything we worked for

Just simply disappeared over a long weekend

A short break

A night after night removal of my heart

Your soul

And there is no going back

To many dumpsters have hauled us

Taken us away from each other

Different directions

Now in different places

And I will remember the loft

The laughter, the yelling, the fun

But I'm afraid I will forget you

Because you are gone

For good

I toss this letter into the void, the abyss between us, this space the keeps conversation from happening.

Sincerely,
Rush Whitacre
740-336-9169

8-9-11

Dear Taylor Swift,

  Ok, this morning I was awoken by a phone call from a number I have no idea who it was… the number was a phone number here in NY, but it wasn't one I have saved in my cell phone, and they didn't have anything to say to me, so, it was just a wakeup call I guess. Then, I was woken up by the landlord who then brought in some man who was looking at the place to see that it was being fixed, and made legal, and then Laura-girl finally woke me up to ask me if I had moved my car today…. I had moved it yesterday to a Tuesday side of the street because it was the only side available to me after driving home after meeting up with Alan. Uggg, luckily I didn't get a ticket… right after I moved my truck I double parked it on a different street for a few moments and then I drove it back to our block and parked it at 1 pm.. this moving my truck thing is getting old… I really need to find a way, or a place where I can park my truck and not have to move it for awhile.. I really just want to park it somewhere and just walk away from it and not have to worry about it needing to be moved. Yeah, like I am going to find that luxury. Actually, if I do move my truck, I am not going to have a way to move my table saw from one place to another.. another thing about my truck.. there are so few gas stations around here, I am wondering why… the supply of cars isn't any less.

  So, I spent all day looking for a job, and working on writing, and watching pawn stars. And cooking food. I don't have much money, and I need to watch what I am doing. I need to watch where I spend my money, because I can get so much more food from the market than I can from a restaurant, or from a street vendor. I hate to say it, but the food from the street vendors is delicious. Well, some of them anyway, like the vendors who have lamb kabobs.

  Tomorrow, I have to really do something different. I have been stuck in a routine and I need to break out of it. I think I really should go to the park to spend the day photographing the different bridges like I have been thinking about doing. I just hope the weather cooperates. I will check that after I get done with writing this next poem. Cross your fingers.

This poem is for the Mashup of things,

"Everybody"

Words

Pasted together

Like photo's in a family photo album

They just make sense

And they just feel right

So I will say them

And you'll hear my pause

My hesitation

And all the weight that follows with it

Will make quite an impression

An imprint

A wrinkle

Like the one in my smile

Like the one in your laugh

Tattooed in my memory

With a gun shooting blanks

Blanketing over me

Visceral chill

I toss this letter into the void, the abyss between us, this space that keeps conversation from happening.

Sincerely,
Rush Whitacre
740-336-9169

8-10-11

Dear Taylor Swift,

    So, I didn't get out of bed until 2 pm… NYC has gotten my sleep pattern all screwed up, just like right now I am writing you this letter and it is 3:30 AM and I am suppose to be at a gallery tomorrow around noon to start planning out the shelves that I am to build for them… Aaah… I blame it on my friend Laura-girl's Coffee.. I started to drink her blend of coffee and it really has quite a punch. I will have to stop drinking it so that I can sleep and get goods nights rest…

    Today I spent watching that's three episodes of Pawn Stars, and now that I have finished up through season three I will have no urge to put the show on Netflix and not get other works done like the painting I have started. I will also have more time to find a job, or just go for a stroll around the park, or times square, or just about at any subway stop there is… I just love riding the subway.

    Laura-girl has been particularly busy writing and drawing up her comic's about her life, and for her caveman commission that she has been asked to make. I am so happy for her. I hope that someone asks me to make them some art for them soon. Laura-girl and I have been talking about becoming professional artists who only make art instead of having low paying crappy jobs and then on the side try to make art and try to promote ourselves. I can say this much. If I ever became famous somehow, or if I came into money and lots of it I am sure that I would make sure my friends were standing right there beside me because I don't want to spend the rest of my life being famous, or being rich and having all of my friends there on the sidelines watching it all go down. I want my friends there, right beside me all the way… lol, not that I will ever be famous, or rich, or have the money to take care of all my friends. That just simply won't happen. But, it is fun to talk to Laura-girl about these kinds of things.

This poem is for the rest of my life,

"For the Rest of my Life"

For the rest of my life

I can't think of any other way to spend it

Than to dance

When the music is playing

Than to laugh

When the jokes are done and told

And when the door is there

Open it

And I will take my time

Loving all of my friends

Like they were family

Yeah, that is how I want to spend the rest of my life

My life

Will never be complete

With an empty feeling inside

Or with a wrong or unjust word still lingering

So I will tell you right now my friends

I will be right by your side

Whenever you need me

And whenever you need a hug, or love

<pre>
              You can count on me
               I'll be right there
             To be your helping hand
       To be your words when you need encouragement
          Yeah, that's how I want to spend my life
              In the presence of great friends.
</pre>

I toss this letter into the void, the abyss between us, this space the keeps conversation from happening.

Sincerely,

Rush Whitacre

740-336-9169

8-11-11

Dear Taylor Swift,

    Today was awesome. I went to the new Viridian gallery today to help out and the decided that they need more shelves built than they originally planned… and I am psyched about it… I think that I am going to be ok. I just need to make really good shelves and start to make some nice, really nice smaller works to display in bars and restaurants.. I don't really want to show in galleries because it costs so much money to just be a member, and I think that I will actually get more people to see my work if I show in a restaurant or bar than I would if I showed in a gallery… Yeah, I know there is the whole exposure thing by showing in a gallery and being represented. Then again, who is representing who if you are having to pay an arm and a leg to be represented… are you representing the gallery, or is the gallery representing you… I am shrugging my shoulders at this point. After we organized the gallery a little we all went to a bar and had some specialty drinks.. Alan, the awesome architect paid the first round, then Vernita did the second round, and then Alan did the third round…. And the fourth round was to be on Laura-girl and I but the bar tender was so awesome.. She didn't charge us for anything… Instead we got the fourth round for free… I had bloody Mary's extra hot, and Laura-girl had Whisky-Coke's. We had a blast tonight.

    While we were waiting for our drinks to be made I got to show off some of my work to the bar tender and she was amazed at my work.. she then approached the owner of the bar and told him that I was looking to maybe show my work in his establishment.. He came up to me, gave me his card and everything… I felt rather special, even if only in a little way.. I mean, I have no problem showing of my work in a bar because I don't have to pay oodles of money for a show, and if I sell my work I am sure the bar will not take 40 to 50 percent of my money. And, the Bar is located right in the heart of Chelsea, it is called Velour at the corner of W27th street. Well, maybe not the heart, but where is the heart anyway, it is close enough.

Ok, I have to go to bed early tonight because I have to be hard at work tomorrow at the gallery building shelves and making some money… But first, I have to find out where the nearest Home Depot is to the Gallery, cause I have to carry the lumber to their… that is going to suck. One board at a time, one board at a time… Oh well, I need the exercise right. Right.

This poem is for collaboration,

How About this

Ok

How about that

And if we tweak that a little

And change this color

And add a tassel

And stop to arm wrestle

Just to be sure the right is right

And the wrong is wrong

And all the in-between is tween

Then I am sure this plan,

A quest of most certain certainty

Less observed by the most seen

And least objective

Many will watch

None will understand

But all will cheer

And this is hope, fear, pleasure, and pain

Wrapped into a ball of wriggling tight-nit pencils

All drawing the same circle

Sharpening the same tip

I toss this letter into the void, the abyss between us, this space that keeps conversation from happening.

Sincerely

Rush Whitacre
740-336-9169

8-12-11

Dear Taylor Swift,

    I just wanted to give you an update on the shelves for the back wall that we discussed yesterday.. I have traveled all over the place today, and I mean all over. First I walked from the Gallery to the Home Depot on 23rd street and they didn't have anything we could use for making the shelves, they don't have a lumber yard and all the shelf making L shaped metal brackets were sold out except the great big ones. I bet that walk was close to a mile, maybe a mile and a half. Which isn't really that far, but it would have been if I had actually bought everything I needed and had to carry it back. So, I went back home, got my truck and drove to the nearest Home Depot that had a lumber yard (indoors), and I got all the supplies except a gallon of extra white flat paint by Benjamin Moore because they don't sell it. I will pick up the paint tomorrow from a Benjamin Moore store tomorrow. The Next small Dilemma I ran into was that the Home depot would not cut anything any smaller than 12 inches in width... So, I had to once again drive back to my Apartment to get my Table saw. This whole ordeal was actually a lot more stressful than I actually thought it would be... Finally I got to the Gallery, unloaded everything, and got it up into the space. I got all set up and then realized that two of the attachments were not with the table saw and which are absolutely necessary for the running of the saw. I just stared at the saw, and then looked around to see if there was anything I could use to make straight cuts with the saw. Not a chance. So, I drove back to my apartment once more and just got here 20 minutes ago. This has been a long day, and I have decided that I will not drive back to the Gallery tonight, instead I will just get up early and head there early in the morning to start on the cutting of the MDF for the shelves. And, that concludes my day's adventures. Oh, and my favorite part, the half of an hour where I sat down and ate Chinese food, right before I realized that my table saw was useless without the attachments that were sitting in my bedroom leaning against the wall... I felt like such a moron, and then I laughed and laughed because of how the day had been going up to this point.

    I can't tell what my roommate Jesse is thinking half of the time. I never get to spend much time with her and I wish that was different. But oh well, I guess I am more afraid that she will decide to move out and that would suck because I don't want to have to worry about paying half of the rent verses a third. I have to tell you though, paying only 450 a month for an apartment that is as nice as this one,,, like, this will never happen again. I am so lucky.

This poem is for Rod,

"My Own Personal Superman"

Sleeping just outside

His snore is light and sober

My eyes glint as I feel safe

And I know I will survive,

Anything

His laugh is the remedy to any miscommunication

And my palace is the tops

And he can fly there

My couch is never empty

His apartment is always naked

And his roommate is lost, a lost soul

As he is flying around my world

Saving all of my friends

All but the lonely graphic designer

For he is behind a wall of kryptonite

And my night, is as dark as my day

As I know my personal superman

Cannot save him

Nevertheless, he can see him

And he tells me that he is safe

And happy

And my superman

Has not let me down again

I toss this letter into the void, the abyss between us, this space that keeps conversation from happening.

Sincerely

Rush Whitacre

740-336-9169

8-13-11

Dear Taylor Swift,

    I didn't sleep at all last night. I was up all night tossing and turning and I just couldn't just fall asleep… I don't know what was wrong with me. I didn't feel hungry, and I didn't have to pee, and those are two things that definitely would keep me awake I am sure..

    On a different note, I got up early and went to the gallery with Laura-girl to work on getting it ready to open… there is a lot to do. I wanted to get up around 8 or 9, but that just wasn't happening today… I got up around 10 to half past and I just got about an hour of sleep between 8 and when I finally got out of bed. I wanted to get to the gallery early because I didn't want to cut the wood in front of the director… I don't know, something about cutting and making a giant mess in front of the person who pays me makes me worry a little.. but, I got it all done, and got half of it cleaned up right before she got there…. I was really surprised when she came in. surprised enough that I had to think about what I was doing during the minute or two she was standing in the gallery. Lol. Just singing and sweeping.

    All in all, I got all the shelves cut, glued and nailed, and I also got a set of shelves set up and in place, and I cleaned out the storage room… that was a full day. A good six hour day.

Tomorrow I have to paint the shelves and the metal brackets that hold them up on the wall. I think that I should be able to hide them better, but, aaah, I don't know.. I will see. First thing tomorrow though, I am going to the park to make some art.. Jesse and I are going to go and make some drawings and maybe take come pictures. I don't really have any wild plans for what I am going to do, I just want to go to the park and just make some art. I think I am going to go and start by taking pics of the bridges like I have been planning on doing. Then, after parking is free by the gallery I will drive there and paint the shelves and the brackets.. that is exciting. Ok, I haven't slept now for at least 36 hours. Time to sleep.

This poem is for Dave/Scott

"Not My Fault Man"

So, for a whole year

Not a minute, not a conversation

But for a whole year you let me call you Dave

You answered me

You talked to me over and over and laughed

And you even came up to my treehouse

Carved your name in it and joined

And still I called you Dave

And then one night

Our friend in an angered spite

Corrected me and called me names

And I forever

Shall know you as Dave/Scott

The man with two names

The man of men who climbed with me

To a summit of peace

A platform of knowledge

And where we shared that drink

Where we made our pact

And where we shall forever be kings

Amongst queens, amongst friends

My dear Dave/Scott

I toss this letter into the void, the abyss between us, this space that keeps conversation from happening.

Sincerely,
Rush Whitacre
740-336-9169

8-14-11

Dear Taylor Swift,

  Today was a great day… I spent the morning painting one of the bridges in the park, and right after painting in the skyline I hopped onto a subway and headed down to the gallery to paint the shelves… and I just got home here around 10:45.. and as I was walking into my apartment the landlord asked me if I wanted to make 15 dollars an hour for awhile putting up drywall… and I thought about it for a minute.. Yeah, I told him… besides the fact that I could work when I needed, I am pretty happy with 15 dollars an hour. I told him about my back and how I couldn't take too much heavy lifting. I don't know, graduating with my MFA degree and I will be using it to put up drywall…, I don't think so, at least not forever.. maybe for a couple of weeks… at least until September so that I can afford to pay for my rent.

  What I am hoping is that someone drops out of their spot for a show so that I can swoop in and take their spot and have a show and make some money off of it… I would love to have a show in a gallery here in NY… that would be awesome. What I need, is to get found…

  Anyway. My roommate Laura-girl just came in here. She always seems to know when to come in when I am laying here in my boxers and nothing else.. lol.. she and I are like (related person who is male and not named) and sister, so, it isn't weird. But anyway, after about 20 minutes of crying, and talking I think she is going to be ok.. Her first love has cancer, he is dying, and I would do anything to take it away, but, I just can't, I am only her friend, not a god… But, I am a damn good friend, even if I must say so myself… lol… either way, I went down to the store to get her some beer. Laura-girl made me a deal that she would make me a painting if I would go down to get her some beer. Lol, totally worth the walk. To get an original painting by Laura-girl for a simple walk down to get her some beer… totally worth it.. lol.. this is my favorite part of the day, the promise of a painting.

This poem is for my (related person who is not named),

    "My (related person who is not named)'s Warm Arms"

     When she broke my heart

     You were so close to me

     Catching all of my tears

And understanding my broken heart

The loss of my first love

As she tore me apart

You mended me

And I think often of it

That night I just cried

And you understood

Why

I don't know, but it means a lot to me

And when I think about our best of times

That is at the top of my memories

That is at the top of my list of unconditional

Unconditional love, respect, caring, simple dignity

And you are my (related person who is not named)

Someone I will always look up to

Always love

Always always want to know about me

Always be close

And I love you mom

And I miss you

I toss this letter into the void, the abyss between us, this space that keeps conversation from happening.

Sincerely,
Rush Whitacre
740-336-9169

8-15-11

Dear Taylor Swift,

    Soooooooo early! That is what was going through my brain as I went down stairs to get ready for a hard laborious day of putting drywall up onto a ceiling at one of the houses that my landlord owns.. He must have a lot of money. I Haven't known anyone to have so many houses with so few tenants. I mean, these aren't the greatest places on earth to live, but they are in nice neighborhoods, and there is a lot of work being done to them. Oh, my back hurts…

    Tonight we are going out to celebrate Jesses Birthday by going to Nancy's to have cheese burgers and play some shuffle board… This should be a nice little retreat from today's labor. I just found out that 'Lady' is not the person who is to give me a reference… Interesting,, I know, that was totally out of place, but I just checked my email and saw that… huh…

    Ok, I have been watching some older videos, right now, Young MC's Bust a move is grooving across the speakers of my laptop... This song is just too good, I just posted it on a friend's facebook page, I hope she likes it.

    ….Ok, we just got back from Nancy's pub where we celebrated Jesse's birthday party. It is now nearly 3:30 am and I am totally so tired. I bet the three of use drank and ate 300 dollars worth of food and drinks..and because it was Jesse's birthday they only charged us 100 dollars,,, I was so stoked. I paid for Jesse's everything.. I can't let a friend, or someone close to me spend their birthday paying their entire way.   That kind of things seems like a given. If it is your birthday, someone should care enough to want to take you out and show you a good time, especially since they claim that they are a good friend.   Either way, Happy Birthday Jesse, it was a blast!! Not to mention, everyone did so well on shuffle board, I was proud of everyone. Lol

This poem is for those highlights,

"So frivolous, so expensive, so worth it"

In the midst of a crisis

That color shines through

It is deep within your being

Stuck on you like carbon to your DNA strands

Not like the color you have spread

On your head

To hide the color you seem to hate so dearly

And I am sure those blonde curls

Are as beautiful, if not more so

Than the fake brown ones you have

And I am washing

Washing with my eyes, my memory

Of a time when I remember blonde curls

Between my fingers

Under my nose

The smell of, the scent of, and touch of,

Beautiful, natural, elegant hair

Something I hold dear and close

Not in reality

But in the memory

Of you

I toss this letter into the void, the abyss between us, this space that keeps conversation from happening.

Sincerely,
Rush Whitacre
740-336-9169

8-16-11

Dear Taylor Swift,

    I don't really want to talk about today, actually, today is quite the surprise, maybe someday I will be asked about today and maybe, if that person is lucky, I will tell them all about it. But, until then, I will leave you with this.

This poem if for the secrets of my life,

"I remember, I forget, and most importantly, I forgive myself"

I remember tape I took when I was 10

And the guilt I felt

But I forgive myself, for I returned it

I remember the money I took from my father's till

And how I cried when I got caught

But I forgive myself, for I learned my lesson

I remember today, and all it means to me

And everything I have done

I shall forgive myself tomorrow

For now, I will sleep

Perhaps to dream

I toss this letter into the void, the abyss between us, this space that keeps conversation from happening.

Sincerely,

Rush Whitacre

740-336-9169

8-17-11

Dear Taylor Swift,

    Today I actually put some of the shelves up at the gallery, the ones that everyone is going to see, the ones that will hold art works from all of the members of the gallery… When I put up the top shelf I discovered that the ceiling is really not level, not at all… In fact it was a foot shorter from one side of the room to the other. Let me see now, I have worked enough hours now to pay for my rent in September, so, I need to make some money so that I can afford food. I guess if I make enough money to afford food, then I shall open a savings account and start to save money back. Yeah, and then when this November comes around and I have to start paying on my loans I am going to be screwed… I am not sure I will be even be able to pay for the interest… that will suck, hmm, what is the interest on 85,000 dollars I wonder…

    Here in about 2 minutes we are going to go to a bar to see Shooter Jennings sing, and play. This is what Jesse really wants to do for her birthday, and she says that this is our chance to get to know each other better. I can't wait… I don't even know what kind of music he plays, so, this shall be really interesting. I will let you know… Ok, I am off.

… Ok, I have never been to anything that Shooter would have put on in the past, but Jesse has I guess… Oh, I just got back from the bar/concert/whatever. It is 3 AM. I think that Shooter would have been more interesting except that he found it necessary to remind us that he had not practiced the songs before playing that night, he called it playing cold. I guess he was right because he forgot the lyrics quite a few times.. I wonder if he wrote any of the songs himself…

    Laura-girl got incredibly drunk, and then fell in love with the bartender… Oh Laura-girl. She really fell head over heels for this guy. My friends will not believe me, that Laura-girl fell for the guy behind the counter… It was so cute how she was acting. Now, I just need to find a girl who will be all fluttered about me in that way… lol. Sure. I hope Laura-girl is ready for work tomorrow. We have an early morning tomorrow.

This poem is for the making of a song,

        "Sing, Practice, write, Erase, Try Again"

        Till I forget about you

        I will write these words

        And my story will be read by those who care

About a love story

Written by the broken hearted

And even if I erase

These lines will always be here upon my heart

Like wrinkles in a paper

Graphite in a pencil

And it is wearing me flat

And in the end I fail, but I don't give up

I try again, and again, and maybe once more

Sharpen my pencil, a little focused but not in grip

And a little focus in my mind

And I will sing this song

And you will write my lyrics

With the actions you take against my heart

And my heart is not like a toy

Something meant to be played with,

Till I forget about you

I shall hold this pencil

The mic of writers

I toss this letter into the void, the abyss between us, this space that keeps conversation from happening.

Sincerely,
Rush Whitacre
740-336-9169

8-18-11

Dear Taylor Swift,

    I am starting to worry about Laura-girl. Her first love has been diagnosed with cancer, and this has profoundly affected her, which it should, and I have no doubt that it would affect me. And I am so helpless to help her, but I want to. I guess the best thing I can do is to just be her friend. I just hope that I can help her to get back to working regularly. Mostly, I just want her to be happy, and I know that she loves the art world. Anyway, I don't know, I am just worried about my friend.

Well, I got all of the shelves put up and now I don't have to worry about doing any more work at the gallery until this coming Tuesday. This has been a really nice little experience, moving the Gallery from 23rd street to 28th street, and now I am building shelves for it. Who knows, maybe Viridian will help me to get an assistants job somewhere, or maybe someone will offer me a job working one on one with another artist in their gallery… that is the amazing thing about NY. So many things can happen to you, so many possibilities to choose from, so many unknown factors. I am looking forward to all of the above.

I think for now though, I am going to just plan on working for my landlord, and Viridian, as long as they shall last. Tomorrow however I am going to paint some. I am really excited about painting, and this is my time to paint. I am a little worried about finding a job, and I am a little worried about getting hired, which I know are the same thing, but I think there is a slight difference.

I wonder what Vernita thinks of me. I have been working with her for awhile, and I wonder if she trusts me, or what. I mean, she did give me keys to the gallery, and to the front door.. all I need is a key to the elevator and I will have them all which is awesome because this way I will be able to do everything I need to do and not have to worry about being locked out…

This poem is for the mix,

"Breaking the News"

A little bite out of my past

Still hurts, still scabbed over

And I pick at it all the time

Making myself not myself

And I am gone, and so are you

It is never easy

And it isn't hard to feel so hard

And try to prop yourself up on air

Just breathing memories

And needing somebody else

On this random afternoon

I don't think thoughts about anything

But the happy moments and the smiles

And I can't figure out this puzzle

Our pieces fell together so fast

> And edges scuffed
>
> I'm moving on, your moving on
>
> Just leave your memories of me on a shelf
>
> And I will put them back into a box
>
> Shake them up later down the road
>
> And maybe, just maybe
>
> Our pieces will fall again.

I toss this letter into the void, the abyss between us, this space that keeps conversation from happening.

Sincerely,
Rush Whitacre
740-336-9169

8-19-11

Dear Taylor Swift,

  There just weren't any jobs worth applying to today. I am really shocked that there weren't any. I guess after spending several hours looking for one I was assuming that I would find a new one to apply to. But, alas, in this concrete jungle, I am stuck here, waiting for a good opportunity to arise. If it doesn't rain tomorrow I am going to the park to take some pictures. I have been planning this for about a month now, and every time I get a moment to go and do this I have to back out because of weather. I just checked the weather for tomorrow and my gizmo on my computer shows rain storms both Saturday and Sunday. So, the odds of a photo session happening tomorrow at the part is nill. I will ask Jesse if she wants to try anyway, she and I have been planning on going there and making some art. I guess I will see how the weather is in the morning. We may go rain or shine, lol, better take my water colors. I bet if Laura-girl doesn't work tomorrow that she will go with us. That would be nice. Three inspiring artists at the park making art. I can see it now, Laura-girl making drawings, Jesse making paintings, and me sketching for ideas of installations, or sketches for paintings. Mostly likely for paintings.

  Speaking of making sketches for paintings. I just found out today that there are 40 bridges in the park, and I shall making a drawing, painting, or sketch of some kind for each one. My ultimate plan is to have 20 paintings for sure. I definitely will take pictures of each one. Hmmm, I just wish I had more than just my cell phone to take pictures will… I am sure that it will die about halfway through the day.

Maybe I should do an anti-rain dance. I don't know much about the steps, nor about the tune, and I certainly wouldn't ask anyone to join me, but I am sure that I could figure out the pace, and the smile upon my face should be alone to keep away the rain.

This is off the topic, but I have been listening to no name singers on you tube all day, and I have to say that there is a lot of talent out there. Then I came across the group Big Time Rush. I just like the name I guess, they are a group of four guys. I am digging the remix of their song boyfriend with Snoop dogg and 1984. Lol, and I just found a BTR mashup that has all of the typical pop singers, and then there you are. Lol.. that cracks me up. Oh well.

This poem goes out to random afternoons,

"Wear this Weight"

I am heading out tonight

Not staying here anymore

All this couch surfing has worn me out

I need a break

And I need to forget about you

I am leaving my phone behind

and my friends have my back

as I have my smile back

and everything seems ok

as I chase down this present

this moment passes

from a moonstep to a concrete over-coat

I can't move

I can't breath

And I need a place where I can lose myself

I don't need anybody else

I just need my good friends

Till I break this news

Bright lights warm me up

And I stand still.

I toss this letter into the void, the abyss between us, this space the keeps conversation from happening.

Sincerely,

Rush Whitacre

740-336-9169

8-20-11

Dear Taylor Swift,

    I did it… I finally got into the park and took pictures of about 24 or 25 bridges. I walked and walked and walked around the park using a list of bridges in order from the internet site that I downloaded and printed off. So, I am pretty happy with myself. I think that I will use more than half of the bridges I took pictures of today to make paintings from. I don't know though, because I don't want to say that and then find out tomorrow that the other bridges I see tomorrow are even better… the best part is that I will have more than double the number of bridges to choose from… I am looking forward to having my NYC central park bridge painting show, even if it means having it in a bar or restaurant verses a gallery. I don't know what will happen, but, I will price everything reasonably and see what happens.

    I saw so many new things today in the park… so many things that I have already seen before but they were changed because of growth, or duckweed, or because of the ambience of the people around… there were so many people in the park, just so many people. I can see how just about anyone can slip into the park unnoticed if they want to go exploring. I know that there are lots famous people who like to walk around in the park and not be bothered, and I can see how it would be possible, there were just so many people there that I can see how just about anyone can go there and not have to worry about being bothered by anyone, everyone is too busy trying to avoid each other. True.

    I got my first mail in the mail today, from Jon Sab!!! He is a professor I had from OU and he sent me one of his paintings for me to work on, or collaborate on with him.. I am not sure what will come of it, but I am really excited to see how it turns out. Right now his painting is in acrylic and it looks like he just watered down some paint and then poured it out onto a surface and then let the layers remain see-through… I am going to keep it a secret as to what I am going to do to his surface….

    Lets see. I have enough money to pay my way through September now, and I am looking heavily for a full time job of any kind, just about anywhere… I am worry about when the Gallery tells me that they don't need my help any more, they have been to kind to me.. I will have to somehow find a way to get a job working with another gallery somehow, or working with an artist… I really need to be working on publishing my book… my fantasy book, I have been so worried about making ends meet that maybe, just maybe publishing my book will make me some money.. lol.. I am such a dreamer.

This poem is for the dreamer inside of me,

> "Head in the Clouds"
> You can dream all you want
> And you can breathe in and exhale
> And live your life
> Fulfill all of your dreams
> And you can do all of that
> But including me
> Is not something you can do
> For this is how that path has been carved
> And there isn't a connection
> There isn't an on-ramp
> Or a crossing
> And this boat does not float in air
> So, keep those fantasies
> Make them real in your mind
> And I will be just fine rowing
> Ride that horse
> And I will walk
> And like the little turtle
> I will keep steady
> I will make my path
> Following no one

I toss this letter into the void, the abyss between us, this space the keeps conversation from happening.

Sincerely,
Rush Whitacre
740-336-9169

8-21-11
Dear Taylor Swift,

So, I have watched this video twice now about how college is a scam, and about how the college bubble is going to burst when kids/students figure it out… meaning, when the price of college finally reaches a point where it is not reasonable to go to college, and the price far outweighs the ability to pay it off, the students will rebel, and hyperinflation will kick into high gear, and the government will have to come up with a way to get the loans paid off, or to come up with a way to bail out the school system… there is a reason gold the silver are being purchased from everyone who has jewelry to be melted down, and that is so that everyone can start to rebuy it who needs the ability back themselves to be able to pay for things in the future.. And, not to mention, china is buying 25 percent of all the gold in the world right now, and with good reason. If it is true that the American dollar is going to drop out, then why not use the American dollar now to buy up all the gold from the American people. At least, I know if I was a country of power and had the ability to do so, I know I would… not to be a hater, or to be mean, but to cover my own butt.

Speaking of covering my own butt, I wish I had the money to buy up gold and silver… you should start and buy up gold and silver, I would but at least a million of each if I were you… and I mean you should buy the physical stuff, not some piece of paper that says you own it… I would have the stuff shipped to me in person… I am not a person who thinks the world is going to end, or that we are all going to die or anything, but I think that those people who can certainly fend for themselves should be doing so… don't think about it, just do it.. how can buying up gold and silver be a bad thing, it can't… the price of it will never bankrupt you, and it cannot be faked… it has to be dug up out of the ground and that takes time and energy which can be measured, not like the printing of dollar bills…

Any way, enough of rant on that crap. I will just leave this letter with this. I am looking forward to hyperinflation because I think that my school loans will be bailed out and I won't have to pay for them, but I am not looking forward to starving to death with all the other artists… sad face.

This poem is for the starving artist,

"Swirling Brushstrokes of Blue"

He never cried as he painted

His love was undeniable, and denied by all

No painting sold in a life time

And no match has yet to come

For there is not match in a broken heart

And no one can push around the color of mud

Like he did

And on a lonely sad night

When tears were sure to come

> He picked up his brush and painted
>
> Landscapes, portraits, and still-lifes
>
> And still, no one appreciated him
>
> No one beyond his brother
>
> The love of his greatest loves
>
> And in a moment of insanity
>
> When you saw the world for what it was
>
> You took your life
>
> And your love
>
> And your passion
>
> And with those went the greatest of all
>
> you

I toss this letter into the void, the abyss between us, this space that keeps conversation from happening.

Sincerely,
Rush Whitacre
740-336-9169

8-22-11

Dear Taylor Swift,

    Well, this day started out with me looking for teaching jobs which led me to the conclusion that the universities are advertising their positions in other places that I don't have access to apparently, like to the Paper, that is when they ever publish it, and in magazines, and on some internet sites that I couldn't find… so, I left the game of searching for a job and went on an adventure today. I strapped on my shoes and I headed out my door with the plan of visiting Laura-girl's work, and to buy canvas. When I got to Laura-girl's work I discovered that she was about to go to lunch, and so I tagged along. I ate at a little deli, had some hot food from the hot bar. I don't think that it will make me sick, but then, what do I know, I haven't lived to see tomorrow… lol. But seriously, I am fine.

    I bought some great canvas at Blick, I got it for more than 50 percent off because I found a flaw in their pricing and they decided to match the price of what I found in their store. I was just simply labeled the wrong price and they decided to honor it.. I was ecstatic, because this means that I will be able to make all of the bridge paintings for a lot less than I previous thought I would be able to. Awesome sauce.

When I got home I got some great news. I got an email from Erica from the BDR Design group telling me that my Ripley's project for Ripley's believe it or not in Hollywood California is a definite thing that will happen, but it is a matter of when because she are pretty busy with some other things at the moment right now. But… It also said in the email that Ripley's will be enlarging the project, so, this could be a good thing right… isn't that the motto for America, bigger is better? Or has that changed to something else? Hmmmm.

I also got an email from Dorrance Publishing about me publishing my Mabast Book. I am not sure when that will happen,, probably as soon as I get my book finished. Then again, I need to have my head examined as to figure out when I think that will happen, because I keep putting it off for a day when I am not so worried about making money from a definite job that I will have in the future.. lol

This poem is for Carlee,

"Carlee's Imagination"

I look around me

And all I see are pictures

Pictures I don't recognize

Places I have never been

People I have never met before

And I can't help but question my own reality

My mind, does she play tricks on me

Or is it just the craft of a young lady

One who's laugh drives me crazy

And makes me wish to be a comedian

To make many more moments

Many more perfect pauses

More tragedies plus time

Just so that I can make her laugh more

Make her smile

Yeah, isn't that good enough

I toss this letter into the void, the abyss between us, this space that keeps conversation from happening.

Sincerely,

Rush Whitacre

740-336-9169

8-23-11

Dear Taylor Swift,

(((Earthquake))) in Virginia was felt here in New York. This was exciting, for three reasons. One, I was driving through Time Square at the time, which was my first time to do so, and two, I got to see the slight reactions of people's faces as I drove by but I didn't know why they were all looking around oddly, and three, I got to hear about it from Vernita after I got back to the gallery from picking up supplies from Home Depot. I guess it was the second home depot that I had visited for the day, but, who is counting... wait, I guess I am.

I had a really busy day, another day of driving all around the place picking up supplies to get ready to build the gallery rack and shelves. I am sure that tomorrow will go much smoother... I visited three different home improvement places in order to get the supplies that I needed. Two home depots, and one Lowes... I just love Lowes, it is my favorite home improvement store in the world.. Mostly because I just can't stand the treatment that Home depot puts their wood through, it is brittle at all the ends and when you put a screw in it, it splits... I don't know, maybe it is just me, but that is my experience with it.

Tomorrow I am to meet Dave at the gallery to build the rack and shelves. This should go pretty quickly since we now have all the supplies. Today started out with an email from Vernita pretty much telling me that it was my fault that we couldn't start building the rack and shelves, to me being the hero and getting all the supplies. It was funny to get the email from her blaming me for not picking a home depot to pick up the supplies from, when it was her who said last that she was going to leave the picking up of the supplies to Dave and I after Dave arrived... hilarious. I didn't get back to the apartment. I drove into Manhattan three times today, that is my record. I really hope I never have to drive a fourth time at any given time. I was very happy when I got back and Jesse was still awake and she giggled about how long it took me to get back, and then she felt a little sheepish as she thought I would have been back faster if she had gone.. I wouldn't, they just closed the Brooklyn Bridge down to work on it from one direction and it took me awhile to figure out how to get on it from the other direction... lol... Oh well, I am learning.

This poem is for my secret admiration for someone.

"I Want to Hear you Smile"

As we sat and tried to talk

It was the world telling us to take that walk

Those woods called our name

And I tried to get you to stay

And I tried to get you to go to the island

But it was not in the plans

I was late, again

And I will not forget you

Not your smile

And your sweet voice

Opinionated like that of any harsh critic

Like my worst enemy

Who only wants to make me a better person

The hard way

And I miss you

And I want you in my life

More than you will ever know

So I will keep walking down this path

Blindfolded

I toss this letter into the void, the abyss between us, this space that keeps conversation from happening.

Sincerely,
Rush Whitacre
740-336-9169

8-24-11

Dear Taylor Swift, I still have to finish up the rack to hold all of the paintings, but, I did get the shelves done which was no easy task. Vernita I think is very happy with them, she even made a comment that they were going to look so professional when I got done. So, I am happy with them, I guess, they are just shelves.

    Later in the day we went to the deli at that corner of 10th and 28th street and had Philly sandwiches and they were the best I have had so far here in New York. Dave is a funny guy.. He is a writer, and apparently he has made money at doing it because after writing just one book he was able to take a two year span and just do nothing but paint and make art. I am kinda jealous, and I think that if I had two years to just sit around and think about what to do with myself, I am sure that making lots of paintings is exactly what I would do…

Tonight I sat and talked David's ear off. I talked to him all about all of my shows, and all about grad school and all of the things that happened. He kept on saying that he wished that he had a recorder turned on because he was loving all of my stories… especially how I was able to get through grad school, the treacherous and cavernous journey from falling in love with the school all the way up to my utter and complete disenchantment with the school once I found out just how full of crap the whole was full of… don't get me wrong, there was a good handful of professors there, and it wasn't all of their fault as to why the program was turned into sour milk. Still, I would say that David got an ear-full from me. Pretty exciting.

Hey, I just found my show pic of a birthday show I did with my friend Gari and my friend Jonas. The two of them share my birthday, and I was just randomly searching through images and found our pic together… how weird is that, as if it were looking for me instead. Just my dumb luck I guess. Uh, I am going to have to look for my truck when I leave tomorrow, I don't remember seeing it on my way back here to the apartment… dang it. I better now have gotten towed.. Maybe I didn't look in the right place, hmmmm, maybe I wasn't looking at all. I just don't know.

This poem is for the non-believer,

"Why Should He?"

He makes everything into a joke

Why should he get the same prize

Why should he get any prize

Should he receive an award?

Why should he receive the same degree

He doesn't participate

He doesn't even say a word

I am sure he will make a joke of all of us

Why should he get the same degree

If we get Celsius, he should get Kelvin

Or Fahrenheit

Just please don't let him graduate

Why should he be so happy

So overjoyed

So ready to laugh

Why should he get the same piece of paper

As we do

      He doesn't deserve it

      "Oh, Look at that

    Is that an installation? A sea I see?

       I feel so tiny now

        So insignificant

      Like the worm I really am

     Don't squash me wave maker

I toss this letter into the void, the abyss between us, this space that keeps conversation from happening.

Sincerely,
Rush Whitacre
740-336-9169

8-25-11

Dear Taylor Swift,

  Well, I finished up the rack, for the most part, putting in three of the shelves, two of which had to have vertical dividers, for paintings to lean against… I am proud of my creation, very proud. It has been a long time coming making this silly little rack, I guess I am celebrating the little things. Then after spending 8 hours finishing up the rack I spent four hours cutting 64 stretcher bars so that I can make 16 paintings. So, I am going to see how much money I saved by making my canvases verses buying. So, I guess I am going to have to go to Blick online and figure out how much all of my sized canvases cost, and compare that to what I actually spent… boring.

  Actually, I don't really give a crap. I know I saved a bundle by making them myself, and that is all I really care about. I must say though, I wondered how David's day was today since he wasn't there to help me finish up the shelves. He seems like a really interesting person, and I am not sure what his motives are, but he is a writing, and all of the notes he was taking, and the video he was taking…. Kinda weird. Oh well, you gotta do what you gotta do to remember stuff I guess.

  Vernita was cussing before I got into the gallery today to do work, which was funny to me, because as I opened the door to the gallery to head into to start the day's work she escalated her cussing and screaming at Verizon until she finally just hung up the phone… I don't know what she was trying to say to me by doing this, other than don't mess with me today… the only point I really took from the whole episode was that Vernita was having a bad day, and then she left almost immediately after I entered the gallery… It was so nice, because I really didn't want her to be there with all of my loud tools blaring away… It is just not a pleasant place to be for 6 to how ever long I am working for...

Oh well, I had a really awesome day, and I think I am going to finish the day with a poem about Laura-girl

I dedicate this poem to Laura-girl:

"A Thousand Troubles When you Leave"

I can't think about this anymore

These tears that you've cried

And his life hangs in a balance

In an equation that has no answer

Something imaginary, maybe in a dream

And I can't make him better

And I can't make you smile

Or laugh, or anything with my words

And when you leave

I am left with all the disasters of the world

All the troubles are mine

A basket of hope

Not left here

A shaky proposition

A plan to make it all legit

But seeking the fountain of truth through lies

Will only bring you full circle

Will only make this dead end

End

I toss this letter into the void, the abyss between us, this space that keeps conversation from happening.

Sincerely,
Rush Whitacre
740-336-9169

8-26-11

Dear Taylor Swift,

  This has been a strange day. I feel like I worked a lot, but I didn't get much done it seems.. And to top it all off, Irene is coming tomorrow, or sometime this weekend… I say Irene as in the Hurricane. I of course use to have a baby sitter many years ago who was also named Irene, but she got fired because she was so mean to my older (related person who is male and not named), something I don't remember. I guess there are some reasons to not remember some things.

  Since I got home I have received so many comments about people who are worried about this silly Hurricane coming to NY. I just can't imagine that it will be that bad. I guess I am having trouble imagining it coming here and causing enough trouble that life will not be possible is something that I am not even considering. It just can't happen. Or, I guess it can, but I hope I am not here to witness that… although, it would be quite a stimulus to the whole city, to have to rebuild half of it from being destroyed from a natural phenomenon. Please don't let that happen… I bet if NY got destroyed by a hurricane I bet the president would respond quite fast unlike the Katrina disaster where nothing happened, no one came to the rescue of those people for a long long time.

  Jesse wrote me earlier and asked me if we had to evacuate and I laughed and wrote her back that I really didn't know, and that I am sure we don't have to, but then again, I do live in Brooklyn, and I don't know what to expect… so.

This poem is for the oncoming threat of a major natural disaster:

"Irene"

And I have been on this journey

This path all of my life

And little did I know the treacherous

Terrible fall

And how I did

When I heard about our meeting

I knew history was in the making

And how I couldn't see this any other way

But an energy released

A fate as slow as a seven day eclipse

One that shall surly be just as covered

As I am invisible

Oh Irene

Our fate is tied together

These slow moves you make

>
> And all I can do is watch from afar
>
> And be told about you by friends
>
> Enemies of yours
>
> And I duck
>
> And you goose
>
> And we miss
>
> Arm and arm we swing
>
> And in the morning I will be with you
>
> And you will be owning all the shores
>
> And I will be owning all the drips
>
> The rain drops as you cry
>
> And crash against my shores
>
> I will soak you up
>
> On these shoulders

I toss this letter into the void, the abyss between us, this space that keeps conversation from happening.

Sincerely,
Rush Whitacre
740-336-9169

8-27-11

Dear Taylor Swift,

    Well, today has really been all about communicating to the outside world from here in my apartment… everyone wants to know what is going on with NY with the on-coming Irene… I have been sitting here just checking out everything I can about whatever. Mostly, I have been looking up remixed hip-hop songs. I just love that YouTube has created so many avenues for expression... so many people, so many artists, so many different people who think they know something about something. There is occasionally someone who comes along on YouTube who has any talent, but, few and far between. My goal is to make some pho-music videos from other famous people's songs. I am trying to recruit Jesse to help me out, because I can't do it all by myself. Or I could, but it would help to have someone watch my equipment while I am filming. I can't imagine trying to film and trust that no one will move or steal my equipment while I am setting it and leaving it for me to do a scene.. lol

Now I am listening to Ja Rule, put it on me.. I love some of his beats, his lyrics are pretty repetitive, but, they make sounds like his beats to add to the rhythm that he is trying to create/manipulate. I have also been listening to black and yellow several times today, and I must say that I really like how he can string together a nice little line up of rhymed words... another song that has been rolling around in my head today has been My Hero by Foo Fighters, but,,, I am thinking about the cover by Paramore. Her voice, and her pauses are just a little more for sticking in my brain. I don't think that all covers can succeed, but I think that this one does. Oh, I just found Will Smith/Linken Park mix, weird. Actually, now listening to it, it really isn't that bad. Hmm. Ok, yeah, this has definitely the day of songs, and searching, and making no work on my paintings... may, I should have been painting all day, what am I doing... God, so many paintings I want to do, and here I have been gossiping about a hurricane all day, and my day has ended and now I must write this poem, and head to bed... there is always tomorrow... of course, tomorrow is Irene day... Oooooh

This poem is for the freeing,

"Release your Inhibitions"

She calls to me

She calls me names

And all of them hurt

And all of them are just spattered air

I hear her speak

Not to me, but to a something

And I lose the touch

The sensitivity of a goose bump

And this cold air removes me from my skin

Taking me down that road

To a place that I can't afford

Yet can't do without

So let this air stream lift me up

Pull me to pieces

And rip out my heart

From this chest that is already bursting

Already as hollow as any jewelry store

A rubyless moment

Not easily covered

By the insurance of a coming love

A coming storm

A tear from this eye

I toss this letter into the void, the abyss between us, this space that keeps conversation from happening.

Sincerely,

Rush Whitacre

740-336-9169

8-28-11

Dear Taylor Swift,

  I just got done walking around the area looking at all the trees that were knocked down by the tropical force winds. I wasn't expecting any really , but there were about a half a dozen and that is pretty surprising to me.. the cars that they landed on really didn't look that damaged.. lol, I guess they are seasoned from all the pressures of being driven around here in NY. I suppose that makes you tough. Jesse and I found a new pizza join in our travels, really good pizza. I think the subways will open either later tonight or early tomorrow. They have to do a complete walk through first just to check to see if there is any water problems… it would suck to drive a subway train into a submerged tunnel… can you say subwaymarine?

  Now, we have snacks galore. I have a feeling the people around here won't be shopping for stuff. Two days ago the grocery store was completely loaded down with shoppers who were panicking about what was going to happen to them. I guess it is kinda scary, because they did shut down the whole transit system, and getting off of an island without transportation is impossible without a boat, or wings.

  I am going to just say this again, well, maybe for the first time in a letter to you, but, I just love the song strip me that Natasha Beddingfield sang. I think I like it more though when Gavin Mikhail sings it and plays the piano. It is pretty powerful, and a pretty simple message, "I'm only one voice in a million, and you can't take that from me."

  You know, I was looking up some videos of the 'most beautiful boy in the world,' Andrej Pejic. He really is amazing in his beauty. The statement is correct, he really is a beautiful man. I am betting he is a very sophisticated individual, someone above gender has to be very sophisticated and has to have quite interesting views of the world. I guess he was discovered accidently one day while he was just walking around, lol, so it does happen…

  This poem is for just plain dumb luck,

                "Did you see that"
           We never know where our paths lead
              Or who is to cross them
                  Or change them
             Or just flat out erase them
               All we can be for sure is
           We are definitely moving forward
            Another second just passed
                And now another
         And all we can do is read these words
        And hope that the message is remarkable
     Maybe another sentence that will strike a nerve
      Or make us fall in love with another person
             Or simply just give us hope
          And sometimes, the good ones, yeah
            They bring us the tears of joy
                  Of happiness
                     Of loss
             Of a sad sad memory
         Tugging us along by our hearts
                      Pluck
                      Pluck
                      Pluck

I toss this letter into the void, the abyss between us, this space that keeps conversation from happening.

Sincerely,
Rush Whitacre
740-336-9169

8-29-11
Dear Taylor Swift,

I did something semi funny today. I hoped on the subway and found my way to the lowes to buy some stuff for the gallery. I bought stuff as if I were going to drive it to the gallery instead of ride the subway there.. so, after I checked out and found my way out into the parking lot it hit me, duh, you ding dong, you can't possibly take all of this too the gallery on the subway, not in a million years. I had purchased boards and several other things that were going to be quite difficult to haul around on my shoulder. So, with a smile on my face I pushed my load back inside and that had them store if for me while I went to get my truck. The guy smiled and wondered what I was doing standing outside the store just shaking my head.

After getting my truck I grabbed my stuff and headed to the Gallery. I really like working for the gallery, I just wish I had a permanent offer there. Today I put up three different portions of the shelves. A little bit in the storage room, some in the kitchen area, and some in the office storage area where a bunch of what appears to be useless paperwork is stored just to keep a record of what has occurred. I honestly can't see a reason for keeping the records in the gallery, they should be taken home, or taken to some other place, or just be thrown away. I don't see anyone writing a documentary on Viridian artist gallery for any reason, but, that is just me.. I actually am going to be very cynical right now, I don't see the art world making too many strides into the future… there seems to be a stand still. A wave needs to come in and crash upon the shores of this empire, to shake things up across the board.

Ok, for the past week I have been a facebookaholic. I have been writing everyone, adding friends left and right. I probably need to take a break. Tomorrow I am going to stretch canvas all day. I need to get all 16 canvases ready for bridges to be painted on them.. I have decided on making the view of the bridges in my own image. I have decided that what they lack I will give them, I will put into my painting what I think will make them truly whole, as far as the vista goes anyway. They are quite beautiful, but, there seems to be something with each of them that could be added…

I am still listening to skinny love, the cover by Gavin Mikhail. He sings it so beautifully, and nice and slow.

This poem is for all the lies,

"Hear what I have to say, then go"

I did it

Is that what you want to hear

I ruined your plans

And I rearranged your project

And my friends helped

It was bad ass

Do you think that is what you want to hear

That I am not your friend

That I am someone to not trust

For I could never just be unjust

I am the reason you are crying

Is that what you want to hear

I am the one who you should blame

Is that better

For I can't think of any reasons why

I just want you to move on

I just want you to be happy again

And I don't want to lose you

But, if I must, then I will

So go, but know this

I wasted time with you, and it has made all the difference

I toss this letter into the void, the abyss between us, this space that keeps conversation from happening.

Sincerely,
Rush Whitacre
740-336-9169

8-30-11

Dear Taylor Swift,

    Well, I got my car moved today, but no one else moved their vehicles… I was rather surprised. So, I moved back to my original parking space because it was a good one. I then went inside and stretched canvas over five of my stretchers. I can't wait. I am really excited about making my paintings come to life. I just really don't want to start on one painting when I can do many at the same time. I have decided to revisit my way of making a painting like I did with my psychic automatistic piece I did at OU. I am going to combine several different methods for making a painting and then have those different elements compete for dominance in the piece. I like this method a lot because I like the freedom of not having to come up with my own style, but rather just combining those from the past. Who knows, maybe I will come up with a new style in the process of making these ones. Yeah, that might happen. I remember when I first showed my piece to Matthew Friday my monster piece I remember vividly saying that he hadn't seen anything like it. That he really hadn't seen anything quite like it and that he was worried about me pulling it all together to make it work, and then he said right there at the end I pulled it together and made it word. Even the graduate student acknowledged this, so, I think I will revisit this piece and make ten paintings using this method. Why not, I have nothing to lose.

Tonight Laura-girl and I went to eat some free food and have a free glass of wine at an opening that followed her opening. When we got there Vernita had taken her 30 percent out of Laura-girl's sold work… which they first discussed 25 percent.. so, that was a little of a surprise. Then the second surprise to follow was the random Karaoke that happened where Vernita rapped to Eminem… it was hilarious… I filmed the entire thing. Eminem was the last person we expected Vernita to rap to, but she did it and she had a ball. It was great fun.

This poem is for the day February 30th

"When will we see you again?"

I heard about you in my past

I was told that you were real

But everyone keeps telling me that you are not

And I am upset

Cranky

And tired of hearing disbelief

Something that makes me crazy

Because a day is actually 23 hours,

56 minutes and 4 seconds

Which boggles my mind

Trying to think about how important

We think exact time is

It doesn't really exist

Unless we want it to

And it won't be until we realize

It's nonexistence

That we will be able to travel beyond it

Past it, and before it

And we will remember

Nothing

Just be in the moment

Silence.

I toss this letter into the void, the abyss between us, this space the keeps conversation from happening.

Sincerely,
Rush Whitacre
740-336-9169

8-31-11

Dear Taylor Swift,

I totally finished building the rack today… I only needed 6 boards and now it is done. All I am waiting for now is for the carpet so that I can cover the wood and make everything a bit more nicer looking, or unified. I am expecting the carpet this coming Friday, we shall see. We painted the trip for the gallery floor/wall. I am sure we will give them a second coat tomorrow. I can't wait to be done with the renovations and fixing up of this gallery. I will miss the work, and the money… that is the only downside.

So, I will go and work with Alan tomorrow at his place putting together metal shelves. He told me that we could discuss me finding a more permanent position somewhere where I can breathe a little easier. I just need someone to give me a chance to prove that I have some skills, something to offer their work, their products, their mojo… if that is such a thing in that world… I really like Alan, and I will like him as a person even more if he finds me some kind of work somewhere. For now though, I am working enough to just make it by. What I need is for Ripley's to call me and tell me to make their showcase piece for the Marilyn Monroe display. Once they pay me I will be set for like two years… I think I can make their money last quite awhile. The only thing I have not made room for is my school loans. I have no idea how much that is going to cost me.. I am a bit afraid… just a little.

My life will never be the same after NY… I just have this feeling that my stay here is going to open doors for me that would never open anywhere else in the world. The night before last I met a woman named Jane who was having an art opening and her work was really small and relatively basic brush strokes that were attempting to make shapes and space. The colors were rather bland and plain and simple and I kept on trying to move my eyes beyond the one that was blue… it was the cheapest one in the room, but its design and its color, and everything about it was screaming the word buy me, I am art, and I know what I am doing here in this room,,, and that is getting your attention… right, isn't that a part of art, to get your attention. Maybe I am wrong, maybe I am not…

This poem is for the willingness to try,

"Fantasy of Mr. Teal"

I want to make a minute last forever

And I want to rip this picture up to make a million new pictures

All different, all radical and avant-garde

Turn heads

Attract a crowd of mini lesions

Sore to the touch of my voice

Yet something they can't live without

Like the rub that raws you

Or the soothing violence that rapes you of vision

Not your eye sight, but the goal, the place you are aiming

And then a bulls-eye moves

And your aim is the same

Offed by the vision you kept

As your eyes closed

And when you finally open them

You too will see

And you will be just as wrong.

I toss this letter into the void, the abyss between us, this space that keeps conversation from happening.

Sincerely,
Rush Whitacre
740-336-9169

9-1-11

Dear Taylor Swift,

    Today was a long and fun day. I drove Laura-girl to the gallery and then I ran to New Jersey to pick up some carpet for the shelves I built. This was quite a trip, because I got to go through an underground tunnel, and I got out of paying the 8 bucks to get back into New York. The guy who was getting the carpet out of the back of the storeroom was hilarious. As I waited I watched him as he harassed one of the other workers who were sitting on a forklift. The guy on the fork life started to cuss him out, it was just so hilarious. And because the guy thought I was such a good friend of Daves that he treated me like gold, it was amazing. Just showed me just how important it is to know the right people. Alan is a funny guy. He is a 65 y/o architect who is looking forward to retirement. He built his company from the ground up and has he has had quite an interesting life.. His wife is a doctor and he has a 14 year old son who I can tell he loves and adores. His sons name is Jonas I believe. After working for 6 hours on some shelves we went to a little family diner that was across the street. It was there that he told me that his son had been taped to be on the Ellen Degeneres show but because Ellen became so famous at her show so quickly his son's episode never made it to TV. He said that he wished he had just a taping for his son to keep, but, alas he said, it just didn't happen. I flipped, I thought it was great. I guess his son was being interviewed because he knew so much about the subway system at such a young age. Pretty cool.

Then I got onto the subway and came back to the apartment. I learned tonight that Laura-girl may have the opportunity to give an artist lecture at a college. I told her to do it, totally do it? She is so shy and timid, I laughed at her doing her nervous dance in her room as I told her she would have 300 people show up to hear her talk.. lol. I would be one of the 300 of course. And I would be nervous for her. Lol.. although, I think that I would be less nervous, I would love to jump at the chance to do such a thing. God that would be awesome.

This poem is for the Architect.

"Brought it to my home"

And out of my window

I could see the fall of two giants

The power of my view

The innocence of my young

And all the while

I stared

The zero became a new beginning

The people pointed

And I saw the accident

And soon

I saw the 'on purpose'

And then a new purpose

For those people

In my office

Were my responsibility

Were my friends

Colleagues

And I knew I had to get to them

To set them free.

I toss this letter into the void, the abyss between us, this space that keeps conversation from happening.

Sincerely,

Rush Whitacre

740-336-9169

9-2-11

Dear Taylor Swift,

    I finished!!! I finally finished all of the work needed to be done on the shelves in the gallery, and to the trim around the base of the wall. So, I am pretty happy about that. I worked hard all day, and then I met this girl. Her name is Molly. I won't mention her last name because I like just writing the name Molly. She just recently graduated from Cal Arts with her Master's degree. Hmm, I guess anyone could find her on their home page I guess with a little search… I guess anyone could find anyone on the internet if they really tried. Kinda sad.

I have been listening to Obadiah Parker's cover of Hey Ya on youtube. It is amazing. I love this man's cover, it is like the right about of wax with the right amount of flame. Just like this light in the haze of the darkness that makes YouTube such an amazing tool for getting 'you' out there to be noticed, to say 'hey, look at me and this greatness I am in at this very moment'. Thank you Obadiah.

Moving on. Like I said a little while ago about the girl named Molly. She was adorable. She came in and walked around me like a person who knew what she wanted to do… and of course, that was to see what I was up to in the gallery space next door. And, to talk to me. I had been eyeing her out of my door, and every time I glance out the door and she was there I noticed that she was looking in at me working, and then would divert her eyes. I don't know if I am just being hopeful, but, it would be nice to find someone interested in meeting me. Lol

Weird, my ex Mandy just wrote me to tell me that my grandma in the nursing home would like to get a postcard from me from New York. So, I guess I will be on my way to the find a really cool postcard tomorrow to send to my grandma. I hope she is being treated well where she is. I am a part of her after all, even if I didn't get my degree in graphic design... lol

So, I am sitting here in my living room right now with five blank gessoed canvases around me, begging me to put paint on them… I might just have to do that, soon. Even if I still have 11 other canvases to stretch and prime first. Maybe…

This poem is for the surprise texter of this night.

"Surprise Friend"

I never meant to lose them

It just happened

And it was most likely in the right

In a world full of haters

And wanna-be's

And people who don't know

What love is

Or how it should be treated

You have somehow passed through the layer

The icing to the cake

To the meat of who I am

> Sticking with me as a friend
> Even if I couldn't forgive you
> For the mess that I most likely caused
> I was, and have always been good at
> Self sabotage
> Self doubt,
> And the crown you place high above me
> I will never wear
> I will never be yours again
> And that is a tear
> That I shall hold onto
> For it is my own
> My love

I toss this letter into the void, the abyss between us, this space that keeps conversation from happening.

Sincerely,
Rush Whitacre
740-336-9169

9-3-11

Dear Taylor Swift,

    Laura-girl and I are goofing off at the gallery. Well, we are working in a goof off kind of way. Right now as we speak I have the computer speakers strapped to the side of my head held there by a single rubberband. I am waiting for it to snap and leave a red mark around my forehead, lol, that would be funny. Wow, and it is so loud clear and the picture Laura-girl is taking is sure to be on the good ol facebook tonight when I get home. We are testing out another theory right now as well. We had one of those air conditioners that can roll around on the floor and they not only put out cold air, but hot air. Actually, more hot air than cold air, so, it is right now heat up the room instead of cooling it down… ugh.. you have to put the hose for the heat out the window otherwise it is pretty counterproductive. I am going to do something about it right now…

    Wow, I spent about an hour making something so that the new in room air conditioner could work properly,,, and then Laura-girl finds that actual parts that are supposed to be used to make the hot air pump out the window. Talk about embarrassing. Here I had taken a box out of the air conditioner box and totally placed it off to the side and then just as soon as I let it go I forgot about… Laura-girl had even written Alan to let him know that the air conditioner was missing pieces. Lol. What a trip. I guess Laura-girl and I were rather tired and not all together with it there towards the end of the night. Lol

    Laura-girl was slightly disappointed because she wanted to catch a glimpse of the girl who I met yesterday. I didn't think she would be there on the weekend, for not too many people work at the galleries during the weekend, I mean, when renovations are being done. It didn't matter to me either way. While we were at the gallery I got a great phone call. I was just working like a little busy bee and then I got a phone call from Blick, and I have a group interview this coming Tuesday at 12:30. I think that I will show up around noon just so that I am there a little early. Oh gosh, that means I need to shave… wonderful.. shaving is the one thing that my face doesn't like…

    Tonight has turned into a marathon of music videos where people have used all different kinds of songs and put them to a conglomeration of the Notebook movie scenes. There are some that work really well, and then there are some that don't work at all.. Such a good movie.

This poem is for the wrong impression,

"Not a Flower for You"

He sat in front of my painting

Talking, talking, helping when he could.

But my wait wasn't as heavy as his

And then, they sat there

Questioning my every move

Talking to me like the night would never,,

Grow old

Yet it did

And then he looked back

His shoulder between him and a sunflower

And my story was robbed of me,

By the words that he read first

And he read them aloud

And he read them twice

Then three times

And when he asked me who she was

I laughed

Until I cried
And I cried until he didn't want to hear it anymore
And I told it anyway
And my story set you on fire
And set me free
My sight cleared
I fear nothing
And you love me for my misunderstandings
A whim not necessary

I toss this letter into the void, the abyss between us, this space that keeps conversation from happening.

Sincerely,

Rush Whitacre

740-336-9169

9-4-11

Dear Taylor Swift,

    I was awoke this morning with a phone call from Russ my landlord. He was in need of my driving services. I was willing to do it for free because I have wanted a new adventure every day since I came to NY. So far, I have almost had a new adventure since I came here, and I love every day. I am excited to see what this winter brings to me. I am hoping for a good hard winter where we may even get snowed in for a couple of days. That would be awesome… just me and the two girls sitting around and making art and telling stories and going outside to make snow things. I can't wait for Christmas.

    I hope that my dad lives long enough to enjoy this coming winter… Beverly has such beautiful winters with such nice little snows. Plus, I don't get to come home until Christmas anyway. I think that I will make it a two week trip if I can manage it. I will see though, because I need to make the Ripley's piece which I am hoping will be something that I get to do well before Christmas. Yikes!!

    This afternoon I stretched all of my canvases except two, and then I painted them. In between the stretching and painting I talked to this girl who used to date Louis, her name is Katie. She and I had what I would call a typical misunderstanding between two people who like to joke around on facebook, but then the emotions of trying to be funny isn't coming across… So, she and I discussed Louis and his doings, and then we discussed my art as she was looking it over. She asked me to make her a mural, and I laughed because I get that so much because my work is so big. I just love it. Then she lost it when she looked over my shadow art. I just love the affect my shadow art has on people… it is awesome. I learned tonight that Louis and Katie actually didn't date, and I am surprised. I thought that they did, and I would have laid money on a bet that they had. Interesting. I can't imagine the two of them seeing each other as much as they did and then they didn't actually have a dating spree… I wonder if he will end up a forty year old virgin… that would be interesting, very interesting. If that is the case then I am sure his friends will make something happen for him… No doubt.

This poem is for Katie

"Breaking the rules"

Making me think things that aren't real

A story I can't tell right

For what I see isn't real

My eyes unable to see the real verses the fake

And I just want to be happy

I just want to be happy for you too

But I can't make the ends meet

The story has now been read once

And as I am having it read to me it sounds so different

So many vague moments.

So many lost gems amongst the dirt

And my detector is set to truth

But all it is picking up on are falsehoods

And again, my mind is tricked

So I fall, I fall for it, fall to the floor,

I've been stuck for so long

And I must admit that I haven't had enough

But don't worry

I will get this story right

I need it

And I want it

And I have been stuck for so long

And I am not content with last place

I toss this letter into the void, the abyss between us, this space that keeps conversation from happening.

Sincerely,
Rush Whitacre
740-336-9169

9-5-11

Dear Taylor Swift,

 I am so excited. Tomorrow I have my first job interview. It is only at Blick, and not at some high almighty fancy place where I could make a lot of money, but it is a job nonetheless, and I shouldn't pass up the opportunity to work. Besides, Laura-girl works there and I really would like to work with Laura-girl, and I wouldn't mind getting the discount either. I don't have anything laid out to wear, and that is unusual for me as when I am this nervous I usually plan things out way ahead and have my clothes picked out and I jump at the chance to be clean cut and shaved… but, for some reason I am really laid back tonight. I am just chilling here in front of my laptop. I have been listening to this one song all day, I just can't seem to get enough of it, and there is something about it, the beat, the video, the words… I don't know, but I am addicted to it. It is called "So Good to You" by Marianas Trench. I have never heard of them before, either on the radio, or on YouTube… I don't know where they came from.

 So, I finally got all of my canvases stretched and ready to be painted on tomorrow. I really need to get them started. The first several steps are relatively easy and I don't need to be careful with them. There is something of a movement to them that I am hoping will catch on. Doubt it, there is so much lacking in the art world, and most of it comes from the heart, and that is where I want to come in, to make art that will tug on people to a place that I create, I want to draw people into my art like they are drawn into a new and fresh and attractive relationship. Not some lousy lust, but a pull from a special place from deep inside where people hide who they really are. I will 'draw' them out, and they will love me… lol, what a line.

 It is now 11:27 and Laura-girl is not home yet. I hope everything is ok. I worry about her when she isn't home when I think she will be home. I guess I just want her to be safe is all, where ever she is. Too many unexpected things could happen to a girl in a big city like this.

 Anyway. I must get off of here and think about what I am going to wear tomorrow I suppose. I can't trust that my cell phone will wake me up… I really need to get a good night's sleep.

This poem is for the girl named Louis,

   "You Don't Need to Ride"

If you are holding back

Thinking like the way you sometimes do

That your way through life is on the fence

you don't have to ride that line

that crack or crevice is dark and deep

and as much as I want to help

Your footsteps aren't heavy enough for me to follow

I only want to see you bloom

Only to take photos

And maybe make you smile

But I can't be that for you

And I don't know who can

And so you keep me guessing

Keep me wanting to catch you from falling

For the wrong guy

From the flash of light

But I shouldn't care that much

For you aren't even aware I exist

That I am alive

And I am here waiting with open arms

My imaginary friend

I toss this letter into the void, the abyss between us, this space that keeps conversation from happening.

Sincerely,
Rush Whitacre
740-336-9169

9-6-11
Dear Taylor Swift,

    Hello world… I had my interview today and I must say that I don't know how I did, just to say that my opinion doesn't matter as much as Laura-girl's pull in the business. I know that because of Laura-girl's pull to get me on board may have more influence on the position that anything I have ever done... so,, thank you so much a Laura-girl for being my friend and for helping me out... right after my interview I went to the gallery to see how it was going and I spent time with Laura-girl and answering any questions that any passerby's had. I was what Laura-girl was calling the spotter, the person who watches the gallery while it is open, looking for anyone who might be interested in what we have to show. IT was fun, but I kept on playing the chess for the Mac computer and I kept on losing,,,, mostly because I just wasn't trying, and it sucked because I was just wanting to have fun, and, I really wasn't wanting to try to win anything just during that time, so, the computer didn't let me win at all... lol.. yeah, next time I will have to really try.

After the gallery, I went with Laura-girl to Nancy's bar to have a bite to eat. We ended up staying there to play "sand" shuffleboard. It was amazing. Laura-girl got so drunk, I ended up chasing her out to a cab and getting In it with her. She fell asleep on the way home... I couldn't believe just how drunk she got. Not really. Laura-girl really was just tired. I think that she works so hard, she needs a break once in awhile. Now, here I am watching video's of Zach Galifianakis and his little funny show called between 2 ferns. Just so funny. I think that people actually thing that he has some big show or something. Zach, you are a hero,,, to who I do not know ,but you apparently have a way of attracting the elite of the elite... good for you.

I am still watching the video by Marianas Trench: Good to you.. it is so good. This singer has something in his voice that makes me want to grab a mike and make a fool of myself. Lol,,, and yeah, seriously, their music is something that my ears have been begging to hear. It is not rap, but, it is still catchy.

This poem is for Jesse,

"You Surprise me Around Every Corner"

I don't read you

But I read you and wrong

I am sensitive

And I am shy

And as a roommate

I must admit I want to be a good one

So I try

And hard I try

Pushing the limits of boundaries

Of privacy without meaning to

Solving for your x

When I should have asked myself y

First

And then there went the kitchen

The idea of stability

Some marker of freedom

Of money

Or lack there of

Just another form of a fire

A fire in a cave

One that has been put out

But we know

We can put in

I toss this letter into the void, the abyss between us, this space the keeps conversation from happening.

Sincerely,
Rush Whitacre
740-336-9169

9-7-11

Dear Taylor Swift,

 Today was a rather stay at home kind of day. I got up, made coffee, cleaned house for about 2 hours, and then I got 7 of my blank canvases arranged throughout the house and started to paint on all of them… I started by painting the lyrics to a poem from one of the letters I have written to you. I don't remember which one it is to be able to relate to any time period of my past year, but, that is ok. The poem's time is called "In the Wake" and I decided that it would be a nice way to start off the series of bridge paintings, that is, to cover all the canvases with lyrics from a poem or two, or may be three, just depends on how much canvas I have to cover and how big I make the letters, and how long each poem is. Lol…

 I am going to write one poem onto these canvas's in one direction in one color, and then turn all the canvases and paint onto them another poem in a different color, and I am going to do this until I have turned the canvases in all four directions and have four different poems in four different colors overlapping each other. After that I am going to start in on the second phase of the paintings, which is the building up of layers of oil paint like that of a drip and pour technique. After that I will head into phase three of the painting, which I won't go into right now because I am playing this process a little by ear to see exactly which direction I go in. After that step there are about a half a dozen more steps involved before I will consider each painting to be done. I am going to work on these as fast as I can, but, they are in oil paint, so, it is up to the drying time of the oil paint really, that is all it is up to. I guess what I really need right now is just a little more room for drying space for the paintings so that I could do more of them on the walls… I had plans on building a drying rack above our stairwell, but I am afraid of taking up that space and regretting it later… I may still make something there, I guess it depends on this other ceiling rack I Have an idea for.. It involves me making a single thin shelf using four I-screws and two tie downs that I use in my truck. We shall see… I just need a place to put wet painting to keep them out of the way. I will figure it out.. I like how things are coming about. I just need to work on my work every day and I will succeed, I have faith in my ability.

This poem is for Carlee,

"For the Waiting"

I remember the smell of the woods

The feel of your hand as you put it out for help

And the sound of your laugh as I was stupid

As I still am

I see that you are happy,

And as my friend I must say that I am happy too for you

But as a man who sees who you are

I am sensitive, and jealous, and wanting

And the wanting goes on and on

Like the weather

Like the blue sky we all share

Long enough that I go blind looking for where we meet again

A day, a week, a month go by

And I hear nothing of you

More silence than can be carried by the void

Of the universe

My palm is open

And your smile is always on

So when you are ready

I am ready

For another adventure.

I toss this letter into the void, the abyss between us, this space the keeps conversation from happening.

Sincerely,
Rush Whitacre
740-336-9169

9-8-11

Dear Taylor Swift,

    This, has been yet another amazing day here in NY. I spent the morning driving into Manhattan to pick up my stuff from the gallery because they had a meeting there, and then on my way back from the gallery I got many texts from this guy named Reamy who I know. He graduated from OU the year before me and went to a much more prestigious grad school than I. but,,, then again his first job for a year out of grad school has been working at an apple store selling ipods and iphones for a year... so, at least I have made the leap to working in a large city that the art world appears to be revolving around. I love it in NY. No offense to my friend Reamy, but, I would have thought that he could have had a much better job than working for apple... but then again I don't want to lay that kind of judgment down without more info to go on.

    I made it to the bank today and opened up a savings account and met some really nice people. I gave the manager at Blick a thank you card and then headed to the gallery to make the meeting where about 8 or 9 of the members showed up to talk politics and the business portion of the gallery. I was really enjoying my time watching the different gallery members talk/debate/argue/confess/brag/etc about the gallery, or their shows, or otherwise... It was just really nice to have the insight into the gallery... I guess in this new location Viridian will be saving a lot, and I mean,,, a lot of money simply because of their move... I am so happy for them. I got so caught up in listening to the gallery that I lost what it was that I was supposed to be doing... and that is going around to the different galleries to look at shows. Duh,,, after all it is Thursday night and it is also fashion week... so all the galleries were extra busy, and extra crowded. Laura-girl and I went around, she read the artist's statements, and I tried to figure out the real statements behind the art. For the most part, I think that most everyone is just trying to be different, trying to do something to get attention. I guess, what else is there really... except that I am making art because it simply feels good to make, and I am really really hoping that people will like it just a little... we shall see.

    I have been trying to call Gari again lately. He is not answering his phone again. I hope he is ok. I think that I will follow up on this whole apple/working for apple/ job with apple thing just to see what it is all about. If nothing else maybe I can get some free training with apple products. I have no idea how to use any apple products... how lame is that. Lol... they just hate me.

This poem is for Louis,

"What the Fuck?"

I can't believe that I just heard that come out of your mouth

That is worse than Zack

And all of his antics are planned

Preplanned in fact,

And all of his victims know pretty much what is coming

But with you Louis

No one knows you are about to bash them

Jokingly of course

But no one knows that you are not serious

So who is the joke on really?

Who has made the joke

What is the stage?

A room in the middle of a complex

Like I am sure the one you carry on your shoulders

The one screaming for you to sleep

To be awake

To lay there for hours with no sleep

And then exhaustion

6 sleeping pills later

I toss this letter into the void, the abyss between us, this space the keeps conversation from happening.

Sincerely,
Rush Whitacre
740-336-9169

9-9-11
Dear Taylor Swift,

    Well, got a lot done today. I applied to work at Apple to sell apple products,, and I don't know anything about apple products… If I get a job at apple it will be a miracle, and I will have so much work to do to catch up with how to run apple products… Wow, I can't believe that I actually applied. My friend Reamy was so sure that I should apply. I am thinking that he is going to benefit from my applying regardless of actually getting accepted. Lol, Ooooh Marcus.

So, I painted for most of the day. Today I finished painting one poem onto all of the canvases… I was nice because the poem was perfectly fitted to work across all of the canvases without leaving any space and without me needing to fill, or to make words bigger, or to make the letters bigger. I was actually very pleased with all the different things I could have done, and instead the poem fits perfectly. Then I started a second poem on the already dry 7 canvases that had the first poem on it in purple. The second poem I painted on in orange. The two colors are really trippy together. I can't wait to get the third poem/third color onto the canvas. I am going to use the color green… I just decided to go with all the secondary colors on these paintings because this series comes from my first painting I did at OU. So, I decided to use poems that I have already used in these letters that I am sending to you, and why not use the secondary colors to paint them onto the canvas with. I am sure that I will continue to utilize this secondary style for the rest of this series. I am not going to really discuss right now what my next step is on this series because my few ideas that I have rolling around in my head I haven't fully decided. I guess I will surprise myself as well. But for the most part, I am just really enjoying the feel of a paint brush in my hand, and the way paint slides across a canvas surface, and the way the canvas's texture grabs little dots of color as I drag the bristles across it. Something tells me that if I just keep painting with the idea that what I am doing is what I want to be doing instead of what I think will be show-able, then everything I paint will at least be a success to me. At least that is how I see it. If I enjoy the making of them, then it doesn't matter what anyone else thinks… thank god I graduated.

This poem is for the sweet sweet ending of grad school.

"Paintings my Way"

There are no students

And no directors, and no professors

Just a canvas, a whole wall of canvases

And a room of paint and paint brushes

No words

A little music

And a void to fill as I've tried with all my works

A void that I have that I keep trying to fill

An emptiness that was ok until I finally noticed it

And since that day, I have thrown everything into it

Trying desperately to fill, over and over

And every new thing I toss into this hole

     Only seems to mask its existence
     And then the hole swallows everything
     Like a raging hunger
     With nothing to satiate it
     A calm I yearn for out of my storm,
     The open arms of the still,
     The unmoving ground,
     The base.
     A form of safety,
     That only time can rob me of
     And here now
     I toss another into the hole
     Eyes closed

I toss this letter into the void, the abyss between us, this space that keeps conversation from happening.

Sincerely,
Rush Whitacre
740-336-9169

9-10-11
Dear Taylor Swift,

  I found a really good Mike Tompkins cover of PYT Michael Jackson. It has simply made my day. On a different note, I washed my towels in the bath tub, which I think was probably a waste of time because here in a little bit I think that Jesse and I are going to go to the laundry mat to actually wash a load of stuff.. lol.. I guess I could rewash them and actually get them dried. This shall be a good time.

  So, last night Jesse and I want to a local bar here in Brooklyn called Denny's I got to watch some real pool sharks play some pretty fantastic pool. There were two actually, and neither spoke a lick of English. I got to play one of them and just almost beat him, I was really really lucky. Jesse was pretty amazed at how close I got to beating the guy. I laughed at how I scratched there at the end… lol I don't know why every time I go places with Jesse I don't notice more about all the guys who are checking her out. It is quite a funny thing to me. I mean, she is pretty, but I can't see past her being my roommate, and that is something that I guess keeps me in my place of mind. Wow.

So, now it is much later in the night, and Jesse and I went to the laundry mat and did more laundry. I washed some of my bedding this time. It is nice to have a l-mat so close, but I am looking forward to the time when our landlord has a washer and dryer right down in the basement. I am planning on keeping our rent low while we stay here. At first I was worried about the transition of going from kitchen to no kitchen, mostly because I was worried that Jesse would bail out on us. Her bailing out I guess wouldn't be that big of a struggle for Laura-girl and I ,but, at the same time I think if she did that would help my argument for lowering our rent a little bit further.

So, while at the laundry mat I bought some baseball cards. I know, it is ridiculous and a terrible investment, but I couldn't help myself, the machine was calling my name, and the cards were so cheap. I am amazed at how much lower cards are these days from 20 years ago. I feel kinda sick to my stomach when I think about the collection I have and how little they are worth.

This Poem is for the difference between

"Boundaries"

Feet, I hear feet clamoring

The little pitter patter of paws

And the drive home I do not remember

Just the painted lines, the guard rails, the bumper guard

And the crayon moves outside the line

A position out of position

And second gear is broken

But the wooden leg is still attached

So break off a piece of this limb

And hand me a pick

So that I can choose

So that I can push the button myself

Even if I just saw you push it

Same floor, same cause, same fall

And I fall, and you don't

And I fall, but you don't know I exist

That my existence is like the air you breathe

There, and all around you

Just search

Just dig

Just do anything but stop looking

For I shall never be the same

A difference that can't be measured

By a mirror,

Or your looking glass

Or goggles

Emotions turn

Emotionless

I toss this letter into the void, the abyss between us, this space that keeps conversation from happening.

Sincerely,

Rush Whitacre

740-336-9169

9-11-11

Dear Taylor Swift,

    Today was a day that reminded me of the good old days with the loft… I got to build a wall in our apartment without getting permission. I guess it is just one of those things that I do, build stuff and not get permission, but beg for forgiveness later. I did it because my roommate wanted to have some more privacy in her little area of the apartment. I don't blame her, but at the same time she is paying a lot less that Laura-girl and I, and I think that is where I keep my mouth shut and see what Laura-girl thinks? Lol. I guess after all this is not my place originally.

    So, today is 9/11, and Jesse and I decided to not go to Manhattan just because of the possible risk of something happening on the ten year anniversary of the… 9/11 attacks. So, that was when we decided to make the wall. I had fun, made many messes, and I found out a lot about Jesse. I think that I know why she works in encaustic art forms that melt, mostly because they dry very quickly, and there is no need to wait for the work to be touchable, to start another layer, to start another piece. I have this part of me that thinks that Jesse is sometimes to impatient for things that take time. Like after we got the wall up I had to sand the one side to make it smooth so that I could paint it. As soon as I stopped the sander she spoke up and asked me if I was going to sweep it up. I just stood there wiping off the dust off of one of the walls and said, "Uhh, I just finished, and now I have to knock off the lose dust before doing that." That was when the whole encaustic art form thing seemed to make sense in my head for Jesse, because she comes across as impatient sometimes. I am not saying that she is, but man, sometimes I get this feeling like she is putting off this vibe of, "this just simply isn't fast enough for me." Oh well.

    I feel really good about my decision to make that wall. It cost Jesse about 90 dollars, and I got to build it, and I get to use the one side to hang paintings on. Hmm, I guess I have to be careful and make sure that if I put a screw in that it goes into one of the stud's and not into nothing… lol

    Tonight I have been listening to good to you by Marianas Trench again. This song is addictive. I have also been listening to Boyce Avenue. They mostly do covers on YouTube, but they have their own songs. I noticed that they actually don't have music videos for their songs. I thought about maybe I should make some for fun… Hmm, just need to come up with a good idea first I guess.

This poem is for me wanting her to know,

"I Thought I was Right"

How blind could I be

My mind taking over

Pixels I can't put together

A grave

And a grave mistake

Flowers left for the son

But picked up by the father

And how the anger ran from your eyes

To your fingers

And then burned into my vision

The hate of your loss

A signal I couldn't understand

Or see

Hear, touch or taste

And when I say I was senseless

I mean I was dead

As I feel I am to you now

As I probably should have always been

May my path to your door

Not leave a trail

For others to follow

And I backtrack,

Over cemetery stones of pain

I toss this letter into the void, the abyss between us, this space that keeps conversation from happening.

Sincerely,
Rush Whitacre
740-336-9169

9-12-11

Dear Taylor Swift,

 Another day of painting. I do this little painting dance where I move half of the paintings out of my room and hang them on the wall and then gather up the paintings that I just took off the wall that also have wet paint. I have to be careful not to smudge the paint, I don't want there to be any unnecessary looking at parts that don't need attention, like a mistake. So now all the paintings have orange and purple, and half have green. Here in a couple of days they will all have the three colors and half will have a fourth color, I think I am going to use baby blue since that is my favorite color. I am having the feeling of gessoing over the entire thing and then painting a completely new painting on the gesso… the reason for doing this is because the places where I have already put the oil paint on would not hold the gesso, the gesso would flake off over time, and this would reveal the maze of different colored words beneath. I think that it is a really neat way of making a painting, but I am not ready to that yet. I will finish this series as I have planned first, and then I will venture off into that world of an ever changing painting. One that reveals more and more of the underneath portions. Huh, I don't know, it is kinda gimacky, kinda unique, kinda overrated. I may do one just for fun. I don't want to waste to much money, so one painting won't hurt me too much. As if 15 paintings is an easy task to come up with the money for… lol

 Jesse came home and Laura-girl came home and we had a photo session. It was fun. Laura-girl laughed at my poses. I might put them on facebook, well, maybe one or two of them… maybe. Doubt it. Anything that goes onto the internet is there forever, period. That is until something happens and the world ends, and I don't see that happening for some time. I wonder what kind of marketing would come out of an end of the world scenario… hmmm.

 There would probably be a lot of churches asking for a lot of money, as if they could really do anything about the end of the world with money. If it happens, it happens. Deal with it as it does, lol.

This poem is for the rapture,

    "Can I Have Two of Those Please"

    With questions comes answers

   Or the long silence which is in itself the solution

Actions with reactions

And transactions from motivational eagerness

The reason we have a left with a right

An up with a down

And if there is to be an ending

There must have been a beginning

So let the ending be the beginning be the ending

All over again, and recycle this cycle

As this wheel is attached to another

And I am sure with every trainer

There is another opposite

So, with this end

Let there be another beginning

And when the world ends

Let that be the best beginning

The moment with one opposite it

And let the sunshine and the rain drop

As every rainbow touches down twice

A curve predicted by the numbers

One and the opposite

And together they make nothing

Enter the balance

I toss this letter into the void, the abyss between us, this space that keeps conversation from happening.

Sincerely,
Rush Whitacre
740-336-9169

9-13-11
Dear Taylor Swift,

This has been a really good day. I got a phone call from Jesse earlier and she has decided to hire me on at Blick… that is a big deal for me. My first job in New York. With this job I should be able to make rent without too much trouble, and I should be able to afford to pay for art supplies when I need them. I was really excited. I then rode with Laura-girl into Manhattan to Blick so that I could fill out the background check paperwork. I was shocked at how little I actually had to fill out. There was nothing to it. I have no worries about getting the job, I have an untarnished history. After visiting Blick shortly I headed over to the gallery to visit with Laura-girl, and we ended up staying at the gallery until almost 10 pm… it was great, and because Laura-girl did stay there that late she doesn't have to go in tomorrow at all. Which is a really good thing.

So, tomorrow I don't think that my paintings will be dry enough to paint over again, so I will resort to writing as usual, and maybe look at the job market a little. Now that Blick has hired me on I can settle down a little. Just a little though. Blick doesn't really pay that much, so I am still on the outlook for another job, another job with benefits and better pay.

A little side note, Louis just messaged me, he just said that he is going to crash on my couch tomorrow… Uh,,,, I don't think that is going to happen because I don't have the room, and because he can't support himself. If you are not willing to make some sacrifices here in NY to make it by,,,, then you probably just weren't meant to live here. That is the truth, I don't see Louis ever moving here again. I guess his mother had to drive here to pick him up and take him home once before because he had lost his mind or something. Personally, I don't think he ever got it back… No, as much as I really care about Louis, I don't ever see him living with me again… He was just too much maintenance. Lol, if that is possible. Love ya Louis, just can't live with ya I guess.

So, this Thursday there are some amazing openings to go to. I think we are going to a Mathew Barney opening, and the Richard Serra, and Jenny Saville. This should be a lot of fun, and I can't wait to see these works in person. Jenny Saville is someone who's work I have enjoyed for awhile. Of course, I have to work with Alan in the morning putting up shelves, but, after that I am probably just going to camp out at the gallery until the openings… I can't wait!!!

This Poem is for edges,

"They Matter so Much"

Blended, rough, and just plain unsure

They are all around us

The meeting of two

The meeting of many

And it is very important

The moment of the merge

A place that we only stare

> If the flaw is greater than the execution
>
> Of greatness
>
> And this moment varies
>
> Contractor, engineer, to artist
>
> All is subjective
>
> And all is wrong in the eyes of the harsh critic
>
> All is right in the eyes of a hardcore fan
>
> And in the eyes of the artist
>
> All is art
>
> And all is worthy of 15 minutes of fame
>
> 15 minutes of connection
>
> Art against the curve
>
> Against the art.

I toss this letter into the void, the abyss between us, this space the keeps conversation from happening.

Sincerely,
Rush Whitacre
740-336-9169

9-14-11

Dear Taylor Swift,

    What a great ending to a slow day. So, all day I worked on my cleaning the house, and then rested on the couch for a little bit, and then I did some writing, and then Jesse contacted me to see if I wanted to go to the Richard Serra Opening at the on 555 W 24th street in Chelsea. I said to her, "why not". Besides, I really needed to get out of the apartment and spend some time with Jesse and just hang out. We got to the show and I found out then that Richard Serra was going to be at the show to greet people, which got me really excited. I am a fan of Serra's work because it is big and impressive, and awe inspiring. Then while we were walking around Chuck Close came into the gallery and I got to meet him and ask tell him that I am a fan of his and how much I appreciate his vigor. He was a rather quiet man, kinda shy at first, but he warmed up. Then we parted ways. I think I will be better prepared to actually ask him some more intelligent questions the next time I meet him verses the awe I felt in the moment. I don't know though, he seemed rather intimidating at first.

Richard Serra has some really nice big work, and I can dig that.. My motto has always been bigger is better, and nothing can be better than to see powerful 2 inch steel plates bent and formed into contours and are really reminiscent of my imagination of a world I have written about. I really had a connection with the Richard Serra Steel and its rust. The Serra piece is much more beautiful that I imagined. In person I could enjoy all the little walkways, and all the variations in the rust patterns and the odd feeling of walls that make me want to walk against gravity. I really couldn't grasp the weight of the structures as they so elegantly flowed from one of the room to the next, making their own little moment, little rooms within the room. And in those rooms I found that no one wanted to stay, no one wanted to be hidden from the crowd of people who were so eagerly eating each others faces off. I say that because everyone wanted to be seen and see at the same time... there was this grotesqueness about the people, all looking and wanting to be looked-at at the same time. Even the models that were having their pictures taken during the show were having a hard time not finding themselves trying to look, verses being looked at. I was finding quite a nice little balance between the show, the showers, and the showees. Something about the eating off of the faces fits, and if you were there, you would know what I am talking about.

This poem is for pressure,

"On Top There is a Mountain"

Two inches wide

Twelve feet tall

And all the metal in the world

And all the scrap yards

Beckon its height of awareness

And a boat of shows aren't sailing

Not like this showboat

This show full of mimes

Full of mysterious box makers

And matches waiting to be lit

And don't raise your voice

Or wait too long in the line

For the turning of the world never ceases

Neither does time

And your time is now, is waiting

Is the only thing keeping you from standing still

Keep the move on

Move on the keeper and make your goal

For the moment shall never pass
Your way again.

I toss this letter into the void, the abyss between us, this space that keeps conversation from happening.

Sincerely,
Rush Whitacre
740-336-9169

9-15-11

Dear Taylor Swift,

    I am really really tired. I got up at 6 and left for Alan's apartment to put up some shelves. The shelves were so easy to put up. Afterwards I got to go up on the roof of Alan's apartment building. Wow, what a great view. I know exactly where I am taking a date if I can round one up, to that roof top. There is a really nice terrace, and a really nice view. Alan is so funny. I found out from him that his son was actually interviewed by Ellen on the Ellen show but it never aired because it just didn't for some reason. Alan told me that he could get a copy of the tape because it never aired. I told him that he needed to write another letter asking them to air it on YouTube, then he could at least see it, and download it using Kepi. Oh well. I am sure that kind of thing happens all the time. I then, while at his place, realized that I somehow broke the protective cover on my phone and had to find a Verizon store to fix it. Uggggh. I bet I walked 3 miles today, which was a really good thing. It was fun exploring and finding new places. Mostly I found out there Verizon stores weren't located. On my way I found a Chipotle, mmm, delicious.

    Alan gave me some photo's to take to the Gallery, and I did. While at the gallery I got a phone call from the Metropolitan Museum for a job offer to work in Security. I have an interview this coming Saturday, and I am a little nervous because they want a copy of my diploma, and it hasn't come in the mail. You have to hear why, because this interview prompted me to find out why. I called UC and found out that they had a hold on my diploma because of a Zero dollar Balance at the health center. This means that my diploma was on hold because I didn't owe them money… How fun is that. So, for about 2 months I have been thinking that they were just really taking their sweet old time to get it to me when really they just had some kind of glitch in their system… lol, wow, what a day. Then…

    Later tonight I went to the Jenny Saville opening.. Wow, so awesome. Finally, someone working big, gesturally, and someone who also shows up at shows to be a part of the scene. It was really nice to see Jenny Saville juxtaposed against the backdrop of her own work. She only showed up for the last ten minutes, but it was well worth the ten minutes. She is a lot shorter than I imagined. I don't know, I guess I see how big her work is and think that someone with a long arm made the sweeping motions that I see. Not only that, but she was a lot skinnier than I imagined. Her flesh paintings through me off I suppose.

This poem is for the decision,

"Two Trains Coming Head to Head"

Time as it would seem

Has caught up with me and my applications

And I applied them all well

A deep well

With an echo

So long I waited for its return

And with it came more than I said

More noise than I made

And I stand here happy, laughing

Waiting for my laugh to echo back

But it doesn't

It just lapsed into walls

Into a cube

Into a space with my mouth open

And my ears open wider

Waiting

Time passes

And the closer I get

The further away my hearing goes

I tap my foot

Bleaker.

I toss this letter into the void, the abyss between us, this space that keeps conversation from happening.

Sincerely,
Rush Whitacre

740-336-9169

9-16-11

Dear Taylor Swift,

Another fun filled day. I spent the morning talking to Jesse from Blick where I just got hired, and then I came home and painted all after noon until heading over to Alan's. What a day. Kristal was fun to pick on a little. The store was started by a man named Dick Blick, and I asked her if it was ok if I wore a shirt that said "I work for Dick" and she just laughed and laughed. I am pretty sure it has already been done before, but it is still a funny maker.

After visiting Blick I had some lunch at Wendy's and then came back to the apartment to paint. I got all the 15 paintings covered with another layer of paint, this time with a poem written about my (related person who is male and not named). The all over pattern I am creating is getting really interesting. I keep looking at the painting in the mirror and trying to decide which I like better, the straight on view, or the reverse from looking in the mirror at it. Right now I have four poems on the 15 canvases, four different colors, the three primary colors, and baby blue because it is my favorite color. While I was finishing up painting the last two paintings Jesse came home. She went into her room and stayed there the rest of the night while I was here. I left shortly after I finished painting to get some pizza, and then I looked at my truck and realized that I had forgotten that I was supposed to be at Alan's at 8 pm, it was now 7:30. So, I hoped into my truck and rushed over to his place and he was so tired.

We ended up driving to his place and picking up a bunch of large boxes of his photography stuff. I got to see Alan's workplace, it was absolutely awesome.. I could just tell that many important things had happened there. I was jealous. I am sure that if I asked Alan he would let spend a day at his work place following him around like an intern just to see what he does, and how things operate. I think it would be a great experience, just like sitting in on the gallery meeting.. I learned so much just from listening. Lol. Oh, I need to have a show up here in NYC… Heck, I need to finish these paintings!!! Lol.

After helping Alan I went up to the roof of his place and saw the beauty of the city from an amazing perspective. From 22 stories up with no buildings around for 360 degrees. I just kept talking to myself and saying to myself how beautiful the city is. I thought I was alone, and then I turned and there was a lone woman on the roof just sitting there.. I had to recap what I said and decide if I should be embarrassed, nope, not me… lol.. I met the woman, her name is Giselle, and she was really nice to talk to. I learned from her perspective what it was like to be in NYC during 9/11. She had a horrible boss. She even quite her job because she learned what a horrible boss she had because of the whole thing. Giselle loved my art, and mentioned that she is related to the people who run a gallery in Chelsea. I don't know what she meant by that, but I am sure it was just a nice friendly gesture.

This poem is for the roof

                "A view less enjoyed, a pity"
                At every edge my mouth drops
                I smile and I walk and walk and walk
                In circles
                How can it be empty?
                I ask myself
                How can it not be enjoyed
                Even the inhabitants are not sure
                The ones who dare to venture
                The ones who know beauty
                The ones who make the effort
                The ones proud of their home
                And I say
                Thank you
                As your stories enchanted me
                I hope I enchanted you
                And my stay was worth your while
                As your while was worth every second
                To me
                Tokens to be dropped
                Wishes to be made
                And I remain
                Eyes glistening.

I toss this letter into the void, the abyss between us, this space that keeps conversation from happening.

Sincerely,
Rush Whitacre
740-336-9169

6-17-11

Dear Taylor Swift,

      Well, I really wasn't that nervous at the interview. The fun was leading up to the interview. 30 minutes before I was to leave for the interview I found out that our subway was shutdown for construction… luckily I have a truck and I could drive to get there on time. I still left an hour and a half early in order to make it. The traffic was awful, just totally packed with people. When I got within two blocks I discovered that I wasn't going to be able to make it to my interview on time.. apparently there was a parade and all the blocks surrounding the museum were blocked off, and I got ushered through the park over to the Natural history museum. Once I got over there I called to tell someone at the Museum that I was going to be late for my interview. I asked for Meredith, but, she wasn't working today, and so, they patched me through to a man named John who was doing the interview. He was so nice. I totally expected him to tell me to not come if I was going to be late, or to tell me that the position was filled and to go ahead home… I don't know why I thought that. Then, I made a mistake and parked in a spot that only allowed me one hour… not much room for error. I don't know why I thought it would only take an hour to interview me.. it was silly. The whole time I was being asked questions I just kept envisioning a tow truck, or a huge fine that I wouldn't be able to pay. Then suddenly the guy asked me if I had any questions. I decided that I might as well ask some. I mean, at figured let what may come to come. If I was to get a ticket, I was to get a ticket.. then the interview was over and I left the building as fast as I could. I must say, that museum is a maze, just a maze. I had to ask three people where the main entrance was in order to get out. I will really have to learn my way around that place if I am really to get a job there. The guy asked me if there was a problem with calling me on Monday, and I said absolutely not, that he could call me any time on Monday. I am working at Blick on Monday, I don't know if he will be able to get me… dang it. Oh boy, when it rains, I get wet… I am pretty sure that I am going to take the position at the museum. That only way I could work at Blick is if they made my schedule so that I could work there Monday, Tuesday, Wednesday. I have this bad feeling that I am not going to be able to work at Blick all the time, or for very long. I guess I will hold out and see what I get. Maybe they won't even call me back. Who knows. If I do get the job at the Museum, I will have to tell Blick, there is no doubt about that. I wonder if they would let me work just three days, Monday through Wednesday, because those would be my only days available. Aaaaaaaaahhhh. I just can't simply cut out all my time, sacrifice it for two jobs can I?? lol we shall see. This will be the determining week.

This poem is for the moment that we all know,

"Once it's Over, it's Over"

Drop the mic

The crowd is cheering

Roaring, clapping, screaming

I dropped my mouth

<pre>
                              Open
                   And those lyrics cut through me
                  My past with someone I once loved
                 I once spent time with, held their hand
                 You dropped my name, without speaking it
                   And across the world I am known
                         And I am so unknown
                      And hated as I hate myself
                   Hated as the drum beats away that tune
                         As you have beaten me
                             So drop the mic
                    Because once the words are written
                        They don't have to be sung
                                Or repeated
                           One syllable at a time
                          and I will drop myself
                            one drip at a time
</pre>

I toss this letter into the void, the abyss between us, this space that keeps conversation from happening.

Sincerely,

Rush Whitacre

740-336-9169

9-18-11

Dear Taylor Swift,

      Today is kinda like the calm before the storm. I start working at Blick tomorrow, and I might have a phone call from the Metropolitan Museum of art about starting there at a security guard, or at least for the training for this upcoming 26th. On a little side note, my roommate is cooking really good smelling food, and I am so jealous. I am down to Ramen… and, luckily for me I bought about 80 packages of Ramen when I had money, because I knew that I could exist on them until I got a job, and the money started to roll in. ha, roll in, as if the jobs will provide me with that much money. I will love my jobs, or I will quite.. I am not going to work a job that carves away at my soul. I simply will not do it. Not to mention, it is easier for me to say this knowing that the met and Blick are interested in me. If I had no opportunities, I would not be so easily suaded.

 I have been hearing a lot from my friend Carlee lately. I think she has taken a little more interest in me since I moved to NY. I must say, so have a few of my other friends. I miss my friends from home, and the few I still have living in Cincinnati. They are a support system, like a little circle of energy all bustling around with things to do and things to say and it is the honest friend who I cherish, the friend who is not afraid to tell me that I am wrong. My friend Andre, who is now in Portugal was that kind of friend. He was awesome, and kind, and sweet, and someone who I think was genuine most of the time, unless he was acting.

 I want to Ikea today with Jesse, it was an experience. I have never been to an IKEA, and I found out that everything there is made in china… well I am assuming this because every label I read said this. Now, I am not a stickler for buy things made here in the USA, but,, man, why can't we make the things like they are making… seriously. It can't be that hard to make those things at a fair and cheap price right?? Most of the things looked machine made anyway. What do I know.

This poem is for the edge of the universe,

"I can't bring you back"

Nothing is as cruel as gravity

And you have defied it all

Your legs have helped you travel beyond reality

And there is nothing worse

Than waiting for you to come home

No fate I would rather endure

Or feelings I would rather have about this place

Than the ones I have while you are not here

As my life is not complete as thin as it is watered down

With all the people seeing your so strong

And this little girl who shined like an angel

And this hole is ever bigger, ever wider

As I am left behind

Behind a wall,

Behind the noise

The flap of an angel's wings

Changes the weather

And whether you like it or not

It is getting colder

And parts of me freeze

And this empty spot beside me

The cursed void

The crushing nothing

Alone and I am your visitor

Nothing more

I toss this letter into the void, the abyss between us, this space that keeps conversation form happening.

Sincerely,
Rush Whitacre
740-336-9169

9-19-11

Dear Taylor Swift,

Yeah! My first day at Blick was a complete success. I even told Jesse up front that I got a job at the Museum and she was totally cool with it. She told me that she was a bit disappointed, but, she understood that only working 24 hours a week would not keep me afloat. I think what I am going to do is ask if I can work 2 twelve hour shifts at Blick so that I can have Wednesday off. I think that would be for the best, this way I can have that time off and still have time to paint for a full day at least once a week. As it is, I will be pressed to work on my paintings every little bit that I get.

Tonight was a weird night. We were planning on talking to Russ, our landlord, about our rent and our new found infestation of mice since he has not fixed our floor. I know the mice are coming up through the floor where he ripped out the kitchen sink and stove. When Russ said that he would have someone come up and finish the floor tomorrow, we agreed to pay the 1,200 dollars. When Jesse found out that that we were going to split the bill up just like before she got upset and walked back into her room quite upset. I was surprised, really surprised. She just comes off sometimes a bit off, I guess we all have those days. I mean,,, who can say they are living up here in NY to the tune of 300 dollars a month with utilities included…. Wow, that is ridiculous. I am sure that there is no one else anywhere within 100 miles with our situation… lol Oh well. She will get over it.

Tomorrow I am going to get fitted for my suit to work at the met.. how exciting is that. And then on the 26th I will be going through orientation. I guess there is a quiz that I have to pass in order to become a security officer, and I also have to go to the DMV to get my NY id… I guess I had better do that tomorrow… hmmm, yeah, I had better do that tomorrow. Lol, maybe I had better do that tomorrow before coming home to go to home depot.. wow.

Ok, here is the best thing that has happened all week. My friend/exroommate has informed me that I am friends with his ex on facebook, and it is really eating him alive. I am surprised by this, because I can't help but to wonder why it matters to him, and why above all of that he is still friends with her on there…. It doesn't add up, how can he get mad at me for something that I didn't know I had done, when he is doing it on purpose??? Weird. There is no code for this.

This poem is for the code, if it were to be written,

"No way of knowing, no?"

You run that way,

And I will run that way

If we end up in the same place

And we are still friends

Then does it matter which route we took

Or what happened in between

Or who we saw along the way

Or how many times we flapped our wings

Only to have the wax melt

And for us to fall

To the ground

Or in love, neither matter

What matters

What does matter?

Does matter matter

Or is it just something to fill the void

The one left behind from your absence

Am I suppose to suppose

Or is the fact just that, a fact

A matter of the mother of all matters

And another void erupts

Dissipates

Evades me

I toss this letter into the void, the abyss between us, this space the keeps conversation from happening.

Sincerely,

Rush Whitacre

740-336-9169

9-20-11

Dear Taylor Swift,

    Well, my visit to the met was actually dualistically unique. I met a man in the basement who just cussed like a sailor, he was a tailor, and I must say that he was old, but his words were bold... ok, enough rhyming. He did cuss like a sailor though. It was a complete reversal from what I was expecting.. I was expecting so much professionalism, and it was a complete comedy of errors. In the end it was decided that I was too tall for any of the suit jackets they had and that I would have to come back in this Monday to get fitted the right way by some professional. I am looking forward to that. Although, I hope that it doesn't affect my day with orientation and all... I hear that we are supposed to get a tour of the entire museum, and I would love to be given a tour of the entire place. That would be awesome.

    Today while I was away from the apartment Russ was suppose to fix our floor in our kitchen. He was suppose to fill in the hole so that a certain mouse would stop coming in and worrying my two female roommates. I haven't seen it, but I have seen its foot prints in the grease left behind in Jesses unwashed greasy pot. Yeah, I am still doing her dishes. She is really upset about having to do her dishes in the bathroom... she considers it as some degree of the 8th deadly sin or something. I don't quite understand it really... I mean, the kitchen had a sink. The bathroom has a sink... and both put out the same water... hmmm. Maybe I am not meant to understand this. I do know that I am waiting until the dishes are uncomfortably overflowing out of a little plastic container we have. Not on purpose, but because I simply don't have as much time as I did when this all came down in the first place.

    Ok, on a different note. I don't know if I am going to be able to keep up my job at Blick. I am going to give it my all, but, in the end, I can get paid better at the museum because of overtime and all...and I would rather be paid over time and make more money faster than I would working two jobs and being miserable. I will have to plan carefully though, because I will need to give Blick a two week notice before I bail on them.. I really don't want to quite Blick because the people who work there are awesome, and there are some pretty important people who shop there who I want to meet, so, we shall see.

This poem is for the puzzle II

"Turning"

When I was turning over leaves

You were learning to walk

And my world was revolving around rules

And yours was about learning them

And when it comes down to lessons learned

And places been

I don't know if I fit

Inside that world

The place that you are trying to see me go

To many suns lighting this side

And none on the other

Maybe that is where I belong

Across the universe

Fading into the dark matter

Where the stars still shine brightly

And the black hole

Is never silent

Is always hungry

And is always consuming

I toss this letter into the void, the abyss between us, this space the keeps conversation from happening.

Sincerely,

Rush Whitacre

740-336-9169

9-21-11

Dear Taylor Swift,

Today was my first long day at Blick, and my first day to close. It is a different world around closing,,, and,,, I am surprised that place doesn't get itself robbed blind, that is all I am going to say about that. I really wish I could say a lot more, but, I also don't really care. The day was really busy, and the stock wasn't put away again. I am surprised that anything ever gets done around there. I just kept on getting pulled aside and asked so many questions, and I was asked to help out so much. I like the job, but I am never going to get all that stuff put away if I keep getting pulled away from my post, my area where I am suppose to be working. I didn't take my second 10 minute break. Not that it would have mattered. I guess I should have. I just really didn't care, I suppose if I thought I needed it I would have taken it. Tomorrow is this thing called Blick Madness. We are having a great big celebration for the sake of selling more stuff, and trying to make more money than usual, or, giving the appearance that we are really trying to make an effort to give good deals on our goods.

You know, I am just going to say it. Why have a security officer if they are not allowed to do anything about stuff being stolen. Why do we have one, I just don't understand it at all. The employees are not allowed to do anything about it, and the security officer is pretty much just allowed to follow people around and keep them from putting stuff in their pocket, but he can't keep his eyes on everyone, and therefore, dozens of people throughout the day simply come in and steal stuff and get away with it. It is nerve racking. I really don't care. Really I don't, it is just one of those facts of life, that stealing in some places is just that easy, just that easy. I have this theory that some places are just simply more worried about their own stuff being stolen by the employees instead of costumers. I wouldn't be surprised.

I have been watching more and more original songs by people, and I have even added some of the people who are singing the songs to my friends list on facebook to ask them if they are interested in making a music video for their music here in NY. I know that NY is not the capital of the world of Music videos, but, it doesn't hurt to have it in the background. And, it really is a beautiful place. Anyone who says otherwise doesn't know any better. My fingers are crossed on the making of a music video. I think it would be really worth my while, something else to add to my list of accomplishments.

This poem is for Leah,

"The Stranger"

You don't know me

But I am sure we were friends in a different life

And I am sure that we were lovers

Or maybe just visitors

To dark places

Where the lights only comes in

To slip the light a token

For just one more moment of sleep

Where day dreams only wish they could journey

To walk amongst the greatest places

The greatest imagination

Clouds

And flight with not reason for hovering

And silly fantasies that come true

Only in the dark and still

Of a restless sleep

A nightmares foe

Is a friends interjection

The sudden lull of daylight

And awaken.

I toss this letter into the void, the abyss between us, this space that keeps conversation from happening.

Sincerely,
Rush Whitacre
740-336-9169

9-22-11

Dear Taylor Swift,

    WOW… Blick Madness was really a mad house. The funny thing about it is that even though it was a mad house I think that that madness actually allowed me to get more stuff stocked and put away than usual. People must run around looking for stuff themselves while I ran around filling in the gaps. It was a really nice day. I think that we should have more madness days, maybe a madness week. I say why not. What could it hurt. One wild crazy week out of the whole year.. that might actually be a disaster. We would surely not be able to keep up with stocking everything. There would have been empty shelves everywhere

    I am really tired. I think that I will call it a night early. I am on the phone with Gari. Gari and I am and Laura-girl have started something that I haven't heard of before… we have a user account on facebook where all three of us actually run the account from three different places. I didn't think it was possible, but it is totally possible. Something similar happened on my laptop once when Louis has logged into his account and then I went to log into my account and instead of logging in on my account it logged in on Louis's account and I could see him navigating his account, and his conversation with Kittie.. and I went to his friend request list and added myself as one of his friends. I was glad that I did, because he would never have, and we would not be in contact right now. Lol.. which is kinda sad to think about, because I do miss him, believe it or not.

This poem is for the multiuser,

"We Are One And Many"
We argue with ourselves
We talk to ourselves
And yet all the while we are not
We are many using one
Many making many comments to ourselves
Making motions
Moving foreward
Yet moving nowhere
Getting nowhere
And our comments are short and swift
Less of an ideal
More of an epicness
Well beyond its time
Someone will take notice
And that person will most likely
Shut you, we, us down
And in this moment
Our moment
Your time is my time is her time
And no one is watching
But I hear you laugh
And that makes me feel good
We feel good

I toss this letter into the void, the abyss between us, this space the keeps conversation from happening.

Sincerely,

Rush Whitacre

740-336-9169

9-23-11

Dear Taylor Swift,

    Hello Hello… I love Blick! The people at Blick make my day worth spending putting away thousands of items for making our government money… because in the end,, I am working for the government right.. I mean, especially since I owe the government around ninety thousand dollars in school loans? Lol. I am still laughing about that.

    Oh well.

    But seriously. I love all the employees who are working at Blick, I really do, and from what I hear from Laura-girl, she says that the management who are working right now are the best she has experienced thus far, so, I am pretty psyched to be working for this company. This is what I have to say about Jesse, Crystal, Melody, and Meg.. totally awesome bosses to be working with. Totally.

    Ok, so, Laura-girl and I have been talking for hours tonight, and laughing and just having a good time. I really just love Laura-girl to death like a sister, like someone I have the utmost respect for.

    Today it rained like it does in the movies. Out back of Blick rain was coming down so hard it was like rain like you see in the movies. Rain was coming down like fire trucks were shooting it up in to the air at us, it was spectacular. We couldn't put cardboard outside for fear that it would fill with water and not be liftable to get into the back of a trash truck. Lol. I can't imagine that the hydraulics wouldn't be able to lift the trash, but I am also sure that weirder things have happened.

    Laura-girl and I worked the same shift today, it was great. She actually came back to where I was working and messed with me for a second. It was funny. Laura-girl and I are so great of friends. I just love Laura-girl so much. Really, she is a great friend. I did so much stocking today, there was a massive amount of stocking to do and I just whipped it all out. It was great. I hope that I didn't make anyone look bad or anything, because I really went through the shipment really fast because I just wanted to get the stuff out there for other artists to find so that they could work with the stuff. I know that I would want the people to have the stuff out there so that I could find it, instead of it being trapped in boxes where I couldn't get to it.

This poem is for French fries,

        "Hmmm, but I need more ketchup"

        So, I ordered a large fry

                    And I asked for a lot of ketchup
                            But, all I got was a lie
                      Because four packets of sauce
                      Doesn't mean that it will last
                  And doesn't mean that I am happy
                        It just means more begging
                              And more questions
                 And more getting up from my seat
                    And leaving my food at the table
                                  Abandoned,
                  Well, for a moment or two anyway
                        All because I like ketchup
                  And you wouldn't give me a handful
                    Or just twice as much as usual
                Such a sad state this world would be in
                If my appetite for ketchup could possibly
                                Bankrupt you
                                And yet you,,,
                    Woud be worse off without me
                          As your costumer
                              Check please.

I toss this letter into the void, the abyss between us, this space that keeps conversation from happening.

Sincerely,
Rush Whitacre
740-336-9169

9-24-11
Dear Taylor Swift,
      Well, I decided to go to the gallery to spend the day with Laura-girl and to get out of the apartment and let Jesse have it to herself so that she could have some free time to do whatever and not have to worry about anything or anyone getting in the

way. We all need that in the apartment, free play time. I know I get it, lol, regardless of who is there.

I have started this new project, besides the paintings, and the fantasy novel, and besides these letters, and besides the drawings, and the fake facebook page, and learning about my new work places, and besides the creative tactics I am using to not starve to death. I have decided to search out really small time musicians who are just using their laptops and an instrument to make music and I am contacting them to see if they want to come to NY to maybe actually shoot a make a music video using their song. I am really excited about this, as broke as I am, I can see making videos for these people as a way to make some great contacts. So far I have found it pretty hard to get through to people because I don't think they are expecting to get someone who honestly just wants to try to make something great, something fun, and not to mention that some of them have thousands of friends on their sites so I am just like a needle in a haystack, I am a needle in a needlestack really I guess. Oh well, at least I am having fun.

Here I sit at this gallery, Laura-girl beside me is actually working, and I am here just because I really wanted a desk to work off of today. And, surprise surprise, molly is next door in the gallery working, making stuff for the gallery. She and I talked for about thirty minutes. Pretty interesting girl. Has a boyfriend, use to do trick rollerblading, and also does work about her illness's mostly her injuries I guess rather. She is an interesting person. I don't know about her work though. She started out with a scholarship to play sports in college and then she blew her knees out and she lost the scholarship and went into art. It is interesting how people come to their decisions. It is unfortunate when the body just simply can't get done what the minds feel it should be able to do…

I think that later I am going to paint at the apartment. My paint in dry and it is calling to me. I just have to finish the blue writing on half of the paintings and then I can start the drip drawings over the words.

This poem is for art snob,

"Tempting Brunette"

Click and clack

I hear you coming

You have a look of a vixen

Tiger tempting the prey

From the tree

From the tall grasses

You will watch me graze

Eat these letters

These words

My foot

And I stick it in my mouth often enough

That I am sure I will trip

I will fall

Consumed by your presence

And all I can do is run

And run

Only to never catch up

And just the same

Never be caught

I toss this letter into the void, the abyss between us, this space the keeps conversation from happening.

Sincerely,
Rush Whitacre
740-336-9169

9-25-11
Dear Taylor Swift,

  Today is Sunday, the day before my big first day at the Metropolitan Museum job. I am only nervous because I don't have a NY ID... and this is a problem because I need it to join the union at the Museum... I need it so that I can get all the benefits that the union guys get... but more importantly, I need the ID so that I can get and keep this job... and here is the irony of the whole thing. I need to get a copy of my social security number... ahhh, ok, things will get better.

  Today I painted for hours, and I took lots of photographs of my work.. I don't know why it is so important to take so many pictures of my work,,, really I don't. I would just as soon do all the work and then just have the work and not that much recorded history. Besides, all people are going to see is the final product... lol. So, it is all I am worried about. I will make it good, I will make it great, and I will be successful. I must keep telling myself this.

  I found a new funky song that I like, called Mr. Hurricane by Beast. It is pretty cool. In the video there is a person made of bees, and I really find it,,, well, rather intriguing, and idea of a man made out of bees... I think the lead singer is a woman, but they use some kind of voice modifier or something and her voice is just as equally intriguing as the bee-man. Watch It if you get a chance.

I have to go to bed here real soon, I have to be at the met tomorrow by 9 am, and that means I have to leave here around 7:30 am… I am not looking forward to this. It is 1 am now. So, ahhhh, what have I done to myself… Oh yeah, I remember now, I watched two episodes of breaking bad, that is what I did. Good show, great show, but I am not sure how it has gone for three seasons though… I have only watched the first two episodes… so, I will have to watch more and see. Ok, good night world.

I am talking to my ex roommate Louis, the one who liked to watch a lot of movies and play a lot of video games. I hope that he is making better decisions for himself, otherwise he is going to not have a very good life ahead of himself. He needs to get in gear and focus on something, something that he is good at,,, something that he likes, something that makes him happy. Ok, enough about that.

This poem is for the empty bottle,

"Shake That Bottle"

This is the explosion I warned you about

There was only a little cap

A lot of mixing

And then a mess, quite a mess

And time is spent, wasted

And the day seems to drag on as I haven't slept

In days, it feels like days

But that is what planes do

They keep you awake

And they decompress everything

And in flight

You won't think about that bottle

That shake, shake, shake

And that plug

That just can't hold

Just can't keep back the pressure

That end is near

And I must sleep

Good night sweet world

Bitter death dreams

Walls, just walls

I toss this letter into the void, the abyss between us, this space that keeps conversation from happening.

Sincerely,
Rush Whitacre
740-336-9169

9-26-11

Dear Taylor Swift,

  I love the Met… I have found a job that I can do a long time and have a different day every day. I really can't even explain the job I have picked up at the met because it is such a secretive society… the people who were talking about their positions actually made a point to shut the door so that no one could hear what they had to say… I feel really good about my job at the met, you have no idea. I just hope that I don't let anyone down. Especially myself. I am really feeling good about this job. I don't know if it is because it is the first job that I have gotten because I didn't have someone find me the job, or if it because it is at the Met… both play a role I am sure.

  Ok, Laura-girl is home, and I feel good about this… I have been so worried about this. She didn't come home last night and I was so worried about her. All the way up until around 2 am last night.. I think I have her convinced to call me the next time this happens, just because if I am expecting her home and she doesn't come home and I am so worried that I can't sleep I think she wants me to be able to sleep… she is a great friend… I just love Laura-girl to death as a friend. I would run through fire for Laura-girl.

  Tonight after I got home I could sense quite a personality change in Jesse and the way she was talking to Laura-girl and I.. I don't know what is going on with her, but I fear that she is thinking about moving out for some reason. I mean, she doesn't like how we don't have a kitchen, even though she is only paying 300 dollars a month for rent including utilities. I think that she is underestimating the great things that are happening, and are going to happen here at our apartment… a new balcony, and new rooms within the year.. I mean,,, wow, this is going to be a great place. I can't wait for all of this to happen.

  Ok, tonight Alan, one of the Viridian Artists took about 20 pictures of me tonight. I am trying to convice him that he needs to be taking pictures of Laura-girl, Jesse, and myself as part of his portfolio… it could be called his starving artist series. And, not to mention, if any of us get famous,,, he would have a record of our time here in Brooklyn as starving artist, the before we were famous pictures. As I see it, every group of famous artist seemed to have their famous photographer friend who took all of their pictures, and why not Alan for us… All that needs to happen is the pictures, we are living the lifestyle for sure in this illegal apartment with no kitchen, sleeping on the hardwood floors. Why are we not photo quality material, or subject matter???

This poem is for the click of the moment,

"Flash, and you are Immortalized"

"Flash"

And there is a click

You see the light

You look up,

And there before you is a person with a camera

Someone who was laying and waiting

Someone who was watching for you to screw up

A picture you were trying to avoid

Is now out for all to see

Is out there for the masses

And all you can do is own it

Say, "yes, that was me"

We were crazy

We were carefree

And we were happy artists

And the world took notice for just a moment

Just fifteen minutes

And poof, we were in the mix

In the talk,

In the vocabulary of history

We were hip

Living the dream

We were alive

I toss this letter into the void, the abyss between us, this space the keeps conversation from happening.

Sincerely,
Rush Whitacre

740-336-9169

9-27-11

Dear Taylor Swift,

My second day at my job was just as exciting as my first… well, the orientation anyways was. I am really excited about finally getting out on the floors to the Met and meeting and greeting all the people and seeing all the art. I watched as some of the guards yawned and stretched and I couldn't help but to think that I could be that person very soon… I found out some other really good news about my job too, about the pay and pay scale, and how it changes… but, I am not allowed to reveal secrets… too bad I suppose. I mean, I want to keep my job, and they told me that revealing their secrets would get me fired quicker than anything ever could. They are all serious about their jobs, and I understand why… they are holding billions and billions of dollars worth of art within their walls.

I am excited about tomorrow, and I can't wait to start working full time at the museum and working some over time and getting a check in the bank so that I can but some real food.. Ramen noodles are not great as a meal everyday and every day and every day. And every day.

Tomorrow I will be eating in the café at the Met. I just need a change, maybe I will eat a salad. I saw their salad bar today and I was jealous at all the people who got one. So, tomorrow, I will simply grow a pair and use my credit card for some food.

It is late again, and I should be getting to sleep here soon. I haven't slept much in the past couple of days, I get so excited about my job that I can't seem to get to bed, that and I want to make sure I don't have any important emails and facebook stuff.

I have decided that since I am not getting a reply from people who I have searched out on YouTube to make music videos with them that I am going to make my own music video using my voice and someone else's instrument skills that I find on YouTube… it should be fun. I have decided, that when I get some time I am going to record myself singing Landslide by Stevie nicks. I remember years ago my brother Randal telling me that it was the perfect song for our dad, because of how our dad was such a rock climber and how he got us all interested in rock climbing, and many others interested. I will use central park as my location for filming. I just need so find some people to watch camera's so that they don't get stolen. Lol. This will be ridiculous.

This poem is for sticking your foot in your mouth

"Louis, What are you Thinking?"

Words words words

And you write without thinking

Consequences my friend

Think about who you are hurting

Who you are writing too

Who is your audience?

The world?

Your mom,

Me?

For I am losing all the corners

This square rounds out

And if you are not careful

It will roll away

It will roll

And you will be left with a blank spot

An empty chair

The tiny room

Colored only by the paint stains

That I left behind.

I toss this letter into the void, the abyss between us, this space that keeps conversation from happening.

Sincerely,
Rush Whitacre
740-336-9169

9-28-11
Dear Taylor Swift,

    Another day on the job in orientation. I guess this Friday we will all be shadowing someone on the floor to see what they do in our area. I am sure I will get the hang of it. Besides, I will be in the same area for 4 months.. I will get really familiar with all the work around me. Part of me sees myself working here in until I retire, only because there is so much room for moving up in this place. With my education, and the possibility to move up, I can totally see myself moving up through the ranks and being quite happy with an ever evolving job at the Met. I just need to keep focused on what will be in demand in the future. I would hate to transfer into a job the then get let go because the demand just disappeared. That would not be a happy day for me. Either way, I work hard at everything I do, I am sure I would just get into a different position in the whole place.

I love my job for several reasons, one of them being something that happens when my shift is over. I get to walk through the park over to the B or C train and take them down to West 4th street to the F train. But, the point is, I get to walk through the park. The last three days I have been able to watch the set up of the concert of the concert for Black Eye'd Peas that is to take place this coming Friday. I don't know if it is free, or if I would have to pay to see it. All I know is that I am going to walk through the park probably during the concert and probably get to see some of it. I am sure it will be fun. I don't know, I have never been to a concert of theirs, so I have no idea what to expect.

I am home now, I just got off the phone with my friend Wester's wife. She told me that their son is getting some really good speech therapy and he is actually putting together sentences and asking for things in full sentences… he is four, and when he started at this speech therapist their son was classified as having the speech of a 18 month year old, and none of the kids would play with him at the child care that he was going to. Now, after three weeks he is starting to make some really good progress. I am sure that when I go home he will be talking up a storm, I am excited to hear what he has to say. It is going to be awesome… Ruby told me that she cried when she heard her son say a whole sentence.

This poem is for Caiden,

"I wANT a pEENUT bUTTER sANDWICH"

"What?"

And the tears start to come

Eye's swelling

And you think I am soo sad,

But I am not

I actually don't know what to say really

I don't know

I have longed to hear your voice

I have longed for this moment

Where I hear you

Listen to you

And you make words

Sentences

And you say to me

Mommy, I love you,

Now can I have that?

And the tears fall

How long I have waited to hear your voice

How long have you been waiting

To tell me

That you love me too.

I toss this letter into the void, the abyss between us, this space that keeps conversation from happening.

Sincerely,
Rush Whitacre
740-336-9169

9-29-11

Dear Taylor Swift,

Today was the first day that I swiped into the Metropolitan museum for work(orientation). It was an experience, and I don't mind being the new guy on the job, because I won't be for long. There are a lot of people at the Met who are great people, and many who are artists. We are a great family, well, I am really projecting this from what I have seen thus far, but there isn't a mean bone in any of the guards that I have seen. There is this one guy named Joel who just came back from Afghanistan, he looks like he had seen some battle. He is a very nice guy, always going out of this way to point things out to me the extra things that will be nice to know about once I am on the job. I must say, I am just excited to be around so much art, so much history, so much to see and read. I am going to apply for overtime this coming Thursday, I should get it since I have the least amount of time on my record...

I just watched the skyscraper video from Demi Lavato, I guess I haven't seen it until today. It brought tears to my eyes because it made me think of 9/11. I have always been an American, but on that day, I became a New Yorker, I became.

Ok, on a different note, Jesse won't be here for the next couple of days because her mother is in town and she doesn't want her mother seeing where she lives because she is too embarrassed I guess... I mean, it is a little place, but, it has artistic charm, and two other great artists living here...., my opinion.

I feel bad for Louis, he has no home,,, he is like a step away from being homeless. He doesn't find a job, and he lives at his moms like one day a week, and then to another place, and then a friends couch... I don't know how he is getting around.

Ok,,, there is this girl at the downtown stop on the F train who plays that accordion so beautifully... I mean, every time I am there she is there, except for the past three times that I have been there… Her music is mesmerizing, simply amazing… I would ask her for her name, but I don't want her to stop playing. I would give her a dollar, but I don't ever have one. I will someday, and I will ask her for her first name, I just want to be able to talk about her with a name to go with her face, her music. It really is great, she does this little sway while she plays, and then gives a little smile and you can just tell that she loves making her music. It is great. For now, she is the "Beautiful Accordion Girl"

This poem is for her,

"Beautiful Accordion Girl"
From the next track away
I hear you
Your music is swaying me, begging me to follow
And so I allow myself to be pulled In your direction,
People pass by like people do
Some stop and drop a dollar
Others change
And I changed
I started to see your world in a different light
In a different world
Where I still don't know your name
Just your music
And the people, they all stop
And tell you
You are so beautiful
And your music is why we have come
Is what makes our day complete
Fingers push
Arms pull

I toss this letter into the void, the abyss between us, this space that keeps conversation from happening.

Sincerely,
Rush Whitacre
740-336-9169

9-30-11

Dear Taylor Swift,

    Today was my last day in training at the Met as a security officer. I am excited that I will not have any more training, but I am also excited that I will be meeting some pretty cool people who will become my friends, or at least I hope they do. I followed a guy named Robert, he is a writer. There are so many artists who work at the met. I learned that he recently graduated from college with a creative writing degree and he has been writing abstract poems of some kind. I am not completely sure that I understand exactly what it is that he does, but, I am sure that I will learn somehow. Anyway, I shadowed him around all day today, just following him and looking at all the art. There is so much art there in the gallery, I love it. I have a pretty good idea of how quickly I will get familiar with the art. I only stood in the American wing for about 3 hours, and I just stood there looking at all the art, just reading labels, and just admiring so many different artists from over the years who have made work for the better.

    I am excited about the American wing's American painting section to open. I guess it has been closed for three years and is set to open in January. I have also found that I really like the viewable storage area… it has some of the stuff that can't be put out in the galleries because there just simply isn't enough space for all of it to be viewed. I also found out that the Museum has like three basements… one below the other. I am really impressed. Really impressed. I am thinking about spending at least two years in the security area, really, I am thinking about this seriously because we were told today that it takes at least that long before many people get promoted. I am going to start to apply for promotion as soon as my opportunity comes because I am curious if I can get it. I am curious if I can get promoted into other sections of the museum, into other areas and have influence over any of this world's greatest collection of art. Like I have said before, I am relentless, I will succeed, I will not stop until I have achieved what it is I am trying to achieve.. lol, mostly, I just want to be a great dad someday to some kids, but until then, I will work hard for what I see as the right thing.

This poem is for the Met,

"Collection"

An army is here to protect you

An army of artists, writers, graduates.

Students of the world, from the dark places of the world

The rejected appreciate you the most

And then there is the public

The mass of electronics, the eyes that only see the collection

Through the lens of a camera

Through the weakness of a printer

A matrix of dots not worth wasting your time on

When you have the real thing right in front of you

Staring at you

Wanting you

Begging you to stop what you are doing

In the greatest city in the world,

In the greatest museum in the world

And in this world

Don't waste your beautiful eyesight

By blocking it with the view of a picture

Of a camera

I toss this letter into the void, the abyss between us, this space that keeps conversation from happening.

Sincerely,
Rush Whitacre
740-336-9169

10-1-11
Dear Taylor Swift,

  Ahhh, this is another Month! October looks to be a great month, I will always remember that I started to work at the Met on a cool day in October. A year from now I shall be still at the Met,,, but it is up to fate, and depends on my ability to apply to different positions available at the museum. So, I am sure that I will be at the museum, but I am going to try out a different hat for sure. They told us that we would just have to keep trying and applying all the time because jobs will come up and it is up to us to apply, but those with more seniority will get the jobs first. I am hoping that it just so happens that at the time I am applying that the stars aligned so that I can be in there… I mean, I am not even sure that I want to curate or manage at the museum, but, I mean, I might as well try. I will never stop making art, creating, even if it means no sleep.

  I sometimes question the authenticity of artworks… I mean, some of these great artists had studio's where they taught others and the students became as good, if not better than the master at hand, and their names are not attached to the work, because their name is forgotten due to the nature of the way history is written… kinda sad, but then again, it happens, and it is kinda your own fault if you are copying someone else, you should not be remembered over the original right? So, I do not copy anyone, I just try to keep to my own original ideas. I can't say that anything I do is good/great/or otherwise, but I can say that it is definitely from me... I mean, I did make some work like that of others, but my designs are my own, and I am sure that no one has copied me... lol, oh, what really is original anymore... from the strum of a guitar, to the brush stroke of a painter, what is original.

This poem is for Jesse's mother,

"Exploding inside"

As plain as day

Written across your face

All your fears spelled out

Fickle little apartment

Where your daughter lives

And two artists mess and mess

And make and make

And your daughter, left and right

And right to left is surrounded

And even though you didn't tally your flush

We have measured it up

Your head may be exploding inside

As this sight you see

Three traps, no kitchen, and what room

None

But you should know,

That your baby girls new friends

Love her to no end, no strings attached

And she is in good hands

So, let go of those fears you may have

As you know me, you will

And can trust what I say

When the words are

She is safe with Laura-girl and me

I toss this letter into the void, the abyss between us, this space that keeps conversation from happening.

Sincerely,

Rush Whitacre

740-336-9169

10-2-11

Dear Taylor Swift,

    First day down, many many more to go. Today was a good day, but I am definitely going to need to get some comfortable shoes if I am to keep this up. My knees were suffering… so, this cannot keep going this way… at the end of the day I cannot be crippled from something simple as bad shoes. My back is holding out so far. I look at it this way I can only get stronger from here on out. The people I work with are pretty cool, and they are already noticing that I am a team player, that I will come back from my breaks on time, and that I am here for the work, not here to goof off. For the most part, I am pretty impressed with the staff. There only looks to be a few people who don't really seem to care too much about their job too much, that or they are so far into their job that they can't really see anything else, not even Humans as humans, they just see moving fixtures within the large scale model of fixtures.

    So, I am soo tired, I think that I am going to go ahead and go to bed early tonight.

This poem is for the smash,

"Island of hard shelled nuts"

They fall,

The tumble,

And they sometimes crack open

But not always

And your space is forever voided

Like your name

Like your face

I toss this letter into the void, the abyss between us, this space that keeps conversation from happening.

Sincerely,

Rush Whitacre

740-336-9169

10-3-11

Dear Taylor Swift

  So, the city of New York failed me in a small little tiny way, kinda in a funny way. I went into Manhattan to apply for a copy of my SSN and after waiting in line for two hours I found out that I had to go to the Brooklyn Branch near where I live.. I of course only went to the one in Manhattan because that is where the DMV sent me over there in Manhattan to the SSN place in Manhattan.. So, I guess this goes to show that a person should do more calling before leaping… even myself. So, rode the subway back into Brooklyn and waited in line again for another two hours. I was so flustered that I forgot to call in and grab the overtime that I was hoping to pick up . I mean, I have nothing else to do tomorrow, and I thought that making a couple dollars would be a good idea, well, that won't be happening because I waiting in line and forgot to call between 12 and 1 pm… It is really nice that they have that rule at the Met, that I have to call in and confirm my overtime for the next day, but it is also a pain if you simply forget and if you really need the money. I really need the money. I have now been living off of Ramen Noodles and vitamins for the past two weeks, and I could really use a nice meal. So, I have the rest of today off, and I have all of tomorrow off… Hmmm, I guess that is ok, I just have to find some form of art to make tomorrow. I think that drawing something with charcoal is in order, maybe splashed with some water color, maybe something from my neighborhood, maybe this place where I Live… that is actually a good idea. I never did draw the place where I lived back home, and I should have. Making works of places I have lived should be a definite thing in my life, but, it just hasn't I guess. Hmm. Yeah, maybe that is what I will do.

  Well, I guess I could do that drawing, but I also have that funny/silly zombie movie I shot last summer, I guess I could work on that. It comes down to how I feel in the morning. Oh, and there is the video of me doing my performance piece where I unwrap myself from inside of a giant present, from inside of the giant cardboard box from school, I totally forgot about that. That is something I could do and post on YouTube and then link it to my artist web page. www.rushwhitacre.yolasite.com I keep hearing from people that I should buy a domain name, but I haven't yet. I hope that no one else buys up my name, that would suck to have to buy it from them. Maybe someday I will, until then, I will just hope that it isn't purchased from right from under me… I am sure I will have it soon enough.

This poem is for Penelope,

"The Red Dragon"
Fire brightly burning
Flames bring down a house
And the love that created it
Is lost

> Separated by the smoke screen of a devil's thoughts
>
> Just an imagination running wild
>
> And she sits and cries
>
> And her knight in shining armor
>
> Says good night
>
> And you say goodbye
>
> And now in different castles you sleep
>
> And dream on it tonight
>
> And this poem is never ending
>
> As it will be read over and over
>
> Until the meaning sinks in
>
> From my ocean's heart of blue
>
> The words come out
>
> That I love you
>
> Mom

I toss this letter into the void, the abyss between us, this space that keeps conversation from happening.

Sincerely,
Rush Whitacre
740-336-9169

10-4-11

Dear Taylor Swift,

    What a day this has turned out to be. I have done relatively nothing all day but text and watch YouTube videos… I was going to make some art, but I have been too involved with just thinking about when I get paid, what I have to eat here in the house, and what it is I will be writing about in this letter I suppose… that is kind of a silly thing to do since I write every day… If all I did was worry about what I was going to write about, all I would write about is worrying… that would be quite silly. I got to see Laura-girl off to work this morning. I slept in until around 9:30 and then I got up and took my usual shower and then started looking at videos. This is my lazy day, a day of just letting my body and mind rest as one… I needed this, as I have needed a break for some time.. I am really hard on myself, on my body, on my mind. I just assume that if I take a break like I have today that I will not matter, that I will have missed something, that I could have done something incredible…. The truth is, without little breaks like this from time to time I would not have had the time to realize that my body was so stressed out. I can feel myself healing today, I can feel myself relaxing, getting ready for the next plunge into work, both art and the museum.

    I don't know if I said this yet, but I called Blick and quit that job so that I could focus on the Museum… they told me that I was now on a nonrehirable status. Oh well… I am above them now. I just have to keep on a good record at the museum and everything shall be fine. I have never had to quit a job so quickly, I kinda felt bad, but only for about a minute. I am sure that Laura-girl is upset with me to a certain degree as well, but she totally understands. She cares about me like a sister would, like family I think that she wants what's best for me too. And Blick just isn't the Met… period

This poem is for Nicholas,

"Cat Fancier"

What a mess, a life of little fixes

All compiled together by a hoarders attraction

The stories of storage gone wrong

Animals upon animals

Feasting on the ankles of another

Old and faded, trashed

Mutated garbage, like gold, collected

And you, the collector of stories

Captured now by your artist's wrist

Brushstrokes telling the history of the keepers

The horrors of hoarders

Spread out on canvases, paper, and boards

Screwed and glued, painted combinations,

Of combinations of a story worth telling

Worth spreading

Worth taking in with eyes of a traveler

So do not be stopped

For a Denise-aged road block

Stands between you and glory

Choose glory

As you to shall capture your experiences

A story teller for the troubled

A humble hero

I toss this letter into the void, the abyss between us, this space the keeps conversation from happening.

Sincerely,
Rush Whitacre
740-336-9169

10-5-11
Dear Taylor Swift,

My second full day at the Museum. I think that I am not completely ready for a 12 hour day at the met,,, but I am working myself up to it. After an 8 hour day my feet are just killing me… it is amazing, all that standing with relatively not much else and my feet are just killing me.. I can't imagine what a 12 hour day will be like. I mean, I will find out really soon, this Friday for instance… and then Saturday… I can hear myself now this coming Sunday night… "thank god thank god tomorrow is Monday",,, that is what I will be saying. But, there is only one problem, and that is, I have picked Monday up as another day for more money on my next pay check… so, as you can imagine, I will be making quite a bit of money on my next pay check. I am really excited about this. But, I am not excited about not having any free time this coming week. I am working up to making a buffer between me and my loans coming due this coming November… I can't imagine what they will be like.. I am still kind of in awe that this government allowed me, an artist to take out over 90 thousand dollars in loans… full well knowing that I could lose my shirt in the whole deal. I mean, the tax alone could be astronomical, or at least it will be if I do not pay my taxes on these loans. I simply cannot allow these loans to go into default. I hate that debt, this is something I didn't take into account when I was just trying to make it through grad school… grad school tells me that I can't have a job on the side, and the government just throws money at me… hmmm, quite easily the worst combination. I mean, what is the government possibly thinking with these loans,,, there was no risk management what so ever calculated as to whether I would even be able to get a job after I graduated… and, I never did get a job in the teaching world. So, go figure.

Not that it matters, I didn't want to teach right out of school anyway. I am quite content with my new job at the Museum, and I am thinking that the museum is quite content with me.

Tonight I think that Nate is coming over, but, I don't know if he is staying here, or if he is going to stay somewhere else. I actually don't know fully what he is up to here in New York besides getting involved with the protest that is going on. I don't understand the protest myself because no one is really solidified on what they are protesting yet… and I guess that is the number one reason I am not joining the protest, that and I just simply don't have time, nor do I really give a crap at this moment. Yeah, that pretty much sums it up. I am sure I will have a story about the Nate who stays here tonight, but that will have to come in tomorrow's letter, and if he stays.

This poem is for Nate,

"Loft Lost"

I let you down brother
And I let you all down
My inability to be there
When my baby came crashing down
When my life's work up to this point
Was taken from us
And the lazy eyed man pressured you
Luckily you got away
As we all did
But I should have been there for it all
I should have somehow taken a fall
But somehow I didn't,
And this is my folly
My penance will be great, and long
And I shall have to beg
Plead and bludgeon myself
Before things are set right
Before you forgive me
And I am so sorry
For I love you like a brother
And I can't forgive myself.

I toss this letter into the void, the abyss between us, this space that keeps conversation from happening.

Sincerely,
Rush Whitacre
740-336-9169

10-6-11

Dear Taylor Swift,

    Well, I got asked to work overtime at work today, and I got accepted. So, today was a really good day, but a really long day too… less time for sleep, something I need going into a long four day work weekend. I also found out that this coming Monday is also a holiday with double time pay, so, I signed up for it. What am I thinking… I guess I really must be that hungry. Not having money for food does something to a person's brain when they first get a job that pays pretty good.

    Tonight, I spent my very last 12 dollars from my checking account on a sandwich and on two small bags of chips… I decided that it is close enough to my pay day that I could afford for my account to be just on the verge of going into the negative's… why not right. Besides, I really needed something else to eat other than Ramen noodles. As much as I love them, I simply can't eat them for every meal every day. So, I will go back to eating Ramen noodles while I am at work tomorrow. But for tonight I will feast on a Philly Cheese steak sandwich… mmm, delicious.

    My friend Nate is over here at the apartment again tonight. He came over last night by surprise and I didn't get the chance to talk about him in yesterday's letter, so, I had better mention this in today's letter… This guy, my friend nearly died this past August and he didn't tell anyone, he didn't tell a soul, not even his family… I got so so sad inside that I couldn't be there for him somehow… I really wish he and I were closer for real. Nate and I were the ones who started the whole "building up" of the place while we were in undergrad, and if it weren't for him I don't think that it would have all really come into existence. Anyway, to make a long story short, Nate is a really good friend of mine, and he had a pretty bad motorcycle accident that probably should have caused him to lose some extremity of his body but he didn't he had and still has pretty bad road rash form the accident. I would say that if he hadn't been wearing his helmet he would have been dead. He described the helmet as having scrapes across it that made him think that his face would have been ripped off, or at least really badly road rashed as well… All he was wearing was a T shirt, carhart bottoms, and a helmet,,, thank god he was wearing a helmet.

This poem is for Ben,

                      "Big Red"

        Why don't you just try a little harder

          Just, push yourself a little further

                And quite working

                At making excuses

                      And quite

       Just stop everything you are doing

> That is keeping you from the making
> Keeping you from the exercises
> For your brain and body
> And just pick up that brush and push around mud
> And pick up that pencil and scribble
> Just make anything
> Anything at all
> Except more excuses
> Our plates are full right now
> And more excuses will just have to stay on the burner
> Burning
> Turning black like your heart
> Rainbow black

I toss this letter into the void, the abyss between us, this space that keeps conversation from happening.

Sincerely,
Rush Whitacre
740-336-9169

10-7-11

Dear Taylor Swift,

    Well, this was my first long day, and I must say that it wasn't as tiring as I thought it would be, even after not getting much sleep. I got paid today, so lets see, I have enough money to pay my rent and have just over 16 dollars for the next two weeks… Hmmm, love it. The next check is going to be glorious. I worked with a great group of people today. I even worked with three or four of my fellow colleagues who were in my orientation with me. I was posted for most of the day in Visible storage and I got so many questions about where the paintings were. There were some really upset and or frustrated people who had visited several times in the past three years and didn't get to see the paintings because they have been put away while the paintings galleries were renovated. I personally can't wait for the galleries to be finished, I in fact am going to try to get a sneak peak of them before if I can. I need to ask one of the really nice guys who was teaching us in our orientation, maybe Jose, maybe Sean, Maybe John himself… we shall see. I really doubt that I will be given permission to see them. Oh well.

I got home really late, well, 10 pm, and when I got here I was alone. It was the first time I had come home and there just wasn't anyone here to meet up with. I guess Jesse was out at some gathering with her work buddies, and Laura-girl is out hanging out with her Buffalo boys. So, Jesse is home now, and so, that is all good. I am not waiting up to see Laura-girl, I am guess she won't be in until really late. Good for her. I hope she doesn't have to work tomorrow. I love NY, I just love it. Now, if my knees and ankles can hold out and get strong enough so that I can stand at work for long periods of time. That is all I need, to get stronger.

When I got home tonight I got three emails asking me to come and be a part of a special audience to see you live at the ABC studios… I am not sure how to feel about this, since I said I wouldn't learn about you on purpose… I replied that Yes I would come to see you live, but, I am having second thoughts. I guess I have a week to fully decide. Ok, I am really tired and need my sleep. Good night world.

This poem is for Laura-girl,

"Thank You, Now, And In The Long Now"

I owe so much to you

Because of you I am able to exist

I am able to thrive here in my new nest

My life is what it is by your word

Without you, I would simply have had to turn around

Begged for help to get home

To an Ohio street

And all alone

And most likely starving

Laura-girl, I can't thank you enough

I can't hug you enough

And I can't take you out to enough nice places

Sure, they are simple jobs,

Simple pay

Easy enough to say

But without each one

Make it this far

I would not

So hugs and kisses to you my friend

And I am always here for you

Always.

I toss this letter into the void, the abyss between us, this space that keeps conversation from happening.

Sincerely,

Rush Whitacre

740-336-9169

10-8-11

Dear Taylor Swift,

    I just can't seem to get enough of the Met. I was on team four for the first half of the day. See, on these 12 hour days' things can get switched around a bit, but hat is ok, because I don't mind getting sent to a new area to look at new art. Today after walking through the same areas all morning my shift got shifted and changed up and I got to spend the afternoon walking through the musical instruments. It was fantastic. So many pianos and other weird stringed instruments. I could only imagine how they would sound, or in some cases be played. My feet are just killing me, but, every pain, and every ache are so worth it.. I just simply love my job at the Met. It is so nice to just help people at random, in the most simple and easy way. I really could not ask for a better job right now. I can totally see myself working this job for a little while just to see where it leads to.

    Ok, so, it is the weekend, and the subways are always a little haywire on the weekends and so on my way home I decided to get out and walk from the 14 street 4,5,6 train stop over to the 14th street F train stop. Today at work I was handed 20 dollars from a coworker because they are tired of seeing me only eat Ramen noodles for lunch, and she is worried about my health, and, probably with good reason I suppose. But, I found a chipotle on my way home and got a burrito in a bowl to go, it was delicious. But, that is not the story I was really trying to get at, on my way home the accordion girl was at the F stop on 14th street and I got to hear her play for a little bit, it was amazing. I then noticed that she was advertised to be friended on facebook, and she was advertising for people to email her. So, being the socialite that I am I emailed her tonight and facebooked her. I she immediately responded and I found out that she is in four bands, and that she wants me to introduce myself next time I come through the 14th street station. So, it will be nice to be able to meet her formally and say Hi, and for me to not feel weird about staring at her while she plays. Yeah, that will be nice, and not to mention if she tells me when she is playing with her bands I could round up my roommates and go to hear her play wherever she is playing her accordion, that will be awesome.

Then,,, when I got home I met Laura-girls friend Dave, who is a really nice guy. I was really surprised that he was here, really surprised, a good surprise, which is why tonight's poem is for him.

For you Dave,

"Good Guys End Up With Broken Hearts"

Be careful my new friend

For I can not

Nor will not talk bad about my friends

But I will throw out this head of warning

Guard your heart like you would your name

Like you would your prized vision

And I love the girl you are hanging out with

Like a sister

But keep in mind

That this sister

Can break your heart into pieces

So don't fall my new friend

Don't stick your hand into that trap

The snap is that worst

And then the memories come second

And again, you snap yourself

And again I say take head

For no one should end up

Broken hearted

I toss this letter into the void, the abyss between us, this space that keeps conversation from happening.

Sincerely,
Rush Whitacre
740-336-9169

10-9-11
Dear Taylor Swift,

Today was a whole new experience in the Met. I was placed in the European paintings area. It was great. I spent the whole day with Vermeer, Carravaggio, Van Dyke, Rubens. It was nice to have all day to just spend standing in galleries at the same paintings and just focus on them, you know, really look at them, how the paint is applied. Oh, and I always did my job of course. This was a short day, actually I was amazed at how fast the time flew by, and I was actually worried a little about making it back to my post on time. I really love the end of the day when we push everyone out of the galleries. Tonight I had a young guy try to slip by me to go into the galleries that were closed and I said to him, "Please Sir, you can exit that way." And without missing a beat the young man said to me with an English accent, "But, I don't want to exit." And I smiled and retorted with, "Oh, I am sorry, but our galleries are closed now." The guy laughed and understood finally why he had to exit. I guess you had to be there… there were about a dozen other security officers around me and it was funny to me that this guy couldn't put two and two together that something was happening that wasn't quite a normal during the day thing. And there were other guards directing people out of the door too which added to the humor of it all in my head… like I said, one of those, you had to be there moments..

I can't wait to make enough money so that I can get some really good inserts for my shoes… My right heal is really hurting from all the standing around, like there is a bone spur or something, but I hope it is just from my poor inserts that I am having this trouble. I am more active now, with all of my moving around, and all of my work, so, maybe I just need to give it a break, maybe…

Tonight Laura-girl took pity on me and bought me 20 dollars worth of groceries. So, now I have a box of cereal to munch on for about a week, so, that will help. That is about one meal for me for a day,,, so, I will have to buy some Ramen Monday night when I get off of work. I just have to remember to buy it before I walk to my apartment, the more I rest this foot that better off I will be. Just when something good happens to me,,, something bad starts to happen… damn it.

This poem is for Francis,

"Twenty"

You are like an amazing flower

On the cusp of beauty

Clipped, vased, and shelved for a day

And there isn't a moment to waste

Not a moment for wondering

Or wander back through a past

So just keep on smiling and trimming

Taking away that which doesn't matter anymore

For you are truly beautiful

>   From the bottom of the bottom
>   Of everything I know
>   I see you in your single state
>   And can't help but be moved
>   Can't help but wish that the difference between us
>   Wasn't a difference
>   But a same
>   And the same's between us even better
>   But then there I go again
>   Wishing
>   And this well wasn't made for that
>   It was made like a looking glass
>   For looking at the past
>   As it hits the surface
>   And replies

I toss this letter into the void, the abyss between us, this space that keeps conversation from happening.

Sincerely,
Rush Whitacre
740-336-9169

10-10-11
Dear Taylor Swift,

    Today was another double day, and I got a vacation day on the books. I decided to not pick up over time tomorrow or on Thursday. I need these few days to just be me, to just not have anything on my mind but to maybe work on some of my art works. I have these paintings to work on further. I really don't know what I am going to do though because I really need to buy a couple of things first, and I don't have any money to do so. I need about three gallons of linseed oil, and at least one jar of Japan drier. So, I will just have to hold out on the painting.

    So, I heard the other day that the show Star Gate Universe was cancelled… if this is true I am very upset about this. It was the best stargate show to date really. There were some very original ideas being explored in this show and I was really getting into it. I guess if it is cancelled I will just have to imagine what it would have turned out being in the third season. I guess I was first turned on to it because I saw the main character was the character who was also the main character from the movie 28 weeks later. Only on the show SGU he is a crazy scientist and not just some survivor who doesn't get infected by some rage virus until later in the movie.

Tonight I spent most of my time on the internet on facebook talking to people. My friend Carlee is going to be sending me some pics of some work she has been doing tomorrow. I am excited to see these pics of her work. I am always excited to see any of my students work. Carlee's especially, she was my favorite student, and then her student career got cut short by her parents getting divorced. Kinda sad how that can happen, and very frustrating.

Laura-girl blocked me from posting things to her facebook directly. Lol. Now she gets to accept what I am writing first. She is so funny. I wonder why she just didn't just ask me not to post stuff to her facebook page. Lol I mean, I only did it two days in a row, and nothing bad or anything. Goofy girl.

Thank goodness I have tomorrow off.

This poem is for Dustin,

"Gatherer of Many Lumbers"

Don't let them critique you into a corner

Or like the structure we tore apart

You will fail

You will never be able to connect the dots

And when they call it a school that starts with a D

Has two A's and a P for an ending

Don't let that get you down

For the world will recognize your work

Before it recognizes the letters of the alphabet

In the case of your education

Alphabet soup

Filled with crackers

Salty bastards

Who they themselves are tasteless

Cardboard to the tongue

Like a dash of salt to the ocean

Unnoticeable

Make your mark young man

Stand your ground
Flag
Your flagship

I toss this letter into the void the abyss between us, this space that keeps conversation from happening.

Sincerely,
Rush Whitacre
740-336-9169

10-11-11

Dear Taylor Swift,

    Ahhh yes, a nice day off where I am laying around and looking up original songs from no named artists. I found a really good one, and he doesn't have that many views either, which surprised me. His name is Mike Stec, and his voice is awkwardly like that of John Mayor's and if I don't watch him play the guitar it really sounds like him because he just does. Ok, on a side note, I just found the Lavato cover by Mike Tompkins and it is awesome, except that he wants me to but it on itunes… something I don't want to do really. Here is also a secondary note on istuff, Laura-girl's ipod died the same day that Steve Jobs died, coincidence…. I think so.

    I think I am getting skinnier since I have nothing to eat here at the apartment. I mean, I would have to right. I have coffee, vitamins, and occasionally some ramen noodles and occasionally some help from people at work or from my roommates. I really don't like owing people money, but now I owe the corner store money, and I owe my roommates, and I owe two coworkers money. I am really excited about getting my next pay check. Then I shouldn't have any more posts like this on my facebook nor be writing about it, but for now, it is something I have to think about all the time until then for I am simply hungry. Hungry in more than one way, hungry from lack of food, and hungry to create.

    My roommates just got home. They are hilarious. We are planning on writing to 2000 flushes and telling them that their 2000 flushes only lasted 303 flushes. We are really planning on doing this as a joke, but in a serious joke kinda way.. I wonder if they will actually send us a free 2000 flushes, or if they will respond at all. I am sure that everyone who has ever recorded the number of flushes has simply written these people to tell them that they product doesn't last for as long as they say it should… actually, 2000 flushes is just a name, let's get real. Just like any of those mountain spring water bottle companies sell their product under the name of a natural spring because that is the actual name of the business and the water isn't actually from a spring at all… irony. Mmmmm, good ol' bottled tap water.

This poem is for Alan the Architect,

"An Artist's Heart"

Carving your way through time

Pencils become drawings

And drawings become blueprints

And blueprints become the places where we live

Where we work

Where we like to go when we are bored

Blue prints are to buildings

As cartoons are to the Sistine ceiling

Master pieces in their own rights

Pieces of paper

Gold leaf, the color of white

The color of blue

And your smile will not be seen

In your scenes

Your photo's of a concrete jungle

Of underground man-made caves

Where man-made monsters roam

Travel down tracks at high speed

Being filled with acclaim

And fame

From your energy

From your mystique for shutter speeds

And for light

Say cheese.

I toss this letter into the void, the abyss between us, this space that keeps conversation from happening.

Sincerely,

Rush Whitacre

740-336-9169

10-12-11

Dear Taylor Swift,

    What an incredible day this has been. I spent the day working at the Met where I was surrounded by people and art and hundreds of questions of where the bathroom is, where the exit is, where the paintings are, the temple of Dender. So many things that I know the answer to, and then many more that I do not.

    This day went by so quickly. Every time I looked down at my phone 15 minutes had passed by, every time I looked down to my phone I found when I looked up the guard who was there to push me to the next post, or to my break was on their way. I think that I was in some kind of time warp. Some kind of mysterious vacuum where time was being ripped from me, second by second, minute by minute, and all I could do is feel it burn through my fingers. I have to do something about this, for my time to me is more precious than this. I do believe that I am going to start and bring a digital voice recorder to work with me and discuss my thoughts, discuss my ideas, discuss what I feel is my motivation for taking the steps I am taking, literally and figuratively. I will also discuss my idea for my next novel, the sequel and prequel to Mabast, my life's greatest work as of now. I have had ideas roaming around in my head, and I am so full of so many new characters, so many new adventures to draw from, so many new places that have become burned into my mind with the delicacy of the flickering flame that has me moving, has me hungry for more and more all the time. I feel that I must be creative all the time, not just when I have free time, and thus, starting this Friday, I will be taking a voice recorder to work with me, to record my life. This shall be interesting, and I hope that I don't get in trouble for taking in my recorder, not that anyone should see it, for I must keep it a secret, I must keep is hidden, and I must keep talking.

    Tonight Laura-girl and I went to Nancy's. Laura-girl and I had such a good time playing shuffleboard. And, to top it all off, I had the best burger I have ever had in my entire life. Amazing, just simply amazing. Nancy's Whiskey Pub is the Art bar to be at, it is the art scene that Laura-girl and I make it. It is where Laura-girl and I are going to start going on a regular basis, every Wednesday night it we will dine like masters, talk like peasants, and love like fools.

This poem is for Nancy's,

"Pub"

Faceless suits fill you for a moment of cheers

And then your empty again

Filled only with those looking for a good time

The regulars

The hardcore artists and writers and unsung heroes

My favorite old guy in the corner

And bartender

And especially Benta the queen of the grill

Making master piece food

And my way to my heart is an easy one

A path simple and pure and honest

As brush strokes fill the light fixtures

And the hours grow small

We linger, alone and wallowing in our sorrows

Our happy moments turned south

And it is off to a bed

To sleep

A machine made for dream making

Goodnight cruel world

I toss this letter into the void, the abyss between us, this space that keeps conversation from happening.

Sincerely,
Rush Whitacre
740-336-9169

10-13-11
Dear Taylor Swift,

Well, my friend Dave wrote me an email this morning telling me that you were in town… interesting, I wonder what for.

So, I spent most of the day messing around the house here,,, totally forgetting that I need to be going to apply to get my license for New York so that I can get a New York ID number so that I can be part of the Union at the Met… aaahhh, I totally forgot, but I have Monday that I can go and get it done. I may check that out later if I get bored, just because it was such a random thing for Dave to write me and tell me this.

Tonight Jesse and I ate at a diner where I ordered a steak and a Pepsi,,, my dad gave me some money, so I won't starve between paying my rent and when my next pay check comes in about a week. I also went out and bought 72 packages of Ramen Noodles so that I have something to eat at work… the food at work is so expensive. I can't afford to eat an 18 dollar meal everyday… I mean, compared to eating Ramen at 33 cents a package, how I can compare with that. Eating Ramen is like the most unhealthiest thing ever, but, I have to do what I have to do in this situation… I am going to end up like the way my dad is with Macaroni and cheese… my dad ate Macaroni and cheese everyday during college and he go so fed up with it that he can't hardly stand to eat it anymore… he just doesn't like that stuff at all. I can totally see myself ending up not liking Ramen after all of this is said and done… although, I do like Ramen a lot,,, we shall see. I may never stop eating them,,,, and my liver would probably be shot too..

  Jesse and I didn't see any famous people out tonight,,, well, famous artists anyway. We only visited ground floor places as well, so, go figure. We really only stayed on the scene for about two hours or so. it was all in all, a really good night. When I got back I was happy to see that Laura-girl was hard at work being an artist…. Something I will be happy to be doing when I get some money to buy supplies. Aaarrrggghhh.

This poem is for the mist in the air tonight,

"Amazing Haze"

Bring about this white blanket to surround me

Make me forget my dreams

And push me into the darkness

Where I have been afraid to go

Where I must go

Where the first I love you was heard

The reason for coming out into the light

Like rains conversation with the window

It is so soft and gently

Dangling drops from roof tops

Surround me

For I am the air

And the mist is like the love from a fallen lover

Surrounding me

Making me feel not so alone

Not so distant from the next

And the pinch not so painful

From the last

I toss this letter into the void, the abyss between us, this space that keeps conversation from happening.

Sincerely,
Rush Whitacre
740-336-9169

10-14-11

Dear Taylor Swift,

Well, this is my second weekend well on its way to being over. And, I have picked up two days of overtime. I found out today that I can have two days of overtime a week and not get into the next tier of taxes, which would make my working not worth it because they would take away so much money. So, for the next pay check I will work four days of overtime and see how much I make. I may have to do this for quite some time to just pay off my loans… or, a miracle will have to happen. That is something that I can't count on. I keep hearing rumors that the government would be better off to just clear the slate of their horrible decision to give out so much school loan money and start to really pay attention to who they give money to. They are creating generation after generation of servants to the system, people who will never pay off their debts, and people who will take their entire lives to pay off their debts… I hear that if there were a debt forgiveness plan for these people then they would be able to spend a lot more money and thus fuel the economy… of course, I don't see how forgiving such debts can actually help anyone except those countries we are buying our goods from… we ship off our raw materials to other countries for them to assemble our goods so that we can buy back really cheap stuff. And if we forgive our loans to our government doesn't that just mean that we will have more money to buy stuff and has even more of our money go overseas? I am not a person who knows these things, but it seems like this kind of thing will only help our corporations, and not us so much. I like the idea of everyone taking their money out of the banks and just not leaving the banks with any other decision other than to meet the needs of the people and not the corporations. I don't know. I am simply just going on and on here for no reason.

Today at the Met I was placed in Modern Art and then into the America's Oceanic and African art sections. I am being placed all over the place to watch the art.

Ok, I have found this trailer for the new movie coming out about Marilyn Monroe and I am sooo excited to see this movie. I really am.. There is this trailer I have put on my facebook that I just keep watching over and over. There is something about this idea, this week with someone, a magical week that just happens, and now here so many years later it has been turned into a movie. I love it.

I guess I am just a sucker for a sucker who wins a little.

This poem is for the song you didn't write part 2,

"Spread thin"

How many hearts do you have

One

And only one that I can see

And in this

You should be aware that it can only be broken one at a time

One at a time indeed

And as you sit and write lyrics

Write your smoke and mirrors

And feel energetic

And the burst of energy

That hits you at 4 in the am

Is not the excitement of being together

But being apart

Being secluded and robbed

Robbing yourself

And the heart of a man

Who has been waiting for so long

I hope he is not too late

I toss this letter into the void, the abyss between us, this space that keeps conversation from happening.

Sincerely,
Rush Whitacre
740-336-9169

10-15-11
Dear Taylor Swift,

    I am going to bed early tonight. By early, I mean before 2 am. Last night I was up so late, and had to get up so early… I can't be having this happen… I don't know what I would blame it on, except that I know that I would not be able to make it stick… I think I was just excited after having a good day at work, and then I stayed up because I feel that I have to be accomplishing more than I am.

I am feeling the click situation at work. Even when I take a break with certain people I don't get invited to sit with them… I don't know, maybe I am being overly sensitive, and maybe they are actually the ones who are wanting to sit with me and just don't know how to ask… I don't know what these people are thinking, and that is ok. I am sure I will win them over with my charm. Eventually.

Thank god my second long day is over. I was looking forward to the end of this day… all day, well, at least for the last hour. I guess, welcome to the good life.

All I have to say is, your all welcome, and I mean, welcome to come to the Met and see what we have. Totally worth your time as always.

I really love the end of the day when all of the guards end up at the great hall… It is quite a site to see all the men and women in uniform standing around swapping stories. Then there is this rush as everyone darts down the first set of stairs they can find to get to the locker room to change to go home. This is a really good job. I can't wait for more guards to be hired. That is a part that I like. I feel very lucky to have gotten this job. Really, because without it I would still be working my butt off or possibly having to move home because I wouldn't be able to afford my apartment. This was a really close call, without this job lets be real, I would have had to move home and find a job in Beverly, or Marietta… and nothing would have made any sense with the back ground that I have. I guess I should also be looking for a job that is better than this one, but, for now. I am content and I don't see myself moving anywhere soon.

Laura-girl won't be home until 1 to 2 am, and I won't see her for a couple of days. She is at Blick doing inventory. I think that they will find that they were robbed quite a bit over the past year.. Which is sad. Come on artist's, have some pride and buy your pens and paint brushes…

This poem is for the one who doubts me,

"Singled Out Liar."

Why must you question what I say

And say you don't believe me

Even when I have proven myself to you

Time, and time again

And time

Is running out for forgiveness

For a tray of tarts to be sweetened

To be less vinegar

And more wine

And this big cheese

Waits for no one

Not you

Not even me

I toss this letter into the void, the abyss between us, this space that keeps conversation from happening.

Sincerely,
Rush Whitacre
740-336-9169

10-16-11

Dear Taylor Swift,

  This was a short day, as Sundays usually are. I now realize the importance of me staying on my 3rd platoon so that I can have three days off and so that I can have time for myself if I need it, and, so that I can have two possible days for double time… this is really important. I guess the Met started a hiring frenzy and because of this I am worried a little that when the newer people get hired that the over time will become more about slim pickens and it will be a bountiful harvest… I will wait for that day to come in first though before worrying about it.. We all went out to a bar after work tonight. It was an experience to say that least. I was the quiet one as usual… there is something about a traditional bar setting that can drone me out apparently.. I am already the quite person, but then when about a dozen people start talking to each other all the time I just sit back and listen, I guess it is what I do.

  Ok, so, I have been watching YouTube videos on Occupy Wall Street, and I have no idea as to why these occupiers are forcing themselves into confrontation with the cops, they should be forcing their way into the media, not into the backs of police cruisers. They shouldn't be cornering themselves on the streets, but in Wall Street Buildings, and they should get more of a following on the internet, and they should recruit other countries to come and take part, simply because it would heighten the risks, and the awareness.

  I really have no idea what I am talking about. I just hope that they don't make plans to come to the Met… you know, if they all snuck in and only paid 1 cent and then all at the same time decided to lay and handcuff each other from wrist to ankle all over the floors, we would have to close the Met, there would be no way to maneuver in that place. Ok, this is silly.

On a more serious note, I am going to start something different for my last month's worth of letters before finishing up this last month to this year of letters into the void, the abyss.

This poem is for uncertainty,

"So Uncertain"

I've never opened myself up

Like this to anyone

And I am now

Fading

I toss this letter into the void, the abyss between us, this space the keeps conversation from happening.

Sincerely,

Rush Whitacre

740-336-9169

10-17-11

Dear Taylor Swift,

I think today I am going to discuss a fear of mine. Actually, I think that for the next 7 days I will discuss a different fear that I have. After that, I guess we shall see.

I would have to say that a common reoccurring theme of a fear that has popped up over and over in my life would be that of losing my dad. I have almost lost him like 4 or 5 or 6 times. Each time I get a little bit tougher, a little bit more tempered against the changing of time, the changing of life to death. I am still though afraid that I simply won't be ready for him to go when he does. He is the most important person in my life as far as how I turned out. I really wouldn't be who I am without him. My dad is a legend, a hero, a force to be reckoned with, someone who deserves to have books written about, movies made of. And, I love him with all my heart. He is the person who believes in me. I don't know what will happen when he dies, I am just so afraid of that day to come because I am not ready for him to leave. But he must.

I have these memories, and these videos I have taken of him from when he was still able to go out to one of his favorite places, rock mountain.. It isn't a mountain at all really, just a sandstone ledge about 65 feet high and about a half of a mile long with several climbs varying in degrees of difficulty. I videotaped my father talking about all of the climbs. It was the first time I met my (related person who is male and not named) now exgirlfriend, and it was the first time that Wester was at our house, and on a random whim we traveled out into the woods and Wester got to hear all about my dad talk about his stories about the rocks. I am actually amazed that I was intuitive enough to think of videotaping my dad at that time. I need to get to those tapes and convert them to digital files to that I can make them into a great video for the family. I think that my brothers and sister would really like to have my memories, my recordings. This is something that I know will be cherished. Yes, losing my dad is something that I definitely fear, even though I know death comes to us all. I will just have to be there, and be strong for the rest of my family, and they will be for me.

This poem is for the raising of a village,

"Old Country Doctor"

His house is a place of healing

A place to go to when you need help

When you are more than broken hearted

But broken

And this man will come to see you

If you can't make your way to his door

He will get out his chains,

His doctor bag, and he will make his way

Through snow drifts, and floods, and hell

To get to you, to help you

To deliver your baby

To poke you with sharp needles

To immunize you from deadly diseases

Why, because he loves what he does

He loves helping people

And he does it without any expectation of repayment

Without any expectation of a thank you

And tomorrow when he wakes

He will wake with new eyes

Refreshed and ready to see you again.

I toss this letter into the void, the abyss between us, this space that keeps conversation from happening.

Sincerely,
Rush Whitacre
740-336-9169

10-18-11

Dear Taylor Swift,

 I guess I will talk about another fear I have. I have this fear about seeing my friends suffer. I do all that I can to see to it that my friends have everything that they need, that is if it is within my power to see to it that they have it. I am not saying that I am the reason my friends are happy, far from it, but I really do try to be a good friend. Sometimes I succeed, and sometimes I fail. Like here not too long ago I realized that I failed my friend Risque somehow. I don't know how, but, that is ok. I am not supposed to know. The point is. I don't like to see my family or friends suffer, and it is a fear of mine that I will be witness to them suffering and I will not be able to do anything about it.

 I am not a freak about worrying about this kind of thing, but it is something that I have looked back and I can honestly say that I have done everything I can for my friends as far as making them laugh, making them comfortable, just being myself and being attentive to what is going on In my circle of friends. I guess that is not something that a completely normal person does, but, I guess I try, mostly on the fringes, mostly when I am not totally consumed in my work. I really do have my moments though where I am doing nothing but problem solving for things that I have no control over, no way to change, for things that have passed, things I will never get to go back and visit to correct, or to do right… and that is just how it is. Lessons learned, education of life.

 "Well, she was precious like a flower." I have been listening to Keith Urban today, and I just caught that line and thought about the connection of my flower paintings and the relationships from my past. Hmmm, interesting. Gosh, I hope that this doesn't make me a stupid boy.

 Anyway, I have lost a few really good friends in my past, and I can't figure out if it was my fault. I will not worry about that tonight, I will not worry too much on it at all really, for I can't make anyone love me, and I can't make anyone want to be my friend, they just are, or they just aren't. period.

This poem is for the 'read'

"Staring into the mirror"

Who I've become

A glance in the mirror won't tell this story

Nor will a photograph

Nor a social network

But my friends, my works, my lover's

And all the ex's of ex's

May be closer in the essence of my other self

My doppelganger in perspective

And when they tell this story

When you hear my words

Coming from their mouths

Whispering hidden secrets, open declarations

Pages will turn

Chapters will form

And a life will come into sculpture

More than just a poke in the eye

Buttercup sprinkled with jazzy lace

And all I can do is shiver at the thought

Of a liar's game

A way to break into a smile and vandalize

Petrifaction of a smile

Of a dance

Dipped in freckles

I toss this letter into the void, the abyss between us, this space that keeps conversation from happening.

Sincerely,
Rush Whitacre
740-336-9169

10-19-11
Dear Taylor Swift,

    I have grown to have a love for NY over the years, and there is a part of me that doesn't want to let her down, or let myself down by failing her somehow. I think that the worst failure would be me having to move back home because I couldn't make enough of a living to support myself. I guess this is my biggest fear about living here in NY, not being able to make it. I don't want to leave this city if I can help it. I really don't want to. Making money as an artist, or simply moving to New York isn't that easy for that matter. I am here to not just make it if I can help it, but to really make it, to live the American dream as an American, lol, the American dream.. what is that any more right?

I guess, when I left home I remember my sister telling me that she would come to my rescue if I needed to be rescued from up here, but she would only do it once. I sat in my little homemade apartment and just thought to myself about how little faith my sister has in me, or about how little anyone in my family may have in me for whatever reason. I guess they don't see me lasting here in NY because it is so expensive to live here, and that they don't see me as being able to reel in a job that will support me... I guess, that could happen, but I am doing everything I can to make sure that I get my name out there so that people see my skills through the work that I am doing. Lol, yeah, sure.

So, yeah, that is one of my biggest fears as of right now. I can't imagine anything worst than having to run back to my home town with my tail between my legs because I failed up here in NY. At one point I would have said that failing out of school would have been my big fears, but I made it through that part, and I am good. Huh, I guess hey, I never thought about this little irony. What if it is my school loans that actually make me fail NY?? Does that mean I failed, or does that mean that my education actually sabotaged me? Hmmm, interesting. I don't think there should be any interest on loans. I think that more money should be paid back to the government, but not a steadily building up of interest...

This poem is for my green and browns part 5

"This Word, This Word, This Word"

Please

Just whisper it one more time

My ears are eager

And your smile

Oh, that way that you showed me

Thy hand upon me

And that room

Where I said

In another world

In a different place

That door would be shut

And those lights would be off

And I would hold you forever

And again

You said that word three times

That word, that word, that word

Maybe someday

> Somewhere
>
> In a different world
>
> In a different place
>
> You too will have that word said to you
>
> Three times
>
> Everyday
>
> And for the rest of your life.

I toss this letter into the void, the abyss between us, this space that keeps conversation from happening.

Sincerely,
Rush Whitacre
740-336-9169

10-20-11

Dear Taylor Swift,

    This is a selfish fear, but a really real one because no one wants to be alone. No one wants to be alone and not have any friends, or to not have any family, or to suffer alone, or to have good things happen to them alone. I guess my fear of being alone comes from my fear of my parents dying. When they are gone that is a big part of my life just gone. So, I guess that my fear of being alone isn't as great as my fear of my (related person who is male and not named) (related person who is male and not named) being alone. Not too many people understand him like I do, or want to help him like I do. I am not a complete worrywart when it comes to (related person who is male and not named), because he is a big boy and can take care of himself, but I guess I always want him to know that I love him and that I never want him to be lonely. Lol

    I guess (related person who is male and not named) has his friend Wester, and I say that he has 'a' friend, because not to many other people become (related person who is male and not named)'s friend. Wester is the only friend that he has, and that is something that I worry about. I try to put myself in either of their shoes and I realize that the friendship is that of a symbiotic one most of the time where each of them benefit from each other,,, most of the time. (related person who is male and not named) gets a friend, and Wester gets a break from reality and gets to delve into (related person who is male and not named)'s world. I consider myself very fortunate to have as many friends as I have. I have lost some along the way, but those I have lost always know that I am here if they need me really. I am just that kind of guy. I hope that I never do anything super stupid that causes me to lose everyone. I can only imagine what I would have to do to lose all my friends. I have some that love me unconditionally, at least I think this, I can't speak for them straight up, but I can say that I have some friends that I love like family, and treat like family, and spend time with like family. Just writing this makes me wish I were home with my friends from back there.

    I guess the reason that I have being alone as one of my fears is that because I have been alone a few times in my life and it sucked. It is no good to be somewhere alone and not have a support system of some kind. I remember when I lived in Tennessee in a dingy dirty old dorm that my old biochemistry got me into during the last few weeks of the quarter. I was placed there because previously I was living with a girl, and that relationship went south, haha, I guess even further south that Tennessee and I moved out with just my truck and a few of my things. It sucked.

This poem is for the one that never was,

"It Reminds me"

The wooden floor in the kitchen is bare

As your things no longer sit there

And I can't feel the cold wood bend beneath me

Spaces echoing my whispers

My endless debates with myself

My worth judged by a wind at the back of my neck

Goose bumps bring me to a new chill

The lights are out

And I lay here alone

Thinking about this ceiling

These walls decorated with vacant spots

And I can still smell you near me

A pillow just sitting there

Just as lonely as I am

And the backs of my eyelids bring me darkness

Bring me my thoughts

My dreams

A vision worth repeating

Worthy of trial

And error

I toss this letter into the void, the abyss between us, this space that keeps conversation from happening.

Sincerely,
Rush Whitacre
740-336-9169

10-21-10
Dear Taylor Swift,

    I can see this letter being shorter than usual. Mostly because this is a fear that I think that I have covered already, but I still have to say it again anyway. I have a fear of losing my friends. I have lost a couple of my friends over time, they haven't passed away, they just fell away from me, and we aren't friends anymore. I miss them, and I hope they are happy where they are in the world. I have this friend who I went to OU with, I won't mention his name, but he and I were really close. We could sit and have these long conversations and these long talks about art and or science, or whatever, it didn't matter. Well, I lost him, we are no longer friends. Sad, you know. This is for him if he would ever happen to read this, I am here for you anytime you need me, period.

This poem is about not writing that song,
        "And how your voice won't make the difference"
        I'm dying here
        Because I can't say what I want to
        And it wouldn't matter anyway
        Just like a song written and not heard
        A voice silenced by the hand
        Words erased by the clock
        And it won't matter what you write
        And it won't matter the tone in your voice
        Say the word, say them, scream them
        They will never be heard
        The pen of love poured out
        And me the empty vessel
        The glass that never passes halfway

> Or the poem that makes you stop
>
> Think
>
> And turn the page confused
>
> Turn the page to yet another blank page
>
> I trust this

I toss this letter into the void, the abyss between us, this space that keeps conversation from happening.

Sincerely,
Rush Whitacre
740-336-9169

10-22-11

Dear Taylor Swift,

 I do a lot of wood working. There is one thing that I always take away with me after I have used my saws, and that is; "Thank God I still have my fingers…" I have this giant fear of cutting off my fingers. I guess that would do me in as an artist, by a lot. I use my fingers for so much, and losing them from some strange or awkward accident would just simply not make my day. I have had a few close calls. I got real close to cutting my left thumb off with a chainsaw once. I actually cut the side of my index finger on my right hand because it got that close to a table saw as I was pushing a board through its cutting blade and the board suddenly gave way and my finger got in the way of the blade. Actually, I would say that the table saw incident was probably the closest I ever came to cutting off a finger. I remember taking a break after that and just sitting and thinking about what a close call I just had. I don't like to think about it, but I must to remind myself that I need to be careful.

 I guess I have many more scars on my left hand than my right. My right hand seems to mostly be holding a tool, or machine, and my left hand is holding something that my right hand is working on and therefore when a tool slips my left hand sometimes is in the way and catches the wrath of the tool… I have several cuts from where a screw driver has slipped and sliced my hand. It just happens. Not lately, but when I was younger. I guess I have become a little wiser.

 Yeah, so, I guess this is my sixth fear that I have talked about. I will probably talk about at least one more before changing topics. We shall see. I may just go ahead and change the topic. I will find out tomorrow.

This poem is for repetition:

> "Just Another Mistake I like to Make"

> I keep falling for the same you
> Keep seeing myself fixing all the same broken parts
> And I still love you I think
> Because you were my best
> My only
> My mistake
> And if I could take it back, I wouldn't
> For the fall is my favorite part
> And the climbing out of this hole
> Makes life worth living
> Makes my heart beat stronger
> My will shaken
> And I see another you on the horizon
> And I am made free
> Free to see with my own blinders
> My own heart
> Calling out to your broken parts
> Willing me into another mistake
> Another moment to fall
> A moment to fly

I toss this letter into the void, the abyss between us, this space that keeps conversation from happening.

Sincerely,
Rush Whitacre
740-336-9169

10-23-11
Dear Taylor Swift,

    I have this one really big fear, and that is,, not going for it when it really matters. I guess I just need to keep my eyes open, I just need to keep working on what I am doing and believe that what I am doing will pull me through, just keep on believing in me. I still haven't had any business cards made, and I think that they are pretty important for my further advancement into the art world. They are just an easy way to let someone take me home with them until they can get in front of a computer to look me up. They are just a reminder of what I would like them to do, and that is to check out my stuff on the internet. I guess that is what I need to do soon then, order my cards. I think I will order a whole lot of them, just because that is what I do. I just do big. Lol.

So, I guess a part of this fear is that I am scared. I sometimes feel all alone here in NY, I sometimes feel like I just might not make it, that I might just not be at the right place at the right time. I need to keep trying I guess. I can't fail unless I just don't try, with no try, I will not, simply will not anything. My (related person who is male and not named) has actually called me several times since I moved up here to NY. He has taken his time and called me and made it clear to me that he wants me to call him, which he wants me to call him and keep in touch with him. I am not sure that I fully understand what my (related person who is male and not named) is going through. He has nothing. He is living out of my mother's farm with nothing, and I am here in NY fighting to have anything, to own anything, to have even my simply name. So, I guess I don't understand my (related person who is male and not named) at the very basic level, at the level of what he is trying to accomplish in his life. Don't get me wrong, I love him, and I want him to call, and I know why he is calling. I am just not exactly sure why, if that makes any sense at all..

Ok, I must get off of here and keep going for it. I must keep trying, and I must keep pushing forward. Things will change for the better, I can feel it happening. I can feel it coming. Please o please let me know the right decision when it is place before me, and let me act quickly.

This poem is for my mother,

"Let's Keep this simple"

This is who I am

And I have done you wrong

As you have done me wrong

And as time passes we seem to try to out do

Each other with hate

And this should have never been a choice

That either of us should have had in mind

But I want you to know

That whatever it is that has come between us

It is not unforgivable

It is not something that will keep me from loving you

Or being able to love another unconditionally

> There are moments that won't leave me alone inside my head
>
> And I am only losing me
>
> Bits of me
>
> And my memory may not let me forget
>
> But my heart has
>
> And I say I love you
>
> And that which we have done
>
> Is not unforgivable

I toss this letter into the void, the abyss between us, this space that keeps conversation from happening.

Sincerely,
Rush Whitacre
740-336-9169

10-24-11

Dear Taylor Swift,

      So, this letter is not about a fear, it is time to change it up, and this letter is the beginning of something new, something about what I feel I am happy about as far as my achievements are up to this point. I guess the first thing that comes to my mind is my Masters degree. I really went through a lot of trial and error in my schooling to get to that little degree, 15 years of schooling.. granted, it was all full time, it wasn't however all in the same direction.. I spent about 6 years getting my Degree in Biochemistry, and then in my last semester I dropped out of Maryville College to pursue art, and took my first art class. And the rest is history. I do however wonder if I should have waited to go to grad school at a different school other than the University of Cincinnati… I guess we will never know. I suppose if I really wanted to I could apply to another grad program and get another masters degree somewhere else in something else, I guess if I wanted to, but I really don't want to. I just want to make art, and make my mark, and move on with my ideas. I just need to somehow make enough money so that I don't have to worry about it anymore. Lol.

      Another part of getting my masters degree that I am proud of is that I can teach college now if I wanted to. I am sure that if I applied I would get my foot in the door and teach here in NY somewhere, but I am taking a year off of college to focus on being a starving artist, which I am truly starving I must admit. I would like to thank the makers of Ramen Noodles, and the makers of vitamins. That is about all I have to say about that. Ramen Noodles actually aren't the worst thing in the world for you, just be sure to get your vitamin pill, and vitamin C every day is all. That is something that Ramen is not known for, nutrition.

This poem is for the missed letter,

"A, B, C, D, Etc."

You are on my mind

Like the wind across a tree

Or a waterfall across a rock face

Your closeness is soothing

A comfort I shall not want to lose

Or take lightly

And I will not let you down

Or take advantage of you

A safety you should take advantage of

As I will let you

Welcome you

A missing sea

And a missing peace in my heart

Has left me empty

And I yearn for your touch

Your gently hand upon my back

Letting me know that I am still alive

As without you

I am just a missing piece

A letter shy

Of the last wor…

I toss this letter into the void, the abyss between us, this space that keeps conversation from happening.

Sincerely,
Rush Whitacre
740-336-9169

10-25-11

Dear Taylor Swift,

    I guess before being thankful for my Master's degree I should at least declare what I think is the achievement that led me down the path towards the master's degree. I would have to say that I am really proud of my paintings series, the LIfeCycle series of flower paintings. They have been a big part of my life, and I shall not stopping painting flowers I am sure, even if I do take break from time to time to paint other things, or to do other things. So, here is a secret about the LifeCycle Series that no one knows, and they might as well know, I started them on the basis of proving a point. I had a girl once tell me that roses are ugly, and I guess that part of me set out to prove this statement wrong. I am sure that she will never know this, and that is fine with me, I wasn't out to prove her wrong, but that I could prove to myself that a rose at any stage of its existence, bud, bloom, and in death could be seen as beautiful, and they are. I of course then extrapolated this idea from just her to making other paintings about other flowers that represent relationships that I have had with other women in my life. The bigger the emotions in the relationship, or at that time in my life, the bigger the painting, and the more vibrant the colors, and the more intense the design.

    I remember when I decided to make the rose paintings. I took pictures of a rose bush right outside of my house. I used film, not digital cameras or anything digital. And I had to wait for the film to be developed and I had no idea if what I was taking would be even usable. The dead rose in particular was a worrisome one. I set up a light and right after I took only one picture the lamp fell over and knocked the remaining petal that I was trying to get a picture of.. I only got one pic of the dead flower, and it was all I needed… it was quite a lucky shot. Quite a lucky shot indeed. Looking back, I should have taken pics of other dead roses on the bush… I guess I was simply shocked at the lamp falling over that maybe I saw it as a sign or something to stop taking pictures… I don't know.

This poem is for mending,

"The Forever Wound"

Somewhere there is a bandage

A wrap for wrapping

Mending

Making me feel like I am together

Not broken in a world full of cracks

And crevices

I trip

I get back up

And I remember to keep my eyes open

This is not where I would say goodbye,

Hello,
Or signal for help by the fires light
This is where I look into the mirror
The looking glass, lakes surface
Ripples make me shiver
And I am once again
Humbled
Silent in my study
Writing these lines
Making up a story as I go
Telling you truths about truths
And helping you to understand
That a lie is a lie is a lie
And a lie is a great story
Asphyxiated by the truth

I toss this letter into the void, the abyss between us, this space that keeps conversation from happening.

Sincerely,
Rush Whitacre
740-336-9169

10-26-11

Dear Taylor Swift,

    This achievement may seem like a rather simple one, but it is a big deal in my life… I didn't let school, particularly grad school change how I love to invent, how I love to make, now I love to investigate art in my own way. I consider this to be quite an achievement because it is one of their things to do, to take you as a student and break you to make you… I just remember them saying that they wanted us to come to some aha moment in our work, and I was thinking,,, isn't that why most of us went to grad school in the first place, because we had some aha moment in our lives and made us all see that we needed more, that we wanted more. That we were not just simply coming to grad school to force come aha moment, but those we had already had this in our lives and that we wanted to investigate it further. I don't know, I guess grad school is different for all of us. For me it was a huge $@#$%^%$##$%^%, and I will just leave it at that.

I can't imagine my life without going to grad school, don't get me wrong, it was one of the best decisions I have ever made. I just wish I would have pushed the envelope even harder. I wish I would have pushed the notion of me making the rules, and breaking their rules to an even greater degree. I mostly spent my time working my butt off to come up with ideas. I was a general think tank all to my own,,, playing in their mud puddle they called an education. I call it, 'myducation' because it was all up to me what I learned and didn't learn, what I wanted to take away from classes. I never spoke up because the arguments being made simply were just not worth picking sides on, and in every great argument there are at least two sides, and I just couldn't find it at 'school' where I went.

Would I do it all over again if I had the chance… absolutely, would I go even bigger on my thesis idea… absolutely… would I make even more enemies… probably,,, but I would gain the respect of many more people. I just do, like I do, have always done, and I will succeed because I will never give up pushing forward in my fight for novelty, or advent guarde'ness. Something worth striving for because it just seems right in the moment, just seems like it will work. I will make it work.

This poem is for Hogan,

"Oh little little boy."

You are so small little boy

I barely see you

In an uncrowded room

And your voice is harsh

Angry words don't make you bigger

But smaller

And less intelligent

And less important.

I can't understand why you would want to waste your time

Making up stories about the leader

For you will only make him stronger

Energy is energy is energy

And the leader absorbs it all

Through space, through time, through shields

There is no stopping that which cannot be stopped

Or that which cannot be challenged

You must break yourself

As you are fractured

Not tempered

Against time

I toss this letter into the void, the abyss between us, this space that keeps conversation from happening.

Sincerely,

Rush Whitacre

740-336-9169

10-27-11

Dear Taylor Swift,

When thinking about my achievements I think about my (related person who is not named), and the things that she taught me… she and I haven't always had a good relationship. In fact I would say that she and I never see eye to eye ever, but there is one thing that I am forever grateful that I learned from her. One of my greatest achievements is learning to love unconditionally. I have friends who I love unconditionally no matter what. I guess I can say that about my (related person who is male and not named)s and my dad and my (related person who is not named) too. But it is important to make the distinction between family and friends because it is not easy to love a friend unconditionally for everyone, or anyone since they are not family, or not associated like a family member all the time. I don't mean that it isn't something that people can't do, but that it isn't something that you hear people talk about, that is, loving someone unconditionally no matter what they do, no matter how bad they are. It is something that actually sounds crazy I guess if you really think about it.

I have friends who I would trust with my life, and they do that same for me. I have an understanding with some of these friends about certain things, things that can't explained in letters, nor explained in novels, but with looks from across the room, a certain kind of nod, a certain kind of smile, or a kind of story that takes place from within a certain kind of group that isn't a verbal story, but one that exists just because it can exist. In other words, it is there irregardless of reason, it is there because it must be there, it must be or else the moments we need would be lost to the unmeasurable, the spinning and ceases to spin. A world that doesn't move, but sits and waits for the singularity to become.

"Here Kitty Kitty"

You are Purrrrfect

And you are loved and adored

By a master

Who is also a master of my friend

And my friend is also a keeper

Who loves your purrrrfect purr

Your meow

And your whiskers

You are a cat

Owned and yet free

And although you walk on a leash

You are not attainable

You are a cat

Vernita's cat

One who loves trips to Ohio

And who loves to claw

And fight

And be just out of control at times

For you are an animal

And you are not just a friend

But you are a friend of a friend

Of a roommate

The keeper

The one who deserves respect

The one who is quietly planning to win

I toss this letter into the void, the abyss between us, this space that keeps conversation from happening.

Sincerely,
Rush Whitacre
740-336-9169

10-28-11
Dear Taylor Swift,

Ok, I just want to make it clear as to one of my favorite things,, an achievement that I have yet to assess on the my scale of things to come that I am proud of... that is the Ripley's project where I will be making shadow art for the company Ripley's believe it or not... I see this as a great chance to show what I can do with my skills and with what I have learned as an artist. I am happy that I was asked to help with their museum, I just wish they wouldn't be taking their sweet old time getting to my project. This is how I see myself.. I see myself as a student who has graduated but owes the world his energy, work, his livelihood. I see myself as an artist who has a grave debt, something that he will not overcome and wants too. I am not just talking my financial obligation, that I hope to pay off in my lifetime,,, but I am talking about my heart... deep inside of my heart I feel like I owe it this world full of people a part of myself, a part of my art, my energy, my love, my everything.. something inside of me thinks that I am not working hard enough, and I am not trying my hardest, or that when I thought I was going to be challenged I wasn't, so I set up my own obstacle course. Things like trying to make things happen where there was nothing, like writing you for a year. I never dreamed that I would write anyone everyday for a year, not anyone, yet here I am closing in on a year.

But, yeah, I just wish that Ripleys would contact me to say, "Go" because I am so ready to start making my work for them, to blow their socks off, to even maybe impress myself. I have so many ideas rolling around in my head, you have no idea. There is one thing that I know for sure, and that is, I will not fail when it comes to working for such a major player as Ripley's, it is just not in my vocabulary, to fail that is... I only have my reputation once, and if I were to screw it up that would be that. So, I will take this thing inside of me and I will make it real, I will make it happen, period.

This poem is for the memory I have instilled in my students minds,

"I remember"

I remember a guy

Nervous and shaking,

One who had never taught before

Who was so afraid that he sent you home

In 15 minutes

Who made you work on assignments

Even he didn't believe in

And I didn't

They were nonsense

And my last wish

Was to confuse you

Or make you make things for the sake

Of making…
A perfectly good waste of time
Not a moment passed
That I didn't want the best for you all
And how I miss you
My little pack of students
Friends from afar
A penny in a jar
And the rattle doesn't make sense
Not like the love I have
Pent up inside
Waiting for a daydream
A sweet sweet fantasy

I toss this letter into the void, the abyss between us, this space that keeps conversation from happening.

Sincerely
Rush Whitacre
740-336-9169

10-29-11

Dear Taylor Swift,

    I guess if I am going to be talking about my achievements I might as well talk about a really big one, and that is my move to NYC… I mean, it is not just anyone who can pack up and move to NYC who has such wonderful friends as Laura-girl and Jesse who were so nice as to let me move in with them… I mean, Laura-girl didn't have to let me move in with her, but I think that she see's that it was a great idea. She has told me several times that she is glad that I moved in with her. This journey has been quite a rollercoaster ride. I even thought for a little while that I was going to have to move back to my home town and get a job working for minimum wage somewhere and be miserable. But I didn't, the job at the Met came through and I have survived.. Like they say, if you can make it here you can make it anywhere.

    I talked to some of my students this year, and they say that they are happy for me, proud of what I am doing… but, I am not here to be proud, I am here to make it, make it as an artist, with my paintings, with my installations, with my work, my artwork, with my passion, with my ability to make stuff happen. I just want to make my art, using everything that I am, everything that I can bring to the table her in NYC, this place that I never thought, imagined I would be living in… I actually told myself after I visited here the first time that I would never want to live here, never want to work here, never want to stay anywhere near this place.. this city is just so huge, so many people, so many opportunities here to take, to miss, to challenge. And, I am here to challenge, to push, to take what I feel I can and make it my own… I can succeed, I just need to keep working hard, keep making my art, and keep soliciting other artists to work with me, to encourage them to want to work together… I feel that is that future, the working together with other artists, like a team, or like a family… with many there is force, with many there is power, and with many there is hope.

This poem is for A.O.

"You are so Beautiful on the Outside"

I know why you are miserable

Your outside is a trick, an illusion

Not that it is not real

But it is so far beyond that which is possible

Which is fooling the fools

The guys who only want a night of you

And not a lifetime

Like time is what matters anyways

Not like hope

Happiness and all the memories

All of the times that make us remember we are alive

The love, the hate, the changes

Changing us inside and out

And we age

Ever getting older

Ever dying, slowly to our long sleep

From our short now

And I don't want to close my eyes

And lose my chance to be with you

Or someone just like you

As I breathe

You breathe

And I sing like I meant to.

I toss this letter into the void, the abyss between us, this space that keeps conversation from happening.

Sincerely,
Rush Whitacre
740-336-9169

10-30-11
Dear Taylor Swift,

    Well, I must say, I have to include into my achievements thus far these letters. I never dreamed that I would be writing letters to anyone, let alone a star like Taylor Swift and for a whole year. I still can't believe that I have been able to keep this up for this long… I am not the kind of person who starts something and then gives up on it,,, but there were a few times during this making of these letters where it was just so late and the time was just so not happening that I actually contemplated on simply not finishing , or leaving out some days, or just giving up completely… Now though, I feel as though I must do something with these letters. I want to make them in to something that may inspire others. I will find a way to show the world these, I just will have to take my ideas to the next level, to the not being afraid of others seeing my written stuff.

    I have read my poems to others and they seem to like them pretty much, and so, on that note maybe I will explore the idea of publishing these in some kind of book… I don't know though, we shall see.

    I just don't want to end up like my friend Louis, or some other artists who never sell a thing in their life. I guess in Louis's case he does it because he is just afraid to take the next step of getting onto a stage to be funny in front of people.

    I believe that I can do anything. I mean, within reason of course, I am not superman, or Spiderman, and I can't move mountains with my own two hands, but I can move people, I can make people fall in love with my work, I can make people love art… so, that is something I guess. Like I said, 365 letters in 365 days is quite an achievement for me, and I hope that someday someone will appreciate these, because I am pretty sure they are being thrown away, definitely not being read by Miss Taylor herself, which doesn't matter to me, I didn't write them for Taylor, I wrote them for me.

Lol

This poem is for 'K', yeah, you know who you are,

"You can try and Take Everything I am"

I am not a mess like I was then

As you made me

And I will not sit blind to your ugly deeds

And your lies will not go unanswered

For my Karma is stronger than your hate

And I will simply go about my days, weeks

And I will forget you

As I have already

Only reminded by the spit upon my window

The twist unexpected

And this leap of faith

Without a prayer of being saved

I can't stop the waves of fate

Of Karma's nasty bite

I will ask my mother

To pray for you

I toss this letter into the void, the abyss between us, this space that keeps conversation from happening.

Sincerely,
Rush Whitacre
740-336-9169

10-31-11
Dear Taylor Swift,

     Since I first started writing my fantasy novel I have had this goal of getting it published, and I think I am going to now start a series of letters that discusses my goals, well, I will most likely only talk about them for a week like the last two subjects. I started my fantasy novel because of this really unfortunate relationship that really didn't go anywhere. I started it by accident in an email to a friend by making up a story that took up four paragraphs. That happened in 2001. In 2005 I expanded the story to 1244 pages, which was way way too much. I have been editing it down over the years to a more manageable book size, and making the story flow better, and changing some things that just needed to be changed for the book to work… I wish I had more free time, because that is the only time I get to work on this thing. I have this dream of it becoming a best seller, but then again, I just don't know. I really need to buckle down and start working on it after I get done writing these letters or something.. it is not like I won't have the time, because I will. I mean, I can have three days off at the Museum, and I can't imagine a better way to get myself motivated to make written works than to be working on the novel I promised myself I would finish. I mean, it has to be finished.

I have used so many people from my life in this book… their personalities, some parts of their names, and I have made up so many characters who's roles in the book with my character are close to scenarios that actually played out in my life, well, but in fantasy form, and out of perspective from what reality can offer and I altered things to make sense and not single anyone out. I guess my fantasy novel is taking a long time because I want it too somehow… really I don't, but I am not taking time to work on it. I am assuming when it comes time to work on it I will, and I will. So, there it is, it will happen, and soon.

This poem is for the imaginary (related person who is not named),

"You have tried your best to hurt me"

There are ledges you can't jump from

And there are punches you can't pull anymore

I am too far away for you to catch up

And I do not nap in this race

Says the rabbit to the tortoise

I hip and hop and hip and hop

And my friends adore me

The long for me to be happy

And I plan on staying happy

I plan on keepin my dignity

My mouth will not utter words

Of despair

And you will know that I am happy

That you can not budge this unmoving

Protected species of man

So send me your hate

Your words of despair

Your utterances of utterances

And I will read them and discard them

With a smile

Knowing that I do not have to live with

Your decisions

I toss this letter into the void, the abyss between us, this space that keeps conversation from happening.

Sincerely,
Rush Whitacre
740-336-9169

11-1-11

Dear Taylor Swift,

 Ok, a second goal of mine,,, and it is really far out there, but I would like to sell out an art show of mine… I know what it does happen from time to time with other artists, but I would like it to happen to me some time. I work hard, I like what I do, and I do it because it feels good to me, and therefore, I am hoping that someone else can see my stuff the way that I do. Maybe I will find someone who wants to collect my stuff. I am just looking for that edge, those buyers, and those interested in my skills. I can do anything, all I have to do is put my mind to it. I know I can. Well, at least right now I feel that way, and this world, art world, is trapped between artists, curators, galleries, museums, and historians who are all trying to label the unlabelable. I can't see a name for this era because enough time hasn't passed. Sometimes, time has to pass and then history can be written… something's can't be forced, and that is ok. Artists just need to keep working, they just need to keep making, curating, being security officers and having shows at galleries. Because the time will come for names, for change, for periods, for ages… trust me, these times, moments will not go unaccounted.

 I am thinking that I may have to just have all of my work priced slightly below what I would consider to be a good price for a work of art. I can't see myself selling out pieces of art at too high of a price because I don't think that anyone appreciates my art that much,,, at least I don't see that there is anyone alive right now at this point. Yet, what do I know. My work is diverse yet it is all tied together through scale, amount of work put into it, through the obviousness of my wanting to fill a space, like I have been trying for such a long time. My reasons are my own for my wanting to fill the voids, wanting to make experiences, installations that are edgy. And I am sure that I am not alone, as much as it excites me to find other artists like me, it pains me just the same. What is unique anymore really… Unique really isn't selling much anymore anyway. Right?

This poem is for the darkness in her path,

        "A Heart that has Stopped"

      Places within me died when I saw that look

        Your eyes couldn't search out mine

         And your face turned to tears

       And I couldn't do anything but imagine

        Imagine what it was that I had done

      And you still to this day haven't told me

         You just cry tears of sad

      Of lonliness, something I can't believe

          I can't let you fall

       For me, or for that state of mind

        As I know you deserve better

      As I am not yours and yours alone

          I am to the world

         As I am to your heart

           Very little

     A speck of sand amongst the pyramids

      A blade of grass amongst the field,

       And you don't notice my tears

          As I cry for you

            For me

          For this moment

I toss this letter into the void, the abyss between us, this space that keeps conversation from happening.

Sincerely,
Rush Whitacre
740-336-9169

11-2-11
Dear Taylor Swift,

This just happens to be something that I want in my lifetime, and thus, might be more feasible than not,,, I would certainly not say that it is possible within ten years, so, I will say a lifetime. Another goal I would like to achieve would be to have my work in ten different museums around the world. Now, can you imagine that… me, with ten different works of art around the world in ten different places with ten different pieces.. well, I guess it could be the same piece just redone ten times,,, but, that would kind of be boring in a way. I would be known as the artist who does X… and nothing else. I want to be known for many things. And, I am motivated enough to make it happen,,,, now I just need to win the lottery of life, the lottery of the 'random win'. Maybe Laura-girl is the reason I get discovered, maybe she becomes famous first and then by the shear fact that she and I are roommates maybe I get discovered and through her coat tails I become what I am suppose to become… this would not be unwelcomed, and I am sure Laura-girl would like it that way, as I do owe a lot of my success to her since I moved up here to NY… well, my finding a job was all me,,, but Laura-girl allowing me to move in was a huge huge step. I would have never been able to move here without having this place here with Laura-girl… the rent is so cheap here…. So so cheap, and the neighborhood is so quiet, so special.

If you can make it here, you can make it anywhere, the saying is true. And I am only begun.

So, I guess I will have to start compiling the names of the different museums that I want to get my works of art into… I will definitely count Ripleys… I would even settle for ten different Ripley's across the world, or even just ten different museums across the US. That would be interesting… me and Ripley's… sounds like a book. "Me and Ripley" Hmmm, I will have to consider that as something of a possibility… I wish I had the patience to learn the piano, or the skills to learn the guitar. I just don't have the time… well, I suppose I have a lot more time to learn those things now that I have graduated from school… I will have to consider trying to tackle that. Maybe that is something I do in my spare time. Hmmm,, I will consider it.

This poem is for the 'love-you' songs,

"Your Words Just Aren't Enough"

Your words just aren't enough

When I am here alone, and you are too

And there is this distance between your lips

And that word you want to say

Where you sing about my downfalls

And my laughter remains in your past

With all the things you like to think about

This fare isn't right as I am the road

And your bus'd lines run me down

> Your stages are lined with classical dismissals
> And your words just aren't enough
> Not enough to you forget me
> Rather project me into the stars
> And these letters are just full of lines
> Meant for the eyes of lovers
> Passionate little nothings of words
> Like whispers in the dark
> Compelling
> Leaving you wanting for more
> For now, nothing
> Like the distance
> Between the fingers of god
> And Adam
> Simply the world's most important use of negative space

I toss this letter into the void, the abyss between us, this space the keeps conversation from happening.

Sincerely,
Rush Whitacre
740-336-9169

11-3-11

Dear Taylor Swift,

    Ok, this next goal I am very serious about. I would like to make enough money to help make the dreams of those around me come true.. I know that this goal sounds l more like a wish, but there are a lot of dreams that can be fulfilled with not that much money… most of the time it comes down to options.. Like my friend Gari. I am trying to get him motivated and get him to move to NY where he can have a real job at the Met. Gari is a great guy, he is funny, motivated, and he has goals and aspirations. What Gari doesn't have is a good record… I am trying to help in that regard. I am stepping in to try to help out with his situation… mostly, he just needs motivation. Gari is like a brother to me. Kind of like a twin brother alone from the fact that he was born in the same year on the same day. Really bizarre. Anyway, I am hoping that I have been a good influence in his life, that I have helped to bring purpose into his life, that I have giving him reasons to want to be motivated. Gari does not live an easy life, he does not have the easy road, and I am trying to flatten out some of the bumps, I am trying to fill in some of the pot holes, I am trying to just be a friend without sacrificing myself, because what kind of help could I be if I am failing myself in the process of lifting him up. I wouldn't do that with anyone. It is easier to help from a position of being able to look across at a situation that it is to be in the middle of it in a crowded fixed position.

 So, maybe within the next year I will have succeeded in getting Gari moved up to NY where he too can be working as an artist, as a security officer at the Met, where he can be making money to support his child back in Ohio. Maybe he will even get full time custody of his kid at some point, this would be amazing. Time is the only thing holding this back… I can only offer myself as far as my friends are able to stretch out their hand asking, seeking help. If I don't see a hand, I don't see a way to be there, I won't know that help is needed… But seriously, I will be there for any of my friends,,, period. I just need to start to make this money-thing happen

This poem is for standardized appraisal,

"Economy-Sized Thanks"

Would you like fries with that

Is that going to be a large?

Its only fifty cents more for the value meal

And in the end

Those words will come back to you

Again and again

As it is easy to pay a little more now

And not realize the actual payment

Over the long now

The energy required to burn it out of you

The activities

The diets

And all the thanks in the world

Will do you nothing

So keep stuffing it in

And putting on the pounds

For the price you will pay

Is likely to be greater than you can bear

Or burn

I toss this letter into the void, the abyss between us, this space that keeps conversation from happening.

Sincerely,
Rush Whitacre
740-336-9169

11-4-11
Dear Taylor Swift,

      I guess if I am looking to have a goal of selling out a show then I should also consider a goal of being written up in different magazines… but of course, that is not a goal I can accomplish alone, that takes several things to happen, such as my show being found and then having a critic come to the show to see the work and then be moved enough to find a reason to write about what I have done… and, my guess is that I will have to get in with the write people to have this happen. I mean, I am trying to get to know some of the critics, and my best chance I think is on facebook,,, facebook seems to help to level the playing field as far as getting to know different people who are not otherwise knowable. I can see myself adding people and them not responding though, simply because they are not the kind of people who add just anyone. Like Jerry Saltz for example, he is an art critic here in New York… now, my two roommates have met him in an elevator and even got him to add them to his FB page. I tried to add him to my page but I was turned down immediately for some reason. I think that his privacy settings must be on high or something.. Add that to the fact that I add lots of people to my FB who I don't know and therefore am probably labeled as a spammer something… I can see why I would be turned away.

      Oh, I just tried it again just now!!!! And facebook told me that I would have to wait for Jerry to add me as a friend… so, we shall see. I guess it depends on how Jerry perceives the connecting friends we have on this god forsaken site… lol. I am sure that Laura-girl is a good connection, I will have to see if who the other five people are,,,… hmmm.

      But, yeah, so I guess I have to get into some shows and advertise in the direction of people who would write up the show.. maybe I will have to write up my own show a couple of times. I am sure I could create a little spark to create interest in the show. I also need to do some public art works that are sudden quick and are not potentially harmful to other public works, but get the attention of New York… something that is a good thing, something that makes people take another look at this city and fall in love with it all over again.

This poem is for the never having to say it,

"What if there is no goodbye"
There is no end when there is no end in sight
And every day is a new beginning
A new horizon
And I look into your eyes and I see
You and I forever
You and I together
This knot that we have tied
Slips through itself slowly
But the rope is long
Too long to ever be undone
And as I pull you in our slack is paid
And the roads are paved
And now I drive
Like a raging horse race
I will be there bridal straps in toe
And a memory more
Less that the trace of a lovers smile
Ear to ear
And this glass of fear
Is never full
As it drains out the bottom
Into places that can't be reached
No return
Mended.

I toss this letter into the void, the abyss between us, this space that keeps conversation from happening.

Sincerely,
Rush Whitacre
740-336-9169

11-5-11

Dear Taylor Swift,

    Here is a goal that really is something I would like to happen to me while I am still alive… This goal is me finding someone to settle down with who wants to raise a family with me… with the understanding that I am an artist though… that is a big deal really, well, I mean having a family is a big deal… I want to find someone to be close to but it seems that every time I get close to someone they end up not being the one that sticks. As far as kids go, I love kids; they are what make living life worthwhile. My dad told me when I was younger that his life really didn't start until he started having kids. I am obviously glad that he had this thought process… lol

    Maybe I will find someone up here in NY, maybe I won't. either way, I will find someone, somewhere who just wants to be with that one guy, not many, and who is faithful and honest and just simply wants to have a good time and live life… life is too short, and too precious for there to be misery in your life… simply put.

    Lets see. I really haven't place a number for how many kids I would like to have. It comes down to how old I am, and how old the woman is who wants to be with me I guess. I mean, seriously, does life have to be so complicated that we are all running around scared of being hurt by the other side, being committed, just being honest… I say,, find that someone who you can trust, trust them without regard to anything they say, but what they do, because actions are more powerful than words, and if the other half of the equation isn't balancing out, then it most likely isn't meant to be and just get out, find another… there is always another. So many fish in the sea, and they haven't all been caught, or been ruined, bruised, or ruined. Just open up your heart and let them in. the truth will always come out of every situation, sooner or later it will be known and everyone is found to be faithful, or not. I guess I choose to side with wanting to believe that who I am with is faithful until proven otherwise.

This poem is for being broke,

"Where has all my money gone?"

I save it, I keep it where I can see it

And still it eludes me

And I somehow think that when I have it

I will be safe, secure, happy

And yet I am not

I am always on the edge of being gone

Having to move

Needing to find a second job

A third one under the table

And all the ends fray

       As does my hair
     As I am unable to afford a haircut
    I just want to stop eating altogether
        So much waste
       This expensive food
   And for what, to taste, to gain weight
    To press forward into the present
     Simply slipping into my past
      And I wait for payday
     As if I really own the check
         For I don't
        The earth does
     My tidings have been tied

I toss this letter into the void, the abyss between us, this space that keeps conversation from happening.

Sincerely,
Rush Whitacre
740-336-9169

11-6-11

Dear Taylor Swift,

  Well, to go along with my goal of having a family I better also throw in the goal of owning my own place where we all can live right… so, yeah this goal is me saying that I want to own my own home someday. I haven't decided where yet, that will be more of a teamwork kind of decision. I am not picky, but I do have to live somewhere where it would be good for kids. Some place with room to play, somewhere there is room to run and let the imagination grow and consume a child until their creativity is loose. I guess I want kids who are free to just have room to be kids and not have to worry about harmful things in the world, because there are a lot of good things to be enjoyed.. some place with a big yard, not too many neighbors, and yet still close to a metropolis so that it can be visited often as needed or wanted.

  I think that I also want a place with lots of windows. My dad's house had lots of windows and I loved to sit in front of them and just look out at the birds that my (related person who is not named) would feed. So many thoughts use to run through my mind sitting in front of that window, so much of my imagination I used to create things inside… there is something about being inside on a cold winters day and being able to see all the would though giant panes of glass and wonder what life could be instead of is, or what it would be if I wanted it to be. I use to come up with so many little fantasy stories about different things while day dreaming. Yeah, giant windows to the outdoors, to the woods, or just to some trees would be nice. Just enough nature to take away the idea of the 'other', who is living close by.

    I don't have a problem with living in the woods for that matter, but I would still want to be close enough to some city, to some civilization where there is a hospital, and there is food, and all the other places I depend on being there in the coming future. Places like Lowes, lol. Well, I have to have power tools too.

This poem is for Tilley,

"Eyes Like a Fox"

When I am around you

I am always on my toes

Always watching where I am stepping

What I am saying

And most of all what I am looking at

For I feel if I do not look you in the eyes

I will miss something important

Or you will simply catch me looking at your shoes

As I watch you walk

From here to there

I step

And you step

And away we go

In this dance where neither of us know left

From right

Neither of us care

So we just stare and look

And the color of your eyes are burned into my mind

Blue as the ocean

Brown as dead grass

And green like algae

Yet always as soft as the petal of a flower

I toss this letter into the void, the abyss between us, this space that keeps conversation from happening.

Sincerely,
Rush Whitacre
740-336-9169

11-7-11

Dear Taylor Swift,

    So, I have been letting out these wishes for myself and I am thinking that I turn the table a bit that says what I wish for others, and I am going to start with you Taylor. First of all, as I wish for all of my family and my friends, I wish for you happiness. There is nothing else more precious, and more sought after that just that, to be happy, to not want to anything, to be content with your life and know that no matter what that you are loved by your family and friends. I simply wish for you, as the recipient of these letters, joy, and happiness. May no one take away this from you, and with this, may all you do bring happiness to others, including those who may or may not feel they deserve to be happy. Let your words bring forth a new era where people no longer look to each other for what they can get from each other to profit from them, but what they can offer to each other free and from the heart. No more dog eat dog, or pioneering for profit for profits sake, for the bottom line. And may your voice be heard. May your happiness stay with you, and shed from you on all your travels infecting all who come in contact with it. That is what I wish for you.

    Now, all of that sounds good and wonderful, and maybe kinds weird, but no matter, for I still wish for you happiness. Period. No one truly deserves to be unhappy, deserves to be thought negatively of or about, or to be treated unfairly. So, may a small bit of happiness from me be shed onto you, and so everyone will have a piece of happiness from each other until we can all look into each other's eyes and see that we are never alone, that we have each other.

This poem is for the block,

"This Begins with I love you"

May what I have to say one day mean something

And may what I say be quoted and never forgotten

As I pass I will leave behind my words

My images

My work shall forever be preserved

And people will know that I fought for what is right

For the left is not wrong either

It is just on the other side

And I will look both ways

To all of my family

My friends

And I will say to them,

I love you all

And with as much as I can

I will provide for you

I will carry you when you cannot walk

I shall hold you up when you start to tumble

This is not the end

But the beginning of something vast

Possibilities stand before us

And we can grab them up and take them for our own

And share them with everyone

For I believe this

And that is all I need

Hope, happiness, and open arms

Where there iare none.

I toss this letter into the void, the abyss between us, this space the keeps conversation from happening.

Sincerely,
Rush Whitacre
740-336-9169

11-8-11

Dear Taylor Swift,

    I wish for you Taylor that your family stays healthy through the years. I know nothing of your family, but like any family I am sure that they are like any other would be with their kids, I am sure they are there for you. I am sure that they support you. I can't imagine that they need a wish like this from me, but, since this is that this letter is about, I will follow through. I wish that your mother and father are good, healthy and remain so for many years to come. It seems like such a simple thing, but, it isn't for anyone who has suddenly found themselves in the middle of a crisis, a health crisis. My friend Laura-girl has experience this a couple of times in her life, as have I, and when loved one comes down ill with something it is something that is first on your mind. I wish for you to not to have to worry about these things. That your family will be good, and healthy as long as possible.

This wish I also apply to anyone who might come into your life as well, may they also be well, and be free from the worries of bad health. May you never take for granted the days while you are healthy, for if that should ever leave you it would be tragic.

This poem is for the first class I taught,

"I will never forget you."

So nervous

I was

Standing before a room filling up from wall to wall

I had never done this kind of thing before

Like the conductor of a symphony

I would have to find my melody

My pages were all out of whack

And my whack was all out of pages

But somehow we found our way through to the end

And I believe, wanted to believe that I actually did some good

Did I do good?

I shall not know for years to come

Maybe not until I am dead.

Did I change the hearts of architects and turn them

Into painters

I may never know

I will say this though

I shall never forget you

My first class of many

My first class of few

And my way home that quarter was filled with doubt

And right when I thought I was losing it all

> You reminded me that I was not lost
>
> But here before you
>
> Right where I belonged
>
> Right where you put me

I toss this letter into the void, the abyss between us, this space that keeps conversation from happening.

Sincerely,

Rush Whitacre

740-336-9169

11-9-11

Dear Taylor Swift,

    Here is another wish for you, and because I can't think of another term for it I am calling it the soothing wish. A wish for you to not have to worry about things that people shouldn't have to worry about. Mostly, I hope that you never have to worry about stupid things happening in your life that shouldn't be there, like crazed fans, or sickness, or strange alien ships from outer space coming down to rob you of your favorite china or something stupid like that. I hope that you are always well protected and that you are always well taken care of. I am sure that as a famous person it is sometimes difficult to go out in public and not be mobbed by people. I will never know what that feels like I am sure of this, and neither would I want to be that kind of famous. I wouldn't mind being known, but I certainly don't want the mob kind of fame. That kind of fame only leads to things like creepy people wanting to follow you everywhere you go, as if they are actually going to accomplish something by doing this. Well, I am assuming things again, actually kind of projecting what I think people are capable of when the worst comes out of us. What do I know… I live in a hole in the wall apartment in Brooklyn. The only people who know my name are some of the guards, some gallery peeps, my roommates, and my ex fellow workers at Blick. But for you, the whole world knows who you are, what you look like, what you sound like. Etc. and that kind of fame is kind of amazing really. There are not too many people out there who have that kind of standing, or who need that kind of projection of themselves. Mostly those who need to sell themselves as a commodity, like movie stars who need the attention. There I go again assuming things, from my podium here in my apartment. I guess this is where I stand on some issues though. And may you never have to worry about not sticking out in a crowd. I am positive that you will always have a smile on the cover of a mag, or have a track in the top 50 if not the top 10 at most times in your life. Just keep doing what you do best, that is all any of us artist can really do. Thanks for listening to this ridiculous rant… I shall not reread it, for I don't want to change this totally off the cuff crap. Lol

This poem is for the musicians who are working the underground on the internet,

"Everyone Will Have Their 15 Minutes"

Point, Click, Play

And everyone on the net will have their fame

Everyone who wants to have their voice heard

Will be made crystal clear

And those who matter the most

Or who have created the most addictive

Will be the most watched

The most listened to

And like all diseases, these virus's will spread

Not making you sick

But making you laugh

Be entertained

Be amazed or stupefied

Meant to inspire all of us to a new level

A new degree of fascination

And we shall as artist's be held

To a new level of professionalism

Raise your glass

And join me in this cheers

This drink is for you

And this wish is for all of us,

Clink.

I toss this letter into the void, the abyss between us, this space that keeps conversation from happening.

Sincerely,
Rush Whitacre
740-336-9169

11-10-11

Dear Taylor Swift

    Here is a wish that many of wish for you, but probably not all for the same reason. I wish for you to find true love. Ok, now I can imagine that many people want you to find this for one reason or another, but I am wishing this for you because I am wondering what will come pouring out of that heart of yours after it has been cranked up to such a high level of emotion that you never worry about not being loved, or mistreated, when you have found your soul mate, if such a thing exists, and to such a degree that you are overwhelmed with satisfaction of life. I mean, nothing is perfect, but here is such a thing as a better than average, and there is such a thing as almost perfect, and that is all anyone can really strive for anyway. If we really could find the perfect person for each of us then we would all be better off, and maybe even the world would be better off, but, I am not wishing that for you, as I know that a little bit of the lip biting, and a little bit of the funny looks across the room are all good for the artistic expression, and energy that helps to make something great. I truly believe that the best artistic expression comes from some kind of struggle, some kind of compromise, some kind of mixed signal, some kind of love that is unexplainable, and this I wish for you… the kind of love that drives you crazy, makes your heart's blossom open, and makes you feel like you just simply could be loved any stronger,,, with lots of laughter and lots of hugs, for those are important. Yeah, lots of hugs.

    Oh, and strange looks from across the room, just to make you feel that certain bit of satisfaction that you are always being questioned and yet answered within the same look… yes, you are worth it all, and worth doing it all over for again. Period. Ok, there is that wish. I am sure that you will be loved, and that you will find it someplace you least expected it. Good luck.

This poem is for the girl at union station at the downtown F stop,

"Accordion Angel"

Even though your basket is empty

You play

You bring tears to the eyes of the emotional

And smiles to those who are wanting

I listen to you

Watch you sway back and forth

Your eyes closed and you love what you do

You look up for a moment to smile,

Say thank you

And continue playing for the passing of people

          Those who don't look like they notice,
                Trust me they do
            As I watch them pass you by
        And then give a look over their shoulder
              And I am mesmerized
             Enchanted by your music
         Your fearless passion to keep playing
        While all the world looks to ignore you
         And not drop into your box a penny
              As I have no money
           I shall pass to you a note
          A token of my appreciation
   For, "your music is so beautiful, as you are"
              Please keep playing
                  For my sake.
             Angel of the subway

I toss this letter into the void, the abyss between us, this space that keeps conversation from happening.

Sincerely,
Rush Whitacre
740-336-9169

11-11-11
Dear Taylor Swift,

    I wish that you never go wanting. I don't think that I need to elaborate on this one. And on top of all of this, I don't think that I want to say anything else on the topic, so I will just let the statement stand as it is, with minds wondering.

This poem is for the Multi-colored haired girl,
                "You Will be Loved"
            Blue, Green, Red, and Purple
    And all the colors of the rainbow could not be decided

And your life's decisions

Have helped the decision he has had to make

As you lay and wither on the subjects from a sad day

Just know that I am out here

Wanting to make you happy

To make you smile

To see you through the tough times

And help to create the best ones

I am alone in this fight though

I am always alone in this battle

For no one knows that I exist.

As I am the one who wants you

And wants you in pieces, or in whole

However I can

However I must

And if I must be in pieces myself,

Then so be it

For I am bursting at my seams

Being ripped apart

Like the dreads you separated

Losing half of it all

Maybe even more than that

For I am already pieces of pieces

I am just not looking in the mirror

For I disgust myself

I hate what I have done

And I am working as fast as I can

To make these mends

Thread and needle

Love through heart.

I toss this letter into the void, the abyss between us, this space that keeps conversation from happening.

Sincerely,
Rush Whitacre
740-336-9169

11-12-11

Dear Taylor Swift,

    I can't imagine a world without Swift songs, and therefore I hope that you continue to write songs far into the future, album after album, word after word. I can see that things will change a bit as time passes, and I can see that you will have some tough decisions to make, but that all will happen with good reason. Yeah, I wish for you to make many many new albums. I don't think you will have any trouble writing more songs or more albums as you are quite the prolific writer as I am sure. I can't imagine that someone like you doesn't write all the time. So, for tonight's poem, for the first time, I will dedicate this poem so you.

This poem is for Taylor Swift,

"Prolific"

And in the middle of this memory

I am losing myself and the aching grows into pain

But I patch myself up and face the music

The strumming of a lone guitar

And field of faceless people

Screaming

Passions to my ears

My adrenaline soars

Takes flight and I am one with this guitar

With this stage

This band

My voice will reach you in a minute

And this minute will last

And turn your heart inside out

Just like my emotions run high from the turn of a dial

My love runs higher, like the sun

So grab this mic from me

And steel away my vocals

> Pinch me for I must be dreaming
>
> This wax can't melt can it
>
> And I can't possibly fall
>
> And yet, as I do, I will write another line
>
> Another jest,
>
> Another stanza for the stands
>
> Pickling anything you thought
>
> And making this wretched vat blossom
>
> A fragrance of cotton candy
>
> Devoured

I toss this letter into the void, the abyss between us, this space the keeps conversation from happening.

Sincerely,
Rush Whitacre
740-336-9169

11-13-11

Dear Taylor Swift,

    This is my final wish for you in my letters, as I only have one letter left after this, and I haven't decided as to what I am going to do with it. So, here in this final wish I can't think of anything more special than to say that I have a wish for you to become a beautiful mother, as I see you as being an amazing mother to your kids, loving them with love ever after. Now that I have pitched this wish out to you I can't help but to wonder what names you already have picked out, as most people, even guys have once in a blue moon thought about what they would name their kids. Maybe I am wrong about this, but, I am also not so foolish either. So. I will let that go, but I will still wish for you a wonder family, and kids, beautiful happy babies. I wish you well.

This poem is for goodbye,

> "How it Goes"
>
> And this is how it ends
>
> My words all twisted up,
>
> And me not making sense
>
> 365 times I have reached out

       And 365 days I have waited

         Not a day longer

        A year in the making

    The greatest, saddest, toughest, most remarkable times

        That's what I have had.

         That's how it goes

I toss this letter into the void, the abyss between us, this space the keeps conversation from happening.

Sincerely,

Rush Whitacre

740-336-9169

Day 365 is the first letter

-ITV-